The Architecture
of the United States

An Illustrated Guide to Notable Buildings
A.D. 1115 to the Present
Open to the Public

The Architecture of the United States

Volume 1
NEW ENGLAND AND
THE MID-ATLANTIC STATES

G. E. Kidder Smith
Fellow, The American Institute of Architects

in association with
The Museum of Modern Art, New York

Introduction by Albert Bush-Brown

Anchor Books
Anchor Press/Doubleday   Garden City, New York
1981

The Architecture of the United States is published simultaneously in hardcover and paperback editions.
Anchor Books edition: 1981
Anchor Press edition: 1981

This book is the first of a three-volume series—*The Architecture of the United States*. The others are *The South and Midwest* and *The Plains States and Far West*.

PHOTO CREDITS

With few exceptions all photographs in this book were made by the author. Jorgé Figueroa of Modernage made—beautifully—most of the prints. For outside photographs in this volume, the author is deeply indebted to the following:

Page 57 Courtesy of James Stewart Polshek, architect; photographs by Nathaniel Lieberman
Page 64 Division of Historical and Cultural Affairs, Department of State, Delaware, photograph by H. Short
Pages 78–79 The Hagley Museum
Pages 122 and 320 *Architectural Forum—The Magazine of Building,* September 1954; March 1964
Page 304 Plimoth Plantation

Library of Congress Cataloging in Publication Data

Smith, George Everard Kidder, 1913–
    The architecture of the United States.

    Includes glossaries and indexes.
    CONTENTS: v. 1. New England and the Mid-Atlantic states.—v. 2. The South and Midwest.—v. 3. The Plains states and Far West.
    1. Architecture—United States—Guidebooks.
I. New York (City). Museum of Modern Art. II. Title.
NA705.S578   917.3'04926
Hardcover edition ISBN: 0-385-14672-8
Paperback edition ISBN: 0-385-14673-6
Library of Congress Catalog Card Number 79–8035

to DFKS

who enriched every page
—and every hour

Foreword

This guidebook was initiated (1967) and first sponsored by the Graham Foundation for Advanced Studies in the Fine Arts, Chicago, under its then-director (now emeritus) John Entenza. In 1978 the Foundation, under the directorship of Carter H. Manny, Jr., FAIA, gave me a supplemental stipend to complete and update my research. The National Endowment for the Arts, first under Roger L. Stevens and then under the ever-helpful Nancy Hanks, assisted by Bill N. Lacy, was co-sponsor with two substantial fellowships, while the Ford Foundation contributed two grants at critical moments and the Museum of Modern Art a grant-in-aid. To the two Foundations, the Endowment, and the Museum, my lasting gratitude: this demanding project would not have been possible without their financial and moral support.

Objective of Book The purpose of this guidebook is to help establish architecture more fully in the cultural life of the United States. For "architecture" is largely unknown to the public, all but ignored in general art courses at our universities, and—with the pioneering exception of New York's Museum of Modern Art—rarely shown in our museums. By pinpointing excellence and introducing the reader and traveler to distinguished building, it is hoped that the book will encourage interest in the heritage of this country's architecture. For unless we develop more discernment regarding urban and architectural quality, we will continue to commission and produce the mediocrity which characterizes most of our cities and buildings today.

This guide does not pretend to be a history of architecture in the U.S.A.—its author is an architect and critic, not a historian. The book is intended to serve as a commentary on a cross section of each state's architectural resources from earliest times to the present. It is by no means an inventory of memorable works—at only twenty buildings per state one arrives at a thousand entries—but it will critically examine structures considered representative of major periods of development. (There are, of course, many more than a thousand notable buildings in this country, but today's book economics severely limits the number which can be included.) Some states, particularly the older and the more populous, obviously have a greater range of distinguished work than the more recent or more sparsely settled.

Selection of Buildings A compilation such as this must reflect the selective process of one individual. However, every building described has been personally examined and, with my wife's perceptive aid, an on-site, preliminary report written. The final choice represents a winnowing of over three thousand structures to half that number. With few exceptions each is at times open to the public.

The lengthy research connected with the preliminary selection of the historic buildings was greatly facilitated by the books and articles of architectural historians and other specialists in the field, to whom I am deeply indebted. Though there is no up-to-date overall history of architecture in this country at present (1980), several promising ones are now in production. There are, however, a number of useful volumes on various periods, regions, and architects, and these are mentioned in the text when quoted. For selecting contemporary examples I relied on my extensive architectural file, which contains speedily retrievable articles on almost all buildings of merit published in the last forty years. Conversations with architects and historians kept matters topical. Because of limits of space, only those engineers, landscape architects, and related specialists who played a major design role arc listed.

As regards choice of buildings, some readers may, of course, harbor favorites which have been irritatingly omitted, while other structures may be puzzlingly included. However, to bring *de gustibus* up to date, the late Mies van der Rohe and the late Walter Gropius—architects and educators of great significance in this country—each thought little of Le Corbusier's chapel at Ronchamp in eastern France, a building many hold to be one of the century's most important. Frank Lloyd Wright's disagreement with much of the architectural profession is well documented.

Omission of Some Building Types No private houses have been included in this guide, though several harmonious streets of such houses are listed. A few private buildings are so stimulating on the exterior that they are mentioned with the cautionary note of sidewalk viewing only. Some contemporary suburban corporate headquarters and similar works of distinction were omitted at the request of their managements. All correctional institutions were bypassed and only a few mental institutions written up. The most sincerely regretted absence is that of a number of fine new buildings which had not been finished when we were last on the scene. More than twelve years were spent on this project and though three updating grants were made, inevitably in a country as large as this we missed some outstanding new work, plus some historic museum-houses which only recently have been opened. Sadly, some buildings discussed here undoubtedly will disappear in the next few years.

State and City Guidebooks Although this book of necessity omits many important buildings, old and new, this lacuna is partly eased by the realization that an encouraging number of comprehensive local architectural guidebooks is becoming available. One hopes every state and major city will eventually have a critical guide to its outstanding buildings. The local offices of the American Institute of Architects—listed in most telephone books—can often be of help, as can state tourist boards. Many cities and towns have an annual house tour, usually in the spring, when homes otherwise not open to the public can be visited.

For all architectural exploration, state and city maps are essential for time-saving travel.

As this book is primarily a field guide and reference source, the photographs are necessarily small. For a "visual data bank" of architecture in the United States see my two-volume *Pictorial History of Architecture in America* (American Heritage/W. W. Norton, 1976).

Caveats The structures described herein generally are open on the dates, days, and hours indicated, but it would be wise to check on these. Admission might range from 25 cents to a number of dollars, and, like hours, is subject to change. If no admission charge is indicated, the entrance is probably free although this, too, can vary.

There are times—a dreary winter day for instance—when even the Parthenon fails, when Pentelic marble cannot inspire. So it will happen that buildings extolled here can disappoint: moreover some might show their years before their due or have undergone serious alterations since last visited. In addition, this book is admittedly a cheerful report, probably at times too cheerful, but I am, for better or worse, an optimist in the first place and, secondly, if a structure was not considered outstanding it would not be included.

Prior to publication, the description of each building was sent to its architect or the appropriate historical body for correction of possible error. The responses were of the utmost help in corroborating and correcting data, and I am deeply grateful to those national and state agencies, dedicated historical societies and curators, fellow architects, and individuals who so generously and constructively helped check the text. I only wish that there were space to list them all individually.

It is well to keep in mind that in some cases even specialists will disagree, often in dating, occasionally even in the attribution of the architect of a historic building. The dates of the buildings given here begin with the generally accepted date for commencement of construction and the finish thereof. Major alterations, when known, are also listed. The facts given here represent the most recent research; in most cases data came from information at the source. The National Register of Historic Places (1976), U. S. Department of the Interior, was also of great help. If there are errors, however, the fault is, of course, mine.

In Summary   The United States with its geographic range, size of population, ethnic richness, and financial means produces more architectural probing, offers more excitement, and achieves a greater volume of outstanding new work than any other single country. But lest this encomium seem comforting, it must be immediately added that for the most part, our town planning lags far behind that in Scandinavia, our land usage both in city and suburb is lamentable, and our low-cost housing generally inexcusable. Moreover I am uneasy about much work now being turned out. A few architects, properly publicized, seemingly are more concerned with conjuring novelty for novelty's sake, or with producing seductive exhibition drawings, than they are willing to be vexed by the tough, three-dimensional realities of a client's program, his money, or the annoying details of site and climate. Professional responsibility—let alone societal responsibility—appears to be of little moment. We are increasingly witnessing what Siegfried Giedion called "Playboy Architecture." Many of these idiosyncratic excursions will look trivial twenty-five years from now when, peradventure, the house or building will be paid for. Architecture should be concerned with creating significant space, not scene painting. Nonetheless we in the United States still have a workshop with a vitality unmatched elsewhere, and if we take a greater interest in what is being built (and torn down), we can create a finer tomorrow. This is what this book is about.

Corrections and suggestions would be appreciated by the author.

G. E. Kidder Smith, FAIA
September 1980

163 East 81st Street
New York, NY 10028

ACKNOWLEDGMENTS

This book would not have been published had it not been for the constant help and encouragement of Martin Rapp, the Museum of Modern Art's spirited and talented Director of Publications. Stewart Richardson, former Associate Publisher at Doubleday—and a friend of long standing—was his stalwart cohort. Both have given me wonderful support. Editors Loretta Barrett, Elizabeth Frost Knappman, and Eve F. Roshevsky, and Harold Grabau, Adrienne Welles, and Patricia Connolly, copy editors, went over the manuscript with many suggestions for its betterment and shepherded a staggering mass of material through production. Marilyn Schulman did a brilliant job of design.

I am particularly grateful to the four eminent architectural historians whose introductions give such illuminating perspective on the background and forces which helped shape the buildings in the three regional volumes. Dr. Albert Bush-Brown, chancellor of Long Island University and co-author with the late John Burchard of the encyclopedic *The Architecture of America,* contributed a superb introduction to the architecture of the Northeast—Volume 1—and also commented pertinently on the text for individual buildings. Professor Frederick D. Nichols of the School of Architecture of the University of Virginia and an author long known for his brilliant studies of Jefferson and the architecture of the South wrote the first introduction for Volume 2. Professor Frederick Koeper, a specialist on the buildings of the Midwest—his *Illinois Architecture* is one of the finest state guides—sets the stage for the second part of Volume 2. The indefatigable David Gebhard, whose guidebooks to the architecture in California and Minnesota are classics, gives great insight to the work of that vast sweep of states west of the Mississippi in Volume 3. To all four I am deeply indebted for their sterling contributions.

But the two individuals who dealt with every word of every sentence—always to their betterment—were my wife and Patricia Edwards Clyne. My wife advised on the field selections of buildings, wrote up almost all of our on-the-spot reactions, navigated when not driving (we covered some 135,000 miles/217,200 kilometers), and shared twelve years of work, most of it under pressure conditions. (She also shared the delights of finding many extraordinary buildings in this extraordinary country.) The material simply could not have been gathered nor the book written without her constant help, judicious taste, and glorious companionship. When travel was over—once forty-seven different motels in fifty-six nights—and I had typed the text with semilegibility, Pat Clyne, the distinguished author and speleologist, took over. She tackled the oft-confused (and sometimes windy) language of 2,800 pages of manuscript, rationalized constructions, minimized malaprops, inserted the forgotten, removed the superfluous, all in a superb editing job. She then typed each page so beautifully that it could be framed. With these two lovely and talented daughters of Minerva the task became not only possible but pleasurable.

VOLUME 1 ACKNOWLEDGMENTS

In addition to those who gave invaluable assistance in checking data on individual buildings, the following were of outstanding help:

Connecticut Dorothy Armistead, Curator, Henry Whitfield House; Wilson H. Faude, Executive Director, Old State House; Stephen A. Kezerian, Director, Yale University News Bureau; Wynn Lee, Director, Mark Twain Memorial.

Delaware The Historical Society of Delaware; Alice Rowan O'Brien and Libba Sevison, The Hagley Museum; Michael S. Shapiro and staff, Division of Historical and Cultural Affairs, State of Delaware; Catherine Wheeler, Winterthur Museum.

District of Columbia Douglas E. Evelyn, Deputy Director, National Portrait Gallery; Jeanne B. Hodges, President, AIA Foundation; The National Trust for Historic Preservation; David Sellin, Curator for the Architect of the Capitol.

Maine Frank A. Beard and staff, Maine Historic Preservation Commission; Mrs. Millard S. Peabody, The Tate House.

Maryland Barbara A. Brand, Hammond-Harwood House; Historic Annapolis Inc.; Mianna S. Jopp, Office of Tourism Development; Karin E. Peterson and Nancy Baker, Maryland Historical Trust; Walter Sondheim, Jr., Martin Millspaugh, and Mrs. Robert O. Bonnell, Jr., of Charles Center—Inner Harbor Management Inc.

Massachusetts Donald R. Friary, Historic Deerfield Inc.; Judith M. Ingram, Plimoth Plantation; Dean Lahikainen, Essex Institute; Bettina A. Norton, Trinity Church; Lynne M. Spencer, Gwen E. Brown, and staff, The Society for the Preservation of New England Antiquities; Leroy H. True, Nantucket Historical Association.

New Hampshire Peggy Armitage, Director, Strawbery Banke Inc.; Ray E. Johns, President, Hancock Historical Society; Elizabeth Lessard, The Manchester Historic Association; Portsmouth Historical Society; Shaker Village Inc., Canterbury.

New Jersey Earle Coleman and A. Melissa Kiser, Office of Communications, Princeton University; Josephine L. Harron, Save Lucy Committee; Marden R. Nystrom, Bergen County Historical Society.

New York State The Cobblestone Society, Childs; Huguenot Historical Society, New Paltz; Louis C. Jones; Mark D. Lyon and staff, New York State Parks and Recreation; Bruce D. MacPhail, Sleepy Hollow Restorations; John D. Randall, Louis Sullivan Museum; Frederick L. Rath, Jr., New York State Historical Association; Norman S. Rice, Director, The Albany Institute; Grace Zuckman, The College at Purchase.

New York City Avery Library, Columbia University, and its Director Emeritus, Adolf K. Placzek; Marshall B. Davidson; Arthur Drexler, Director of Architecture, Museum of Modern Art; Margot Gayle, Friends of Cast Iron Architecture; Ludwig Glaeser, Curator of the Mies van der Rohe Archive, Museum of Modern Art; Harmon Goldstone, FAIA; Wallace K. Harrison, FAIA; David M. Kahn, National Park Service, Manhattan Sites; Leon Katz and Mario V. Salzano, The Port Authority of New York and New Jersey; Walter Killam, Jr., FAIA; Majorie Pearson, New York City Landmarks Commission; Michael T. Sheehan, Snug Harbor Cultural Center; Staten Island Historical Society.

Pennsylvania Richard J. Boyle, Director, Pennsylvania Academy of the Fine Arts; W. Eugene Cox, Valley Forge National Historical Park; Edith Feld, Girard College; Nancy D. Kolb, Pennsbury Manor; John Maass, architectural historian, Philadelphia; National Trust for Historic Preservation; Pennsylvania Historical and Museum Commission; David Wisdom, architect.

Rhode Island Antoinette F. Downing and David Chase, Rhode Island Historical Preservation Commission; Leonard J. Panaggio, Director, Rhode Island Tourist Promotion Division, and staff; The Society for the Preservation of New England Antiquities.

Vermont Rev. Wallace W. Anderson, Jr., The Congregational Church, Middlebury; Charles H. Ashton, Division of Historic Preservation, State of Vermont; Emily Gyllensward.

Contents

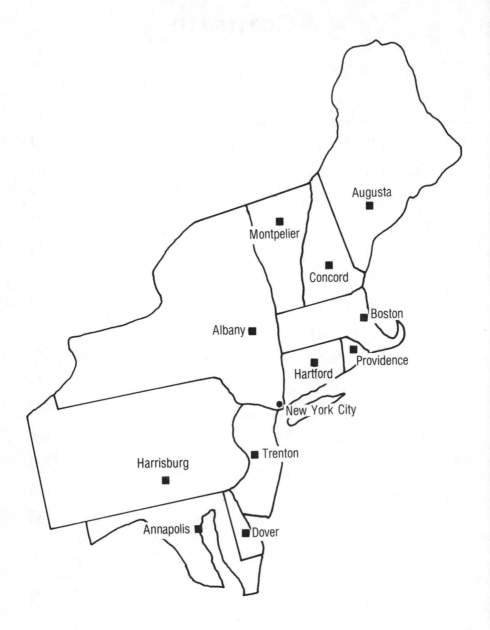

Introduction

You are fortunate indeed when Kidder Smith guides your journey into architecture.

He leads you to encounter buildings wholly and expects you to let architecture surround you until you yourself are quickened to his enthusiasm for space and the magnificent play of light and shade on form.

He informs the encounter with bits of history. Whether he has found a fine meetinghouse for a remote religious community or an air-supported shelter for a transatlantic communications station, he delights in sharing his discovery. He insists that he is neither historian nor engineer but his descriptions of wooden trusses in covered bridges and the leap of suspended steel across rivers might make you think so.

He is not the sort of critic who only examines esthetic trends and social influences. He loves buildings themselves, as only architects do, applauds success quickly, and is even quicker to discard any puerile performance. But, first and last, it is the buildings he loves, not abstract theory about them or their clients.

To find such moments of visual brilliance, Kidder Smith studies carefully and travels far. Accept his invitation to see what is remarkable and wonderful. Our companion is the best of guides, the best of interpreters.

We take the guidebook from the glove compartment and swing our automobile off the expressway to find Wickford, Rhode Island, or Ephrata, Pennsylvania. Guidebook in hand, we walk through the campus of Princeton or Yale or Harvard. We visit Boston's revived Faneuil Hall Marketplace, the dramatic new City Hall (1969), and the historic Kings Chapel. A Saturday morning in Newport lets us enter the Touro Synagogue; later, we can visit the Redwood Library and Trinity Church; a picnic luncheon along the Cliff Walk is the best prelude to the Breakers. Kidder Smith's text recites the origin of each building, judges its quality, points out an elegant pulpit or spiral stair, regrets a misplaced window or offensive proportion, and keeps us alert to functional satisfactions and disappointments.

The reader will sense that American architecture has been the subject of some great, continuing debates. We have differences in taste: Do we prefer Colonial or Georgian over modern architecture? We are divided about land: should we have dense apartment clusters in open fields or single-family houses spreading across the landscape? Should we adore the machine, including our automobiles, or keep the machine out of the garden and living room, even exclude automobiles from cities?

If our new neighborhoods lack a center, with no sense of community, should we build a center around a church, a school, a shopping mall, a town hall, or none—or all—of these? Those questions are part of persistent themes of which three can be introduced here: style, taste, and urbanity.

The question of style has been a recurrent theme. Is there a distinctly American style? Should there be one? Or is the American landscape too varied, the special character of our people not really identifiable? Are Americans (and their architecture) distinguishable from Europeans or Latin Americans or Canadians? If not, if style instead is an international phenomenon, should it be traditional or modern or an eclectic combination of both, as Americans declare in suburban houses: the clipper ship weathervane above an electronically operated overhead door; a tall Gothic grandfather clock with electric works inside?

Clamor for a distinctly American architecture appears whenever we assert our national self-consciousness. It was not important to Colonial builders nor to the eighteenth-century Georgian architects of Portsmouth, New Hamsphire; Salem, Massachusetts; Wethersfield, Connecticut; nor, to introduce a more southerly example, Annapolis, Maryland. Georgian buildings followed English precedent which was derived from Italian, especially Palladian, antecedents. The Georgian Style graced most seaboard cities and towns from 1730 through the decade after the Revolution. It was often elegant and the interiors could be elaborate, as in McIntire's work at Salem.

The following decades summoned a sense of national purpose and called for an American architecture. An ornamental response appears in Latrobe's tobacco and corn leaf capitals in the Capitol at Washington, D.C. More basically, he insisted upon sequential, segmental composition of a building's elements, a series of volumes and masses shaped by useful purpose, without any Georgian unity or formality. By displaying articulated masses in his Cathedral at Baltimore (before the additions), Latrobe broke from the international Georgian tradition to achieve distinctive buildings that expressed their purposes. The Federalist buildings of Bulfinch show his search for an American architecture, as do the critical essays of Emerson and Greenough, who, in the 1840s, called for an architecture as well adapted to our institutions as our clipper ships were to wind and sea.

But other architects, often led by amateurs and critics, argued that an American architecture must follow Classical precedents. Latrobe might help with the innovative plan for the University of Virginia but Jefferson insisted that the porticos should be Roman and the library should be a replica of the Pantheon. Jefferson's respect for Roman example was practical: a young republic must heed Pliny's precepts on agriculture, study the law and government of the Roman Republic, and learn architecture from Vitruvius. The lesson often produced inventive buildings in Classical Style, such as Providence's Arcade (1828).

The Roman Revival of 1820 to 1850 also had a Grecian counterpart.

It was popular among amateurs like Nicholas Biddle, who admired ancient Greek architecture and democracy and sympathized with the
modern Greeks in their struggle for independence from the Turks in the
1820s. Biddle's Second Bank of the United States (1824) and his
Andalusia (1836) show the Grecian Revival in Philadelphia.

But if the Grecian Parthenon suggests the imagery for American
democratic institutions, what models would serve Christian churches
and colleges? Upjohn gave the answer at Trinity Church, New York,
begun in 1841, in the first of three stylistic phases of Gothic Revival in
America. James Renwick's Grace Church (1846) in New York and the
Smithsonian Institution (1847–55) in Washington are venerable re-
minders of our first Gothic romance.

Thus, American architects from 1810 until about 1860 were proponents of "associationalism," the theory that a historic style conveys the
national, political, or religious meanings associated with its origins.
Most of the discussions within the American Institute of Architects
when it was formed in 1857 debated which of the styles—Greek,
Roman, Romanesque, or Gothic—best expressed America's continuity
with the past.

After the Civil War, the desire for expressing historic continuity
through Classical and medieval architecture conflicted with increasing
practical needs. What Grecian temple or Gothic cathedral could be a
model for a vast railway terminal or for a factory producing cotton
goods? New industrial and commercial institutions required new architecture. The American responses from 1865 to 1890 had an essential
dichotomy: for industry and manufacture, it was sufficient to build utilitarian, expedient buildings devoid of style; the result could be strong
and picturesque, like the factories along the Merrimack River or the
mills at New Bedford, both in Massachusetts. The Amoskeag mills in
Manchester, New Hampshire, show the reliance on utilitarian, structural design from 1838 until World War I.

But for modern cultural institutions, it was necessary to be monumental, historical, ornamental, and inventive. The English critic John
Ruskin captivated America with his advocacy of innovation in the
Gothic manner. Hearkening to Ruskin, Charles Eliot Norton urged
Harvard to build the Victorian Gothic Memorial Hall, an example of
our second romance with Gothic Style. Other critics and architects favored the mansarded, Classical Style, as seen today in Washington's Executive Office Building (1871–88), Boston's Old City Hall (1865),
and Philadelphia's City Hall (1872–1901). The new president of Harvard after 1869, Charles W. Eliot, disliked such taste; a scientist, he
wanted useful laboratories, not monuments, and in this respect was an
early advocate of plain functional buildings such as the ward pavilions

erected by an engineer for the hospital at Johns Hopkins University in Baltimore about 1876. But Eliot was exceptional.

In the centennial year, Philadelphia displayed the Corliss engine and vast spaces covered by glass and iron, to the delight of engineer, scientist, and industrialist. The centennial exhibition also had Victorian Gothic and Renaissance pavilions which pleased the literary, historical, and artistic amateurs. They cherished their Gothic Street School of the Arts at Yale and Chancellor Green Library at Princeton. From the Philadelphia exhibition they returned to Providence and Baltimore to build Victorian Gothic churches and schools in cities and suburbs. Old Grand Central Station in New York showed the dichotomy: wonderful glazed roofs over the tracks, ornamental masonry architecture over the terminal. Most Americans in 1885 did not recognize the schism or that it could be bridged.

Intimations of a resolution were achieved only sporadically before 1885. Philadelphia offers a hint in Frank Furness' Pennsylvania Academy of the Fine Arts (1876). Boston offers several, beginning with Austin Hall at Harvard and the suburban railroad stations of Henry Hobson Richardson. While Richardson's Trinity Church at Boston and his Allegheny Courthouse and Jail (1888) at Pittsburgh reveal his love of the Romanesque, they, too, show his passion for exposing structure and expressing strength through stone and brick and wrought iron. From Richardson's warehouse in Chicago for the Marshall Field store, architects learned how the utilitarian and the ornamental might proceed together from a single esthetic.

Louis Sullivan learned the lesson from Richardson, and his tall office building, the Prudential in Buffalo, of 1895, was developed accordingly. Its verticality and internal organization were framed in piers, recessed spandrels, and marvelous new ornament. Here, some architects and historians believe, is the seed of a truly original American architecture. Sullivan came to believe so. So did Frank Lloyd Wright after 1920 and he railed against his colleagues for having neglected Sullivan in favor of importing one more European imperial style, which he thought to be baleful to America.

What caused Wright's wrath was the Chicago Columbian Exposition of 1893. There, New York architects created a fashion for the beautiful city with monumental white buildings in generally Roman Style. Its axes, fountains, and Classical buildings inspired Philadelphians and Washingtonians to revive and extend their boulevards and plazas. Washington built Union Station (1903–7) to Burnham's plans; New York City gained the Public Library (1898–1911) and new gateways in Pennsylvania Station and Grand Central Station; Boston built the Public Library (1895) on Copley Square. At its best, as in Paul Cret and Albert Kelsey's Pan American Union (now Organization of American States) (1908–10) at Washington or in McKim, Mead & White's Library at Boston, Beaux Arts architecture gave American cities a scale and dignity they needed. What would Washington lose if it did not have the Lincoln Memorial (1914–22)? What new building and sculpture on that site could mean as much? Recognition of that service is dawning, even among modern architects who were brought up to decry Beaux Arts architecture. Wright was only partly right. The best practitioners were neither servile to French precedent nor slave to Roman example. They, too, sought a national architecture.

Still, whether classical or modern, a national architecture might not be wanted. Instead, or so many architects argued in the period 1910 forward, there should be regional differences. New England architects rediscovered Georgian models at Salem and Newburyport, Massachusetts. Philadelphians revived the styles of Independence Hall and Bucks County farms. Californians discovered a Mission Style. New Mexico tried a pueblo revival. Occasionally, Frank Lloyd Wright was called East. We now cherish Fallingwater (1937) in Pennsylvania, and his much earlier houses in Buffalo, although we destroyed his pioneering Larkin Building there. Wright lectured at Princeton University in 1929 but Princeton did not give him a commission; nor did any other university, so happy were they with the "collegiate Gothic" quadrangles of Princeton and Yale and the new Georgian houses at Harvard. Such revivalism, whether for religious and educational connotations or for reasons of regionalism, became increasingly difficult to defend but the mode remained fashionable until 1950 at least.

Then, even though they avoided Wright, universities and national industrial corporations became tentative, eventually avid clients of a new, essentially European architectural movement. Begun in Germany and France between the two world wars, modern architecture stressed social, economic, and moral needs, especially in housing and industrial buildings, insisted upon functional spaces and efficient circulation, with masses expressed cubistically without any ornamentation save the textures and color imparted by materials themselves. Even high elegance—the precision and polish of metals, together with the transparencies of glass walls—was achieved in the residences designed by Mies van der Rohe.

In 1947, the Massachusetts Institute of Technology retained the Finn Alvar Aalto. Harvard commissioned the German Walter Gropius, and, much later, the Swiss-French Le Corbusier. Mies van der Rohe designed a new campus for the Illinois Institute of Technology in Chicago. Yale's campus today is a mecca for students of contemporary design. There are many explanations for this phenomenon, including the sudden growth of universities after 1950, the rising influence of scientists and engineers within universities, and the revolutions in costs, materials, and labor.

But paramount among the reasons is the prestige modern architecture won for industrial and commercial corporations after 1950. In Manhattan, Lever House (1952), the Manufacturers Hanover (1954), the Seagram Building (1958), and the Chase Manhattan Bank (1961) established new symbols, offered a fine premise for urban amenity, and also set standards for sculpture and paintings in their buildings. Like Rockefeller Center in the 1930s, these buildings and the United Nations Secretariat (1950) helped to change corporate taste.

Not every architect today rejoices in the corporate image of the 1950s and '60s. Within Skidmore, Owings & Merrill, who helped to establish it nationally, there are innovators, as revealed by Gordon Bunshaft in the Beinecke Library (1963) at Yale and by Walter A. Netsch in the Engineering Laboratories at MIT and the Library at Wells College, New York. Benjamin Thompson achieved a vivacious and elegant architecture in the Design Research Store (1950) at Cambridge and the Quincy Market restoration in Boston. Robert Venturi at the Franklin Court in Philadelphia (1976) and Ieoh Ming Pei in the new wing for the National Gallery in Washington (1978) proposed wonderful departures from what the public expected as the 1980s approached. But modernism had won the day, and even public buildings like Boston's City Hall, the Brydges Library (1974) at Niagara Falls, and the New York City Police Headquarters (1974) confirmed that debates about a national architecture were over.

Now the questions for contemporary architects hinge on America's future. We surely have achieved enormous competence in modern architecture. From New York, Cambridge, Chicago, San Francisco, and the recently successful offices in Houston and Atlanta our architects export modern architecture to Africa, the Middle East, and the Far East. But what about opportunities here? Is modern architecture a mere style, a new cosmetic symbol; or will clients, both governmental and private, seek it for what it promised in 1925: to solve urban problems through modern technology and design?

A second theme enlivens the debates about American architecture. Should an egalitarian taste prevail? Should each citizen possessed of property be entitled to exercise his own taste with full right to use his land and resources as he sees fit? Or, even in a democracy that prides itself on having laissez-faire commerce (or once did) and an ever expanding frontier of land (now nearly exhausted), should there be limitations upon egalitarianism, some subjugation to the neighbor's rights, some concession to the commonwealth, before you or I decide what we shall do with our piece of land?

Obviously, whether an egalitarian taste or an elitist possibly aristocratic taste should prevail has divided Americans for a long time. Disputes over restrictions upon what we can do with our land disrupt villages and cities today. In the 1890s, Cleveland's attempts at imposing regulations upon factory smoke and river pollution excited resistance from industrialists and journalists. Not many cities can boast of success today, although Boston, Pittsburgh, and Baltimore have reason to be proud of recent progress in their waterfronts.

Americans have not wanted any high priest of culture. For a while they did not need one. The Georgian towns of New England and the Mid-Atlantic States reveal agreement upon design: streets, trees, commons, and houses with compatible scales, shapes, and rhythms. The scene was interrupted in the nineteenth century by a cacophony of scales, intrusions of commercial and industrial buildings, and the prevalence of tenements and slums with no urban amenities.

The American Institute of Architects in the 1860s asked how architects might curb the amateur builder and assert themselves as professionals. The same question was being asked a century later. Not more than 10 per cent of American construction today is guided by architects. In 1963, when Congress was studying the proposed National Endowment for the Arts, a principal concern was whether its director and council might become a "Czar of the Arts." What Congress overlooked was the devastation created by their own National Highways Act, which laid 42,000 miles/67,500 kilometers of expressway across America (more construction than the entire Italian Renaissance had produced) without benefit of architectural, urban, or regional planning.

Not permitted to become an arbiter of taste, the elitist artist and patron tried to educate by example. When the architects McKim, Mead & White served a Morgan, the resulting Pierpont Morgan Library (1906) in New York City set a model for emulation. When Seymour Knox struck a friendship with Gordon Bunshaft of Skidmore, Owings & Merrill, the partnership produced more than the admirable addition to the Albright-Knox Gallery (1962) in Buffalo. Bunshaft's Marine Midland Building (1968) and Beinecke Library (1963), not to forget his abandoned design for the Amherst campus of the State University of New York at Buffalo, are witness to Knox's directorships and benevolent interests. The Museum of Modern Art (1939; 1953–64) became a tastemaker of extraordinary influence and helped publicize widely the new buildings of the Connecticut General Insurance Corporation, IBM, Polaroid, Chase Manhattan, Lever, Seagram, Citicorp, and many other corporations. With bountiful monies and a need for corporate identity and advertisement, they could not risk the pushcart buildings or vulgarities of many lesser entrepreneurs.

Even they have no sure defense against the American proclivity to spoil town and landscape and to allow private interest to turn each Main Street and highway into a commercial strip for fast foods, cut-rate sales, and gasoline pumps, often mixed in among houses, churches, and schools. The example of Lever House and the Seagram Building was ignored by most of the builders of upper Park Avenue; the open terraces and plazas of the Lever and Seagram buildings are still coveted for taxes.

Given the urge to develop each property as its owner sees fit, America's architectural heritage is always vulnerable. Too often the venerable building is knocked down by the wrecking ball, or it disappears through obsolescence and neglect. That so many fine historic buildings remain is a tribute to the historical conscience, scholarship, and philanthropy quickened by historical societies, the restoration of Colonial Williamsburg, and the National Trust for Historic Preservation. One of the better restorations is the Saugus Ironworks (1646) in Massachusetts. Among more than two dozen other examples of seventeenth-century houses, those in Topsfield, Massachusetts; Cutchogue, Long Island; Croton-on-Hudson, New York; and New Castle, Delaware, show the regional variations. Portsmouth's Strawbery Banke restores much of an entire seaport. More than four dozen Georgian houses are presented here, including Boston's best, for which great credit must go to the Society for the Preservation of New England Antiquities. The citizens of Philadelphia, Newport, Baltimore, and Providence have preserved entire neighborhoods.

Only recently have Victorian and Beaux Arts buildings won protectors. See the imaginative conversion of the Mount Clare Railroad Station for the Maryland Art Institute in Baltimore. Rejoice at the restoration of the Quincy Market in Boston. Admire the addition made to Boston's Public Library by Philip Johnson in 1972. Join those who rallied to save the Grand Central Station (1903–13) in New York and the Pension Building (1882–87) in Washington, which had been threatened periodically with destruction.

By 1895, during the romance with the City Beautiful, there were esthetic codes for building heights and use of police powers to limit billboards. The most significant of the early laws to control development of land was the set-back zoning law enacted in 1916 to restrict high buildings in New York City. With the post–World War II appointment of city planning commissions and federal funding of urban development programs, zoning and planning gained greater influence, as can be seen in the examples cited in Worcester, Boston, New Haven, Philadelphia, and Baltimore. The architecture is often distinguished and meets urgent needs for housing and civic functions.

Yet the American taste is often amateurish and anecdotal when it is not vulgar. To find the buildings described in this guidebook, you will travel past many others that are offensive, banal, and meretricious. You will drive on few Merritt Parkways where sculptured grades and curves open pleasing vistas to shrubs and trees. You are best advised to reach the Triborough Bridge when Manhattan sparkles under clear night skies and a full moon. You will ignore much visual, aural, and nasal pollution to sense the wonderful thrust of industry as you speed over the New Jersey marshes among ships, railroads, airplanes, trucks, and colossal petroleum refineries. When you enter the side streets of cities and towns, you will be provoked to ask whether man-made America supports our human potential or subverts it.

That observation raises questions about urbanism and ruralism—a third theme, which has excited American debates for almost two centuries. Is the city vile, anonymous, and vicious, while the village is personal, healthy, and virtuous? Is the factory injurious to family life and to skills and pride in workmanship? Which supports political and economic well-being? Can cities nurture culture and urbanity? Can cities achieve a sense of community?

Such questions start from assumptions about the village. You can see village virtue celebrated in Mystic Seaport, Connecticut; The Farmer's Museum, Cooperstown, New York; and Sturbridge Village, Massachusetts. Village scale and values were not threatened when Slater built his Mill beside the waterfall at Pawtucket, Rhode Island. Nor were those of early cotton manufacturing settlements, such as Lowell, Massachusetts, which was laid out to be a model village. Unfortunately mining and drilling industries made no similar plans. Pittsburgh in the 1880s was a soot-blackened jumble of wooden shanties scattered among colossal furnaces and railyards. The later factories at Lowell, Waltham, Chicopee, and Manchester brought immigrant and farm populations into new large aggregations where the village social order did not fit.

From 1820 onward but especially after 1850, American reformers expressed fears about the industrial city. They feared industrialization, immigration, laborers' mobility, family disruption, religious change, emancipation of women, and deepening divisions among economic classes. We still see towns where the mansion is on the hill, the mill in the valley, and wooden tenements cling to the hillside. Reformers attended to the poor, the immigrant, the orphaned, and the unemployed in the 1880s. They established schools, churches, hospitals, parks, and playgrounds, the YMCA and YWCA, the Henry Street Settlement House, and many poor farms. That so few of those institutions summoned great architectural talent suggests much about the architectural profession and much about the reformers who were too few to influence the growing industrial city.

One aspect of urban reform gained powerful allies in the decades from 1890 to 1930. The City Beautiful movement evident at the Chicago Fair of 1893 inspired Eastern cities to make grand plans and to build fine boulevards, new gateways, and new buildings for their municipal and cultural institutions. Prior to 1895 symphony orchestras were founded in New York, Boston, and Philadelphia. Art museums were started, as were museums of natural history, women's colleges, hospitals, botanical gardens, and zoological gardens. The city was to be made into a vast resource of public educational and cultural institutions. It was all to be done by the elite from their own European taste.

But Americans had made several big decisions about cities. One was to separate place of residence from place of work. That was decided when railroads and trolley cars were the chief conveyances. It has meant that districts within cities are specialized, which gives distinct character to New York's Wall Street or Garment District, to Boston's Government Center, and to Washington's Mall. Like Philadelphia's Penn Plaza, most governmental and commercial districts are vacant at night. People move to specialized urban and suburban residential districts, which exhibit divisions among races, nationalities, and incomes. Between work and residence, most Americans today commute by automobile and bus, having decided that the rail shall be removed from the streets of Providence and the elevated from New York City's Third Avenue. It is by no means clear that all the recent efforts with the subways in Boston, New York, and Washington will be successful. For Americans have made an irreversible decision to live in suburbs, to decentralize and therefore to depend upon individualized mobility even at demonstrably higher costs in fuel, depreciation, and time and at incalculable losses in environmental quality.

While we may not choose to live in our cities, they hold enormous fascination for us. What combination of spectacle and speculation accounts for Manhattan's century-long competition for the emblematic tall building: the Woolworth (1913), American Radiator (1924), Daily News (1930), Chrysler (1930), Empire State (1931), Chase Manhattan Bank (1961), General Motors (1976), World Trade Center (1977), and Citicorp (1977)? Midtown Manhattan from Forty-second Street to Fifty-ninth Street is seldom silent or free from high-rise construction, while Queens, the Bronx, Brooklyn, and Manhattan's West Side summon no comparable investment or massing of people.

All the attitudes and technology needed to fulfill an antiurban premise were ready and proven well before 1950, but the decades after World War II accelerated the flight from the city. The American ideal was to own a single-family house in a suburb, to fill it with the products and machines that advertisements heralded, and to rely upon the automobile for shopping, commuting to work, and connections with friends. Populations spread wherever cables and wires could be stretched to carry electric power. Scattered households and distant families shared a network of communication by telephone, radio, and television, which leaped the distances and relieved the absence of neighborly contiguity.

Then, for suburban neighborhoods, the public school became a singularly common concern. A high school, and we built some fine buildings, offered a plural focus that the denominational church, the commercial shopping center, or the economically or socially segregated club could never provide. School and village drew commuters from the radial and circumferential highways built in metropolitan regions in the 1950s. The State University of New York built new if not fine campuses in suburban Buffalo and Purchase. Commercial corporations, like Connecticut General Life Insurance (1957), were quick to move from Hartford to rural land. The new electronics companies leaped from Cambridge to Route 128. Only uncommon leadership within the other insurance companies remaining in Hartford resisted the flight from the city and reinvested in downtown Hartford, where Constitution Plaza stands today.

Hartford's example helped to spur other cities to urban revitalization. Boston's Government Center, Baltimore's Charles Center and Inner Harbor, and Philadelphia's redevelopment are cited in this guidebook.

Some fine, small urban parks were created, such as Paley Park (1967) in New York. Washington and Manhattan struggled to maintain their older parks, especially Central Park (1857–76), which experiences devastatingly heavy use. You will see a few worthy examples of low-cost housing, where we have had many high-rise failures. But most of the cited housing is for middle- and high-income families, beginning with Radburn (1928) in New Jersey and Chatham Village (1932–36) in Pittsburgh. Recent examples include Pei's Society Hill apartments in Philadelphia (1964), and Davis and Brody's Waterside apartments in New York (1974). Still, construction did not keep pace with the deterioration of urban districts. It was by no means certain that 1980 would see the inner city flourish. Years after the Lincoln Center for the Performing Arts (1959–68) was built, we had every reason to wonder whether the city's population was prepared to support its opera, symphony, ballet, and theater.

Such doubts raise many themes beyond the three mentioned here: America's quest for identity, taste, and urbanity. Yet those three most affected the American architect during the past two centuries. Sometimes he interpreted them one way, sometimes another, but he seemed to work best when he and his client proposed an ideal that society valued. Perhaps the best proposals appear in the buildings Kidder Smith urges us to see. Those he selected make an admirable case for American purpose, quality, and civic pride.

Albert Bush-Brown
CHANCELLOR
LONG ISLAND UNIVERSITY

ORGANIZATION OF BOOK

The three volumes of this guidebook describe the architecture of three geographic regions with approximately the same number of buildings in each: Volume 1—New England and the Mid-Atlantic States; Volume 2—The South and Midwest; and Volume 3—The Plains States and Far West. The states in each volume are arranged in alphabetical order, and each state begins with a map showing by numbered dots the geographic location of cities containing buildings described in that state. The cities are also listed alphabetically and if there is more than one building in a city they appear in approximate chronology. As is explained, the structures which are in boldface in the state indexes are of general interest, whereas the others are more for architects, architectural historians, and other specialists. An index and glossary appear in each volume. Pertinent books and reference sources are listed in the text.

Connecticut

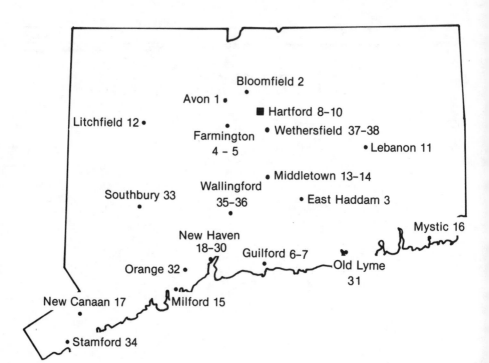

Bloomfield 2

Avon 1

■ Hartford 8-10

Litchfield 12

Wethersfield 37-38

Farmington
4 - 5

Lebanon 11

Middletown 13-14

Wallingford
35-36

Southbury 33

East Haddam 3

Mystic 16

New Haven
18-30

Guilford 6-7

Orange 32

Old Lyme
31

New Canaan 17

Milford 15

Stamford 34

CONNECTICUT

The buildings in boldface type are of general interest. The others are for the specialist.

Avon	1 Avon Congregational Church (1818–19)—David Hoadley
Bloomfield	2 Connecticut General Life Insurance Co.—South Building (1954–57)—North Building (1962–63)—Skidmore, Owings & Merrill
East Haddam	3 **Gillette Castle** (1914–19)
Farmington	4 **Stanley-Whitman House** (c. 1660) 5 **First Church of Christ, Congregational** (1771–72)
Guilford	6 **Henry Whitfield House** (1639–40) 7 Hyland House (c. 1660)
Hartford	See also Bloomfield and Wethersfield 8 Old State House (1792–96)—Charles Bulfinch 9 **Mark Twain House** (1874)—Edward T. Potter 10 **Unitarian Meeting House** (1963–64)—Victor A. Lundy
Lebanon	11 Trumbull House (1735–40) and First Congregational Church (1804–9)
Litchfield	12 **Village Green and First Congregational Church** (1828–29)
Middletown	13 The Honors College, Wesleyan University (1827–29)—Ithiel Town 14 **Center for the Arts, Wesleyan University** (1972–73)—Roche/Dinkeloo
Milford	15 First United Church of Christ (1823–24)—David Hoadley
Mystic	16 **Mystic Seaport Museum** (mid-19th century)

Southbury	33 Heritage Village (1966–75)—Callister, Payne, and Bischoff
Stamford	34 **First Presbyterian Church** (1956–58)— Wallace K. Harrison
Wallingford	35 Paul Mellon Arts Center (1970–71) —I. M. Pei
	36 Upper Campus, Choate Rosemary Hall School (1971–72)—James Stewart Polshek
Wethersfield	37 **Buttolph-Williams House** (1686)
	38 **The Webb-Deane-Stevens Museum** (1752–88)

1 Avon Congregational Church (1818–19)
6 West Main Street
Avon, Connecticut

DAVID HOADLEY, ARCHITECT

The Avon Congregational Church presents an expertly detailed facade
with triple, fanlighted portals, four Ionic pilasters, and well-projected
pedimented front. These are topped by a tower (a bit high) and a delicate, three-stage steeple. Note that the pediment's entablature ties
cleanly into that of the main body of the church, wrapping the two intimately together. The relation of tower base to projected front and to
nave roof is also good. The front is of flush boarding, while clapboards
(replacements after a fire in 1876) enclose the rest. In plan the tower
and entry are now combined in axial alignment, not separate and
conflicting as in many eighteenth-century places of worship (such as
the Farmington Church, q.v., with door in middle of longer wall and
tower at end). Much of this can be explained by the phasing out of the
secular, that is town functions, of the earlier meeting houses, a process
which began a decade or so after Independence and attained legal separation later (1811–20, varying in the New England states). It can also

be argued that "competition" of the churches of other faiths undoubt-edly was an influence on the Congregationalists, successors to the theocratic Puritans. In any case around 1800—which date also corre-sponded with the sharp rise of Unitarianism—the meeting house more and more resembled Church of England examples.

The Avon interior, unfortunately, is not of the caliber of the outside due to changes made in the last century. J. Frederick Kelly in his *Early Connecticut Meetinghouses* (Columbia University Press, 1948) points out evidence that the present pulpit wall once had two windows on each side of the rostrum and a fifth above it, while the pulpit itself (1854) was undoubtedly higher originally. (Edmund W. Sinnott's *Meet-inghouse & Church in Early New England,* McGraw-Hill, 1963, is also highly recommended.)

Open Mon.–Fri. 9–3, except July–Aug. and holidays: apply at office

---

2   **Connecticut General Life Insurance Co.—South Building**
    (1954–57)—North Building (1962–63)
    900–950 Cottage Grove Road
    Bloomfield (Hartford), Connecticut

SKIDMORE, OWINGS & MERRILL, ARCHITECTS

The first Connecticut General Building was pivotal in establishing large-scale corporate headquarters in the suburbs (here 5 miles/8 kilo-meters northwest of Hartford). This complex and the Reynolds Metals Building in Richmond, Virginia (q.v.)—each designed by Gordon Bunshaft of SOM within a year of each other—changed both city and country. (The central business district has now "regrouped" and is fighting back, in many cases successfully.) While Connecticut General is important from a socio-economic-urban standpoint, its ar-chitecture is equally cogent. Of three-story design (with separate but attached five-story executive block) the building represents the early "classic" development of SOM and is carried out with their usual thoroughness, which ranges from overall philosophy of structure (here the curtain wall) to its detailed realization. Its flexible interiors open outward to the countryside and inward to six garden courts designed by Isamu Noguchi. The main building was expanded approximately 50 per cent in 1971 and a low but three-level garage built unobtrusively across the street and cleverly bermed into the site. The North Building, origi-

nally designed for Emhart Manufacturing Company five years after Connecticut General (and acquired by them in 1977), lies directly across Cottage Grove Road and shows graphically the progression of the firm toward more structural expression (especially in concrete). The South Building remains, however, one of the key buildings of its period, while its 280-acre/113-hectare, beautifully landscaped site with red granite sculptured group by Noguchi looks better every year.

A serene detachment characterizes Connecticut General's North Building. Poised on stilts along the brow of a hill amid a well-tended, 100-acre/40-hectare lawn, the drive toward it curves so that the 378-foot/115-meter long building only gradually reveals itself. This introduction is intensified close up by the spatial magnet of the atrium, or entrance court, framed on three sides by an elevated wing of executive offices and on the fourth by the mass of the main building. As all but the central block is poised on stilts, the lawn seemingly flows through, integrating the building with nature. The elevation of the office floor above grade also permits parking for employees under the building, removes an unsightly array of cars, minimizes walking and provides weatherproof access. The towering concrete "umbrellas" on which the office part is supported form floor sections 42 feet/13 meters square. Windows are set back 3 feet/.9 meter from their edge for sun protection—and, of course, for design richness. One of the country's most impressive headquarters buildings. Gordon Bunshaft was, again, design partner in charge.

Grounds and reception area open during office hours

---

3 **Gillette Castle** (1914–19)
State Park
**3 miles/5 kilometers E of East Haddam on CT 82, then 1.7 miles/
2.7 kilometers S on local road**
near East Haddam, Connecticut

William Hooker Gillette (1853–1937) as playwright and actor achieved enormous success both in this country and in England, particularly in the role of Sherlock Holmes. He married in 1882 but his wife died of a ruptured appendix six years later, and, being childless, he poured much of his considerable fortune into this gloriously bizarre hobby house, a building which he himself "designed," and on which he and a cadre of carpenters and masons worked for five years. Obviously

impressed by the possibilities of droplets of fieldstone instead of sand to
construct his castle, Mr. Gillette—who was born in nearby Hartford—
produced a building which, while not of celestial architectural importance, certainly belongs among the lovable foibles. Outside and in, fieldstone preempts the place, even hooding the windows. In 1943 the
castle and its extensive grounds were acquired by the state, and it is
now a state park. Unique, and the view of the river is sylvan.

Open Memorial Day–Oct., daily 11–5: admission

4   Stanley-Whitman House (c. 1660)
37 High Street
Farmington, Connecticut

Its weathered oak clapboarding (restored and now protected by a stain), its diamond-pane triple windows, massive central chimney, and its projecting "framed overhang" with heavy pendants are all typical hallmarks of one of the best-preserved seventeenth-century houses in the United States. This external quality carries over to the inside, particularly in the hall to the right and the bedrooms above. The entire building was restored by J. Frederick Kelly in 1934–35, some rooms to their original three-hundred-year-old condition, while the parlor has eighteenth-century paneling and the lean-to addition contains an eighteenth-century kitchen, kitchen bedroom, and buttery. Roof changes were made with this addition to create a straight line from ridge to eaves and thus give the house its saltbox shape. (A fireproof wing was added to the rear during the late nineteenth century to accommodate additional items of local interest.) The plan of the house embraces its central chimney with two rooms per floor each with sizable (and original) fireplace, a tiny staircase (restored) against the chimney giving access to the upper level. Although the "purity" of the house is somewhat

compromised by its additions—compare the Parson Capen in Topsfield, Massachusetts, for example—the main body of the Stanley-Whitman remains one of the classics of its type. The framed overhangs that are so prominent in both front and gables of the house—as in the Capen as well—stem from the medieval tradition which some feel arose because houses were taxed on the amount of ground they covered. Other medievalists trace overhangs to cramped town lots. (Finances walled up many English windows from 1696 to 1851 [!] because of the tax levied on them. And, of course, François Mansart's [1598–1666] Mansard roof not only provided more under-roof space, it also avoided the tax per floor on French buildings.) The horticulturist visiting the Farmington Museum will want to see the herb and flower gardens at the rear.

Open Apr.–Nov., Wed. and Sat. 10–12, 2–5, Tues., Thurs., Fri. and Sun. 2–5; Dec.–Mar., Sat. 10–12, 2–5, Fri. and Sun. 2–5: admission

---

5   **First Church of Christ, Congregational** (1771–72)
Main Street (CT 10) at Church Street
Farmington, Connecticut

In contrast to the nave-dominant, altar-accented houses of worship of the Virginia Colony (usually of brick)—virtually all of which belonged to the Church of England—the great majority of the late-seventeenth- and eighteenth-century meeting houses of the Northeast were simple, gabled boxes with at times a stair hall attached at the end but often without towers and steeples. In plan they formed a compact rectangle with three doors, the main entry being on the longer side facing the pulpit. This arrangement delivers maximum contact between parson and congregation (as the New Liturgy seeks today). The prominent pulpit was elevated so that the divine could oversee the gallery, which wrapped around three sides. Most of the early New England colonists were, as has been pointed out, anti-Church of England, and their architecture logically and functionally reflects this. Whereas house building —in all the Colonies—closely followed the designs and trends of the areas of England from which the early settlers came, the meeting house, which combined both religious and secular functions (in some cases as late as the early nineteenth century), having almost no prototypes, evolved its own form independent of Europe. Some consider it to be the only "American" architectural contribution until the balloon frame for

house building of the mid-nineteenth century or the skyscraper from the latter part of that century.

One of the finest meeting houses—the third for its members—is this at Farmington on the southwest edge of that comfortable town. The church's relation to its green-carpeted site, the tower's relation to the church, and the joyfulness of light within mark this as one of the outstanding eighteenth-century ecclesiastical examples. The rectangular body of the church bears resemblance to others of a similar size (it measures 74×50 feet/23×15 meters), but the belfry and spire atop its tower (150 feet/46 meters high) are superior, the open octagon of the belfry repeated above and then fairing with a curve into the graceful spire (which was built on the ground and somehow hoisted into place). Towers were very rare in the early part of the eighteenth century, but later on they began to sprout in many New England towns as this example proclaims (many, indeed, were added to existing churches). However, when tower and steeple abut the end of a meeting house—as here—a visual dichotomy is set up because the tower outpulls the main door: where does one enter? It might be said that the Farmington shrine epitomizes and terminates an architectural era, while doing so with uncommon style. For the American Revolution began shortly after it was completed and there then followed a period when virtually no building was undertaken. When matters perked up, financially and otherwise, in the last decade of the eighteenth century, the new plans—under a variety of influences—became distinctly longitudinal with tower unambiguously over and proudly marking the entry, with the result, as has often been said, that the Puritan meeting house "became a church."

The Farmington interior is as rewarding as the outside. Suffused with light, it has been accurately restored. Until 1952 the 1901 organ dominated and almost threatened the pulpit: it has now been put in its correct place, and the whole east wall attended to. Other earlier changes had been made—the Greek Revival portico dates from 1834—but today all is in proper order. Captain Judah Woodruff was the designer-builder.

Open Mon.–Fri. 9–4, except holidays

---

6 Henry Whitfield House (1639–40)
S on Old Whitfield Street at Stonehouse Lane
Guilford, Connecticut

Said to be the oldest stone house still standing in New England, this ancient dwelling carries a suggestion of England's Cotswolds though most of Master Henry Whitfield's Puritan group were from Surrey and Kent (south and southeast of London). Stone was surprisingly little used in rocky New England, for wood was cheaper, easier to work, and offered better insulation. Moreover lime for mortar was scarce. Though what we see today represents less than a third of the original Whitfield House, the dwelling remains a fascinating example. It was built to serve not only as a home but for meeting place and "fort." The outer walls range in thickness from 18 to nearly 30 inches (46–76 centimeters), with most of the ground floor taken up by the Great Hall, some 33 feet/10 meters long and 15 feet/4.6 meters wide. An unusual overhead hinged partition—which was also used to cut the cross draft set up between opposing fireplaces—can be lowered to divide this lengthy room. The wall and giant chimney at the north end, with fireplace almost the full width of the room, are almost all original, as are about half of the facade and part of the east wall. Most of the rest is restored.

Adjoining as an ell to the main room is the Hall or Parlour Chamber and the Stair Hall, while above are three other rooms. The whole is topped by a roof sharply pitched at an angle of 60°. Additions and changes were made to the house by its various owners through subsequent centuries, stucco covered its walls from an early date, fires demolished parts of the house at least three times but it was always rebuilt—the last time under private ownership in 1868. The state of Connecticut acquired the Whitfield dwelling in 1900. An architect of the time, Norman Isham, prepared the building for use as a museum, removing the second floor to make a large exhibit hall, but it was not until the 1930s that the late J. Frederick Kelly, a leading expert in old New England architecture, completed (1937), with a minimum of conjecture, the restoration we now see. The furnishings, some English and some American, cover a time span of well over one hundred years. A fine herb garden is adjacent to the house showing plants that were in common use in the seventeenth century.

Open Apr.–Oct., Wed.–Sun. 10–5; rest of year, Wed.–Sun. 10–4; except holidays; closed mid-Dec.–mid-Jan.

---

7   **Hyland House** (c. 1660)
84 Boston Street
Guilford, Connecticut

Several features of the exterior of the Hyland dwelling are immediately noticeable. First is its ruddy red color which gives it distinction amid so many white examples; most authorities feel that paint in the Colonies

was rarely used before 1700, but when it was, the preferred exterior colors were red, blue, and yellow. White was not employed until the latter part of the eighteenth century. Even interior hues were generally pastel. Another unusual feature of the Hyland House is its chamfered overhang on three sides with the butts of its hewn posts visible. Instead of pendants or drops for decoration we have structural expression. The double-hung windows are neither original nor correct, but the casement central opening on the second floor, which measures approximately 25×14 inches/64×36 centimeters, represents the exact sash which was originally installed: it is a copy of one found in the attic when restoration was undertaken. Double-hung windows were almost unknown in the Colonies until the beginning of the eighteenth century—the Capitol in Williamsburg (1699—q.v.) is generally cited as the first example. The interior with its five fireplaces, the main one 8.4 feet/2.6 meters wide, and with good paneling (some original) gives a sturdy impression with its proper seventeenth- and eighteenth-century furnishings. The lean-to across the back dates from 1720: the house initially had a two-room over two-room plan. It is owned by the Dorothy Whitfield Historical Society.

Open mid-June–early Sept., Tues.–Sun. 10–4:30: admission

8   Old State House (1792–96)
800 Main Street at State
Hartford, Connecticut

CHARLES BULFINCH, ARCHITECT

The Old State House will, of course, recall Bulfinch's Massachusetts State House in Boston (q.v.), designed in 1787 but not built until 1795–97, the time when this much smaller sister in Hartford was constructed. Many of the same basic architectural elements are common to each (but at different scale): brick loggia on lower floor of projected center bay or pavilion, classic portico above, and golden dome atop. In Hartford the dome is vestigial on a small cupola and was added in 1827—possibly not by Bulfinch. And, as in Boston, English influence —here Federalized—is apparent. (Harold Kirker's encyclopedic *The Architecture of Charles Bulfinch,* Harvard University Press, 1969, illustrates this graphically.) Whatever the inspiration the result is skillful. The State House became the City Hall (1879) following the building of the new capitol, then underwent a period of decline when municipal functions moved out in 1915. A partial restoration—which stabilized the

building—was undertaken in 1921. Much of the original interior had been so drastically altered that the restorers had to go to the Boston prototype for details. Then in 1978–79 a complete renovation, including both structural and mechanical updating, took place, spurred and largely financed by the non-profit Old State House Association. (Roger Clark was the architect.) The building now shines brightly, serving as a Visitors' Center and for exhibitions, concerts, and other cultural activities. The chambers for the House of Representatives and the Senate with their Adamesque detail provide its interior highlights: they are as close as possible to Bulfinch's original design. Designated a historic landmark in 1961, it is the nation's oldest state house after Maryland's.

Open year round except holidays, daily 10–5: admission

---

9   Mark Twain House (1874)
351 Farmington Avenue
Hartford, Connecticut

EDWARD T. POTTER, ARCHITECT

Mark Twain's house synthesizes a period of architecture which is only now being properly appreciated. Its Stick Style fancifulness probably hints of the Bernese Oberland in Switzerland, a touch of hill station in Simla, India, and H. H. Richardson and his compariots in the U.S.A. For roughly two decades (the 1870s and '80s) the style gloried in an expression of wood, particularly with structural outrigging, and in a prominent covering of shingles. When structure became more contained and shingles more prominent it was then termed the Shingle Style. Though Edward Potter specialized in churches, primarily in a Romanesque vein, here he persuaded Mark Twain to let him design "a poet's house." After Louis Comfort Tiffany and Associated Artists added their embellishments to the interior (1881), the result became one of the key dwellings of its period: it is indeed a form of Stick Style fireworks. A servants' wing was also added in 1881 under the direction of Alfred H. Thorp, Potter's assistant. Reputedly all of the Clemens family dearly loved and rejoiced in this house, and the care, affection, and money which they lavished on it can be seen today. Note, incidentally, the picture window through the dining room fireplace. Because of heavy personal debts, the house was sold in 1903 (Mark Twain died in 1910), and for a long time was used as a private school, warehouse, apartments, and a branch public library. Threatened with destruction in 1929, it was purchased by friends, but it was not until 1955 that sufficient funds were raised to undertake the complete restoration necessary, including the restenciling of the Tiffany decorations. (In the basement will be found the typesetting machine on which Mr. Clemens lost a fortune.)

Open June–Aug., daily 10–4:30; Sept.–May, Tues.–Sat. 9:30–4, Sun. 1–4, except holidays: admission

---

10   Unitarian Meeting House (1963–64)
50 Bloomfield Avenue, off US 44 at CT 189
Hartford, Connecticut

VICTOR A. LUNDY, ARCHITECT

An extraordinary church both structurally and esthetically. The structural frame, precisely expressed without and within, is based on twelve irregularly spaced reinforced concrete piers that rise from the ground to form an uneven crown. At their top these semitriangular piers are in-

terlaced by a series of steel cables that uphold the wooden "tent" over
the sanctuary. (The selection of twelve radial walls had nothing to do
with disciples or tribes; it resulted from an economic reduction from
the fifteen originally projected.) The interior, which the brochure
describes as "a symbolic and lyrical interpretation of Unitarian faith,"
centers, literally and figuratively, on the sanctuary, over which an inverted calix of wooden strips or gills hovers like an escape hatch to
heaven. This centrally placed sanctuary is surrounded by church school
rooms, offices, and lounge on the outer periphery. As the whole church
is encompassed under the sweep of the one roof, and as the inner walls
of all the outer rooms are topped with Plexiglas, the high central roof
over the chancel—the calix—can be seen throughout. This also brings
to the center of the church a halo of outer daylight, supplementing that
from the clerestory and that which filters through the fantastic web of
slats. A 7-foot/2.1-meter-high wood enclosure encircles the worship
room, lending it preciousness while encouraging spatial flow (and
some acoustic problems). A fellowship hall and classrooms occupy the
basement.

Generally open weekdays: inquire at office

11 Trumbull House (1735–40) and First Congregational Church (1804–9)
S edge of The Common
Lebanon, Connecticut

The quiet and seemly village of Lebanon, which was settled in 1700, has roughly the population today (c. 3,800) it had two hundred years ago. Then it was an important center during the Revolution, being on one of the main roads between New York and Boston. The Common, which lies to the northwest of the village center, presents an unusually lengthy, totally informal greensward decorated with several architectural rewards. The Jonathan Trumbull Sr. House, which the former governor—the state's first—himself designed, is a good early Colonial dwelling which was moved by oxen from the corner to its present site in 1830. Used and misused, and occasionally added to by the successive families which occupied it, it was willed (1908) to the Connecticut Daughters of the American Revolution with life use of the occupants. However, it was not until 1930 that the DAR took possession. Restoration was then begun and the house, except for a rear addition now inhabited by the caretaker, has been taken back to its early design. It was opened to the public in 1935. The DAR also collected suitable furnish-

ings including some Trumbull items which have been loaned or given. The interior is simple and comfortable, while the front of the house merits notice for its neat pediments over both entry and the double-hung windows beside it.

A hundred or so yards away toward the village rises the First Congregational Church (often open, inquire at adjacent hall), designed by Colonel John Trumbull, the governor's son and one of the country's finest artists. This, the colonel's only building, has a unique facade with its deeply inset, ellipsoidal entry between two solid brick sides, each framed by attenuated and attached Doric columns of white-painted brick, the whole topped by a London-inspired steeple. In 1875, following the fashion of the times, the interior was transmogrified into two floors of Victorian obliquity, and there are those who aver that the hurricane of 1938, which caused so much devastation throughout the Northeast, had an especial eye out for this latter-day desecration, for it lifted the steeple and hurled it through the roof of the church, demolishing all except the front end. Restoration was undertaken though not completed until 1954 (due to World War II), but the entire meeting house was rebuilt precisely as Trumbull designed it with proper assembly room and raised pulpit. (The adjacent, overly stated Fellowship Hall dates from 1962.)

House open May 15–Oct. 15, Tues.–Sat. 1–5: admission; church open by applying at adjacent office

---

12 Village Green and First Congregational Church (1828–29)
CT 202 and The Green at Torrington Road
Litchfield, Connecticut

Litchfield, its hilltop location (1,100 feet/335 meters) sparing it the blessings of a main-line railroad and nineteenth-century industrial development, merits its reputation as one of New England's few unspoiled towns, as this Common and church attest. The town was founded in 1719 and platted the same year with Common at center: note that North and South streets are offset, not continuous, defining thus a small green central square. Each of these two streets merits a stroll, for both have buildings (private) of merit. (It must be added that The Green fades away into commercialism at the west end.)

The church was carefully placed to command the uphill approach to the village while its facade proudly holds down The Green spaciously outstretched in front.

The church's exterior is marked by its massing and sharp detail, with good harmony between portico, tower directly behind, octagonal belfry rising above, and conical steeple (restored) atop. It is the three-dimensional merit of these parts which lends the exterior distinction both when approaching from the hillside angle or directly across The Green. The outside of the Litchfield Church has relatives around the state, the closest being those in Milford and Cheshire, designed by David Hoadley. A church booklet suggests that Levi Newell and Selah Lewis may have had a hand in its design, but nothing definite is known about the architect. The interior, though flooded with light from windows on both sides of its longitudinal plan, falters at the sanctuary; centrifugal forces pull the eye from the spidery mahogany pulpit to those corners where the side galleries merge into doors on the chancel wall. Almost unbelievably the church was moved from its original site to one several hundred feet up Torrington Road (where it once operated as a movie house), and a new Victorian edition erected (1873) in its place. When truth dawned this upstart was demolished (1929) and the old meeting house put back where it first sat and restored (1930) to pristine condition by Richard H. Dana, Jr.

Church open daily 9–4

13   The Honors College (1827–29)
Wesleyan University
High Street at Washington
Middletown, Connecticut

ITHIEL TOWN, ARCHITECT

An example of the Corinthian in the Greek Revival era by one of this style's most prolific practitioners. Built as a house for Samuel Russell (it is also known as the Russell House), its airy, powerful portico of six elaborately capped columns—which portico fills the entire width of the building—sets a stately presence. A wing was added in 1860. In this century it was made The Honors College by the university. The well-preserved interior, though now occupied with new functions, still exhibits fine detailing. Talbot Hamlin in his *Greek Revival Architecture in America* (Oxford University Press, 1944) mentions that Town & Davis were the architects. University records—unofficial—state that "It shows that Ithiel Town designed the house, presumably prior to Davis' association with him (which began 1 February 1829)." David Hoadley, according to these records, was the builder.

Main floor area open Mon.–Fri. 9–5, during school year

14 Center for the Arts (1972–73)
Wesleyan University
Wyllys Avenue
Middletown, Connecticut

KEVIN ROCHE/JOHN DINKELOO & ASSOCIATES, ARCHITECTS

The small (c. 2,400 students), selective, handsomely endowed Wesleyan possesses one of the most complete art complexes in the country, housing art studios, drama, cinema, and music in a series of eleven buildings or pavilions that solemnly step along the tree-lined campus edge. Each unit rises as a limestone cubic box linked in sequence by a limestone wall, its parade of cropped white forms suggesting an Appian Way for the arts. These sedate exercises in solid geometry march in procession from the partially underground 548-seat theater at the top of the mall to the Recital and Gamelan halls along Wyllys Avenue. There is little spontaneous greeting or invitation to enter, but they exert a finely tuned and subtle group suggestive in spatial rhythm of Jefferson's pavilions at the University of Virginia (q.v.). The Wesleyan Center is possibly even more Classical than Mr. Jefferson's. The interiors of the theater and the art gallery are particularly fine.

Gallery open daily 12–4 during school year, theater and recital hall as programmed

15   First United Church of Christ, Congregational (1823–24)
West Main and West River Streets
Milford, Connecticut

DAVID HOADLEY, ARCHITECT

The First United Church of Christ, Congregational, bears striking similarity to the Congregational Church in Avon by the same architect. Being several years later in design, it shows a bit more sophistication, the chief difference lying in the fact that the Milford example has a portico of freestanding Ionic columns, instead of pilasters as at Avon, and

a tower with clocks on three sides versus a single false window on the earlier. The meeting houses at Cheshire and Litchfield (q.v.) are also similar, but the Milford steeple is better. Exterior detailing matches and at times exceeds that at Avon in its delicacy, the former being, in effect, a refinement of the earlier. Note, for instance, the fanlights over the Milford portals and the alternate louvered openings on the second stage of the belfry. The interior is not as satisfactory. A 15-foot/4.6-meter extension was made in 1868 with more recent modifications to the original design—points for which we cannot blame Mr. Hoadley.

Open Mon.–Fri. 9–12:30, 1:30–4, except holidays

---

16   Mystic Seaport Museum (mid-19th century)
Greenmanville Avenue (CT 27), c. 1 mile/1.6 kilometers S of IS 95
Mystic, Connecticut

Mystic Seaport Museum establishes a superb re-creation of the Age of Sail and the town that supported it. The early and middle nineteenth century provided the first peaceful period in which the stripling United States met Europe on its own terms (the sea) and conquered it both in commerce (the famous clipper ships) and in sport (America's Cup with the *America* vs. *Aurora* et al. in 1851). Based on sail and its chief commercial enterprise—the whaling industry which this country once dominated—the Seaport creates with admirable fidelity the architectural backup which made whaling possible and whaling towns intriguing. It captures the atmosphere of both land and sea with a village of appropriate land units that then introduce us to its water-borne delights, two major ships and over two hundred smaller vessels including the famous *Charles W. Morgan,* launched in 1841, the only surviving sailing whaler. (One obtains a new appreciation of *Moby Dick* by examining the *Morgan's* functionally crowded decks.) Most of the buildings were moved to this site from nearby towns and seaports. They range from the utilitarian (the 250-foot/76-meter-long Ropewalk of 1824 and the Mallory Sail Loft of around 1840, etc.) to the filigreed New York Yacht Club of 1845, whose neo-Gothic fantasy was designed by Alexander Jackson Davis (of Town & Davis). Having been moved several times in its career, the building now rests permanently in its third state (New Jersey, New York, and Connecticut). Several dwellings open to the public also merit attention: the Buckingham

House of 1768, the Edwards House of around 1820, and the Thomas Greenman House of 1842. All have been restored and furnished. A large model (in Building #6) shows the town of Mystic as it appeared 120 years ago, giving a good orientation for the visitor. (Unfortunately it is not near the main entry, where it could better serve this function.)

The layout of the Seaport proper, which covers 37 acres/15 hectares, is divided into two basic sections: one, the historic with the waterfront and buildings concerned with servicing ships; and two, a somewhat fractionalized formal museum section where focus is on objects and history. The general public will find atmosphere in the sailing end and historic information in the museum part: both should be seen, for they offer a marvelous insight into a great period of America, its skills, and its seaport allure. Mystic Seaport Museum is no static repository but in summer a very bustling "living" port, and, most important of all, one of the world's leading centers of ship geriatrics, an intensely active and concerned art/science that seeks to preserve for the future the remaining sailing glories of the past.

Open daily 9–5 in summer, 10–4 winter; closed Jan. 1 and Dec. 25: admission

17 First Presbyterian Church (1970)
178 Oenoke Ridge Road (W on Main Street)
New Canaan, Connecticut

PHILIP IVES, ARCHITECT

Starting with an 1899 mansion surrounded by 5 acres/2 hectares of well-treed lawn, the architect has skillfully inserted into this domestic milieu an engaging new church. This is placed sufficiently in front of the house to accommodate a connecting link containing reception area, large practice room, and office. (The house recently served as the church itself and still provides administrative offices and church school.) The new church, built of salmon-reddish brick and dark stained wood outside and in, engages in spirited roof and wall angles. These planes and their massing are also effective on the outside (except for a few awkward moments at the entry). They express a positive religious conviction with no-nonsense clarity, an affirmation as commendable as it is rare.

Within, the ceiling plane at the chancel rises to the left to a dramatic height that stops short of the acrobatic as it admits a flood of light via the towering sanctuary window. Because of the clearly defined planes there is no architectural confinement yet no spatial indecision. Daylight, in addition to that from the tall chancel window, also arrives from win-

dows along both sides so that this key element in church design—natural illumination—is well taken care of. All windows are set in wooden reveals so that little glare results: more depth here would not, however, have hurt. The prominent artificial lights—white metal globes of seven spotlights per unit—are hung from angled ceiling fixtures. The sanctuary is understated yet eloquent with a well-scaled black wooden cross, the simplest of freestanding altars and accessories, and a minimum pulpit topped by an expressive, wire-suspended sounding board. Part of the east sector of the nave is given to the choir and organ, an unusual disposition but one that enables the 60 voices of the choir, being almost in the middle of the congregation, greatly to encourage the singing. This imaginative choir location also encourages liturgical participation from the 560 parishioners alongside. Future plans include a large common room and kindergarten grouped around a courtyard.

To visit inquire at parish house

---

18   The Green and Its Churches (1813–15)
Temple Street between Elm and Chapel
New Haven, Connecticut

The three churches lined up like so many saints on New Haven's Green underscore the stylistic dichotomy in nineteenth-century (and, indeed, twentieth-century) Protestant approaches to the house of God, while delighting us with their serenity amid the moil of central city. Encompassed by today's downtown chaos, this New England common develops a unique contrast of the years. The space and visual peace of the Green are even more valuable now than when laid out—with strict biblical planning precepts and a single church—as the center of nine squares in 1638. It is still the essence of New Haven. (The eight surrounding squares [i.e. blocks], measuring 825 feet/251 meters—roughly 500 Old Testament royal cubits—on a side, were then further subdivided by other roads. Strangely, both harbor and river were almost ignored.)

The dichotomy mentioned stems from the fact that Trinity Episcopal at the southwest end of the Green is neo-Gothic—and one of the country's earliest essays into this style—while the other two, with their more independent (i.e. Congregational) background, are basically Georgian. All were finished within a year or so of each other (1815), Trinity and the Center Church being by the same architect-builder, Ithiel Town.

(As an index of versatility—aided by his library, which reputedly had over eight thousand books—Town became famous with his subsequent partner, Alexander Jackson Davis, for their Greek Revival work.)

The first of the trilogy, **Trinity** (open Mon.–Fri. 10–3, Sat. 10–12), has been so drastically changed both outside and in since it was finished in 1814 that it is scarcely recognizable as the church seen in early watercolors and engravings. Part of the exterior initially was of wood (upper tower, etc.), hence replacement in stone became advisable. However, further liberties, simplifications, and expansions continued through the years. When built Trinity was, as mentioned, one of the first examples of the Gothic Revival in the U.S.A. and Ithiel Town was extraordinarily precocious with its original design.

Ithiel Town's relation to the erection of the second, or **Center Church** (1813–14), as the First Church of Christ in New Haven is generally called (open Tues.–Fri. 9:30–12, 1–4, Sat. 10–12:45), remains somewhat unclear but most authorities feel that Town himself designed the building probably with a plan assist from Asher Benjamin in Boston, to whom Town had been early apprenticed. All agree that he was in charge of construction. The National Register of Historic Places (1976) states that its design "was initiated by Asher Benjamin and completed by Ithiel Town." (Isaac Damon, who had probably worked in Town & Davis' New York office, actually received the church commission.) In any case the results are splendid, by far the handsomest church of the lot. It was called a meeting house for its first few years until the separation between church and state in Connecticut in 1818. Its rich portico and pediment, confident well-engineered steeple (bit of Gibbs here), and urn-topped parapet make this one of Connecticut's finest buildings. The interior—used until 1895 for Yale's commencement exercises—does not live up to the exuberance of the facade, being somewhat tame. Also, it underwent changes and counterchanges with the years while the 1894 Davenport Window in the pulpit wall is simply anachronistic. The crypt with its 135 ancient tombs is, however, intriguing. Its genesis arose through the fact that the present church (the fourth on this same site) not only covers more ground than its predecessor but part of its cemetery as well.

The third of the group, the **United Church** or Old North (open Tues.–Thurs. 10–4:30), was built under the supervision of David Hoadley, who, as seen, also designed a number of competent churches throughout the state. However, the architect of this meeting house remains somewhat a mystery: it is generally supposed that Ebenezer Johnson, Jr., produced the final plan, very likely aided by preliminary work by John McComb in New York and Asher Benjamin in Boston (especially on the interior). Of the same red brick and Federal Style as Center Church, the United Church suffers by propinquity with the richness of the latter. The audience room (i.e. nave), its pulpit wall originally flat, underwent a series of changes through the years.

But see them all. The churches and their Green are an incalculable visual and spiritual asset to the city.

Churches open as indicated plus Sun. morning services

19 Grove Street Cemetery Gates (1845–48)
227 Grove Street at Prospect
New Haven, Connecticut

HENRY AUSTIN, ARCHITECT

This diverting foray into ancient Egypt is a nostalgic example of a little-seen style. Henry Austin (1804–91), who got his start working for Town & Davis (see Index), evolved into a facile designer on his own, establishing, in the process, a long and successful practice. He favored first the Greek Revival when it was popular (up to the 1840s), then espoused the newly imported Tuscan Villa or Italianate Style, ending with Ruskinian neo-Gothic and the Mansardic. These gates represent probably his only excursion into the land of the pharaohs. Measuring approximately 48 feet/14 meters wide×25 feet/7.6 meters high and constructed of red sandstone, their two pylons rightly battered, their columns with reasonable lotus-bud capitals, and the whole topped by solar disc and protective vultures, the gates provide a Nilotic entry to the cemetery. The burial ground itself was opened in 1797, and is locally held to be the earliest in the country to be laid out in family lots. Richard G. Carrott's book *The Egyptian Revival* (University of California Press, 1978) offers an excellent survey of the style.

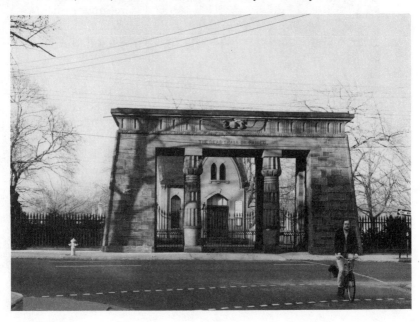

20   Yale Art Gallery (1951–53)
Chapel Street at York
New Haven, Connecticut

LOUIS I. KAHN, ARCHITECT; DOUGLAS ORR, ASSOCIATE

The architectural revolution which shook the Gothic and Colonial mantles off Yale University's conservatism came largely during the presidency (1950–63) of the late A. Whitney Griswold, who died in office at fifty-six. The vitality he encouraged brought many of the finest architectural talents in the country to the campus with resulting buildings (some two dozen) that make Yale a mecca for architects from all over the world. A limited cross section of their work is included here— the process of excellence continues.

The structure which inaugurated Yale's new approach is this four-story Art Gallery—really an addition to Egerton Swartwout's 1927 building—by the late Louis I. Kahn (1901–74). Appropriately, his posthumously finished Yale Center for British Art (1972–77) (q.v.) stands directly across the street.

The Chapel Street facade and entry of the Gallery are quietly stated —the late Philip L. Goodwin's pioneering project for the museum in the 1940s (halted by the war) was more inviting—but once inside Kahn's building excitement begins. The chief impacts come from the flow of space and the intriguing tetrahedral ceiling. The ceiling, 2.2 feet/.67 meter deep (and possibly inspired by Buckminster Fuller's geometric excursions), delivers a marvelously textured, triangulated canopy that hovers over exhibition and work floors. Its alternately open, alternately closed tetrahedrons enable all spot- and down-lights to be recessed yet installed and projected at will (instead of dangling helter-skelter from the ceiling), and also allow the air-conditioning ducts to be laced through with appropriate acoustic insulation above. Equally important, almost complete flexibility in installing partitions is assured, as opposed to many new museums where the right angle is mandated. There is, however, one problem in the Art Gallery: the "busy" diagrammatic ceiling can distract from the works of art. On the main floor this impingement rarely occurs—depending somewhat on the type of exhibition beneath—because the ceiling height is sufficiently high. Here it works wonders. But in the upper galleries where the ceiling is lower, the geometric "pressure" tends to compete with the art below. But linger on the main floor, stroll into the small garden behind: rewards are there. Henry A. Pfisterer was the structural engineer.

An addition containing 2,000 square feet/186 square meters of exhibition space and a lecture hall was added in 1976 (Herbert S. Newman Associates, architects). In 1979 the Gallery was the recipient of the prestigious "25-Year Award" of the American Institute of Architects.

Open Tues.–Sat. 10–5, Sun. 2–5, except holidays

---

21   Yale Center for British Art (1972–77)
      Chapel Street at High
      New Haven, Connecticut

LOUIS I. KAHN, ARCHITECT; PELLECCHIA & MEYERS, SUCCESSOR ARCHITECTS

The architect of the British Art Center had to solve a difficult site problem. He had to incorporate lines of shops on the ground floor so that the museum, as an extension of Yale University, would not preempt a section of two of New Haven's important shopping streets. The handsomely scaled but for Kahn curiously boxlike exterior of pew-

ter finish stainless steel and poured concrete is thus on the quiet side, its 200-foot/61-meter-long inset of dignified shops (which eases the juncture with Chapel Street) adding a note of restrained activity. On entering the Center via the low corner portico, one is greeted by an austere but almost breathtaking four-story-high lobby, skylit and lined with superb white oak panels, with some openings allowing a glimpse of the paintings above. But one is then shunted—under a 40-foot/12-meter-long beam—into a one-story hall containing information stand, checkroom, and elevators, with lecture room and stairs almost hidden behind. This progression into the building is not elating; moreover the location of the art is only vaguely sensed.

The building is organized on a grid of 20 feet/6.1 meters (expanded in the shops and courts) with gallery divisions flexibly based on this. Two courts open up the interior vertically and provide internal foci, a four-bay square at entry and the six-bay Library Court. The latter, also sky-lit, rises three floors on top of the lecture hall. The Library Court displays a fine series of large-scale paintings, as opposed to the purposefully clean-walled entry, but it is marred by an intrusive concrete stair tower. (The architects wanted glass here but were overruled by the fire marshal.)

The most satisfactory method of approaching the art is to take an elevator to the top floor (as in Wright's Guggenheim Museum in New York—q.v.) and walk down. All of the galleries are freely adjustable within their square grid division. The fourth-floor exhibition space is top-lit via ingenious truncated pyramids containing square double acrylic skylights with internal baffles angled against direct sun and furnished with ultraviolet filters. The joy of light was one of Lou Kahn's credos, but here, while it has its rewards, for some viewers the geometric cadence of deep pyramids, each topped with bright oculus and each heavily structured, can distract the eye from the art. (It is useful to compare this treatment with Kahn's less insistent daylighting in his beautiful Kimbell Museum in Fort Worth—q.v.) The use of natural light at Yale, including of course some windows, has the additional advantage of imitating the light in the English mansions where the pictures were orginally. This analogy of provenance is carried further in the entertaining, antiformal Study Gallery along the south wall of the top floor; here the paintings are marvelously crowded together in the fashion of the eighteenth–nineteenth centuries.

An unexpected pleasure of the galleries on all three floors can be seen in what might be called the variety of spatial options. One can observe the art at comfortable, almost domestic, range, then find visual "relief" through the rectangular openings between many gallery and gallery-courtyard divisions, and finally enjoy occasional views out. Detailing throughout is impeccable. Benjamin J. Baldwin was primarily responsible for interior design; Richard Kelly was consultant for lighting—particularly the skylights; Pellecchia & Meyers, as indicated, completed the building after Kahn's death (March 17, 1974); David P. Wisdom was project manager. The building, its collection of 1,500 paintings, 30,000 drawings and prints, 30 pieces of sculpture, and some 20,000 rare books were the princely gift to the university from Paul Mellon, Yale Class of 1929.

Upon leaving, cross Chapel Street to Kahn's older Art Gallery (1953 —q.v.)—his first major work and facing his last. Here the dark, reticulated ceiling tends to disappear (particularly in the loftier ground floor), as its spotlights explode onto canvases hung on white walls. The paintings here leap forward, whereas in the Center—as perhaps befits their more domestic nature—they are more "possessed" of the wall. The British Art Center, it should be explained, is as much a research institution as a general museum. See them both.

Open Tues.–Sat. 10–5, Sun. 2–5, closed major holidays

22   D. S. Ingalls Hockey Rink (1956–58)
Yale University
73 Sachem Street at Prospect
New Haven, Connecticut

EERO SAARINEN & ASSOCIATES, ARCHITECTS

Take one gigantic arched "spine" of reinforced concrete 228 feet/69 meters clear span, abut a horizontal concrete arch on either side just above the ground, stabilize them with three guy cables per side, lace the three frames together with catenaries of steel cables 6 feet/1.8 meters on center, and on this lay a wood roof deck. The result is a brilliant tension structure with a plan of optimum shape for 2,900 spectators. Moreover the building's graceful profile makes it acceptable in its near-campus location, where the typical barrel-vaulted rink would not be relished. With chairs in (and ice out) the Ingalls Rink can seat up to 5,000 for commencements and even dances and concerts (acoustics excellent). It is also used by club groups for ice skating on weekends.

The esthetics of entry are worth noting as one moves through low front doors, sheltered under the sweep of the projected roof, advances under the still low lobby, and then confronts the dramatic plenum of

the interior. The rink is set 10 feet/3 meters below the entry level, while the arched spine rises to 75 feet/23 meters above the ice. Precast concrete bleachers envelop the 200×85-foot/61×26-meter rink with maximum number of seats near center line (and with dressing rooms beneath). The underside of the cable-supported, neoprene-covered roof was left its natural wood "boat construction" but with a plaster soffit immediately over the peripheral spectator area for fire protection. Fred N. Severud of Severud-Elstad-Krueger Associates worked closely with the architect in developing the tension structure. Douglas W. Orr was associate architect. Oliver Andrews designed the lighting fixture projected boldly over entry.

Open to public for hockey games: admission

---

23   Married Students Housing (1960–61)
292–311 Mansfield Street
New Haven, Connecticut

PAUL RUDOLPH, ARCHITECT

Fifty-one apartments in five tightly packed units step down a steep site with an imagination that utilizes every opportunity for developing three-dimensional relations. An Italian hill-town analogy might come to mind especially if one looks at Rudolph's incredible early drawing of the project. (All of his drawings show dazzling draftsmanship.)

Designed for graduate students with small children, the site plan places two- and three-story, standardized two-bedroom units toward the center of the lot with two parking areas on the periphery so that no child will be menaced by cars. The remaining open space is tight, the apartments minimal and without sufficient storage, but on the positive side the intimate scale, the utilization of grade, respect for existing trees, and the spaces and walks between buildings—the interlock of solids and voids—are excellent.

Grounds open daily

---

24   Stiles and Morse Colleges (1960–62)
Yale University
Broadway at Tower Parkway
New Haven, Connecticut

EERO SAARINEN & ASSOCIATES, ARCHITECTS

Unlike "Renaissance" buildings whose facades can be grasped from a one-point perspective, Stiles and Morse demand that the viewer move about them to realize their progression of spaces. They do not proclaim their entity, they unfurl it. This space-time aspect—Le Corbusier's "architectural promenade"—can make a stimulating venture, and if the backdrop here appears medieval, this evolved because Saarinen sought carefully to tie his group to John Russell Pope's potent neo-Gothic Payne Whitney Gymnasium tower (1930) at one visual "terminus," with James Gamble Rogers' neo-Gothic Hall of Graduate Studies (1930) rising at the other. A singularly well-scaled conspiracy of four buildings, two old, two new, results via this walkway. The passage numbers among the country's most subtle developments of open-air linear footage. As one walks through this spatial conduit, snatches of towers (old and new) appear above, while at eye level bits of strategically placed sculpture and reliefs, mostly by Constantino Nivola, enliven the *passeggiata*. Throughout, angled walls of stone and concrete (walls made by

dumping loose stones in grout, not laid-up masonry) jump in and out of
sun and shadow. This excursion does not, however, constitute the total
architectural interest; it is only one of them. Each college provides accommodations for 250 students, mostly in single rooms, with master's
residence for each and two excellent dining rooms with a single, underground connecting kitchen. From the exterior many of the students'
rooms seem underwindowed, but in actuality few are (and those mostly
north-facing). The chief student complaint centers on the inadequacy
of commons areas and lounges. Though some observers feel that
Saarinen went too far with his stage-set neo-medievalism, there are lessons here.

Grounds open during school year

25   Art and Architecture Building (1961–63)
Yale University
180 York Street at Chapel
New Haven, Connecticut

PAUL RUDOLPH, ARCHITECT

Whirlwinds of both praise and damnation have been flung against this "furiously ambitious building" (Vincent Scully). Yet both proponents and opponents are right. It stands castle-like on its corner, its seven-story form proudly holding down its urban and campus functions. It is a good neighbor considering the architectural equivocation on several sides; and its great two-story drafting room was, until a fire heavily injured the interior (1969), one of the inspired spaces of its time. However, this emotionally demanding building (with entrance seemingly for initiates only) solved only some of its problems: architecture was dominant and painters, sculptors, and printmakers were shunted to spaces in either attic or basement. Yet the interior, until post-fire partitioning, offered almost electric three-dimensional exploration: it still has powerful moments.

Lobby open during school year

26 Beinecke Rare Book and Manuscript Library (1961–63)
Yale University
High Street and Wall
New Haven, Connecticut

SKIDMORE, OWINGS & MERRILL, ARCHITECTS

Beinecke is sandwiched between the neo-Roman of the University Dining Hall and the neo-Gothic of the Law School: its designer, not unexpectedly, simply ignored both except for cornice lines. The resulting
building, though impeccably chilly—almost arrogant—on the outside
(compare Rudolph's Art and Architecture Building and Saarinen's dormitories), possesses one of the most sumptuous interiors to be seen. It
is actually two buildings in one, an outer shell harboring an inner core.
The exterior "wrapping" consists of four Vierendeel trusses, whose
granite-covered steel grid rests dramatically on four corner bronze
"hinges." Enclosing the walls are squarish panels of 1.3-inch/33-
millimeter-thick marble, whitish on the face but chameleon-like via
their translucency within.

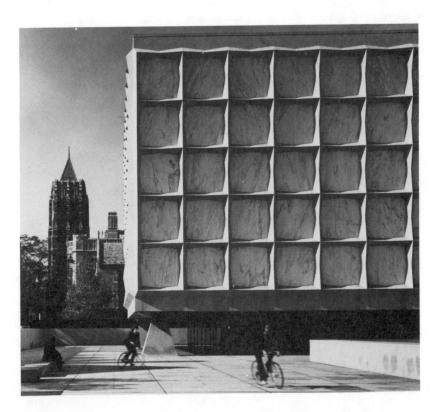

Arising serenely and detached in the middle of the outer box stands a six-story glass cage of rare books, their spines of varying colors creating a gigantic tapestry. This glass showcase lends preciousness to the books, although interestingly enough it was first planned to leave them unenclosed. As the ancient volumes require a temperature of 68° F/ 20° C and a humidity of 45 per cent, the glass enclosure was needed to maintain this index for the books while a less humid one was required for the reading room to keep the marble shell from sweating inside in cold weather. The Vermont marble panels provide a stunning veil around the building, and when the sun moves in the sky and clouds move over the sun the opalescence of the walls comes alive, then subsides. At night the building shines outward. (Onyx had been sought but could not be found in sufficient size—approximately 4 feet/1.2 meters square.)

A second-floor mezzanine surrounds the central shrine of books: comfortably furnished and with separately air-conditioned vitrines for special exhibits along its walls, this provides an excellent spot for witnessing one of our most exciting interiors. Expansion for the library can take place in the excavated but unfinished basement. There are at present some 23 miles/37 kilometers of stacks and over 300,000 books. A sunken courtyard with geometric sculpture by Noguchi gives light to the study rooms and offices grouped about. Gordon Bunshaft was chief of design, Paul Weidlinger consulting engineer.

Open Mon.–Fri. 8:30–4:45, Sat. 8:30–12:15 and 1:30–4:45, Sun. 2–4:45, except weekends in Aug.

---

27   Kline Biology Tower (1964–66)
Yale University
Upper Campus, N end of Hillhouse Avenue (or via Prospect Street)
New Haven, Connecticut

PHILIP JOHNSON ASSOCIATES, ARCHITECTS

The Kline Tower dominates the science (i.e. north) end of the Yale campus both by its own height and its "precinct" hillside location. Its sharply etched seventeen-story-plus-roof-deck profile commands respect on the urban silhouette, yet acts as a good neighbor to the Hillhouse Avenue flow of spaces by standing offset, instead of centric. It is also kind to the fifty-year-old, neo-Gothic laboratories at its feet by

repeating their purplish-brown color. Kline's unusual, highly packaged exterior stems from the thirty-two demi-cylindrical (in places cylindrical) columns which prominently line the building's periphery. These are partly structural columns but within each (except at inset end walls) there is a circular exhaust shaft 20 inches/51 centimeters in diameter which vents the laboratory directly behind. Each lab has a vent hood that can tap into this stack, which then expels the noisome gases above the roof. The architectural expression of these suave shafts, their undulations emphasized by the flat spandrels, takes a potent turn both as monumental cylinders at ground level and as they erupt with rooftop flourish above the working floors. At the time Johnson admitted to being under the influence of H. H. Richardson—"the greatest American architect." (*See* Cook and Klotz's provocative *Conversations with Architects,* Praeger Publishers, 1973.) The second through the eleventh floors of the tower accommodate some 320 laboratories and offices— the number varies, as lab areas can be combined around a central utility core—with a 250-seat dining room and lounge on the twelfth floor, and cooling tower, water tank, and mechanical equipment grandiloquently perch above. The Kline Science Library occupies the lowest floors, with business offices on the second. The building, in relation to its site, and its detailing show the architect's usual fine hand. Richard Foster was associate: Zion & Breen were the landscape architects.

Grounds and reception area open during school year

The architecturally related **Kline Geology Laboratory** (1963), also by Philip Johnson, lies down the hill to the east at 210 Whitney Avenue. (Its half-rounds, however, contain no vents.) Adjacent to this is an admirable parking area, designed by Bruce Adams, with berms and landscaping that render its dreary rows of automobiles invisible from the avenue.

---

28 Knights of Columbus Headquarters (1968–70)
1 Columbus Plaza (Church Street between George and North
   Frontage Road)
New Haven, Connecticut

KEVIN ROCHE/JOHN DINKELOO & ASSOCIATES, ARCHITECTS

Until the Knights of Columbus Building, the skyscraper consisted of a skeletal cage of steel or concrete or both. The bones could be on the inside or the out but they almost invariably necessitated a grid system with a geometric network of columns wrapped by repetitive bays of windows. The twenty-three-story K of C Building boldly broke away, in most respects, from this relatively small-scaled, thickly metronomed skeleton. Instead of utilizing a steel cage for its structure, it employs four mighty concrete cylinders, 30 feet/9.1 meters in diameter, set in a "square" and well spaced from each other, with a concrete elevator core in the center. These five independent structures were then connected to form floors by 36-inch/.9-meter-deep steel spandrel beams that bridge the 72-foot/22-meter space between towers, with secondary floor beams framing into these outside beams and the central core. The cage is gone: there are only five vertical "solids" per floor, the round towers and the square internal elevator block. The towers, which are tangential to the enclosed volume and barely nip the corners of floor area, contain the services: toilets and air conditioning on one diagonal, with fire stair, storage, and mechanical equipment on the other. The windows on each floor (above the third) consist of continuous end-butted ribbons of glass sealed with mastic.

The function of steel in the Knights of Columbus Building is readily grasped from the exterior, for—like Gothic buttresses—it provides structure inseparable from esthetics. The yard-deep main beams that connect the midpoints of the towers stand 5 feet/1.5 meters in front of the glazed walls so that the steel could be completely exposed yet not constitute a fire hazard, a pioneering and ingenious engineering technique. (In virtually all other skyscrapers the steel must be protected against fire by concrete or other casing even though this might also be wrapped in a metal jacket.) It should be added that the piercing of the tile towers by the steel beams at K of C is visually discomforting. The floor beams that frame the center rest their outer ends directly on the large spandrel beams, as can be seen. A horizontal steel sun-screen fills the space between spandrel and outer frame, forming also a platform for window washing. All of this steel is of the weathering variety, taking on a brown velvety color that oxidizes to blackness. With the purplish color of the silo tile which revets the concrete towers, and with the dark bands of window glass, an overall somberness results, but it is an intentional—and effective—one.

Inasmuch as this is a one-organization building, except for the bank on the inset three lower levels, many of the floors become open work spaces without room divisions or high partitions. Thus the resulting sense of space and freedom both within the office area, and looking outward from the offices, creates spatial exhilaration of a high order.

The "para-military" (Scully) statement of the building as a gateway on the cityscape has been criticized as being on the strong side, but Knights of Columbus is full of the traditionally non-traditional ideas which one expects from Roche/Dinkeloo.

Building open to public only by prearrangement

---

29 Veterans Memorial Coliseum (1970–72)
between North Frontage Road and George Street, immediately SE of Church Street
New Haven, Connecticut

KEVIN ROCHE/JOHN DINKELOO & ASSOCIATES, ARCHITECTS; LeMESSURIER ASSOCIATES, STRUCTURAL ENGINEERS

The Memorial Coliseum, an arena for multipurpose entertainment, nests under a startlingly elevated, quadruple-decked parking facility. Two helical ramps (one up, one down) provide automotive access to its aerial garage. Cars not only dash frantically (and conveniently) by on the Oak Street Connector just outside, they drive right through the building itself and, of course, invade its roof. Considering that the midtown road pattern could not be interrupted and that ground-level parking space was unavailable (and underground garaging too expensive because of high water table), the solution of storing cars on top of the arena and maintaining the street layout—plus putting the inside attractions closest to the outside sidewalk—was resourceful. A less difficult site on the far edge of the city would, of course, have been easier and cheaper, but the Coliseum's downtown location was purposefully chosen to revitalize the central business district after working hours. A major hotel, department stores, and shops are all only a short stroll away. Moreover the parking facility, which holds 2,400 cars, could (and does) serve as a much-needed—and profitable—adjunct during the day. A convention hall was included in the initial plans but was eliminated temporarily—its space exists—because of cost.

The resulting structure is not so much a building 560 feet/170 meters long×454 feet/138 meters wide as a staggeringly articulated framework concerned with supporting the massive weight of four decks of automobiles. (Three decks are covered, the roof provides open parking.)

On the interior eleven rows of seats in each of four sections frame the rectangular arena floor. This level lies just below grade with an access-circulation corridor across the top near the seating midpoint. Above this aisle are twenty more rows on long sides and nine on the ends. Truck loading, dressing rooms, and services are located under the main (elevated) floor level. The Coliseum's flexibility enables it to accommodate the usual panorama of sports and entertainments including ice hockey (the rink is also popular for skating by the public), basketball, the circus, orchestras and singers, etc., with a seating capacity of 9,000 to 11,500 depending on use of main floor. Much of the structure and all utilities are prominently visible, the ceiling suggestive of a ship's engine room, with brightly color-coded seats to enliven the mechanistic ambience.

The Coliseum relates closely in color and materials to the Knights of Columbus tower (q.v.) next door, designed by the same architects. The piazzetta on Church Street forms an introduction to both.

Open to public during events

---

30   Dixwell Fire Station (1975)
Goffe Street at Webster
New Haven, Connecticut

VENTURI & RAUCH, ARCHITECTS

To the casual eye this small building a few blocks northwest of the Yale campus might seem routine. There is, however, little of the casual or routine about it except materials. Understatement is manifest but an almost fey touch can be seen in the sign which "peels off" at the right end to proclaim the unity of the two formerly separate engine companies and the rescue group within. The lettering over the apparatus doors sits directly at lintel level. The scale of the four horizontally emphasized doors, of the entry, and of the narrow strip of windows above are all in tension, the flagpole providing the proper vertical catalyst. The buff brick running across the low base (in front) keeps the facade from heaviness, while the rich red brick above, unified with red mortar, acts almost as a banner. Look again.

Can only be seen from street

31 First Congregational Church (1816–17/1908–9)
Lyme Street at Ferry Road
Old Lyme, Connecticut

One of the most elegant churches in New England, First Congregational sets high standards. Colonel Samuel Belcher constructed the meeting house and the contract of 1815 says "That the said Belcher for the consideration hereinafter specified, covenants and agrees with the said Society to build a Meeting House . . . 57 feet [17.4 meters] in length and 47 [14.3 meters] in width." It is almost inescapable, thus, that he designed it as well and "in all respects equal to that of the meeting house in Ellington." Other specifications included "the pulpit and stairs in the style of those in the North Brick Meeting House in New Haven." Unfortunately the church we see today is not the original, which burned in 1907, but as exact a copy as could be made at the time when full documentation was not available. Some liberties were of necessity taken by Ernest S. Green, who was in charge of the reconstruction of 1909. But the overall profile and the imaginative geometry from triangulated portico to balustraded octagonal spire—with circles and half circles in between—are still very fine.

Open 9–12 weekdays: apply at parish house behind church

32 Harvey Hubbell Corporate Headquarters (1966/1972)
Exit 56 S'bound on Wilbur Cross Parkway onto Grassy Hill Road,
Turkey Hill Road, L on Derby-Milford Road
Orange, Connecticut

ORR-deCOSSY-WINDER ASSOCIATES AND BRUCE CAMPBELL
GRAHAM, ARCHITECTS

A corporate headquarters hidden in a woodland retreat which was first
designed (by Edwin William deCossy) for another client. Planned
about a one-story square courtyard, which was wrapped by offices, corridors, offices, and outside loggia, the resulting building created a close-
in-touch-with-nature yet smoothly efficient block. This core was then
almost doubled in size—by Bruce Campbell Graham—for the Hubbell
Corporation. The process was made easier by enclosing most of the 18-
foot/5.5-meter-wide loggia surrounding the original structure, then
adding an executive extension to west and a computer wing at east. A
new elevated road was put in with parking beneath, the metal fascia,
which develops more power but less finesse, added, and further landscaping undertaken. The result is a congenial, functional place to work.
The landscaping of the 165-acre/67-hectare site, first by Marianne
MacMaster and then by A. E. Bye, focuses on a large man-made pond.
It is as sensitively done as the building.

Grounds and reception area open during business hours

33 Heritage Village (1966–75)
off Exit 15 of IS 84, N on CT 67 to Heritage Road
Southbury, Connecticut

CHARLES WARREN CALLISTER, JOHN M. PAYNE AND JAMES
BISCHOFF, ASSOCIATED PLANNERS AND ARCHITECTS

Land usage is the most dismal quality of most housing developments in
the United States. Here southeast of Southbury, attentive planning and
architecture both preserve and take advantage of the rolling site so that
every house enjoys space and views. A 1,005-acre/407-hectare retirement village (minimum purchasing age, fifty; minimum age for permanent occupancy, eighteen) has been laid out in informal clusters of
eight to twelve individual units, most of which are of one-level design.
Each grouping is well separated from those adjacent, with unfenced
greenery flowing between and all utilities underground. A neighborly,
non-structured atmosphere results.

The community is given a strong pedestrian emphasis, placing the
cars in small-scaled auto courts for each cluster of houses. The walking
approach to each dwelling is through a landscaped central court around
which neighborhoods are loosely arranged. All houses—of vaguely
mixed California-New England architecture—are of wood (vertical
Idaho cedar siding and cedar shingles even on the chimney boxes), but
with enough variation to prevent monotony while keeping homogeneity,
and enough standardization of detail to maintain economy of con-

struction. Two thousand seven hundred units are completed. The Village is condominium-owned to cover exterior upkeep of the dwellings and all ground maintenance, plus communal—and safety—facilities. (No owner may alter the outside of his or her house or grounds.) A twenty-seven-hole golf course meanders through the center of the site with a wildlife preserve across the top and a 12-acre/4.8-hectare garden along the Pomperaug River where the residents can obtain a plot and grow their own flowers and/or vegetables (over five hundred have done so). The full range of communal facilities includes a professional building, conference center, recreational facilities, clubs and workshops for men and women, meeting house, library, etc. A 400-foot/122-meter-long bazaar—a covered, multilevel shopping center—is placed near the entry alongside a 129-room inn and theater. The architecture and colorful graphics (by Barbara Stauffacher) offer a tempting invitation to part with money.

Office open 10–6

---

34 First Presbyterian Church (1956–58)
1101 Bedford Street off Hoyt Street
Stamford, Connecticut

WALLACE K. HARRISON, ARCHITECT

The exterior of First Presbyterian is curiously angled, but its 670-seat nave (plus 50 in balcony) envelops its parishioners and visitors in a glorious colored-glass mantle that produces a unique glass experience. Almost the entire body of the church from the floor to the very ridge itself is enclosed by walls and roof made of multicolored pieces of glass set in 152 precast concrete panels (which also form the supporting structure). The effect of the sun shining through these 22,000 chunks of 1-inch/25-millimeter-thick betonglass is stunning. As the glass is faceted (on its inner face), the moving sun brings some elements to intense life that dart jeweled rays into the building while others fade to shine again later, an effect observable in motion when one walks down the nave and the colors pulsate with every step. Gabriel Loire of France, working in close cooperation with the architect and his overall design, produced the glass with eighty-seven colors, and although there is abstruse symbolism in each of its sections (for example, the Crucifixion on right when entering, Resurrection at left), one's enjoyment of this multicolored canopy is not impaired by not knowing about

it. (A folder giving an explanation of the symbolism is available at the church.) A few details are questionable, and the plan might be too attenuated for liturgical intimacy, but the nave of the First Presbyterian is highly moving. Sherwood, Mills & Smith were associate architects, with Willis N. Mills partner-in-charge of both church and the adjacent educational complex. Felix J. Samuely was consulting engineer; Bolt, Beranek & Newman, acoustic consultants.

Open daily 9–5

---

35   Paul Mellon Arts Center (1970–71)
Choate Rosemary Hall School
Christian Street
Wallingford, Connecticut

I. M. PEI & PARTNERS, ARCHITECTS

Linkage architecture or "the linear conquest of space" is one of the functions of the Mellon Center. The two-part Center acts as a staging point between the old and new sections of the Choate Rosemary Hall campus. Besides this conjunctional campus function, the Mellon building comprises theater, gallery, and instructional unit, making possible a wide range of curriculum offerings in the visual and performing arts.

The main theater, which accommodates 400 to 840, depending on type of production, flexibly provides for both theatrical productions and concerts, its curved outside wall and lobby reflecting the rows of seats within. The glass-enclosed art gallery opposite provides an animated exhibition space and lounge that tempts all who parade by this nexus to stop in. With open balcony and floods of light from its glazed roof, the building encourages both art and camaraderie. A small experimental theater is placed in its basement, with studios and seminar rooms above. Overall the Arts Center is good when one is static, stimulating when one moves in, by, and through. George C. Izenour was theater consultant.

Gallery open Tues.–Sat. 10–5, Sun. 2–5, when school is in session, theater during performances

---

36 Upper Campus (1971–72)
Choate Rosemary Hall School
Christian Street
Wallingford, Connecticut

JAMES STEWART POLSHEK, ARCHITECT

When Rosemary Hall moved to Wallingford to coordinate with Choate, the well-known preparatory school for boys, it needed a new, complete, and adjacent campus. The site chosen occupies a hilltop overlooking

the "old" Choate campus and is "connected" to it by a path which bisects the Paul Mellon Arts Center. The architect divided the Rosemary buildings into two groups with administration and school functions forming one cluster and the dormitories, symbolically detached, another, each following the changing contours of the hillside and each almost secreted in trees. Administration building, dining hall, and classroom block form a near-symmetric central axis as they step down the grade with library on one side and gymnasium on the other, all related by 45° angles. This triangulation continues in the plan of the class block. The open spaces flow easily into one another. The three new dormitories, which house two hundred girls, loosely define a triangular central court with the buildings stepping back in groups of six single and double bedrooms to create a non-dogmatic scale. The classroom block contains the English and foreign-language departments, thus all students, regardless of where their rooms are, traverse the campus once each class day and they have the option of eating in either the old or the new dining hall. All units are of reinforced concrete frame—exposed in the major grouping—and red brick walls with, on the interior, a spritely use of color and well-designed furniture (by the architect). Geometry at times becomes complex (in the scholastic group) but Choate Rosemary can boast of a distinguished new campus.

Grounds open during school year

---

37   Buttolph-Williams House (1686)
249 Broad Street at Marsh
Wethersfield, Connecticut

An illuminating revelation of architectural development in the Colonies can be seen in the medieval Buttolph-Williams House when compared with the sophisticated Webb, Deane, and Stevens houses (q.v.) not distant in space nor overly in years but miles apart in maturity of design and statement of Colonial progress. Buttolph-Williams gives an authentic picture of the primitive dwellings of the end of the seventeenth-century period; the other three show the maturity of the Georgian, though little more than a half century later in time. Altered through the years, the Buttolph-Williams House was rescued from a dismal past, and beginning in 1947 thoroughly restored. When the late pine clapboarding was stripped off, it was found that the 4-inch/10-centimeter overhang was hewn, not framed, its posts rising the full two stories. Sections of the framing of the original casements (which had been replaced in the last

century with large double-hung windows) were also discovered so that they could be properly installed. The chimney and four fireplaces, the usual one per room, needed only moderate repair. The new oak clapboards copy the originals, sections of which were found on the back wall. Note that the entire rear of the house is windowless against northerly exposure, Indian attack, and the high cost of glazing. The interior has been carefully restored and beautifully furnished—the kitchen is outstanding. Even the plastering was carried out with the original formula of clay mixed with cattle hair. The house is owned and operated by the Antiquarian & Landmarks Society, Inc., of Connecticut, an organization which is doing much to preserve the state's historic heritage. In December 1978, a construction account book was found which fixed the date at 1686, not 1692 as previously thought.

Open May 15–Oct. 15, daily 1–5: admission

---

38   The Webb-Deane-Stevens Museum (1752–88)
203, 211, and 215 Main Street
Wethersfield, Connecticut

Wethersfield, some 40 miles/64 kilometers up the Connecticut River from the sea—and today a suburb of Hartford—was the first settled community in the state (1634). Its river location and fertile soil soon attracted land-hungry families—the first from Watertown, Massachusetts—and in a bit over a hundred years it became a prosperous

town and river port. Having been bypassed by the industrialization of the last century, the city today retains—in part—a relaxed domestic flavor of old New England. One of the town's greatest assets is this lineup of three adjacent museum houses from the latter half of the eighteenth century, all three fortunately in the possession and care of the National Society of the Colonial Dames of America in the State of Connecticut. The gambrel-roofed Joseph Webb House (1752), in the center, was the first purchased (1919), and though it is the oldest it is also the most elaborate. Its interiors are particularly fine. The other two, acquired in the 1950s, are administrative "dependents" of the Webb House, which should thus be seen first. The Silas Deane House dates from 1766 and the Isaac Stevens, 1788. All three have undergone very careful restoration and refurnishing, including research into original paint colors, the varieties of herbs, and the design of fences. Be sure, too, to see the privies out back: that behind the Stevens House is family-sized (a five-seater of graduated diameters). Altogether the three houses form a splendid group of Colonial architectural achievement. Each has been designated a National Historic Landmark.

Open Tues.–Sat. 10–4 throughout year except holidays: also Sun. 1–4 from May 15–Nov. 1: admission

Delaware

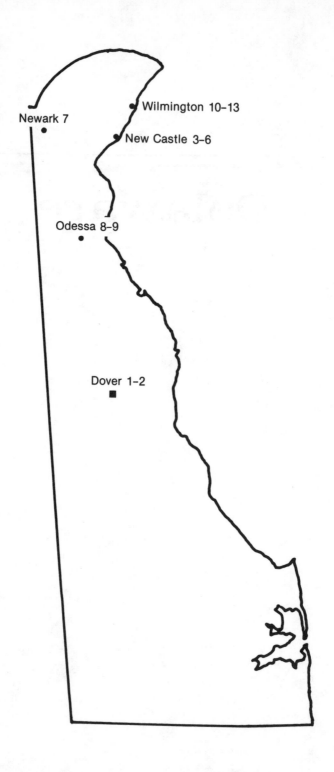

Wilmington 10–13

Newark 7

New Castle 3–6

Odessa 8–9

Dover 1–2

DELAWARE

The buildings in boldface type are of general interest. The others are for the specialist.

Dover
1 **Swedish Log House** (mid-18th century)
2 **John Dickinson Mansion** (1739–40)

New Castle
3 **The Green and Its Buildings**
4 **Amstel House** (c. 1707/1730s)
5 **George Read II House** (1797–1801)
6 Buena Vista (1845–47)

Newark
7 Christiana Towers, University of Delaware (1971–72)—The Luckman Partnership

Odessa
8 **Corbit-Sharp House** (1772–74) Wilson-Warner House (1769)
9 Old Drawyers Church (1769–73)

Wilmington
10 **Old Town Hall** (1798)—Pierre Bauduy
11 **The Hagley Museum Complex** (19th century)
12 **Grand Opera House** (1871/1976)— Dixon and Carson
13 **Garden Pavilion** (1961/1966)—V. and S. Homsey

1 Swedish Log House (mid-18th century)
Delaware State Museum—Building #3
316 South Governors Avenue
Dover, Delaware

Swedes introduced the log cabin into the American Colonies in Delaware in 1638. Strangely such construction, so logical for wood-rich frontier settlements, was either unknown to or unused by the slightly earlier English settlers in the South or New England. (The Swedes were also the first to establish a permanent outpost in both Delaware [1638]—at Fort Christina [now Wilmington]—and Pennsylvania.) The New World Swedish settlers had ample opportunities to practice the building art which they had been employing at home since before Christ was born. (Vitruvius, the Roman architect who lived at the time of Caesar and Augustus, wrote in his *De Architectura,* Book II, about "log cabin" construction in Asia Minor.) After its introduction to the Colonies by the Swedes (and Finns) the log cabin quickly became our "standard" pioneer home type.

The small log dwelling we see here was rescued from the elements and brought to the museum, where it was carefully restored and furnished, providing us with a good insight into the primitive building conditions of the early settlers. The glass in the window may or may

not be authentic: oiled paper or sliding shutters would seem more likely for such an unpretentious house. Note the saddle notching at the corners and the heavy shell-mortar chinking required to weatherproof a structure of uneven round tree sections. (In Sweden and some sections of America, a log building can be accurately dated by its type of corner joinery.) Log constructions, even though they were unspiked, were immensely strong—they often had to serve as blockhouses—and were, because of 6 to 8 inches (15 to 20 centimeters) of wood insulation, warm in winter. Though not evident in this example, the early Swedes often placed their fireplaces in the corner.

Open Tues.–Sat. 10–4:30, Sun. 1:30–4:30, except major holidays

---

2 John Dickinson Mansion (1739–40)
**Kitts Hummock Road, .3 mile/.5 kilometer E of US 113, 5
  miles/8 kilometers SE of
Dover, Delaware**

A plantation built by Judge Samuel Dickinson—a distinguished Delaware patriot—which is noted, overall, for its ambience and, in detail, for the high quality of the Flemish-bond brickwork of the house, where

glazed headers add a bright note to the texture of the exterior walls. The dwelling, which faces southerly toward the St. Jones River, at first consisted of a rectangular box with wide central hall. However, two large additions on the west end were made during the original builder's lifetime, the dining room dating from 1752 and the summer kitchen, with unusual arcade, from 1754. (The main kitchen has always been in the basement.) There are but few windows on the north side (only one and a door in the original ground floor), showing logical grasp of the winter elements in this flat, exposed landscape. A major fire in 1804 destroyed most of the roof and much of the interior of the house. When John Dickinson, the first owner's son, had it rebuilt it was on slightly simpler lines and with a gable instead of (probably) a hip roof. After many years of neglect the National Society of the Colonial Dames of America in the State of Delaware raised sufficient money to purchase the house in 1952 and to present it to the state. The interior was then restored to reflect its more prosperous era, and appropriately furnished. A formal, but theoretic, garden has also been added. A good example of Middle Georgian house and grounds.

Open Tues.–Sat. 10–5, Sun. 1–5, except major holidays

---

3 **The Green and Its Buildings**
Delaware, 2nd, 3rd, and Harmony Streets
New Castle, Delaware

The Green in New Castle and the sympathetically scaled buildings which demark it provide one of the unspoiled enclaves in the United States. It is a square where urban civility makes up for the lack of individual architectural brilliance. Supposedly, the Green was laid out in 1651 by Peter Stuyvesant of New Amsterdam fame. The Old Court House, or State House—this was the state's first capital—faces the Green on Delaware Street; its central section dates from 1732, but there were numerous additions and changes through the years (east wing added in 1802, west wing in 1845, etc.). It is thus more a building of architectural accretion than architectural purity. For years, until 1936, the entire exterior had been covered with nineteenth-century yellow stucco but this was then taken off, revealing reasonable brickwork and an unusual "stepped" belt or stringcourse which runs across the flat arches of the window heads and jogs twice around the corners. The overprominent balcony above the front door was also added at this time. In 1957 the New Castle Historic Buildings Commission took

charge of the Court House and was active in restoring it: presently it is under the care of the Delaware Division of Historical and Cultural Affairs. The nearby Old Town Hall (1823), at Delaware and 2nd Streets, is an unusual building, square in plan, and dominated by the large arcade on the ground floor. This arch led to the wooden market which stood behind the Hall until 1880. The building is now used by the Town Council. The Old Academy (1798–1811), which occupies the northwest corner of the Green at 3rd and Harmony Streets, is a two-story abbreviated descendant of Nassau Hall in Princeton (q.v.). This "formula" developed in the early twentieth century into a semi-prototype of the New England "Georgian" prep school with its projected central bay and pediment, Palladian window, belfried cupola, and symmetrical wings. Planned as a school itself, it is now used by the adjoining Immanuel Church (1705) for parish and community activities.

The Old Dutch House at 32 East 3rd Street lies just west of and down the street from the Academy. Considered by some to be the oldest house still standing in the state—built about 1690—it gives us a semiauthentic souvenir of the several hundred houses built by the Dutch in New Castle before the English captured the town in 1664 and before the latter's culture began to predominate. Its low lines are accentuated, first, by the overhang of its extended roof, and, second, by the spread of its broad, solid shutters. Together with the steep slope of its roof and its large chimney we have a good example of a simple, Dutch-derived dwelling, whose interiors, however, reflect the growing English influence. The house is now owned and operated by the New Castle Historical Society, which acquired and restored it in 1938.

The only buildings lining the Green which are open to the public—other than during "A Day in Old New Castle" (end of May) are: the Old Court House (Tues.–Sat. 10–4:30, Sun. 1–4:30, except major holidays) and the Old Dutch House, 32 East 3rd Street (Apr.–Oct., Tues–Sat. 11–4, Sun. 12–2: admission).

Buildings open as indicated

---

4   Amstel House (c. 1707/1730s)
NW corner of Delaware and 4th Streets
New Castle, Delaware

The Amstel House is so called in memory of New Amstel, the town's earlier name. The dwelling's first-built section, on Delaware Street, comprises the unpretentious wing at the rear, while the imposing, gable-

ended front on 4th Street carries the house's architectural distinction. Note especially the rich quality and relationship of the prominent door and its white-shuttered windows. An unusually bold coved cornice tends to isolate the tympanum. In plan a central hall divides the front of the house into two slightly uneven rooms with the earlier kitchen wing at back. The interior has been carefully restored, after years of neglect, beginning with the paneling in the fireplace, all of the music room or parlor (at right), and extending to the well-furnished kitchen at rear. The house and grounds were acquired by the New Castle Historical Society in 1929 and made into a museum.

Open Wed.–Sun. 11–5, except major holidays: admission

---

5 George Read II House (1797–1801)
The Strand
New Castle, Delaware

The George Read II House is one of the most handsome late-Georgian, early-Federal-Style dwellings in the state. It is set off by its garden on one side and the Delaware River in the front. The property was

acquired in 1975 by the Historical Society of Delaware and opened to
the public the following year; it is still undergoing meticulous restoration on the interior and exterior. The most striking feature of the well-
detailed exterior is the compact richness which is achieved by the
woodwork of the entry and the window above. The flair of the angled
lintels above the windows gives an upward lift to the facade. (The shutters shown have been removed as they were not original to the house.)
Two slender dormers and the captain's walk on the roof (note the
urns) are contained to tautness by the broad chimneys (one doubled)
at each end. There is a slight heaviness of detail in the Palladian window above the entry, which heaviness is in part due to the fact that the
molding which defines the half-round of the upper section is approximately the same width as the molding around the much wider doorway
directly below. On the interior an elegant arched double doorway divides the reception room from the drawing room. The detailing of its
framework and fanlight (by one Peter Crouding according to the pamphlet) is superior. The plaster work should also be noted. George Read
II designed the house himself and supervised its construction. The garden, which occupied the site of a house which had earlier burned, was
laid out in 1847. It has been attributed to landscape architect

Andrew Jackson Downing, and has been closely reconstructed to the original design of three divisions with a vegetable garden at the rear.

Open Tues.–Sat. 10–4, Sun. 12–4, except major holidays: admission

---

6   Buena Vista (1845–47)
off US 13, 1.3 miles/2 kilometers S of fork of US 13 and US 40,
**   c. 4 miles/6.4 kilometers SW of New Castle**
near New Castle, Delaware

An avenue of ancient trees winds up to this house, one of the relatively few major residences in the state which shows influence of the Greek Revival in its architecture. The five-bay central portion, set behind a one-story Doric veranda, is illuminated by sizable windows on both floors. The end walls and a low pediment, or fronton, project above the eave. The wings to the rear and to left are later additions. The house's furnishings are primarily Empire. It is operated by the Delaware Department of Administrative Services.

Open Tues.–Sat. 10–4:30, Sun. 1–4:30, except major holidays

7   **Christiana Towers** (1971–72)
    University of Delaware
    **off DEL 896, .5 mile/.8 kilometer N of Main Street, entry on
      Pencader Drive**
    Newark, Delaware

THE LUCKMAN PARTNERSHIP, ARCHITECTS

The two Christiana Towers dormitories and the commons are handsomely designed, carefully related buildings. Beyond visual pleasures
their philosophy of housing and feeding students then probes advanced
construction techniques. The design philosophy reflects the independence of today's university students, who tend to rebel against the
rigid concept that provides a bed, closet, and desk, with bathroom
down the hall and mandatory eating in one place at specified times. The
provoked response of many has thus been to live off campus (especially
if married). At the University of Delaware, all apartments, whether of
one or two double bedrooms, contain living room, bath, and small
built-in kitchen. The apartments are also individually warmed by electric heat combined with air conditioner. Such facilities would normally

be more expensive per student than a routine dormitory, but this was offset by the towers' completely prefabricated modular construction. As a result the 255 one-bedroom and 197 two-bedroom apartments (accommodating 1,298) are much sought after. (They also provide a distinct architectural attraction for the university.)

The towers, one of fifteen floors and the other of seventeen, flank the one-story commons, the three dispersed over rolling ground. The advanced construction technique mentioned utilizes the British-developed Bison system of prefabricated concrete wall and floor panels. The prestressed, hollow-core slabs measure 8 inches/20 centimeters thick, 8 feet/2.4 meters wide, and 15 and 27 feet (4.5 and 8.2 meters) long. Wiring conduits are run in horizontal, dry-packed mortar joints between walls at each floor, and the only ductwork needed is for bath and kitchenette ventilation. The facade panels are of sandwich construction with white fluted concrete on the exterior, foam polystyrene insulation in the center, and a structural concrete inner face. The prefabricated window framing and spandrels are of aluminum.

In addition to dining facilities, the commons provides rooms for meetings, seminars, and recreation and is arranged so that it and the dormitories can be used as a conference center in summer. The project resulted from a small competition won by Charles Luckman Associates working with Frederic G. Krapf & Son, who suggested the Bison system, as general contractor. Severud-Perrone-Sturm-Bandel were the structural engineers.

Public rooms in commons open throughout year

---

8   **Corbit-Sharp House** (1772–74)
Main Street at 2nd (turn E off US 13 at Main)
Odessa, Delaware

A sophisticated city house—directly inspired by the original owner's stay in Philadelphia. If it seems urbane in its country-town setting it is nonetheless extremely handsome outside and in, the finest Colonial house open to the public in Delaware. The house remained in the family of William Corbit, for whom it was built, until 1938, when it was purchased by H. Rodney Sharp, who meticulously restored and refurnished it with Delaware Valley antiques. In 1958 Mr. Sharp gave it to the Winterthur Museum, which now administers this and the adjacent David Wilson Mansion. The Corbit House presents a refreshingly lively facade, and much of this vitality stems from its details. Note, for

instance, the paneled blinds: the lower four windows which bracket the front door have solid shutters painted white, while the upper five have louvered shutters—which permit ventilation with privacy in the upstairs rooms—and are dark green, a solution as logical as it is handsome (and is seen often in the state). The bold slash of the granite belt course adds a strong accent to the facade which is echoed by the key-stoned lintels and the prominent mutule blocks of the cornice. The end of the house nearest the road is wisely windowless. Four dormers, the two in front differing slightly from the two at left, transfer the eye to the delicate Chippendale balustrade of the roof-deck. The two-story kitchen wing at left was added in 1790, the first kitchen having been in the basement. Robert May, a master carpenter, is credited with the overall design, aided without question by Swan's *Collection of Designs in Architecture* (1757) and *The British Architect* (1745).

The interior lives up to the front of the house. It is well proportioned and discriminately detailed, the upstairs "long room" with its pediments, pilasters, and paneling being the most elegant single chamber. The other rooms, while simpler, make their own contribution. An inventory of the original furnishings enabled Mr. Sharp to approximate the ambience of the interior as it stood almost two hundred years ago. And in recent years descendants of William Corbit have donated to the house some twenty-five pieces of the original furniture. A geometrically laid-out herb garden, designed in 1938 in the Colonial style, extends from the kitchen wing. It, too, is well worth seeing.

Open Tues.–Sat. 10–5, Sun. 2–5, except holidays: admission

Be sure to visit the **Wilson-Warner House** next door, which was built shortly before the Corbit House (1769) by Corbit's brother-in-law (joint admission with Corbit-Sharp). It also is administered by the Henry Francis du Pont Winterthur Museum. Parenthetically, much of the town of Odessa merits a stroll.

---

9   **Old Drawyers Church** (1769–73)
on US 13, .8 mile/1.3 kilometers N of
Odessa, Delaware

A stalwart, squarish Presbyterian church crowning a hill above a cemetery. There is a firmness in the overall proportions and mathematics in the openings of the church which give it distinction. Note the lightly arched lower windows versus the flat lintels above, then the return of cornice at the gable ends. Robert May—of Corbit House fame (q.v.) —was its designer, and for this building it would seem that the simplicity of Quaker meeting houses impressed him. The white-painted interior (to judge from photographs) is as clean-cut as the outside. The church is open for a special service on the first Sunday in June. It is regrettable that the interior thus can be seen only rarely. Old Drawyers is listed in the National Register of Historic Places.

Unfortunately almost always closed but still worth an exterior look. Group tours can be arranged by the curator of the Corbit-Sharp House one week in advance: telephone (302) 378-2681

---

10   Old Town Hall (1798)
512 Market Street between 5th and 6th
Wilmington, Delaware

PIERRE BAUDUY, POSSIBLE ARCHITECT

A superior building fortunately preserved amid a welter of downtown commercialism. It is the city's sole public structure of the eighteenth century. As the Town Hall is set back from the street one can readily assay the salient features of its facade: the four round-headed windows of the lower floor—with springpoints and keystone accented in white marble against the red brick; the round-headed door, which carefully does not match the height of the windows on either side; the five unusual marble plaques or cartouches in the belt course; and the rectangular twelve-over-twelve windows. With the refinement of these elements and the accent of the slight projection of the pedimented central bay, a fine orchestration results. Only the cornice of the pediment and its clock seem overly large and out of key. The space of the ground floor, which was formerly the judges' chambers, takes one completely by surprise, for it consists of one great room flooded with light and air. The upper floor is more routine. The building was designed, at least according to Eberlein and Hubbard in their book *Historic Homes and Buildings of Delaware* (Public Archives Commission, 1963), by a French-born, West Indies-based painter and amateur architect named

Pierre Bauduy. Bauduy had come to Delaware with his young wife in 1790 as a refugee from uprisings in what is now the Dominican Republic. This, however, is disputed by other specialists, who feel that there is little or no evidence for this attribution. In 1916 the Hall's muncipal functions were moved to a new public building, and the former was acquired by the Historical Society of Delaware.

Open Tues.–Sat. 10–4, except holidays and Aug.

---

11 The Hagley Museum Complex (19th century)
N off DEL 141 (New Bridge Road), E of DEL 100, and 3
miles/4.8 kilometers NW of
Wilmington (Greenville), Delaware

The Hagley complex centers on a fascinating museum which traces early industrial development of the U.S.A. It also comprises an impressive group of structures concerned with the manufacture of black powder plus an imposing 1803 manor house and ancillary units. The community's wooded site of 190 acres/77 hectares along the Brandywine River was the birthplace of the Du Pont Company's original black

powder industry which was started by Eleuthère Irénée du Pont in 1802. (The Brandywine also powered scores of other non-Du-Pont-related industrial enterprises—papermaking, flour milling, power looming, etc.—along its swift-flowing banks.)

Pierre Samuel du Pont and his son Eleuthère Irénée, having been arrested for criticizing "revolutionary efforts" in their native France, lost faith for their future in that country, and upon release fled (1799) with their families to the United States. There was an urgent need for quality powder in the developing nation for building roads, excavating foundations, etc., and Irénée, having studied its manufacture under the great French chemist Antoine Lavoisier, and later having obtained financial backing and machinery in Europe, set about revolutionizing quality-controlled powder production in the U.S.A. (His up-to-the-minute methods were of great help in the War of 1812.) Settling on this Brandywine site he established the Du Pont Company, which soon

became the nation's preeminent explosives producer, expanding later into other chemical fields as the century progressed.

To mark the company's 150th anniversary, the Hagley Museum was planned in 1952. The three-story, local granite building which acts as the main exhibition structure was built in 1814 as a cotton spinning mill, then later remodeled into a metal keg factory for packing black powder. Upon its total interior reconstruction as an industrial museum —it also had suffered several times from fires—it was opened to the public in 1957. The museum's intriguing series of exhibits, as has been pointed out, depicts much of the development of this country's early industry—primarily along the Brandywine—not just powder production.

Stretched along the river just north of the museum stand the sturdy remains of the twenty-one early black powder mills, once the largest manufactory in the country. They remained active until 1921. Each of these small units was constructed with three immensely thick (up to 6 feet/1.8 meters) walls in a squared-U plan facing the river with the stream-side and roof only lightly enclosed. They were designed in this fashion so that in case of an explosion the water side would receive the blast. The river, of course, furnished the power. At the water's edge in front of the Black Powder Exhibit Building (1858) stand the Eagle Roll Mills. Here, a demonstration via a reconstructed water turbine shows how the force of the stream was transmitted to move the 10-ton, cast-iron wheels which pulverized the saltpeter, sulphur, and charcoal to make the powder. The restored Birkenhead Mills (1822–24) at the

far end of the twenty-one units show the more primitive wooden waterwheel.

On the hill beyond stands Eleutherian Mills, the 1803 house mentioned, designed by Pierre Bauduy and expanded in 1853 (and donated to the museum in 1958). Nearby are the office (1837), Lammot du Pont's workshop (1858—where several important developments in explosives originated), and a large nineteenth-century garden. All are recommended.

Open Tues.–Sat. and some holidays, 9:30–4:30, Sun. 1–5; closed Jan. 1, Dec. 25, and Thanksgiving: admission

---

12 Grand Opera House (1871/1976)
on the Market Street Mall between 8th and 9th Streets
Wilmington, Delaware

THOMAS DIXON AND CHARLES L. CARSON, ARCHITECTS

Wilmington's old Masonic Hall has been totally restored outside and in as Delaware's Center for the Performing Arts, forming the jewel of the city's new pedestrian mall (1974—David Crane & Partners, landscape architects). The building is a notable addition to the city, its late nineteenth-century Parisian-inspired facade projecting a particularly rich and well-composed example of cast-iron work. Built by the Masons as a performance hall (their offices and recreational facilities still occupy the top floor), there are Masonic details throughout: note, for instance, the eye in the pediment of the central bay. The ground-floor shops, all brightly refurbished, were, of course, part of the original design, as was the prominent filigree of cast iron capping the slate of the Mansard roof. Whereas the exterior needed only a moderate amount of cleaning and restoration, including the recasting of some pieces of cast iron, the interior, which had been cannibalized, also required a complete technical updating, fire protection, and general amenities. These improvements have been done—with the aid of the original drawings—including the replacement of the frescoed ceiling. The 1,100-

seat horseshoe-shaped auditorium is now used by the Delaware Symphony, the Wilmington Opera Society, plus a number of both nonprofit and corporate groups. Grieves-Armstrong-Childs were the architects of the restoration; Steven T. Baird, consulting architect for cast iron; Roger R. Morgan, theater consultant; and Klepper, Marshall, King, acoustic consultants. A fine facility of which city, citizens, and the professionals concerned can be proud. It is listed on the National Register of Historic Places and is a charter member of the newly formed League of Historic American Theatres.

Open for performances

---

13   Garden Pavilion (1961/1966)
     Henry Francis du Pont Winterthur Museum
     E off DEL 52, c. 6 miles/10 kilometers NW of
     Wilmington, Delaware

VICTORINE AND SAMUEL HOMSEY, ARCHITECTS

A multiple-use orientation, lecture, and luncheon center which is the first stop for visitors to the famous museum. Simply but sympathetically designed, it abides comfortably in its 60-acre/24-hectare landscape, not a bush of which was unnecessarily touched. The interior is flooded with daylight from its double-height central bay; the use of natural materials is admirable, and the overall effect is delightful. A 360-seat lecture hall was added in 1966. The problems of landscaping, particularly the handling and screening of a large number of automobiles, have been dexterously taken care of.

It is from this pavilion that one takes a bus, or walks (recommended), to the Winterthur Museum (original house built in 1839). With its incomparable collection of well over a hundred American rooms from 1640 to 1840, each furnished as though momentarily expecting its owner, the museum gives a unique insight into our architectural inheritance. (Open Tues.–Sat., except holidays: admission. Reservations needed for main museum but not Washington wing: write Winterthur Museum, Winterthur, Delaware 19735.)

Pavilion open—with cafeteria—Mon. 8–2, Tues.–Sat. 8–4, Sun. 11–4: museum separate

District of Columbia

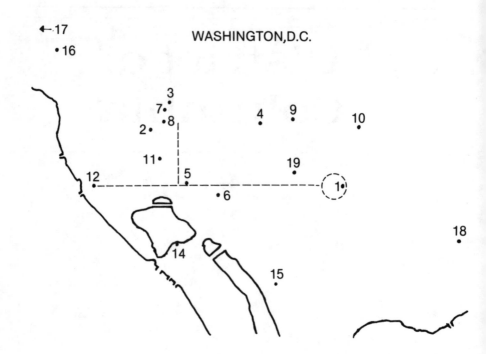

WASHINGTON,D.C.

DISTRICT OF COLUMBIA

The buildings in boldface type are of general interest. The others are for the specialist.

Washington

1 **United States Capitol** (1793–1863)— Thornton, Latrobe, Bulfinch, Mills, Walter

2 **The Octagon** (1798–1801) **and AIA Headquarters** (1971–73)—Thornton/ The Architects Collaborative

3 Decatur House (1818–19)—Benjamin H. Latrobe

4 National Portrait Gallery (Old Patent Office: 1836–67)—Elliot, Town, Mills, Walter, Clark

5 **Washington Monument** (1848–85)— Robert Mills

6 **Smithsonian Institution Building** (1847–55)—James Renwick, Jr. Arts and Industries Building (1879–81) —Cluss & Schulze

7 **Renwick Gallery** (1859–60/1974)— James Renwick, Jr.

8 Executive Office Building (1871–88)— Alfred B. Mullett

9 Pension Building (1882–85)—General M. C. Meigs

10 **Historic Union Station—National Visitor Center** (1903–8/1976)—D. H. Burnham

11 Organization of American States Building (1908–10)—Cret and Kelsey Folger Shakespeare Library (1930–32) —Paul P. Cret

12 **Lincoln Memorial** (1913–22)—Henry Bacon

13 **Greenery and Water** (1791–   )

14 **Jefferson Memorial** (1939–43)—John Russell Pope, Eggers & Higgins

15 Southwest Washington Redevelopment (1959–69)—Various architects

16 **Wing for the Robert Woods Bliss Collection of Pre-Columbian Art** (1963) —Philip Johnson

17 Embassy of the Federal Republic of Germany (1962–64)—Egon Eiermann

18 **Buchanan School Playground** (1968)— Pomerance & Breines and M. Paul Friedberg

19 **National Gallery of Art—East Building** (1971–78)—I. M. Pei **National Gallery of Art—West Building** (1938–41)—John Russell Pope, Eggers & Higgins

1   United States Capitol (1793–1863)
Capitol Hill
Washington, D.C.

WILLIAM THORNTON, B. H. LATROBE, CHARLES BULFINCH, ROBERT MILLS, T. U. WALTER, ARCHITECTS

The United States Capitol—"the spirit of America in stone"—achieves greatness in spite of its oft-troubled and interrupted history (which includes burning). Its Classical influence and its spirit of boldness—even its use of cut stone instead of brick—were of enormous importance in the development of the young country, and the lengthy evolution of its construction is itself fascinating. As Glenn Brown put it in his monumental two-volume *History of the United States Capitol,* "the Capitol is not a creation, but a growth, and its highest value lies in the fact that it never was, and it never will be, finished" (Government Printing Office, 1900 and 1902). Moreover as the father-image of most of our state capitols, it was, of course, seminal.

The construction of the building covered four major and several minor stages. The first step occurred in 1791 when Thomas Jefferson, with President Washington's approval, proposed a competition for a capitol. The winning design was that submitted (late) by William Thornton, a West Indies-born, Edinburgh-educated, non-practicing doctor with an impressive range of interests, including a surprising (for a self-taught amateur) grasp of architecture. Jefferson said of the winning project, "It is simple, noble, beautiful, excellently arranged" and "had captivated the eyes and the judgment of all" (*They Built the Capitol,* I. T. Frary, Garrett and Massie, 1940).

The principal element of Thornton's sophisticated design was a prominent porch with eight Corinthian columns, simple pediment above, and low dome on stepped rings—highly similar to Rome's Pantheon (A.D. 124). But as Thornton was not a professional architect, troubles arose to plague the building's erection, many continuing to the present day. Stephen (Etienne Sulpice) Hallet, a capable French-born architect, who had won second prize, was appointed superintendent of construction and he immediately attacked the technical inadequacies in his rival's plans. He was discharged in November 1794 for taking "excessive liberties" with Thornton's design. George Hadfield, a promising English architect, succeeded Hallet but he lasted only until May 1798. Work, however, continued and Congress occupied one wing (the north) in 1800. Dr. Thornton himself was Architect of the Capitol for

less than a year (1793–94), and the building's construction was managed by three commissioners—of which Thornton was one—until 1802.

Stage Two commenced in 1803 when Benjamin H. Latrobe, a highly trained English architect and engineer, was made Surveyor of Public Buildings with the chief responsibility of completing the Capitol. Though he had some architectural disagreements with Thornton—the two were not friends—these were not serious. Latrobe completed both the House and Senate wings, which at the time were only connected by a covered walkway with no central portion built. He also introduced his imaginative "corncob capitals." Then in 1814 (during the War of 1812) the British burned the building, and the next year Latrobe was charged with repairing what he termed "a most magnificent ruin." As Talbot Hamlin remarked, "The burning of the Capitol . . . was architecturally far from an unmixed catastrophe. It gave Latrobe a free hand in rebuilding much of the interior, while preserving Thornton's exquisite walls" (*Greek Revival Architecture,* Oxford University Press, 1944). Latrobe redesigned the Hall of Representatives (now Statuary Hall), completed the two wings, as mentioned, changed sections of both east and west projected facades, and made drawings for the central domed mass and added cupolas—really low domes—over each wing. However, he, too, encountered disagreements and resigned in November of 1817, dying three years later of yellow fever while supervising engineering work in New Orleans.

Stage Three began in 1817 when President Monroe, on seeing Charles Bulfinch's famous Massachusetts State House (q.v.), persuaded Bulfinch to come to Washington as Architect of the Capitol at Washington. Bulfinch first finished some repairs needed on the Senate and House (Congress moved back into them in 1819), and then constructed the central portion, thus joining the hitherto lonely wings to make one substantial building, the Rotunda link being finished in 1825. Most of the work that Bulfinch designed followed Latrobe's earlier sketches, but when it came to the dome that Thornton had originally drawn up—and which both Latrobe and Bulfinch also liked—Bulfinch was pressured by the Congress to make it higher. This was done with results that vaguely suggest an unhappy compromise between Rome's Pantheon and Bulfinch's own dome atop his Massachusetts State House. Bulfinch also added a front on the west or Mall side that recalls his State House, and landscaped the grounds. The Capitol then entered a tranquil phase from 1825 until the mid-1850s. Robert Mills, who had won the competition (1833) for the Washington Monument (q.v.), became Architect and Engineer for the Government in 1836, his main concern with the Capitol being that of heating, ventilating, and lighting.

By 1850 the rapidly growing country needed more space for its governmental offices, and Congress approved a competition for the Capitol's extension. Though four prizes were awarded for this, the results were unsatisfactory and President Fillmore appointed Thomas Ustick Walter direct (as was his prerogative). Walter designed the two large additions for the House (completed in 1857) and the Senate (1859), placing—with great skill—their axes at right angles to the main axis of the building and connecting them with proper hyphens. Equally important, he replaced the copper-sheathed masonry and wood dome, which Bulfinch had designed, with one far higher and bolder (1855–63). Walter realized that his broad extensions, which almost doubled the building's length—to 725.8 feet/221 meters—and nearly tripled its size, demanded a higher dome to maintain proper proportions. For maximum profile buildup, he placed the dome on a pilastered circular gallery which rests on a prominent column-girt drum. Walter, with Montgomery Meigs his engineering consultant and August Schoenborn his assistant, wanted to build the dome's structure of iron for fire protection. However, as Carl Condit points out, "The only example of an iron-framed dome in existence at the time was that of the Cathedral of St. Isaac in St. Petersburg, Russia" (*American Building Art,* Oxford University Press, 1960). Walter, Meigs, and Schoenborn therefore carefully studied the documentation on the Russian structure and came up with their daring result. They also were highly influenced by St. Isaac (1817–57) in the design of their drum with its multitude of freestanding columns. It should be added, however, that William Rumbold's cast- and wrought-iron dome atop the Old Courthouse in St. Louis (q.v.) "was the forerunner of many similar ones to be seen on capitol buildings throughout the land and predates that of the Nation's Capitol by two years" (National Park Service folder). Rumbold's dome, for which he received a patent in 1862, measures 57.3 feet/17.4 meters in diameter with a height of 42.5 feet/12.9 meters.

The Washington dome, beautifully engineered, consists of two cast-iron shells, a high one for exterior silhouette nesting over a low one for interior scale—the usual concept of the Italian Renaissance. The Capitol dome, while a structural triumph, is for some finicky on the interior, especially the coffering. It lacks the boldness of concept of its hidden structure. Except for a few details the Capitol was finished in 1863 and Walter—in another power problem—resigned two years later. The building remained basically untouched until 1959–62, when the East Front was extended 32.5 feet/9.9 meters. The length of time taken to complete the Capitol is underscored by the fact that there are four cornerstones laid by an equal number of Presidents: Washington—Senate Wing, 1793; Monroe—center section, 1818; Fillmore—lateral extensions, 1851; and Eisenhower—East Front extension, 1959.

Frederick Law Olmsted was in charge of landscaping the Capitol grounds from 1874 to 1892, the work including the addition of plazas and terraces. Thomas Wisedell, an architect, worked with Olmsted on the design of the great stairways and terraces.

Chief among the artists who decorated the interior of the building was Constantino Brumidi (1805–80), an Italian who spent twenty-five years working on the Capitol, most conspicuously in the Rotunda. His fresco entitled *The Apotheosis of George Washington,* which fills the concave canopy of the dome, was very enthusiastically received upon its completion in 1865. Brumidi also began the great 9-foot/2.7-meter-high frieze around the top of the Rotunda. This depicts highlights in the history of the nation from its "discovery" by Columbus (who almost certainly never saw the North American continent), to *Penn's Treaty with the Indians,* planned by Brumidi but finished after his death by his assistant Filippo Costaggini. Allyn Cox completed the frieze in 1953 with a representation of the Wright Brothers at Kitty Hawk. Some of the corridor decorations away from the Rotunda tend to flamboyance and—for some—even malgusto. (Each state was empowered to select its own artists and subject.) And if, as Talbot Hamlin wrote, Statuary Hall is marred "by some of the world's least appealing sculpture" (*Greek Revival Architecture,* op. cit.) they rank as details. Architecturally there are many moments of grandeur in the Capitol of the United States.

Open daily 9–4:30, tours every 15 minutes; closed Jan. 1, Thanksgiving, Dec. 25

---

2 **The Octagon** (1798–1801) **and AIA Headquarters** (1971–73)
   18th Street NW at New York Avenue
   Washington, D.C.

WILLIAM THORNTON, ARCHITECT OF THE OCTAGON; THE ARCHITECTS COLLABORATIVE, OF AIA HEADQUARTERS

The American Institute of Architects regards as its hallmark this chaste early Federal Style building. One of the first substantial houses in the new city, it was planned for Colonel John Tayloe III by Dr. Thornton, who had won the competition for the design of the Capitol six years earlier. During the War of 1812 when the White House was burned, the Tayloe mansion served briefly as the home of President Madison. (Incidentally, the city was not incorporated as "Washington" until 1802.) The brilliance of Dr. Thorton's work can be immediately grasped when one sees how the building dovetails onto its difficult, 70° angled plot. Although the site was open country when the dwelling was put up, the street pattern had already been laid out by L'Enfant. The splayed flat sides of the house parallel the two streets, while the wider front bay breaks out with a near semicircular entry. The commanding result is unorthodox but masterful. (The plan is, of course, not a pure

octagon as one face is arced.) The partially raised porch (eleven steps) leads to a circular vestibule—note fanlight—with dining room at left, stair hall on axis, and drawing room at right. These front rooms are virtually identical in size (they differ by a few inches), measuring 20×28 feet/6.1×8.5 meters. Each has an "inset" fireplace at the far end so that the windowless rear walls could be flush on the outside. The ground-floor room disposition is repeated on each of the two upper levels. Kitchen and wine cellar occupy the basement.

After the death of Mrs. Tayloe in 1855 and the departure of the family, the house was used as a school and as offices, and eventually deteriorated into a tenement. In 1897 the American Institute of Architects, then located in New York City, rented the building—in the process removing ten indigent families—and therewith transferred its headquarters to Washington. After thorough cleanup and repair, the Institute moved in (1899) and found the accommodations so suitable that it purchased the entire property three years later from the Tayloe family who had retained ownership. The old smokehouse in the back and the garden behind the house were also renovated.

With the growth of the Institute from roughly 3,000 members in 1940 to 8,374 in 1949, long-standing plans were implemented and all staff offices were removed from the Octagon (1949) to a nearby office building and limited restoration of the house undertaken. With the explosive increase of members in the 1960s (there are approximately 33,500 today) larger headquarters became essential. The new building —described subsequently—stands on the same property as the Octagon, which, for administrative reasons, was acquired by the AIA foundation (1968). The house was then meticulously restored (1968–70) from bottom to top by the firm of J. Everette Fauber, Jr., of Lynchburg, Virginia, and reopened to the public (1970) as a museum. (The museum was officially accredited in 1973.) The restoration took the building back as near as possible to its original condition, with furnishings from the 1785–1820 Adam-Federal period. The first floor and basement serve as a museum, the second for museum and exhibitions, and the third for staff. The Octagon represents the early Federal Style at its best, with a simplicity of wall statement, a delicacy of detail, and a quiet elegance that evolved as a reaction to the increasingly rich late Georgian Style—and its English connotations. Funds are now being raised to redesign and rebuild the present garden.

Octagon open Tues.–Fri. 10–4, Sat.–Sun. 1–4, except major holidays

Headquarters of the American Institute of Architects (exhibition area open during office hours). One of the most difficult tasks for an architect is to design a building that serves as a harmonious backdrop for an existing historic structure. However, The Architects Collaborative has produced here an example of architectural sensitivity at its best, a well-conceived office block that states its own restrained authority yet does not intrude upon the domain of its graceful Federal neighbor. Historic continuity is achieved, preserving the past while growing to meet the future.

The seven-story Headquarters, completed in 1973, shares the same corner lot and garden with the Octagon, and its architects achieved a deft transition of spaces between the two. The new structure was designed to focus attention on the old and was put as far back as possible

on the lot to open up the space between, thus making a landscaped garden the connecting link. In addition, the curved facade of the office building—which frames its neighbor in a semicircular embrace—the glazing of its two lower floors, and the setback of its top floor to lessen visible height all indicate respect of the new for its smaller, older neighbor. The boldly expressed conference room on the second level is cantilevered on the New York Avenue side to act as a scale transfer and to provide a covered entrance. Red brick, similar to that used in the Octagon and the garden wall, paves the terrace and extends into the new building itself as the ground floor. Two-story, tinted glass with glass mullions makes the interior of the Headquarters building visible from the courtyard. From the first-floor lobby and the mezzanine these walls of glass provide a fine view of the dignified Federal structure outside. The exterior of the Headquarters building is of precast concrete in a warm gray color, with bands of solar gray tinted glass stretching across much of the curving facade. (In 1979, the AIA, a vocal supporter of energy conservation, completed an energy retrofit of the building with the goal of reducing energy consumption by more than 50 per cent.) The reception foyer on the first floor and an open social gallery on the second have public exhibition spaces—open during regular business hours—which play host to various exhibits throughout the year. Besides exhibit space, the first floor accommodates the library and some offices, while the second floor houses the boardroom, conference rooms, and executive offices. General offices occupy the third floor, while the four upper floors are for leasing and future AIA expansion. Two underground levels accommodate the garage and services. Norman C. Fletcher was in charge of design with Howard F. Elkus associate; Knox C. Johnson and Hugh T. Kirley were the landscape architects.

---

3   Decatur House (1818–19)
748 Jackson Place NW
Washington, D.C.

BENJAMIN H. LATROBE, ARCHITECT

A simple but distinguished example of Federal architecture, the two lower floors of which are open to the public. Previously serving as headquarters for the National Trust for Historic Preservation—which moved to larger offices in 1979—the building is now a house museum under the aegis of the Trust. Facing Lafayette Square, which the White House also fronts, Commodore Decatur's residence brings discrimination to the domestic scale of the neighborhood. (Much of the square's frontage, including this house, was once threatened with demolition to make way for two substantial federal office buildings.) The Decaturs lived only briefly in their new home: they left shortly after the Commodore died in 1820 from wounds received in a duel. The dwelling subsequently accommodated a series of legations, congressmen, and diplomats, with the expected changes taking place through the years. In 1944 Mrs. Truxtun Beale, the owner and last resident, asked Thomas T. Waterman to restore the house. Latrobe's original drawings, stored in the Library of Congress, facilitated restoration. On Mrs. Beale's death in 1956, the house was bequeathed to the National Trust. The well-furnished bedroom lies at right on entering, with the study and dining room at left, with the usual dependencies in the back yard. The ground floor was restored to the Decatur era, while the second floor with its drawing room is of the Victorian period, reflecting the tastes and changes made in the 1870s.

Open daily 10–4, except major holidays: admission

4 National Portrait Gallery (Old Patent Office: 1836–67)
F Street at 8th NW
Washington, D.C.

W. P. ELLIOT, ITHIEL TOWN, ROBERT MILLS, T. U. WALTER,
EDWARD CLARK, ARCHITECTS; FAULKNER, KINGSBURY &
STENHOUSE, ARCHITECTS OF RENOVATION

The Parthenon's carefully copied end was the model for the Old Patent
Office's south wing, which was the first section built (1836 and 1840).
Its design is credited to Elliot, who represented Town in Washington.
Mills—who had considerable experience in fireproof building—
directed its construction, using a system of masonry vaults and adding
an elegant central circular stair. Mills also designed the east and west
wings (1849), which were completed in 1853 and 1856 respectively,
under Walter assisted by Clark. Their modifications included increased
use of iron and its total substitution for masonry vaults on the top floor
of the west wing. Clark designed the north wing (1856–67), incorporating iron beams on all floors, to produce a building covering a full
city block with a garden court 260 feet/79 meters long in its center. A
fire in 1877 damaged the top level of the west and north wings, which
were then renovated by Cluss and Shulze, along with the adjacent floors
of the original south wing. This area actually had not burned, because
its older masonry construction—by Mills—had blocked the fire, but
was renovated to make better use of its interior space. Besides the Patent Office, the building housed various bureaus of the Department of
the Interior, and, after 1932, contained the Civil Service Commission.

The south portico had a monumental flight of stairs until 1936, when
they were removed so that F Street could be widened. The resulting
amputation, cleverly camouflaged by rusticating the raised basement,
amusingly makes the present pavilion resemble in principle Thornton's
original design for the center bay of the Capitol. If the General Services
Administration had had its way, instead of just the shearing of the
steps, the whole building would have been demolished in the 1950s to
create a parking lot. However, David Finley, Director (1941–56) of
the National Gallery of Art, with President Eisenhower's backing,
stopped this incipient destruction and the then empty structure was subsequently given to the Smithsonian to house the National Portrait Gallery and National Collection of Fine Arts. Faulkner, Kingsbury &
Stenhouse (now Faulkner, Fryer & Vanderpool) did a superb job of restoring the vandalized hulk (1968) to its original flowing assortment of

inner spaces—from Mills's entry hall and stairs on the south side to the stunning Lincoln Gallery above. In addition to its value as a museum, the National Portrait Gallery shows dramatically that we do not have to tear down every elderly building that might have lost its original purpose. Moderate monies and large skills can convert many of them to rewarding new uses.

Open daily 10–5:30, except Dec. 25

5 **Washington Monument** (1848–85)
The Mall, off Constitution Avenue or 15th Street
Washington, D.C.

ROBERT MILLS, ARCHITECT

Senmut, Queen Hatshepsut's architect, commissioned more obelisks than anyone before or since. However, he probably never dreamed that this polished marble symbol would, some 3,400 years later, stand 555 feet/169 meters high on a green-swathed hill. But what more noble monument to the Father of Our Country? The Washington Monument as erected is superb in its simplicity. It is the least-quarreled-with memorial that one will encounter. However, the purity one sees today was not of the original drawing. Mr. Mills, who won the competition—organized by private citizens—for its design (1833), planned to have an obelisk 600 feet/183 meters high atop a 100-foot/30-meter-high circular Greco-Roman temple 250 feet/76 meters in diameter! (Mills, incidentally, had won an earlier competition for a monument to Washington in Baltimore, one in the form of a modified Tuscan column atop a large base that was also vastly simplified between original design in 1815 and completion in 1824.) The Monument in Washington got off to a slow start because of almost total lack of cooperation from Congress. The cornerstone was not laid until 1848 and its height had only reached 150 feet/46 meters when lack of funds and subsequently the Civil War postponed construction. Moreover, its location at the intersection of axes south from the White House and west from the Capitol (which L'Enfant had suggested) had to be moved 371 feet/113 meters east of the north-south axis and 123 feet/37 meters south of the Capitol axis because of unsatisfactory soil conditions (the Potomac then being much closer). The west-east axis was reshifted by the McMillan Report of 1902 so that Capitol, Monument, and site would align for a proposed major memorial. One hundred years after the Declaration of Independence work on Mr. Washington's needle was again commenced, this time under the direction of Lieutenant Colonel Thomas L. Casey of the Army Corps of Engineers, who found the obelisk out of plumb, necessitating further delays to shore it up and install a 13-foot/3.9-meter-thick pad of concrete underneath. Also at this time, due to the researches of G. P. Marsh, then U. S. Minister to Italy, the height was fixed at 555 feet 5⅛ inches (169.3 meters) to match the usual ancient Egyptian proportions of ten modules of height to one of base, the base line being 55 feet 1.5 inches (16.8 meters). And through

Marsh's enlightenment, Mills's flattish capping was changed to a proper pyramidion, and the "temple" desecration at its base omitted—causing one critic of the day to term the result a "stalk of asparagus . . . the refuge of incompetence in architecture." Mark Twain wrote that "It has the aspect of a factory chimney with the top broken off."

The resulting slender, hollow shaft has walls which taper in thickness from 15 feet/4.6 meters at base to 18 inches/.46 meter at top. Marble facing with rubble masonry fill was used for the first portion (completed prior to the Civil War), and marble with granite backing above except for the last 103 feet/31 meters, which is all marble. The exterior is sheathed with Maryland marble to the 150 feet/46 meters line, then Massachusetts marble for 26 feet/7.9 meters (the earlier not at that time being available), then back to Maryland stone again, hence the mismatched "band" around the middle. There are 897 steps inside plus elevator and entry ramp for the handicapped. It is the highest all-masonry (i.e. no steel) structure in the world; and certainly our finest legacy from Egypt. More sensitive landscaping is needed, but the Washington Monument itself might well be the world's finest memorial in the pure, albeit impersonal, sense. One of the best times to ascend it is at dusk.

Open daily 9–5, except Dec. 25; summer 8 A.M.*–midnight: small elevator charge*

---

6   **Smithsonian Institution Building** (1847–55)
    The Mall, 1000 Jefferson Drive between 9th and 12th Streets SW
    Washington, D.C.

    JAMES RENWICK, JR., ARCHITECT

James Renwick was catapulted into national prominence when at the age of twenty-three he won the competition for the design of Grace Church (q.v.) in his native New York, a church considered by many to be the finest example of Gothic Revival in the country. In 1846, a year after its completion, he was commissioned architect—over a sizable number of firms consulted—for the Smithsonian Building. James Smithson, an Englishman who died in 1829, left to the United States the munificent bequest of a bit more than half a million dollars for "the increase and diffusion of knowledge among men." After years of inexcusable delay the government accepted this, but it was not until 1846 that Congress finally chartered the Smithsonian Institution. (Mr. Smithson's only trip to America was to be in his coffin to be buried in the museum he had made possible.) The Institution's many functions are now housed in a potpourri of scattered buildings, but this whimsical pile—a "red stone castle"—strung along (and intruding into) the Mall, remains its administrative and sentimental heart. The building is "in 12th-Century Italian Lombard Romanesque style"—reputedly the first such in the country—but with hints of the Gothic which launched Renwick at Grace Church. But the rich, red sandstone "medieval

confusion" of the Smithsonian (Horatio Greenough) is a free interpretation of an architectural period which has only recently evolved from ridicule. This was an era when the Victorian taste preferred the complicated to the simple, the picturesque or "artful" to regularity, the variegated to the plain—in other words, a total rejection of the formal Greek Revival period it superseded. The plan, it is surprising to note, is almost completely symmetrical: it stretches 447 feet/136 meters. Nathan Reingold characterizes the Smithsonian as "early Robin Hood."

A fire destroyed part of the building only ten years after its completion (1865), and what we see today was partly rebuilt by Adolph Cluss, who finished the job in 1867. Numerous changes were made through the years, the final alteration dating from 1967–70 when the entire building was mechanically updated and restored (Chatelain, Samperton & Nolan, architects). The Smithsonian is architecturally one of the delights of its improbable period. There is generally an informative exhibition inside (free to public). For Smithsonian Associates there is a Members' Lounge and dining room.

Open daily 10–5:30, except Dec. 25

Be certain to visit the polychromed brick "modernized Romanesque" **Arts and Industries Building** (1879–81—Adolph Cluss and Paul Schulze, architects) adjacent to 900 Jefferson Drive—same hours as Administration Building. The finely engineered dome over its four 56-foot/17-meter-high "naves" and the colorful confusion of the interior spaces hold great excitement, as, of course, do its displays. It came

into being largely because the Smithsonian had been offered many of the exhibits from the Philadelphia Centennial Exhibition of 1876, and had no existing space available. The peripatetic General Meigs was consulting engineer. The entire interior was sparklingly restored (1974–76) for the nation's bicentennial by the Smithsonian's Office of Facilities, Planning and Engineering Services with Hugh Newell Jacobsen architect. The exhibits themselves reflect those of the 1876 Centennial Exhibition.

---

7   **Renwick Gallery** (1859–60/1974)
17th Street at Pennsylvania Avenue
Washington, D.C.

JAMES RENWICK, JR., ARCHITECT

The facade of the Renwick is one of the most exuberant of its Second Empire period—and its first example of consequence in the United States. It is also probably the first building in the U.S.A. to be designed as a museum. The skill evident in this rich and assured structure can be seen on the exterior by the power buildup. This is evident in the prominent curved Mansard roof of the central pavilion versus the small straight-sided flanking Mansards, and in the emphasis of the pedimented entry bay where paired, freestanding "Corinthian" columns

(with corn motif capitals) are used instead of the flat corner pilasters on the second floor. (A facade influence of the Paris Louvre has been noticed by most historians.)

On entering one pushes open the etched glass front doors (restored) and marches straight up red-carpeted stairs to the Grand Salon. This sedate chamber, top-lit best to show its pictures, offers an imposing background for the art on its mulberry walls. Originally built to house the collection of William W. Corcoran, the gallery was used as a warehouse during and after the Civil War (1861–69), and it was not fully restored and formally opened to the public until 1874. In 1897, Mr. Corcoran's collection having outgrown its premises (he built the "new" Corcoran down the street), the building was sold to the federal

government. The U. S. Court of Claims occupied it from 1899 until
1964, inflicting some damage in partitioning the major spaces. In 1965
it was added to the Smithsonian Institution's "family of national museums" and full restoration was undertaken (1972) as a public institution. (The windowed entry level, originally the sculpture hall, is
devoted to crafts and the decorative arts.) John Carl Warnecke & Associates were charged with repairing the fabric of the building, including
replacing most of the time-eroded exterior ornament. Universal Restoration, Inc., played a very active role in this. Hugh Newell Jacobsen &
Associates restored the interior in the spirit of its day. They did an admirable job, the American Institute of Architects' Honor Award proclaiming it "a masterpiece of creative restoration." And how appropriate to have the building renamed in honor of its architect.

Open daily 10–5:30, except Dec. 25

---

8   Executive Office Building (1871–88)
Pennsylvania Avenue at 17th Street NW
Washington, D.C.

ALFRED B. MULLETT, ARCHITECT

The former State, War and Navy Building is not open to the public except on official business. However, as its prime architectural attraction lies in the almost palpitating outside walls which encompass this vast pile, much of the building can be appreciated by strolling by. Symmetrically and composedly holding down a whole block with a vigor that would do credit to Europe or America, the English-born Mullett's scale buildup, modulation, and handling of site make this rank high among this country's Second Empire-inspired buildings (*le style Napoléon III*). There are, reputedly, nine hundred Tuscan columns on the outside and 2 miles (3.2 kilometers) of corridors within. Moreover, it is claimed that this was the largest office building in the world when built. (Mullett, who was Supervising Architect of the Treasury Department, 1865–74, also designed the somewhat similar Post Office in St. Louis [q.v.]. In ill health toward the end of his life, he committed suicide in 1890.)

Can be seen from street only

---

9 **Pension Building** (1882–85)
4th–5th and F–G Streets NW
Washington, D.C.

GENERAL MONTGOMERY C. MEIGS, ARCHITECT

Sangallo's and Michelangelo's Palazzo Farnese in Rome (1534) obviously inspired the facades of this aged delight. However, Montgomery Meigs replaced stucco and travertine with 15,500,000 red bricks, and belted the building's enormous girth with probably the longest (1,200 feet/366 meters—and certainly the most tedious—sculptured frieze known to mankind. Its terra-cotta panels by Casper Buberl depict scenes from the Civil War: note even the covered wagons. But whereas the exterior is semiarcheological, the titanic inner court (159 feet/ 48 meters to ridgepole) stuns with a space all its own. Nine Presidents have held inaugural balls here. Eight freestanding Corinthian columns 89 feet/27 meters high—each, supposedly, of 55,000 bricks—uphold the central portion of the roof, their stucco-covered massiveness playing against the delicacy of the rod and wood trusses (which should also be noted). Three floors of offices surround this core with arcaded clerestory crowning the top of the court and flooding the interior with light. Note that the arch motif carries through the entire interior. From

any level the effect is mighty. The future use of this great building is now under a feasibility study to house "the National Museum of the Building Arts." This would be a superb adaptation.

Open Mon.–Fri. 9–5, except holidays

---

10 **Historic Union Station—National Visitor Center** (1903–8/1976)
Massachusetts, Louisiana, and Delaware Avenues NW
Washington, D.C.

DANIEL H. BURNHAM, ARCHITECT

Daniel Burnham was one of the founding architects of, and chief of construction for, Chicago's World's Columbian Exhibition of 1893—an exhibition both famous and infamous for its influence. (Louis Sullivan

said of its neo-Classic architecture, "The damage wrought by the
World's Fair will last for half a century"—*Louis Sullivan* by Hugh
Morrison, Norton, 1935 & 1962.) Burnham's Union Station was obviously influenced in its design process by the Roman classicism of the
Fair that he had had so much to do with, but Burnham also carefully
studied important depots in Europe and saw to it first that his design
for Washington be a splendidly working railroad station. It would be
Classical obviously, but not a building plucked from the pages of ancient architectural history with today's functioning compromised accordingly.

The setting was also designed by Burnham, who with Charles F.
McKim, Frederick Law Olmsted, and Augustus Saint-Gaudens comprised the laudable McMillan Commission (Senate Park Commission),
whose Report of 1902 did so much to shake up a laissez-faire Washington. The Report forcefully pointed out that a full return to L'Enfant's
original plan should be made, and, despite considerable opposition, this
was largely effected. The new station and its plaza relate completely to
the L'Enfant concept, providing a stimulating and immediate view of
Official Washington from the main entrance. Moreover, the reverse is
also true: the building holds down its position with dignity as one
approaches it. (The previous station, 1873, incredibly, penetrated with

its tracks the very Mall itself—at 6th Street—almost at the foot of the Capitol.)

The monumental Burnham facade is dominated by three almost triumphal arches, with statues by Louis Saint-Gaudens on top of its Ionic columns and with long, lower arcaded wings on either side. Burnham's Union Station functioned extremely well, particularly its main terminal level, where canopied platforms along its tracks once led to a 760-foot/232-meter-long (now 630 feet/192 meters) concourse with an airily vaulted roof. Its circulation pattern was spontaneously clear to any traveler. The great, deeply coffered, barrel-vaulted waiting room (now reception and information)—reminiscent of but not a slave to the tepidarium of a Roman bath—provides one of the country's few monumental interior spaces.

With the decline of rail travel the station lost much of its traffic and was remodeled at vast expense (1976) as a controversial National Visitor Center, Aram H. Mardirosian, architect. This provides a "Welcome to Washington" orientation, a Hall of States, two small theaters, information center, and facilities for the tourist. However, in 1977 the Secretaries of Transportation and Interior—in a preliminary report—"have decided that two-thirds of Union Station will be returned to transportation purposes, and the rest will remain a visitors center" (*P/A*, 11:77). Hopefully this will be implemented in 1981–82. This change sagely reflects the burgeoning interest in high-speed rail traffic in the BoWash corridor—and appreciation of Dan Burnham's claim that "this station [is] superior to any structure ever erected for railway purpose" (ibid.).

Open daily 8–8, except Dec. 25

---

11   Organization of American States Building (1908–10)
(formerly Pan American Union)
Constitution Avenue at 17th Street NW
Washington, D.C.

PAUL PHILIPPE CRET AND ALBERT KELSEY, ARCHITECTS

The Lyons-born Paul Cret was fresh out of the Paris Beaux-Arts when called to the University of Pennsylvania, and barely settled there when he and Albert Kelsey won the competition (over seventy-seven other entries) to design this building, which now houses the headquarters of the Organization of American States. The purpose of the structure is to

be "a permanent center of information and of interchange of ideas among the republics of this continent as well as a building suitable for the library in memory of Columbus . . . the home of the American Republics in the highest sense of the word." Cret and Kelsey interpreted this mandate with welcoming scale, and it is their achievement "of stately domesticity" which makes the Pan American Union/OAS Building still so agreeable outside and in. Measuring approximately 160 feet/49 meters square (without subsequent annex), the headquarters (of white Georgia marble) is approached by a short flight of stairs presided over by statues of draped females representing North America (Gutzon Borglum, sculptor) and South America (by Isidore Konti). In panels above are low reliefs by the same artists depicting momentous events in the history of the two continents: among them Washington's farewell to his generals and San Martín's meeting with Bolívar in 1822. Because the patio "was regarded as exceptionally desirable, owing to the important part which courts play in Latin American architecture"— one was even specified in the competition rules—the Washington building centers on a large, lofty, and richly planted forecourt which sets a characteristic entry to the great hall above and the facilities around it. Extensive ornamentation throughout the public areas rewards detail study. Altogether the OAS Building provides one of the more relaxed, less didactic highlights of the Beaux Art School that was to dominate so much U.S. architecture for half a century. Andrew Carnegie provided approximately three quarters of the sum needed to construct it.

Open Mon.–Sat. 8:30–4, except holidays

Many Cret admirers will also be interested in the **Folger Shakespeare Library** (1930–32), 201 East Capitol Street SW, by Paul P. Cret with Alexander B. Trowbridge consulting. (Open Mon.–Sat. 11–4:30, Sun. in summer, except major holidays.) The exterior typifies its early 1930 period with its "shaved classicism," while the Tudor interior contains a beautifully reproduced Elizabethan theater. The library contains some 250,000 volumes on the sixteenth and seventeenth centuries, one of the greatest collections in the English-speaking world.

12　Lincoln Memorial (1913–22)
23rd Street NW and the Mall
Washington, D.C.

HENRY BACON, ARCHITECT

The Lincoln Memorial so epitomizes the interrelation between architecture, landscape architecture, and sculpture that it must not be considered an isolated building, but one that synthesizes a meridian of talents closely working in respectful harmony. And just as the setting of axis, reflecting pool, and built-up acropolis of green ennoble the building, so the building within bows discreetly to the majesty of Daniel Chester French's statue. However, it should be pointed out that this is not a Greco-Roman temple, as often termed, but a rectangular marble box peripherally framed by thirty-six Doric columns. It presents its broad side as its entry and does not have the mandatory Greek gable roof, while the cella, or enclosing, walls rise in a straight projection "through" the embrace of its columns and entablature. The columns do not support the roof in a Classical statement of structure, nor does the entablature frame its eaves. Thus Henry Bacon inventively—many think brilliantly—modified a Greek prototype.

　　The Memorial stands at a spot that was once a swamp, but which at the urging of the McMillan Report of 1902 had previously been filled in from 17th Street to beyond 25th to form West Potomac Park. The Lincoln Memorial Commission pinpointed the building's precise spot (1913) over other proposals for a location near the Capitol or the Union Station.

　　The reflecting pool, recalling those at Versailles and the Taj Mahal.

projects the image, if not the substance, of the Memorial into the Mall, further binding building to nature. Finished in 1923, the pool measures 2,027 feet/618 meters long, 160 feet/49 meters wide, and 3 feet/.9 meter deep. As mentioned, the shrine itself rests on a man-built earth mound. (The importance of the landscaping of the eastern approach to the Memorial can be seen by comparing it to the western side via McKim, Mead & White's Arlington Memorial Bridge—1926–32: the building from there stirs few souls.)

Initially, in a signed drawing dated September 29, 1911, Mr. Bacon proposed to place the building on a rectangular stepped "pyramid" of thirteen steps, each of which he named for the original states. The proportions were so awkward, however, that he used instead the traditional stylobate of three giant steps of 7.8 feet/2.4 meters total height, with eighteen normal risers at entry. The "temple" thus rests on a terrace with retaining wall 15 feet/4.6 meters high, 256.9 feet/78 meters long ×187 feet/57 meters wide made of North Carolina granite. Its twenty-three steps (note slightly darker color) are directly in line with the marble ones above. The thirty-six white Colorado-Yule marble columns which give the building's periphery such chiaroscuro and spatial interaction are 44 feet/13 meters high, and though rumor has it that they represent the number of states at the time of Lincoln's death, the fact is that this happened to be the number which Mr. Bacon rightfully thought architecturally desirable—twelve on the long sides, eight on the short (corner columns being common to each side). Bacon himself wrote "the frieze above it bearing the names of the thirty-six states existing at the time of Lincoln's death": frieze only is mentioned, not columns. The "attic" on top carries plaques for the forty-eight states existing when the Memorial was completed. The listing is in chronological order of joining the Union. (A proposal to add Alaska and Hawaii—additions requiring more than casual changes—was dropped, fortunately, due to the dedicated work of Leslie N. Boney, Jr., FAIA.)

It is interesting to note that the prefluted columns of nine drums each do not stand precisely perpendicular, but tilt in slightly toward the wall, those on the corners tilting 3.5 inches/89 millimeters, the second ones 2 inches/50 millimeters. Moreover, the end columns are closer together than the others—to compensate optically for the bright light usually showing between them—while the two marking the center entry are farther apart; optical refinements reminiscent of the Parthenon. The outer wall, too, has a slight inward tilt. The naos, or "shrine" proper, measures 60 feet/18 meters wide and high, and 74 feet/23 meters deep, and is finished with Indiana limestone.

French's majestic statue, resting in that monumental chair, faces the rising sun, supplemented by a built-in "sun" that artfully spotlights Mr. Lincoln throughout the day and much of the night. (The ceiling is of thin slabs of Alabama limestone made translucent with beeswax. Above it are skylights and a battery of artificial lights.) Though constructed of twenty-eight blocks of white Georgia marble, the chair and figure seem almost monolithic. The statue, incidentally, was originally proposed to be only 10 feet/3 meters high but was later—and wisely—enlarged to 19 feet/5.8 meters. It was carved over a four-year period by the Piccirilli Studio in New York's Bronx, utilizing a 5-foot/1.5-meter clay model from French and assistance by him, and its 175 tons/159 metric tons were sent (1922) in eleven freight cars to Washington. On either side of this main room are less satisfactory chambers, that at left of entry with a plaque with the Gettysburg Address, that at right with Lincoln's Second Inaugural Address (each difficult to read). Their allegorical murals on canvas, measuring 60 feet/18 meters long, were painted by Jules Guerin.

There are, of course, those unmoved by both building—"this white dream of a forgotten Acropolis"—and its setting. Robert Lowell writes of "the too white marmoreal Lincoln Memorial" (*Notebook 1967–68*); some hold the landscaping to be old-fashioned, the architecture a refuge of Classic design, and the statue unimaginatively realistic. Moreover, what is a man of Lincoln's reputed warmth and concern for humanity doing wrapped up in these cold white walls—or do they represent what he was up against? Even Lewis Mumford queried, "Who lives in that shrine—Lincoln, or the men who conceived it?" (*Sticks and Stones,* Dover, 1955). However, such stray thoughts tend to vanish for most when one is wrapped in the magic of Mr. Bacon's creativity. It is unquestionable that this building has added appreciably to Lincoln's position in our history. With gracious thoughtfulness, President Harding, on the steps of the Memorial, presented Henry Bacon with the Gold Medal of the American Institute of Architects upon the dedication of his masterpiece (May 30, 1922). Bacon died less than two years later, deeply grateful for the building's reception and justly proud of the results in which he had put so much care and ten years of his time—contributions far beyond normal professional duties.

Open daily 8 A.M.–midnight, except Dec. 25

---

13 Greenery and Water (1791–   ) Washington, D.C.

MAJOR PIERRE CHARLES L'ENFANT, BASIC PLAN

The Mall provides its informal formalization, Potomac Park spreads its greenery artfully between waters, then ascends its miraculously untouched river, while Rock Creek Park meanders until it blossoms northward. Close at hand dozens of ellipses, squares, triangles, and circles add geometric testament. When these are combined with the prodigality of trees, the infinite trees, and the grasses and unspoiled waters, Washington (in public areas) becomes the country's loveliest city. And when we regard the bowered residential streets of the ancient (1751) port of Georgetown, the numerous lessons of mid-city openness, grass, flora, and shining waters should drive home to every visitor the realization that cities are brutal without man working with nature downtown, midtown, and uptown.

Williamsburg in 1699 and Washington not quite a hundred years later (1791) offer us perhaps the only, and certainly the earliest, urban plans which fixed on a major scale their capital status, with monumental avenues, cross-axes, and terminal vistas and locations for important buildings. Major L'Enfant's greatest contribution in planning the Federal City was that he sought to create an interrelation between town and nature (including the Potomac). Indeed, he thought first not of broad avenues but of parks, "two coordinate axes of parks," which stretch from the Capitol to the Potomac to form, as mentioned, the Mall, and from the White House to the river, with the Washington Monument at their axial intersection. By this the "park" imprimatur—the glory of the city—was set. He then laid out the diagonal Baroque ge-

ometry of the rest of the city, influenced by Williamsburg, by Wren's bold but never achieved plan for London (1666), and by the work of Le Nôtre in France, particularly at Versailles. (The major had spent much of his youth at Versailles as his father was a royal artist.) The theory is herewith advanced that the cross-axial plan of Williamsburg could have been a factor in developing the layout for Washington: Capitol for Capitol, Duke of Gloucester Street for the Mall, William and Mary College for the Lincoln Memorial (here obviously a perhaps questionable hypothesis, as the swamp area had not been filled in), and, on the cross-axis, the Governor's Palace and Green for the White House and its green. L'Enfant's inability to work with others, however, soon caused the word *terrible* to be coupled with his name and he was fired (January 1792); thus only the name of Andrew Ellicott, his successor, appeared on their famous plan later that year.

Although Ellicott, an engineer and highly regarded surveyor, stayed faithfully with the Frenchman's plan (until he, too, was replaced, by J. R. Dermott in 1797), Washington itself, as it burgeoned through the years, did not. There was, seemingly, no real authority in charge. President Jackson had the new Treasury Building so placed (1836) that any expansion would block the view of the Capitol from the White House, while the Smithsonian was allowed to poach on the Mall, and much of the rest of the city simply accreted. In the middle of the nineteenth century, President Fillmore laid the cornerstone for the lateral extensions of the Capitol (1851) (q.v.) and about the same time retained Andrew Jackson Downing, then the country's outstanding landscape architect, to pull together the Mall in front of the Capitol and the grounds around it. Downing's school of "natural style of Landscape Gardening" was small in scale, romantically oriented, and was, as a consequence, in conflict with L'Enfant's broadly classical urban layout. Thus it is fortunate that upon Downing's death in 1852 relatively little of his plan had been put into effect. The Civil War then curtailed all activity.

In 1871 Mayor A. R. Shepherd (also a builder and a part-owner of the Washington *Star*), abetted by C. S. Noyes, another owner of the paper, was made head of the newly appointed Board of Public Works and began a furiously active campaign to spruce up the city with new roads, sidewalks, sewers, water supply, "scores" of new parks, and thousands of trees. Visual "holes" are apparent and scale at times got out of hand, but Washington was enormously improved by Shepherd's efforts until they were halted by the depression of 1873. The Senate Park Commission later took over and its Report of 1902 reestablished L'Enfant's plan and the development of the Mall area—"then no better than a common pasture" plus planning the nearly 1,800 acres/728 hectares of Rock Creek Parkway, whose valley had been purchased in 1890, and the Potomac Park. President Kennedy's Council for Pennsylvania Avenue (1964) currently offers hope for this potentially great street. The National Capital Planning Commission and the Capital Regional Planning Council have already brought out a book on *A Policies Plan for the Year 2,000* (National Capital Planning Commission 1961). But forget the names, the dates, and the incidences, and lose yourself in those lovely sections of Washington which equate nature with man in determining our cities and suburbs. In what other city— here or abroad—can one encounter canoeing, jousting on horseback, field hockey, and polo, to say nothing of minor diversions, on a half-mile walk along the river of a Sunday afternoon?

14   Jefferson Memorial (1939–43)
     S edge of Tidal Basin off 14th Street (US 1)
     Washington, D.C.

JOHN RUSSELL POPE, ARCHITECT, OTTO R. EGGERS, DANIEL P.
HIGGINS, ASSOCIATES

Mr. Jefferson was architecturally enamored with Rome, which he never
saw; Mr. Pope (1874–1937) was likewise inclined (he was the first architecture fellow—1897—at the newly formed American Academy in
Rome). And though the former wrote—as the plaque within states—
that "Institutions must advance . . . to keep pace with the times," it
was inevitable that Pope should turn to ancient Rome as an inspiration for this Memorial, and that that city's best preserved and perhaps
most compelling monument, the Pantheon (27 B.C.), should be its inspiration, as it was with Jefferson's Library at the University of Virginia
(q.v.). However, it would be wrong to dismiss the Jefferson Memorial
merely as warmed-over classicism, a twentieth-century anachronism.
While it is certainly this, it also solves several problems—siting and
architectural—with distinction. (The general site was one selected "for
a great memorial" by the Senate Park Commission—the McMillan
Report—in 1902.) Beginning with the building's subtle projection into
the Tidal Basin, and continuing with its cunning ambulatory that in

Parthenon and Oriental fashion makes one traverse half the perimeter to reach the entry, a controlled circulation with a careful relation between building, land, and water was established.

The architectural element of distinction lies in the fact that the building's Vermont marble walls were designed in quadrants, separated at the four cardinal points, so that from the outside one can see into and through the rotunda, much as one visually pierces some contemporary sculpture. The building and the statue within become in effect welded into a gigantic spatial interpenetration. Inside, because of these same four interstices, no feeling of enclosure—only shelter—attends the visitor. More importantly the interior reaches out to the setting to extend a hand, as it were, to welcome the water of the basin, the trees, and even the distant Washington Monument.

The interior, walled with white Georgia marble and measuring 86.3 feet/26.3 meters in diameter, is dominated by the bronze standing statue of Jefferson, 19 feet/5.8 meters high, sculpted by Rudulph Evans. This height is precisely that of Lincoln (seated) in his Memorial. (John Pope was also asked to submit a design for the Lincoln Memorial, the commission for which was eventually won by Henry Bacon.) On the surrounding walls of the Jefferson Memorial are four well-lettered (and well-edited) statements by the third President: would only that he had been able to implement the one on the wrongfulness of slavery.

The overall diameter of the stylobate on which the Memorial rises is 183.9 feet/56 meters. The colonnade is composed of twenty-six Ionic columns 41 feet/13 meters high with an octastyle portico entry facing the basin. (The sculpture in the pediment is not notable.) The building was dedicated on April 13, 1943, the two-hundredth anniversary of Jefferson's birth. Otto R. Eggers and Daniel P. Higgins completed the architectural design and supervision on the Memorial after Mr. Pope's death.

The Jefferson Memorial was born amid considerable controversy—political (Democrats versus Republicans), economic (the Depression), but most of all esthetic. The Commission of Fine Arts, indeed, initially turned down both Pope's design and his redesign, while the uproar of the modernist against this "applied archeology" was highly vocal though ineffective. Frank Lloyd Wright termed it "Pope's arrogant insult to the memory of Thomas Jefferson" (*Frank Lloyd Wright on Architecture,* edited by Frederick Gutheim, Duell, Sloan & Pearce, 1941). Finally after Pope's death in 1937, Eggers & Higgins modified the original design and this was accepted by the Fine Arts Commission in March 1938, and by Congress in June of that year.

Open daily 8 A.M.*–midnight, except Dec. 25*

NOTE: John W. Reps's *Monumental Washington* (Princeton, 1967) is a highly recommended book on the city's development, as is Daniel D. Reiff's more limited *Washington Architecture, 1791–1861* (U. S. Commission of Fine Arts, 1971).

---

15 Southwest Washington Redevelopment (1959–69)
S of G Street, E of Maine Avenue
Washington, D.C.

VARIOUS ARCHITECTS

The 427 acres/173 hectares of the Southwest Redevelopment were once burdened with slums, largely of wooden shacks with backyard privies—a view of the neighboring dome of the Capitol rewarding the occupants. Though its rehabilitation has been termed "the finest urban renewal effort in the country," to its critics the Redevelopment's plan is coreless, with little urban identity and with inadequate community facilities, while its promising river site is almost neglected. Moreover, its street layout, especially M Street, cuts most of the area into bits. Its plan, in short, was hampered by bureaucracy and the semi-abandonment of overall objectives. The 1959 Webb & Knapp/I. M. Pei plan was far superior, particularly as it tied the Redevelopment closely to L'Enfant Plaza and the South (10th Street) Mall to the Mall proper, an area now also butchered. It is to point out for yet unborn urban renewal efforts the absolute necessity for proper social, economic, and urban goals, a complete master plan, and coordinated architecture of a high level that this Redevelopment is included here as an abject object lesson. It should be mentioned, on the positive side, that several good building groups partially redeem matters: 1) I. M. Pei's Town Center (1962), 512 smart upper-bracket apartments in four identical buildings, two on 3rd and two on 6th Street between I and M. 2) Harry Weese's Arena Stage (1961), directly across the street. Neatly expressed on the outside, it features prominent mechanics over its four-sided theater-in-the-square auditorium of 752 seats. Weese's Arena Stage II, or Kreeger Theater (1970), ties directly onto the lobby of the earlier complex, and in plan forms a quarter circle with ten rows of seats in orchestra and five in balcony to accommodate 500. 3) Tiber Island Apartments (1965), 4th and N streets, by Keyes, Lethbridge & Condon; ingenious combination of 4 eight-story apartments containing 368 units, intermixed with 85 two- and three-story row houses. Care-

fully related to each other and to the central plaza and pool, and with garaging underneath, they form a top-flight group, weighted only by heavy-seeming balconies. 4) Harbour Square (1966), 4th Street at N, by Chloethiel Woodard Smith & Associates, a high-rise (420 units) and row house group facing the river and cleverly incorporating several ancient residences.

16 Wing for the Robert Woods Bliss Collection of Pre-Columbian Art
(1963)
Dumbarton Oaks
1703 32nd Street NW
Washington, D.C.

PHILIP JOHNSON, ARCHITECT

This wing of the Dumbarton Oaks collections is a showcase for small, exquisite pre-Columbian objects (many of gold), hence wall space becomes secondary to atmosphere. With this program in mind, Philip Johnson designed a setting of intimacy which is almost more precious than the exhibits. The basic plan consists of eight interconnected tholoi, or cylindrical chambers, geometrically interlocked about an open fountain court. The spaces of these eight "rooms" flow down their axes and across the diagonal of the court so that one has visual relief and freedom from confinement. Moreover, this "escape" is intensified outward into the gardens through floor-to-ceiling windows. Each of the eight "pavilions," which are 25 feet/7.6 meters in diameter, is supported by eight marble-revetted columns, capped with bronze, which alternate with curved plate glass panels. The carefully laid sunburst floor is of teak. The ceilings are slightly domical within, but prominently so on the exterior—appropriate for a structure attached to a Byzantine Research Center. (It should be mentioned that a minor acoustic reverberation

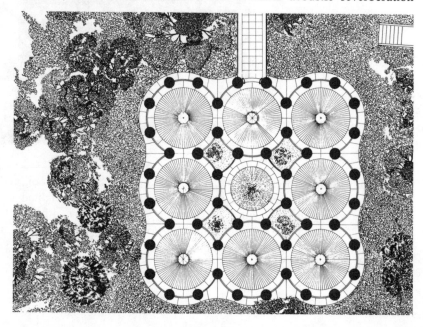

problem results under these domes.) The objects on display are shown in freestanding Lucite and Plexiglas cases which enable one to inspect them from all sides. Though the building tends to make these containers "incidental," and even to dominate them and their objects, it does create a sumptuous ambience even if it has been termed more of a "garden pavilion" than an art gallery. This is probably the most superbly detailed and maintained building of our time.

Open daily except Mon. 2–5; closed July–Labor Day

---

17   Embassy of the Federal Republic of Germany (1962–64)
4645 Reservoir Road NW
Washington, D.C.

EGON EIERMANN, ARCHITECT

The Embassy of the Federal Republic of Germany by the late Professor Eiermann is probably the only diplomatic building of contemporary architectural consequence in the U.S.A. Instead of being hindered by a sharply sloping, narrow site—plus the need to respect a residential neighborhood—Eiermann placed the building at right angles to the road and used the grade conditions to generate the stepped design of the chancellery. Not only does this step-up and step-back fit the site, it presents minimum exposure to the road (two stories 50 feet/15 meters wide), maintaining thus a reasonably domestic scale. A tiered profile results, with two large and two small roof terraces toward Reservoir Road (and two small "terraces" at rear). These serve as occasional open-air meeting spots, and are surrounded by an "outrigging" which, if desired, can be used to support awnings. The floor slabs of the building are cantilevered outward for sun protection (the building is oriented roughly NE-SW), and to keep its mass from becoming ponderous. The slender natural pine "blinds" and the white-painted pipes of these side projections, which form almost a vertical trellis, lend color touches to the gray of the steel frame, while the perforated steel deck or catwalks add an animated, see-through horizontal "web" against the solid building. At times there is a suggestion of constructivist sculpture. These projections also double for emergency exits. (Because the chancellery is a diplomatic building it did not have to conform to restrictive U.S. architectural codes, hence could use exposed steel on its "balconies.") The 300-foot/91-meter-long embassy varies in height from three to eight stories (including

basement), and as almost all of the floors are of different lengths they pancake atop each other as they build up, diminishing in length, toward the center. The ground floor contains a fine entrance hall with glass on its two long sides. A two-hundred-seat auditorium (with overly insistent exterior grille of pine) lies directly adjacent to the reception area, so that public and official spaces are completely separate. Detailing and workmanship are exemplary. The outer approach is slurred by the usual lineup of automobiles, but the building itself adds a skillful and imaginative note to the Washington scene. A previously existing residence at the back of the lot houses the ambassador. An underground garage is placed beneath the approach drive. Altogether a beautifully conceived embassy. Eberhard Brandl was associate architect; Lublin, McGaughy & Associates prepared the working drawings.

Reception hall and auditorium open by appointment

18 Buchanan School Playground (1968)
13th and E Streets SE
Washington, D.C.

POMERANCE & BREINES, ARCHITECTS; M. PAUL FRIEDBERG, LANDSCAPE ARCHITECT

Here at last is a playground for young children which is both a challenge and a delight, fun and games, foreign lands, a trip to a nether and another world. The imagination shown here in the stacks of vertical blocks, the webs of horizontal rods, the jungle "trees" for swinging through, the pyramid for inching up, the cave for slithering into, desert sands for crawling across—instead of concrete—has created an astonishing collection of recreational sculpture. Most of these elements, whether of wood, stone, piping, concrete, or cable, are cleverly coordinated to produce a unity instead of random equipment. Note the in-

geniously sculpted "totem pole," which can be climbed upon with suitable risk. An open court for organized games for older children stands parallel to the playground, its basketball court sunk so that built-in seats line one side to transform the area into an outdoor gymnasium—or stage. The other side is occupied by a simple shelter for adult recreation. The playground forms, thus, a community relaxation center in a part of town where such amenities are woefully inadequate—though not many blocks southeast of the nation's Capitol. Mrs. Vincent Astor, through the Vincent Astor Foundation, generously made it possible.

---

19   East Building—National Gallery of Art (1971–78)
Constitution Avenue at 4th Street
Washington, D.C.

I. M. PEI & PARTNERS, ARCHITECTS

The requirements for the new East Building of the National Gallery were formidable: extensive galleries, research center, library, staff offices, auditorium, cafeteria, connecting link with West Building (underground), and services, the whole shaped, it should be stressed, by a difficult trapezoidal site bounded by the ritual Pennsylvania Avenue and Madison Drive in the Mall. Moreover, the new building obviously had to be a good neighbor to its highly respected parent—and to the Capitol down the street—while not exceeding a cornice limit of 111 feet/34 meters along the avenue. To solve this the achitects evolved a plan of two opposingly faced but conjoined triangles, with secondary parallelograms at the corners, all proportionally related. The larger isosceles triangle shelters most of the public area, while alongside an attenuated right triangle contains offices, library, and Center for Advanced Studies in the Visual Arts. The major triangle provides entries to both sections across its base; this side also opens onto a plaza which it semiframes with the West Building opposite, the two structures' axes precisely aligning. A granite-paved fountain "court" (of some irresolution) joins them. The point of the secondary triangle which houses staff and research touches this plaza, and its acutely angled (19°) marble edge forms a daring and superbly constructed detail. The base of this triangle is parallel to the plaza side but faces east (toward the Capitol), and its main facade overlooks the Mall.

The elevations resulting from this dynamic combination of geometry

and function vary as they reflect internal needs. The entry off the plaza on 4th Street welcomes one with a vast expanse of glass and a glistening, multivisible Henry Moore bronze *Knife Edge Mirror Two Piece* (1978), commissioned for this spot and a gift of the Morris and Gwendolyn Cafritz Foundation. The adjacent staff and research entry discreetly proclaims private versus public. The 405-foot/123-meter Pennsylvania Avenue side with one long low window seems scaleless, even dry, from a distance but it is given a sidewalk accent by the sculpture (at present *Adam,* 1970—by Alexander Liberman). Adjacent, behind a low parapet, stretches a 135-foot/41-meter-long reflecting pool which mirrors a spirited Dubuffet. The east elevation is a straightforward, largely glass statement of six floors of offices with an inset seventh floor marking the president's, director's, and assistant director's rooms. The long facade on the Mall is comprised of a series of interlocked, complex geometric forms mostly containing offices; because of its fracturing and because it faces the southerly sun, it is the most alive. The same carefully graded pinkish Tennessee marble (here 3 inches/76 millimeters thick) was used in the new building as in the old; it was even selected by the same expert.

Entering the East Building we find a skylit interior brilliant with an eruption of light and shade and spaces. This develops the most exhilarating introduction to the visual arts which one will encounter. Its explosive quality—beginning with low entry to lofty release—the dartings of sun and shadow, and even the accent of full-grown trees inside constitute art in themselves. This great central atrium almost vibrates, intensified by the multilevel choreography of visitors, particularly those on the high passerelle which bisects the midriff. Several large-scale specially ordered works of art complement this glass-roofed agora, particularly a magnificent 86-foot/26-meter Calder mobile (1977—completed just before the artist's death). The triangular steel and aluminum space-frame skylight is made up of twenty-five tetrahedrons, each measuring 30×45 feet/9.1×13.7 meters, with an overall dimension of 225 feet/69 meters on two legs and 150 feet/46 meters across the base. Sunscreens are placed below and injurious-ray filters are placed between its double glazing.

Some ambiguity arises as to where the major collections are located, for they are not immediately apparent, and herein, perhaps, lies a weakness. However, the visitor soon discovers the building's fascinatingly varied series of galleries. Some of these are almost closet-like, others capable of displaying large works, but virtually all establish intimacy between observer and art. One is never overwhelmed by walls of paintings, and thus a domestic atmosphere results (which recalls the Frick Museum in New York). The 20,000 square feet/1,858 square meters of galleries on the upper level—there are four exhibition floors altogether—establish a continuum via their off-center junctures, their spatial flow intensified by the fact that almost no rooms are rectangular. The experience of going from gallery to atrium to gallery is very quickening. The top level also provides an inside terrace for very large works and a cafe overlooking the Mall. Like New York's Guggenheim Museum (q.v.) and to a certain extent Berkeley's University Museum (q.v.), the East Building's basic concept groups the collections around a self-orienting open core. And perhaps also like Frank Lloyd Wright's Guggenheim, the East Building is so exciting that people swarm to see it—and stay for the art.

Artificial light is used as the primary source of illumination but the three top galleries are (or can be) skylit. This flood of daylight is particularly effective in the tiered northwest upper room, where David Smith's *Voltri XVII* (1962) are stunningly installed. Whereas the entire museum is highly flexible, both ground and (below grade) concourse levels are primarily for loan (i.e. changing) exhibitions, with two medium-sized galleries on the former and an 18,000-square-foot/1,672-square-meter area for "special" exhibits on the latter. Besides workshops and services, the concourse level also includes a 442-seat auditorium, a 90-seat lecture hall, with a moving walkway connecting East and West Buildings and a 700-seat cafe/buffet in between. (This is open to the public Mon.–Sat. 10–3:30, Sun. noon–6; longer in summer.) A 37.5-foot/11.4-meter-long waterfall entertains diners. Altogether there are 604,000 square feet/56,100 square meters of new exhibit and service space.

The West Building of the National Gallery of Art (1938–41), John Russell Pope and Eggers & Higgins, architects, forms an instructive contrast to the new. One might summarize this as elegant rigidity versus explosive informality, the volumetric versus the kinetic. The main entry to the old is circuitous, up the stairs and almost arcane; that to the new is immediate, welcoming, and at ground level. The rotunda of the old is of subduing impressiveness: the atrium of the new bursts with sunny vitality and excitement. In the impeccably detailed, always rectangular galleries of the Pope building there is an architectural "insistence" in many galleries with an emphasis on wainscoting and elaborately framed doors and paneling—the walls would look almost as handsome without the paintings; in the Pei wing the plain angled walls exist for the art alone. But see them both, for each epitomizes a period —it might be said from elitist to popularist—and each building is a tribute to the extraordinary generosity of one great American family. Andrew W. Mellon gave the West Building (and with incredible foresight reserved the plot to the east for future expansion), and his son, Paul, and late daughter, Ailsa Mellon Bruce, together with the Andrew W. Mellon Foundation, provided construction funds for the new. Almost four hundred donors—including, of course, Mr. Mellon, who gave 126 paintings—have contributed works of art and collections to the nation's magnificent National Gallery. It should be mentioned that only maintenance and administration are paid by the federal government.

I. M. Pei was design partner in charge for the East Building; Leonard Jacobson project architect; Weiskopf & Pickworth were the structural engineers; Kiley, Tyndall, Walker, the landscape architects. Superb.

Open in winter Mon.–Sat. 10–5, in summer Mon.–Sat. 10–9, Sun. noon–9, except Jan. 1 and Dec. 25

Maine

Bangor 2 •

Columbia Falls 5 •

Andover 1
•

Ellsworth 9 •

• Waterville 20

South Andover 17
•

■ Augusta

Dresden 8
•

Waldoboro 19 •

Deer Isle 7

Wiscasset 21
•

Bath 3 •

Damariscotta 6

Sabbathday Lake 16 •

North Edgecomb 12

Brunswick 4 •

Portland 13–15 •

• South Berwick 18

• York 22

Kittery Point 10–11

MAINE

The buildings in boldface type are of general interest. The others are for the specialist.

near Andover	1	**Comsat Earth Station** (1962)
Bangor	2	Morse Covered Bridge (1881)
Bath	3	**Washington Street** (19th century)
		Crane at Bath Iron Works (1972)
Brunswick	4	**Coles Tower** (1964)—Hugh Stubbins
Columbia Falls	5	**Thomas Ruggles House** (1820) —Aaron Sherman
near Damariscotta	6	**Old Walpole Meeting House** (1772)
Deer Isle	7	**Haystack Mountain School of Crafts** (1962)—Edward L. Barnes
near Dresden	8	**Pownalborough Court House** (1761)
Ellsworth	9	John Black Mansion (1824–27)
Kittery Point	10	**Fort McClary** (1690/1812/ rebuilt 1844–45)
	11	**Lady Pepperrell House** (1760)
North Edgecomb	12	Fort Edgecomb State Memorial (1808–9)
Portland	13	Tate House (1755)
	14	**McLellan-Sweat Mansion** (1800–1)
	15	**Victoria Mansion** (1859–63)— Henry Austin
Sabbathday Lake	16	**Shaker Village** (1794–1847)

South Andover	17 Lovejoy Covered Bridge (1868)
South Berwick	18 **Hamilton House** (1787–88)
Waldoboro	19 Old German Church (1772) and Cemetery
Waterville	20 **Colby College Dormitories** (1967)—Benjamin Thompson
Wiscasset	21 **Nickels-Sortwell House** (1807–8) **and Village Green**
York	22 **Jefferd's Tavern** (1750) **and Historic District**

1 Comsat Earth Station (1962)
E of town off ME 120 (c. 90 miles/145 kilometers N of Portland)
Andover, Maine

BIRDAIR STRUCTURES INC., ENGINEERS

This stupendous, air-supported bubble—210 feet/64 meters in diameter and 161 feet/49 meters high—cannot fail to impress the visitor when he wheels around the corner and encounters its non-negotiable shape nestled in the Maine woods (which woods once furnished the area's wealth). A remote valley site was selected so that the peripheral mountains would screen surface interference from its Telstar duties of relaying television, telegraph, and telephone communications across the Atlantic. Built in 1962 by AT&T for Telstar experiments, three years later it became the world's first commercial satellite station and is now operated by the Communications Satellite Corporation in joint ownership by five communications companies. Its .06-inch/1.6-millimeter-thick skin of opaque Dacron and synthetic rubber covers the complicated receiving and transmitting antenna inside, yet remains transparent to radio signals. Only one tenth of a pound of air pressure per square inch (.7 gram per square centimeter) is needed for support. An air lock

gives personnel access. In spite of harsh winters, winds, and snow the air-supported velum has given no trouble. (Its high-profile, uninsulated pneumatic form lets the snow melt and slide off.) The sphere itself is almost as impeccable as Euclid: unfortunately the same cannot be said of its architectural base.

The visitors' enclosed observation room gives an excellent view of the fantastic 380-ton/345-metric-ton antenna within, whose mouth alone covers 3,600 square feet/334 square meters. It is through this that microwave signals are transmitted and received via a satellite 22,300 miles/35,900 kilometers above the earth, establishing an electronic "bridge" between the U.S.A. and Western Europe. The adjacent Visitors Building offers an illuminating audiovisual presentation of operations. Nearby stand two large communications antennae, with one "dish" 97 feet/30 meters in diameter (1973) and the larger 105 feet/32 meters (1976). Very impressive.

Open Memorial Day–Labor Day, daily 9–5

The **Lovejoy Covered Bridge** (q.v.) near South Andover merits the small detour from the Comstat Station.

---

2   Morse Covered Bridge (1881)
off Harlow Street—behind Federal Building
Bangor, Maine

A well-maintained Howe-truss span which at 212 feet/65 meters is the longest in the state and reputedly the only one still standing in a New England city. It bridges the Kenduskeag Stream just above its entry to the Penobscot River. The truss type which William Howe invented and patented used the diagonal wood bracing (the X-bracing or lattice pattern) of the Long truss but employed wrought-iron rods, adjustable with turnbuckles, for the vertical tension members, greatly increasing bearing capacity and ease of maintenance. It was an immediate success, especially with the railroads, because in addition to strength it could also be erected in a few days with precut standardized parts. The reason for covering—in this case almost totally enclosing—wooden bridges was, of course, to give them all-weather protection. Rain and melting snow would soon rot their timbers if they were not shielded.

3 Washington Street (19th century)
Bath, Maine

Beginning two blocks north of US 1 with the chocolate-painted former church, now headquarters for the Performing Arts Center of Bath, and continuing .75 mile/1.2 kilometers to Cedar, Washington Street unfolds (with lacunae) a courteous succession of structures. The street forms the spine of the Bath Historic District. Although only a few buildings are of architectural significance, their collective impression is one of low-keyed pleasure, revealing a variety of architectural styles and revivals through the years. Halfway along the Washington Street promenade at №880 stands the former Congregational Church (1843–44), which was saved from destruction in 1973 and now houses the Winter Street Center of the Marine Museum (open mid-May–mid-Oct., Mon.–Sat. 10–5, Sun. 1–5: admission). Designed by Anthony C. Raymond, a local builder, its wooden Gothic Revival exterior merits inspection, but the interior is not strong. The parent Bath Marine Museum at 963 Washington Street (open same hours and admission) oc-

cupies the gracious, Federal-influenced Sewall Mansion with, oddly enough, a rear addition (1902) by the famous Addison Mizner, who "blessed" Florida after World War I by vastly broadening the Spanish Revival architectural beachhead originally established there by Carrère & Hastings in the 1880s and '90s. Both museums in Bath are of interest, for Bath-built ships have been famous since the beginnings of the Colonies, reaching a peak during the last third of the nineteenth century when Bath turned out almost half of the sailing vessels constructed in the U.S.A. The museums limn this still active industry.

(A site 16 miles/26 kilometers south of Bath, the Popham colony, was founded the same year as Jamestown, 1607—and built its first ship in 1608, a 30-ton pinnace—but the community lasted only a bit over a year because of the discouraging severity of that winter, deaths, and hostile Indians. Bath itself was established permanently in 1630.)

The superb **crane,** maximum height 400 feet/122 meters, boom 240 feet/73 meters, towering over the Bath Iron Works along US 1, is a fittingly contemporary terminus of Washington Street. (Iron works not open to the public.) The largest shipbuilding-way crane in the country, with lifting capacity of 220 tons/200 metric tons and unique level-luffing power, it was fabricated and painted at Bath Iron Works in 1972.

4   Coles Tower (1964)
College Street off Maine Street
Brunswick, Maine

HUGH STUBBINS & ASSOCIATES, ARCHITECTS

Like most urban colleges Bowdoin is being forced to the high-rise to remain compact and coherent while expanding on its increasingly cramped campus. However, few tall academic buildings can equal this sophisticated sixteen-story tower (one of the tallest in Maine). Around the high dormitory, which accommodates 202 students and 2 faculty members, are grouped a low commons-lounge and a university office. The three buildings are enfolded by an ingenious berm, grass-covered on the outer face, which gives identity and privacy to the buildings and definition to the peripheral circulation. This cincture is particularly useful in "closing" the small plaza in front of the Admissions Office (formerly the home of the resident director). Other subtleties can be seen in the slight lateral bowing outward at the midpoint of the tower—to eschew rigidity—and the small splay at the bottom of the tower's brick piers. The angled "bays" of the tower are not capricious but resulted from forming alcoves for the students' desks, the act of study thus generating the facade. Lounges occupy the corners with four

single bedrooms per side in between. The tower also has a penthouse for seminars and small meetings and accommodations for visiting lecturers. Materials are the same red brick with white trim which have characterized most Bowdoin buildings since the college received its charter in 1794. Interiors match the high quality of the exterior.

Grounds open daily

---

5 Thomas Ruggles House (1820)
Main Street, .25 mile/402 meters S of US 1
Columbia Falls, Maine

AARON SHERMAN, DESIGNER

A simple house but intriguingly—and sometimes quaintly—detailed, the work of a little-known "architect" from Massachusetts. It was excellently restored in 1951, and one should note fence, porch, swags over the window, the cornice, and, within, the divided "flying" staircase and mantels. The drawing-room mantel, reputedly carved by an English craftsman with a penknife, almost dazzles with its combination of natural mahogany and white-painted wood, all with Adam-like delicacy. Of the stair the brochure states, "The most famous craftsmen

of modern times, the most noted architects of the country, have stood before it in amazement, and declared that nowhere have they seen its like." The house has been well furnished of the period, and is proudly maintained by the Ruggles House Society.

Open June 1–Oct. 15, Mon.–Sat. 8:30–4:30, Sun. 10–4: admission

---

6   Old Walpole Meeting House (1772)
3.7 miles/6 kilometers S of Damariscotta off ME 129
between Damariscotta and Bristol, Maine

The simplest of wooden boxes, domestic in appearance, set amid oaks, and several miles from any contemporary town. Although rarely used today, it has been constantly maintained, and its unusual hand-shaved, white-painted shingles—instead of clapboarding—seem almost new: they are, in fact, the original ones. Generally the meeting house is locked, but the key is available nearby, as a note explains. The interior follows the usual pattern of a two-story space with box pews below and balcony on three sides above facing a raised pulpit on the center of the long side. In the balcony there is also a row of boxed pews with a row of benches for the servants. The elaborate pulpit, with its sounding board, and with glaring windows directly behind, forms the focus. The

church—"the oldest in Maine still serving as a place of worship," as the bulletin claims—was built for Scotch Presbyterians and served them for twenty-four years, but became Congregational because the latter's headquarters were much closer.

Open June 15–Labor Day, daily 9–5: services every Sun. at 3 P.M., *July–Aug.: donation*

---

7   Haystack Mountain School of Crafts (1962)
Extreme E end of
Deer Isle, Maine
(Get local map at Chamber of Commerce Booth on Little Deer
    Isle)

EDWARD LARRABEE BARNES, ARCHITECT

By rearranging a few planks after they have been through the sawmill lightly, placing them vertically, horizontally, and at 45°, then giving them a silvery coat of cedar shingles, Ed Barnes has evolved an admirable low-keyed summer camp-school. Stepped skillfully down the steep, south-facing side of the hill, with Penobscot Bay at the bottom, a score of buildings has been integrated with nature in a way that could scarcely be more felicitous—nor could the relations between building and building as they cascade down the slope. Continuity and flow along the horizontal level are equally commendable. The buildings themselves are of inexpensive summer construction, yet site deployment, mutual relations, and roof angles are keenly sympathetic.

Visitors welcome June–Sept. by appointment: telephone (207) 348-6946

---

8   Pownalborough Court House (1761)
on ME 128, c. halfway between Augusta and Bath
near Dresden, Maine

Many of the extant buildings that are revelatory of eighteenth-century Maine have been bypassed by population shifts and are now far removed from any settlement. Among these lonely relics is this 1761 courthouse, built by Gershom Flagg, a Boston housewright, on the banks of the Kennebec River, now 2 miles/3.2 kilometers from any existing town, but well situated when river communication formed the colonial highway system. It was constructed within the grounds of Fort Shirley (1752—long vanished), which was even then no longer a military strongpoint. The 45-foot/14-meter-square courthouse itself, the earliest still standing in Maine, is a fine example of civic rural vernacular of two hundred years ago. Its white-painted, three-story exterior is in excellent condition. The pine interior, with tavern on ground floor, courtroom on second, and transient accommodations above, is in process of full restoration. Well worth a detour.

Open June 15–Labor Day, Mon.–Sat. 10–5, Sun. 12–5: admission

---

9   John Black Mansion (1824–27)
West Main Street (US 1)
Ellsworth, Maine

One of Maine's most handsome houses, the John Black Mansion shows the influence of the famous Asher Benjamin, whose books, especially his *American Builder's Companion,* were very popular in setting early-nineteenth-century architectural standards. The Black House—the estate was also called Woodlawn—is situated on a hill back from the

road and stands well preserved, having been lived in by descendants of the original family until 1928, when, on the death of the owner, it was willed to the city. Its Georgian-early-Federal red brick and white wood exterior with its triple-hung windows and well-detailed balustrade and porch (the latter added later) are commendable. Note, too, the offset one-story wings flanking each side. The carriage house and contents behind are also worth a look. The formal garden, which was laid out in 1903, is now being restored. The interior, unaltered since the house was bequeathed to the public, is "livable" but jam-packed with furniture and memorabilia from many periods. The elliptical stair is outstanding. The house is operated by the Hancock County Trustees of Public Reservations.

Open June–Oct. 15, Mon.–Sat. 10–5: admission

---

10 Fort McClary (1690/1812/rebuilt 1844–45)
off ME 103 on Kittery Point Road, W of
Kittery Point, Maine

The British constructed the formidable granite lower bastion, calling it first Pepperrell's Fort, then Fort William—both after Sir William Pepperrell. It did not receive its current name until after the Revolution, when it was named for a Major McClary, who fell at Bunker Hill. A workmanlike quaintness characterizes the restored wooden hexagonal blockhouse which rests on top, a copy of the 1812 original. Perched on

its rocky base, it peers meaningfully toward the mouth of the Piscataqua River, which here separates the tips of Maine and New Hampshire, yet its compass surveys land approaches as well. Repaired and activated during the Civil War, the impressive granite outworks are slowly being restored today.

Open Memorial Day–Oct. 15, daily 10–6: admission

---

11   Lady Pepperrell House (1760)
on ME 103, c. 2 miles/3.2 kilometers W of
Kittery Point, Maine

The Pepperrell House, overlooking the Piscataqua River (and 4 miles/6.4 kilometers distant from Portsmouth, New Hampshire), stands in somewhat lonely grandeur outside the town. It attains a high patrician quality through a central pedimented pavilion that is boldly delineated by two-story Ionic pilasters whose richness is reemphasized by the simplicity of the sides and the dormer-less roof. (An open porch stands at left end added by John Mead Howells in 1923.) Though this Georgian mansion is built entirely of wood, the smooth clapboarding of the pavilion and the quoins at the corners both imitate stone, as was

often the fashion of the day. The Lady Pepperrell House was given to the Society for the Preservation of New England Antiquities in 1942, the house donated by Mrs. Lovell Hodge, the contents by Mrs. Hodge and Miss Catharine Parry. The fireplaces, mantels, and woodwork are outstanding. "This truly elegant house may be counted as one of the very finest Colonial mansions ever built in Maine." (*Maine Forms of American Architecture,* Deborah Thompson, editor, Downeast Magazine, 1976. This book is a highly recommended survey of Maine's notable buildings.)

Open May and Oct., Sat.–Sun. 1–5; June–Sept., Tues., Thurs., Sat., Sun. 1–5: admission

---

12   Fort Edgecomb State Memorial (1808–9)
.7 mile/1.1 kilometers S off US 1
North Edgecomb, Maine

An octagonal blockhouse, 27 feet/8.2 meters on a side on lower floor, 30 feet/9.1 meters above, of heavy oak timbers covered with shingles. Built to protect Wiscasset's then busy deep-water harbor, and patterned on medieval English forts, it never was fired on—though it probably could have withstood the cannon of that day. The blockhouse itself has required only routine repairs but the stockade was rebuilt and earthworks tidied in 1961. The site is panoramic and there are picnic facilities with tables for military buffs. Town and fort were named for Lord Edgecomb, an English friend of the budding colonies.

Open Memorial Day–Labor Day, daily 10–6: admission

---

13   Tate House (1755)
1270 Westbrook Street (c. 2.6 miles/4.2 kilometers W of downtown Portland via Congress Street/ME 22)
Portland (Stroudwater), Maine

An unusual house in part inspired by Tate's London town house; here, however, built of wood. Among other elements it is made distinctive by the treatment of its gambrel roof and its "indented" upper windows on the main facade. Having never been painted, the narrow feather clapboarding—with some original boards and handmade nails—has weathered to a hoary gray, offset by white and slightly heavy doorframe and windows. The enormous L-shaped chimney contains flues from eight fireplaces. Built for George Tate, an Englishman whose job it was to supply the Royal Navy with masts—a length of 72 feet/22 meters was routine—the construction of the house and the size of some of the planks are, not unexpectedly, impressive. Fortunately its heavy timber framing can be seen in both basement and attic. (The taking of the area's finest trees was in measure responsible for Maine's espousal of the Revolution, though it was part of Massachusetts until 1820.) Notice, within, the paneling, especially the width of the one piece over the fireplace in the room at left of entry. Long abused as a tenement and in shabby condition, the house was purchased for $2,500 in 1932 by the National Society of the Colonial Dames of America in the State of Maine and given what was for the time (1932–36) a proper restoration. However, it was not until 1951–56, following archeological and related research, that the meticulous restoration by Walter M. Macomber was carried out. Now being correctly furnished, the house, a National Historic Landmark, is one of the important architectural resources of Maine.

Open July–Sept. 15, Tues.–Sat. 11–5, Sun. 1:30–5: admission

---

14   McLellan-Sweat Mansion (1800–1)
Portland Museum of Art
111 High Street, corner of Spring Street
Portland, Maine

A chaste Federal-period house, erected under the direction of John Kimball, Sr., a Portland master builder of note. Local sources feel that Alexander Parris, who later achieved fame in Boston, was probably designer of the front portico. (Both men had excellent architectural libraries.) Of restrained elegance both outside and in, the house establishes a striking stylistic counterpoint to the nearby Victoria Mansion (q.v.). The half-round entry porch, the fanlighted door, the Palladian window above, and the balustrade are expertly detailed. Note the balustrade and its urns, whose rhythm is picked up by the fence and

hand-carved urns in front. (The influence of Bulfinch can be seen here.) Within, the almost floor-to-ceiling windows, with sizable nine over nine panes of glass on the main floor, flood the airily proportioned front rooms with light. (These windows were lengthened in the 1820s.) The most notable feature of the interior—aside from the exhilarating flood of light—is the divided flying stair. The house was willed to the Portland Society of Art as the basis for a museum in 1908—to which the house now forms an adjunct. It has been carefully restored and fitted with furnishings of its time in addition to housing the Swan Collection of Portland Glass.

Open Tues.–Sat. 10–5, Sun. 2–5, except major holidays: admission

---

15 Victoria Mansion (1859–63)
109 Danforth Street at Park
Portland, Maine

HENRY AUSTIN, ARCHITECT

"The finest and least altered example of a brown stone Italian villa town house in the United States" (as the plaque proclaims) was acquired (1943) by the Victoria Society of Maine Women and is operated by them. Long in need of repair, the roof and the once scaly exterior were restored (1974–79) with matching funds from the Department of the Interior, the National Park Service, and the Maine Historic Preservation Commission. This is one of the greatest of Victorian mansions and it must be seen to be believed. Designed as a summer home by Henry Austin of Yale Library fame (1842), a variety of ideas and motifs—with a deep bow to the bracketed Italianate—have been hurled at this two-story brownstone, but hurled with accuracy—and $400,000! In spite of the prominence of individual parts, it forms a marvelous unity. (The reddish stone, incidentally, was shipped in from Connecticut.) The hurricane of 1938 flung a limb through the great central

skylight, destroying its colored panes, but the interior still offers an astounding parade of mid-nineteenth-century opulence all in a variety of
"styles," with many walls and ceilings painted by Giovanni Guidirini
and eleven assistants. The lofty entrance hall provides an unexpected
spatial welcome—and a prominent, freestanding hand-carved mahogany stair—but the real delights are found in the rooms, particularly
the music room to the right, where every square inch, including the
ceilings, has been properly attended to. The interior of the square
tower, which rises imposingly above the well-modeled, well-articulated
facade, was furnished in Sheik of Araby style. Also known as the
Morse-Libby House, it is incuded in the National Register of Historic
Places.

Open mid-June to Labor Day, Tues.–Sat. 10–4: admission

---

16   Shaker Village (1794–1847)
**on ME 26 (c. 3 miles/5 kilometers S of Poland Springs) E off Exit
    11 of Maine Turnpike, N on ME 26 at Gray**
Sabbathday Lake, Maine

Austerity has always marked Shaker activities, in personal life to the
point of celibacy. (The growth of the movement, which reached a peak
of more than six thousand members in the middle of the nineteenth
century, was by conversion and adoption.) Shaker architecture and furniture naturally reflect this purity and pared directness, and it is unfortunate that of the nineteen settlements which descended from Mother
Ann Lee and her Band of Eight, who landed in New York in 1774, this
is the only active Shaker group which still exists. Several notable
Shaker communal villages, which are discussed in this book, can be
seen, but these have by now passed into other hands. The unadorned
meeting house (1794) at Sabbathday Lake—the only building of the
group of sixteen which can perhaps claim architectural merit—constitutes basic response to isolated, even primitive building conditions
shaped by liturgical demands. Moses Johnson, of New Hampshire, reputedly built it along with ten other meeting houses in New England
between 1785 and 1794, each with gambrel roof, two separate but
equal doors (for brethren and sisters) and an upper-floor apartment.
Though these buildings are not of "stylistic" significance in architectural terms, they give good insight into the "Purity and Plainness" of
Shaker design. Note, too, the wonderfully sinewy furniture.

One of the most successful commercial products of Sabbathday Lake—as in other Shaker communities—was the extensive herb industry; here the activities were housed in a separate clapboarded Herb House (1824). Though trade is of course not as active as it was one hundred years ago, it is still carried on with a resident herbalist in charge. It is worth mentioning that the United Society of Believers in Christ's Second Appearing celebrated their bicentennial two years before that of the U.S.A.

Tours June–Sept., Mon.–Sat. 10–4:30: admission

---

17   Lovejoy Covered Bridge (1868)
on Ellis River off ME 5
South Andover, Maine

A fine example of the Paddleford-truss bridge—a type derived from the X-shaped members of the (Stephen H.) Long truss but strengthened by paneling. It represents the same engineering directness as the Comsat

installation (q.v.) a half-dozen miles (10 kilometers) away, and is proudly maintained by the community and the Maine Department of Transportation. The shortest covered bridge in Maine, its span is 65 feet/20 meters with a width of 20 feet/6 meters. It is listed in the National Register of Historic Places.

---

18   Hamilton House (1787–88)
Brattle Street and Vaughan's Lane, c. 2.5 miles/4 kilometers S of
    town via ME 236
South Berwick, Maine

Superbly situated overlooking the Quamphegan River, a branch of the Piscataqua, the Jonathan Hamilton House and garden add a sophisticated note to Maine's domestic architecture. Squarish in plan, the dwelling's two main floors are topped by a prominent hip roof with four towering square chimneys and elaborate dormers. The exterior, sheathed in narrow clapboarding, is light gray in color with white trim and greenish roof. The interior has been carefully furnished to match its late Georgian architecture with some pieces reflecting the subsequent Federal period. The beautiful gardens with view down the river—where Colonel Hamilton's ships once tied up—are lovingly maintained. This is one of the few great houses outside the South where a distant view is part of the overall design. The mansion was willed to the Society for the Preservation of New England Antiquities in 1949 and after thorough refurnishing opened to the public. (The house was "a very sad object" at the end of the nineteenth century, before initial restoration.) Much of the surrounding land, including a forest of pines, was left to the state of Maine as a park, ensuring the untroubled peace of the estate.

Open May–Oct., Tues.–Sun. 10–5: admission

**19　Old German Church (1772) and Cemetery
W off ME 32, c. 1 mile/1.6 kilometers S of US 1
Waldoboro, Maine**

The church, which is one of the oldest in Maine, was built by German
Lutherans, many of whom found the region less gladsome than they expected upon their arrival from their native land (as a tombstone amusingly attests). The central-aisle church, though not of great architectural importance, creates a comely scene with its yellow clapboards
and white trim set in a picturesque ancient graveyard. Remarkably, the
church was moved to its present location twenty-two years after being
completed. Inside, box pews and high pulpit (added in the 1790s) are
of natural unfinished wood. The building has been recently restored
and is well maintained. Memorabilia of the early parishioners are on
display.

Open Sundays in summer, grounds always open

20 Colby College Dormitories (1967)
West central edge of campus, reached via Washington Street from Waterville, Maine

BENJAMIN THOMPSON AND ASSOCIATES, ARCHITECTS

Onto a steep and uneven hillside covered with birch and pine, the architect has eased four dormitories and a fraternity house. Although the buildings are staggered vertically and laterally over a demanding north-facing slope, Thompson has left subtle spaces between so that each can adapt to its microtopography and breathe its own space yet help to form a coherent group. The buildings are constructed with a reinforced concrete frame, left its natural gray, with white-painted brick walls—so painted as companion to the birch trees of the site. Common rooms, lounges, and studies occupy most of the ground floors, three of them interconnecting, with bedrooms above. Within, the raw concrete, red tile floors, natural wood, and bold colors in the furnishings combine to pro-

duce a series of resilient and cheerful rooms. Individual bedrooms are
in many cases divided by movable wardrobes and partitions which can
be changed to suit the student's wishes. Outsize numerals (6 feet/1.8
meters high!) of blown-up Clarendon typeface (designed in 1848)
punctuate each stair landing. The meticulous preservation of the setting
—landscaping by Carol R. Johnson is excellent—and the quality of the
architecture outside and in mark this a distinguished addition to a
hitherto neo-Georgian campus.

Grounds and common rooms open during school year

---

21   Nickels-Sortwell House (1807–8) **and Village Green**
Main Street (US 1) at Federal
Wiscasset, Maine

A three-story house in the Federal Style (and Boston influence) with facade of exceptional detail. The high entry portico, bracketed by arcaded side windows, with a Palladian window above and a strange half-round window on the top floor, combine with narrow Corinthian pilasters and "novelty" (i.e. flush) siding to produce a sometimes elegant, sometimes naive front. The door is straight out of Asher Benjamin's *American Builder's Companion,* published the previous year. The delicacy of the tracery in the fan and side lights should be observed, as should the cornice and low-pitched roof. The interior—notice the elliptical stair with domed skylight—is well furnished and maintained. The house was purchased (1900) and completely restored by Alvin F. Sortwell after it had suffered for years as a hotel. His family generously willed it (1957) to the Society for the Preservation of New England Antiquities.

The Village Green, the lower end of which just touches the house, ranks high among low-keyed New England commons. Though neither its white-painted church (c. 1773) nor its brick courthouse (1824) numbers among the architecturally elite, their relaxed positions at the top of the hill and their collective impression with the houses that frame the common create overall unity.

Open June–Oct., Tues.–Sun. 10–5: admission

**22 Jefferd's Tavern (1750) and Historic District
US 1A at Lindsay Street
York, Maine**

Jefferd's Tavern expresses well the saltbox domestic architecture of early New England, showing, too, that other regional trademark: a single color for the entire exterior including the window muntins. The maroon used here produces a subdued effect—belying, no doubt, the stagecoach passengers' activities within. The building was dismantled in 1939 and moved from nearby Wells to York, where it was reerected (1939) and restored outside and in by Howard Peck, vandals having done much damage. Note the narrow (2.7 inches/69 millimeters) clapboards, a sign of early construction.

York itself, one of the earliest continuously settled towns in Maine having been founded in 1624 (as Agamenticus), is well worth exploring. It also boasted the Colonies' first sawmill (1633). The stone- and oak-walled Old Gaol (1653), reputedly "the oldest existing English public building in America" and since 1900 a local history museum, lies just up the street. The kitchen and cellar date from 1736, the second floor from 1763–99. (Open mid-June–Sept., Mon.–Sat. 10:30–5, Sun. 1:30–5: admission). The First Parish Congregational Church, across the street from both tavern and jail, was begun in 1747.

Tavern open Memorial Day–mid-Sept., Mon.–Sat. 9:30–5, Sun. 1:30–5: admission

Maryland

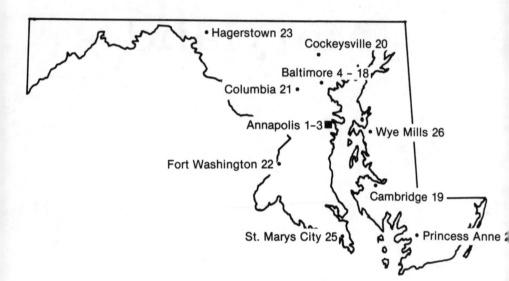

• Hagerstown 23

Cockeysville 20
•

Baltimore 4 – 18

Columbia 21 •

Annapolis 1–3 ■

• Wye Mills 26

Fort Washington 22 •

Cambridge 19 —

St. Marys City 25 •

• Princess Anne 2

MARYLAND

The buildings in boldface type are of general interest. The others are for the specialist.

Annapolis

1 **Maryland State House** (1772–79)
   Old Treasury Building (1735–37)
2 **Chase-Lloyd House** (1769–74)—
   Buckland and Noke
3 **Hammond-Harwood House**
   (1774–75)—William Buckland
   William Paca House and Garden
   (1763–65)

Baltimore

4 **Mount Clare** (c. 1763)
5 **Hampton National Historic Site**
   (1783–90)
6 **Basilica of the Assumption of the
   Blessed Virgin Mary** (1806–21/
   portico 1863)—Benjamin H.
   Latrobe
7 First Unitarian Church (1817–18)—
   Maximilian Godefroy
8 Baltimore Stoops (late 19th–early
   20th century)
9 **College of Art, Maryland Institute**
   (1894–96/1966)—Baldwin &
   Pennington/Cochran, Stephenson
   & Donkervoet
10 Highfield House (1963–65)—Mies
   van der Rohe
11 **Charles Center** (1957–69)—Various
   planners and architects
12 **Morris A. Mechanic Theater**
   (1966–67)—John M. Johansen
13 Two Charles Center Apartments
   (1965–69)—Conklin & Rossant
14 Greater Baltimore Medical Center
   (1965)—RTKL and CN&A
15 John Deere Office and Warehouse
   (1967)—RTKL

16 Blue Cross/Blue Shield of Maryland
(1970–72)—Peterson & Brickbauer

17 **Inner Harbor Redevelopment**
(1970–80s)—Wallace, McHarg,
Roberts & Todd, planners; various
architects

18 **Coldspring New Town** (1973–   )—
Moshe Safdie & Associates

Cambridge   19 **Old Trinity Church** (c. 1675)

Cockeysville   20 Noxell Office Building (1967)—
Skidmore, Owings & Merrill

Columbia   21 **Columbia New Town** (1966–81)—
Morton Hoppenfeld, chief planner;
various architects

Fort Washington   22 **Fort Washington** (1814–24)—Pierre
Charles L'Enfant

Hagerstown   23 Jonathan Hager House (1739–40)

Princess Anne   24 Teackle Mansion (c. 1801/wings
1803)

St. Marys City   25 **Old State House** (1676/1934)

Wye Mills   26 **Old Wye Church** (1721)

1 Maryland State House (1772–79)
State Circle
Annapolis, Maryland

The Maryland State House—the oldest in continuous legislative use in the U.S.A.—was for a brief period (November 26, 1783–August 13, 1784) the Capitol of the new country. It is the third to grace this site, the first having burned (1704); the second was torn down (1771) because of its inadequate size and deplorable condition, Thomas Jefferson remarking that "judging from its form and appearance, [it] was built in the year one." The architect of the present State House was, most authorities feel, Joseph Horatio Anderson, whose design produced an eleven-bay, two-story building with a three-bay central pavilion with porch, the whole topped by a hip roof. The domed octagonal cupola, which we now see pushing heavenward with brave if overambitious effort, is the second (1788), the first having been torn down in 1785

(possibly 1786) because of rotting timbers. Its design, supposedly 60 feet/18 meters higher than the original, is the work of Joseph Clark, a local architect understandably not found in most history books. Unfortunately a huge "annex" at the back was added by Baldwin & Pennington in 1902–5, which, being larger than the State House itself, overwhelms the latter.

Within, the finest room is the Senate Chamber, a simple room highlighted by its large windows, a pedimented niche, and excellent carving. The gallery at rear was probably added after the room was completed. It is likely that William Buckland, who designed the Chase-Lloyd and Hammond-Harwood houses down the street (q.v.), had a hand with the interior of the Senate Chamber. The whole building has been completely restored.

Open daily 9–5, except major holidays

The delightful **Old Treasury Building** (1735–37), which stands on the State House grounds, should also be seen (open daily 9–5, except major holidays). It now serves as headquarters for the walking tours conducted by Historic Annapolis Inc., a private organization concerned with local preservation. (Tours mid-June–Labor Day, 10, 1:30, and 3: by appointment rest of year: fee.) In spite of the sophistication of the building, the architect is not known; one Patrick Creagh was the builder.

2 Chase-Lloyd House (1769–74)
22 Maryland Avenue at King George Street
Annapolis, Maryland

WILLIAM BUCKLAND AND WILLIAM NOKE, ARCHITECTS

Rising magisterially above Maryland Avenue, the unusually high (three stories and basement) Chase-Lloyd House presents an austere facade. Comeliness, however, is found at the elaborate entry to which a prominent picket fence escorts one. The house was begun by Samuel Chase, who ran out of money when only the outer walls were in place, and its shell was purchased in 1771 by Colonel Edward Lloyd IV. Lloyd immediately employed William Buckland, an English-born master-joiner-architect, to complete the house—Buckland was thus not responsible for its mass—and Lloyd then set about pouring a good deal of his substantial money into the task. Buckland's imprint lies in the details, beginning with the handsome, raised entry mentioned. Inspired by Palladian elements, the entrance takes the usual two windows and a roundheaded door, but combines them freshly in a broad, columned, pilastered, and pedimented whole reached by a half flight of stairs. Buckland then opens his front door into the entrance hall, which is equally handsome and which leads directly to the stairs at rear. The

large Palladian window which illuminates the landing of this stair is one of the finest, outside and in, to be seen. Note that its central, arched opening and two side windows call on the same elements as found at the entry, but here they are knit compactly together. Carving and details throughout the house are superior. The building was left to an Episcopal Board of Directors in 1889 to be used as a home for elderly ladies, hence the upper floors are not open to the public. (The Episcopal Church itself does not own the building.)

Open daily except Wed. and Sun., 10–12, 2–4; closed Thanksgiving, Dec. 25: admission

---

3   Hammond-Harwood House (1774–75)
19 Maryland Avenue at King George Street
Annapolis, Maryland

WILLIAM BUCKLAND, ARCHITECT

Considered "without doubt one of the finest medium-sized houses of the world," Hammond-Harwood represents the ultimate contribution of William Buckland, who, as we saw, did much work on the Chase-Lloyd House directly across the street. It also represents his ultimate in breadth of concept and fastidiousness of detail. Unfortunately Buckland died in 1774, when only forty, just before the Hammond House was finished. Unlike Chase-Lloyd, this house was totally planned by Buckland and supervised by him. It is unlikely, however, that any of its wondrous woodwork was carved by him. The dwelling forms a provocative contrast to the Chase-Lloyd House, having a finer sense of scale, proportion, and even detail, while the almost pulsating profile of its three sections, connected by hyphens, carries far more sophistication than the towering cube opposite. The dependencies on either side— note the semioctagonal front ends—were designed for Hammond's law office (left) and kitchen (right). The almost square central block smolders with quiet understatement except for the intensely rich but impeccable front door, the framing of the window above it, and the bull's-eye window in the pediment (the latter inspired by a plate in Gibbs's *A Book of Architecture,* 1728). The entry ranks as one of the finest in U.S. Georgian architecture. Note that it garners extra attention because the windows alongside are quiet (with the upper central exception) and shutterless. On entering one finds a front hall lit only by fanlight, hence one with none of the spatial elation that characterizes the Chase-Lloyd

House. However, a few steps farther on, beyond the smallish front rooms and the strangely closeted stairs at right, one enters—better, encounters—the superb dining room, Buckland's master chamber. The wood carving here reaches an apogee, beginning with the framing of the doors, windows, and interior shutters up to the intricate cornice encircling the ceiling. Note that one of the windows also doubles as a door to the garden, its lower section being hinged to form a jib door. The ballroom on the second floor is almost as fine as the dining room, as, indeed, are the airy bedrooms. There is an Adam influence in the plasterwork, but historians disagree as to whether this was by Buckland's design or was an addition after his abrupt death. Although the monumentally pilastered garden facade of the Hammond-Harwood House cannot equal the elegance of the front, mostly because of its heavy pediment, altogether it can well lay claim to being "the most beautiful town house in America" (*Great Georgian Houses,* Dover edition, 1970). Fortunately it has been superbly restored.

As for Matthias Hammond, who commissioned the house for his intended bride, it is said that he became so fascinated by the house he neglected the young lass, who then ran off and married someone else. The Harwood family—descendants of architect William Buckland— occupied the house for the latter half of the nineteenth century, while St. John's College owned it and used it as a Colonial Museum until 1938. The Hammond-Harwood House Association, organized in 1940, purchased the property from St. John's and has cared for the mansion ever since.

Open Apr.–Oct., Tues.–Sat. 10–5, Sun. 2–5; Nov.–Mar., Tues.–Sat. 10–4, Sun. 1–4; closed Jan. 1, Dec. 25: admission

The nearby **William Paca House and Garden** (1763–65), 186 Prince George Street, should by all means be visited. The thirty-seven-room house was once engulfed in a hotel while the garden was used as parking lot and bus station. Both mansion and garden have undergone long and complete restoration (1965–76) after intense archeological and architectural research. The architect is not known. The house is a Historic Annapolis Inc. project, while the garden is managed by Historic Annapolis Inc. for the state of Maryland. (The house is open Tues.–Sat. 10–4, Sun. 12–4, except major holidays; the garden also on Mon.: admission.)

---

4 **Mount Clare** (c. 1763)
Carroll Park, Monroe Street (US 1) and Washington Boulevard
Baltimore, Maryland

Mount Clare—Baltimore's only remaining pre-Revolutionary mansion —does not fall into the routine pattern of Georgian tidewater plantation houses. On the north side it projects an unusual central bay with open portico below and enclosed room above emblazoned with a large Palladian window, and, on the river front, it carries four two-story, two-toned brick pilasters. (The awkward lunette on the river pediment dates from the last century.) The original wings and hyphens on either

side of the house disappeared well over a century ago, and it was not until 1906 that they were replaced as we see them today. (One of the wings or "cottages" might well have been the first part built.) The interior, much of it in plaster in imitation of wood, still possesses many of the early furnishings. It also contains a magnificent collection of eighteenth-century china, silver, and crystal.

The property was acquired with its extensive grounds by the city in 1890—the land for use as a park. Since 1916 Mount Clare has been under the custody of the National Society of the Colonial Dames of America in the State of Maryland, and is maintained jointly by them with the Baltimore Department of Parks and Recreation.

Open Tues.–Sat. 11–4, Sun. 1–4, except holidays: admission

---

5   Hampton National Historic Site (1783–90)
535 Hampton Lane—Exit 27N of IS 695, N 1 Block, E on
  Hampton Lane
near Baltimore (Towson), Maryland

This extraordinary house north of Baltimore takes a simple but sizable basic form, (175×55 feet/53×17 meters), of local stone stuccoed, embellishes it with exuberantly projected porticos front and

back, adds dormers and urns on each side of the pediments, runs up coupled chimneys at the ends, and plants a beyond-belief domed-and-glazed cupola atop the ridge. Two-story dependencies, laterally not on axis with the one-story hyphens, complete the scene. It is the Georgian gone Baroque. Surrounding this splendid pile are terraced formal and herb gardens and 45 acres/18 hectares of well-tended land. (Note the cedars of Lebanon.) Fourteen additional acres (5.6 hectares), including overseer's house, slave quarters, and plantation outbuildings were added to the property in 1980. The vastly scaled interior matches the enthusiasm of the outside. The central hall alone is 22 feet/6.7 meters wide and 53 feet/16 meters long, and doubled as banquet room (seating fifty), gallery, and ballroom, which it could easily do, as the stairs are in a separate hall. Charles Ridgely, its wealthy builder, probably designed the mansion with the help of a master carpenter named Jehu Howell, aided by the usual array of books available from England. (Mr. Ridgely unfortunately died the year the house was finished.) There is, thus, an amateur imprint on the house, obviously so in the exterior elements mentioned above, but it is so determinedly opulent, and the whole picture is so entertaining, that the house is well worth the approximately 10-mile/16-kilometer trip from downtown Baltimore. Much of the furniture is original, as the house never left the Ridgely family (for six generations) until the Avalon Foundation purchased it and gave the mansion to the National Park Service in 1948. It has since then been completely restored.

Open Tues.–Sat. 11–4:30, Sun. 1–4:30, except Jan. 1, Dec. 25: admission

6 Basilica of the Assumption of the Blessed Virgin Mary (1806–21/ portico 1863)
Cathedral Street between Mulberry (US 40) and Franklin
Baltimore, Maryland

BENJAMIN HENRY LATROBE, ARCHITECT

This, the first Roman Catholic cathedral in the United States, calls on ancient Rome (mostly) for its architectural inspiration with imposing results. It is a church which broke the English-inspired Colonial pattern of church design which had dominated most religious architecture— other than meeting houses—in the northeast part of the country in the seventeenth and eighteenth centuries. Its importance thus is mighty, and the great Pevsner calls it "North America's most beautiful church" in *An Outline of European Architecture* (Penguin Books, 1943 et seq.). The Baltimore Co-Cathedral, its second name, was designed by the British-born (1764), English- and German-educated architect and engineer Benjamin Latrobe, who came to the U.S.A. in 1796, becoming one of our most distinguished early architects; Talbot Hamlin called him "the father of the American architectural profession" (*Benjamin Henry Latrobe,* Oxford University Press, 1955).

For the Baltimore Cathedral, Latrobe submitted—gratis—two designs, one Gothic-derived, the other Roman. A cross section of the design chosen reveals a strong parallel with his earlier (1798) Bank of Pennsylvania in Philadelphia: classic portico, low entry, high-domed central chamber. The cathedral is, of course, much larger and more imposing than the bank, but the basic arrangement of parts is the same. (The church's portico was added in 1863 by Eban Faxon.) The awkwardness with this layout for a church is that, whereas it generates a potent development of spaces on the interior, it is primarily addressed to those worshipers seated under the brilliantly engineered dome. The buildup of spaces is good as long as one is walking down the center aisle, but when one is seated in the "nave" (as opposed to the circular crossing) the lateral spaces are dissipative and semi-isolated. Moreover, in 1890 the chancel was extended to the rear to make it almost double the size Latrobe had designed, and one with open side aisles instead of the original closed niches, vitiating further the spaces at what should be the climax of the church. (The onion-shaped domes atop the towers —not like Latrobe's proposal—were added in 1832.) But don't let these criticisms restrain you: visit the cathedral and enjoy what Professor William H. Pierson, Jr., calls "one of the most extraordinary moments in American architecture" (*American Buildings and Their Architects*, Doubleday, 1970).

Open daily 6:30–6:30

7 First Unitarian Church (1817–18)
Charles Street at Franklin
Baltimore, Maryland

MAXIMILIAN GODEFROY, ARCHITECT

The French-born Godefroy (c. 1765–1845) is little known in the United States but his impact as architect and architectural professor (among the earliest) was strong in Baltimore, to which city he fled (1805) after Napoleon proclaimed himself emperor. Chief among his few surviving works is this church, which confidently occupies its corner site. The three arches of the pedimented entry bay on Franklin Street are echoed by the arched windows on Charles. The unusual and effective burnt-clay Angel of Truth in the pediment was sculpted by Antonio Capellano (and upon its deterioration was renovated in 1954 by Henry Berge). Note the bold geometric simplicity of the attic above the cornice line. The nave, 53.5 feet/16.3 meters square, is no longer as Godefroy designed it, its Pantheon-inspired dome producing unfortunate acoustics. Thus in 1893 a false barrel-vaulted ceiling was installed by J. E. Sperry, a prominent Baltimore architect of the time, and the church rededicated. The chancel and six side windows were (unfortunately) installed between 1895 and 1904. The exterior remains essentially as originally built.

In addition to Sun. service, open Mon.–Wed., Fri. 9–3, except holidays: apply at 1 West Hamilton Street

8   Baltimore Stoops (late 19th–early 20th century)
NW of downtown: W of Wilkens Avenue, S of Calhoun Street
Baltimore, Maryland

Distinctive stoops of four or five steps have been a trademark of Baltimore since the last century. Among the earliest was a group of twelve houses with stoops designed by Robert Mills in 1815, now vastly altered. Other cities, notably Philadelphia and New York, have stepped approaches to front doors, but they lack the extraordinary seriatim dance which bounces down so many of Baltimore's streets. A slightly elevated entry to a house is, of course, desirable as it makes possible a windowed basement or semibasement. But whereas the generator might be said to have been space-derived (i.e. a ventilated cellar), the sociological use of stoops, especially today when security is of concern, is virtually part of the life-style of many inhabitants, both young and old. For instead of sending children to a park where there is little or no

supervision—and at times unpleasantness—youngsters can play many sidewalk games in front of the house with a grown-up observing from the stoop or from within. While for the adults after work of a summer evening, a block-long parade of neighborly stoops provides a casual socializing forum with no need to leave the premises. From the urban planning point of view, there has thus been too little consideration of the multiple recreational uses of stoop-fronted row houses: it could affect the width and design of sidewalks and even neighborhoods. That Baltimore's stoops are a proud extension of the homes is shown by the shining upkeep of most of them, the majority indeed being of a local (once inexpensive) white marble. Reputedly the longest continuous row (fifty-four units) is the 2600 block on Wilkens Avenue. The photograph above was taken on Fulton Street. "Many Baltimore row-house owners do not own the land on which their houses stand but rent it for a nominal sum" (*Comparative Atlas of America's Great Cities,* University of Minnesota Press, 1976).

---

9 College of Art, Maryland Institute (1894–96/1966)
Mount Royal Avenue at Cathedral Street
Baltimore, Maryland

BALDWIN & PENNINGTON, ARCHITECTS OF ORIGINAL STATION; COCHRAN, STEPHENSON & DONKERVOET, ARCHITECTS OF REMODELING

Few of our no longer used railroad stations have been put to such imaginative use as the old Mount Royal, which now houses the city's famous art school, a block from the parent Maryland Institute. The Romanesque-inspired exterior—showing a touch of Richardson—was left intact except for the enclosure of the southeast end for a sculpture workshop, but the lofty old waiting room was skillfully sliced horizontally in half to make two floors, with a 250-seat auditorium and gallery at ground level and library above. All characteristic details, including the former waiting room ceiling, were saved where possible. The old train shed doubles as a first-rate open-air (but covered) sculpture shelter. A sparkling adaptation, it preserves the affectionately regarded old, while serving economically the new.

Decker Gallery open—except between shows—June–Aug., Mon.–Sat. 10–3; Sept.–May 10–4, Sun. 1–4, except holidays

10   **Highfield House** (1963–65)
4000 North Charles Street at Highfield Road
Baltimore, Maryland

MIES VAN DER ROHE, ARCHITECT

Mies' impeccable taste is, as usual, smartly expressed in this fifteen-story, wide-bay, reinforced-concrete apartment house. It is, in form, a simple slab, well set back from the road on a sloping site, airily raised a precise double floor above the entrance level. By this elevation Mies enables the sun to sparkle through the two-thirds-open, largely glazed ground floor, so that instead of approaching a shadowy mass, which would obtain half the day—the building being oriented north-south—one is greeted by sunshine and a view of the garden beyond. (Le Corbusier's famous Unité at Marseilles, 1952, pioneered this rationality.) The terrace under the tower block extends laterally a few feet to the lot line on either side, then projects to the rear (westward) at the same lobby level to form a garden "plaza" over the garage, which, because of the drop-off in grade, was readily fitted underneath. An 80×100 foot (24×30 meter) "well" opens in the center of the terrace, revealing a circular swimming pool with fountain and recreation area on the lower deck. The recreation room wall can be opened to the pool in fine weather. The building's 165 apartments range in size from efficiencies to three-bedroom units. Each is glazed from wall to wall and from ceiling to the 2-foot/.6-meter-high sill (which contains air conditioning and utilities). The buff-colored bricks in the spandrels lend a domestic touch and engage in a subtle color play with the exposed white concrete structure and the black metal sash.

Entry lobby only open to the public

11   Charles Center (1957–69)
Charles Street, Lombard Street, Hopkins Place and Liberty Street
Baltimore, Maryland

DAVID A. WALLACE WITH KOSTRITSKY & POTTS OF THE
PLANNING COUNCIL OF THE GREATER BALTIMORE COMMITTEE;
RTKL, COORDINATING ARCHITECTS-PLANNERS

Baltimore, like most cities in the middle of the twentieth century, was
faced with the deterioration of much of its central area in the post-
World War II period. By the late 1950s business, shopping, and entertainment were moving away from downtown, leaving in many blocks a
shuttered, blighting residue. The city's business leaders realized they
must do two things if they wanted to keep the city alive: one, reverse
the drain from the central business district (CBD) by making it so attractive and convenient that no one would want to leave; two, coordinate any potential new work for overall urban betterment. Most American cities operated in the mid-fifties as they generally operate today:
strictly laissez-faire, with few if any long-range planning objectives for
the CBD. Baltimore's leaders—and it took leaders to push through
their plan—sought to rejuvenate a 33-acre/13-hectare plot between the
business-financial section (to the east) and the retail shopping district
(to the west). Part of this acreage had several substantial skyscrapers,

which had to be kept, but most of the rest was occupied by old lofts and obsolescent structures which could be readily cleared. An awkward street pattern presented a problem, but it was found that several minor avenues could be eliminated to the disadvantage of no one. The grade drop of 68 feet/21 meters could be used for visual variety. The site, thus, was no bulldozed urban dream, but a tough, workaday area into which the new would have to be dovetailed. Baltimore's businessmen and planners realized, too, that this should not be a precious enclave to which one made the proper pilgrimage to admire the sights but should instead be a lively round-the-clock living, working, playing, and shopping core in the fundamental sense. In addition, they reasoned, the car must not only be separated from the pedestrian, but it should have its own house under the street. On these two laws hung all of the undertaking. A few of the early dreams of the developers, planners, and architects have not worked out, but most have, and Charles Center is without question one of the great CBD developments in the country, one replete with lessons—many good, some bad—for all cities. Moreover, it was commenced and largely realized with private (and some city) funds. The pleasures of the Center can be seen in its day-night vitality, a veritable forum by day, often with activity after 5 P.M. The units include a spirited but logically related amalgam of apartment houses at the north end (q.v.), a six-hundred-room hotel in the middle, a theater (q.v.) near the south, the Federal Government Building athwart (but bullying) the south boundary, and general office blocks in between. In addition the city's auditorium-exhibition hall rests (agitatedly) across Hopkins Place.

The whole Center is laced with plazas and elevated pedestrian walkways so that one rarely has to cross a street. The planners had hoped that these aerial sidewalks would have played a more prominent, more gracious role, but one building owner refused to cooperate fully and others were unable to market retail space at two levels instead of one, thus the scope and visual quality of the walkways, while good, has not achieved the full potential that was originally hoped for. (Compare Minneapolis' success in this regard.) On the other hand the early-morning-to-late-at-night vitality and street cheerfulness have—in general and sometimes only seasonally—turned out satisfactorily. This animation finds its epicenter in the plaza by the theater, where by day office workers, in dulcet weather, sit in its terraced and well-planted "park" at lunchtime, and in the evening the theater crowd takes over. The fountain, while not the world's most glorious, does spout cheerful gallons of water per minute, and is, at night, properly illuminated. A quiet corner of the park (east end of Federal Building) enables those seeking a retreat to find a shady refuge.

The weaknesses of Charles Center lie in its lack of spatial conse-quence—it does not "unfold" smoothly—and in its lack of archi-tectural integration. Not only are the buildings all different, most are indifferent with the exception of the two apartments at the north end (q.v.), the dignified twenty-four-story One Charles Center (1962) by Mies van der Rohe, and the Mechanic Theater (q.v.). There is too lit-tle architectural cohesiveness: the group therapy of building harmony, such as at New York's Rockefeller Center, got lost along the way.

But for urban planning, conditioned by important existing buildings (and with the 68-foot/21-meter drop in grade profile mentioned), for open spaces, pedestrian lib, and for a measure of urban vitality into the night, Charles Center makes a great contribution. It is not only significant for itself but for the stimulation it has brought the entire sur-rounding area. (See Inner Harbor Redevelopment.) It is rightly the focus—and pride—of Baltimore. Moreover, it helped change the na-tional trend in the design of the CBD from what might be termed the "monumental approach" of endless walls and grids to one with a rich mixture of human-scaled spaces and buildings.

---

12 Morris A. Mechanic Theater (1966–67)
Charles Center—off Baltimore Street
Baltimore, Maryland

JOHN M. JOHANSEN, ARCHITECT

Baltimore's Charles Center (q.v.) transformed a worn-out urban sector into an alive and bustling core of the city. A good share of the Center's vitality comes from this theater, which is named for its generous bene-factor and theater buff. It is a building which by its functions attracts the populace to the Center after dark and thus helps keep it alive, and by its architecture establishes an intriguingly sculptured accent for all to see throughout the day. The architect had a problem keeping his low —and economical—building from being smothered by the skyscrapers on all sides. Thus instead of wrapping a smooth package about a com-plex theater form, he took the theater's actual and latent projections and divisions (including stairwells), exaggerated them—within logic— and evolved the concrete stronghold whose functional expressionism we see. As Johansen has said: "the outside is the other side of the inside." Aggressiveness is evident but it is lively, at times even dramatic, never offensive. One of the chief reasons the theater ingratiates itself so com-pletely into the square is that it meets the square halfway, so to speak,

by means of its broad terrace surrounding the front. The terrace then extends to join the elevated walks that flow down from the upper end of the Center, tying the building to the setting. This open-air platform overlooking the plaza finds considerable use at intermission and doubles as an emergency exit: when occupied it presents a visual inducement to enter the theater itself. The auditorium of the theater is placed on the second level so that the ground floor can be devoted to revenue- and activity-producing shops, plus a restaurant and ticket office—wise use of a very expensive site. Seating is approximately evenly divided between orchestra and balcony. A two-hundred-car garage lies directly underneath with other parking nearby. The theater level is reached by escalators, stairs, and elevator. The concrete and glass lobby is so restricted that it serves primarily as a corridor to the lounges at either end. The original stage concept, desired by the first theater manager, was for a flexible thrust type. However, in 1976 a complete technical renovation was carried out under the direction of Roger R. Morgan, the theater designer and consultant, who preferred the conventional proscenium. One hundred and seventy-five seats were removed to improve lateral sight lines (leaving 1,554), the sides closed with new walls to improve acoustics, and new mechanical facilities installed. The results, reportedly, are most successful. Cochran, Stephenson & Donkervoet were the associate architects for the original structure.

Open for performances

---

13 Two Charles Center Apartments (1965–69)
Charles, Saratoga, and Liberty Streets
Baltimore, Maryland

CONKLIN & ROSSANT, ARCHITECTS

Restrained and quietly self-confident, these two brown brick and glass apartment towers, one twenty-seven stories high, the other thirty, provide that medium-to-upper-bracket residential ingredient that downtown must possess if complete urban rejuvenation of our cities' cores is to take place. In a field dominated by the flashy or the sterile, these well-tailored and expressive-of-plan buildings highlight the north end of the Charles Center development. That they are amost always fully rented convincingly demonstrates the advantage of a return-to-downtown living option, both from the investment point of view for their builders, and from the vitality—if not survival—of all central business districts. Directed primarily to young married couples, the single, and the elderly, the towers, which contain 400 apartments, offer nearly instant commuting, being a few hundred steps from almost everything. At the tenants' feet at ground level range a tantalizing variety of shops, a restaurant, and a 510-seat cinema, while at their feet from the upper floors lies much of Baltimore. The individual apartments are thoughtfully planned, and range from efficiencies (combined

living-sleeping room), to two-bedroom, two-bath units. Apartment sizes developed the various bay modules seen on the exterior—with results much more imaginative than a straight-line, internally divisible-at-will rectangular plan. Windows almost completely fill the outside walls. Tenant attractions include a sizable community room, swimming pool and cabana, and five-level underground garage. George Patton was the landscape architect for the attractive mall. A handsome couple.

Ground floor and shops open to the public

---

14   Greater Baltimore Medical Center (1965)
North Charles Street (MD 139), c. 7 miles/11 kilometers N of
Baltimore, Maryland

RTKL ASSOCIATES AND CHRISTIE, NILES & ANDREWS,
ARCHITECTS

The most unusual architectural feature of the Greater Baltimore Medical Center is that it is upside down, with kitchen and services on the top floor. Food and supplies are transported from the top level by an electric train which travels on a central service ramp to the other four levels. The very uneven topography of the site mandated a pavilion layout with each of the five floors offering entrance from the outside. The hospital is divided into three main areas: General Medical; Ear, Eye, Nose, and Throat; and Obstetrics. Two of GBMC's eleven nursing units follow the Kaiser plan (pioneered by the Kaiser Hospital in Oakland, California), where there is total separation between visitor and professional circulation. This is established by a visitors' corridor around the outside wall of these units and, in the center, a completely open area with a highly automated nursing station for doctors, nurses, assistants, and therapists. Between this area and the visitors' corridor are clusters of four single-patient rooms. The advantage of this system lies in the uninterrupted open-access work area completely restricted to professional personnel. Moreover, patient rooms are a minimum distance from nursing stations and other medical care. However, there can be a disadvantage in that the patients' rooms lose privacy, having circulation on both sides and no direct contact with the outside.

Seventy-five per cent of the Center's 399 rooms are private and designed with emphasis on self-help, being laid out so that the patient can be in maximum charge. The wall beside the bed contains a stainless-steel washbasin and towel rack, ice-water faucet, lockup depository,

bookshelf, and a shelf for toilet articles. A grab bar is accessible for help in getting to the adjacent toilet and shower. A clothes compartment stands next to the service wall with a tackboard for get-well cards next to it and suitcase storage under the lavatory. An electronic control and communicaions panel swings out to operate the call bell, telephone, radio, and television. It also controls the room lights and even the window draperies.

GBMC is currently in the midst of a major expansion of services. Two new buildings—a central stores warehouse and an outpatient/laboratory building—comprise phases one and two of the project. Substantial interior renovation in the third phase will provide additional space for support services and also establish a separate eight-bed Coronary Care Unit. The late E. Bruce Baetjer designed the excellent landscaping. An innovative, attractive hospital.

Public reception areas open daily

15 John Deere Office and Warehouse (1967)
E off IS 83 onto Padonia Road and Greenspring Drive (2.8 miles/4.5 kilometers N of Beltway—IS 695) ne: r Baltimore (Timonium), Maryland

RTKL ASSOCIATES, ARCHITECTS; SEVERUD, PERRONE, FISCHER, STURM, CONLIN & BANDEL, STRUCTURAL ENGINEERS

A 304-seat auditorium-showroom, office, cafeteria, and warehouse located a few miles north of Baltimore. Its curved and sloping site suggested the slightly fan-shaped plan, and the need for inner flexibility prompted the unusual cable-suspended roof. At the uphill back of the building there are 18 massive underground concrete "anchors," and from these 1.5-inch/38-millimeter-diameter cables (102 altogether) space out to create the steel web which carries the roof. The far ends of the cables are attached to a hefty horizontal concrete beam which is

supported by the angled concrete piers that line the front of the building. From these cables hangs the roof of concrete planks which were precast with special suspension hooks. Inclined steel columns form rear supports for the non-bearing rear wall, with two interior rows of "matchstick" columns carrying the intermediate loads. This produces in cross section a three-catenary "tent" of concrete via rear anchors, inner columns, front beam. The interior of the warehouse has a minimum area of structural support with maximum flexibility. Expansion can readily be effected. A rugged building for rugged products. Note the supergraphics on the west side.

Reception area open during business hours

---

16   Blue Cross/Blue Shield of Maryland (1970–72)
700 East Joppa Road
Baltimore (Towson) Maryland

PETERSON & BRICKBAUER, ARCHITECTS; BROWN, GUENTHER, BATTAGLIA, GALVIN, ASSOCIATE ARCHITECTS

Mirror buildings are not to everyone's taste, but this frangible cube on the north edge of Baltimore engages in such spirited reflecting games with its red brick utility annex—also a cube—that it well merits a look. Moreover, the demarcation of floor levels of the glazed block are not slurred over or camouflaged but directly stated. In addition its "invisible" form makes it a better neighbor in a residential part of town. The angled relations between the two cubes, and their reflective feedback, were minutely worked out to establish tensions and changing images. The building was set near the top of its hill site on leveled ground, but with a sunken entry and limited visitors' parking occupying the lowest level, invisible from the street. The Belgian-block circular forecourt between main building and mechanical cube sports six 12-foot/3.7-meter-high water jets. Undercover parking for 234 cars occupies much of the area behind the lobby, with additional parking, bermed from view, nearby. Above rise eleven floors of office space for some one thousand employees, with three-hundred-place cafeteria located on the sixth floor. Planned on a 6-foot/1.8-meter module, the steel-framed office cube overall measures 134 feet/41 meters square and high, the brick service block 42 feet/13 meters on a side. The double solar glazing of the offices produces well-lit interiors with vertical blinds installed against the low sun.

Ground floor lobby open during business hours

---

17   **Inner Harbor Redevelopment** (1970–80s)
West end of Baltimore Harbor
Baltimore, Maryland

**WALLACE, McHARG, ROBERTS & TODD, PLANNERS AND
LANDSCAPE ARCHITECTS; ARCHITECTS AS NOTED**

Baltimore has undertaken one of the most extensive—and one of the most promising—programs of downtown urban renewal in the United States. As we have seen, the Charles Center development, which arose largely in the 1960s, created a nucleus which proclaimed with almost magnetic force that the central business district was here to stay. Moreover, it gave this CBD breadth and depth with the presence of middle-upper-income apartments which enrich the Center, and a fine theater to make it more viable at night. This splendid work has now been extended as the Inner Harbor project by the same capable and imaginative business, civic, and government interests which, with the planners and architects, created Charles Center. This team is working on the long-range (twenty–thirty-year) development of a once run-down site of 240 acres/97 hectares within a few blocks of the Center and hugging three sides of Baltimore's historic harbor. With its wonderful openness, its views over the water, and access by automobile, bus, and subway (phase one—1982 target date), the Inner Harbor has enormous urban possibilities. And it is important to add that the Charles Center-Inner Harbor program was approved eight times by voters when bond issues were raised; citizen interest and endorsement, plus private enterprise, have been vital to Baltimore's success.

Because of its enormous scope, the program will be constructed in several stages, the first concerned with the physical transformation of the south, west, and north sides of the harbor basin, along Key Highway and Light and Pratt streets. Many buildings have been completed along the north and western sides of this C-shape with WMR&T responsible for the plan. The green swath, parks, and promenades around the water's edge have blossomed into a folk-park, highlighted by numerous festivities including an annual and joyful City Fair (in mid-September) with multitudes of ethnic celebrations reflecting the city's pridefully multinational and multiracial background. A key accent is the restored U.S. frigate *Constellation,* the first ship commissioned for the United States Navy (launched in 1797)—and the oldest ship in the world continuously afloat. Tied up at Constellation Dock, it lends a proper nautical touch to the country's fourth busiest port. (The ship is open to the public May–Labor Day, Mon.–Sat. 10–6, Sun. and holidays 12–6; Labor Day–Apr., Mon.–Sat. 10–4, Sun. and holidays 12–5: admission.)

The following structures and facilities are thus far complete or will soon be under construction (beginning at the southeast corner of the Inner Harbor):

Joseph H. Rash Memorial Park (1976), Key Highway—RTKL Associates, architects. A waterside park which provides game and recreational facilities and acts as a coordinated spatial transfer from historic Federal Hill, directly behind, to the harbor's edge. It has two standard athletic fields and a track which are also used by the nearby Southern High School. Spectator seating for 3,500 is carefully incorporated in the slope on two sides.

Maryland Science Center (1976), Light Street at Key Highway—Edward Durell Stone, architect. (Open Mon.–Thurs. 10–5, Fri.–Sat. 10–10, Sun. and holidays 12–5, except Jan. 1 and Dec. 25.) The Science Center holds down the southwest corner of the harbor rehabil-

itation, its angled brick exterior developing a positive, not pompous, scale and its terraces extending politely out to greet the view. The exhibitions within are superior. Nes, Campbell & Partners were associate architects, *see photo above.*

Christ Church Harbor Apartments (1972), directly across Light Street from the Science Center—Don M. Hisaka & Associates, architects. (Grounds open daily.) Elevated in the Le Corbusier fashion—thus creating spatial lightness and revealing the far garden side from the street —this nine-story block provides moderate-income housing for 288 elderly (over sixty-two) with 32 efficiencies, 256 single bedrooms. Each apartment has a balcony, those on the east facing the Science Center and harbor (and street), those to the west the quieter but less spectacular small plaza and garden. Every floor has a lounge with large reception room at entry level. The apartments were built by and are affiliated with nearby Christ Lutheran Church, *photo p. 192.*

The John L. Deaton Medical Center (1972), at 611 South Charles Street, stands directly behind the apartments—Cochran, Stephenson & Donkervoet, architects. (Reception area open daily.) Like the housing, the Medical Center was conceived, developed, and is supported by Christ Lutheran Church. The five-level building stands adjacent to the old; thus, to be a good neighbor, it is discreet in design and of brick similar to that on the church (built 1935, extended 1956). The center accommodates 220 patients in private and semiprivate rooms. Polite outside, it is efficient within. The congregation of Christ Lutheran Church should be proud of the results of their social and architectural involvement with and support of both the Medical Center and Harbor Apartments, *photo p. 193.*

The Otterbein Homesteading Area (early and mid-nineteenth century), Barre, Hanover, Sharp, and Hughes streets, comprises a three-block precinct where 112 run-down but redeemable houses—slated for demolition—were sold for $1.00 each to purchasers (chosen by lottery). The new owners then contracted to rehabilitate their new homes under guidelines set by the city and to occupy them for at least eighteen months. Over half of these row houses have been restored (1979) at an average cost of $37,500. Land Design/Research were the landscape ar-

chitects. The nearby **Otterbein Church** (1785–86) stands on Conway Street near Sharp—Jacob Small, architect. Though much changed inside through the years—it is Baltimore's oldest standing church—it adds flavor to the urban scene outside and in.

Inner Harbor West, west of Charles Street and surrounding Otterbein on the north and east, is an urban neighborhood of 10 acres/4 hectares providing new dwellings for up to 450 families. The first building (1979–80), with Louis Sauer Associates as architects, is a 196-unit midrise apartment for moderate-income elderly.

The McCormick & Company Building (1921), Light Street, between Barre and Conway—Edwin Tunis, architect—is the only substantial industrial structure remaining in the area. Its tea room on the seventh floor provides a panoramic view of the harbor: one can also enjoy the aroma of its spice blending.

The Baltimore Convention Center (1977–79), Pratt Street at Charles—Naramore, Bain, Brady & Johanson and Cochran, Stephenson & Donkervoet, architects. The most spectacular new building of the Inner Harbor Redevelopment is this crystal and spacious structure which gives the city prime exhibition and assembly facilities. In addition to meeting rooms accommodating fifty to two thousand people, there are four main exhibit halls measuring 140×180 feet/43×55 meters, each of which can be used with total flexibility. It is one of the finest of its kind in the country. Skilling, Helle, Christiansen & Robertson were the structural engineers for the unusual post-tensioned pyramidal domes of bridge-like form, *photo p. 194.*

The Hyatt Regency Hotel (1979–81), Light Street at Pratt, will face the harbor—A. Epstein & Sons of Chicago are the architects with RTKL of Baltimore associates. It will stand next to the **C & P Telephone Building** (1976) by RTKL.

Two two-story pavilions (1979–80) known as **Harborplace** occupy (with some crowding) the intersection of Light Street and Pratt under the aegis of the James W. Rouse Company, with Benjamin Thompson & Associates architects. Housing approximately 150 small shops, these pavilions were inspired by the extraordinary Rouse-Thompson success at Boston's Fanueil Hall Marketplace (q.v.).

United States Fidelity & Guaranty Company (1971–74), 100 Light Street—Vlastimil Koubek, architect. (Lobby open during business hours.) Besides being a handsome forty-story skyscraper—Baltimore's tallest—USF&G acts as urban pivot for Inner Harbor, its height and podium position turning the corner from Light Street to Pratt where the Redevelopment continues. In addition it acts as a liaison with nearby Charles Center. The building's slip-form elevator and utility core are of concrete, while its piers and framing are of steel. A taut Henry Moore sculpture, *Conception* (1974), adds a powerful note to the railed podium. Enis Y. Baskam was the structural engineer, *top photo p. 195.* Immediately across Light Street stands the **IBM Building** (1975)—Pietro Belluschi and Emery Roth & Sons, architects. Note its fenestration.

World Trade Center (1976–77), Pratt Street between South and Gay streets—I. M. Pei & Partners, architects. (Ground floor open during office hours.) This thirty-story, pentagonal building in effect visually ter-

minates, at least for the present, the sweep of the Inner Harbor Redevelopment, its beacon-like form turning its back on no one, its position being of the sea as well as land. The building is also of structural interest in that five massive clawlike piers of reinforced concrete uphold the corners, with a pentagonal concrete inner core for elevators and services, no intermediate columns being necessary. Henry N. Cobb was design partner; Richter, Cornbrooks, Matthai, Hopkins, associate architects; Weiskopf & Pickworth, structural engineers, *bottom photo p. 195.*

The Baltimore Aquarium (1979–80), Pratt Street on Pier 3—Cambridge Seven, architects. The Aquarium's boldly fractured geometry of concrete is topped by a glass pyramid containing a complete tropical rain forest. Circulation around its great ocean tanks is one-way. Four levels of galleries supplement the tanks. LeMessurier/SCI were the structural engineers.

It is hoped that a series of high-rise residential towers will be built on the piers adjacent to the Aquarium. Medium-upper-income apartments would attract many citizens who have fled to the suburbs to return to the city. The superb pier site and the proximity to business and government could scarcely be improved upon.

Non-profit Charles Center—Inner Harbor Management, Inc., is primarily responsible for all rental and related negotiations and for supervising "the design and construction of public facilities and coordinating the activities of the various city agencies and private developers. The corporation serves as liaison between the City and private business interests to expedite completion of the projects." Their work has been admirable thus far—full of urban lessons for all our cities. Let it also be noted that a brilliant, overall plan was prepared before any ground was broken.

---

18   Coldspring New Town (1973–   )
take Cold Spring Lane exit W off Jones Falls Expressway
   (IS 83), N off first right onto Springarden Drive
Baltimore, Maryland

MOSHE SAFDIE & ASSOCIATES, ARCHITECTS AND PLANNERS

The City of Baltimore, which has been extraordinary first in revitalizing its central business district, then in implementing its broad-ranged Inner Harbor Redevelopment, has been engaged since 1973 (date of construction commencement) in one of the country's most imaginative housing undertakings. The basic aim of this is to provide such attractive residential options at reasonable prices that the city will retain within its borders moderate-to-upper-income—and taxpaying—families. This

New Town in town took actual root when it was found that 375 acres/152 hectares of almost unbuilt-on land in the western part of the city was available. Located between two wooded parks—one of which is a wildlife preserve—its lovely site had been bypassed earlier because grade conditions were too steep and uneven for routine development. It was just this condition of difficulty, however, which inspired the architects and planners to arrive at their clever solution. The Euro-Middle Eastern tradition of building on the hills and farming the flatlands was part of the inspiration. It should be mentioned that though federal funds under the urban renewal act helped acquire the land, the town houses (1978–) and apartments are being erected by a private builder following specific plans of the architects. The developer then sells the condominium units at a fixed profit. The land itself, which is owned by the City of Baltimore, was carefully organized to keep its unspoiled qualities—"a community in a park." A network of pedestrian walkways provides that essential classification of circulation to keep cars and children separate.

The program for housing at Coldspring consists of three main types: 1,023 deck town houses in groups of fifteen to thirty units; 1,727 hillside cluster housing of six or seven units; and 1,030 units in high-rise apartments. An imaginative twenty-story residential building will be built against the face of an abandoned quarry. Altogether it is expected that 3,780 units (70 per cent condominum "homeowners," and 30 per cent rental) will accommodate approximately 12,500 people. A neighborhood shopping center with an elementary school will be established in each of two centers with a third town center between them, dramatically bridged over Cold Spring Lane. This latter will provide wide shopping and cultural opportunities, offices, a middle school, and housing for the elderly.

Though only the beginnings of this promising project thus far have been realized, they augur as much for the future as any housing in the United States (124 condominium deckhouses in stage 1-A had been built and occupied by early 1979). The deckhouse apartments rest on "platforms" which neutralize grade differentials, interlink with adjacent decks, and on the entrance level create an agreeable "deck neighborhood" and playground for children in the apartments which surround them. Underneath there is a high-clearance service area (garbage, etc.) and room for two automobiles per unit. Not only is the car out of sight, the owner can drive directly to his apartment under cover. One side of the deck is framed by two-story town houses, with vertically stacked maisonettes or duplexes on the other side. The lower of these and the town houses opposite have fenced patio gardens, while the upper units have broad terraces and planting boxes on the roof of the apartment below. Thus all enjoy not only immediate contact with nature—"a garden for every house"—but sweeping views as well. Though tightly concentrated, there is reasonable privacy, and through ingenuity of design almost every owner enjoys that rare feeling of identity. Extensive use of prefabrication, primarily in reinforced concrete, makes the above attractions reasonable financially in spite of difficult ground. The construction techniques first used by Moshe Safdie in his "Habitat" at the Montreal Expo '67 are being perfected here.

Coldspring New Town Corporation is a subsidiary of the F. D. Rich Housing Corporation of Stamford, Connecticut. Consultants were Lawrence Halprin & Associates for intitial environmental analysis and landscaping; Tadjer Cohen Associates, structural engineers; Burdette, Koehler, Murphy & Associates, mechanical and electrical engineers; the Department of Housing and Community Development, City of Baltimore; and the Delta Group, Philadelphia, for final infrastructure and landscaping design.

Grounds open daily

19 Old Trinity Church (c. 1675)
.9 mile/1.4 kilometers W of Church Creek, off MD 16, 6.3 miles/10 kilometers SW of
Cambridge, Maryland

A gem of a small church (nave 38×20 feet/12×6 meters) which is set amid an ancient cemetery and along the water which served as high-

way for most of the early congregations. One of the oldest churches in the country in continuous active use, it is one of the finest buildings open to the public on Maryland's Eastern Shore. The exterior, though possessed of a certain quaintness, carries little distinction, being primarily a simple rectangle with steeply gabled roof. A small semicircular apse (note neat wood shingle pattern) stirs up this geometry, while the burnt headers of the brick add a touch of interest, but the framing and mullions of all windows, while authentic, are weighty. The interior, however, is a pure delight, with a towering, natural wood pulpit in the midst of the congregation on the left wall, surrounded by unpainted box pews. A delicate brass chandelier hangs over the aisle, a fine complement to the wood, to the square bricks of the floor (mostly original), and to the white plastered walls. The church suffered grievously in the 1850s when it was "modernized in the Gothic style," but from 1953 to 1960 it was meticulously restored to its seventeenth-century condition through the generosity of the late Colonel and Mrs. Edgar W. Garbisch, who formerly lived nearby. The restoration's architectural consultant was Louis Osman of London.

Open Jan.–Feb., Sun. only 10–4; Mar.–Dec., Mon., Wed.–Sat. 9–5, Sun. 1–5

---

20 Noxell Office Building (1967)
York Road (MD 45), c. 5 miles/8 kilometers N of IS 695, and just N of
Cockeysville, Maryland

SKIDMORE, OWINGS & MERRILL, ARCHITECTS

Introduced by a serpentine driveway—the site had previously been a well-laid-out nursery—one rounds a curve to come upon a pristine glass box with prominent roof upheld only by four external columns on each side. Four enormous steel girders rest on these to span the width of the building, creating a completely column-free interior 115×300 feet/35×91 meters. (Air conditioning and other utilities are strung through the girder webbing.) The freestanding reinforced concrete columns and the white-painted muscular fascia dominate the outside with the gray-tinted glass walls tucked under the roof's overhang. The main floor is used for administrative headquarters while labora-

tories occupy the lower level which notches into the sloping grade. Executive offices line the two long walls of the entry floor with an open secretarial pool between. A glazed court, open to the sky and well planted, punctures the center. Penetrating to the lower level, it also brings light and visual liberation to the cafeteria and some of the laboratories. The boldness of the structural concept, the contact with the landscaping which one sees from the lateral offices as well as from the central work space (the end walls being all glass), and, within, the colors of walls and furnishings combine to make this a first-rate headquarters. All services are placed underground to the west, their wing punctuated on top by a tall black cylindrical stack of sculptured impact. Manufacturing and warehousing are located in a large building nearby. William S. Brown was partner-in-charge.

Reception hall open to visitors 9–5 on business days

21   Columbia New Town (1966–81)
US 29 (c. 17 miles/27 kilometers SW of Baltimore, c. 20 miles/32 kilometers NE of Washington, D.C.
Columbia, Maryland

THE HOWARD RESEARCH & DEVELOPMENT CORPORATION, DEVELOPER; MORTON HOPPENFELD, CHIEF PLANNER; VARIOUS ARCHITECTS

No city in the United States has been planned with more conscientious expertise or with more determination to make the city work as a social organism than Columbia, Maryland. Located off a major highway between Baltimore and Washington, but nearer the former, occupying 22 square miles/57 square kilometers of former farmland (an area larger than Manhattan Island in New York), this "new town" was planned as a coalescence of "villages." These will eventually reach a total of seven, with an overall population of 110,000. (In 1980 its six existing villages housed approximately 50,000.) Columbia's actual planning is of overwhelming importance, but much of the thinking behind it is even more meaningful for the future of America's urban development and the sheltering of man and his family. For Columbia's "planning" did not begin with a "plan" at all, but with a search for objectives which aimed at a pragmatic urban utopia within the framework of private enterprise. A lengthy series of conferences and consultations with experts far removed from land usage conceived Columbia's goals. Sociologists, administration and government specialists, economic researchers, human relations professors, ministers, recreational commissioners, women's sociologists—before women's lib—transportation experts, behavioral scientists, city managers, doctors and public health people, psychologists, educators, even a historian, were among those in the preplanning think tank. They sought an approach which would "lift community life to a new level of dignity and inspiration" and make Columbia, to quote James W. Rouse, the city's messianic brains, progenitor and father, "a garden where people grow."

The ideas which evolved suggested an interlocking series of villages, each approximately a mile (1.6 kilometers) in diameter and accommodating ten thousand to fifteen thousand people. These would all have the full facilities of a small town. The fully integrated villages would be broken down into relaxed, non-grid "neighborhoods," three to five per village, with three hundred to five hundred families in them. The focus of the neighborhood unit would be the communal buildings—assembly

hall, elementary school, day-care facilities, swimming pool, shops, etc., virtually all of which could be reached by walking. A major Town Center, surrounded by a greenbelt, would provide the nexus for the whole development, with office buildings, a large shopping center, including a department store, hotel, theaters, and all the necessities and amenities of a medium-sized city. ("Downtown," as a spontaneous cultural and commercial core, has not yet fully materialized.) A band of clean industry, well isolated on the periphery, would establish a base for employment. (At present—1980—some twenty thousand jobs are provided by about eight hundred concerns. Many of these, however, are filled by non-residents. Almost all who work in Columbia can afford to live there.) Nature would everywhere be protected and would interpenetrate neighborhoods and villages, offering direct contact to all for outdoor recreation and intergroup activities. Dammed-up streams would create several lakes, while golf courses, riding trails, and even a game refuge would be part of the picture. As regards personal health, comprehensive services would provide a master health insurance plan which would cover all contingencies for those who subscribed to it. These, then, were the objectives. What is the reality?

Wonderfully enough, reality—at least in land usage—mirrors theory. Columbia's location between two of the East's most important cities, and straddling one of its major highway linkages, with an interstate on one border, establishes a viable location with excellent communications. Its respect for the rolling terrain is admirable, probably the finest in the country, while its own road network is sensitive to every opportunity of its uneven topography. No bulldozer transgressed, no slaughter of the trees was permitted. Moreover, lot pattern and disposition were not cranked out of a musty duplicating machine, but reflect and fit the terrain and its natural features so that few houses face onto a thoroughfare and most open at the rear onto an unspoiled park setting. As a consequence, children can play unmenaced by cars, and can in many cases walk to school without crossing a road. All of this constitutes a planning paradigm almost unique (with Reston, Virginia —q.v.) in the United States, though often seen in much of Scandinavia and some of the British New Towns. The manifold lessons of land usage, almost land worship, at Columbia should be on the desk of every real estate developer in the country.

The weakness of Columbia lies in the less than sparkling quality of its architecture. When the planning is so superb—and planning here means the concept of urban living as well as its reality—it is unfortunate that the buildings are not of the same caliber. Some are good, such as the exciting shopping center (1971—Cope, Linder & Walmesley), the Merriweather Post Music Pavilion (1968—Frank O. Gehry & Associates, architects), the very handsome Rouse Company Headquarters (1974—also by Frank Gehry), but many public buildings are routine. Moreover, the houses, all of which were designed and erected by speculative builders, generally repeat the dismal level of architecture seen in every suburb. It should be added that all houses are built on specific sites planned by the corporation, which also laid out the roads and installed underground utilities. Builders buy this "prepared" land and erect their houses which are in theory subject to "design review," but apparently control is not strict. If only the buildings matched the quality of the land on which they stand.

Lack of architectural quality was virtually built in at those early sessions which formulated the philosophy and scope of the new city. Wrote *House & Home* then (December 1964): "Builders who locate in Columbia will have to conform to design standards when they build, but architecture will not be an over-riding consideration. Says Rouse: 'I don't think we're going to create anything new in design in Columbia.'"

Economics are, of course, a prime consideration in building, but good design can be just as good marketplace as poor design; the payoff is not so much what a building costs as what it's worth. Top planning and high-level architecture are essential ingredients for any large-scale undertaking that houses people; let our bankers, insurance companies, and major corporations heed this when they start their next New Town. Columbia is so rich with lessons on its use of the ground, let us hope that its subsequent architecture will be more of consequence on top of it.

Public welcome at all times

---

22   Fort Washington (1814–24)
4.3 miles/6.9 kilometers S of intersection of IS 495 and MD 210, S on MD 210, then 3.5 miles/5.6 kilometers on Fort Washington Road
Fort Washington National Park, Maryland

PIERRE CHARLES L'ENFANT, ARCHITECT-ENGINEER

George Washington himself picked the site for this fort (1794)—it is, incidentally, almost directly opposite Mount Vernon on the Maryland side of the Potomac—and the first redoubt, called Fort Warburton, was built in 1809. During the War of 1812 the fort was abandoned upon

the capture of the city of Washington, and its guns blown up by the American forces to keep them from coming into the hands of the British. However, on the cessation of fighting and with the lesson of war just behind them, L'Enfant, who had finished his famous plan for Washington, was commissioned to design a new and more formidable fortification to protect the water approaches to the capital. L'Enfant used a star-shaped design based loosely on the famous works of Sébastien Vauban, the great French military engineer (1633–1707). (See also the Castillo de San Marcos in St. Augustine, Florida.) Rising over 70 feet/21 meters above the Potomac, with stone and brick walls some 7 feet/2.1 meters thick, it forms a substantial bastion whose guns could be trained to sweep both angles of the river. A dry moat separates the protecting outer walls from the river. The well-designed officers' quarters near the sally port and the enlisted men's barracks beyond face onto the parade ground.

L'Enfant, it should be added, was replaced (temperament again) by Colonel W. K. Armistead and his assistant, Captain T. W. Maurice, who finished the fort in 1824. Twenty-five years later its firepower was substantially increased when eighty-eight gun platforms were added, and the previously weak wall of the land approach was strengthened. However, it was abandoned as obsolete as a defense measure in 1872, though the 341-acre/138-hectare reservation was later fitted with concrete batteries and 10-inch/25-centimeter rifled guns. After World War II it was returned to the Department of the Interior, which now administers it under the National Park Service. Besides being a robust and well-preserved example of early river fortifications, the fort and extensive park make a pleasant excursion from Washington (S on IS 295 and E on IS 495). Picnics are encouraged: the views of the river are unequaled.

Fort and park open daily 9–5; afternoon tours daily in summer, weekends only rest of year

---

23   Jonathan Hager House (1739–40)
19 Key Street adjacent to City Park
Hagerstown, Maryland

A simple but sturdily built fieldstone frontier house on a rustic site. Note the asymmetry of the openings and the fact that the stone under the porch is whitewashed to reflect more light into the dwelling. The walls are thick so that the building could serve as a fort against Indian attack, while two inside springs ensured water. The basement floor was used as a fur trading post. Numerous artifacts are on display in the interior, most of them found during the excavation and restoration of the building in 1953. The rooms themselves have been authentically furnished.

Open May–Sept., Tues.–Sat. 10–4, Sun. 2–5; Oct.–Apr. by appointment only: admission

24   Teackle Mansion (c. 1801/wings 1803)
Prince William Street at Mansion Street
Princess Anne, Maryland

Somerset County (founded in 1666) and Princess Anne Towne, the latter fortunately bypassed by the freeway, retain much Eastern Shore atmosphere. The Teackle Mansion—which is said to have been inspired by a Scottish manor house which Littleton Dennis Teackle had seen when in Europe (dubious)—constitutes the town's chief architectural attraction, its nearly 200-foot/61-meter-long facade dominating the street. The five-part brick Federal house is in the Classical tradition of central block, hyphens, and wings, the latter originally designed for a law office and gatehouse when they were added two years after completion of the central section. The left (south) wing and main house are owned by Olde Princess Anne's Days, the right by the Somerset County Historical Society. There is both a land and river entrance. The interior, long in disrepair, is now undergoing restoration, as are the extensive gardens. The north wing was once used for a "Female Academy." The Adam decorative detail and ceiling should be noted. Though not in the topmost architectural category of the major Maryland and Virginia plantations, the Teackle Mansion definitely merits a look—as does the town of Princess Anne. The house is on the National Register of Historic Places.

At present open only on Sun. afternoon 2–4, and by appointment

---

25   Old State House (1676/1934)
off MD 5
St. Marys City, Maryland

Maryland, under the famous Calvert family, was established as a colony in St. Marys City in 1634 when some hundred and fifty weary souls stepped ashore from the *Ark* and the *Dove*. They had left England in November and did not reach their destination until March. St. Marys thus became the capital of the new colony and remained such until the government was moved to more accessible Annapolis in 1695. Isolated geographically near the end of the peninsula where the Potomac enters Chesapeake Bay, and bypassed politically when it lost the seat of power, St. Marys City entered into a long period of amiable desuetude. When Maryland celebrated its tricentennial in 1934 one of the most laudable functions of this birthday was the reconstruction of its first statehouse. The original Jacobean building (1676) had partially burned and was razed in 1829, its locally made bricks being used to construct Trinity Church. The adjacent cemetery was eventually to

cover the site of the early building. The present reconstruction (1934), therefore, sits near, not on, the spot on which the first structure arose, but it is precisely of its dimensions (from measuring the existing foundations) and appearance (from early documents). Much of the hardware was copied from appropriate prototypes in Annapolis. The two-story result, of modified Greek cross plan and slightly medieval exterior, forms one of the handful of distinguished buildings of the Colonies that survived (or, as here, derived from) the seventeenth century. The large ground-floor assembly hall (some 45×30 feet/14×9 meters) dominates the interior. (It even served as a chapel when the capital was moved.) The top floor holds a replica of the former Council Chamber and a room which was probably originally a waiting room but which is now devoted to an imaginative exhibit which traces the beginnings of this outpost in the New World. With hospitable Indians, rich soil, and—thanks to Lord Baltimore (Cecilius Calvert)—unprecedented religious freedom (as long as it was Christian—the good Lord was probably also motivated by a desire for more colonists), Maryland was—and is—a favored land, and the well-laid-out "City of St. Maries" a picturesque palimpsest of its beginning. Plans are under way to continue preservation and restoration, including a reconstructed *Dove*.

Open Apr.–Oct., daily 10–5; Nov.–Mar., Tues.–Sun. 10–4, except Jan. 1, Dec. 25

26   Old Wye Church (1721)
on MD 662 (just W of US 50), immediately S of town
Wye Mills, Maryland

Maryland's famous Eastern Shore is fortunate in having two historic churches of significance, this and Old Trinity (q.v.). Old Wye was built over forty years after Trinity, and its exterior proclaims its greater mastery of details as in its neat roundheaded, shuttered windows, capable front entry, and superior brickwork. Wye's interior, however, with its routine pulpit, lacks that almost medieval delight of Trinity. But see them both—they are not far apart—each has its rewards. The Wye Church was beautifully restored, really rebuilt, in 1949, through the generosity of Arthur A. Houghton, Jr. The adjacent Vestry House was also reconstructed. Perry, Shaw & Hepburn were the architects.

Open Mon.–Fri. 10–1:30, except holidays; often open Sun. afternoon

Massachusetts

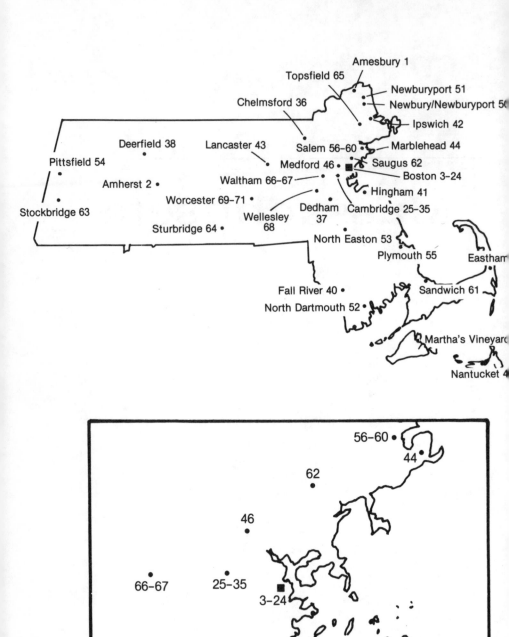

Amesbury 1
Topsfield 65
Newburyport 51
Chelmsford 36
Newbury/Newburyport 5(
Ipswich 42
Deerfield 38 Lancaster 43 Salem 56–60 Marblehead 44
Pittsfield 54 Medford 46 Saugus 62
Amherst 2 Waltham 66–67 Boston 3–24
Hingham 41
Worcester 69–71 Dedham Cambridge 25–35
Stockbridge 63 Wellesley 37
Sturbridge 64 68 North Easton 53
Plymouth 55 Eastham
Fall River 40 Sandwich 61
North Dartmouth 52
Martha's Vineyarc
Nantucket 4

56–60
44
62
46
66–67 25–35
3–24
68
37
41

BOSTON AREA

MASSACHUSETTS

The buildings in boldface type are of general interest. The others are for the specialist.

Amesbury   1 **Rocky Hill Meeting House** (1785)

Amherst   2 University of Massachusetts (1966–74)—Various architects

Boston   Note: in Greater Boston area see Cambridge, Dedham, Medford, Saugus, and Waltham

3 Paul Revere House (c. 1676)

4 **Christ Church** (Old North—1723–24)

5 **Faneuil Hall Marketplace**—Hall by Smibert and Bulfinch (1742/1806); Market by Alexander Parris (1826), rehabilitated by Benjamin Thompson & Associates (1976–78)

6 **King's Chapel** (1749–54)—Peter Harrison

Christ Church, Cambridge (1759–61)—Peter Harrison

7 **State House** (1795–98)—Charles Bulfinch

8 **First Harrison Gray Otis House** (1795–96)—Charles Bulfinch

9 Louisburg Square (1826/1830s)

10 **Lewis Wharf Rehabilitation** (1838/1972)—Carl Koch & Associates

11 120 Fulton Street Building (c. 1850)

12 Old City Hall Rehabilitation (1862–65/1972)—Bryant & Gilman and Anderson Notter Finegold

13 **Trinity Church** (1874–77/ 1897)—H. H. Richardson

14 **Copley Square Redesign** (1970) —Sasaki Associates

15 **Central Library Building** (1888–95)—McKim, Mead & White
Public Library Addition (1967–72)—Johnson & Burgee

16 **City Hall** (1963–69)— Kallmann, McKinnell & Knowles
New England Merchants National Bank Building (1969) —Edward Larrabee Barnes

17 Residential Complex at the Children's Hospital Medical Center (1968–   )—The Architects Collaborative

18 **New England Aquarium** (1967–69/1971)— Cambridge Seven

19 Warren Gardens Housing (1969) —Hugh Stubbins; Ashley, Myer

20 **Christian Science Center** (1969–72)—I. M. Pei
Church Park Apartments (1970–72)—The Architects Collaborative

21 Boston Five Cents Savings Bank (1971–72)—Kallmann & McKinnell

22 **State Service Center** (1971–   )— Paul Rudolph; M. A. Dyer; Desmond & Lord; Shepley, Bulfinch, Richardson & Abbott

23 John Hancock Building (1969–76)—I. M. Pei

24 **Federal Reserve Building** 1974–78)—Hugh Stubbins

Cambridge	25	**Longfellow National Historic Site** (1759)
	26	Memorial Hall (1870–78)— Ware & Van Brunt
	27	Baker House (1947–48)— Alvar Aalto
	28	Harvard Graduate Center (1949–50)—The Architects Collaborative
	29	**The Chapel,** Massachusetts Institute of Technology (1953–55)—Eero Saarinen
		Kresge Auditorium (1953–55)— Eero Saarinen
		Stratton Student Center (1965) —Eduardo Catalano
	30	**Carpenter Center for the Visual Arts** (1961–63)— Le Corbusier
	31	Holyoke Center, Harvard University (1960–66)—Sert, Jackson & Gourley
	32	**F. G. Peabody Terrace** (1962–64)—Sert, Jackson & Gourley
	33	**Crate and Barrel Shop** (1969–70) —Benjamin Thompson
	34	George Gund Hall (1969–72)— Andrews, Anderson, Baldwin
	35	Undergraduate Science Center (1970–73)—Sert, Jackson & Associates
Chelmsford	36	Chelmsford Junior High School (1966)—The Architects Collaborative
Dedham	37	**Fairbanks House** (c. 1637–54)
Deerfield	38	**Historic Deerfield** (18th and early 19th centuries)

Salem	56 **Jonathan Corwin House—the Witch House** (c. 1642)
	57 **John Ward House** (1684)
	58 **Peirce-Nichols House** (1782)— Samuel McIntire
	59 **Gardner-Pingree House** (1804–5)—Samuel McIntire Crowninshield-Bentley House (1727/1790)
	60 Chestnut, Essex, and Federal Streets (mostly 19th century)
Sandwich	61 **Old Hoxie House** (c. 1665) and **Dexter Mill** (1654)
Saugus	62 **Saugus Iron Works National Historic Site** (c. 1648/ reconstruction 1948–54)
Stockbridge	63 Mission House (1739)
Sturbridge	64 **Old Sturbridge Village** (primarily 1790–1840)
Topsfield	65 **Parson Capen House** (1683)
Waltham	66 **Gore Place** (1806)
	67 Brandeis University (1955–68)
Wellesley	68 Science Center (1975–76)— Perry, Dean, Stahl & Rogers
Worcester	69 R. S. Goddard Library (1969)— John M. Johansen
	70 Plumley Village East (1970–71) —Benjamin Thompson
	71 Downtown Redevelopment (1971–74) Mechanics Hall (1855–57/ 1976–77)—Elbridge Boyden/ Anderson Notter Finegold

1   Rocky Hill Meeting House (1785)
   **SE out Elm Street to Portsmouth Road, c. 1.4 miles/2.3 kilometers
   from town (or c. .5 mile/.8 kilometer N of IS 95 Amesbury exit)
   Amesbury, Massachusetts**

The Rocky Hill Meeting House is not only a prime example of its type, it is properly accessible, being open in summer four days a week— unlike most of its cloistered sisters. Thus the spartan interior of one of the finest and most characteristic New England places of worship can be fully savored. Worship, however, as is well known, was only one function of these bare-boned, heatless boxes: they also served the secular. Rocky Hill was first used to inaugurate a town meeting and its last years of public activity were also for this purpose. The interior, which measures 61×49 feet/19×15 meters, follows the usual pattern of balcony on three sides with organ and choir in the center of the gallery facing the magisterial pulpit. The design of this properly elevated rostrum, topped by well-turned sounding board and with table and deacon's seat in front, ranks high among its peers. The marbleizing of the pulpit's pilasters and of the columns upholding the balcony should be noted, as should the warm (in color) unpainted pine pews. The church with its spireless, simply gabled, almost clinical exterior resembles the slightly earlier (1773) and bit smaller meeting house at Sandown, New Hampshire (q.v.), as do the interior handling and details. Some authorities feel that one Timothy Palmer, a master carpenter, was responsible for both. Though the last services were held over a hundred years ago (in the 1870s) and town meetings ceased in 1886, Rocky Hill miraculously managed to survive as built, unmolested by later stylistic foibles or recent vandalism. In 1942 it was given to the Society for the Preservation of New England Antiquities, which now carefully guards it. One of the greats.

Open May–Oct., Tues., Thurs., Sat., Sun. 10–5: apply at parsonage: admission

---

2 University of Massachusetts (1966–74)
N edge of town off MA 116
Amherst, Massachusetts

ARCHITECTS AS NOTED

The University of Massachusetts has burgeoned from a 4,000-student agricultural college to a university with an enrollment of almost 25,000 students. The university was blessed with a sufficiency of land and having sought expert planning and architectural guidance (Pietro Belluschi was architectural consultant to the university; Hideo Sasaki produced its master plan), a group of new buildings has been and is in the process of being built.

The most substantial development is the **Southwest Quadrangle,** *top photo p. 223,* North Hadley Road at University Drive, a residence group for 5,500 students by Hugh Stubbins & Associates (1966), who designed both area plan and its buildings. To achieve an acceptable scale for such a number, the architect combined five twenty-two-story towers (four oriented EW, one NS) with eleven four-story "row" dormitories about the periphery. So that the high-rise buildings would not bulk too large he then sliced them into clearly demarked sections of three or six floors of bedrooms between three layers of common rooms (on the fifth, twelfth, and nineteenth floors). A further loosening of scale can be seen in the "random" window treatment in both high and low dormitories: few windows directly line up with those above or below. Two commons and a student union complete the complex. Though the stair towers in the low dorms are, perhaps, insistent, the spaces between buildings, changes in site levels, and scale are outstanding.

The Murray Lincoln Campus Center (1972), off Campus Center Way, by Marcel Breuer and Herbert Beckhard, provides in powerful form facilities for students, faculty, guests, and continuing education. It contains a series of well-designed public rooms, chief of which is the 650-seat auditorium, plus numerous bedrooms for guests of the university. Note that the various functions are expressed in the lively facades, with bedrooms on the fourth to seventh floors, offices on eighth and ninth, topped by catered dining and banquets on tenth, and further dining and cocktail lounge on top floor. The last two floors are protected on the south side by a grille to keep off too much sun. Two underground floors were necessitated by the constricted site. The building's elevation on pilotis minimizes heaviness. Construction is of reinforced concrete and precast concrete panels, *bottom photo p. 223.*

The Fine Arts Center (1974), off Massachusetts Avenue, by Kevin Roche/John Dinkeloo & Associates, is unquestionably the most dramatic building on campus, though some find its 650-foot/198-meter length overwhelming. A centric opening in this great facade helps break its extent and leads to covered entries to the 2,200-seat auditorium and the 668-seat theater. These two facilities also serve as regional cultural assets and the divisions between public-access and university teaching areas were one of the programmatic problems. To develop coherence, in view of this public/private division, and to make the building in effect a gateway to the inner campus, the architects mounted a "bridge" across the entire front, supporting it on V-shaped piers—the better to

play with the sun—stretched a reflecting pool along much of its colonnaded length, and topped it all with thirty-three studios. They then attached on the "back" side the groups of instructional functions (library, studios, recital halls, etc.) required by the university's arts program.

The extraordinary auditorium interior, with its faceted concrete walls and its tiers suspended from the ceiling trusswork, is potent. LeMessurier Associates were structural engineers; Bolt, Beranek & Newman acoustic consultants.

Reception areas open during school year, theaters as programmed

---

3   Paul Revere House (c. 1676)
19 North Square
Boston, Massachusetts

There are few city houses of the seventeenth century left in New England largely because most were of wood, hence combustible. As Boston's fire of 1676 had its turn, this rare example is of architectural interest despite suffering a series of manipulations and changes. The front facing North Street presents a compact facade with its second floor framed out over the lower in the late medieval fashion of England and the Continent. The court side, however, rambles with an L-plan and facades of little coordination. The interiors have been properly restored, the kitchen and living room on the ground floor carrying the most interest. The house was originally of two stories, but when Paul Revere bought it (1770—after it had stood for a century) it probably had three. When acquired in 1908 by the Paul Revere Memorial Association, it was taken back to its late-seventeenth-century appearance, the house in the meantime having served—and suffered—as a shop.

Open daily 10–6 in summer, 10–4 in winter, except major holidays: admission

---

4   **Christ Church** (Old North—1723–24)
193 Salem Street at Hull
Boston, Massachusetts

When the non-Puritan churchgoers in Boston outgrew the first King's Chapel—which was their earliest Anglican parish—and sought to build a second church, they turned to Christopher Wren and James Gibbs for inspiration. Christ Church resulted and it shows the typical English U-shaped, long-aisle interior with balconies, but one tempered by New England simplicity and marked by a primitiveness of detail. Note, incidentally, the cheerful quality of daylight compared to that in most of Boston's churches of any period. The building measures 51 feet/15 meters wide×70 feet/21 meters long. In the approved Church of England manner, Old North's pulpit stands at left—as opposed to the centric Puritan tradition—its height enabling those in the balconies and the high box pews to see the minister (and vice versa). The pew "boxes" were tall to ward off drafts, and square in plan so that the occupants could share the foot warmers they brought with them in winter, the church being unheated. The brass chandeliers, which are still used in some services, were made in England; the organ is a 1959 restoration of the 1759 original.

Christ Church today suffers urbanistically, being closely hemmed in by a packed neighborhood, but the well-tended Washington Garden at

its side does let it breathe a bit. It was from this church's superior steeple (190 feet/58 meters high) that Robert Newman hung the celebrated lantern for Mr. Revere. The wooden steeple was several times damaged by gales and/or fire, and in 1954 was totally destroyed by hurricane. Charles R. Strickland restored it to the original design the following year. The church, probably, and unquestionably the steeple, were designed by William Price, a local draftsman who reputedly had studied Wren churches when in London. However, the extensive parish records reveal no known architect. Thomas Tippin and Thomas Bennett were the "master builders."

Open daily 9–5

5   Faneuil Hall Marketplace (1742/1978)
Dock Square between North and South Market Streets
Boston, Massachusetts

JOHN L. SMIBERT AND CHARLES BULFINCH, ARCHITECTS OF
HALL; ALEXANDER PARRIS, ARCHITECT OF ORIGINAL MARKET;
BENJAMIN THOMPSON & ASSOCIATES, OF MARKET
REHABILITATION

Fan'l Hall and its market have for years formed a spontaneous brows-
ing and shopping spot for Bostonians and visitors alike, and the buildings' brilliant restoration for the bicentennial makes this area even
more enticing. The group is located just east of the Government Center
(City Hall, q.v.) and extends to the Fitzgerald Expressway, which
cruelly slashes through the edge of the city. The city fathers have shown
wisdom in recognizing and rehabilitating their heritage to the advantage
of today and tomorrow. There is a vitality in this ancient section of
town which in no small part stems from the stimulating variety of its
buildings and the intriguing, oft unexpected spaces between them.
Faneuil Hall (1740–42) itself was first designed by the Edinburgh-
born Smibert, the fashionable painter of American notables (one of the
earliest), who this once applied himself to architecture. The accomplished result burned in 1761, leaving only the outer walls, but work
was immediately commenced on its rebuilding, a task finished two years
later. In 1805–6 Bulfinch came on the scene to effect a vast enlarge-
ment of the Hall by doubling the gable end from three bays to seven,
adding a third story, and enclosing the previously open ground-floor
market. And with the new interior height Bulfinch created a taller and
more handsome Assembly Room. However, from the exterior the
Bulfinch edition, although copying Smibert's structure for the two lower
floors, is less elegant than its prototype (to judge from an old engrav-
ing): the three-by-nine-bay original simply could not expand with
grace to seven-by-nine plus a 50 per cent increase of height. Lumpiness
results. It should be added that the Bulfinch Hall was completely
rebuilt of fireproof materials in 1898–99.
   The Greek Revival **Quincy Market** (1824–26) was designed by
Alexander Parris, a Maine-born (1780–1852) architect who did much
work in Boston. (The flanking North and South Markets—the three
once on the water's edge—were not directly drawn by Parris.) With
Doric porticos clamped on each end and a low domed block rising at
center (dome added in the 1880s), the Quincy Market puts up a val-
iant struggle to maintain cohesiveness over its 535-foot/163-meter

length and 52-foot/16-meter width. However, its design and its granite construction—one of its initial backers was a granite contractor—command respect after over a hundred and fifty years of strenuous usage. (The one-piece column shafts were the largest then quarried in the U.S.A.)

The sparkling restoration, really more a recycling than a restoring, by Benjamin Thompson & Associates (1974–78) took the formerly run-down area, jammed with automobiles and lined with often untenanted buildings (the markets having moved to new suburban quarters), and transformed it into a tree-lined pedestrian mall bordered with a series of bright and attractive restaurants and shops. The central "backbone" market (Quincy) expands laterally via glazed and awninged enclosures which in summer open onto the mall as sidewalk cafes. The numerous benches under locust trees extend the munching possibilities and add to the informal, do-it-yourselfness and jollity which characterize the whole development night and day. (Note the multiple 20-watt lamp standards, also the graphics). Pushcarts—Thompson-designed—and occasional entertainers contribute to the scene.

On the Quincy interior the architects and developer were careful to maintain the market heritage and to establish "non-arty" speciality shops and restaurants, generally ethnic (almost all family-owned), without supermarket domination. They also kept Parris' central colonnade to maintain bazaar atmosphere and circulation ease, established strict rules for signs, and opened up the floor under the restored dome. Tempting sights and redolent smells contribute no small part to the atmosphere. The two flanking buildings are primarily devoted to shops (clothing, jewelry, luggage, etc.), with several upper-bracket restaurants and offices floors above.

Significantly, the architects not only wanted to make the three-block enclave alive and festive, plus, of course, commercially viable: they also sought to create a pedestrian isthmus, the whole acting as an active link between the Government Center at west, the new skyscraper development on several sides, and the residential waterfront sector being rapidly developed—much of it by rehabilitating old docks—to east. It represents enlightened urbanism and a marvelous use of the old. The Rouse Company of Columbia, Maryland, was its wise and sympathetic developer, while the Boston Redevelopment Authority had a very contributory hand in both planning and financing, with preservationists eagerly backing the project. As Ben Thompson has said, "Bringing people and vitality back into the city . . . That's what Quincy Market is all about." A glorious urban metamorphosis.

Hall open Mon.–Fri. 9–5, Sat. 9–12, Sun. 1–5, except holidays; Market never closed

6 King's Chapel (1749–54)
58 Tremont Street at School Street
Boston, Massachusetts

PETER HARRISON, ARCHITECT

The truncated exterior of King's Chapel with 4-foot-thick (1.2 meters)
dark granite walls (the first in the Colonies of stone) and highly serious
near-black portico is not inviting. But within one finds a lustrous, ambitious nave aglow with chandelier, cream-colored walls, ornate coupled
Corinthian columns and entablature, vaulted galleries, a fine canopied

pulpit (pulpit 1717, canopy later), red damask-lined box pews, and red curtains in the "windows" of the apse. A lack of architectural coordination characterizes the chancel, but the nave, which set out to be the most splendid in the Colonies, wears well. Some historians consider it our finest Georgian church interior. The original parish was established in 1688 as the first Church of England parish in the Massachusetts Colony, and the earliest building was of wood. (The Puritans held organized religion solely in their control until that time.) In the mid-eighteenth century Peter Harrison designed the present structure, influenced by Gibbs's work in London, building the new church around the old, which was then "thrown out through the windows of the new stone building!" Plans for a towering steeple had to be abandoned when funds ran out: even the construction of the wood Ionic portico came later (1785–87—but to Harrison's design). The cemetery alongside gives a good contrast to the crowded site around the building. The American Revolution caused, understandably, a period of crisis for the Church of England, and King's Chapel was briefly closed during that war, to open in 1789 as the first Unitarian church in the United States.

Open Tues.–Sat. 10–4, services Sun.

Peter Harrison also designed the less satisfactory **Christ Church** in Cambridge (1759–61); of wood, it has been added to (two bays in 1857) and tampered with.

---

7   **State House** (1795–98)
   Beacon Street at Park
   Boston, Massachusetts

   CHARLES BULFINCH, ARCHITECT

A series of elements make up the famous State House, a building designed by America's first native-born professional (really semiprofessional) architect, and one who was born in Boston (1763) and educated at Harvard. (Peter Harrison, 1716–75, is generally considered our first architect, but he was born in Yorkshire, coming to this country in 1740. Charleston's Robert Mills was born in 1781.) London influences via Palladio were obviously influencing Bulfinch in the design of the State House as he himself was the first to admit. We find here a boldly stated structure crowning a hill and proclaiming via its

dazzling gilded dome that democracy dwells within. (The dome was originally shingled, then copper-clad by Paul Revere in 1802, and gold-leafed in 1874.) The horizontally expressed main block of the building might well have been more correct architecturally uncapped by a pedimented element rising behind, with a golden dome towering above this; although we would have gotten a less busy building we would also have a less dashing capitol. The State House was for many years the most important public building in the United States, and was directly responsible for Bulfinch's being made architect of the Capitol in Washington, D.C., in 1817 (q.v.). The projected central block is flanked by two Federal wings and topped by a continuous balustraded cornice (which was neither continuous nor fully balustraded in the first design). Note that the seven arches of the loggia are more widely spaced at the two ends than in the center, this extra and subtle feature being coordinated above by coupling the wooden Corinthian columns for the end bays of the open porch. On either side of the porch recessed, roundheaded windows, the central ones Palladian, marry the arches below, unifying the 172-foot/52-meter-wide facade. The pediment of the upper portion with its frustrated verticality disagrees, as mentioned, with the horizontal satisfaction of the columned porch directly beneath, while the dome obviously seems ready to take off and ascend heavenward. But though the separate elements may play too much their separate games, there still remains a very stately quality.

As soon as one enters the building and crosses the Doric Hall one encounters the frippery of the 1889–95 addition to the State House. However, hasten up the steps to the domed Senate Chamber (until 1895 the House of Representatives) and the barrel-vaulted Senate Reception Room (the former Senate Chamber): both are basically untouched since Bulfinch's day (a few fireplaces and back windows filled), and both are elegant public rooms. The 55-foot/17-meter-square Senate Chamber was, as Professor Buford Pickens has pointed out, greatly influenced by James Wyatt's London Pantheon of 1772. In addition to the enormous extension to the rear of 1895, the white wings on either side were added in 1917 (Chapman, Sturgis & Andrews, architects).

Open Mon.–Fri. 8:45–5, except holidays

---

8 **First Harrison Gray Otis House** (1795–96)
   141 Cambridge Street (enter from Lynde Street)
   Boston, Massachusetts

CHARLES BULFINCH, ARCHITECT

The restrained, almost severe facade of the Otis House—the first of three in Boston for the growing wealth of the same appreciative client —proclaims with dignity the emerging Federal Style of planar red brick front, white marble stringcourses, and discriminating touches of Classic detail. Both the entry and the Palladian window above semiwithdraw into the wall while the other openings are almost flush with it. The cornice which traces the top is a model of discretion. Even the blinds are inside, not out: the statement of the wall is paramount. It is an architecture of sophisticated proportions that reaches a climax in McIntire's Pingree House at Salem (q.v.), a dwelling inspired by the Otis House here (as it in turn had been inspired by work in Philadelphia and London). The Society for the Preservation of New England Antiquities purchased the house in 1916—it had fallen on evil days, having been used as a tenement—and began restoration. There are a few details of the exterior, such as the second-floor windows, which do not match Bulfinch's elevation drawing, but it is generally agreed that economy dictated the double-hung versus the "French style" he favored. The restoration of the museum rooms of the Otis interior is now substantially complete: one should notice in particular the delicate mantels of the

dining room, the delightful 1826 painting in the hall, and the with-drawing room on the second floor. The Society, which has done so much to preserve the area's enormous heritage, uses the Otis House as its headquarters. Its museum occupies a wing at rear.

Open Mon.–Fri. 10–3, tours at 10, 11, 1, 2, and 3 only: admission

---

9   Louisburg Square (1826/1830s)
Beacon Hill
Boston, Massachusetts

A good slice of Boston, some 2,944 acres (1,200 hectares) it is es-timated, is "filled" land as John W. Reps succinctly put it in his *Town Planning in Frontier America* (Princeton University Press, 1969). He

adds that "Today every point on the waterfront extends well beyond the original shoreline." Much of the area along the Charles River Basin had been tidal bog and to convert marsh into vendible real estate an early group of entrepreneurs began the systematic leveling of Tremont or, as we know of what is left today, Beacon Hill. The inspiration for this can be traced to 1790, when considerable ground was removed to make way for Bulfinch's nearby State House (q.v.): obviously it would be advantageous to live near this masterpiece. The views, too, were topping. Thus by 1826 much of the hill had been reduced to a mishmash of lots, almost all of them platted without a suspicion of imagination—except for Louisburg Square. This small retreat, modeled on London prototypes, is well worth a stroll with its bay-windowed, generally Federal-inspired houses, all serviced from rear alleys and most of them speculatively built in the 1830s. The fenced central green is maintained by the residents, not the city. (Bainbridge Bunting's *Houses of Boston's Back Bay,* Belknap-Harvard University Press, 1967, gives an illuminating and encyclopedic history of the area.)

10   Lewis Wharf Rehabilitation (1838/1972)
32 Atlantic Avenue
Boston, Massachusetts

CARL KOCH & ASSOCIATES, ARCHITECTS OF REHABILITATION

Boston since its founding in 1630 has, because of its natural advantages, always been one of New England's chief seaports. Early in the nineteenth century it was the leading port in tonnage in the nation. To accommodate the then almost unending flow of ocean traffic—highlighted by the famous clipper ships (from 1833)—the city constructed a series of wharves, the most impressive of which were stone fingers jutting into the harbor. Generally avoiding wood piling with its

problems of rot, sensitivity to ice pressure, and periodic upkeep, Boston occasionally opted for granite. However, it is reported that the granite often rested on deep wood pilings whose sub-surface placement enables them to last almost forever. Atop the Lewis Wharf rests the **Granite Building**, a former warehouse and shipping office 400 feet/122 meters long×80 feet/24 meters wide. The economy of this rigorous six-story building—a landmark in nineteenth-century industrial architecture—suffered, however, with changing commercial tides, primarily deep-draft steam vessels. The wharf gradually lapsed into decline then cessation (1915), South and East Boston having better facilities. Imaginatively realizing its potential for transformation into upper-bracket apartments and ground-floor shops, the architect and his financial associates bought the building and its 10.5-acre/4.2-hectare site, and converted the former warehousing and food processors into shops and restaurants, the second floor into offices, and the top four floors into ninety-four condominium apartments with one to four bedrooms. With the outer granite walls ranging in thickness from 16 to 30 inches (41 to 76 centimeters) and with 14×14 inch (36-centimeter-square) beams forming the framework (and left exposed in the renovation), structural basis existed for almost any adaptation needed. Within a few minutes' walk of much of downtown, with lovely views, and with both one's car and boat outside the window, the Lewis Wharf rehabilitation represents a highly creative step in attracting back to the city the income brackets it needs most. Moreover, it is restoration full of talent and respect for what was there before.

Shops and restaurant open during business hours

---

11   120 Fulton Street Building (c. 1850)
120 Fulton Street
Boston, Massachusetts

In tracing briefly the state's architectural development it is appropriate to include this well-detailed, five-story, cast-iron-front building a few blocks NNE of City Hall (just beyond the Fitzgerald Expressway). It is one of the city's, indeed the country's, finer structures of its period and material. It was possibly built by Daniel Badger, who, though born in New Hampshire (1806), got his start in Boston before moving to New York in 1846. Badger claimed (erroneously) to have given Boston in

1842 "the first structure of Iron ever seen in America." The building was occupied for 112 years by the George T. McLauthlin Elevator Company, which made a number of changes in it before moving to the suburbs in 1977. In 1978 the exterior was carefully restored and the interior converted to condominium offices and apartments: first-rate adaptive use.

Can only be viewed from street

12   Old City Hall Rehabilitation (1862–65/1972)
45 School Street between Tremont and Washington
Boston, Massachusetts

**BRYANT & GILMAN, ARCHITECTS OF ORIGINAL; ANDERSON
NOTTER FINEGOLD, OF REMODELING**

This is one of the country's cleverest adaptations of an aged but sturdy
municipal building, here turned into highly desirable office space and a
top-flight restaurant. The boldly modeled Second Empire facade, vibrant with light and shade, has been scrupulously maintained and
cleaned. The interior has been thoroughly updated mechanically and of
necessity substantially changed, to provide competitively priced banking
and office facilities. Would that more cities would thus recycle their
"old-new" architectural heritage. But, it must be added, this School

Street metamorphosis did not come about without a struggle. Even the Boston Arts Commission had recommended the building's destruction, feeling that it would be too expensive to turn it to commercial advantage. However, a young group of developers, keen on salvation, took over and the result is a profitable lesson for all—including its entrepreneurs. The small plaza in front with statues of Ben Franklin and Josiah Quincy—two of Boston's greats—develops a welcome breathing space in its tight street. George M. Notter, Jr., was principal-in-charge.

Open during business hours

---

13   Trinity Church (1874–77/1897)
Copley Square
Boston, Massachusetts

HENRY HOBSON RICHARDSON, ARCHITECT

The stalwart ruggedness, even majesty, of Trinity rightly places it among the country's signal churches. Although its commission was won in an invitation competition in 1872, many changes—fortunately—evolved before the church was completed. Its front porch (not by Richardson but based on his design) was not finished until eleven years after the architect's untimely death (at forty-eight) in 1886. Trinity's exterior reaches an almost thundering climax of masses via a series of scale buildups that culminates in the enormous turreted tower at the crossing. Richardson wanted a strong central tower—"the main feature," as he put it—to hold down the visual approaches to the church from any angle. His studies, after winning the competition, continually enlarged the tower's bulk, in the process changing it from an octagon to a more compelling square form. In the meantime the engineers—and HHR was a keen mathematician—said that the filled land on which the church stood could not support the reputed 18 million pounds/8,165,000 kilograms to be placed upon it in spite of 4,500 piles already (1873) driven into the ground. Though some weight was pared from the tower, most reduction was achieved by lowering the walls, a move that caused Mr. Richardson proper anguish. Not until 1875, after the adjacent parish house had been completed, did the tower's evolution reach its final form and aboveground construction was commenced on the church itself.

In the design of Trinity references to medieval France are obvious: its Louisiana-born, Beaux-Arts-trained architect, who spent five years

in Paris, wrote that "The style of the Church may be characterized as a free rendering of the French Romanesque, inclining particularly to the school that flourished in the eleventh century in Central France" (*Trinity Church in the City of Boston, 1733–1933*, Boston, 1933). However, Ann Jensen Adams writes in *The Art Bulletin* (September 1980) that HHR was also impressed by G. E. Street's description and illustration of the Old Cathedral of Salamanca in his book *Gothic Architecture in Spain* (London, 1865), a copy of which Richardson possessed. But these influences constituted no mere copying. In an age of architectural eclecticism the introduction of "new" architectural forms, freely adapted from eleventh–twelfth-century Europe, occasioned an esthetic revolution in the U.S.A., one which gave a vivid—if at times overworked—imprimatur known as the Richardsonian Romanesque. This was, it should be added, a unique American development, one refreshingly untouched by influences from Europe. As Wayne Andrews wisely put it, "Richardson . . . brought order out of chaos" (*Architecture, Ambition and Americans,* Harper, 1955).

The interior of Trinity, in plan a compact Greek cross plus apse, proclaims a unity—once one adjusts to its dim level of natural light (compare early meeting house radiance)—which surprises by its "oneness" and by its sweep upward. This stems from the prominence of the inner void of the square tower, which gathers the spaces together from nave and transepts, pauses before the chancel (refurbished by Charles D. Maginnis in 1938), then shoots heavenward 103 feet/31 meters. This

three-dimensional journey is enlivened by polychromy (of complex iconography) by John La Farge, and magnetized by the stronger light from the tower windows. The "color church" which results forms one of the most successful collaborations between architect and artist in this country. (It should be added that the famous Phillips Brooks, the rector, also made many suggestions.) It is extremely important to note that the interior is totally transformed when the artificial lights are turned on: without them the church approaches the gloomy; with them it almost bursts into song. The boldness of the inside (restored in 1956–57) thus matches that of the exterior—and Richardson was always bold. Hugh Shepley, of Shepley, Rutan and Coolidge, completed the west towers and the porch in 1897.

Open daily 8–4, except some holidays

14 **Copley Square Redesign** (1970)
Copley Square
Boston, Massachusetts

SASAKI ASSOCIATES, LANDSCAPE ARCHITECTS

Copley Square, the front yard for Trinity Church and the Boston Public Library, was originally bisected on the diagonal by Huntington Avenue. A competition for its redesign was won by Sasaki Associates (formerly Sasaki, Dawson, DeMay) in 1966, with a project that transformed an urban aggravation, which isolated two of the city's great buildings, into an urban pleasure. Their plan took full cognizance of the necessity to adjust from the on-axis symmetry of the library to the off-center placement of the church. Changes in level (gentle near the edges), sight lines, scale, planting (which along the north side helps screen Boylston Street), the frolicsome fountain, and day/night use are exemplary.

15   Central Library Building (1888–95)
      Copley Square
      Boston, Massachusetts

McKIM, MEAD & WHITE, ARCHITECTS

The late Talbot Hamlin, one of our noted architectural historians, said
of McKim's library, "its perfect harmony makes it one of the best loved
of all modern American architectural masterpieces" (*The Enjoyment
of Architecture,* Duffield, 1916). Charles Follen McKim of McKim,
Mead & White was partner-in-charge of the building. And as it sits facing Richardson's Trinity Church, completed just eleven years before, it
asserts more than "perfect harmony": it heralds the beginning of a new
era in American architecture. The Boston Library was the first expert
public building in this country to espouse the neo-Italian Renaissance:
Richardson's gutsy neo-Romanesque was doomed by the strictly ordered new style. (McKim's Paris-trained, neo-Classic Style reached its
ultimate five years after the library was finished in the Chicago World's
Columbian Exposition of 1893, in which he played a leading role.

Drolly enough, he also worked with Richardson on the design of Trinity.) It might be pointed out that in addition to the challenge of the new Renaissance-inspired style made popular by the library, Richardson's magnificent labors in stone were also "threatened" by constructional steel, then becoming an economical material. If he had lived how would he have handled it?

Under the library's quiet green tile roof a caravan of thirteen arched windows marches across the facade—and picks up the arch motif of Trinity—expressing well that one great room, the reading room, lies behind. As has been pointed out, the facade of the library was based on the Italian Renaissance and specifically on Labrouste's Bibliothèque Sainte-Geneviève (1843–50) in Paris—on which Richardson himself worked—though McKim's has more panache (on the exterior) than the Bibliothèque. However, William H. Jordy brings out that the side wall of San Francesco in Rimini, which Alberti transformed c. 1450, was also of great influence (*American Buildings and Their Architects, Progressive and Academic Ideals,* Doubleday, 1972). At each of the two stringcourses the building steps back a few inches to lessen visually the overall mass. The chief points of interest within are: the sumptuous stairway and quiet Roman courtyard at entry level, the great (218 feet/66 meters long) reading room—inspired by a Roman bath—the Chavannes and Abbey rooms on the second floor, and the muraled Sargent Room on the third. After this elegant effort Boston puzzlingly dozed and did not produce another building of distinction for almost eighty years, until its new City Hall of 1969 (if one excepts Welles Bosworth's classical MIT complex in Cambridge of 1912–15).

In 1969–72 the adjacent **Public Library Addition,** Boylston Street at Exeter, was built to the design of Philip Johnson and John Burgee. It forms a smoothly working circulating library addition (holding 750,000 volumes) to Mr. McKim's 1895 palazzo, the earlier now used primarily for research. The new building of nine structural bays, nearly square in plan, does not eschew monumentality outside or in, the exterior favoring a muscular scale while the center of the structure, the granite-revetted Great Hall, rises through seven floors to a skylight at top. (The new does pick up the cornice and stringcourse line of the old.) The entry level, mezzanine, and second story are devoted to open stacks, with staff occupying the third and book stacks the fourth to seventh floors. The third through sixth floors are hung from 16-foot/4.9-meter-deep trusses to eliminate all interior columns. The lower-level concourse houses picture and record collections, a paperback section, lecture halls and public lavatories. The Architects Design Group were associates, William LeMessurier the structural engineer.

Open Mon.–Fri. 9–9, Sat. 9–6, Sun. except in summer 2–6; closed holidays

16   City Hall (1963–69)
     Government Center Square
     Boston, Massachusetts

KALLMANN, McKINNELL & KNOWLES, ARCHITECTS; CAMPBELL,
ALDRICH & NULTY, ARCHITECTS; LeMESSURIER ASSOCIATES,
ENGINEERS

The 1962 competition for the design of the Boston City Hall (which
drew 256 entries) was won by a firm of young architects—Kallmann,
McKinnell & Knowles—in the first major competition for a comparable
civic building in the United States supposedly since that of 1912 for the
San Francisco City Hall. (In much of northern Europe competitions
are held by law for almost *all* public buildings.) But more important
than the means are the results, and the results established a powerful,
tantalizing direction in American architecture. Before discussing
the building, however, Boston's fathers are to be commended for the
boldness with which they attacked the large-scale rehabilitation of
the skid-row area where the City Hall now stands. Several years before
the competition (1960) the Boston Government Center Urban Renewal
Project retained I. M. Pei and Associates to prepare a master plan for
the 60 acres/24 hectares of moribund downtown which they wished to
rejuvenate and much of which they had already cleared. Pei's subsequent plan not only stipulated such matters as traffic patterns and vehicular circulation, it established locations and heights for most buildings. Moreover it even demanded that an arcade be included in the
projected skyscraper adjacent to the delightful old State House* (State
Street at Washington, open Mon.–Sat. 9–4, except holidays: admission) so that this could be seen from the new City Hall. The plan also
required that the decorative 1841 Sears Crescent at the southwest
corner of City Hall be maintained and renovated—work carried out by
F. A. Stahl & Associates. Unfortunately Pei came on the scene too late
to save other historic buildings in the area, and equally unfortunately

---

* The old State House, built in 1712–13, rebuilt in 1748, was plastered with
billboards a hundred years ago, shrieking with the importance of the shops and
offices within. Scheduled for demolition in 1881 because of the value of its land,
it was saved just in time by the Bostonian Society and restored in 1882 by George
A. Clough, the city architect. It now serves as a museum.

no residential development was mandated, thus leaving the sector deserted (except the Quincy Marketplace—q.v.) after five o'clock.

The City Hall itself, though it was kept purposely low (six stories on the plaza side, nine on Congress Street), attains a virile monumentality in concrete, a grandeur with which the exterior is invested and the interior invaded. The influence of Le Corbusier's La Tourette is strong in its design, as reference to the "top-dominating" cantilevered floors of each will attest (and as most critics point out). The contrast of strict mathematics with the irregular—as seen also in Corbusier's Chandigarh —is prominent in the Boston building where the modular window grid of the upper floors gyrates against irregular sculptured, hooded projections. In all cases this remarkable three-dimensionality is *épatant*.

The architects of the City Hall tied the plaza in front to the very heart of the building with a continuous carpet of red brick, Boston's historic building material even before the Great Fire of 1872. The entrance, which because of the grade is at the third level, leads to a staggering series of spaces and floors that terrace upward around one: some are anticipated horizontal ones, several spaces shoot up five floors to the roof. The lobby creates a dynamic atmosphere of tempting circulation as opposed to the static; it is fluid, not fixed. Moreover this great chamber and its surrounding balconies double as an auditorium, serving functions from the Boston Pops (excellent acoustics) to fashion shows. Above and reached by wide flights of stairs are exhibition galleries and access to the mayor and the city council. The top three floors, which form a rectangle around a central lightwell, accommodate departmental offices, the dominating regularity of their fenestration— the module mentioned above—stating cellular offices versus multisize public areas. Below and generally entered direct from the Congress Street side are the tax, registration and licensing bureaus in a four-story semiseparate brick wing whose daily contact with the public is acknowledged and expressed architecturally on the exterior.

There are complexities and extravagances of space in the City Hall that are dubious (as in the 126-foot/38-meter-high light shafts), the circulation within is sometimes confusing, a soullessness is often apparent, while the all-concrete finish could stand a few color touches (banners, anyone?). There are, however, few civic interiors of today which carry the City Hall's excitement. On the exterior, though the plaza (its basic size and location taken from the Pei plan) is most welcome (in non-snow, non-wind conditions) and is carefully detailed, a dryness and lack of focus can be seen except near the pool. In the building elevations one can question the emphasis of the top, the projecting, hooded members of the midriff are capricious, and the loggia spaces to the north are of little use. But enough nit-picking: this is one of the great contemporary buildings. And like all great buildings—and herein lies an understandable "danger"—it is spawning a dismal collection of weak imitations, which is hardly the fault of its clever architects.

Open twenty-four hours a day

Directly south of the new City Hall rises Edward Larrabee Barnes' forty-story **New England Merchants National Bank Building** (1969—open during business hours). In addition to being a very handsome building, the bank insets (as per the Pei master plan mentioned earlier) a two-story arcade along its entire west side to establish a splendid conversation between the old State House and the new City Hall. This pedestrian street with its variety of contrasts—including, of course, the bank itself—offers one of downtown Boston's most interesting strolls: true urbanity. The bank's lobby, entered from either end of the arcade, is unusual in that it not only provides elevator access but acts as overlook for the two-story banking room, with tellers under this "balcony" and officers' desks lining the far wall. The ends of the granite-faced room, which extends the full length of the building, carry paintings by Larry Rivers. The top of the building is occupied by a terraced restaurant-club and mechanical services. The steel-framed structure is faced with reddish granite veneered onto precast concrete panels to make spandrels only 6 inches/15 centimeters thick. Emery Roth & Sons were associate architects; the Office of James Ruderman, structural engineer.

---

17 Residential Complex at the Children's Hospital Medical Center
   (1968–   )
Longwood Avenue at Brookline Avenue
Boston, Massachusetts

THE ARCHITECTS COLLABORATIVE, ARCHITECTS

Hospitals are among architects' most difficult design problems. Large complexes involve a staggering number of general and specific functions both interrelated and local, all of which must be carefully coordinated. The reconciliation of often conflicting medical theories and

treatments, and the distillation of ever changing technical aspects of actual medical care, often become so paramount in hospital design that the unfortunate patient, often the staff—and even architecture itself—are frequently lost sight of. This facility for the Children's Hospital Medical Center is part of an expanding group of buildings in the vast medical complex around the Harvard Medical School, on which The Architects Collaborative has been working for two decades. The residential group noted here represents an effort to ameliorate part of the total hospital-health problem, that "beyond medicine" concern, to which all large medical complexes must give more attention. One of these new buildings (the long low mass on Longwood Avenue) serves primarily as a "private" hotel where the parents of children being treated can stay, lessening the trauma of separation at a time of crisis, which in the young especially can be acute. It is hoped to use this hotel also for children (with parents) who have semigraduated to out-patient care yet must be close to medical services in emergency. Such a move would free beds in the hospital proper, hence substantially reduce costs. In addition commercial rentals at street level help financially. The second building of this residential complex is a twenty-two-story apartment tower for staff and employees, a facility which has been of great importance in attracting and holding doctors, nurses, and personnel. Both structures have been carried out with solid architectural know-how via an approach that emphasizes where possible the horizontal over the vertical and never forgets why hospitals exist.

Grounds open daily

---

18   New England Aquarium (1967–69/1971)
Central Wharf—Atlantic Avenue at Central Street
Boston, Massachusetts

CAMBRIDGE SEVEN, ARCHITECTS; LeMESSURIER ASSOCIATES, STRUCTURAL ENGINEERS

The reserved exterior of the aquarium betrays little hint of the excitement hiding within. But on entering, the visitor is nearly transformed into a fish himself as he strolls up the blue-lit straight ramps that define the outer walls, studies the enticing display tanks and back-lit graphics, and arrives at the top of a gigantic circular Ocean Tank. Here he pauses before coiling in descent to wrap around the tank and view its piscatorial activities at intimate hand. This giant vessel, 40 feet/12 meters in inner diameter and holding 260,000 gallons/984,000 liters of seawater, forms the obvious focus of interest, but the exhibits on all four levels are full of inventive and resourceful techniques which make 74 per cent of the earth's surface more intelligible. Note, too, that the circulation is programmed and all one-way, a highly important element of crowd control particularly under dim light conditions. The aquarium also constitutes a dramatic stage in the rehabilitation of Boston's waterfront. Until roughly a decade ago this once proud area was considered gone-to-seed, an urban embarrassment. Today its ancient wharves and warehouses (see Lewis Wharf Rehabilitation) are being rapidly

converted to luxury apartments and shops, while new construction such as this stimulating aquarium are adding contemporary spice. In addition to being the architects, the Cambridge Seven were also the exhibition designers. Francis Associates were the mechanical engineers.

Open Mon.–Fri. 9–5, Sat.–Sun. 10–6, except major holidays: admission

---

19   Warren Gardens Housing (1969)
Warren Street at Circuit
Boston (Roxbury), Massachusetts

HUGH STUBBINS & ASSOCIATES; ASHLEY, MYER & ASSOCIATES, ARCHITECTS

Though this low-income development faces a commercial strip along one side of Warren Street and had to deal with rough terrain, it manages to create a family-scaled series of town houses of considerable appeal. Two hundred and twenty-eight two- and three-story units form clusters and groups with a rarely seen intimacy, the individuality of each emphasized by the slight projection of concrete-block party walls,

which define both walls and roof and give fire protection as well as acoustic insulation. Taking advantage of the sometimes sharp drop-off of grade, some efficiency apartments are half in the hillside with a duplex above and entrances on opposite sides. Almost all families have their own small garden with most of them planned so that the kitchen work-center overlooks children at play outside. The clapboard construction nicely reflects the New England background.

Grounds always open

---

20   Christian Science Center (1969–72)
Huntington Avenue at Massachusetts Avenue
Boston, Massachusetts

I. M. PEI & PARTNERS, ARCHITECTS

One of the main problems the architects faced in designing this Center was to make it an urban pleasure for the public after answering the practical demands of the private. To achieve this a vertical Office Tower for administration, a horizontal Colonnade Building, and a

separate Sunday School Building were summoned together about a long
and broad reflecting pool, landscaped on the avenue side, the whole
producing a tranquil retreat on this southwest edge of downtown. It
provides a place, as intended, where it is wit-collecting to stroll or sit,
to read, mull or pray. The twenty-eight-story Administration Building
acts as a vertical accent for the motorist and pedestrian on Huntington
Avenue, while the five-story horizontal block for clerical staff and
cafeteria closes the space opposite and via a vigorous colonnade leads
directly to the Christian Science Mother Church. The quarter-circular
Sunday School Building of muscular bent (containing classrooms,
offices, and an auditorium seating 1,100) stands detached at the far
end of the pool. Measuring 670 feet/204 meters long×110 feet/34
meters wide and 2 feet/.61 meter deep, the pool serves as recirculator
for the air-conditioning system and suspends enough antifreeze so that
it does not ice up in winter. Note its elegant edge detail. A 550-car
garage lies underneath. The architecture, smartly cast in reinforced
concrete, is overly monumental for some but it sets the stage for the

Romanesque Mother Church of 1894 and the large neo-Roman addition of 1904. The expansive pool, the garden with benches, and the triple rows of 108 linden trees make definite contributions to the city: altogether a careful orchestration of buildings old and new, one which is exerting a salutary upgrading of an entire urban area. Cossutta & Ponte were associate architects; Sasaki, Dawson, DeMay Associates were the landscape architects.

Grounds always open: tours Mon.–Fri. 10–5, Sat.–Sun. 12–5

Facing the Christian Science Center (but having no fiscal connection with it) stretches the eleven-story **Church Park Apartments,** 199–255 Massachusetts Avenue, designed by The Architects Collaborative (1970–72). This works in visual coordination with the Center in closing an urban space, but its 700 feet/213 meters uninterrupted expanse seems overly lengthy. The individual bays, however, are beautifully designed, planned, and detailed. One quarter of its 508 apartments are for the elderly.

21 Boston Five Cents Savings Bank (1971–72)
10 School Street at Washington
Boston, Massachusetts

KALLMANN & McKINNELL, ARCHITECTS

Facing the historic Old South Meeting House and a minute triangular park, with the old City Hall (q.v.) a half block up School Street, this new addition to the bank's headquarters occupies a fortunate location. (Old South Meeting House, 1729–30, Robert Twelves, architect, is open daily 9–5, except Sun.: admission.) The bank's site, however, was made difficult because of its awkwardly curved semitriangular shape. The architects ingeniously fanned their building around its plot, and utilized a freestanding exoskeleton of reinforced concrete (note detail) to form a "colonnade," and simply enclosed the rest with plate glass. They achieved a crowd-stopping four-story showcase with a not inconsiderable invitation to enter, nickels in hand. This fun corner to walk by is especially effective at dusk. The bank, incidentally, paid for the small park.

Open during business hours

22   State Service Center (1971–   )
Cambridge, Staniford, Merrimac, and New Chardon Streets
Boston, Massachusetts

PAUL RUDOLPH, COORDINATING ARCHITECT, WITH M. A. DYER, DESMOND & LORD, AND SHEPLEY, BULFINCH, RICHARDSON & ABBOTT

An extraordinary complex, as yet unfinished, which shelters a miscellany of state functions and services. These range from Health, Education & Welfare, a twenty-three-story tower originally designed by Paul

Rudolph and M. A. Dyer, later redesigned to double floor area by Shepley, Bulfinch, Richardson & Abbott and Desmond & Lord, along New Chardon Street, to Mental Health (Desmond & Lord) on Merrimac Street, to the C. F. Hurley Employment Security Building (Shepley, Bulfinch, Richardson & Abbott) on Staniford Street. That the four firms of architects involved were able to produce an articulated group for diverse needs speaks well of their cooperation and the overall planning and design contribution of Paul Rudolph. The roughly triangular disposition of buildings, all of which are connected, and the large pedestrian plaza they frame sit atop a parking area made feasible by changing grade conditions. Thus the staff can go directly from car to office under cover. The complex is still without the focal "pinwheel" tower for Health, Education & Welfare, and without most of the fantastic swirls of terraced levels which Rudolph has designed—both key symbolic and visual elements in the overall plan—but galvanic reactions can yet be felt in this more than unusual civic group. Monumentality abounds, often under control, at times of complexity. The Merrimac Street approach with its nautilus ramps, sculptured forms, and framed vistas sums up both intent and achievement. As the *Architectural Record* (July 1973) put it, "The State Service Center is a hymn to enclosure: the freedom of protection, the sweeping spaces of a defined openness, and the reassurance of massive pylons." Let us hope that the tower will soon be authorized.

Grounds and lobbies open during business hours

---

23   John Hancock Building (1969–76)
Clarendon Street at Copley Square
Boston, Massachusetts

I. M. PEI & PARTNERS, ARCHITECTS

The John Hancock forms a pure, prismatic parallelepiped of assurance and elegance. Stages of the evolution of architecture for the last hundred years can be seen in its juxtaposition with H. H. Richardson's granitic Trinity Church and McKim, Mead & White's neo-Renaissance Central Library across Copley Square. It should be brought out, however, that the initial proposal to inject so huge a building mass (and number of office workers) into this low-scale, historically precious area aroused intense opposition, chiefly among the distinguished architects of the

Design Advisory Committee of Boston's Redevelopment Authority. Some felt that it would "reduce the square and its buildings to leftover Victorian toys" (*AIA Journal,* June 1968). A zoning variance nonetheless was granted, and as the *Architectural Record* observed upon the building's completion eight years later, the tower "though maligned as an incursion, has turned out to be a strong, energetic, civil presence—giving the Square, if anything, more closure, definition and even delight" (June 1977).

John Hancock's use of reflective glass sheathing might not be to everyone's taste—and technical problems were not unknown—but here glass, which refracts approximately one third of the light striking it, has been employed with finesse, the inverted V at the ends giving interest that does much to enliven the overall mass. The angling of the plan to a rhomboid also lessens the feeling of bulkiness which otherwise might have been generated and minimizes the building's size when seen from Copley Square. The scale of the slender mullions versus the heavier structural indications (of floor levels) is also good. The three-story-high lobby—which parallels the length of the building—sparkles with polished stainless-steel columns, excellent supergraphics, and a 14×17 foot/4.3×5.2 meter copy of the Declaration of Independence, also on stainless steel, suspended from the ceiling. Five acrylic domes mark the entries. Henry N. Cobb was design partner; the Office of James Ruderman were the structural engineers.

60th-floor Observation Deck open Mon.–Sat. 9 A.M.*–10* P.M.*, Sun. noon–10, except Dec. 25: admission*

---

24 Federal Reserve Building (1974–78)
600 Atlantic Avenue between Summer and Congress Streets
Boston, Massachusetts

HUGH STUBBINS & ASSOCIATES, ARCHITECTS

The dominant structure on Boston's waterfront is the Federal Reserve Building, its power deriving in part from its location but far more importantly from its geometry of smooth verticals versus "ribbed" horizontals. (Note, in passing, Shepley, Rutan & Coolidge's South Station of 1896-99 across Summer Street.) In developing the Federal Reserve the architects have taken the special character of the building and emphasized its separation of "money handling" from general office space, using an elevated tower for the latter sphere and a spread-out four-story unit for high-security areas, with two additional levels belowground. (Cf. Gunnar Birkert's Federal Reserve Building in Minneapolis.) The "void" under the tower underscores this dichotomy of function and also proclaims the structural independence of the tower while moderating ground-level wind disturbances on an exposed site. Utilities, such as vertical circulation and toilets, were placed at the ends of each floor in the towers (windowless for fire protection and efficient wind bracing), with 143 feet/44 meters of flexible, open office space between. The floors are supported by two rows of four columns each inset from the slab edge: they are carried below by monumental trusses, at 36 feet/11

meters deep among the largest ever fabricated. From the exterior the horizontality of the floors is emphasized by their spandrels, which are angled outward to help screen the hot, high summer sun yet welcome its warmth in winter. The .75-inch/19-millimeter-thick glass is end-butted and mullionless. Bright aluminum is used for both towers and spandrels. Two mechanical floors, one at bottom (and also receiving the trusses) and one at top, give horizontal framing to the tower.

In addition to the thirty-two floors in the high-rise, there is, as mentioned, a four-story unit branching behind the double-height lobby. This contains a museum and a four-hundred-seat auditorium (often open to the public—inquire) on the front part of the ground floor, with vault and some bank operations behind and above, and employees' cafeteria on top overlooking a roof garden. A small plaza gives welcome at entry. Detailing and colors throughout—by the architects—are very superior. Hugh A. Stubbins was principal-in-charge and designed the two large lobby murals; LeMessurier Associates/SCI were the structural consultants.

Lobby and museum open during business hours

---

25 Longfellow National Historic Site (1759)
105 Brattle Street
Cambridge, Massachusetts

High Georgian flair characterizes the mansion built for John Vassall which dominates Brattle Street with Longfellow Park across the way providing perspective. The house's projected and pedimented pavilion is framed by two-story Ionic pilasters, and these are repeated to terminate and bind the ends of the facade. A well-balustraded hip roof with prominent chimneys crowns this performance. The addition of the ell at

rear and, almost certainly, the two side porches were made by Mr. Andrew Craigie. Henry Wadsworth Longfellow, who made changes himself, lived in the house from 1837 to his death in 1882 and most of the furnishings date from his occupancy. A few authorities feel that Peter Harrison of Newport fame and the architect of King's Chapel in Boston (q.v.) designed the house. For many years known as the Vassall-Craigie-Longfellow House, it is now called the Longfellow National Historic Site and is administered by the National Park Service under the Department of the Interior.

Open daily 9–4:30, except major holidays: admission

---

26 Memorial Hall (1870–78)
Harvard University
Cambridge, Quincy, and Kirkland Streets
Cambridge, Massachusetts

WARE & VAN BRUNT, ARCHITECTS

This piquant pile—a former dining hall—epitomizes the High Victorian era which once cloaked England with buildings of assembled "Gothic" motifs capped by roofs of wondrous multicolored tiles. (Use of color had been ardently pushed by Ruskin in his many influential books, especially *The Stones of Venice* of 1851–53.) Memorial Hall— its transepts are a memorial to Civil War dead—though not lovely, is loved, a mammoth ugly duckling, an almost fanatic statement of the taste of its time. If it is open be certain to see the former refectory: its hammer-beam trussed roof and its Victorian windows are superior. In 1956 a fire removed the upper, more Gothic, tower; however, there is hope that this will be rebuilt. For a time Mem Hall itself was threatened with destruction to make way for a new building, but this danger has passed. The hall is now a National Historic Landmark for it is not matched on these shores. (Peripherally, its co-designer, William R. Ware, 1832–1915, in 1865 set up the country's earliest School of Architecture at neighboring MIT and is generally ascribed to have been our first fully trained professor of architecture.)

Lobby open weekdays

---

27   Baker House (1947–48)
Massachusetts Institute of Technology
362 Memorial Drive
Cambridge, Massachusetts

ALVAR AALTO, ARCHITECT

The late, great Aalto's preoccupation with the curve—always functionally generated—began with the ceiling of his library in Viipuri (1935). Here lyric undulations which were used for acoustic betterment, continued in the memorable Finnish Pavilion at the 1939 New York World's Fair, and reached a climax—at least in scale—in MIT's Baker Dormitory for 353 undergraduates. Wishing to give each student a view up or down the Charles River flowing in front of the building, yet circumscribed by a plot of limited length, Aalto insinuated his building onto the site by calling on a double bend. This graceful curved facade contrasts with the refreshingly angular entry side, where an extraordinary V of projected stairs steps down to the front door with unabashed utilitarianism. Down with the uniform, tidy box—and this in

1948. In front (on the Memorial Drive side) rises the two-story dining hall, squarish in plan. Perry, Shaw & Hepburn were associate architects.

Can only be viewed from outside

---

28 Harvard Graduate Center (1949–50)
off Massachusetts Avenue at Everett Street
Cambridge, Massachusetts

THE ARCHITECTS COLLABORATIVE, ARCHITECTS

The buildings belong to an earlier—and pioneering—generation of the modern movement but the spaces between them are generationless. This great effort by TAC, with the late Walter Gropius as "job captain" as he called it, advanced educational architecture in this country immeasurably by demonstrating that our oldest university could call on

one of our most advanced architectural firms. Harvard previously—like its confreres—had dusted off the past. The Center is composed of seven dormitories housing approximately six hundred students with its Harkness Commons able to feed over a thousand at a sitting. Note that although the space is limited, no dormitory faces its neighbor. A milestone in the development of the modern movement in this country.

Grounds open daily

---

29 The Chapel (1953–55)
Massachusetts Institute of Technology
off Massachusetts Avenue and Amherst Street
Cambridge, Massachusetts

EERO SAARINEN & ASSOCIATES, ARCHITECTS

The problems which the late Eero Saarinen (1910–61) had to face in designing this small (130-seat) chapel—a building which ranks high in his memorable output and from which he himself was buried—involved creating a "religious atmosphere" to accommodate a variety of faiths or no faith at all. Instead of an interior which homogenizes active and pas-

sive religion into a bland, multifaith convertible box, we find a spiritual retreat, a retreat directed mostly to "a place where an individual can contemplate things larger than himself," yet one with no references to organized religion. (A cross or other symbol can be used or not, as desired.) Saarinen walled off the busy, traffic-heavy world outside with a "windowless" cylinder of deep red brick that rests on light arches in an encircling moat. The inner wall, also of brick, instead of assuming the pure circle of the exterior, undulates rhythmically against the outer so as to lessen any psychological feeling of geometric compaction or acoustic feedback. Both outer and inner walls rest on the same low arches (in the water), and they extend sufficiently beyond the circumferential bench-high "base" of the chapel to allow the insertion of a narrow glazing strip between inner wainscot and the encircling walls. Through this "reverse clerestory" (which might have been wider) reflections bounce from the sun shining on the pool, delivering thus an evanescent light. The main illumination (daylight and artificial), however, pours down from a shielded roof oculus and onto a masterful reredos whose short, flat, multiangled gold facets play with and reflect the light. This grille by Harry Bertoia represents a consummate example of the rewards of architect and sculptor working together. A simple cube of marble standing on a low circular dais in front of the screen serves as altar. A forceful aluminum spire by Theodore Roszak tops the chapel. Landscaping beside it is good, the combination superb. Anderson, Beckwith & Haible were associate architects.

Open daily 8–8

Facing the chapel to the west stands Saarinen's **Kresge Auditorium** (1953–55—open during performances), an unnecessarily warped building; the chapel utilized old means to attain a new spirit, whereas the auditorium employs new means to cover an old shape. Eduardo Catalano's boldly scaled **Stratton Student Center** (1965—Co-Op shop open during business hours) closes the plaza on the north and gives coherence to the grouping.

30 Carpenter Center for the Visual Arts (1961–63)
Harvard University
Quincy Street between Broadway and Harvard
Cambridge, Massachusetts

LE CORBUSIER, ARCHITECT

Space-time progression via ramps—the visual excitement of walking aloft—has characterized many of Corbusier's most provocative buildings from Poissy to Chandigarh and Ahmedabad. The use of an elevated ramp at the Carpenter Center sought to tie two parallel streets, Quincy and Prescott (and future campus expansion), to the very center of the Center and its upper-level galleries, to inject the student and

public into the activity of the building as they moved from one thoroughfare to the next. As Carpenter is an art facility for the non-art major (providing studios, galleries, lecture hall, etc.), this concept of injection, of making the building and its glass-lined art showcases intimately, indeed inescapably, tied to the very path of the students, carries logic. The resulting building is somewhat of a tour de force with its aggressive multiplicity of elements and its almost rude scale, while lately the need for greater security has compromised some of its native élan as the ramp galleries now have to be locked much of the time. Moreover the building proper cannot be called a conciliatory neighbor —Corbu, incidentally, never saw it personally—but then the visual arts are not conciliatory either. Logic and rationalization aside, a stroll across the ramp and through the building, with spaces being manipulated at each step, provokes a potent reaction. Albeit not from the Swiss-French maestro's top drawer, it is a product of one of the greatest architects who ever lived, and the only one we have completely by him in the United States. (See, also, the United Nations in New York, whose skyscraper was to a large degree Le Corbusier's design.) Technical realization of Carpenter Center was in charge of Sert, Jackson & Gourley.

Perhaps of equal importance with the material building is the educational concept. Carpenter seeks to sensitize the process of perception— in both intellectual and psychic terms—for students, many of whom will eventually be called upon to help commission future environments. And unless our bankers, insurance men, and developers can "see," in addition to knowing mortgage rates, there will be little hope for a finer physical tomorrow.

Ramp always open: galleries on occasion

31　Holyoke Center, Harvard University (1960–66)
　　Massachusetts Avenue, Dunster, Mount Auburn, and Holyoke
　　　Streets
　　Cambridge, Massachusetts

SERT, JACKSON & GOURLEY, ARCHITECTS

The Holyoke Center contains a complex of functions for Harvard, chief among them being student health and infirmary, various offices for admissions and departmental use, plus a ring of ground-floor shops. Lo-

cated just south of Harvard Square, the Center occupies a tight urban
block hemmed by assorted buildings. It largely fills this block yet
minimizes its own bulk by concentrating its tall H-shaped mass at the
center and sending out low wings to meet the avenues. Though dominating its unregenerate neighborhood, it is urbanistically a reasonable
neighbor, performing a valuable linkage between two important streets.
Taking a cue established by Belgiojoso, Peressutti and Rogers in their
famous Torre Velasca in Milan (1958), the architects of Holyoke
realized that a building with so many diverse functions could not be

clad satisfactorily with a rigid pattern of fenestration. They therefore evolved a flexible wall module (26 inches/66 centimeters wide) of clear glass or translucent panels, the latter a British-made fiber glass and glass sandwich. The module can be of one, two, or three units, with each section put where internal needs (of light, privacy, etc.) demanded, not in a straitjacket of external symmetry. The result has worked out to be an efficient solution with design stability maintained—in spite of some choppiness—by the strongly emphasized horizontal of the spandrels and by the slightly projecting vertical fins between modules. Variety occurs in the non-aligning windows and in the use of color which is correlated with the window module. The 268-foot/82-meter-long arcade which penetrates the building from Massachusetts Avenue to Mount Auburn Street, and which does much to tie these thoroughfares together, ends in a welcome piazzetta on the former, where the need for a lateral breathing space was acute, and in a smaller park on Mount Auburn Street.

Pedestrian arcade open daily

---

32   F. G. Peabody Terrace (1962–64)
Married Students Housing, Harvard University
Memorial Drive at Sterling Street, N of Western Avenue
Cambridge, Massachusetts

SERT, JACKSON & GOURLEY, ARCHITECTS

The vertical village for housing married students is now a fact of life for most urban universities, and while there are those who claim with theoretical justification that young children are better off digging up the garden outside their own kitchen window, such an ideal will rarely be possible. This cluster for married students seeks to humanize as far as possible the high-rise: its search has been for the most part very successful. Three-, five-, and seven-story terraced units, their height building up from the Charles River and Putnam Avenue sides to maintain a residential scale along the roads, are combined with three twenty-two-story towers to provide 499 rental apartments (efficiencies to three-bedroom) with garaging (off Putnam Avenue) for 352 cars, plus a small shopping center and an even smaller community room. The spatial relationship between high and low units is admirable, the lower buildings knitting the tall into the overall fabric and at ground level defining circulation and molding local areas. Pedestrian experiences—

one of the firm's strong points—are stimulating throughout; the scale of the courts (and their landscaping) is excellent. Although the buildings vary in both height and shape, they are all based on a standardized reinforced concrete three-story unit, three bays wide with a central stair in each. In the towers this economy-producing "module" is made possible by corridor access from the north or east side on each third floor with skip-floor elevators. Such an arrangement also permits cross ventilation in almost all apartments in addition to cross-connection and joint elevator sharing by the lower buildings. As the main views of two of the three towers are westward over the Charles River, rotatable, vertical louvers are installed to control low sun yet permit vistas. On the south side the windows are generally hooded by the balconies above. The visual play of the louvers and the juxtaposition of balconies make for intriguing facades and break up any tendency to aerial boxiness on the part of the twenty-two-story masses. The individual apartments are tightly planned because they had to be competitively priced. Moreover the community rooms and facilities (laundries, etc.) are far too slighted. Nonetheless this is probably the finest group of its kind in the country. Sasaki Associates were the landscape architects.

Grounds open daily

33 Crate and Barrel Shop (1969--70)
Brattle Street at Story
Cambridge, Massachusetts

BENJAMIN THOMPSON & ASSOCIATES, ARCHITECTS

A minimum of building with a maximum of effect: slender slabs of concrete wrapped in the thinnest of glass walls. Actually an entirely new (for the United States) technique of glass detailing had to be evolved, for these exterior walls are *totally* of glass, no metal mullions upholding or enframing or interrupting their diaphanous skin. The tempered-glass plates (.39 inch/1 centimeter thick by 5×7 feet/ 1.5×2.1 meters in standard size) are end-butted, fastened in place by tiny stainless steel clips, and braced by internal steel arms. The effect, especially at dusk, is seductive as one observes the activities on different levels, the colors of the displays, and the movement of people in this total show window. But dusk or day or night: very stimulating. Note that the building is not a simple prism, hence a simple answer, but one with breaks and angles to give divertimento to its near invisible form, and especially to create greater transparency via a series of open corners and to emphasize the horizontal interaction of floor levels. The building was originally known as the Design Research Shop.

Open during shopping hours

34 George Gund Hall (1969–72)
Quincy Street between Cambridge and Kirkland
Cambridge, Massachusetts

JOHN ANDREWS, ANDERSON, BALDWIN, ARCHITECTS

Harvard's Graduate School of Design syncretizes under one stupendous and steeply slanting roof its hitherto scattered major Departments of Architecture, City and Regional Planning, Urban Design, and Landscape Architecture, plus Computer Graphics and other minor divisions. The philosophy of its evolution, one fiercely debated by faculty and students alike, was that "space" design today is so complex that it must be interdisciplinary. To bring these curricula together where the students of each could—hopefully—stimulate one another, the architects evolved a series of four slightly overlapping and stepped terraces or "trays" extending the width of the building. The almost fantastic teaching agora which results, rising upward and backward in platformed splendor under one gigantic roof, corrals all concerned with the design process into visual proximity, if not into the embrace of intellectual camaraderie. It is a startling space. Overhead (a bit close overhead) seven magnificent, sharply canted tube-trusses 134 feet/41 meters long and 11 feet/3.4 meters deep span the column-free area, with heating and ventilating conduits paralleling the trusswork. (There have been student complaints about both ventilation and noise level.) As the roof rises, long narrow bands of windows fit vertically between the angled trusses—from direct rear elevation one sees almost all glass—and from these skylights pours a flood of daylight. The four major instructional levels are flexibily divided longitudinally, depending on enrollments, with the broadest "terrace" on the second floor, the three others narrowing as they rise. Across the bottom and down six steps stretches the student lounge, open, of course, to the entourage.

Gund represents a startling architectural concept of intense dedication to an idea; but the resulting floating yet visually related platforms are more persuasive in theory (and model form) than in walk-in space where their identities in use are blurred by furniture, tracing paper, and coats. Moreover this prodigious canopied chamber, while exciting to some, can lead others toward a hankering for privacy in their lonesome search for personal identity. Overcrowding in recent years has not helped matters. However, whether the individual exults as a participator or suffers as a cog from the building's overriding philosophy, Gund is an audacious and highly provocative addition to our architectural thinking.

Staff offices wrap in an L-shape around the front and the north side. The main floor contains the two-level Frances Loeb Library at left and the W. T. Piper Auditorium at right. In the basement are the second level of the library (cleverly visible from the outside), audiovisual rooms and services. Unfortunately only the lobby is open to the public except on tours. The exterior has a few awkward moments (as with some angles along Cambridge Street), but circumnavigation, particularly when the building glows at dusk, produces exciting contrasts. Edward R. Baldwin was partner-in-charge; LeMessurier Associates were the structural engineers.

Lobby open during school year

---

35 Undergraduate Science Center (1970–73)
Harvard University
immediately N of Harvard Yard at Oxford and Kirkland Streets
Cambridge, Massachusetts

SERT, JACKSON & ASSOCIATES, ARCHITECTS

The Harvard Science Center rises as an incredible series of sometimes disparate elements, but the overall result is forceful and on the inside the public spaces are cheery. As the complex faces the Yard—the university's historic core—the architects were careful to build up the mass required from a low profile in front to the seven- and nine-story units at

rear. (The mall in front was created at the same time by lowering Cambridge Street to an underpass.) Thus the mathematics department rises, at slight angle to the Johnston Gate (McKim, Mead & White—1889), in five broad, stepped-back terraces to its ninth floor. At left, and angled because of pedestrian circulation pattern and the intersecting geometries of the Yard with the North Campus, rises the fan-shaped main lecture hall, its roof somewhat self-consciously upheld by nine weathering steel triangular trusses and stainless steel cables. Across the rear and at right angles to the stepped mass of the mathematics department extends the laboratory block, with physics at left and chemistry at right, and biology, geology, astronomy, etc. interlarded.

Though the exterior is on the restless, even aggressive, side, the inner passageways, particularly the pedestrian "street" along the laboratory axis, are filled with light and visual stimulation. Glass, often overhead and at times in greenhouse form, is the key to much of this effervescence, with shafts of sun probing corridors and creating a sense of nonconfinement. The fully exposed structural framework also plays a role in this alive progression. (The precast concrete perforated beams seen are 60 feet/18 meters long and 3.8 feet/1.2 meters deep.) In addition an excellent use of color and color accents enlivens the entire building inside and out. The molded-sand relief in the hall behind the auditorium was executed by Constantino Nivola and formerly graced the Olivetti showroom in New York; it was given to the university by the Olivetti Corporation.

Lobby open to public during school year

---

36   Chelmsford Junior High School (1966)
.9 mile/1.4 kilometers on Westford Exit of MA 3 Rotary
1st R fork then L on Graniteville Road
Chelmsford, Massachusetts

THE ARCHITECTS COLLABORATIVE, ARCHITECTS

The outstanding contribution of the school—one not apparent at the entry—lies in its ingenious use of a difficult terrain. A "ravine" and small stream separate the front and rear sections of the limited site. Instead of regarding this as a liability the architects have turned it to an asset and projected across the small canyon two wings of classrooms whose one to three floors mirror the defile. These connect the front part of the school, most of which is devoted to administration, library, and crafts, with the rear part across the ravine, which is given over to workshops. An open square results with the twenty-five classrooms for 1,200 pupils framing the two sides and enclosing an inner court, one distinguished architecturally by the cantilevered levels of classrooms and enhanced by the unspoiled nature. A semidetached building for a 500-seat cafeteria and for a gymnasium stands at right. A highly developed TV system, complete with teaching studio, has piped connections with each classroom, obviating (supposedly) the need for a central assembly other than cafeteria. Though there is a lack of spontaneous gathering areas and the library is isolated, the terrain adaptation and the atmosphere of its inner court (which is visible to half the classes) live up to the usual standards of sophisticated simplicity for which TAC is noted. The school was built on a limited budget.

Grounds and lobby open during school hours

---

37 Fairbanks House (c. 1636–54)
Eastern Avenue at East Street, SE off US 1
Dedham, Massachusetts

The original house of Jonathan Fayerbanke, now the central section, began as a two-story compact medieval dwelling hugging a large double chimney. Some claim its main beams were precut in England. This kernel was first expanded by a lean-to across the rear, then by a wing at east, and later (possibly as late as 1680) by the small addition to west. The much-altered result, with some work probably in the early eighteenth-century, tends to the haphazard and from some angles to the awkward, but from the northwest we find a highly picturesque accretion. Though a few historians feel that a date as early as the 1630s is "rash," Dr. Abbott Lowell Cummings, director of the Society for the Preservation of New England Antiquities, confirmed this dating (in 1977) by dendrochronological research. Dr. Cummings' book *The Framed Houses of Massachusetts Bay, 1625–1725* (Harvard University

Press, 1979) gives an enlightening series of drawings and photographs of the Fairbanks House showing the construction techniques used in it. The book is enthusiastically recommended to all interested in early New England architecture.

Open May–Oct., daily except Mon. 9–12, 1–5: admission

---

38   Historic Deerfield (18th and early 19th centuries)
Deerfield, Massachusetts

Beginning at the north end of The Street with the Ashley House (wood —1730) on one side and the Wright House (brick—1824) opposite, and unrolling for almost a mile (1.6 kilometers) to the Wilson Printing Office (wood—1816), the main street of Deerfield provides us with a memorable series of architectural and urban impressions. The architecture ranges from the generally excellent to the occasionally intrusive as it covers well over two hundred years of building (and renovation). The urban delight stems from the variety and quality of "enclosure" of the street, those elusive spaces between buildings and the buildings' relation to each other and to the village that establish the avenue. Planting and trees are obviously strong factors here.

There are twelve Historic Deerfield Houses (including the Ashley, Wright, and Wilson houses mentioned), which are open as listed below. Each of them merits inspection. A useful free guidebook is readily obtainable. The entire village, which was platted in 1670, and which suffered terribly from Indian massacres in 1675 and 1704, is a Registered National Historic Landmark, a distinction more than well deserved on both urbanistic and architectural grounds. The epitome of New England.

Museum houses open Mon.–Sat. 9:30–4:30, Sun. 1–4:30, except major holidays: combination tickets available

---

39   Captain Edward Penniman House (1868)
Fort Hill Road via Governor Prence Road, .5 mile/.8 kilometer
**   E of US 6**
Eastham (Cape Cod), Massachusetts

According to legend Captain Penniman brought from Europe the plans for his small but not too humble home. It is not likely that this voluptuous Victorian-Second Empire abode sprang from the brow of a local architect. Measuring 40.5×34.7 feet/12.3×10.6 meters, it is a gaudy

and wonderful dwelling which will gladden any visitor. It is now owned by the Cape Cod National Seashore (National Park Service), an agency of the U. S. Department of the Interior, and though its survival is assured, being listed in the National Register of Historic Places, the restoration of the interior awaits funding. The whale jawbone gateway is an old Cape Cod seafaring memento.

Grounds always open: house at present closed

---

40 **Textile Mills** (19th century)
flanking IS 195
Fall River, Massachusetts

The granite textile mills of Fall River comprise a sterling chapter in the history of American industrial building, the post-Civil War era sparking its most prolific development (1865–80). The uniqueness of their appearance stems from the fact that the city rests on an extensive granite ledge, and the cheap availability of this stone has bequeathed us a series of enormous mills of this handsome material instead of the often

depressing brick found almost everywhere else at this time. Though
only the specialist will be concerned in a detailed inspection of the individual buildings—most of which have now lost their textile manufacturing—even the hurried motorist will be impressed by them as he
drives along the Interstate which cruelly bisects the city. The Interstate,
it should be added, was formerly the Quequechan (i.e. "falling water")
River from which the mills once drew their power as it stepped down to
Mount Hope Bay. (To see them in detail, turn off on Pleasant Street or
Plymouth Avenue and Rodman Street.) Rarely will one encounter such
non-industrial-appearing industrial buildings: with their gray granite
walls, white-trimmed windows, and dark roofs, many resemble gigantic
barns. Technically they are put together with precisely cut blocks to
build up their 3-foot/1-meter-thick lower walls and the vibration-
damping bases required for heavy machinery. The large looms usually
occupied the first two floors, with carding, spinning, and "dressing"
above. With such expert workmanship, general feeling for proportion,
tower accents, 400 feet/122 meters or more of length, plus often good
spatial interaction, they also come up with fine architecture.

Mills themselves not open to the public

41   Old Ship Meeting House (1681–1755)
90 Main Street
Hingham, Massachusetts

As the only surviving relic of the squarish, clapboarded meeting houses of the late seventeenth century, Old Ship ranks high in importance historically and esthetically. It is, moreover, the oldest wooden church in the United States as well as claiming to be the oldest in continuous use. (The seating plan of its 1681 dedication still survives.) The exterior enjoys its hillock location, with diamond-paned windows on its broad sides (the top sashes meeting the eaves), hip roof with gently up-curved ridges, and railed platform at top with belfry spire that carries heavenward the sweep of the ridges. Yet it is the interior which is most fascinating, an interior far more "Gothic" than is suggested by its clapboarded sides.

Squarish in plan and surrounded by balconies on three sides, the inner space rises in the center via a magnificent framework of three oak trusses and knee braces that uphold the roof with a display of Gothic wood engineering that gave the meeting house its name: inverted, the upper part would resemble the ribs of a ship. This medieval structuring —the most efficient means then of spanning such an ambitious width— defines its spaces to create a memorable interior. The original meeting house, now demarked by the columns upholding the balconies and roof trusses, measured 45×55 feet/14×17 meters and was entered from the southwest. In 1729–31 the church was extended 14 feet/4.3 meters to the northeast, and in 1755 an equal distance to the southwest, making it 55×73 feet/17×22 meters overall. This, of necessity, involved a new roof extending above and beyond the old, creating thus a dead "attic" between old roof and new. In 1930 the church was completely restored (by Edgar T. P. Walker of Smith & Walker), and the dropped ceiling which had been installed only fifty years after completion was taken out so that the interior structure now stands revealed as it was almost three hundred years ago. (The low ceiling had been installed to reduce the frigid air volume in a stoveless room, particularly with the new lateral expansion.) The restoration left the expansions, pews, and pulpit—all of the mid-eighteenth century—as is. A hundred years after its completion, the meeting house became completely religious (1780), the town's civic gatherings having removed. In 1791, the parishioners, feeling that their church was old-fashioned compared to the new Wren style, voted to tear down the building, a vote that happily was counter-

manded a year later. They did vote, however, to add the 10×10 foot/3×3 meter vestibule in front which we now use. One of the nation's finest early buildings.

Guided tours July–Aug., daily except Mon. 12–5; other times by appointment

42   John Whipple House (c. 1640/1670s)
53 South Main Street
Ipswich, Massachusetts

In the Whipple House we find a good evolutionary example of the
"growing" house so often seen in early New England. Initially the
dwelling started life as a two-and-a-half-story box with one room per
floor (probably two above) covered then as now by a steeply pitched
roof in the medieval English tradition (but originally thatched). Some
years later (in the 1670s) the right-hand, slightly larger section was
added to make four rooms, with a lean-to ell at rear following around
1720. Considering its very early date, its two main rooms are unusually
spacious, its Great Room being outstanding. Note, however, that the
enormous summer beam, which longitudinally bisects the older part, is
recklessly supported by cross bracing above the end windows instead of
having its weight transferred directly to the ground by an upright post,
a structural peculiarity puzzlingly present in a number of houses of this
period. Note also that there is no overhang across the front of the house
—resulting in a close-croppedness—but two at the east gable end. The
house (in deplorable shape) was purchased by the Ipswich Historical
Society in 1898, restored on its original site and opened to the public

the next year. In 1927 it was moved from across the river to the present location and completely rehabilitated together with the garden. The latter was redesigned in the early 1950s by A. A. Shurcliff of Williamsburg fame and seeks to include the typical flowers and herbs raised domestically in the seventeenth century when gardens were basically for function (remedies, seasoning, dyes, etc.), not looks. Shurcliff's work was greatly assisted by research by Ann Leighton Smith, plus a 1683 inventory of the Whipple House which included its garden "products" then on the shelf. John Fawn was the original builder. Dr. Cummings in his book *The Framed Houses of Massachusetts Bay, 1625–1725* (Harvard University Press, 1979) gives 1655 as the probable date of the "original" half of the house but the National Register and the official folder favor circa 1640.

Open Apr. 15–Oct., Tues.–Sat. 10–5, Sun. 1–5: admission

---

43   First Church of Christ (1816–17)
Village Green on Main Street
Lancaster, Massachusetts

CHARLES BULFINCH, ARCHITECT

One of the great Federal Style churches in the country, this masterpiece by Bulfinch—rather Bulfinch and his job captain Thomas Hearsey—should be seen by all interested in the architectural developments of the early nineteenth century. It established a new creativeness in church building, reflecting the architect's increased sophistication, plus, it must be added, the design changes effected by Hearsey, who went out from Boston to supervise the job. (See Harold Kirker's encyclopedic *The Architecture of Charles Bulfinch,* Harvard University Press, 1969.) Bulfinch himself supposedly never visited the church. Hearsey's most prominent changes involved making the three arches of the portico of equal height, adding the volutes on the tower base, and reducing the size of the cupola—all design changes for the better, particularly the equalization of the portico arches. (Bulfinch had proposed one large arch flanked by two smaller.)

The church stands parallel to the street, facing a well-kept green, which it shares with several spatially disjoined municipal buildings. The proportions of the well-projected portico—which boasts an arch on each side to match the three in front—the exquisite thinness of its brick piers, and the refinement of its white-painted pilasters and entablature are masterful. The knifed flatness of the arches and their interaction with the shadowed spaces behind and with the black-faced clock above (only a touch smaller in diameter than the arches) create a rhythm unmatched by any other church entry. A vestibule, not quite as wide as the nave proper, stands directly behind the portico, with a modest brick tower, almost a cube, atop this, with identical clocks adorning its three sides. White wood volutes marry the tower's narrow width to the vestibule on which it rests. A temple-like cylindrical wood cupola, capped by a small dome, weighs (heavily?) on the tower base. Altogether a facade liberated from prototypes, one bringing fresh design wind into the young country. Unfortunately the interior does not share this architectural venturesomeness, following the usual squarish meeting house plan and following it without the distinction seen outside. The balconies, for instance, push themselves into the space of the worship room instead of being as one with it, and while the north wall does boast an elaborate, almost magisterial, high pulpit, the elements of the sanctuary end do not work harmoniously together. Some of this is due to the fact that this end of the church was changed when the chapel was added in 1881, necessitating the closure of its chancel windows; plaster decorations also date from this period (and probably the prominent stovepipes). Strangely enough there was no artificial lighting until indirect broad-beam lamps were installed in the balconies (c. 1970). These reflect off the ceiling.

Open Sun. services: to visit at other times consult notice board

44 Colonel Jeremiah Lee Mansion (1768)
161 Washington Street
Marblehead, Massachusetts

The New England shipbuilding carpenters of the eighteenth century were a skilled lot, and here in this three-story late Georgian house they achieved a convincing imitation of stone using wood, accented by "putting sand in the final coat of limestone gray paint" (to quote the Lee Mansion booklet), a procedure doubted by some authorities. This waggery gains special credence in the white-painted quoins and keystoned window lintels, which are boldly set off against the gray painted walls. The boxy exterior is also marked by a minutely projecting central bay, topped by a pediment, and accented by a well-stated portico. Whereas the exterior is merely rich, the interior is sumptuous, from its 16-foot/4.9-meter-wide entrance hall, half taken up by its broad stair, with mahogany wainscoting and extraordinary Pannini wallpaper, to the almost Rococo carving of the woodwork in the Banquet Room. Note, too, the mantel (which as Morrison, Pierson, and others have pointed out was copied from Abraham Swan's book *British Architect* of 1745).

The upper rooms are equally elaborate, even including the glassed-in cupola from which Colonel Lee could keep lookout for his returning vessels. This very New England example of Georgian architecture served as a bank for over a century (beginning in 1804)—during which time the Banquet Room's pine walls were grained to resemble oak. It was bought in 1909 by the Marblehead Historical Society, restored, and refurnished in the period.

Open mid-May–mid-Oct., daily except Sun. 9:30–4: admission

---

45   Methodist Tabernacle (1879) **and Campground
Oak Bluffs, via Circuit Avenue or Dukes County Avenue
Martha's Vineyard (Oak Bluffs), Massachusetts**

The Wesleyan Grove Camp Meeting was inaugurated in 1835 as an evangelical center—starting thus the first summer trek to this famous island. Its open-air Methodist tabernacle (1879)—note its delicate steel construction—sits encompassed by a century-old ring of neo-

Gothic wood cottages, largely from the 1860s, built to replace the tents that had earlier sheltered the faithful. Although many of these story-and-a-half houses are of no interest architecturally, there are enough jigsaw examples to make the whole entertaining, while the sight of scores of their gable ends nudging each other is unique. (More than three hundred cottages remain, some now winterized. Often the front porches were added later.) On Illumination Night in August cottages and grounds are decorated with thousands of candlelit lanterns.

Grounds always open

---

46   Isaac Royall House (1732–37)
15 George Street at Main
Medford, Massachusetts

A highly unusual house—for one thing each facade is different—offering fresh insight into early Colonial domestic architecture. The original farmhouse, now incorporated in the rebuilding, dates from 1637 and its brick silhouette can still be seen in the lower part of the all-brick south end. This two-and-a-half-story farmhouse was enlarged in 1690, then totally rebuilt (1732–37) by Isaac Royall in the three-

story form we see today. (He also acquired some 504 acres/204 hectares of land, much of which he left to Harvard.) The most extraordinary facade is that at the east where the windows and their spandrels are "framed" into continuous vertical panels from sill to rich cornice, their strong white-painted divisions alternating with the gray clapboarding to produce a uniquely spirited front. The west facade (1747–50) is more routine except for the pedimented windows and the prominent pilasters at each end. Another unusual feature—for a New England mansion—is the slave quarters at rear, Colonel Royall having brought twenty-seven slaves to Medford from his earlier home in Antigua. A succession of families, some not always attentive to the house, occupied it through the years until its condition became so parlous that local concerned individuals organized the Royall House Association in 1905 and in 1906 were able to buy the property. Its well-paneled and well-carved interior has been thoroughly restored and refurnished in the mid-eighteenth-century style. In addition to the woodwork, note, too, the colors. The house is a National Historic Landmark.

Open May 1–Oct. 15, daily except Mon. and Fri. 2–5: admission

---

47   Old Town (mid-17th century)
Nantucket
Nantucket Island, Massachusetts

This quaint and historic town—one of the best preserved in New England and since 1956 under design control—has rescued its crumbling edges by sympathetic surgery and imaginative, non-neon, non-cottagey planning for its future. (The waterfront redevelopment was designed by The Providence Partnership in 1968.) Much of the ancient core of the town—but not all of the 15-mile/24-kilometer-long island—has been preserved, and along historic, cobbled Main Street one can stroll as far as the residential area with much pleasure. The Nantucket Historical Association, Old Town Building, 2 Union Street, has helpful data for the visitor.

Nantucket Island, some 30 miles/48 kilometers at sea, was chosen (1659) by its first European settlers (mostly Baptists with Quakers later on) to escape the "Puritan severity" of the Massachusetts Bay Colony. Before the Revolution and after the War of 1812 it was one of the greatest whaling ports in the world, its far-reaching sailors pioneer-

ing deep-sea whaling. Whaling died out in the late 1860s, largely due to the discovery of oil at Titusville, Pennsylvania, in 1859 (plus, here, a silting of the harbor), but the island soon became known as an ideal summer retreat, a reputation that has rocketed since World War II. The Nantucket Conservation Foundation was set up in 1965 and matters seem to be in reasonable control. It would be tragic if Nantucket's magic atmosphere was sullied by commercialism.

48 Jethro Coffin House (c. 1686)
Sunset Hill Lane
Nantucket, Massachusetts

Often called the oldest house on Nantucket, the one-and-a-half-story Coffin saltbox on a hillock northwest of town is of interest because of its plank, as opposed to stud, construction. Wide planks were nailed vertically to either side of the sill and to the plate or girt at the eave, while the space between the two was "insulated" with clay and straw (seaweed was also used for this purpose). On the exterior, and possibly

at a later date, cedar shingles were laid. The inner face of the outside walls was plastered; the room partitions were merely a single thickness of planks. A substantial chimney fills the center of the house, serving fireplaces on both floors, each of the four rooms boasting one. The interior, almost all of it whitewashed (but not, it is safe to say, in the seventeenth century), was completely restored in 1926. Note, also, the plank front door with its sturdy strap hinges.

Open June–early Sept., daily 10–5: admission

---

49   The Atheneum (1847)
India Street at Federal
Nantucket, Massachusetts

The Greek Revival aficionado visiting Nantucket Island will want to see this surprisingly competent library, an unusual stylistic excursion for Massachusetts, where Classic "temple" forms were little used. Nantucket itself suffered a devastating fire in 1846, and as its whaling wealth was then great and the Greek Revival still fashionable from New York to Charleston—ports visited by the whaling captains—much of the island's rebuilding shows this influence. (Note, also, Main Street.) The Atheneum's most striking feature is the double-pedimented front with, in the projected portico, two well-turned Ionic columns flanked by two attached columns of delicate detail. The portico's entablature merges with that of the main building block to produce a well-knit fa-

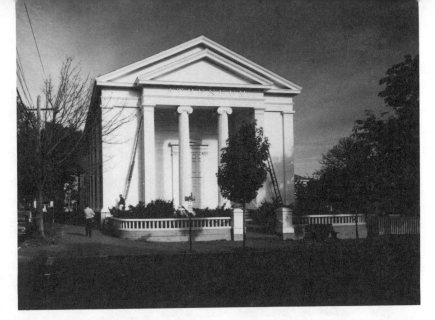

cade with fine recessed porch. Although the interior is, of its atheneum nature, filled with book stacks, hence almost invisible architecturally, the Great Hall on the second floor is of technical interest for its hung ceiling. Appropriately, the library houses an extensive collection of books and paintings on whaling and early sailing days. Reputedly designed by Frederick Coleman, and built entirely of wood, the building was put together with a whaleboat concern for workmanship. Thoroughly restored in 1955—following a serious fire—it has been maintained in pristine condition.

Open summer, Mon.–Fri. 9:30–5:30, Sat. 9:30–12; winter, Mon.–Fri. 2–5:30, Sat. 9:30–12

---

50   High Road/High Street Houses
Newbury/Newburyport, Massachusetts

High Road/High Street (US 1A), which runs around the southwesterly edges of Newbury and Newburyport (hence the name change), flourishes a number of important homes, several of which are open to the public, while many private ones merit the drive by. The Information Booth by the old Court House in the Bartlett Mall, High Street at top of Green Street, in Newburyport provides the visitor with a useful map, though it slights Newbury. The Chamber of Commerce at 76 State Street also provides a guide. The oldest house is the **Tristam Coffin** (c. 1654 plus later additions—c. 1785) at 16 High Road in Newbury,

which is of interest for the changing construction techniques revealed in its several expansions. The exterior is not prepossessing. The **Short House** (c. 1732) just down the road at 39 High is intriguing for its almost medieval (and rare) brick ends with flush chimneys but with dark clapboarding (a replacement) sheathing front and rear. The front door is a reproduction but the interior paneling, fortunately, is not. Both of the above are now owned by the Society for the Preservation of New England Antiquities and both are open, with small admission fee, June–Sept., Tues., Thurs., and Sun. 1–5. The **Cushing House** (c. 1808) at 98 High Street in Newburyport forms a chronological climax to this parade of dwellings, being a good example of the brick Federal Style then coming into fashion. Three stories high and well detailed throughout, the house was given (1956) to the Historical Society of Old Newburyport, and now serves as a museum concerned primarily with the way of life and the artifacts of the late eighteenth and early nineteenth centuries when the port town flourished as a shipbuilding center. The museum is open May 1–Oct. 31, 10–4 except Mon., Sun. 2–5: admission. The garden at the side should also be seen.

Houses open as indicated above

51 Unitarian Church (1801)
Pleasant Street
Newburyport, Massachusetts

The Church of the First Religious Society of Newburyport gives eminent satisfaction outside and in. Though difficult to grasp fully because
of its crowded mid-urban site (try viewing it from the public parking
area directly behind), the exterior shows careful detailing from its fanlit
door to its finely chiseled cornice and its elaborate spire. The famous
church architect Ralph Adams Cram (1863–1942) described the four-
stage steeple—to quote the church pamphlet—as "the most beautiful
wooden spire in New England." Note, also, the neat parish house to the
right of the entrance. The long-aisled interior is typical of its early-
nineteenth-century Federalist period with extended balcony on two
sides and with its prominent and very accomplished Palladian-inspired
pulpit on axis. The nave itself with low box pews is full of graceful light
and space. Ships' carpenters undoubtedly were active both in the construction and in the delicate carving. Though Timothy Palmer is
thought by some to have built the church—as is also the case with the

Amesbury (Massachusetts) and Sandown (New Hampshire) meeting houses (q.v.)—Samuel McIntire had a hand in it, as church records show that he was paid for the carving. (There is also a similarity with McIntire's now destroyed South Church in Salem.) In any case the result is very, very fine.

Open weekday mornings; apply at adjacent parish house

Newburyport commenced in 1973 a long-range downtown rehabilitation (behind the church), with architects Anderson Notter Finegold as prime consultants and coordinators and Sasaki Associates designing the Inn Street Mall and waterfront promenade (1978). Though not completed when last seen, the fabric of the old city has been maintained, storefront restoration taken place, graphics coordinated, pedestrian circulation facilitated while automobiles have been accommodated. Restitution has been carried out with well-scaled regard for the existing town.

---

52   Southeastern Massachusetts University (1965–72)
off Old Westport Road, 1.4 miles/2.3 kilometers S of US 6
North Dartmouth, Massachusetts

PAUL RUDOLPH AND DESMOND & LORD, ARCHITECTS

A university which is architecturally brilliant in many facets, less so in others. It was primarily planned, designed, and detailed by Paul Rudolph. Located between Fall River and New Bedford, just south of Interstate 195, the university was originally intended to be the state's technical college. However, after the completion of many of the class units the curriculum was changed to embrace a fully rounded university, with five undergraduate colleges and a graduate program. Basic to the overall site planning was the decision to confine all vehicular circulation, including trucks, to the outer periphery of the academic area with small service roads direct to the buildings. Dormitories, service and athletic facilities are located outside the peripheral drive. As most of the staff and students arrive by car, parking was a major concern; it has been smartly handled by a series of parking lots placed around the university but bermed and treed so that they are almost invisible.

The academic complex fronts on an undisturbed grass mall, lined by classroom buildings at the upper end, with communal and adminis-

trative units loosely but carefully composed below. As the approach is from the north one initially comes upon the buildings from the sunless side, an unfortunate introduction but one whose cheerlessness is soon dissipated on encountering the vigorous play of sun and shadow, light and shade, and intermeshing building forms of the two class rows which define the mall. Relatively close together at the north end, these three-story instruction units splay outward and step back as they proceed southward down the slight grade, their horizontal sweep punctuated at the end by a 180-foot/55-meter television tower (by Grattan Gill). The space between the two rows escapes westward via a surprise right-angle vista that pivots around tower and library and carries the eye to a distant lake. This vista is framed by an amphitheater to the north and a fine arts building to the south. (The fine arts building, library, auditorium, and administration building were designed by Desmond & Lord.)

The classroom rows are composed of clusters of six "bays" each, the clusters stepping back in three stages to total eighteen units. All are of reinforced concrete frame with walls of ribbed concrete block. Lecture and general-purpose classrooms are located on the ground floor and are inset to provide a covered, open-air circulation arcade along the edges of the mall. Other classrooms, including some specialized laboratories and studios, are found on the second floor, with offices on the top. These office units are placed at right angles to their access corridors and to the axis of the class block, and from the outside can be immediately recognized by their prominent cantilevered projections along the mall. At each nodal point between the three clusters there is a spacious hall which not only serves vertical circulation, but doubles as a spot for spontaneous gatherings and study nooks. These spaces range in size from small stages to intimate corners and are most popular. An elaborate system of hollow piers sets the structural module; they are sufficiently large to accommodate all utilities. Rigidity can be seen in the locked-in divisions of the three-story class blocks, their eternal concrete surfaces are not continually sympathetic, few of the windows can be opened, and an agitated complexity are too evident in design. But in overall plan SMU is conceptually excellent, its spatial experiences from covered conversation pits to outdoor arenas to building relations are stimulating, while strong design continuity ties all together.

Grounds open daily

---

53   **Ames Memorial Library** (1877–79)
Main Street
North Easton, Massachusetts

HENRY HOBSON RICHARDSON, ARCHITECT

Richardson combined at North Easton three elements: one, his subsequently famous, almost Dantesque arched opening (here used by him for the first time); two, an offset tower which forms a vertical agglutinator; and three, an extended horizontal wing with a row of clustered windows. Generated by plan requirements, these elements have been put together to form a simple but skillful hillside composition. Even more important, the building works well inside. Note in approaching that the only breaks in the solidity of the granite base beneath the stringcourse (on which the windows "rest") are the deep-set entry flanked by two slit windows: a powerful introduction which monumentalizes penetration. The profusion of sandstone-framed windows that light the stack at left combine with those in the entry projection to roll across the facade, with the openings in the tower joining in by repeating at smaller scale their roundheaded (i.e. Romanesque) framing.

The interior's finest feature is the stack with its barrel-vaulted butternut ceiling with applewood strapping designed by Stanford White, who started his architectural career with Richardson and worked with him for six years (1872–78). White also helped with the design of the library fireplace and, outside, of much of the carving. The Ames Library

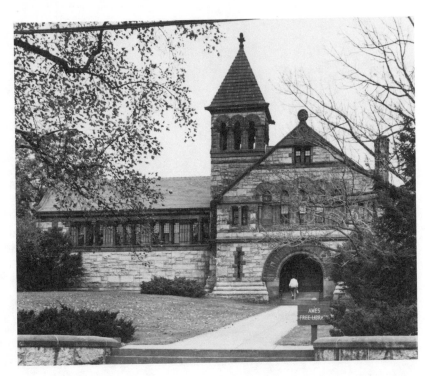

with its clarity, strength, and monumentality, combined with directness of function, numbers among the key small buildings of the 1870s and '80s. Frederick Law Olmsted was the landscape architect.

Open Mon.–Sat., generally 12–5, except holidays

The **Oakes Memorial Hall** (1879)—disjoined Richardsonia—stands adjacent.

---

54 **Shaker Village** (1790–1864)
US 20 just W of MA 41, 5 miles/8 kilometers W of
Pittsfield, Massachusetts

Shaker building, as can be seen in Maine, New Hampshire, and Kentucky, has always been characterized by an appealing directness and simplicity. It has, on the other hand, only occasionally risen to the architectural distinction that Shaker furniture attained in its design field. However, the Round Barn (1826, roof and interior rebuilt in 1864 after fire) is one of the great functional examples of early American ag-

ricultural building, a structure of timeless rightness, even eloquence. A three-level cylinder of local gray limestone 95 feet/29 meters in outer diameter molds this vernacular bastion, topped by a twelve-sided, white-painted wooden clerestory and lantern, the latter replacing the pre-fire conical roof. (A red brick abutting wing, tacked on in the late 1860s, is a sore intrusion.) The simple mathematics of stone cylinder and dodecagonal clerestory erupt inside with a startling geometric fanning of chestnut rafters, beams, and posts. The barn's round shape was chosen so that hay wagons could enter, deliver their load from the ramped top level to a central hay deposit, then exit at the same door. Fifty-two cows occupied the wedge-shaped stalls on the floor below with circumferential manure pit on the lowest level, wide enough for wagons. This tri-level functional design created a farming sensation, and creaking copies (in wood) can be seen to this day in the Plains States. When (in 1932) Massachusetts law ruled that the cows must go as the barn did not have a concrete floor (which could be properly cleaned), the warmth which the cows had until then brought to the interior also vanished and in winter freezing weather attacked and seriously cracked the walls, a process already inaugurated by inadequate footings.

The rest of the seventeen buildings of the community, which is the third Shaker settlement, merit a look even if the exteriors are not inspiring. (The last Shakers left in 1960 and the village was officially closed, to be reestablished as Shaker Community Inc.) Forget, for instance, the outside of the four-story Brick Dwelling (1830) but do sample its authentically furnished period rooms. The 1793 Meeting House, moved here from Shirley and now across US 20, should also be seen—as should the extensive gardens. When leaving look back at the Round Barn: it is one of the country's greatest autochthonous examples. Its existence today is due to the generosity of Mr. and Mrs. Frederick W. Beinecke, who donated a substantial sum to save it from collapse, and to restore it (1968) to its condition of over a hundred years ago. Terry F. Hallock was architect of the restoration.

Open June–Oct. 15, daily 9:30–5: admission

---

55   Plimoth Plantation Re-creation (1627/1957–76)
off MA 3 via Plimoth Plantation Highway
3 miles/4.8 kilometers S of
Plymouth, Massachusetts

No archeological foundations or historic graphic material existed for this re-creation of the first Pilgrim settlement (as was the case, for instance, at Williamsburg and Tryon Palace—q.v.); there were, however, copious and invaluable inventories. And, as has since been proven, research for the first buildings in the village is now outdated. As the administration puts it: "In historical accuracy, the most recently constructed dwellings at Plimoth Plantation have a considerable advantage over earlier attempts due to new research. This research, done by Richard Candee and Cary Carson, combined with archaeological information gathered by Dr. James Deetz, has revealed that the most probable design for the better houses of 1627 would have been the 'posthole' style of construction. This construction uses a frame of heavy oak timbers with sunken corner posts and studs between them that support a wattle-and-daub cladding on the walls, a chimney of the same material, and a heavy reed thatch roof. The clay daub walls are protected from New England weather by an outer layer of riven cedar clapboards fastened to the studs. Other village structures such as the fort, with its thick sawn boards, or the new frame barn, display other techniques, and plans are being made to construct a simpler sort of early structure, a 'palisado' house whose walls are simply four sections of pale, identical to that which surrounds the village, with a thatched roof. This village is a living example of 17th century rural life with animal houses,

pens and gardens inhabited by animals and costumed individuals who take on the identities of the original settlers."

With regard to Plymouth Rock (at Water Street in the town), the Colonies' first Thanksgiving was not given here, as claimed, in 1621, but in Berkeley Plantation (q.v.) on the James River in the Old Dominion in 1619, where "the day of our ships arrival . . . shall be yearly and perpetually kept as a day of Thanksgiving." To quote the *Virginia State Guide* (Oxford University Press, 1964), "Virginia narrowly escaped an invasion of the Pilgrim Fathers . . . Thrown off their course, the Pilgrims set foot on a rock off the coast of northern Virginia." The *Guide* errs somewhat in that the destination *was* northern Virginia, then near the mouth of the Hudson River: actually the Pilgrims set foot in the New England Grant. To conclude matters, it was not until 1789 that the first national day of Thanksgiving was inaugurated. President Washington proclaimed the day "not in response to the bounties of the harvest but in gratitude for the establishment of the Constitution of the United States" (*Plimoth Plantation Bulletin*). However, not until Lincoln's time—1863—was the last Thursday of November properly set aside.

Open daily Apr.–Nov. 9–5: admission

---

56   Jonathan Corwin House—the Witch House (c. 1642)
Essex Street at North
Salem, Massachusetts

For well over three hundred years, the two-story, four-room gabled Corwin house has been standing on this site. While the exterior has been completely restored and in places altered, and the large windows which had been added in the nineteenth century replaced by appropriately sized sash and diamond panes, most of the interior, including all posts and beams and even much of the floor, is claimed to be original. The steeply pointed gables, framed overhang, and "paneled" chimney recall the medieval English house-building traditions of many of the settlers. It is worth mentioning when examining its darkened clapboards that most historians feel that few, if any, houses in the colonies were painted before 1700. The interior of the Witch House with its great fireplaces on the ground floor and surprisingly spacious two bedrooms above has been furnished in the period. The house's name comes not from the building's appearance, though this might seem likely, but

from the investigations—concerning potential or actual witches—held in the house of Judge Jonathan Corwin as part of the infamous Salem trials of 1692–93, when some nineteen souls lost their lives. The house was deeded to the City of Salem in 1948 and is administered by the Park Department.

Open Mar.–Nov., daily 10–6: admission

---

57 John Ward House (1684)
enter via Essex Institute
132 Essex Street
Salem, Massachusetts

A carefully restored, late-seventeenth-century house with lean-to addition containing an apothecary shop and weaving room. The oldest section (to left) originally comprised only two rooms, one above the other in the typical manner of the time, but as Mr. Ward prospered and his family grew he added the second half containing the hall or kitchen to the east, and around 1732, probably earlier, his son attached the lean-to across the entire back. In 1910 the Essex Institute, a local historical museum (with a superb library on the China trade), acquired the house, which was then in dilapidated condition, moving it two blocks from St. Peter Street to its present site. The restoration (1910–12), by George Francis Dow of the Institute (who also restored the Parson Capen House, q.v.), presented many difficulties in that the dwelling had been used as a bakery in the early nineteenth century and as a tenement in the latter part. Moreover, the twin gables which structural archeology showed had previously existed had been eliminated and the windows undoubtedly enlarged when inexpensive large panes became available. With 1700 as a date, Mr. Dow restored the house outside and in (including gables), with, as mentioned, parlor on one side and kitchen-hall on the other, and with the lean-to fixed up as a slightly later weaving room and apothecary. The Ward House gives an edifying picture of its day. As Hugh Morrison mentions, "No house better illustrates that the Colonial builder cared nought for symmetry: he accepted it if the plan called for it, but he never regarded it as an aesthetic necessity as did his Georgian successors" (*Early American Architecture,* Oxford University Press, 1952).

Open June–Oct. 15, Tues.–Sat. 10–4, Sun. 1–4:30: admission

58 **Peirce-Nichols House** (1782)
80 Federal Street
Salem, Massachusetts

SAMUEL McINTIRE, ARCHITECT

Samuel McIntire (1757–1811), with a background of master wood-carver and carpenter, matured from a craftsman to become one of the great architects of the period. Though he was self-taught and worked exclusively in Salem, McIntire designed houses for the wealthy that not only put Salem on the architectural map of New England but epitomized the Federal Style, spawning imitations as far away as Wilmington, North Carolina. Two of McIntire's finest houses which are open to the public are described here: the first which he designed for Jerathmeel Peirce in 1782, and the second for John Gardner (now the Gardner-Pingree House, q.v.) in 1804. McIntire was only twenty-four years old when he undertook the Peirce House: there are few architects

of any time who did so well so early. The house is of ocher-colored clapboarding accented by dark blinds. It is a box—one might say a typical New England Federal Style box—whose facade is framed on the ends by strong pilasters (with awkward entablature), and around the top by a prominent balustrade. A smaller balustrade behind encloses the captain's walk atop an almost invisible roof. The fence in front is also by McIntire. The interiors show the architect's transition from late Georgian to the Federal, the rooms on the right having been remodeled by him in 1801. The carving—by McIntire himself—of the mantels, door framing, and cornices throughout is superb, while the decorative work in the remodeled east parlor possesses an exemplary Adam-inspired delicacy. The garden in back formerly extended to Mr. Peirce's dock, where his ships tied up. One of the country's great wooden houses, it is owned by the Essex Institute, which acquired it by subscription in 1917.

Open all year, Tues.–Sat. 2–4:30; also Sun. 1–4:30 from June to mid-Oct., except major holidays: admission

---

59   Gardner-Pingree House (1804–5)
128 Essex Street
Salem, Massachusetts

SAMUEL McINTIRE, ARCHITECT

McIntire at his peak—as he is here with the brick Pingree House—attained an architectural sophistication which few practitioners, before or after, ever reached in domestic design. The exquisitely tensioned elements of this facade represent nothing less than perfection. The understated semicircular portico quietly pulls one to the dwelling, its cornice picked up to embrace the house via the lower stringcourse. A second stringcourse above completes the division of the front into three horizontal elements, each a bit narrower than the one below. Into these bands are set three rows of windows, the bottom two of identical size, the top smaller. Their proportions, their white keystoned lintels, and their dark shutters make them memorable accents in this pinkish brick front. A white wood balustrade across the top ties it all together. Some of this is influenced by Bulfinch's Harrison Gray Otis House of 1796 (q.v.) in Boston, but the orchestration here is on a far purer plane. The

almost severe elegance of the exterior relaxes within, and opulence, still in check, can be seen throughout. The most memorable feature lies in the wood carving for which McIntire was justly famous. The carved framing of the sliding doors between the two parlors is to be noticed but the finest work resides in the mantels, where the rhythm of elements is often overlooked by one's admiration of their technical virtuosity. One of the finest houses in the United States, it was given to the Essex Institute by the Pingree heirs in 1933.

Open all year, Tues.–Sat. 10–4, also Sun. 1–4:30 from June to mid-Oct., except major holidays: admission

The **Crowninshield-Bentley House,** 126 Essex Street, stands adjacent to the Pingree, and is also owned by the Essex Institute. Its right half was finished in 1727, the left in 1790, the progression of years showing in its design. The Georgian dwelling was moved to this site in 1960 and completely restored, the kitchen being its most interesting room. (Open June–Oct. 15, Tues.–Sat. 10–4, Sun. 1–4:30: admission.)

60   Chestnut, Essex, and Federal Streets (mostly 19th century)
between North Street and Flint
Salem, Massachusetts

Westward from Hamilton Hall (1806–7) at 9 Chestnut Street (by
Samuel McIntire; second floor particularly good), Chestnut unrolls
with an urban comity that can still instruct. The polite relationships between houses, many of which date from the 1830s and '40s, the planting, the street profile, all combine to produce what President Van
Buren reputedly called "the most beautiful street I have ever seen."
Essex and Federal streets, parallel to Chestnut on the north, lag not far
behind in felicitousness and each has an increasing number of houses
open to the public. The Chestnut Street District is listed in the National
Register of Historic Places.

Most houses private; consult local guide

61   Old Hoxie House (c. 1665) and Dexter Mill (1654) on MA 130 at Shawme Lake, S edge of Sandwich, Cape Cod, Massachusetts

The Hoxie House is a shaggy, shingled saltbox without and a dramatic spatial experience within as its main room rises to the full height of the roof. This, the oldest of the Cape's dwellings, was fully restored down to its inner vertical boarding after the town purchased it in 1959. Though all of the exterior is of relatively recent date, some 70 per cent of the interior is supposedly original. In any event, the house is an unusual example of the seventeenth century, its restoration centering on the 1680–90 period. All of the furnishings are original and authentic of the time with five pieces on loan from the Boston Museum of Fine Arts.

Just across the small lake stands the Dexter Grist Mill (group admission with the house), built around 1654 and restored to working condition in 1961. The additions of later years have been removed to leave a simple but informative example of the Colony's early milling operations.

Open mid-June–Sept., Mon.–Sat. 10–5, Sun. 1–5: admission

62   Saugus Iron Works National Historic Site (c. 1648/reconstruction
       1948–54)
       **244 Central Street, .3 mile/.5 kilometer N of monument
       Saugus, Massachusetts**

This reconstruction of the earliest ironworks in the American Colonies,
one generously financed by the American Iron and Steel Institute,
stands high on the list of historic re-creations of our industrial beginnings. (An earlier ironworks at Falling Creek, Virginia, was ready to
begin operations in 1622 but the workers were killed by the Indians
and the project abandoned.) Restored by the same firm of architects
who were responsible for the rebuilding of Colonial Williamsburg—
Perry, Shaw & Hepburn, Kehoe & Dean—buttressed with technical con-

sultants, and utilizing the archeological thoroughness that distinguished the firm's work on the former Virginia capital, the ironworks at Saugus gives an illuminating insight into the earliest industrial groundwork of this country. Though the ironworks itself lasted only some twenty years —high production costs, low capital, and lack of skilled labor occasioned its downfall—the foundation of the future nation's iron and steel industry was here established. For this reconstruction six years of patient research and informed conjecture were needed for the complicated technological facets, as excavations revealed only limited traces of the original. However, today, when wheels are wheeling and forges forging in simulated operation, the results are fascinating.

In addition to the technological restoration, the nearby **Iron Works House,** which has been standing on this same spot since around 1680—and continually lived in until 1915—is itself very worthy of a visit. Radically altered through the years, it was restored by Wallace Nutting beginning in 1915. The ironworks and house are now under the aegis of the National Park Service. The dwelling was earlier known as the Appleton-Taylor-Mansfield House.

Open Apr.–Oct., daily 9–5; Nov.–Mar. 9–4, except Jan. 1 and Dec. 25

---

63   Mission House (1739)
Main Street at Sergeant
Stockbridge, Massachusetts

Stockbridge village was founded in 1734 and incorporated in 1739 as a mission for the Muhhekanuk tribe of Algonkian (Algonquin) Indians with only four white families as residents. Of the four the most famous was the Reverend John Sergeant, the first missionary, who devoted much of his life to Indian education and to establishing better white-Indian relations. His Early Georgian dwelling housed the mission: it is now a summer museum with relevant exhibits, and is operated by the Trustees of Reservations in Stockbridge. The two-and-a-half-story house was moved to its present site and reconstructed in 1928.

Open Memorial Day–Columbus Day, Tues.–Sat. 10–5, Sun. and holidays 11–4: admission

64   Old Sturbridge Village (primarily 1790–1840)
**SW of junction of Massachusetts Turnpike and IS 86, just W of
Sturbridge, Massachusetts**

Old Sturbridge Village, a private, non-profit organization, re-creates
with admirable authenticity and homogeneity a village of late-
eighteenth- and early-nineteenth-century rural New England, particularly
the half century following independence. Though the layout of its 200
acres (81 hectares) of land and its fine Common are of necessity hypothetical, the Village plan is typical, while the buildings themselves are
all original structures moved to this site. They range in date from 1704
(the unpainted Fenno House on the Common, restored in 1952) to two
examples of the Greek Revival (the Baptist Meeting House of
1832—vesper services on summer afternoons—and the Thompson
Bank of 1835, both also on the Common). There are thirty-eight major
structures in all, those facing the Common forming the comely core,
with paths branching off to establish and depict the agricultural and re-

lated rural life of the time. Included here are a working historical farm, an active blacksmith shop, a carding mill, a grist mill, pottery, one-room school (c. 1810), an operating cordwainer's shop, and a covered bridge, all well woven into the landscape. These modest structures are as important to an understanding of this ethos as the more pretentious houses around the Common, for most early New England village inhabitants had a legacy in the soil. All houses and buildings, incidentally, are completely and accurately furnished. In addition there are specialized displays discretely tucked in separate buildings in the northeast corner (beyond the Museum Gift Shop): the collections of clocks, glass, firearms, and lighting devices are excellent. (A first-rate guidebook to all major structures is available.) Although only a few buildings are of historic architectural importance—the Federal Style Towne House (1796) at end of the Common being the finest—the collective Village provides us with an altogether remarkable picture of early New England vernacular. Preserving the past, it educates for the future. It is not to be missed.

Open daily, Apr.–Oct. 9:30–5:30, Nov.–Mar. 10–4, except Jan. 1, Dec. 25, and Mon. between Dec. 4 and Mar. 26: admission

---

65   Parson Capen House (1683)
Howlett Street, NE edge of Common
Topsfield, Massachusetts

Built in the medieval fashion of its day, and nestled on a low ridge with an enormous ash tree in front and oaks and maples on the side, this picturesque house on a storybook site numbers very high among our slender remains of seventeenth-century wood architecture. (Its precise date of erection, June 8, 1683, is carved on one of the beams.) If its windows were replaced by smaller ones with the diamond panes, which some historians think it had originally, it might well be our finest example of its time. The unencumbered directness, even purity, of its basic shape is authoritative. To this firm profile can be added the attraction of its framed overhang that projects the second floor 16 inches/41 centimeters over the lower along the front and, at the gable ends, the third floor over the second. Stimulating what would otherwise have been a simple box form—and visually tying the house closer to the ground by emphasizing horizontality—these overhangs also demonstrate the

skilled heavy carpentry that came to the northern Colonies from southeast England. The carved pendants under these overhangs—which also
mark the framing of the rooms astride the chimney—are noteworthy.
The enclosing clapboards, or weatherboards as the English call them,
were well known in the mother country, particularly in Kent and Essex.

In plan the house is divided, slightly unequally, into two rooms on
the ground floor which abut a large central chimney fancifully paneled
in Tudor fashion above. A sizable parlor—as demanded by a parson's
duties—occupies the left-hand end while a "hall" that is kitchen and
family room takes up the right. (A reproduction of the kitchen with its
8.3-foot/2.5-meter-wide fireplace was for many years in the American
Wing of the Metropolitan Museum.) Bedrooms, reached by narrow
stairs (original), occupy the second and third floors; a basement runs
beneath. The interior was restored (1913–14, by George Francis Dow)
to its original (if somewhat theoretical) Puritan condition. Necessarily,
much woodwork and all shingles and clapboarding are new. A small
museum annex extends at rear. The house is owned by the Topsfield
Historical Society.

Open June 15–Sept. 15, Tues.–Sun. 1–4:30: admission

66   Gore Place (1806)
52 Gore Street, S off Main (MA 20)
Waltham, Massachusetts

New England society, with wealth based primarily on shipping, manufacturing, and finance, was largely urban-oriented as opposed to the
plantation (i.e. agricultural) South. One finds thus relatively few rural
or semirural mansions, at least until the nineteenth century. Outstanding among them, and one of the finest Federal houses in the country, is the stretched-out (204 feet/62 meters) Gore Place. The Gores,
who lived in England for eight years while Mr. Gore was commissioner
under Jay's Treaty, had been impressed by the south facade of Heaton
Park, a house reconstructed by James Wyatt in 1772. However, as
Charles Hammond, the curator of Gore Place, writes in a personal letter (November 1978), "The house was designed by the Gores in collaboration with Jacques-Guillaume Legrand (1743–1807) as Gore's
letters dated 1801 from Paris indicate."
   The central block of the mansion bows out gracefully to mark the
story-and-a-half oval dining room with the governor's study above
(Christopher Gore was elected the Massachusetts governor in 1809).
Hyphens, one for the billiard room, the other for the servants' hall, ex-

tend from either side of the main structure to be terminated by right-angled pavilions housing the music room at one end and the kitchen at the other. Note in these wings the fine geometry of the lower windows and their shutters with the half-round windows above, both tightly contained in shallow arched recesses. The overall result is elegant though there is confusion at the entry with one door leading to the front hall and its twin to the butler's pantry. Used and somewhat abused as a country club in the 1920s, the mansion was purchased by the Gore Place Society in 1935 and thoroughly restored and furnished. The once extensive grounds are down to 76 acres/31 hectares from an original 400 acres/162 hectares, but the spaces are wide and invitingly open—with an obvious influence from the work of Humphry Repton (1752–1818), the famous English landscape architect.

Open Apr. 15–Nov. 15, Tues.–Sat. 10–5, Sun. 2–5, except holidays: admission

67   Brandeis University (1955–68)
entrance on South Street (get campus plan at gate)
Waltham, Massachusetts

Although Brandeis with a new campus on an unspoiled site disappoints in the overall, it does possess several buildings of note. Its most imaginative achievement is the symbolic grouping of three chapels (1955)—Protestant, Catholic, and Jewish—around a common pool: a design of inspired pansectarianism. Harrison & Abramovitz were its architects. The Architects Collaborative's well-composed Academic Quadrangle, made up of the Shiffman Humanities Center, the Olin-Sang American Civilization Center with Shapiro Forum, and the Golding Judaic Center (1960), comprises one of the highlights, as does the Heller-Brown complex by Benjamin Thompson & Associates (1968) just across the street.

Campus open daily

---

68   Science Center (1975–76)
Wellesley College
S off Central Street (MA 135)
Wellesley, Massachusetts

PERRY, DEAN, STAHL & ROGERS, ARCHITECTS

Though technically a major addition to the vaguely Gothic Sage Hall of 1926 (itself thoroughly renovated), this new Science Center carries a potent statement of its own. From the design point of view the most obvious impact is the building's expression of structure and technology. The four fire-stair towers are each inset within a concrete frame of gutsy trabeation, the beams project with punch-card rhythm across the facade, while the whole is topped by over forty stainless steel cylinders which vent the fume hoods of the laboratories. A touch of exaggeration might be seen in this performance, but it is carried out with gusto and intensified by the use of color: blue for the steel members supported by the natural concrete, green for steel handrails resting on steel, and orange for grilles, stairs, and mullions. An angled path leads to the structure, providing access to both library and—because of sloping grade—the raised main floor.

The new building, which measures 100×300 feet/30×91 meters, is attached to the old to form a roughly triangular court between the two. This 60-foot/18-meter-high roofed atrium is flooded with light from both a clerestory at top and a glazed wall at end, with three passerelles adding spatial intensification—aided by openings (i.e. ex-windows) in

the former exterior of the old building, much of which is now used for office space. The library occupies most of the two lower floors with two levels of tightly packed, windowless laboratories above. Special research labs and some offices stretch across the front of these two floors, their functions marked by fiber glass or clear glass; mechanical services are placed on the roof. Internal flexibility has been stressed throughout.

Wellesley, which has always emphasized the sciences for its 1,800 student body (all female), has brought together—to synthesize and cross-fertilize—eleven scientific disciplines in a superb new building, one, it might be noted, which carries with its structural expressionism and carefully built-up scale sequences more than a hint of its "Gothic" confreres on the lovely campus about it. Charles F. Rogers II was chief of design.

Main floor open during school hours

---

69 R. S. Goddard Library (1969)
Clark University
Downing Street at Woodland (out West Main Street)
Worcester, Massachusetts

JOHN M. JOHANSEN, ARCHITECT

With projections, angles, and facets almost tempting logic, the exterior of this library puzzles. There are too many agitating elements to form a satisfactory design entity, no matter how rationalized—or nonrationalized. The architect himself says, "In general aspect, the building certainly is anti-perfection, anti-master work, anti-academic, and I hope successful in being sensitive to its purpose and its time, without pretensions to architecture" (*Architectural Forum,* January/February 1966). He further adds, in a personal letter, that "The angled walls projecting from the exterior are to prevent direct sunlight from entering the study spaces. These projections take different attitudes on East, South and West and are absent on the North. This is not only essential to any library but represents in architecture the biological reference to an organism responding to various stimuli."

High among the building's virtues is land usage; the library's bulk is in large part raised above the ground so that it does not block visual or physical communication with the surrounding buildings: it acts, indeed, as a sheltered crosswalk establishing books as the circulation pivot of the campus. (Its site had been earlier selected by The Architects Collaborative, who had drawn up the university's master plan.) A second provocative concept can be seen in the relation of the three-story stack to the book users. Surrounding this inside "treasury," but separated and linked to it only by small bridges, rises the outer structure for reading spaces which contains open study stations on the inner "balcony" side and directly faces the stack but is separated from it by light wells. Other carrels, study areas, and special rooms are located along the out-

side face. The skylight which surrounds the stack pours natural (and at night, artificial) light down four flights to the main floor. As can be imagined, one meets with a series of often dramatic open spaces between stack and surrounding balconied floors. The main level, which is reached from the ground by a winding ramp, contains control desk and catalog in addition to the rooms around the edges mentioned above. Three open-air reading terraces, an Exhibit Room of Goddard's pioneering rocket work, and a small Rare Books Room occupy the ground floor. Ducts and utilities are painted black, while a differently colored carpet enlivens each floor.

Goddard Exhibition Room open Tues.–Sat. 9–5, Sun. 1–5

70   Plumley Village East (1970–71)
adjacent to IS 290 at Laurel Street off Summer Street
Worcester, Massachusetts

BENJAMIN THOMPSON & ASSOCIATES, ARCHITECTS

A well-laid-out, topographically sensitive, architecturally imaginative housing development for 430 low- and moderate-income families, many of whom had lived in the area before redevelopment. Land clearing and construction were phased so that minimum disruption of the neighborhood would occur at any one time. A sixteen-story highrise on Laurel Street provides one- and two-bedroom-apartment living for those singles and families who choose to live in the air, while its height injects a vertical focus and lends cohesiveness to the "village." A community room, day-care center, and shopping center occupy its base. Around this hub, with freedom from rigidity, are clusters of three-story walk-up housing, primarily two- and three-bedroom units (124 and 197 respectively), but with a number (97) of larger ones for families with many children. Each group centers on a playground with parking lots adjacent (450 cars total). Created with friendly, even intimate, scale, the housing establishes a civilized non-institutional decency rarely seen in such shelter. Solid panels of dark salmon brick with metal-framed and metal-spandreled windows produce "facades" which are angled and fractured to keep matters domestic. Shopping and community facilities are probably inadequate—however, downtown is within walking distance—and it is unfortunate that a preexisting road bisects the development. But in architectural terms, this development is

one of the finest. Plumley Village was built by the State Mutual Life
Assurance Company with FHA 236 financing.

Grounds always open

---

71   Downtown Redevelopment (1971–74)
The Common
Worcester, Massachusetts

ARCHITECTS AS NOTED

Worcester, a city which once suffered an identity problem, has recently
undergone a healthy—and attractive—metamorphosis of its central
business district. The buildings on two sides of the seventeenth-century
Common behind City Hall (1898, designed by Richard H. Hunt, the
son of Richard Morris Hunt) have been redone into the **Worcester
Center,** an L-shaped group of buildings judiciously surrounded by a
vast arc of garages with undercover parking for 4,300 automobiles.

(Interstate 290 lies directly behind.) A seventeen-story office block dominates the west leg along with Filene's department store, with a low-rise building framing the square on the south. Behind this are clustered the Jordan Marsh department store and a series of some one hundred shops and restaurants disported along a cheery, Plexiglas-roofed galleria 475 feet/145 meters long and 60 feet/18 meters high. Works of art and planting are found throughout. Some of the details are unnecessarily heavy (the second-deck crossovers for instance), but the Center is convenient to reach and fun to use throughout the year. Welton Becket & Associates were the architects (1969–71). Consultants were Chermayeff & Geismar, graphics; M. Paul Friedberg & Associates, landscaping; and the late Annie Damaz, art.

Clearly prominent on the other side of City Hall at Main Street and Pleasant, and helping further to stabilize the CBD, rises the **Worcester County National Bank**—Worcester Plaza—by Kevin Roche & John Dinkeloo (1971–74). It is a bifurcated but conjoined building (compare Mies' 1919 skyscraper project for Berlin's Friedrichstrasse), one part rising twenty-four floors, the other twenty-two, its sides branched to parallel the streets, the two sections thus splayed at an angle (11.5°) to each other. The architects have enveloped the structure in 10-foot/3-meter-wide panels of three shades of pale green mirror glass which indicate at least obliquely the floor levels within, the lightest (and most transparent) band being at eye level. A more important— and more eye-catching—revelation of structure is stated by the clear glass of the central elevator-stair hall which joins the two sections. The glass here enables one to look through the building and to observe its people walking back and forth, while the division of the skyscraper into two slightly uneven "halves" (one five bays on the side, the other four) gives it a kinder scale. The banking area projects along Pleasant Street from the wider unit. With its airy skylit roof—the architects' well-loved "greenhouse" atmosphere—it makes an exotic corner particularly on the interior. A private club occupies the top two floors; a 600-car garage (of depressing insistence) is at the rear. Altogether the bank forms a key element in downtown's renascence: "the cathedral tower for the city of Worcester."

Open during shopping hours

Although its restoration was not complete when last seen, **Mechanics Hall**, 321 Main Street, should certainly be noted. This Renaissance Revival building (1855–57), designed by Elbridge Boyden, is outstanding of its type. Long in danger of demolition, it was splendidly restored and technically updated (1976–77) by architects Anderson Notter Finegold and now serves a variety of civic events.

New Hampshire

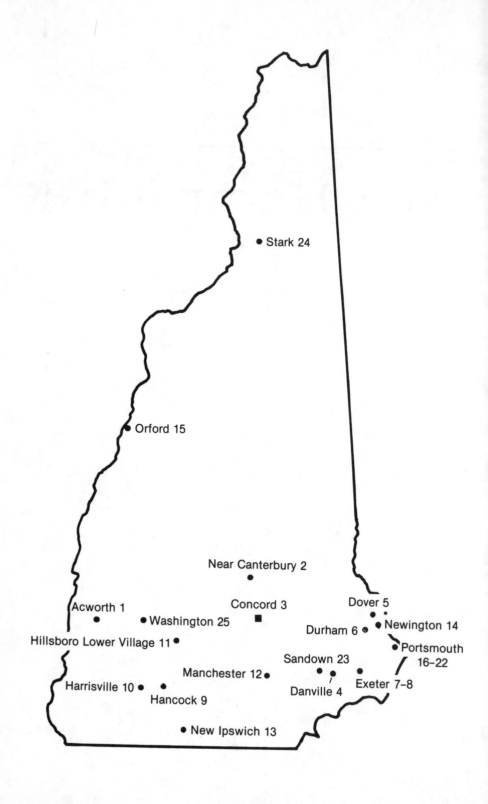

Stark 24

Orford 15

Near Canterbury 2

Acworth 1

Concord 3

Dover 5

Washington 25

Durham 6

Newington 14

Hillsboro Lower Village 11

Portsmouth 16–22

Sandown 23

Manchester 12

Danville 4

Exeter 7–8

Harrisville 10

Hancock 9

New Ipswich 13

NEW HAMPSHIRE

The buildings in boldface type are of general interest. The others are for the specialist.

Acworth	1 United Church (1821)
near Canterbury	2 Shaker Village Inc. (1792–mid-19th century)
Concord	3 214 North Main Street (1826)
Danville	4 **Meeting House** (1760)
Dover	5 **William Damme House** (c. 1675) Friends Meeting House (1768)
Durham	6 Christensen, Williamson, and Philbrook Halls (1969–72)— Ulrich Franzen
Exeter	7 Physical Education Facilities (1967–69)—Kallmann & McKinnell
	8 **The Phillips Exeter Academy Library** (1969–71)—Louis I. Kahn
Hancock	9 **Meeting House** (1820) **and Village** —Elias Carter
Harrisville	10 **Mill Village** (19th century)
Hillsboro Lower Village	11 Franklin Pierce Homestead (1804)
Manchester	12 **Amoskeag Manufacturing Complex** (1838–1915)
New Ipswich	13 **Barrett House** (1800)
Newington	14 Town Meeting House (1712)
Orford	15 **The Orford Row** (late 18th/early 19th centuries)
Portsmouth	16 **Richard Jackson House** (c. 1664)
	17 **Macpheadris-Warner House** (1718–23)

18 John Paul Jones House (1758)

19 **Wentworth-Gardner House** (1760)

20 **Moffatt-Ladd House** (c. 1764)

21 **Governor John Langdon Mansion** (1784)

22 **Strawbery Banke Inc.** (18th–19th century)

Sandown   23 **Meeting House** (1773–74)

Stark   24 **Covered Bridge** (c. 1852) **and Union Church** (1853)

Covered Bridge (1852), Groveton

Washington   25 Civic Group and Village Green (18th–19th century)

1 United Church (1821)
on hill on W edge of
Acworth, New Hampshire

The small, high (1,540 feet/469 meters), semi-isolated village of Acworth, its population now around 500 from the 1,500 of a century ago,
boasts a meeting house whose exterior is one of New England's most
elaborate. The church was constructed, it is said, for $6,000 and sev-
eral barrels of rum: one Elias Carter put it together undoubtedly
guided by handbooks. The projecting central bay and square tower are
well handled and well related to the block of the church, while the steeple and its detailing are very competent. Unfortunately the lofty nave
was framed over in 1886 to make two floors instead of one, and the
upper, or worship room, totally "Gothicized," complete with Victorian
glass in the windows—which was, of course, the fashion of the times.
The vestry on the lower or entry floor is used today as the parish hall.

*Open Sun. mornings, June–Sept.; otherwise apply at post office
at rear*

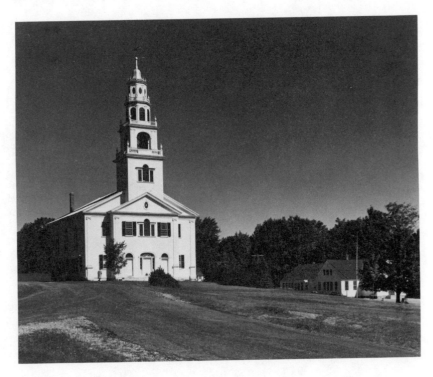

2   Shaker Village Inc. (1792–mid-19th century)
take Exit 18 from IS 93, bear E, and follow signs (7.3 miles/12
kilometers)
near Canterbury, New Hampshire

The Canterbury Shaker sisters (all brethren are dead and this celibate
group is moribund) have turned over their land and buildings to Shaker
Village Inc., a non-profit organization which will preserve and restore
the "village" as a museum. It comprises a number of dwellings and
farm buildings some of which date from the end of the eighteenth century. (Another Shaker settlement is at Sabbathday Lake, Maine; two
Shaker communities which have been turned into fine museums can be
seen near Pittsfield, Massachusetts, and at Shakertown, Kentucky—
q.v.) The oldest and architecturally most important building at Canterbury dates from 1792, and its characteristic gambrel roof can be seen at
the end of an avenue of maples. (The small windowpanes are also typical.) Formerly the meeting house—note its symmetrically placed doors,
one for sisters, the other for brethren—it now serves as a museum, and
should be seen first for the orientation it provides. It is highly likely

that it was built by Moses Johnson, who also constructed the meeting house at Sabbathday Lake. The large (fifty-six-room) building adjacent and at right angles was started a year later (1793) to serve as quarters, kitchen, and chapel. At its peak some four hundred members lived at Canterbury. There are today no more converts or "poor or orphaned children" to replenish its celibatory ranks but at it height this was one of our great utopias. The Shakers also contributed substantially to early agricultural developments in the United States in cattle breeding, seed improvement, and herbs.

Open mid-May–mid-Oct., Tues.–Sat. 9–4: admission

---

3   214 North Main Street (1826)
Concord, New Hampshire

A compact Federal Style building—one of the few non-residential ones in the state—which graces the downtown of New Hampshire's capital. The influence of Bulfinch's state houses in both Boston and Hartford (south side) can be seen in the facade with its shallow arcaded bays: observe that the central bay is wider than the two on each side. Note, too, the unexpected (for its late time) stepped gables at each end. Built as the Merrimack County Bank, the building has come down to us well preserved on the exterior (the entry dates from 1921) but with modernization (1978) within to fit the needs of the law firm of Gallagher, Callahan & Gartrell, who now own it. Former President Franklin Pierce (see Franklin Pierce Homestead) once had his law office in the building.

Open during business hours

---

4 **Meeting House** (1760)
   on NH 111A, 1.9 miles/3 kilometers N of
   Danville, New Hampshire

The seeker of total simplicity in a religious building—"ostentatious austerity"—need go no further. This mid-eighteenth-century wood-frame, ridge-roof, towerless, symmetrical box is almost irreducibly plain, but withal it exerts a fundamental appeal. When seen from the cemetery side it synthesizes the backwoods New England meeting house. The only hint of elegance is the almost reluctantly revealed Classic framing of the front door and, within, the pulpit with its sounding board. The graduated width clapboarding, which is original, should be noted. The interior, with the traditional three-sided balcony, is as frugal as the exterior except for the spindle-topped pews and the pulpit. The church declined when a new one was built in 1836 in the town itself, though town meetings took place until 1878 (when a separate Town Hall was constructed). However, in 1935 it was carefully restored (the pews had been taken out but fortunately saved) and it is now solicitously maintained as the property of the Old Meeting House Association. As the building is almost always locked, squint in the windows or through the keyhole.

Open Memorial Day and the fourth Sun. in August: can be peeked

---

5 **William Damme House** (c. 1675)
The Woodman Institute
182 Central Avenue (NH 16)
Dover, New Hampshire

A frontier "garrison" house three hundred years old and surprisingly well preserved. The ground floor, which measures 40×22 feet/ 12×6.7 meters, contains two rooms embracing a central chimney, with a large garret above. Though primarily designed as a single-family dwelling, such garrison houses doubled as semifortified refuges in time of danger. The heavy, rough-dressed oak logs of which this is built (and never subsequently clapboarded as many were) still bear witness to Indian attack. The corners are mortised, not notched as were the log cabins introduced earlier in the seventeenth century by the Swedes in Delaware. Details of this joinery can be best seen at the rear of the Damme House (also spelled Damm) and in the crossbeams which project from the garret floor. The present windows were, of course, much smaller originally. The house—which was once surrounded by a

stockade—was moved from nearby Back River in 1915, refurbished, and encased (a touch too tightly) in a shed for protection from weather and vandalism. Although the furnishings are not all of the seventeenth century, the building gives a substantially accurate picture of an important house type of early New England frontier settlements.

Open mid-May–Nov., Tues.–Sun. 2–5, except holidays

The **Friends Meeting House** (1768) is located just down the street at 141 Central Avenue, and though generally closed (and altered within) will interest the specialist. It has the characteristic twin doors.

---

6 Christensen, Williamson, and Philbrook Halls (1969–72)
University of New Hampshire
S off Main Street on Mill Road, SW edge of campus
Durham, New Hampshire

ULRICH FRANZEN & ASSOCIATES, ARCHITECTS

Good scale, sensitive relation of buildings to each other, and proper landscaping set apart this dormitory and dining group for 1,000 students. The buildings range from the one-story Philbrook Dining Hall, divided into small-scale, non-institutional nooks, to several four-story and one ten-story dormitories, all in reddish brick. The fenestration of the latter may seem unnecessarily small but it evolved from the desire to give each student in tiny double bedrooms his or her corner with a well-separated desk and private window to look out and thus comfortably identify with self and nature. This is no small philosophical and architectural achievement in minimum-size, minimum-cost university dormitories. Study-lounges are provided for the twelve rooms which make up each typical floor. Public lounges, seminar room, and quarters for the housemaster fill the ground floor of the main unit.

Grounds and lounges open during school year

---

7   **Physical Education Facilities** (1967–69)
The Phillips Exeter Academy
Court Street at Gilman
Exeter, New Hampshire

KALLMANN & McKINNELL, ARCHITECTS

This lavish complex for physical education is one that most colleges would envy. Two hockey rinks, pool, gymnasium with three basketball courts, and a dozen squash courts comprise the major facilities. These are attached to the fifty-year-old Thompson Gym and Thompson Cage, altogether providing year-round facilities for as many as a thousand boys and girls (including in summer some use by the community). The architects had a minor problem in tying on to the existing buldings and a major one in creating giant spans over the rinks and gymnasium. Elevated pedestrian links solved the first, while the second was resolved by a dramatic series of fifteen exterior weathering-steel, three-dimensional trusses (up to 130-foot/40-meter span) from which the roofs are hung. Such outside support also created neater interiors. The right-angled inner hall, circulation for the public, and the spectator gallery create a festive atmosphere, at times a dramatic one. It has been called "a building invested with life—in which activities are sequentially visible to visitors and athletes as they move through the complex along its multi-level spine" (*Architectural Record,* November 1975). William LeMessurier was the structural engineer.

Open to public during games

---

8   **The Phillips Exeter Academy Library** (1969–71)
Front Street between Elm Street and Tan Lane
Exeter, New Hampshire

LOUIS I. KAHN, ARCHITECT

Quiet without, the new Exeter library erupts within. In plan it forms a simple square 108 feet/33 meters on a side, its corners carefully lopped, left "open," and its planar facades projected to emphasize the separation of outer brick from inner concrete. A ground-level enclosed arcade (evocative of those in Asolo and Bern) surrounds the building, masking, it should be mentioned, the main entrance on the north side: should not a library be the most inviting to enter of any building on campus? The exterior walls are of locally made traditional Exeter brick and untraditional teak spandrels. Note the subtle widening of the flat-arched windows as the building rises to its open terrace at top: this progression not only lightens the mass but relieves any tendency toward rigidity. (The small windows in the spandrels of the second and third levels open onto study carrels.)

It is on the inside, however, that the building springs to life. As one winds up an arm of the twin-curved stair past mighty concrete beams, one encounters the startling climax of the second-level Great Hall. Here Kahn's famous play of geometry and equally celebrated play of light—"Light, the giver of all presences"—create stunning sequences, plus a monumentality reminiscent of his work in Dacca and Ahmedabad. The geometrics begin with the square plan of this central concrete-framed "court," which flings its open core up six floors to the prodigious X-bracing at top. High on all four sides a circular opening 29 feet/8.8 meters in diameter liberates lateral enclosure and enables one to realize the books behind. Above the X-bracing a peripheral skylight pours light into the Great Hall. It is no casual experience. The concrete inner frame also supports the stacks, which embrace the core on all sides: they have a capacity of 250,000 volumes. An outer wrapping of brick surrounds the concrete book area, providing on the second and third levels the study carrels mentioned earlier (204 in all). Thus the student can retreat from the monumentality of the Hall to the intimacy of his or her shielded desk, and can view either the world of nature by opening a wood panel or the private world of books. The roof terrace (in effect the ninth floor) offers an open-air reading spot. The interiors were furnished with distinction by Benjamin J. Baldwin. The difficult structural problem of combining a concrete frame with a brick bearing wall structure was solved by Kahn's consultants, the Keast and Hood Company.

Open daily during school year

---

9 Meeting House (1820) and Village
Village Green (NH 137)
Hancock, New Hampshire

ELIAS CARTER, ARCHITECT

A panorama of New England meeting houses might not include this example in its pantheon. Its three sharply stated doors with single lintel—representing the Trinity—are dark hence insistent, the Palladian window above them small, and the tower bulky though the steeple attains delicacy. (Note the painted "windows" at top of lantern. The bell, incidentally, dates from 1820 and came from Paul Revere's factory.) Moreover the interior was altered in 1851 when the church was moved across its green, and an upper floor inserted to create a separate worship area (renovated in 1966), while the lower part was turned to town offices (removed in 1973). But if the church itself has limitations, it does not stand alone: it faces a relaxedly unstructured green and is backed by a carriage shed that curls around the back, witness of an

earlier day. Moreover the town itself, settled in the last half of the eighteenth century, provides a nostalgic example of an off-the-path New England village. It breathes an unhurried atmosphere. Along Main Street several buildings, including a 1793 inn and the Hancock Historical Society House (c. 1809), are open to the public in summer.

Meeting House open June–Sept., daily 9–5

10 Mill Village (19th century)
3.6 miles/5.8 kilometers N of NH 101 and Dublin
Harrisville, New Hampshire

The self-contained, isolated village, complete with mills, employee housing, and public buildings, should not be confused with the oft slum-productive mainstream industrial complexes which dominated many New England river towns in the last century. The small villages were established at remote sources of waterpower, and their modest industrial undertakings had to provide not only plant facilities but adequate shelter to attract and hold employees—preferably families with

numerous employable children. The resulting communities, an effort epitomized at Harrisville, form some of the finer chapters of early U.S. industrial history in spite of their inevitable paternalism and child labor. Harrisville, whose woolen mills expanded from the early 1800s to 1860, and which had additions as recently as 1946, tumbles up and down its little valley. Brick and local stone sheathe all its human-scaled buildings, giving homogeneity to the logical layout of work, living, and worship. Public buildings (the Congregational Church dates from 1842) face the small lake at the top of the valley, with housing spreading off from this core and the mills stretched along the Nubanusit Creek. Architectural distinction will not be found, but the prober into industrial vernacular will be rewarded by this almost totally unspoiled community. However, the future of Harrisville's well-being and even existence was seriously threatened in 1970 when the Cheshire Mill, which had been in operation for almost 170 years and which owned over half of the town's buildings—as well as being by far its largest employer—shut down. With a grant from the National Historic Preservation Fund, Historic Harrisville Inc. was established (1971) and the Filtrine Manufacturing Company (water coolers and filters) moved in, with others, hopefully, to follow. The village's future is now fortunately secure as the Harrisville Historic District has been placed on the National Register of Historic Places.

---

11   **Franklin Pierce Homestead** (1804)
on NH 31 just W of intersection with NH 9
Hillsboro Lower Village, New Hampshire

A compact, white clapboard home—one of few in the area open to the public—which gives a good insight into the simple but comfortable Federal-influenced houses found in even inland New Hampshire at this early date. The interior contains some good French wallpaper— Dufour's "Bay of Naples" adorns the parlor (c. 1824)—but is some- what sparsely furnished. A 60-foot/18-meter-long ballroom extends across the front of the second floor: note both its cornice and wide- planked floor. At the rear of the house is the keeping room and summer kitchen with barn attached in the typical northern New England fashion of the period. The property was given to the state (1925) and the State Recreation Division took possession in 1950 and fully restored it to its present sparkling condition. Franklin Pierce (1804–69)—the four- teenth President—lived here until his thirty-fourth year.

Open mid-June–early Oct., daily 9–5: admission

12   Amoskeag Manufacturing Complex (1838–1915)
E bank of Merrimac River
Manchester, New Hampshire

To the student of American socioindustrial economy the Amoskeag
plants represent possibly the most extraordinary statement of the
nineteenth-century manufacturing scene in this country. Stretching in tiers
for almost a mile along the Merrimac River and tapping its Amoskeag
Falls—named by the Indians, "a place of much fish"—an integrated
and continuingly abutted series of factories proliferated for some
seventy-five years. (The first building on the east side of the river dates
from 1838, the last from 1915.) Moreover, from the beginning the concept embraced decent workers' housing, here placed at right angles
across from the upper canal. (Compare the lack of these amenities in
most European and American industrial slums in the nineteenth
century.) As growth of the Amoskeag plant and subplants had been
planned as a full community by Ezekial Straw as engineer, with Samuel
Shepherd and John D. Kimball generally cited as the first architects, the
resulting industrial, even urban, unity is unique. In effect an instant city
with all amenities for ten thousand people sprang up. Water supply and
transportation ingeniously keyed the basic layout, with two lines of canals and two of railroad sidings dividing the ranks of buildings paralleling the curves of the river. Although products included such hardware as rifles and locomotives, the Amoskeag enterprise was known

primarily as being the largest manufacturer of cotton textiles in the world, turning out 50 miles/80 kilometers of cloth an *hour* at peak production! The company collapsed in the Depression. The multiple lines of red brick factories, simple in form and highlighted occasionally by a Victorian tower, angle and curve along the river, and still create a powerful scene, although many units are not in top shape. Steps are now being taken to prune out some older buildings (unfortunately including some of the finest), rehabilitate the sturdy ones, and resuscitate the city —also largely designed by Amoskeag. Whether this surgery will kill or cure is uncertain: obviously esthetic death will come if rows of river frontage are destroyed, canals filled in, and 90 of 139 buildings razed for parking lots. (Many canals have been filled, the upper laid over with railroad tracks, the lower with roads.) Amoskeag was the greatest of the key enterprises that developed the industrial might of New England: a substantial portion should be maintained for posterity. Or is it even now too late?

Contact the Manchester Historic Association, 129 Amherst Street, regarding tours of millyard: Tues.–Fri. 9–4, Sat. 10–4: donation

---

13   Barrett House (1800)
Main Street, off NH 124, .5 mile/.8 kilometer S of
New Ipswich, New Hampshire

A majestic Federal mansion with attached carriage house on the south side (the wing to north was added in 1900) located outside a tiny textile village. Charles Barrett built the house—also known as Forest Hall—as a wedding present for his son and daughter-in-law (whose father furnished it). Three-story Tuscan pilasters establish the geometry of the facade with slight projection of the pedimented central bay: only the entry lacks determination. On the third floor a ballroom stretches across the entire front of the house. (The top-floor location for a ballroom was common as roof trusses permitted a non-partitioned dancing space.) Many original furnishings, including valuable musical instruments, survive, together with those of subsequent periods. A spinning and weaving exhibit is featured in the carriage house and is well worth seeing—as is the Gothic Revival summer house at rear. The property since 1948 has been owned by the Society for the Preservation of New England Antiquities.

Open May–Oct., Tues., Thurs., Sat., Sun. 10–5: admission

14 **Town Meeting House** (1712)
between Portsmouth and Durham, W of Spaulding Turnpike
Newington, New Hampshire

A compact church, which though altered in 1839 (height, windows, tower) still carries considerable personality. The sizable roundheaded windows, three on the sides and two in front, are echoed by the roundheaded front door and, again, by the windows of the squat belfry tower, a geometric progression and cadence which knit the whole engagingly together. A Paul Revere bell hangs in the belfry. Note the lathe-turned miniature "pinnacles" at each corner of the two stages of the tower. At rear stands the carriage shed, while the saltbox parsonage (1725) nearby should also be noted. This is the oldest meeting house in New Hampshire and is regarded as the oldest in the country in continuous use by Congregationalists.

Open for services Sun. or apply at Town Hall to visit

15   The Orford Row (late 18th, early 19th centuries)
NH 10
Orford, New Hampshire

Orford, a picturesque town along the Connecticut River, boasts seven
Federal Style houses disported along a low ridge back from the main
street. It provides an excellent example of urban land usage, and illustrates the difference between a New England village and a European
one. On the Continent the houses themselves (or their garden walls)
define the street: here the dwellings are set back several hundred yards
from the thoroughfare (and from each other), but the street is given
visual continuity—and the privacy of the houses more assurance—by
the lawns, the planting, and the fences which line property edges and
highway. The influence—but not the direct hand—of Bulfinch can be
seen in some of the architecture, and though the houses themselves are
not open to the public a drive through the village, which Washington
Irving reputedly called the most beautiful he had seen, is well worth-

while. Note that the supports for the white wooden fences are granite, appropriate for the ground—and the Granite State.

Can only be seen from road

---

16 Richard Jackson House (c. 1664)
Northwest Street (NE off Maplewood Avenue)
Portsmouth, New Hampshire

This black and hoary delectation is the oldest house still standing in New Hamsphire. Its elfin roof, at rear, sweeps down to within a few feet of its hillside site, while its two-storied front surveys the lawn and the North Mill Pond where the Jackson shipyard was once located. Descendants of the family occupied the house for two and a half centuries. The saltbox central section reflects the medieval building traditions of southeast England (from which so many New Englanders emigrated) with its sharp roof lines, three-part diamond-paned windows, and unusually heavy oak framing probably fashioned by shipwrights. To this block around 1764 were appended two picturesque but not alto-

gether sympathetic ells, one of which was used as an office for the ship-yard. The house interior has been carefully restored and fitted with the primitive furniture and artifacts of its day. Since 1924 the property has been owned by the Society for the Preservation of New England Antiquities.

Open May–Oct., Tues.–Sun. 10–5: admission

---

17 Macpheadris-Warner House (1718–23)
150 Daniel Street at Chapel
Portsmouth, New Hampshire

The Macpheadris-Warner House is considered by many as "perhaps the finest early-eighteenth-century brick dwelling left in New England." With its thick Flemish-bond walls—its brick possibly brought as ballast from Holland—it would be distinguished early Georgian anywhere. (It should be remembered that brick, not wood, was the favored building material at this time throughout the South.) The roof originally had a double gable with two ridges and was dormerless. The valley formed by

the gables filled with snow and ice in winter, and as there was no metal flashing to prevent structural rotting, the roof was redesigned as now seen. (The anachronistic cupola was a later addition.) The Chapel Street end of the house (at left) is crowded by two large chimneys; the opposite end uses only one because the fireplaces are conjoined at the inside corners. Attention to detail can be seen in the segmental pediment over the front door, a shape which is softly echoed by the relieving arches over the windows on the lower floor and the alternate dormers on the roof.

The notable features of the interior are the fascinating, semiprimitive murals of the stairway, the large size of the rooms (the parlor measures 19.5 feet/6 meters across), their pine paneling, the marbleization (in dining room), the furnishings (few original), and the portraits: an impressive assembly. In 1931 the dwelling was purchased from Warner descendants by the Warner House Association so that it could be maintained and opened to the public. Some restoration, particularly in the kitchen, was carried out by Norman Isham and William Perry, and proper refurnishing begun. The fence along Daniel Street was designed in 1953 by Mr. Perry (who did much work at Williamsburg).

Open end of May–mid-Oct., Mon.–Sat. 10–5, Sun. 2–5: admission

18   **John Paul Jones House** (1758)
      43 Middle Street at State
      Portsmouth, New Hampshire

Good basic New England clapboarded Colonial with gambrel roof sprouting three dormers (over three groups of five windows on second floor). The segmental (i.e. arched) front door is also of merit, as is the interior hall. The furnishings and collections are first-rate. Hopestill March, a housewright, reputedly designed the house; Joseph Everett Chandler was responsible for the 1917 restoration. The admiral boarded here while supervising construction of his ship *America*.

Open June–mid-Oct., Mon.–Sat. 10–5: admission

19   Wentworth-Gardner House (1760)
140 Mechanic Street at Gardner
Portsmouth, New Hampshire

Locally held to be "one of the most nearly perfect examples of Georgian architecture in America," this wood riverfront house was once owned by the Metropolitan Museum. Its ocher facade sports a flat "blocked front" of pine—that is, wide boards cut in imitation of stone —a lapidary presumption accentuated by the white painted quoins. Clapboards sheathe the other three sides. The plan measures 46.8×36.6 feet/14.2×11 meters. The magnificent Baroque entry, the neatly pedimented shutterless lower windows, and the hip roof with dormers create a quietly positive presence. The original garden extension to the river has been severed by the road. The interior is noted for its exuberant late Georgian carving—done by local artisans—and by its scenic wallpaper, particularly the hand-painted paper in the dining room. The spacious upstairs hall reels with a parade of pilasters, architrave, frieze, cornice, and cove ceiling. The kitchen should also be seen,

for, among other items, its 6.5-foot/2-meter-wide chimney. The four rooms of the first floor, each with fireplace, some with original Dutch tiles, are directly mirrored above. The whole house was beautifully restored some years ago by a former owner, Wallace Nutting, who removed the non-original clapboards from the front and even discovered its lovely stair in another house. It has been well furnished and was opened to the public in 1940.

Open May 1–Oct. 31, Tues.–Sun. 1–5: admission

---

20   Moffatt-Ladd House (c. 1764)
154 Market Street
Portsmouth, New Hampshire

Though it was built only three years after the Wentworth-Gardner House, the Moffatt-Ladd expresses on the exterior far more "New" England than England with its foursquare, unpedimented, "uncapped" bulk surmounted by balustraded captain's walk. Its box form hints of the Federal Style which reached its zenith years later in the famous

town houses of Bulfinch and McIntire. (See McIntire's Peirce-Nichols House of 1782 in Salem, Massachusetts, et seq.) Moffatt-Ladd establishes a unity with setting which is masterminded by the picket fence angling to the very front door, and by the extensive garden in the rear. Formerly the house enjoyed a splendid sweep of the Piscataqua River in front—its captain's walk was an active one. The most distinctive features of the light mauve facade—the first of three stories in the town— are the theatrically pedimented line of second-floor windows and the subdued portico with flanking windows at entry level. The top-floor windows abut and almost disappear into the cornice. A spacious and elaborate stair-hall occupies the northeast corner instead of the routine central divider of the house, a location more of English than Colonial inspiration. Paneling, cornice, and stair are outstanding. The French wallpaper (1815–20) should be noted, as should the detailing and carving throughout. While digging (1963) for a new water main, the city found a secret passageway leading from the kitchen down to the wharves. Be certain to see the garden and the separate Counting House (1831–32—off Market Street). The National Society of the Colonial Dames of America in the State of New Hampshire owns the house, having first leased it from the heirs in 1913 and having purchased it in 1969. As with the Macpheadris-Warner and the Wentworth-Gardner houses, there is no record of an architect for the Moffatt-Ladd.

Open May 15–Oct. 15, Mon.–Sat. 10–5, Sun. 2–5: admission

---

21   Governor John Langdon Mansion (1784)
143 Pleasant Street
Portsmouth, New Hampshire

The elaborate exterior of this house—its fanciful portico, its idiosyncratic Corinthian pilasters on the corners, its scrolled pedimented dormers, and its high Chippendale rail around the captain's walk— place it late in the Georgian movement. This effusiveness is carried over within, beginning with the entry hall and continuing to the fireplaces in the two front rooms. (Their mantels were directly inspired by plates in Abraham Swan's *The British Architect,* 1745.) All of which seems proper if you, as owner, were the first president of the Senate of the United States and if you entertained not only General Washington but the future king of France (Louis Philippe, in 1798). It is a house of splendor outside and in. Its master builder was Daniel Hart, assisted by

Michael Whidden III, while Stanford White of McKim, Mead & White added a polite dining room wing at the rear in 1906. The house and its extensive gardens are now owned by the Society for the Preservation of New England Antiquities.

Open May and Oct., Sat.–Sun. 1–5; June–Sept., Tues., Thurs., Sat., Sun. 1–5: admission

---

22   Strawbery Banke Inc. (18th–19th century)
Follow "Strawbery" signs: main gate on Marcy Street at Hancock
Portsmouth, New Hampshire

The historic domestic architecture of Portsmouth ranks among the most notable in the nation. Some claim, indeed, that it has more distinguished eighteenth-century buildings than any other city in the country. By virtue of its being a provincial capital, having a deep-river location and thus active in sea trading and shipbuilding—with a supportive countryside—the city became one of the wealthiest in the Colonies by the mid-1700s: a century later, its economy undermined by the expan-

sion of the railroads (later the highways), and its capitol removed to Concord, decline set in. (This at least saved the houses from being wiped out by "progress," though a fire in 1813 destroyed much of the oldest part of town.) Before stagnation and conflagation occurred a pageant of domestic opulence arose with, strangely, relatively few good churches, though this was a Church of England colony, not a Puritan one. (Some early churches no longer exist.) As might be expected, ship's carpenters worked on many of the houses. In addition to the gracious individual homes of Portsmouth, many of which are open to the public as we have seen on preceding pages, a broad-scale approach known as the Strawbery Banke Restoration (incorporated in 1958) is under way to restore the earliest section of the city's entire seafaring community as it existed in its prosperous days. (Strawbery Banke was the town's genial name until 1653.) In 1957 much of the historic but by then seedy part of Portsmouth was threatened with destruction through downtown rehabilitation proposals, a draconian possibility here because to qualify for financial aid state law required complete razing of all structures. An alarmed group of citizens then banded together as in Savannah and Charleston, and with the help of the Urban Renewal Administration established by 1964 title to some 10 acres/4 hectares of land and twenty-seven old houses, the Sherburne House, the oldest, dating from 1695. Many buildings were in poor condition and several were of no significance whatever and have been removed. The remaining houses, shops, and related structures are being fully restored or adapted, generally on their original sites, a process which will take years. The long-range aim—possibly the largest effort in the nation today—is heartening, the beginning auspicious, and all should wish them well. Perry, Dean, Hepburn & Stewart, the architects from Boston who were principally responsible for the reconstruction of Colonial Williamsburg, were initially in charge. At the main gate and at the Information Center the visitor can get full orientation and a printed guide to those buildings which are now open to the public. The Sherburne House is treated as an architectural study development via its exhibits. Altogether one of America's greatest projects.

Restoration area always open, museum buildings from mid-Apr.–mid-Nov., daily 9:30–5: admission

23   Meeting House (1773–74)
on Fremont Road off NH 121A
Sandown, Rockingham County, New Hampshire

Only a few miles from the Danville Meeting House (q.v.) and a few years later in date, Sandown represents a more sophisticated, indeed elegant, achievement. The late H. W. Rose in his comprehensive *The Colonial Houses of Worship in America* (Hastings House, 1963) terms it "the finest colonial meeting house in New Hampshire and one of the finest in America." Its interior with box pews and wineglass pulpit closely resembles that of the Rocky Hill Meeting House of 1785 in Amesbury (q.v.) just over the Massachusetts line. The gabled exteriors, too, are similar except for the two-story portico on the latter. In any case Sandown achieves a taut, squarish authority with overall simplicity highlighted by unusually capable detail in doors and exterior cornice. (The plan measures 44×50 feet/13×15 meters.) Although abandoned as a church in the 1830s, the meeting house served town secular needs until 1929. Rescued from gradual destruction, it has been handsomely restored and maintained by the Old Meeting House Historical Association.

Open second Sun. in Aug. for service; at other times custodian has key and will show on request

---

24 Covered Bridge (c. 1852) **and Union Church** (1853)
NH 10
Stark, New Hampshire

Among the surviving covered bridges in New Hampshire none is more evocative than this 151-foot/46-meter example at Stark. Spanning the Upper Ammonoosuc River in the northern reaches of the state, the bridge enjoys a calendar-art setting alongside a simple, indeed homely, church. Note the spatial tension between the two. The bridge is of Paddleford truss and its visual strength stems from the fact that the roof overhangs sufficiently to shelter the non-structural pedestrian walks on either side, thus the interior is opened up, not boxed in, to reveal the spatial transparency of the structure. (Covered bridges, as has been mentioned, were roofed to protect them from the weather.) The arches at Stark were added later for additional strength.

The **covered bridge** at nearby Groteton, built in 1852, is likewise worth a look. It is also a Paddleford type, spanning 136 feet/41 meters, and was recently "retired" to its new park site. Colonel Peter Paddleford, incidentally, was born in New Hampshire. The Paddleford

truss was based on laminated wood arches and a complicated series of vertical members with angled bracing. It was not widely used.

---

25 Civic Group and Village Green (18th–19th century)
NH 31
Washington, New Hampshire

Although no architectural grandeur will be found at Washington (the second U.S. town to honor the first President, the earlier being in North Carolina), its three public buildings—Town Hall, school, and church —lining its ridge and facing its small green offer a bonny scene. Several fine private houses, a bevy of maples, a Civil War memorial, and a sweeping view over the forested Monadnock region enhance this New England panorama. The Town Hall (1787–89) stands as the dominant member and architecturally anchors the group (and serves as school overflow). Built as a simple rectangular box to serve both civic function and worship for its Congregational community, it was spruced up in the early nineteenth century by the addition of a tower and steeple at one end and a porch at the other. The open octagonal, double-decked

belfry shows the influence of Asher Benjamin's widely used book and carpenter's crib *The Country Builder's Assistant,* first published in 1797. Benjamin himself, as mentioned before, started as a carpenter and on maturing as an architect realized the need for a handbook which would help the untutored. The book's influence in New England was widespread. (The cribs today are the latest issues of the architectural magazines.) When the nearby church was completed in 1840—plain on the outside and plainer within—the Town Hall/meeting house was divided into two separate floors and used only for civic affairs. The interiors are architecturally unimportant.

New Jersey

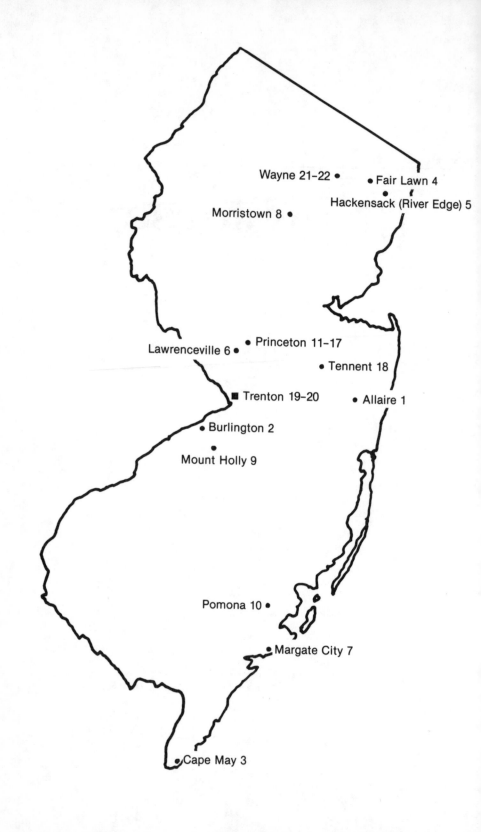

NEW JERSEY

The buildings in boldface type are of general interest. The others are for the specialist.

Allaire   1 Deserted Village (early 19th century)

Burlington   2 New St. Mary's Church (1846–54)— Richard Upjohn

Cape May   3 **Seashore Vernacular** (mid- and late 19th century)

Fair Lawn   4 Radburn (1928–31)—Henry Wright, Sr., and Clarence S. Stein

Hackensack (River Edge)   5 **Ackerman-Zabriskie-Steuben House** (c. 1700–52)

Lawrenceville   6 **E. R. Squibb & Sons World Headquarters** (1970–72)— Hellmuth, Obata & Kassabaum

Margate City   7 **Lucy, the Elephant** (1881)

Morristown   8 **Ford Mansion/Washington's Headquarters** (1774)

Mount Holly   9 Burlington County Court House (1796)

Pomona   10 **Stockton State College** (1973–76)— Geddes Brecher Qualls Cunningham

Princeton   11 Stony Brook Meeting House (1727/rebuilt 1760)
12 **Nassau Hall** (1754–56)— Robert Smith and William Shippen
   Campus Tour and Art
13 **Blair Hall** (1897), **West Campus, and Collegiate Gothic**—Cope & Stewardson and Ralph Adams Cram
   Alexander Hall (1894)— W. A. Potter

14 **L. Stockwell Jadwin Gymnasium**
(1966–68)—Walker O. Cain &
Associates

15 **Stanley P. Jadwin Hall** (1968–69)—
Hugh Stubbins & Associates
Henry Burchard Fine Hall
(1968)—Warner Burns Toan
Lunde

16 Spelman Halls (1973)—
I. M. Pei & Partners

17 Academic Building and Dining
Hall (1970–71)—Geddes
Brecher Qualls Cunningham

Tennent

18 Old Tennent Church (1751)
and Cemetery (1731)

Trenton

19 William Trent House (1719)

20 **Old Barracks** (1758–59)

Wayne

21 **Dey Mansion** (c. 1740)

22 Union Camp Headquarters
(1969–70)—Schofield & Colgan

1 Deserted Village (early 19th century)
Allaire State Park
Exit 98 (North and Southbound) of Garden State Parkway, W on
   NJ 524
Allaire, New Jersey

Those interested in early industrial buildings in the U.S.A. will want to see the remains of the Howell Iron Works and its village. Although the furnace (1830) itself has largely disappeared, leaving only a partial stack, many of the other structures are intact with restoration being undertaken as funds become available. The Howell Works utilized bog ore and charcoal—bog furnaces had been in use in this part of the state since 1674—producing a variety of iron goods from scissors to stoves. With the discovery of richer iron deposits in the Alleghenies, then with coal and coke for fuel, bog production phased out (1846) and the vil-

lage was eventually abandoned. Mrs. Arthur Brisbane, whose husband had acquired the site in 1907, gave it to the state (1941) with some 1,200 acres/486 hectares of land. In 1954 Allaire State Park was established and restoration of the ironworks and its community of buildings slowly commenced.

Open Apr. 15–Sept. 15, daily 10–5: admission. Park open all year

---

2   New St. Mary's Church (1846–54)
West Broad Street between Wood and Talbot Streets
Burlington, New Jersey

RICHARD UPJOHN, ARCHITECT

Having outgrown its original church, built in 1703 and still standing adjacent to the New St. Mary's, the congregation in 1846 asked Upjohn —the apostle of religious Gothic Revival—to design a larger house of worship. Upjohn responded handsomely, producing an example of the

mid-nineteenth-century fashion very much in the English tradition. (Upjohn himself was born in England in 1802, coming to the States in 1829. He was, incidentally, a founder and the first president of the American Institute of Architects.) Surrounded by an ancient church-yard, the church rises gracefully from it, using its ashlar sandstone not only for the walls and square tower base but for the steeple (144 feet/44 meters high) as well, creating thus an unusual exterior harmony. (Note the fairing and broaching of the spire, which changes from a square to an octagon.) The most impressive features of the interior are the four powerful stone piers which support the tower and steeple. Marking—even jostling—the four corners of the crossing of nave and transept, these give tremendous structural and visual strength to the church.

The church was severely damaged by fire in 1976, with most of the interior woodwork being destroyed. Basic reconstruction, under the direction of architect Richard Murphy, was completed in 1979. The stained glass, polychrome painting, etc. are scheduled as funds materialize.

---

3 Seashore Vernacular (mid- and late 19th century)
Cape May, New Jersey

Long before the railroads reached Cape May in 1868, steamboats brought summer visitors from Philadelphia, Wilmington, and even New York and Washington to this point where the Delaware Bay meets the Atlantic Ocean. Cape May claims, indeed, to be "the Oldest Seashore Resort in the United States." (It was first settled in 1631 and named for a Dutchman, Cornelis J. Mey, who in 1621 had explored the area.) After a heyday in the nineteenth century, when it had some fifty-seven hotels—one claiming to be the world's largest—the town began to lose out to Atlantic City's gambling. By the mid-twentieth century Cape May was bypassed by the public, which sought among other features greater automotive access. With the opening of the Garden State Parkway and with the modernization of the Cape May-Lewes (Delaware) ferry, a potential for revitalization was at hand. The townspeople diligently assessed their heritage and their future, and—prompted by historian Carolyn Pitts—decided (1965) to preserve and where necessary rehabilitate. For Cape May possesses possibly the largest concentration of wooden Victorian buildings (supposedly over five hundred) in the East. Its citizens had seen what chrome-striping and

tawdriness had done to most of the Atlantic littoral. Cape May even bought 139 ancient gas lamps from Baltimore to lend atmosphere. Not only is there a master plan, but a Historic District Commission of five with an architectural historian adviser which must pass on any proposed changes in the "Victorian Village" (centered around the three-block Washington Mall) before the building department even gets the plans. A solid program of maintenance and reconstruction under expert direction is proceeding, and the future augurs well. Among the richer examples open to the public are Victorian Mansion (1856), today a guest house, 635 Columbia Avenue at Stockton Place, and the Chalfonte Hotel (1876), Sewell Avenue at Howard Street. The private houses along Congress Place, back of the Congress Hotel (1878), are also good in parts. Virtually the whole town of five thousand permanent residents is now a National Historic Landmark.

NOTE: The Cape May City Chamber of Commerce, Box 109, Cape May, NJ 08280, issues a free pamphlet on "Victorian Cape May," complete with street map. There are also information booths on the parkway and in town.

---

4   Radburn (1928–31)
Plaza Road North, Radburn Road, Howard Avenue
Fair Lawn, New Jersey

HENRY WRIGHT, SR., AND CLARENCE S. STEIN, ARCHITECTS
AND PLANNERS

The planning/architecture team of Henry Wright, Sr., and Clarence Stein did much to influence the development of urbanism in this country. Their example would have been of greater impact if the Depression had not occurred shortly after the birth of Radburn, their foremost work. Influenced by Ebenezer Howard (1850–1928), Raymond Unwin (1863–1940), Patrick Geddes (1854–1932), and the Garden City movement which commenced in England at the turn of this century, Wright and Stein fought valiantly—generally against municipal and corporate indifference—to make large-scale professional planning an essential ingredient of urban expansion. The most famous of their efforts is, as mentioned, the modest-sized community of Radburn—approximately 670 families/3,000 population—"the town for the motor age," located about 12 miles/19 kilometers WNW of the George Washington Bridge.

The layout—which was initially intended to be much larger—was based on a half-dozen premises: the superblock; a community center (library, gymnasium, senior citizens room, youth provisions, etc.), with shopping facilities adjacent; residential cul-de-sacs with clusters of houses placed away from the noise and danger of automobiles; separation of the wheel and the pedestrian; the park rather than the street as the core of the neighborhood; houses turned "outside-in" to face the park, not the access road. The houses are reached by car from the "rear" or garage-kitchen side via a short cul-de-sac, the street servicing two rows of houses. There are 430 single-family houses, 92 apartment units, 60 town houses, 30 row houses, and 54 duplexes. (A single built-in, narrow garage and no curb parking create problems with today's two-car families.) Circulation on foot occurs on the other side where the houses open onto gardens, with a walkway in the center which leads both to a private park and to (Ebenezer) Howard or

(Robert) Owen avenues. An underpass between the superblocks allows children to walk to school or their numerous playgrounds or sports facilities without crossing a street. This dual system of circulation becomes increasingly necessary as the automobile begins of preempt movement, but this elementary lesson is almost totally ignored today even though Radburn's message has been with us for fifty years. (It is not ignored in much of the new European work, nor, fortunately, in our own Reston and Columbia—q.v.) Radburn today is a well-treed community, comfortably lived in. Twenty-three of its 149 acres (9 to 60 hectares) form interior parks, all well maintained by a house assessment. Its lots are small, hence the houses (of non-scintillating architecture) close together. However, this cluster "compaction" makes economically feasible the surrounding parks. Even the pedestrian walks and the driveways (18 feet/5.5 meters, no sidewalks) are tight. But for the seeker of a basic pattern for a superior environment for family life, for the historian of the suburb, and for planning enlightenment,

Radburn stands as one of our precious few planning contributions of the early twentieth century. Frederick L. Ackerman worked closely with Wright and Stein in developing the basic idea of Radburn. Clarence Stein, though he died in 1975 (Henry Wright in 1936), will also live on via his book *Toward New Towns for America* (currently available as an MIT Press paperback), while Henry Wright's literary contribution can be seen in his *Rehousing America* (Columbia University Press, 1935).

5 Ackerman-Zabriskie-Steuben House (c. 1700–52)
1209 Main Street, c. .5 mile/.8 kilometer N of NJ 4 at River Edge
Hackensack, New Jersey

The history of the von Steuben House began around 1700 when David Ackerman erected what was probably a one-room cottage on the site. It is believed that some of the walls of the first house remain, but starting about 1720 and up to 1739, Johannes, Ackerman's son, put up three quarters of the stone house we now see incorporating the earlier structure. By 1745 Jan Zabriskie had bought the home and its lovely land which extended along the river, and in 1752 put on a piazza and raised and changed the roof into a modified gambrel. This roof covers the split-level series of spaces at the rear which still intrigue the visitor. Shortly after the Revolution—in which General von Steuben distinguished himself—New Jersey confiscated "loyalist" Zabriskie's property and, in gratitude for the general's service, gave it to him. (However, it is quite possible that the famous soldier and drillmaster never lived there.) In 1788 it was sold and subsequently went through a series of owners—plus some maltreatment—until 1911, when the sister of William Randolph Hearst acquired it. Lying untenanted, the state of New Jersey bought house and grounds in 1928 and in 1931 began desultory restoration. However, in 1938–39 a careful rebuilding under the direction of Wesley S. Besslel was commenced, work that was not finished until 1958, having been interrupted by World War II. The house forms an important unit of our meager Dutch Colonial inheritance.

Open Wed.–Sat. 10–12, 1–5, Sun. 1–5, except major holidays

---

6   E. R. Squibb & Sons World Headquarters (1970–72)
on US 206, 3 miles/4.8 kilometers S of Princeton, 2.2 miles/3.5 kilometers N of
Lawrenceville, New Jersey

HELLMUTH, OBATA & KASSABAUM, ARCHITECTS

An international administrative and research facility for the pharmaceutical branch of the famous Squibb corporation. With a wide swath of 273 acres/110 hectares of landscaped property (two thousand new trees) fronting the highway, and a 12-acre/4.9-hectare artificial lake between road and building cluster, the setting is dignified yet friendly. The building in plan consists of eleven interconnected three-story modules irregularly branching from both sides of a central circulation spine. Across the front—and facing the lake—are five office modules, each 90

feet/27 meters square, two on the left side of the large lobby-garden and gallery-dining block, and three to the right, each slightly offset axially relative to its neighbor(s). Set back at the left of the entry are two more 90-foot/27-meter-square units for administration office and library, with two larger laboratories beyond on opposite sides of the circulation spine, and a lab support building at rear, all three being squarish in plan. Construction is of limestone-revetted steel frame with brick used for the circulation towers. The interior of each of the office blocks is color-coded to give identity and spriteliness, the color accents enlivening the basic white of walls and cabinets. The most dramatic part of the building is near the entry where spaces and planting intertwine horizontally and vertically to produce a striking reception area. The skylit "garden" with towering scheffleras and ficuses leads to an art gallery (87×62 feet/27×19 meters), where a series of month-long exhibits is programmed from September through June. The restaurant, seating 662, and located just below the art gallery, provides a relaxing view of the lake. All interiors were by the architects, David Suttle designer, with Gyo Obata principal in charge of design; the Office of Dan Kiley was landscape architect; Earl Wall Associates were laboratory consultants. Expansion along two axes was anticipated in the original planning. A fine setting-oriented headquarters for one thousand employees, almost half of whom are research scientists.

Garden-lobby, art gallery, and pharmaceutical museum open to public during business hours and on Thurs. until 9 P.M., Sun. 1–5

7   Lucy, the Elephant (1881)
9200 Atlantic Avenue at Decatur Avenue
Margate City, New Jersey

Man-made elephants for "living" have been popular since the Trojan Horse suggested zoomorphic possibilities. It is said that Ptolemy sported one on wheels around the streets of Alexandria; Henry II entered Rouen "with several elephant automatons" (see Clay Lancaster's delightful *Architectural Follies in America,* Charles E. Tuttle Co., 1960); a gigantic one was proposed for Louis XV but never built; and New Jersey has Lucy. Lucy was commissioned by James V. Lafferty, a real estate promoter, to house—unforgettably—a restaurant (soon called a "hotel") and office. William Free was its designer. However, financial problems overtook Mr. Lafferty and in 1887 he sold the elephant (which he had patented in 1882) to John Gertzen, who "ran" it as a tourist attraction, at one time renting it as a "cottage" and subse-

quently using it as a bar. Several storms caused damage, one removing
the original howdah in 1928, and Lucy's condition became increasingly
parlous. In 1970 Mr. Gertzen's son and daughter gave the elephant—
which faced imminent demolition—to the city of Margate on condition
that they move it two blocks away (to make way for an apartment
house), and at this time the private, non-profit Save Lucy Committee
was established to undertake a complete restoration. Built of heavy timber framing (12×12 inches/30×30 centimeters) covered with a tin
skin, the elephant measures 75 feet/23 meters long, 29 feet/8.8
meters wide, and 60 feet/18 meters high. In the patent drawings
(#268,503) one vast domed inner space is shown, with access via circular stairs in its 10 feet/3 meters in diameter rear legs (one up,
one down). Ten curved-wall "closets" transform the bulging elephan-
tine profile into a properly rectangular Main Hall within, a space that
witnessed other partitioning (now removed) through the years.

This marvelous bit of American "architecture" was designated a National Historic Landmark in 1976, and its exterior, including the howdah, has been restored (1977) through the mighty efforts of the Save
Lucy Committee and its dedicated co-chairwomen Mrs. Josephine L.
Harron and Mrs. H. Sylvia Carpenter. John D. Milner was architect of
the restoration. It is hoped that funds can be raised to complete the
refurbishment of the interior and create a South Jersey History Museum; after all, it is the only patented pachyderm we have.

*Open Memorial Day–June, weekends 10–4:30; July–Labor Day,
daily 10* A.M.*–9* P.M.*; Labor Day–Oct., weekends 10–4:30:
admission*

---

8   Ford Mansion, Washington's Headquarters (1774)
230 Morris Street at Washington Place
Morristown, New Jersey

The Colonel Jacob Ford, Jr., Mansion, or more popularly Washington's Headquarters, stands prominently situated on one of the main
streets of this arbored town. Aside from its historic importance as the
general's winter headquarters in 1779–80, the house provides us with
an excellent example of late Colonial architecture in wood. The richness of the exterior detail greets one at the front door, where an ex-

traordinary Palladian entry beneath a Palladian window (with bold cornice on top) stands out against the flush siding. (Clapboarding sheathes the other sides.) The set-back wing at right contains kitchen below, with servant quarters above. Furnishings throughout are of the period with some pieces coming down direct from the Ford Family. The kitchen, especially, is of interest. The mansion was sold after the death of the last Ford resident (1872) to four gentlemen who organized the Washington Association of New Jersey to preserve the building. This public-spirited group then gave the house to the National Park Service (1933), which instituted a complete restoration and refurnishing. A Historical Museum is located in a separate building (1935–37) at the rear, John Russell Pope, architect, in collaboration with the National Park Service Branch of Plans and Design.

Open daily 9–5, except holidays: admission

---

9 Burlington County Court House (1796)
Main Street between Garden and Union
Mount Holly, New Jersey

"Non-official," indeed almost domestic in appearance, well situated and well detailed, this small-town courthouse is a fine late Georgian-early Federal example of New Jersey's architectural development. The prominent doorway and its flanking roundheaded windows—which repeat the fanlighting of the entry—create with the half-roundheaded blinds a subdued oscillation across the lower floor. A plaque on the stringcourse adds an official note. Above rises a busy, amateurish pediment with octagonal cupola on top. The interiors, which continue to serve court functions, are of less interest.

Open during business hours

10   Stockton State College (1973–76)
Exit 44 off Garden State Parkway, S to College Drive
Pomona, New Jersey

GEDDES BRECHER QUALLS CUNNINGHAM, ARCHITECTS

An innovative and extremely interesting suburban college layout. The
basic plan consists of a central, two-story, covered circulation spine
with academic facilities deployed on either side. This generous "street"
angles near each end as it steps up the slight gradient of the site—the
angles reducing apparent length—and in addition to providing clearly
oriented circulation, the spine creates a series of bustling indoor forums
along the way. The gallery's width was made sufficient to allow for casual groupings of sturdy chairs and benches for much of its length; these

settings are enhanced by banners, supergraphics, views out, and the parade of students. The college units which "attach" to the corridor, six on one side and seven on the other, are basically two stories in height, while their shapes are, of course, free to house properly their various functions (administration to swimming pool). Construction is based on a 5-foot/1.5-meter module, and was carried out with speed and economy by using a "systems" technique of prefabricated components almost all of metal. All of the inner partitions can be readily changed. The office and classroom wings, which project at right angles from the central spine, have their glass walls shielded from the sun by deep overhangs and vertical fins which also give rhythm and character to their facades. The small courtyards between the projecting wings are well developed and landscaped. The college is equally designed for both commuting and residential students, with about two thousand accommodated in the nearby apartments and dormitories. All parking is grouped adjacent to but screened from the college itself, with vehicular access limited to service machines only. Robert L. Geddes and Warren W. Cunningham were partners-in-charge. Very provocative.

Campus open daily

11 Stony Brook Meeting House (1727/rebuilt 1760)
Quaker Road, just E of NJ 583, SW of
Princeton, New Jersey

For those interested in the early meeting houses which radiated with the Quaker faith from Philadelphia, this tiny example—the first house of worship built in Princeton—will prove of value. Although almost always closed except at Sunday worship, when visitors are welcome, it is worth a detour for a view of its basic architecture of local fieldstone walls and wooden porch typical of the area and period. Note, too, its relation to the attached cemetery, in which, among others, Richard Stockton (the famous jurist and signer of the Declaration of Independence) lies buried. The interior possesses an unusual high curved ceiling with natural wood finish throughout, including the original wood floor. Fireplaces stand at each side. The first meeting house on the site was constructed in 1725–26, but was nearly destroyed by fire in 1759: its rebuilding utilized as much as possible of the old (primarily the west end). The Battle of Princeton, in which Washington defeated Corn-

wallis in 1777, took place adjacent to the meeting house, which was used for a while as a hospital. After years of disuse, the building was reconditioned in 1949 and has been open for services ever since.

Generally open Sun. morning service only

---

12   Nassau Hall (1754–56)
Princeton University
Nassau Street at Witherspoon
Princeton, New Jersey

ROBERT SMITH AND WILLIAM SHIPPEN, ARCHITECTS

When Nassau Hall (named for William of Orange and Nassau, who later became William III of England) was finished in 1756 it was "the largest academic building in the Colonies"—and contained the entire facilities of the college. Shelled and injured in the Revolutionary War, it has served such various non-academic functions as a barracks and, for a brief time, as the capitol of the fledgling United States. The building was designed primarily by Robert Smith, who, fresh from his native Scotland, was working in Philadelphia. Nassau Hall was his first independent commission; Dr. William Shippen was his associate. The building displays a dignified, straightforward facade highlighted only by its projected entry, or pavilion, and pediment. It is simply built of local stone, a material more informal than the Hall's Georgian symmetry would normally suggest but one which creates a sympathetic ambience. Following a fire in 1804 it was repaired by Benjamin Latrobe. The cupola was remodeled (and overly enlarged) in 1855 when the building was rebuilt (John Notman, architect) after another serious fire which destroyed much of the interior. Two of the original three front doors were also then removed. The Faculty Room, which was formerly the chapel, projects at right angles to the building at the rear: it possesses a particularly handsome interior. Nassau Hall was, for its time and the experience of its designer, a surprisingly competent and original building. It exerted considerable influence on New England college building in the late eighteenth century from Harvard (Hollis, 1763), to Brown (University Hall, 1771), to Dartmouth (Dartmouth Hall, 1791).

Guided tours of Nassau Hall and campus Mon.–Sat., Sun.

*afternoon, except holidays: inquire Stanhope Hall, immediately W
of Nassau Hall*

A **campus tour** is much recommended, not only for the buildings but
for the magnificent collection of open-air works of art—the Putnam
Collection. Seventeen sizable pieces, forming one of the finest assem-
blages of contemporary outdoor sculpture in the country, dot the
campus, an anonymous gift ($1 million) in memory of John B. Put-
nam, Jr., a class of 1945 sophomore who left Princeton to join the Air
Force as a fighter pilot and was killed on his sixty-sixth mission. Outstanding among the works is Henry Moore's tension-racked *Oval with
Points* (1969), just a few yards south of Nassau and Stanhope halls.
Other artists include Calder, Lachaise, Lipchitz, Nevelson, Noguchi,
Picasso, Pomodoro, and David Smith, altogether a sterling group. Take
a look, too, at the lovingly maintained grounds, their upkeep subsidized
by other friends of the university.

13 Blair Hall (1897), West Campus, and Collegiate Gothic
Princeton University
E of University Place
Princeton, New Jersey

COPE & STEWARDSON, ARCHITECTS OF BLAIR; RALPH ADAMS
CRAM, OF GRADUATE SCHOOL AND UNIVERSITY CHAPEL

Pure Gothic for universities, as paradigmed by Cambridge and Oxford, began in this country in the late 1880s, not, it should be pointed out, as a continuation of the much earlier Gothic Revival, an altogether different matter of Victorian eclecticism. The so-called "Collegiate Gothic" was the outcome of a movement which sought to return to the traditions of medieval humanism and learning, where the scholars could enjoy close relations with their masters in a setting conducive to contemplation and freedom from architectural rigidity. Walter Cope and John Stewardson were among the pioneers of this style, and their work for Bryn Mawr (c. 1886) probably its first significant essay. (The slightly earlier designs by William Burges for Trinity College in Hartford and Henry Ives Cobb for Rockefeller University in Chicago were similarly directed but less pure and only finished in part.) Princeton's Blair Hall, however, immediately estabished the Collegiate Gothic movement for decades to come, a movement which reached a "spiritual" climax in Cram's memorable Graduate School for Princeton (1913)—and perhaps chilled with his University Chapel (1928). Ralph Adams Cram, not unexpectedly, was architect of the university from 1904 to 1927. James Gamble Rogers' notable Harkness Quadrangle for Yale (1921)—plus others to follow—and Horace Trumbauer's Duke University Campus (1923–32) were of the same ingratiating—and in their day even functional—persuasion.

But back to Blair and the quadrangle it faces. Far more permanent than the building's initial impact—and with a force that will outlive any cycle of architectural fashions—is the molding of its architectural spaces, not the accuracy of its archeology. There are vertical spaces in the changes in levels via the almost theatrical steps at the arch and in the landscaping, and horizontal spaces in the pulsations of Blair and the buildings extending from it. The Blair Hall family of structures narrows closely at the south end (falters a bit at the southeast corner), then the spatial continuum broadens into the elongated, eminently relaxed quadrangle framed by a series of dormitories (all from the early 1920s). This three-dimensional excursion is climaxed by the sen-

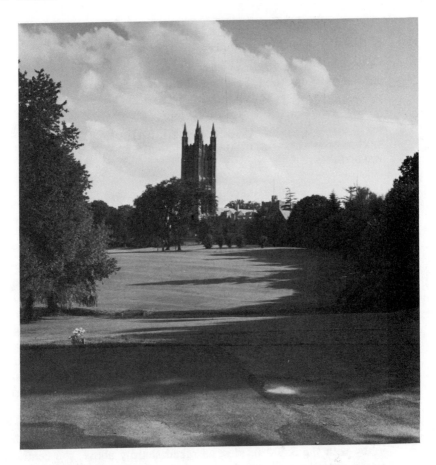

sitive Dodge Memorial Gateway (1933—Day & Klauder). Through the years these buildings were interwoven to produce a masterful three-dimensional experience, one with unforgettable spatial, textural, and landscaping lessons: even the geometry of the paths is important. Altogether an exhilarating experience. Blair Hall, *bottom photo p. 388;* Dodge Memorial Gateway, *top photo p. 388;* Graduate School, *photo above.*

Alexander Hall stands diagonally to the northeast from Blair Arch. Its Richardsonism by W. A. Potter was this movement's swan song, for it was dedicated in 1894, just three years before the new Collegiate Gothic rose to reduce the neo-Romanesque's once-prominent role to stylistic limbo.

Campus open daily

14   L. Stockwell Jadwin Gymnasium (1966–68)
     Princeton University
     off Washington Road, SE edge of campus
     Princeton, New Jersey

WALKER O. CAIN & ASSOCIATES, ARCHITECTS;
SEVERUD-PERRONE-STURM-CONLIN-BANDEL, STRUCTURAL
ENGINEERS

Jadwin Gym is a breathtaking example of the new generation of spaces molded by computer-derived technology in steel space-framing. This extraordinary complex devoted to indoor sports—"The Cage"—grew from its needs, and its needs are manifold. As the Princeton *Alumni Weekly* wrote (April 23, 1968), "The Gymnasium is a single building reconciling the intricate and often conflicting requirements of virtually every intercollegiate sport played at a large University. The 10,000,000-cubic-foot building [283,168 cubic meters] will house track, tennis, basketball, baseball, football, soccer, lacrosse, squash, fencing and wrestling." It goes on to add that "Since there are only 3,600 permanent seats the space can be arranged in any fashion accommodating as many as 9,800 people [with the use of rollaway seats], thus transforming the hall from a basketball court to a ballet theater or concert hall overnight."

The Jadwin Cage is made up of three interlocking shells with a clear span of 368 feet/112 meters. The north or entry segment contains the lobby with the 3,600 fixed seats raked sharply above; the central part wraps over the basketball courts and is a truncated conic section in form; while the third shell shelters, and in its shape reflects, the oval of the running track and structurally forms a half dome. The three independent geometric forms—looking like "the carapaces of a lobster's tail"—are separated by two north-facing glazed strips and upheld by two 19-foot/5.8-meter-deep edge trusses. Tripartite without, the space within is unitary and it is awesome. The lower level, which burrows into its hillside site, and thus helps mask the tremendous size of the building, has only one massive central column to support the upper floor. Infield baseball (dirt floor), tennis, and sundry events, with superb facilities for squash, fencing, and wrestling in the mezzanine, fill this lower section of the gym. Major activities take place on the main floor.

The exterior is covered with diamond-shaped and triangulated panels (protected by Neoprene-Hypalon) which roof the three sections. These

are handsomely expressed and lend excellent scale. (Only the introduction at the entrance of a new material—small-scale brick—seems unnecessary.) The gymnasium was named for Leander Stockwell Jadwin, '28, a noted athlete who was killed in a motor accident shortly after graduation from Princeton. The architectural firm is now called Cain, Farrell & Bell.

Open for events

---

15   Stanley P. Jadwin Hall (1968–69)
Princeton University
E off Washington Road, opposite Palmer Stadium
Princeton, New Jersey

HUGH STUBBINS & ASSOCIATES, ARCHITECTS

The Stanley Palmer Jadwin Physical Laboratory—made possible, along with the Jadwin Cage (q.v.), by the unrestricted $27 million bequest of the late Ethel S. Jadwin—is a fitting structure for what is generally considered one of the finest departments of physics in the nation. With its courtyard, the plaza in front, and Fine Hall opposite, an out-

standing college grouping rises on the eastern edge of the Princeton campus. The design of the six-story Jadwin had to accommodate the contrary demands of eighty-five staff offices opening outward and ninety laboratories with no windows at all. Thus many of the labs are aligned along the outer perimeter of the blank-walled upper floor, while rooms on the other side of the corridor overlook the central courtyard. This beautifully developed court is one of the most attractive features of the building and the non-rigidity of its design a key factor. On the approach side Jadwin is elevated on columns, sweeping the broad plaza in front into the space of the court—and easing the inner confinement outward—while a substantial tower (for vertical circulation and toilets) keeps the court's "layers" from becoming too horizontal. Several well-planted terrace set-backs add their contribution to three-dimensional suavity, with Antoine Pevsner's *Construction in the 3rd and 4th Dimension* appropriately occupying the center. The basement level contains lecture halls, shops, and a 160-foot/49-meter-long cyclotron.

The plaza between Jadwin and Fine also serves as a campus "agora" in addition to doubling as the roof of the two-story combined physics-mathematics library. Near the center of this marketplace for ideas rises Alexander Calder's monumental (28 feet/8.5 meters) stabile *Five Discs: One Empty* (1969), which brings tremendous dynamism to the space between the two buildings. (Calder's father in 1904–5 sculpted statues on Henry Hall and Foulke Hall on campus.)

Courtyard open daily

Henry Burchard Fine Hall (1968), designed by Warner Burns Toan Lunde, faces Jadwin and relates to it and to the plaza between them in sensitive fashion. Part of the entry level of its low wing is elevated to allow a flow of space underneath, tying the building more securely to the campus beyond. Fine's thirteen-story tower, primarily for faculty offices, gives good vertical punctuation to the entire group and also politely recalls the Collegiate Gothic of much of the university, especially the Graduate tower and that at Holder Hall. The three-story wing adjoining the tower contains class and seminar rooms, large lounge, and—projecting toward Jadwin Hall—the rectangular two-story "colloquium." The more formal, squared architecture of the "colloquium" reflects the simple geometry of Jadwin. An exceptional complex.

---

16 Spelman Halls (1973)
Princeton University
University Place at College Road
Princeton, New Jersey

I. M. PEI & PARTNERS, ARCHITECTS

The Spelman Dormitories were plannned to form a connecting link between two sections of the university: the main campus and the Princeton Inn residential college. Progression is the key element of their concept. As one moves toward the campus from the college and nearby railroad station, the angled (and from this approach, blank) walls of Spelman form an open-air arcade framed by six of its eight units, through which dart bands of sun and shadow. Though this "spine" might be said to be confining vertically, space leaps out laterally between the angled ends of the buildings. Two other minor axes spark the spatial flow, the more successful leading eastward by the tennis courts.

The dormitories themselves are similar in design, differing only in their capacity, and all are triangular in shape. A standard "housing unit," of which there are fifty-eight altogether, provides a living room, kitchenette, and bath with four single study-bedrooms (behind the strip windows—reminiscent of Corbusier's apartment at the Weissenhof Estate at Stuttgart). The communal rooms each have a tiny balcony at the

corner of the building plus excellent views through end-butted plate glass windows. (There is also a limited number of single-bedroom apartments for married students.) Overall capacity is 220 under-graduates. Construction is of a prodigious series of prefabricated panels of concrete post-tensioned together by tie rods (note their ends). There is a total of 979 panels, generally 8 inches/20 centimeters thick and measuring up to 57 feet/17 meters long, meticulously fitted together. The lovely, traditional Princeton sandstone has long ceased to be used by the university because of expense and a tendency to leak. It should be added that there has been some criticism of the complex for its centrifugal "passageway" quality as opposed to the centripetal "community focus" characteristic of the older quadrangles. These keenly designed halls were given by Laurance S. Rockefeller, Princeton '32, in memory of his grandmother, Laura Spelman Rockefeller. LeMessurier Associates were the structural engineers; Clarke & Rapuano, landscape architects.

Grounds only open to the public

---

17   Academic Building and Dining Hall (1970–71)
Institute for Advanced Study
W end of Nassau Street, SW on Mercer, S on Olden
Princeton, New Jersey

GEDDES BRECHER QUALLS CUNNINGHAM, ARCHITECTS

The work of GBQC has developed within an unusual frame of intellectual consistency and ongoing inquiry. Influenced by Le Corbusier's liberated spaces and by Mies' philosophical constancy, they have produced for the Institute for Advanced Study an imaginative solution to an unusual program. (Though the Institute, founded in 1930, is "organically and administratively" separate from Princeton University, it maintains close academic ties with it.) The building's requirements were to provide for dining facilities, boardroom, staff offices, seminar rooms, and lecture hall on a site made difficult by drop in grade. The solution consists of two units separated by a wide and well-planted courtyard (which is closed at both ends), with the buildings joined by a bridge. The first unit contains elevated entry, overlooking the double-height, two-hundred-seat dining room, with small lounge and large boardroom at the far end. This entry level also leads directly to the bridge, which, because of grade difference, marches straight to the second floor of the academic wing. This sense of flow is continued in the development of the garden court separating the two wings. These are marked by the planting mentioned, by numerous outdoor tables for fair-weather dining, and by use of water. The inner quality of the commons is also good, with the quadrant balcony containing lounge edging

into the high room, and with carefully calculated windows expanding the hall outward. Commons and garden court offer quietly relaxed forums for the interchange of ideas, or as the architects put it, "a major part of the building task was in influencing or enabling the inhabitants' social interaction" (*Forum,* October 1972). A strong Corbusian flavor can be seen in the deep brise-soleil which shields much of the building from sun and glare, the louvers on the west wall of the office block being angled for maximum protection. Though built of poured-in-place concrete instead of traditional brick, the new respects the old by its siting, by utilizing the same 10-foot/3-meter grid, and by repeating eave heights. Robert Geddes was chief of design; Zion & Breen were the landscape architects.

Public section open during academic year

18   Old Tennent Church (1751) **and Cemetery** (1731)
NE of town off NJ 522 and Tennent Road
Tennent, New Jersey

The church, though rich in years (and some changes), is one of simple dignity rather than architectural distinction. However, its setting on a low hill surrounded by an almost endless panorama of ancient gravestones—some well worthy of design notice—is memorable. Many of the stones date from the Battle of Monmouth (1778), when General Charles Lee's American forces were saved by the timely arrival of reinforcements under Washington and von Steuben.

Church open only for Sun. services

19   William Trent House (1719)
15 Market Street
Trenton, New Jersey

A distinguished two-story Queen Anne-early Georgian house, four
rooms per floor, which measures 40×48 feet/12×15 meters and which
reflects the Philadelphia background of its owner. The house is set in a
sizable garden on the edge of downtown Trenton—and provides welcome historic counterbalance to the new work nearby. It is the oldest
home still standing in the city, its garden in the early days reaching
down to the Delaware River. Judge Trent's overall estate of more than
800 acres/324 hectares eventually became the township which he

graciously called Trent's Town. Several years after his death the house was sold (1729) and underwent a succession of owners and changes. The last private owner, Edward Ansley Stokes, gave the residence and garden to the city of Trenton in 1929, but it was not until 1934 that restoration (by Samuel Mountford) was undertaken and not until 1936 that it was completed. The house as it now stands is approximately 80 per cent original. Upon being handsomely refurnished, a process greatly aided by a 1726 inventory, it was opened to the public in 1939. The fine arts collection is outstanding. The grounds were restored (1938) by the Garden Club of Trenton, with plans by landscape architect Isabella Pendleton Bowen.

. *Open May–Sept., Mon.–Sat. 10–5, Sun. 1–4; Oct.–Apr.,*
Mon.–Sat. 10–4, Sun. 1–4, except holidays: admission

---

20   Old Barracks (1758–59)
South Willow Street at West Front, near Delaware River
Trenton, New Jersey

Housing for the military has rarely been known for its comfort; thus in centuries past when soldiers were billeted in private houses they enjoyed rare amenities for themselves but were a burden for the owners.

In the mid-eighteenth century in the Colony of New Jersey, the citizens, wearying of putting up troops during the French and Indian War and receiving almost nothing in return, petitioned the governor to build a series of barracks to be used especially in the winter months when most fighting stopped and troops retired into the towns. Of the five built throughout the state only this remains—and a handsome structure it is. Accommodating three hundred officers and men, built of local field-stone, well laid out and proportioned, it provides us with an outstanding example of military architecture of the period and of the region. During the Revolution the building was occupied by British, Americans, and Hessians, serving as a hospital in the war's latter stages. After the war the building was sold (1786) and turned first to private houses and then to a home for destitute women. In the meantime, a 40-foot/12-meter section was lopped off for a road extension. Saved from complete destruction by a group of farsighted ladies in the early part of this century, the building was eventually purchased by the state and completely restored in 1917. The exterior looks largely the way it did some two hundred years ago. The interior has been transformed into a colonial museum.

Open May–Oct., Mon.–Sat. 10–5, Sun. 1–5; Nov.–Apr., 10–4:30, except holidays: admission

---

21 Dey Mansion (c. 1740)
199 Totowa Road, Preakness Valley Park (off US 46 N onto Riverview Drive, then E on Totowa Road, or N off IS 80 onto Union Boulevard, L on Totowa)
Wayne, New Jersey

A comfortable lack of pretension characterizes the Dey Mansion in which Washington's headquarters were located in 1780. A gambrel roof caps its simple rectangle, but note that the walls beneath it vary, with brick on the front, accented by stone quoins, while the other three walls are mostly local brownstone with the windows and doors framed in brick. (The front brickwork is laid in Flemish bond, the attic in English—an unusual combination.) With its separate kitchen attached by a covered walk, and with its grounds visually "expanded" by the adjacent Passaic County Golf Course (which initially formed part of the estate), the exterior possesses a relaxed domesticity. The interior, which is the finest part architecturally speaking, has been fittingly restored and furnished of the period. The halls, both upstairs and down,

are extra wide to accommodate festivities. The stair is almost invisible, being enclosed. The Dey family sold their home in 1801, a long succession of owners taking over until the Passaic County Park Commission acquired the house and its extensive grounds in 1930, restoring the residence (1933) and developing most of the 56 acres/23 hectares of the estate for the golf course mentioned.

Open Tues., Wed., Fri. 1–5, Sat. 10–12, 1–5, Sun. 10–5 except holidays: admission

22   **Union Camp Headquarters** (1969–70)
     **1600 Valley Road (via IS 80, S briefly on NJ 62, W briefly on NJ
       46, N on Riverview and Valley Roads)
     Wayne, New Jersey**

SCHOFIELD & COLGAN, ARCHITECTS

A beautifully situated, wisely designed corporate headquarters on a 50-acre/20-hectare rolling site in northern New Jersey. The architects took meticulous pains to ease the building onto its tree-filled milieu—Union Camp's activities are forest-generated—preserving every possible bush. In plan the five-story structure forms a precise rectangle with the upper

three floors slightly cantilevered over the lower, while the one-story cafeteria projects from the ground floor on the southerly side to edge the large artificial lake. This fully glazed, handsome cafeteria and its adjacent terrace—which also serves as an open-air lunch spot—are plus values in making the workday more cheering for the company's over five hundred employees. The upper three floors, which are for general offices, are shielded from most of the direct sun by a projected, well-designed, precast brise-soleil. Their cantilever helps shade the lower two floors. The entry level is primarily occupied with the company's many visitor-related activities, while the bottom floor, partly in the sloping grade, is filled with technical and mechanical facilities. A four-story, 40-foot/12-meter-square light-well over the reception lobby develops a strong feeling of vertical space as one steps inside, and ties the work floors in unity. Parking is carefully confined out of sight in a landscaped lot. Robert H. Schofield was partner-in-charge; A. E. Bye Associates were the landscape architects. Expansion has been foreseen.

Grounds and reception lobby open during business hours

New York
State

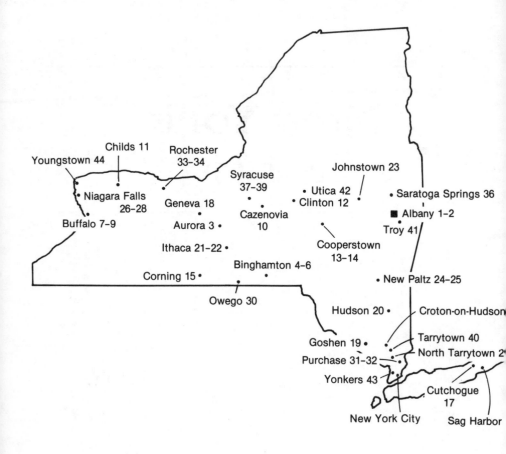

Youngstown 44

Childs 11

Rochester
33-34

Johnstown 23

Niagara Falls
26-28

Syracuse
37-39

Utica 42
Clinton 12

Saratoga Springs 36

Geneva 18

Albany 1-2

Buffalo 7-9

Cazenovia
10

Aurora 3

Troy 41

Ithaca 21-22

Cooperstown
13-14

Corning 15

Binghamton 4-6

New Paltz 24-25

Owego 30

Hudson 20

Croton-on-Hudson

Goshen 19

Tarrytown 40
North Tarrytown 2

Purchase 31-32

Yonkers 43

Cutchogue
17

New York City

Sag Harbor

NEW YORK STATE

The buildings in boldface type are of general interest. The others are for the specialist.

Albany	1	**Schuyler Mansion** (1761–62)
	2	Joseph Henry Memorial Building/Old Albany Academy (1815–17)— Philip Hooker
		State Education Building (1908–12)—Henry Hornbostel
		State Capitol (1867/1879/ 1899)—Laver, Fuller, Eidlitz, and Richardson
		City Hall (1881–82)— H. H. Richardson
Aurora	3	Louis Jefferson Long Library (1968)—Skidmore, Owings & Merrill
Binghamton	4	Ely Park Houses (1971)— The Architects Collaborative
	5	**First-City National Bank** (1971–72)—Ulrich Franzen
	6	**Science Complex, SUNY** (1972–74)—Davis, Brody
Buffalo	7	**Prudential (ex-Guaranty) Building** (1895–96)—Adler and Sullivan
		St. Paul's Episcopal Cathedral (1850–51)—Richard Upjohn
	8	**Albright-Knox Art Gallery Addition** (1962)—Skidmore, Owings & Merrill
	9	Shoreline Apartments (1973–77)—Paul Rudolph

Cazenovia	10	**Town Hall** (c. 1847) **and Historic District**—Andrew Jackson Downing
Childs	11	**Cobblestone Church** (1834), **School** (1849), **and Ward House** (c. 1840)
Clinton	12	**Kirkland College** (1968–72)— Benjamin Thompson
Cooperstown	13	**Farmers' Museum and Village Crossroads** (1783–1861)
	14	Hyde Hall (1817–35)— Philip Hooker
Corning	15	**Corning Community College** (1964)—Warner Burns Toan Lunde
Croton-on-Hudson	16	**Van Cortlandt Manor** (c. 1680/1750–1815)
Cutchogue	17	**Old House** (1649)
Geneva	18	**Rose Hill** (1837–39)
Goshen	19	**Orange County Government Center** (1968–70)—Paul Rudolph
Hudson	20	**Olana** (1870–74)—Calvert Vaux
Ithaca	21	**Bradfield Agronomy Building** (1968)—Ulrich Franzen Research Laboratory (1973)— Ulrich Franzen
	22	Elm Street Housing (1971–73)—Werner Seligmann
Johnstown	23	**Johnson Hall** (1762–63)
New Paltz	24	**Jean Hasbrouck Memorial House** (1692–1712) **and Huguenot Street**
	25	Concourse Development, SUNY (1963–68)— Ballard Todd Associates

Niagara Falls	26 Earl W. Brydges Public Library (1973–74)—Paul Rudolph
	27 **Convention Center** (1973–74)—Johnson/Burgee
	28 Rainbow Center Mall and Winter Garden (1976–77)— Gruen Associates
North Tarrytown	29 **Philipsburg Manor, Upper Mills** (c. 1683/1720–50)
Owego	30 Tioga County Court House (1871–72)—M. F. Howes
Purchase	31 **Pepsico World Headquarters** (1967–70)—Edward Durell Stone
	32 Purchase Campus, State University of New York (1971–78)—Edward L. Barnes, planner, and various architects
Rochester	33 **First Unitarian Church** (1961–63)—Louis I. Kahn
	34 Rochester Institute of Technology (1968–)— Various architects National Technical Institute for the Deaf (1975)—Hugh Stubbins & Associates
Sag Harbor	35 First Presbyterian/Old Whalers' Church (1843–44)— Minard Lafever Suffolk County Whaling Museum (1846)
Saratoga Springs	36 New Campus of Skidmore College (1966–)—Ford, Powell & Carson
Syracuse	37 S. I. Newhouse School of Public Communications Building I (1964)—I. M. Pei

Building II (1973)—Skidmore, Owings & Merrill

38 **St. Mary's Complex** (1966–68)—Sargent-Webster-Crenshaw & Folley

39 **Everson Museum of Art** (1966–68)—I. M. Pei

Tarrytown

40 **Lyndhurst** (1838/1865)— Alexander Jackson Davis

Troy

41 Julia Howard Bush Memorial Center (1834–36)—J. H. Dakin

Utica

42 **Munson-Williams-Proctor Institute** (1960)—Philip Johnson

Fountain Elms (1850–52)— W. J. Woolett

Yonkers

43 **Hudson River Museum** (1967–68)—SMS Architects

Youngstown

44 **Old Fort Niagara** (mid-18th century)

1 Schuyler Mansion (1761–62)
27 Clinton Street at Catherine
Albany, New York

It is difficult today to believe that the grounds surrounding the Schuyler Mansion were once so generous in their swoop to the Hudson River that the house was called The Pastures. The house, however, ranks among the state's finest, even though its exterior carries a strange octagonal vestibule added—reputedly—by Philip Hooker around 1816. General Schuyler himself, it is thought, designed the dwelling, encircling the top of its English-bond brick walls with a Chippendale-inspired "eaves balustrade" which Fiske Kimball considered probably the earliest in the Colonies. But it is the interiors which most impress, especially the four major rooms on the ground floor and the spacious halls on both. Their detail is generally exemplary, their colors far from somber (though—like some interior work—possibly dating from early in this century), and their furnishings (of the period but only infrequently original) are appropriate. Though the outbuildings—kitchen, barns, stables, etc.—have disappeared with the pressure of the city's growth,

the house itself—which had once served as an orphanage—was saved when it was purchased by the state in 1911. Its initial restoration was completed in 1917, with thorough redecoration in 1950. An outstanding example of middle Georgian domestic architecture.

Open Wed.–Sun. 9–5, except holidays

---

2 Joseph Henry Memorial Building/Old Albany Academy (1815–17)

Academy Park, off Eagle Street, adjacent to State Capitol Albany, New York

PHILIP HOOKER, ARCHITECT

The Old Albany Academy, also known as the Joseph Henry Memorial for the great scientist who was educated and taught there, is one of a handful of buildings of architectural character in the city. Its reserved lines, two-story pilasters, red sandstone ashlar walls, and copper-topped cupola give quiet, Federal Style distinction to the exterior. Built as a boys' school (which moved to larger quarters in 1931), it has been owned since 1930 by the Albany City Board of Education. In 1935 it was thoroughly restored and remodeled by Marcus T. Reynolds. Though the rooms on the main floor are of little interest, being crowded with offices, the former chapel on the second floor is very dignified with its two-story height, cove ceiling, and Corinthian pilasters. It is now used for public gatherings. Strangely, one Thomas C. Taylor—of whom little is known—was, according to some official records, the architect of the Academy, while Seth Geer (also spelled Gier) is quoted by another state source. However, the dedication stone is inscribed "Ph. Hooker, architect," and there are receipts for payments to him for his services. Geer, it seems, was the "master builder" while Taylor submitted an earlier design which Hooker—it is thought—substantially changed and improved upon. As Edward W. Root tantalizingly put it in his book *Philip Hooker* (Charles Scribner's, 1929), "Whichever way it was we have no means of telling."

Open during office hours

Directly behind the Academy on Washington Avenue stands the **State Education Building** (1908–12—lobby open during business hours), designed by Henry Hornbostel. It flourishes a parade of thirty-six

enormous Corinthian columns (hollow) with a terra-cotta entablature which represents the apotheosis of cooked earth in the Americas.

Just across Washington Avenue from both Education Building and
Academy rises the cheerless bulk of the **State Capitol** (tours daily in
summer, Mon.–Sat. rest of year), begun in 1867, partially occupied by
1879, but not completed until 1899. Augustus Laver and Thomas W.
Fuller—both English-born—won the competition for its design but this
was subsequently changed (above lower floors) by Leopold Eidlitz
and H. H. Richardson, and finished by Isaac G. Perry. Though the exterior is bedeviled, parts of the interior are very rewarding, the most
notable being Richardson's smashing Senate Chamber (1881–82) with
young Stanford White his assistant. This colorful, baronial, near-square
room was brilliantly restored in 1978–79 by architects Mendel-Mesick-
Cohen and now shines as a city highlight.

Diagonally across the park on Eagle Street stands Richardson's **City
Hall** (1881–82—open during business hours), competent but not sparkling.

3 Louis Jefferson Long Library (1968)
Wells College
NY 90
Aurora, New York

SKIDMORE, OWINGS & MERRILL, ARCHITECTS

A university library should not be a morgue for books: it must be a place of architectural wonder to match the miracle of its contents. Walter A. Netsch of SOM (Chicago), who designed this library—his tenth and each different properly to reflect local "environmental problems"—has created at Wells, a distinguished mid-state college for girls, a building whose architectural envelope makes it the impulsive magnet for the campus. (Henry Wells, who founded the college in 1868, was also William Fargo's partner in the "express" and banking business.) From the outside one sees a series of fractured shapes in red brick, dark wood, and canted white roof planes that step down the hillside in a seemingly disjointed manner. However, an elaborate (at times over-elaborate) geometry underlies their disposition, one comprised of nine "rotated" squares—a square within a square, the second at 45° to the first (Netsch's Field Theory). This fracturing becomes architecturally

complex on the exterior, but on the inside its explosion of irregularities in plan and section—hence in space—intrigues the beholder. Under "a wild tumbling roof," engineered in wood, there descends a cascade of levels, some broad and open, some secret and intimate, to meet the varying demands for research and study.

Stack space is provided for 250,000 volumes; seminar and special study rooms occur on each of the library's three floors; and an art gallery opens off the ground-floor entry. Overelaboration of means at times takes over, a directional puzzlement on entering confuses the visitor, and lack of control would be fatal in other than an isolated girls' college; these, however, are minor carpings concerning a stimulating structure.

Gallery and main floor open during school year

---

4 **Ely Park Houses** (1971)
N off US 17 on Glenwood Road, NW edge of Binghamton, New York

THE ARCHITECTS COLLABORATIVE, ARCHITECTS

An unusual Urban Development Corporation "town house" approach, set in a wooded suburb, for 414 low- and moderate-income families. Comprised of attached houses, all of cedar, the project takes maximum advantage of the many and often sharp grade changes, providing, in the process, views over city and valley. The units are laid out with group parking areas, inset as clusters from the main street, so that minimum roads have to be crossed by children. The split-level apartments vary from one to four bedrooms, but all have both front and rear entrances, generally a half flight apart because of grade conditions. The ground floors have large sliding glass doors which open onto the lawns in front of each unit. (The projected fences for the front lawns suffered budget cuts.) The houses were constructed of factory-built panels shipped in and erected on prepared sites. The architecture is commendably straightforward and well detailed, with a spaciousness little seen in limited-income housing. Community buildings and the shopping facilities are (or were when last seen) inadequate, but the architects, working with minimum funds, have acquitted themselves—and their clients —handsomely.

Grounds open daily

5   First-City National Bank (1971–72)
2 Court Street at Hawley
Binghamton, New York

ULRICH FRANZEN & ASSOCIATES, ARCHITECTS

Downtown U.S.A. is finally discovering one of the most valuable assets
of many of our cities—water. Long blocked from view or arrogated by
highways, our riparian banks have rarely been done justice. They have
here. The architect has terraced his building to enjoy the visual delights
of the Chenango River, at the same time extending the pedestrian

promenade to continue to new structures downstream. As one crosses the Court Street Bridge, either in car or afoot, one is immediately impressed by this sociability with nature. Moreover, the land side of the building with its bold, partly elevated form establishes an important anchor for the central business district. On the inside the white two-story-high banking room tends to be on the restless side with its prominent projections, but note the 49-foot/15-meter-long tapestry depicting Binghamton around 1900. This was designed and woven by the Swedish artist Helena Barynina Hernmarck. There is parking for 120 automobiles under the building, plus both a drive-in and a sidewalk teller. The building forms a major element in the rehabilitation of downtown Binghamton.

Open during business hours

6 Science Complex, SUNY (1972–74)
Vestal Parkway E (S off NY 434)
Binghamton, New York

DAVIS, BRODY & ASSOCIATES, ARCHITECTS

This large complex, a Master Plan for Science, dominates a major entry to the campus. Three new buildings interlock with older ones on a sloping grade to set up an unusual interplay of solidity and transparency. A bristling efficiency characterizes their architecture, and when to this is added the dynamic "bridged" space between the upper structures, then the handling of levels to the lower, a walk through the grouping becomes rewarding. The buildings themselves have many fully glazed exterior corridors, thus revealing the near-continuous animation of people moving within. This quality of "aliveness" provides the main design contribution but logical form-making in space is not far behind. The

library stands at top of the slope, adjoining and serving two older structures, and is laid out so that expansion can easily take place. The Biology Building is planned so that its numerous laboratories are placed in the inner core for maximum precision of environmental (heat and humidity) control. Classrooms and professors' offices on either side tap in, so to speak, where needed and thus produce freely developed facades. The Psychology Building stands as pivot at bottom near the campus entry, with an Interdepartmental Center below the terrace which connects the two lower buildings. Glazed connecting bridges (part of the original design) will be constructed when funds become available. Concrete, brick, and glass—especially glass—have been used here with expertise.

The sensitive, comprehensive site-plan of the university was developed by the Moore & Hutchins Partnership (1965–68).

Grounds open daily

---

7   **Prudential (ex-Guaranty) Building** (1895–96)
Church Street at Pearl
Buffalo, New York

DANKMAR ADLER AND LOUIS H. SULLIVAN, ARCHITECTS

There are many Prudential buildings across the United States—some still abuilding—but none commands the elegant serenity of this 1896 masterpiece by Louis Sullivan. He was the country's first "modern" architect (*form ever follows function*, etc.), designer of several of our greatest early skyscrapers, Frank Lloyd Wright's *lieber Meister*, yet a man who died in 1924 spurned and neglected—an American Mozart. The thirteen-story Prudential—until 1898 the Guaranty (but planned as the H. L. Taylor Building)—possesses a unity, a "wholeness," which few of today's even modest skyscrapers carry. Note, first, the doubling of the bay expression on the two lower floors. On the street level the structural columns are explicitly revealed behind huge sheets of plate glass: the second floor, being devoted to walk-up selling and not offices, carries its own statement. Above this two-story base rises a ten-story cage of multidivisible offices. At top the combined office-and-utility floor, illuminated by startling round windows (oval on Pearl Street), "terminates" all via its glorious cornice. The terra-cotta skin needed for fire protection projects earth colors high above the earth when most ar-

chitects were opting for white. (The facade does not, however, state which pier is a structural column.)

Sullivan's famous ornament, rather Sullivan's and George Elmslie's ornament (Elmslie worked for Sullivan for twenty years), was used with elaborate skill on the Prudential Building; terra-cotta and steel never have been so artfully wedded. As the famous Montgomery Schuyler (1843–1914) wrote, "I know of no steel-framed building in which the metallic construction is more palpably felt through the envelope of baked clay" (*Architectural Record,* February 1896, as quoted in Jordy and Coe's edition of *American Architecture* by Schuyler, Harvard University Press, 1961). However, it should be noted—and deplored—that Sullivan used "conflicting" decoration on the *piers* of the Prudential, whereas on the earlier Wainwright in St. Louis (1891— q.v.) he wisely left these vertical structural elements in pure brick with slight edge mold. While ornament in today's architecture is inchingly fashionable—some feel that it is making a revival—today's architects find Sullivan's ornament an unparalleled achievement. (As regards terra-cotta, Karl Friedrich Schinkel, 1781–1841, with his Berlin Academy of 1835 is generally credited with its first "contemporary" use—its origins go back at least to Assyrian times.)

Sullivan parted with Adler (1895) and finished the Prudential Building alone. Similar, as mentioned, to the Wainwright Building, the taller Prudential carries greater unity and sophistication, in spite of its decorated piers. It is one of the nineteenth century's most significant structures. As Henry-Russell Hitchcock has written, "Almost miraculously one genius, Louis Sullivan, was able to cope with the skyscraper, in the fullest architectural sense, functionally, technically, and aesthetically" (*Architectural Review,* July 1937). In 1974, a fire damaged the top floors, and although it caused little exterior damage, it helped push the building into receivership. After a five-year preservation campaign it has been saved and is now being restored. In 1975 the Prudential was made a National Historic Landmark.

Lobby open during business hours; Louis Sullivan Museum open erratically

St. Paul's Episcopal Cathedral (1850–51, spire 1870) stands directly across the street (Pearl and Erie) from the Prudential; it is one of Richard Upjohn's finest churches. (Open 9–5 daily.) Gutted on the interior by fire (1888), it was restored—freely—by R. W. Gibson. Somber on the exterior in its Gothic Revival brownstone, it is bedecked with banners within (reconditioned in 1953), proudly proclaiming that the downtown Episcopal church need not wither.

8   Albright-Knox Art Gallery Addition (1962)
1285 Elmwood Avenue
Buffalo, New York

SKIDMORE, OWINGS & MERRILL, ARCHITECTS

It would be difficult to imagine a more "classic" addition to Buffalo's stately Greco-Roman museum (1900–5—Edward B. Green, architect) than this taut structure by SOM's chief of design in New York, Gordon Bunshaft. He was born, it so happened, only a mile away. The new is tied to the old by a long, one-story-high white Vermont marble wall, and behind this windowless palisade lie the lateral galleries of the new building. An open-air sculpture court is located near their center facing

the entry. The major gallery is at the far end, and above it rises the dark mass of the auditorium, its deep gray half-inch/13-millimeter-thick glass walls describing a boxlike shape that provides a sophisticated contrast to the Ionic complexity of the old building. The experience of rising upward from the gallery level by twin flights of stairs to the glass-wrapped 350-seat auditorium is inviting. For slide and/or cinematic presentations, curtains can be pulled to darken the lecture hall and its stage. The galleries are all artificially lit, and whereas the two lateral ones are, in effect, stretched corridors, the main rooms (under the auditorium) provide flexible areas for the showing of works of art.

Open Tues.–Sat. 10–5, Sun. 12–5, except major holidays

---

9 Shoreline Apartments (1973–77)
Niagara Street between Caroline and West Mohawk
Buffalo, New York

PAUL RUDOLPH, ARCHITECT

Undogmatic and polite as street expression, and sympathetic in scale, the 613 units of this housing development constitute provocative hous-

ing. Built within sight of Lake Erie—a visual advantage but at times a winter liability—and within easy walking distance of downtown, the basic setup is, in the main, good although the Thruway and railroad edge the lake itself. The architectural response might be described as "familial," for its plan of staggered rows of back-to-back houses creates a sense of identity. This is augmented by the "extended" balconies or enclosed patios of each unit—assets which add enormously to the attractiveness of the apartments. The majority of the earlier buildings were two-story town houses, with three-to-four-story apartments for the elderly properly integrated with the whole. Phase III has several buildings of seven stories admixed with lower ones to keep an undulating rhythm and human scale. A slight temporary weakness at Shoreline lies in its present lack of focus. This will be eliminated when the well-studied proposed town center is built; it is, of course, an essential element in the overall plan. Granted the limits of the program and the funds available, this is one of the country's most imaginative low-cost housing developments. Built under the aegis of the Urban Development Corporation, it is privately owned.

Grounds open daily

---

10   **Town Hall** (c. 1847) **and Historic District**
      7 Albany Street (US 20)
      Cazenovia, New York

ANDREW JACKSON DOWNING, PROBABLE ARCHITECT OF TOWN HALL

A modest domestic version of the Gothic Revival School—and one open every workday, as it houses town offices. The batten and board walls recall Downing's dictum that planks should be applied vertically, as trees grow that way. The steeply pitched roof and gables and the crocketed barge boards are all hallmarks of a period of building which flourished roughly between 1840 and 1865 (with regional variations and delays). The interiors have been adapted (1969) to working offices, hence offer few rewards, but the exterior is excellent. It was previously the Henry Ten Eyck residence. The attribution to Downing is not 100 per cent but local authority so ascribes it.

Visitors are welcome and can purchase for a token amount a guide to other architectural attractions of this picturesque—and preservation-

minded—village, including a Greek Revival library and several out-standing homes. Almost a half mile (.7 kilometer) of Albany Street—on which the Town Hall fronts—has been declared a National Historic District (1978).

Open during business hours

---

11 Cobblestone Church (1834), **School** (1849), **and Ward House** (c. 1840)
US 104
Childs (near Albion), New York

Buildings of fieldstone are naturally found throughout the morainal parts of the world. However, in northwest New York State a "cobble-stone cult," based on the use of small water-smoothed fieldstones, evolved between the 1820s and 1850s which, though it has relatives in

Europe (mostly France and England), attained an apogee unequaled elsewhere. (There are also a few good examples in Illinois and Wisconsin.) The expertise in New York occurred because, in addition to the natural abundance of stratified rocks and pebbles of the region, the building of the Erie Canal, which was finished in 1825, attracted many masons to the area, a number of whom settled permanently. As the builders were skilled and the material freely at hand, the art flourished. The Greek Revival being then in vogue, traces of this style can be seen in many examples. The Cobblestone Society, an energetic body formed in 1960, claims that even today there are approximately 270 cobble-built houses, stores, and churches between Niagara Falls and the land east of Rochester—and possibly 600 in the U.S.A. The earlier cobblestone buildings were made of fieldstones 3 to 6 inches (76 to 152 millimeters) long, and were solid stone throughout; the later—and more refined—ones were built of carefully chosen, uniform "lake-washed" stones of no more than an inch or inch and a half (25–38 millimeters) in diameter and were often merely a veneer over a wooden frame—but what a veneer! Sizes of stones, sizes and directions of joints, kinds of mortar, etc., were all elements to be considered. Of the cobblestone buildings open to the public (at least during the summer months) the tiny village of Childs offers a Universalist church, a one-room school, and a house, all, fortunately, owned by the Cobblestone Society. **The church** dates from a relatively early period when large semifield-stones were used, and is not outstanding in either proportion or detail, but it has been nicely restored and boasts a "diverting" painting (1874) in the chancel and a museum in the basement. **The school** stands a few hundred yards/meters east of the church on Route 104, and, having been built fifteen years later, and with the small water-washed stones, shows greater finesse. Though a veneer over a wooden frame (like today's brick veneer), the exterior is an excellent example of cobble work, while the interior has been faithfully restored to its one-room school genesis. On the outside note the careful integration of cobble coursings with quoins. The **Ward House** was acquired by the Cobblestone Society in 1975 and has been redecorated to the Eastlake period of the 1870s: even the privy has an Eastlake interior. The cobble art waned with the rise of the industry and few cobble buildings can be dated after the Civil War. Those interested in further information on the Cobblestone Society can write to it at Albion, New York 14411.

Open June–Labor Day, Tues.–Sat. 11–5; Sept.–Oct., Sun. 1–5: inquire at church for admittance: admission

---

12   Kirkland College (1968–72)
off College Street, 1.6 miles/2.6 kilometers W of
Clinton, New York

BENJAMIN THOMPSON & ASSOCIATES, ARCHITECTS

Concrete for frame and panel walls determined the design of Kirkland's buildings, as it represents maximum durability and low upkeep. The dormitories and the classroom and public units are two or three stories high. Since they are of one material a certain insistence would be evident if not relieved by the landscaping and by a series of sensitive spaces and building relationships aided by the slightly rolling site. This spatial fluidity is emphasized by the fact that one of the buildings is a firm rectangle in shape. Chromatic notes are found in the curtains and venetian blinds and in the colors of both furniture and graphics. All

common rooms are bright and spacious, and the dormitory rooms carefully thought out. Five years after completion financial problems beset
Kirkland and in 1978 it merged with Hamilton, a venerable 850-
student college for men only a few blocks away.

Campus open daily

---

13 **Farmers' Museum and Village Crossroads** (1783–1861)
    NY 80, N edge of
    Cooperstown, New York

Brilliantly focused on the re-creation of early nineteenth-century village
life, basically of farmers working in a demanding climate with an ob-
durate soil, the Cooperstown Museum and Crossroads reveal poig-
nantly a segment of our history that is too comfortably forgotten today.

Concerned with the agrarian shelter needs of upstate New York, the Museum and Crossroads rise to expository heights in giving a socioeconomic depiction and understanding of a vanished era. The Museum, established in a capacious stone dairy barn (1918, Frank Whiting, architect), provides an enlightening, even exciting, introduction to the village with its "live" exhibitions (broom-making, weaving, etc.), its chronological depiction of the seasons, and its evolution of tool design. One then strolls onto the Green and the "Crossroads" of this microcosmic village. Its "highway" is an engaging path lined with thirteen buildings, all of which are original, all from the upstate area, and mostly pre-1840. These are not dead relics but buildings actively staffed with knowledgeable attendants. The major units are the prominent Bump Tavern, at left (built in 1796 but with Greek Revival porch from 1840); the sprawling Lippitt Farm of 1797, which has been miraculously preserved, meticulously restored, and is energetic with appropriate animals; and the church (finished in 1821, remodeled in 1861). The latter forms the strategic terminus, architecturally and otherwise, of the village. A country store, well stocked with the miscellany of its time (1820), a one-room school (1810), and a blacksmith shop (1827—in use until 1934) are among the other units. Note that an unusual number of the buildings are of stone, rather than the more normal wood, reflecting the nearness of local quarries.

Diagonally across Route 80 from the museum stands Fenimore House (1932—Harry St. Clair Zogbaum, architect), the headquarters of the New York State Historical Association. Its superb collection of folk art complements the Museum and Crossroads, and should by all means be visited. Together they provide "a major force in the rising interest which Americans are taking in their own country."

Open May–Oct., daily 9–5; Nov.–Apr., Tues.–Sat. 9–5, Sun. 1–5, except holidays: admission

---

14   Hyde Hall (1817–35)
Glimmerglass State Park
c. 10 miles/16 kilometers N of Cooperstown on Country Road 31
(4.4 miles/7 kilometers S of NY 80 at East Springfield, also on 31)
near Cooperstown, New York

PHILIP HOOKER, ARCHITECT

It comes as a distinct surprise to find an early-nineteenth-century mansion as sophisticated as this in an area which was then barely settled. But then George Hyde Clarke, its owner—and probable co-designer with Hooker—was no ordinary squire. The first part, the so-called Stone House, was begun in 1817, then extended in 1819 northward, along what is now the rear. The office, kitchen, and service wing date from 1819–23. The foundations for the main dwelling—the distinguished structure which now dominates the mass—were put in during 1819, but it was not until eight years later that Hyde Clarke was able to afford aboveground construction and not until 1835 that it was completed. There is a puzzling scale about its Federal-influenced exterior—especially in the fenestration—but within the drawing room and dining room, which line the front, are beautifully proportioned. Though a touch primitive in detail, they exhibit great vigor. Hyde Hall had been lived in continuously by Clarke heirs until shortly after World War II, when the family found that it could no longer sustain a house of this size. Fortunately, the state purchased it in 1963. Rot and mildew had taken their toll and a long-term program of restoration began in 1971, the roof rightly receiving top priority. As rehabilitation depends to a large degree on state funding, it is not certain when the house will be open to the public. However, Glimmerglass State Park—of which Hyde

Hall is a part—offers rewards itself. Designed by the Central New York State Parks Commission and opened in 1966 (bathhouses, 1968—admission to both), the park provides spacious facilities for picnicking, boating, swimming, etc., on grounds which once belonged to the mansion.

House under restoration; at present only exterior can be seen: admission to park

---

15 Corning Community College (1964)
   E on Dennison Parkway (NY 17), S on Chemung Street, c. 2.8
      miles/4.5 kilometers S of
   Corning, New York

WARNER BURNS TOAN LUNDE, ARCHITECTS

A well-situated, well-laid-out community college for approximately 1,800 commuting students. The 275-acre/111-hectare site caps a hill with views to the south, and allows generous spacing between

buildings. Parking for the numerous cars is accommodated in several peripheral lots, leaving the central campus to pedestrians. Four major buildings—administration/liberal arts, library, science, and student center—make up the core of the college with the gymnasium on the west edge. Space has been allocated for future buildings to be added adjacent to the existing central group. Architecturally, the college is domestic in scale, its one- and two-story designs creating an inviting atmosphere. White concrete frame with brick panel infilling typifies the construction of most buildings. The exaggeratedly angled and projected "cornice" seems capricious but does lend a cohesive idiom and helps keep rain and snow off the walls. Altogether a quiet family of buildings working well together.

Campus open daily

16 Van Cortlandt Manor (c. 1680/1750–1815)
off NY 9A, South Riverside Avenue, .3 mile/.5 kilometer S of Croton Point Avenue
Croton-on-Hudson, New York

The early Dutch settlements along the Hudson River, which the Lowlanders craftily preempted as far as Albany, provided that lovely region's earliest and most picturesque domestic types. (Henry Hudson anchored in the river in 1609, while Fort Nassau was built in 1614.) However, the Treaty of Westminster in 1674 gave New Netherland to the English, creating an Anglo-Dutch cultural influence, and a century later, when the lower Hudson became a battleground during the Revolution, the fighting destroyed and injured much including the Van Cortlandt Manor itself.

The earliest part of the house (c. 1680) with 3-foot/.9-meter-thick sandstone walls probably stems from a pre-Van Cortlandt trading post at the confluence of the Hudson and Croton rivers. Then beginning in

1749 Pierre Van Cortlandt and his wife added a second floor and other improvements and the house was made a permanent Van Cortlandt home instead of a hunting lodge and trade station. The porch wrapping three sides dates from the same mid-eighteenth-century period. During the Revolution the family had to flee Tory attacks, and when able to return after the war they found the house ill served and in immediate need of attention. Much of the finer work which we see today (the paneling in the main rooms, for instance) dates from this period. The house remained in the family for 250 years (until 1945), and through the generations, changes and additions were made, so although there is not purity in the Van Cortlandt Manor, there is unusual continuity—and appeal. The house, much original furniture, outbuildings, and gardens were purchased through the generosity of John D. Rockefeller, Jr., in 1953, and all has been put back (1953–59) into lustrous shape of the 1750–1815 period. Be sure to see the grounds and the reconstructed Ferry House.

Open daily 10–5, except major winter holidays: admission

---

17 Old House (1649)
Cases Lane, 1 block S of NY 25
Cutchogue, Long Island, New York

Eastern Long Island, puzzlingly, never developed in the Colonial period as did much of New England. With good harbors at Greenport and Sag Harbor, excellent soil, and a sea-moderated climate, it is surprising that greater advantage was not taken of these natural blessings. A number of settlers from the New Haven Colony—of which Cutchogue was a part—and from Connecticut (which absorbed the former in 1665) came over but their influx, seemingly, was never great. The oldest dwelling which they left, probably the oldest still standing in New York State, is this venerable number: one of our major examples of English-inspired domestic building. It is also known as the Horton-Wickham-Landon-Case House. A rakish quality attends the facade which stems from its slight cant to the windward, the small wave of its shingled roof and eave (reflected in the curved door lintel), the untethered character of its clapboards (no "framing" by corner boards), plus a

doll's-house window over the front door. It epitomizes a wood skin
pierced for openings. A massive paneled chimney of New England inspiration and three-division, diamond-paned windows complete the exterior scene. (Two original triple casements were found in the north
wall.) Sea grass and clay were used for insulation. About a hundred
years ago barn doors and large windows were cut in its 40-foot/12-
meter side (it is 20.5 feet/6.2 meters deep) and it was used as a barn
until 1939. At that time the Case family sold the property to the Independent Congregational Church and Society of Cutchogue with the express provision that the house be given to the people of the town. The
village itself paid none of the costs. The house, with its well-chimneyed
interior, was then completely restored and furnished in 1939 to com-
memorate the town's tricentennial in 1940. Reputedly built in 1649 in
Southold, 5 miles/8 kilometers to the northeast, it was moved to this
site in 1659 as the wedding present of the then owner to his daughter.

Open July–Labor Day, daily 2–5, weekends in May and Sept.

18   Rose Hill (1837–39)
NY 96A, 1.5 miles/2.4 kilometers S of US 20, just E of
Geneva, New York

Rose Hill faces Seneca Lake across an ample lawn, the classic rhythm
of its six stately Ionic columns echoed by the balustered fence in front.
The pedimented central portico of two stories (with typical upstate
New York cupola on top of the roof) is flanked by one-story wings,
also with Ionic columns, the whole developing an excellent scale progression. The front and back porches are notable on the outside, while
the freshly renovated interior should be seen, from the carved door-
frames with their fanciful soffits to the French wallpaper in the dining
room which recalls Napoleon's campaign in Egypt. Reasonably un-
harmed through the years, the house was admirably restored in

1968–69 and appropriately furnished. One of the finest Greek Revival houses in the state.

Open May–Oct., Mon.–Sat. 10–4, Sun. 1–4: admission

NOTE: Main Street in Geneva (at right angles to and bridging above US 20) contains a collection of houses and churches from the early part of the last century protected by a city-created Historic Zone. Though privately owned, they can be seen on the outside by a walking tour. The Geneva Historical Society in the 1825 Prouty-Chew House, 543 Main Street, publishes a handy inexpensive map giving names and dates of the best of these. The Geneva community has been exemplary in preserving its splendid inheritance.

---

19 Orange County Government Center (1968–70)
265 Main Street between Erie Street and Scotchtown Avenue
Goshen, New York

PAUL RUDOLPH, ARCHITECT; PETER P. BARBONE, ASSOCIATE

The Orange County Government Center shatters the prim box concept inside and out with a building of extraordinary plasticity. One does not stroll quietly into this public facility, one progresses into its vigorous combinations of forms, a process which does not cease until one gets one's driver's license or takes one's jury seat. Few large planes of unbroken exterior walls exist: walls are pushed in and out to proclaim a design approach that veers toward the sophistic but operates (mainly) in the context of function. These carefully composed multiplanes moreover present completely blank facades on both east and west sides: windows dominate only on north and south. The scale buildup of the exterior of the County Center is thus both provocative and substantial, while, within, the central halls are filled with power, an effect that was achieved by space and light, not luxury of materials; these are economical, at times austere. (The top light floods in from north-south-aligned clerestories.)

The Center is divided into three interconnected buildings grouped around an elevated, terraced entrance court: note the spatial role played by the canopy extending as a semiframe to the courtyard. County and Supreme Court stand at right (north); the Family Courts behind; and the County Executive, Legislative, Clerk's, and other Mu-

nicipal Offices are in the unit at left (south). Each building is complete within itself but structurally interconnected by passages on first and third floors and by outdoor passage across the court. Public access and public areas face the plaza side of each building, with administrative areas to the rear. As the eight courtrooms from Supreme (125 seats) down to Family (24 seats) required windowless walls, Rudolph placed these near the center of the buildings and wrapped the ancillary chambers about them. Though little or no flexibility was permitted for the standardized courtrooms, their mutual relation and the formation of halls and circulation areas could be developed freely. Breaks, changes of levels, and shafts of sunlight have all been fused. The smooth reinforced concrete of the structural frame is clearly stated, while the walls are finished with sand-colored, ribbed concrete blocks; its warm color is abetted within by appropriate orange carpeting. A prickliness appears in the smaller areas of the interior with so much unrelieved ridged surface, but the effect in the major spaces is rugged, the natural lighting dramatic. Though complexity (and some inflexibility) appear—a monumental variety of rooms had to be synchronized—the structural system is basically simple and modular, with column spacing regular. Beams are 4.8 feet/1.5 meters×2 feet/.6 meter, spaced 18 feet/5.5 meters apart, and span up to 50 feet/15 meters. Lev Zetlin Associates Inc. were the structural engineers.

Open Mon.–Fri. 9–5, except holidays

20 Olana (1870–74)
E off NY 9G, .8 mile/1.3 kilometers S of Rip Van Winkle Bridge
(NY 23)
Hudson, New York

CALVERT VAUX, ARCHITECT, WITH FREDERIC E. CHURCH

Olana's opulent architecture matches its spectacular site some 500 feet/152 meters above the Hudson River. This thirty-seven-room mansion is one of the key houses of that freewheeling "Oriental" School of the latter part of the nineteenth century. In an era when anything went, everything happened at Olana, at least everything which a lover of the Near East could contrive, collect, and attach to vertical walls. Kublai Khan himself could hardly have outdone Frederic Edwin Church, professionally aided by Vaux. (Church added the studio wing and gallery himself in 1888–90.) Fortunately the heirs of this century-old house lived in it until recently so that its emblazoned interior has been well maintained. All the furnishings are original; there are even ancient photographs to show the furniture arrangements. Fortunately, also, the

state of New York, together with concerned private individuals, purchased the house, its contents, and the inspiring hilltop site of 250
acres/101 hectares on which the mansion rests. (Also included were a
substantial number of Church's unbelievably popular paintings of the
geographic majesty of many sections of the world.) In 1967 it was
opened to the public. A fetching melange of a "Personal Persian" era.

Open Memorial Day–Oct., Wed.–Sun. 9–5

---

21 Bradfield Agronomy Building (1968)
New York State College of Agriculture at Cornell
Tower Road
Ithaca, New York

ULRICH FRANZEN & ASSOCIATES, ARCHITECTS

Punctuating the skyline above Cayuga's famous waters, the Bradfield
Building might well be termed a cathedral to agronomic research. The
thirteen-story, virtually windowless tower is completely filled with
laboratories and attached offices, plus library and a large classroom on
the top floor. A low block with central entry stands adjacent for staff
offices, with a four-story separate classroom and lab building for under-
graduates adjoining this. In plan the tower forms a simple near-square
c. 90×100 feet/27×30 meters. One north-south corridor divides this
down the middle with offices opening on either side, then a line of adjacent laboratories attached to the offices, and beyond these service corridors lining the outer (east and west) walls. Though the three parallel
circulation divisions which run the length of each floor—the two outside service corridors or galleries and the central hall—are "fixed," the
lab-office rows which are sandwiched between them are longitudinally
flexible.

Fresh air is pumped up from near the ground via the quarter-round
towers at the north and south ends; noxious air is dissipated above the
roof through the four prominently projecting "snorkels" with hoods on
the east and west sides. The building's reinforced concrete floor structure, being based on parallel T-beams 18 inches/46 centimeters deep,
permits flexibility in utility layout, air ducting, lab service modules, and
lighting, alternating as needed between the flanges. A windowless solution was purposefully sought so that freedom from contamination, plus
precise light/temperature/humidity could be attained over growing

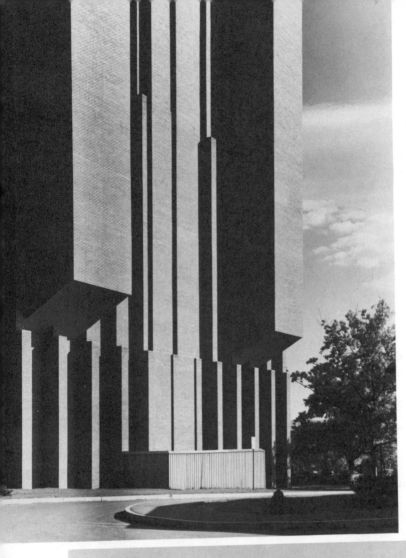

plant experiments. It is a plant-generated plan, and if visual relief is desired there are small (too small) lounges at the south ends of the main corridors. The exterior, sheathed in rust-colored brick, carries well its strong silhouette on the horizon, yet maintains an impressive sense of scale near-to—a difficult feat for a windowless bulk. Though there is an influence from Kahn's Richards Medical Laboratory in Philadelphia (q.v.)—one of the most germinative buildings of our time—the Agronomy Building stands firmly on its own feet.

Lobby open during school year

Ulrich Franzen's **Research Laboratory** (1973) for the College of Veterinary Medicine, at the east end of Tower Road, will be of interest to the architect. (Lobby only open during school hours.) Its north wall is largely of dark-tinted glass; the south wall, where the labs are concentrated, is of windowless brick. This powerful facade, topped by hooded ventilators, proclaims a striking, if at times formal, statement of the dramatic possibilities of one of man's oldest building materials.

---

22   Elm Street Housing (1971–73)
Elm Street at West Village Place (from downtown, W on Buffalo, Seneca, or State, up hill on Elm)
Ithaca, New York

WERNER SELIGMANN & ASSOCIATES, ARCHITECTS

Deftly conceived, low-rise, mixed-density, terrace housing. (Cf. the Halen Development of 1961 near Bern, Switzerland.) Across the top of its hillside site stretches the 534-foot/163-meter-long five-story major building containing 80 two-bedroom duplexes and 20 one-bedroom apartments for the elderly. Behind this are parking areas on two levels on the northwest side, the lower range at the ground floor serving duplexes, the upper parking connected by two ramps to the balcony-access top units so that little vertical effort (with packages, babies, etc.) need be made. Stepping down the hill to the southeast are eight rows of two-story, laterally connected dwellings, each with its own front door and private patio-terrace onto the view and the sun as it overlooks the lower building in front. These terrace apartments contain 28 one-bedroom and 72 three-bedroom "atrium" accommodations. Parking is either on the street which divides the eight rows or on the

street below. Across the lowest section rise four duplex groups containing 17 one-bedroom and 18 four-bedroom apartments. Several laundries, a meeting room (inadequate), and a store complete the grouping, with a total of 235 apartments. Much of the development was factory-fabricated in box modules and shipped to the site. Colors throughout are bright and cheerful (particularly so in the five-story building). Overall, this stands as a distinguished chapter in Urban Development Corporation housing. More public facilities and playgrounds are needed, but these were victims of the budget cut. Perhaps Elm Street's most extraordinary contribution is that it offers individual privacy within a compacted, low-cost cluster. As *Progressive Architecture* (5:73) wrote, "the direction it takes must surely rank it among the most encouraging public housing one is apt to see." There are not many modest-cost developments that provide the majority of its tenants with their own star-viewing platform.

Grounds open daily

23   Johnson Hall (1762–63)
Hall Avenue, .9 mile/1.4 kilometers NW of town via William and West State Streets
Johnstown, New York

Johnson Hall was built by the British colony's Superintendent of Indian Affairs for the Northern Colonies, Sir William Johnson, a brilliant soldier and man of enormous (and deserved) influence with the Iroquois Six Nations. His Georgian house was made architecturally important to attract settlers to this recently pacified central New York area. The wood frame dwelling probably was designed by Sir William himself and built by Samuel Fuller. Note that the windows and shutters are contiguous, creating two powerful "ribbons" across the facade, the lower broken only by the pedimented front door. A hip roof with prominent flat deck tops it off. The wood siding throughout is flush, scored to imitate stone. A 15-foot/4.6-meter-wide hall bisects the building with two rooms on either side, a plan basically repeated on the second floor. The basement, which should also be seen, contains the kitchen and a museum of the life of the region—including its wars—two hundred years

ago. A flanking stone house, used originally as a servants' quarters, stands at the back and contains an exhibit on the settlement of Johnson's land purchases. This and the dwelling are the only original structures on the site. The state purchased the Hall in 1906 and fully restored and refurnished it in 1952–55. House, grounds, and "museum" make a fine expedition for the family and a memorial to an extraordinary man.

Open Wed.–Sun. 9–5, except holidays

---

24 Jean Hasbrouck Memorial House (1692–1712) **and Huguenot Street**
Huguenot Street at North Front Street (Exit 18 on N.Y. Thruway, W on NY 299/Main Street)
New Paltz, New York

Interspersed along Huguenot Street above the Wallkill and the Hudson rivers is a group of wonderfully unaltered houses built at the end of the seventeenth and early in the eighteenth centuries by French Protestant refugees. Highlighted by the Hasbrouck House (1692 beginning, 1712

major part) at the end of the street (a museum-house which has been open to the public since 1899), the collection comprises a vignette from a too-little-known period of early American architecture. Even the street—"the oldest street in America with its original houses"—was designated a National Historic Landmark in 1960.

Architecturally the houses show a northern France-Rhineland-Dutch influence with local limestone walls, steep medieval roof, and (often) wood gable ends. (Many Huguenots spent some years in Germany and the Netherlands before fleeing to the New World.) The houses are directly and simply expressed, but at times, as in the Bevier House, sport an almost fey fenestration. The interiors impress structurally, especially the roof trusses framing the attic where grain was stored, and where enormous hand-hewn beams are revealed. Be sure to notice, also, the unusual open-hearth fireplaces.

House open mid-May–mid-Oct., Wed.–Sat. 10–4, Sun. 1–4 (in July–Aug. 10–4); tours from 6 Brodhead Avenue: admission

---

25 Concourse Development, SUNY (1963–68)
off Maine Street (NY 299), W off South Chestnut Street (NY 208)
New Paltz, New York

BALLARD TODD ASSOCIATES, MASTER PLAN AND ARCHITECT, WITH DAVIS, BRODY & ASSOCIATES, AND FORDYCE & HAMBY

New York State in the 1960s was almost frenetically active in building new and enlarging old university facilities. Considering the enormous scope of the program and the quality of the architects selected, results in the main have been disappointing. Several outstanding campuses have surfaced and a number of individual buildings of distinction have been created, but overall expectations have faltered. Among the finer developments is this concourse at New Paltz, planned by Ballard Todd Associates and molded by five buildings designed in their office plus two excellent science units, one (✳I—1965) by Fordyce & Hamby, the other (✳II—1968) by Davis, Brody & Associates. The Ballard Todd buildings include the ten-story Faculty Tower, which acts as a fulcrum for the mall. Stretching from the tower—in a consciously unregimented line—are Classroom Building, Communications and Lecture Hall, and Library (all finished in 1968), and an earlier Fine Arts Building (1963) by Ballard, Todd & Snibbe. This latter is set back and semi-

facing the others to develop an unexpected small square which terminates this agreeable mall excursion. Highlighting the visual end of the
concourse is a piece of outdoor sculpture by a graduate student in fine
arts, a work that is periodically changed.

Concourse open daily

---

26   Earl W. Brydges Public Library (1973–74)
1425 Main Street between Pierce and Lockport
Niagara Falls, New York

PAUL RUDOLPH, ARCHITECT

The roof, that once docile and oft-ignored parasol over a building, is
currently achieving an architectural renascence as a design element.
When properly handled—as here—this direction though perilous, can
animate both building and site. The 350-foot/107-meter-long Brydges
Library will, for some, outreach itself on the exterior, but within it un-

folds a spatially inviting, well-organized plant. The main reading rooms provide a businesslike learning center, the children's room is jolly, the staff setup good. All floors are occupied by the public library system, balconies around the three-story main reading room providing upper access and spatial flexing. Total book capacity is 325,000 volumes. An auditorium seating 246 opens off the second-floor entry hall.

Open Mon., Wed. 9–9, Tues., Thurs. 9–6, Fri., Sat. 9–5, Sun. 1–5, except holidays

---

27 Convention Center (1973–74)
4th Street at Rainbow Center
Niagara Falls, New York

PHILIP JOHNSON/JOHN BURGEE, ARCHITECTS

The city of Niagara Falls in recent years has been making a determined effort to revitalize its downtown business center, which 5 million annual visitors—en route to a spectacular nature—have largely avoided. The city fathers wisely want people to tarry, to rest up after viewing

200,000 cubic feet/5,663 cubic meters of water per second dashing
madly overboard. They also want a broader base of fiscal magnetism
than a quick trip to the Falls alone. This concinnous Convention Center is the city's most dramatic achievement to date. As Philip Johnson
wrote it "is an attempt to create an automobile-oriented processional
experience" (*Forum,* January–February 1973), "processional" being
one of his key concerns in design (as it is with many other distinguished
architects). Not only do this 4th Street approach and entry create an
"experience," they provide near-total weather protection under an elegant
series of open steel-arched trusses engineered by Lev Zetlin. Within,
and parallel to the entry side, stretches the full-length main foyer with
cocktail lounge and 418-seat theater at right. Set back at left is the
ballroom with two balcony levels and movable seats for 2,100. (It can
also be used as a banquet hall.) Facing the entry and directly tapping
onto the circulation foyer is the multipurpose arena. This bright, lofty,
and airy space, its rainbow form strikingly free of utilities, can be used
for a variety of activities, from ice shows (6,784 seats), to basketball
(8,796) and concerts (11,766)—and for most indoor festivals in between, including, of course, conventions. The fully upholstered seats
used here are on portable platforms, or risers, hence can be set up to
meet the needs of any function. Parking, both open and by garage, lies
nearby, but it is thought that most guests will arrive on foot from the
Rainbow Center pedestrian mall (ex-Fall Street) with its hotels and
restaurants. The master plan for this resort complex and six-block mall
—which leads directly to the Falls—was prepared by Gruen Associates.

Open for events

28   Rainbow Center Mall and Winter Garden (1976–77) off Rainbow Boulevard Niagara Falls, New York

GRUEN ASSOCIATES, ARCHITECTS

A fanciful castle in botanical garden guise well designed to add non-commercial delight—there are no concession stands within—to downtown Niagara Falls. This glass and steel, jauntily angled pleasure dome terminates the city's East Mall, with the Johnson/Burgee Convention Center (q.v.) at the other end of the 1,500-foot/457-meter landscaped promenade. An all-weather arcade parallels the Mall with a new hotel at midpoint. The gesture of the city and its Niagara Falls Urban Renewal Agency in commissioning the Mall and Winter Garden was in-

trepid, the results by the architects brilliant. The Garden magnetizes by day with its intriguingly airy structure, and radiates light and welcome by night when it is aglow. Filled with an exotic collection of trees, bushes, pools, and an indoor observation "tower," it graciously offers itself as urban refreshment. Though measuring only 175×155 feet/ 53×47 meters, it contains almost secret retreats within. Picnics are encouraged, even weddings have taken place. When the proposed shopping center is built the Winter Garden will act as urban conflux, the shops being attached at either side to form a second mall at right angles to the existing one, while at the same time the building will double as gateway to nearby Prospect Point and the famous Falls.

The structural problems in designing this glass palazzo—which might be described as a cross between London's Crystal Palace (long gone) and Milan's Galleria—were considerable. This fragile-surfaced building 107 feet/33 meters high must contend with heavy snow and wind loads and a temperature range that easily encompasses 100° F/38° C. To create a dynamic elevation profile and to establish tension with the symmetrically arced Convention Center down the Mall, the architects evolved the notched and angled frame we see. The structural system employs four rows of cylindrical concrete columns, twenty in all, with horizontal and angled steel lattice trusses resting on top. Glass, clear vertically and generally tempered (shatterproof) otherwise, encases the roof and side walls. Heating is by electricity. Cesar Pelli was in charge of design; M. Paul Friedberg & Partners were landscape consultants; DeSimone & Chaplin, structural engineers; Cosentini Associates, mechanical-electrical engineers; and Herbert Levine, lighting consultant. A transparent delight night and day.

Winter Garden open 10–10 daily

---

29   Philipsburg Manor, Upper Mills (c. 1683/1720–50)
US 9, N edge of
North Tarrytown, New York

Philipsburg Manor was once part of the enormous holdings of Frederick Philipse (1626–1702), a Dutch carpenter-immigrant turned miller, burgher, and entrepreneur. It was preserved and restored by a concerned neighbor, John D. Rockefeller, Jr., who purchased the 20-acre/8-hectare site in 1940 on hearing of its probable subdivision. The plain but sturdy manor house, begun around 1683, had been added to

and tampered with through two centuries. However, its central stone core remained basically intact, and after meticulous study it has been taken back (1943) to its authentic condition of the mid-eighteenth century. A 1750 inventory listing the contents of all rooms facilitated refurnishing. The second-floor kitchen-dining room is of particular interest. The gristmill, small wharf, and dam had disappeared long before, but archeological excavations uncovered the original foundations, so that general outlines are precise even if aboveground appearances are somewhat hypothetical. Even the beams in the reconstruction of the mill were hand-hewn and the nails handmade. Be sure, incidentally, to see the interior of the gristmill: its heavy timbers and wooden gears are fascinating. The dam itself is of oak with stone infilling. The millpond and its birds complete a pastoral scene.

Reputedly a century ago there were around fifty thousand operating water mills in the U.S.A. Though relatively few are left today, "free" energy may soon increase their number. Philipsburg Manor offers a fine model.

Open daily 10–5, except major winter holidays: admission

30   Tioga County Court House (1871–72)
NY 17 and the Green
Owego, New York

M. F. HOWES, ARCHITECT

This near-classic village Victorian courthouse is properly guarded by a brave Civil War statue (1890) and a sturdy stand of elm. Note the horizontal stringcourses and the prim verticality of the slightly mismatched towers with their coupled windows. Note, too, the inset central entrance bay, arced for prominence. The interiors are of less interest. The building was placed on the National Register of Historic Places in 1972 and received a grant in 1976 from the New York State Council on the Arts for inner repairs. Let us hope that it will long be with us: we need these vestiges.

Open during office hours

31   Pepsico World Headquarters (1967–70)
Exit 28 of Hutchinson River Parkway, N c. 1 mile/1.6 kilometers on Lincoln Avenue, E on Anderson Hill Road Purchase, New York

EDWARD DURELL STONE ASSOCIATES, ARCHITECTS

A posh corporate headquarters sympathetically tied to its carefully preserved 112-acre/45-hectare site (an ex-polo field). The complex is divided into seven square and equal-size units which connect only at corner "towers" and which frame, somewhat formalistically, three well-landscaped, slightly sunken courts. Each of the upper floors of the three-story structure overhangs the one below to prevent sky glare and to reduce sun load on the uninterrupted strips of windows. There is a slight patterning in the precast concrete panels of these exterior wall overhangs. Continuous planting boxes are placed outside the windows, and the free growth of their ivy keeps the buildings from being rigid in this shepherd's setting. The landscaping, which included the planting of some three thousand trees of thirty-eight varieties, is not only excel-

lent (and beautifully maintained), but the grounds boast well over a dozen top-flight pieces of sculpture (Moore, Lipton, Calder, Lipchitz, Pomodoro, David Smith, etc.). In addition there is also an inside gallery with changing exhibitions. A fountain in the central court welcomes and a *jet d'eau* in the 4.5-acre/1.8-hectare lake—whose waters are seasonally preempted by several hundred Canada geese—gives an outdoor accent. Be sure to take the road around the edge of the site. Edward D. Stone, Jr. & Associates were the landscape architects.

Visitors welcome during office hours; get map of outdoor sculptures from receptionist

---

32 Purchase Campus
State University of New York (1971–78)
Exit 28 of Hutchinson River Parkway, N on Lincoln Avenue, R on
  Anderson Hill Road 1 block to entry
Purchase, New York

EDWARD LARRABEE BARNES, MASTER PLAN; ARCHITECTS AS
NOTED

The Purchase campus, one of New York State's four completely new universities—here with an emphasis on the arts—contains a number of buildings by distinguished architects. (The original enrollment mix has been recently revised to establish a balance between arts and liberal arts. In addition, a significant program for the community has been established.) Purchase is important architecturally in spite of what many consider its surprising Beaux Arts plan. This centers on a paved mall 300 feet/91 meters wide×900 feet/274 meters long with a spine of buildings in the center showing few windows or visible entrances—just relays of darkish brick, *top photo p. 454.* Along the two flanks the various faculties are dispersed behind lateral arcades and "can never be seen either in their entirety or in isolation." (There is an obvious suggestion of Jefferson's University of Virginia plan here but without the trees or the lawn of Charlottesville.) Each academic building stands on a 130-foot/40-meter-wide lot with a 32-foot/10-meter-wide pedestrian "street" separating structures, and each must use the same gray-brown brick, gray glass, and gray anodized aluminum. Mall and arcades (with service tunnels under) are, it should be pointed out, the domain of the pedestrian, with only service vehicles allowed. Closed at the west end by the theater complex, the mall opens eastward over the rolling countryside.

The **Library** (Edward Larrabee Barnes, architect—1974) properly occupies a central location between the mall's two lines of arcades and class buildings but its entry is clandestine and its lobby not finished as designed by the architect. Library expansion takes place underground. The **Humanities Building** (Venturi & Rauch—1974) accommodates a series of lecture halls, classrooms, and offices on the ground floor with classrooms and faculty offices above. It is a quiet, respectful, efficient building. Note the open-air amphitheater at the east end, *bottom photo p. 454.* The plan of the **Roy R. Neuberger Museum of Art** opposite Humanities (Philip Johnson/John Burgee—open as indicated) provides a wide straight spine of circulation 300 feet/91 meters long off of which on either side five equal-size rectangular galleries, aligned like pistons, alternate with outdoor sculpture courts. These flexible spaces are supplemented by a large second-floor gallery (top-lit) which is basically used for Mr. Neuberger's famous collection of contemporary American art. The architects carried the brick of the exterior inside the museum to form its walls, and on all "hanging" walls they applied panels which can be painted as needed. It makes for an unusual and effective binding of outside and in. Being a teaching facility, the building forms an integral part of the university. The **Natural Science Building** (Paul Rudolph—1975) is set back from the arcade of the north side of the mall to create a sense of freedom from regimentation plus the opportunity to develop a facade. (Most buildings are entered directly from the arcade, hence in effect have no facades.) The intriguing building next door to Science is the **Dance Instructional Facility** (Gunnar Birkerts— 1976). It, too, is set back and, moreover, edges out of the all-brick squared mold with some controlled angularity and color. Its plan is generated by a central lineup of dance laboratories and warm-up rooms with the two long sides filled with offices and lounges (the former with small windows, the latter marked by the projecting bays). Oblique skylights angled over the offices bring floods of light to the corridors and borrowed light to the dance studios along with a view out of the sky—plus isolation from occasional airport noise.

The most impressive structures are those of the **Performing Arts Center** (Edward Larrabee Barnes—1978). They are the focus, symbolically and physically, of the liberal arts at Purchase and are located so that ample parking for the public surrounds them. The 1,400-seat Opera House tops the layout of the four houses, with the 750-seat Hanamachi Theater immediately adjoining at south, a 600-seat Theater of Music and Dance opposite, and a 100–500 seat Experimental Theater on axis with the Opera House and projecting eastward into the mall. A common lobby forms a nexus for the foursquare, cross-sited group, with a convenient drop-off road directly underneath for automotive access and egress. This is one of the most outstanding multipurpose theater groups in the country. Other academic buildings—are the stimulating **Social Science Building** (Venturi & Rauch—1978) with "quiet" east wall to frame the entry to the campus along with V&R's Humanities Building opposite; the **Musical Instructional Building** (Edward Larrabee Barnes—1978) with ingenious separation of functions—both on the north side of the mall; and the **Visual Arts Instructional Build-**

ing (The Architects Collaborative—1977) with serrated roof for north-lit studios on the south side. All buildings are designed to be expanded outward (away from arcade end) if necessary.

Near the open end of the mall there are two campus residential buildings, one on each side of the central spine. A large **Dormitory Group** housing eight hundred students lies to the southeast of the plaza. Built in a U-shape around three sides of an open square, it was designed by Gwathmey, Henderson & Siegel (1973), as was the apartment complex for four hundred students symmetrically facing it at northeast. The dining hall is particularly attractive.

Campus open daily; museum open Tues.–Sat. 11–5, Sun. 1–5, except holidays

---

33 First Unitarian Church (1961–63)
220 Winton Road South
Rochester, New York

LOUIS I. KAHN, ARCHITECT

Kahn has expressed unequivocally for the Unitarians that faith's thesis that education must accompany intelligent worship. Therefore he nests the congregation in the center of the church and surrounds it with two floors of classrooms. By top-lighting its solid-walled, unsentimental worship space in dramatic fashion he has created a vigorous interior. The square nave (in early studies a dodecagon) is dominated by a concrete roof forming a Greek cross, as it were, with its undersides splayed upward. This "cross" being set within a square leaves the corners open, and the nave at these four corners continues upward to receive a downpouring of light from each of the four roof monitors. From these near-invisible sources the natural light floods down, producing a corner-brightness and, inevitably, a corresponding lack of emphasis on the altar: indeed the brightness of the angles distracts the eye from the sanctuary. But as Kahn wrote prior to his death in 1974, "I felt that getting the light from above and down a well into the corners of the space gave expression to the form, to the shape, of the room chosen" (*Perspecta* Seven). The visual dryness of the natural concrete-block inner walls and the raw concrete ceiling and upper sections is relieved —chromatically and acoustically—by a spectrum of sixteen banners hung on the two sides. The exterior, of red brick, clearly reflects the in-

terior division, its hooded classroom windows developing a two-story, lateral, in-and-out rhythm, while four "light towers" project upward to create a strong silhouette. Dr. August E. Komendant and the Keast & Hood Company were structural consultants.

Open Mon.–Fri. 9–5, Sun. service

---

34 Rochester Institute of Technology (1968–   )
Jefferson Town Line Road at East River Road (N off IS 90 on US 15 c. 2.6 miles/4.2 kilometers, then L on Jefferson Road)
Rochester, New York

ANDERSON, BECKWITH & HAIBLE, CORGAN & BALESTIERE, E. L. BARNES, ROCHE/DINKELOO, HUGH STUBBINS, AND HARRY WEESE, ARCHITECTS; DAN KILEY, SPACE COORDINATOR AND LANDSCAPE ARCHITECT

The extensive (1,300 acres/526 hectares) all-new campus of RIT, located just southwest of the city, contains a number of good buildings plus a few groupings which are less satisfactory. The $60 million campus reflects a coordinated attack on the physical planning of a univer-

sity in today's changing world. Its impressive team of architects achieved an excellent feeling of architectural unity but a puzzling line of pedestrian communications in a climate not advertised for its benignity. It's a long, unprotected haul from the residential section of the campus to the academic. (The dormitory isolation does provide privacy for some two thousand residents, who are vastly outnumbered by evening and special students.)

One approaches the campus center down a divided-lane "memorial" drive to an antiformal grouping of administrative and recreational units closely facing each other. These create a visually uncomfortable cul-de-sac, busy with automobiles, while the tightness of space is intensified by the "confederation" of the buildings. The Administrative Tower (the campus anchor at seven stories) and the colleges of Business and Continuing Education form a cluster facing the gymnasium and hockey rink whose uninterrupted brick wall is mighty. The Alumni Union (on axis as one drives up) is one of the rewarding individual buildings, its relation to its neighbors and its sky-lighted corridors within achieving high marks. Perhaps the most competent single structure overall is Hugh Stubbins' enormous Arts Complex (see its Bevier Gallery).

Belden iron-spot brick—some 7 million of them—sheathes all buildings, producing a family homogeneity which is echoed by the sharply cut openings, some softened by splayed profiles. The finest site design feature lies in a series of dramatic and unexpected—but carefully plotted—vistas between buildings. Anderson, Beckwith & Haible were responsible for the College of Applied Science, the College of Science, and the services buildings; Corgan & Balestiere—married student housing; Edward Larrabee Barnes—residential and dining complex; Kevin Roche/John Dinkeloo—Administration, Physical Education, College of Business, College of Continuing Education, and Alumni Union; Hugh Stubbins—College of Fine and Applied Arts and College of Graphic Arts and Photography; Harry Weese—Wallace Memorial Library and College of General Studies. Lawrence B. Anderson was coordinating architect.

The **National Technical Institute for the Deaf** (1975) stands adjacent to RIT at Jefferson Road and John Street, Hugh Stubbins & Associates, architects. It is carefully designed to provide not only all of the technology needed—the hardware—in the education of the deaf, but to establish an architectural background of space, light, and color so that the visual scene will be particularly cheerful for its 750 students. The Institute is composed of three separate (but connected underground) groups: a two-story 300-foot/91-meter-square administration-academic building containing a series of advanced lecture and media halls (including a 542-seat theater), a commons built over the road and forming a "gateway" with RIT across the street, and housing in both low- and medium-rise units.

Both campuses open daily

---

35   First Presbyterian/Old Whaler's Church (1843–44)
Union Street at Church
Sag Harbor, Long Island, New York

MINARD LAFEVER, ARCHITECT

Wooden Egyptian architecture for a Christian church conjures a droll anachronism—"agonizing," writes Norton—but here we are not disappointed. Minard Lafever (1798–1854), that always entertaining eclectic and the author of *The Beauties of Modern Architecture* (1835—mostly Greek details!), instituted a Pharaonic beachhead on eastern Long Island—a style then widely in vogue—and we are all the better for it. Note the batter of its semipylon facade and the blubber-spade motif in the squared-off cavetto cornice. However, the church would be even more fascinating if its fantastic steeple—shaped (more or less) like a sailor's spyglass—had not been carried away by the 1938 hurricane.

As the church folder proclaims, "The lowest section was Christopher Wren, the middle section was Phoenician and the top section was in the style of the Chinese pagoda." Built by skilled carpenters and cabinet-makers, the steeple towered 185 feet/56 meters above the ground and long served as a navigation fix for sailors. Oxen and windlasses were used to lift each section up through the lower one. The interior of Old Whalers' has been termed late Greek Revival. (The Corinthian capitals come from Lafever's book of 1833, *The Modern Builder's Guide*.) The outstanding organ, built by Henry Erben in 1845 (restored 1978), recalls the facade of the church with its whale teeth and blubber spade details. The entire building (except the steeple) was restored and rededicated in 1951. It is rightly on the National Register of Historic Places. The New Jersey-born Lafever, it should be mentioned, moved on to the Gothic Revival.

Open June–Labor Day, two to three afternoons a week—church telephone (516) 725-0894; Sun. services all year

Lafever's friends will also want to see the nearby **Suffolk County Whaling Museum** (1846) at Garden and Main streets (open mid-May to mid-Sept., Mon.–Sat. 10–5, Sun. 2–5: admission). The building was constructed as a private residence in an opulent Classic Revival Style and later used as a Masonic temple (note emblem in the pediment). The ground floor now serves as a well-stocked whaling museum, recalling the days when Sag Harbor was Long Island's most famous whaling port.

---

36 New Campus of Skidmore College (1966–   )
Third Street, W of Broadway
Saratoga Springs, New York

FORD, POWELL & CARSON, ARCHITECTS AND PLANNERS

This beautifully thought-out campus, 1.5 miles/2.4 kilometers north of the original grounds, serves the well-known women's college (which is now sprinkled with men). The relation between buildings and their subtle play of heights are extremely well done. Moreover, every tree which could be saved was saved. The buildings are constructed with a reddish-brown common brick, accented with copper detailing, and marked throughout by a vertical expression of squared bay windows, maintaining homogeneity with each other and the nature about them. O'Neil Ford was chief of design; Samuel Zisman, with Catherine Boone Powell, developed the basic site plan.

Campus open daily

---

37 S. I. Newhouse School of Public Communications
Syracuse University
Building I (1962–64), **University Place at University Avenue**
I. M. Pei & Partners, architects
Building II (1972–73), **Waverly Avenue at University Avenue**
Skidmore, Owings & Merrill, architects
Syracuse, New York

"The world's most advanced center in mass communications, including journalism, radio and television, audiovisual, and other media of communications" proclaim the brochures issued on the dedication of the first of these two correlated structures. Certainly no university can touch such extraordinary facilities, nor is anyone likely to match the munificence of Mr. and Mrs. Newhouse's gift of $15 million to make it possible.

Building I, foursquare and formalistic—and showing hints of Wright's Unity Temple (q.v.)—stands directly across the street from the oldest building (1873) on the main campus. It is set back on an inviting podium-plaza, and is inviting itself, particularly its bright, skylit, three-story Dedication Hall. Lipchitz' *Birth of the Muses* highlights its main wall. A public lounge, a student services area, and the dean's office frame three of its sides with entry on the fourth. Classrooms and offices fill the two floors above, while special classrooms fill the lower

deck which extends partially under the plaza. One room includes an electronic "yes/no" examination grader: you get your grade on handing in your paper. Photographic studios, darkrooms, and heavy equipment services are also placed here. Actually, these below-grade facilities constitute almost two thirds of the building's square footage. At plaza level the 15-foot/4.6-meter-square piers in each corner are of precast concrete with post-tensioned girders on top (clear span 58 feet/18 meters) supporting the mammoth roof (113 feet/34 meters square). Two piers contain stairs, one an elevator, and the fourth toilets. King & King of Syracuse were associated architects; Kellogg Wong of the Pei office was architect-in-charge.

Building II by SOM closes the far side of the podium (but with the main entrance off Waverly Avenue), and houses electronic media and film studios in a four-story L-shaped structure. (Building I houses print media.) Construction had not commenced when last visited, but the results should be up to the firm's usual high standards.

Dedication Lobby of Building I open weekdays during school year

38   St. Mary's Complex (1966–68)
Van Buren Street facing IS 81
Syracuse, New York

SARGENT-WEBSTER-CRENSHAW & FOLLEY, ARCHITECTS

This unusual group of buildings (on the site of a deconsecrated cemetery) is as interesting philosophically as it is architecturally, for it purposefully combines two normally antithetical groups: the aged and
college undergraduates (of Syracuse University). The complex comprises Toomey Abbott Tower for 400 elderly (sixty-two years and
older) in a twenty-four-story building, which includes communal and
medical facilities in addition to its apartments; Boland Hall for 300
undergraduate women in an eight-story block; Brewster Hall for 450 men
in a twelve-story dormitory; and Brockway Hall, a three-story "service"
unit with cafeteria, theater, bookshop, library, etc., open to all. Underground parking is supplemented by outdoor lots. With such an age mixture, the old will not feel shunted off from youth while the cycle of life
rolls on with the two together. In the years that St. Mary's has been
open this age interaction of town and gown has been, in the main, use-

ful all around, stimulating to the elderly and eye-opening to the young. After all, both are groups which feel somewhat "isolated" socially, both are "poor," and both need communal facilities. The architecture of this unusual social experiment is first-rate, from overall site planning which deals with a hillside location (50-foot/15-meter change in level) to great advantage, to mutual building interplay, to the tough, raw concrete of which it is built. The handling of the variety of levels is commendable, as is the ground terrace in front. The university's Medical School is nearby, which is good, while the Interstate highway roars along at the property line, which is not. The architects have created a stimulating complex on a site so steep that it had hitherto been deemed "unbuildable."

Grounds open daily

---

39 **Everson Museum of Art** (1966–68)
401 Harrison Street at South State Street
Syracuse, New York

I. M. PEI & PARTNERS, ARCHITECTS

Sculpting with four powerful cantilevered blocks of galleries and the spaces between them in a manner vaguely suggestive of the work of Henry Moore (whose *Reclining Figure #3* rests outside the entrance), the architects have created an external tension of form which, though not inviting, is tantalizing. Architectural mystery more than architectural invitation pulls one into the building, an effect intensified by its concrete windowlessness. But once within the towering central area— which forms a 50-foot/15-meter-square sculpture core-court—one encounters an exercise of solids and voids and a dance of lights and shadows that are stimulating. Shafts of light from roof "windows" and from glazed bands between the four "blocks" of galleries dash in and out, bounce off the floor, and are carried upward again by a superb spiral stair: a tempting museum introduction. Several small ground-floor rooms open off this entry hall but the stair entices one to the four main galleries on the second floor which are deployed around the sculpture court and project, as mentioned, over its base. Windowless in themselves—for maximum exhibition flexibility—these interconnect with each other and maintain an orientation liaison with the two-story entry hall by means of strategic balconies or passerelles. The spectator

approaching the museum thus moves from an "enclosed" exterior to an "open" light-shafted interior, from "open" balconies to "closed" galleries, a progression of intensity which alerts one's receptivity to the art displayed. (A museum becomes a dull warehouse or a puzzling labyrinth unless it animates the visitor.)

The galleries, which have a large turnover of traveling exhibitions, are completely flexible, artificially lit, and neutrally respectful of the art on their walls. A low administrative wing projects at the east, and the upper part of the 320-seat auditorium/theater frames the entry at the west. Both can be entered directly from the outside and from the lower gallery floor. Note that the walls (of bushhammered concrete with reddish granite aggregate) have the same finish outside and in. The first stage in a downtown rehabilitation, the Everson Museum—municipal sculpture itself—is a tremendous civic asset. The building was named for Helen S. Everson, the museum's principal benefactor. Pederson, Hueber, Hares & Glavin were associate architects; Pietro Belluschi was consultant to the board of trustees; Max W. Sullivan, the first director.

Open Tues.–Fri., Sun. 12–5, Sat. 10–5, except holidays

40 Lyndhurst (1838/1865)
635 South Broadway, off US 9 just S of Tappan Zee Bridge
Tarrytown, New York

ALEXANDER JACKSON DAVIS, ARCHITECT

Lyndhurst was one of the first and is probably the greatest of our neo-Gothic mansions. Set on undulating acres which drop down to the Hudson River, and unrolling the proper mixtures of vistas, lawns, and trees, the original house was begun in 1838 but was substantially expanded between 1864–65 by the new owner, who fortunately used the same architect, the famous Alexander Jackson Davis. It is typical of their times that Davis, with his also illustrious partner, Ithiel Town, was active in both the neo-Classic and neo-Gothic movements in this country a century and more ago. The interior of the house, after the somewhat restrained exterior, bursts on one with rich intensity, an effect accented by the "vaulting" of most ceilings. The rooms, with the exception of the second-floor gallery (once the library), seem surprisingly small, an

effect intensified because they are intricately decorated and are full of furniture and pictures which have come down from each of the three families that lived in the house (the last until 1961), thus displaying a cross section of the tastes of the occupants. The dining room, especially, should be noted. Davis himself designed much of the furniture. Also on the grounds was an enormous (380 feet/116 meters long) and once stunning greenhouse which, hopefully, will be rebuilt in scaled-down size. The house was left to the National Trust in 1964, was fully restored where necessary, and is immaculately maintained.

Open May–Oct., daily 10–5, Nov.–Apr. 10–4, except Dec. 25: admission

41   Julia Howard Bush Memorial Center (1834–36)
Russell Sage College
Congress Street at First
Troy, New York

JAMES H. DAKIN, ARCHITECT

The Greek Revival, so popular in the early nineteenth century in the United States—stemming in part from the Greek War of Independence (1821+) and Byronic inspiration—served many uses. Here it is seen in hexastyle (six-column) Greek temple form built originally to house the First Presbyterian Church. In 1973 the church was purchased by Russell Sage College and used as a concert and lecture hall, and in 1978 thoroughly renovated. The exterior of the building, in downtown Troy, is accurately detailed and proportioned and its stuccoed brick manages to remain in fine shape to this day. The seven enormous pilasters—almost squared columns—on the sides should be noted. The interior is also of a superior mold, if on the startling side, with a ceiling dominated by a circular near-flat dome that practically fills its confines. Except for the memorial Victorian windows of 1885–1905, the detail of the inside equals that without, even with the heavy remodeling of 1873. The Bush Memorial Center is a little-known delight by a too little-known architect, here on his own a year after leaving Town & Davis.

To visit inquire at College Administration Building, Plum Hall

---

42   Munson-Williams-Proctor Institute (1960)
310 Genesee Street
Utica, New York

PHILIP JOHNSON ASSOCIATES, ARCHITECTS

The Munson-Williams-Proctor Museum of Art is a windowless granite box (atop a glass-lined basement), square in plan and broken externally only by its bronze-wrapped structural exo-frame. However, on entering this slightly austere building one is pulled forward from the low doorway into a double-height Renaissance *cortile* sparkling with sunshine that pours through its 121 coffered plastic domes by day, and which is ablaze from artificial lights by night. This unexpected spatial effervescence creates an ingratiating introduction to the art, highlighted by pieces of sculpture. Smaller galleries, basically for temporary exhibitions, open off of the main floor; one takes an elevator or the meticulously detailed double stairs to visit the main galleries above. There two lateral galleries—suspended from the structural frame—open directly onto the courtyard from opposite sides, furnishing orientation and vantage points for viewing court exhibitions and thus "participating" in the total free volume of the museum. The major exhibition spaces—not im-

mediately apparent—run across the front and back of the building. Windowless, they can be partitioned as desired.

An auditorium seating 271, staff offices, and services, accessible from the rear, occupy the lowest floor, which would be semiunderground except for the sloping site and the fact that a dry moat encircles the building. Though at times rigid, the building is compelling, superbly equipped, and full of expertise. It has, indeed, been called "the perfect professional museum" (*Architectural Forum,* December 1960). Bice & Baird were supervising architects; Lev Zetlin, structural engineer.

Open Tues.–Sat. 10–5, Sun. 1–5, except holidays

Be sure to visit **Fountain Elms** (1850–52) next door, 318 Genesee Street, designed by W. J. Woolett, Jr.; its rich Italian Villa exterior offers a foil to the architectural austerity of the museum, of which it is an active part. Early American decorative arts and temporary exhibitions are shown on the second floor.

---

43 **Hudson River Museum** (1967–68)
Trevor Park
511 Warburton Avenue
Yonkers, New York

THE SMS ARCHITECTS, ARCHITECTS

This combined museum, planetarium, library, and art teaching facility forms three sides of a central open-air court with the fourth provided by the craggy 1877 Trevor Mansion which had housed the earlier museum (on a site which the city had purchased in 1923). The relationships between old and new and between new and nature are, in spite of a steeply angled site, ingeniously worked out. The grade is so sharp that the museum has only one story at entry but two additional floors below,

notched in the hillside. The low, covered entry leads to the library wing at right and museums at left, with the open court and sculpture garden directly in front. An excellent wrought-iron gate allows one visually to tie the whole together even when the gate is closed. The 25,000-volume library, which is in effect a separate building, has reading rooms for both adults and children. The entrance level of the museum contains sales desk and some exhibition space but much of this floor is taken up by the 140-seat planetarium, which injects itself into the rear (and whose dome can readily be seen from the outside). The upper-level exhibition floor is cleverly tied to the major gallery space directly below by an open well in the center, establishing a needed visual liaison. The lower exhibit floor flows with one major and two minor spaces, including a surprise view out over the Hudson River. On both of these floors the quality of light, both natural and artificial, complements the art. The lowest level, which can also be reached by an outside stair (when, for instance, the galleries are closed), contains an all-purpose hall that can be used for theater and lectures, with lunchroom, terrace, and kitchen, and three studios beyond. The sculpture court and open-air exhibition space (shown in photograph) serve not only as a background for sculpture, but as an introduction to the old house. Outdoor concerts are also given here. Structural frame is of smooth concrete, walls of lightly striated concrete. The museum combines thoughtful use of the old with splendid creation of the new. Willis N. Mills, Jr., was partner in charge of design.

Open Tues.–Sat. 10–5, Sun. 11–5, except holidays: admission on weekends

44   Old Fort Niagara (mid-18th century)
Fort Niagara State Park
Robert Moses Parkway
Youngstown, New York

At the mouth of the Niagara River where it flows into Lake Ontario—
and approximately 14 miles/23 kilometers north of the famous Falls—
first the French, then the English, and finally the Americans struggled
for this military outpost. By holding it each sought to exercise control
over the Great Lakes route and the potentially hostile Indians. It was of
martial significance through the War of 1812. The earliest fortifications,
of logs and long vanished, were erected by the French under La Salle
and dated from 1678. A second wooden fort was constructed in 1688.
Subsequent masonry rebuildings in 1725–26 and 1750–57, also by the

French, established much of the fort which we see today. Seemingly designed by a Norman familiar with Vauban, this well-preserved—in some cases well-reconstructed—fort provides us with one of the most extensive French architectural remains in what is now the U.S.A. The oldest, most important building in the compound is the French Castle, constructed in 1726. Disguised as a manor house and trading post, so as not to alarm the Indians, it was in effect a thick-walled fort designed by Louis XV's chief engineer in Canada. Even the dormers could be used as gun decks. The castle has been fully restored, offering an excellent impression of a French semimilitary building of 250 years ago. The windowless Powder Magazine (1757) also rears an impressive bulk, while the Storehouse (1762) displays a model and historical data on the area. The chief British constructions—after their capture of the fort in 1759—are the storehouse mentioned and two redoubts, one near the entry and the other in the northeast corner. The Americans added the North and South Casement Galleries (1863–71), whose excellent brickwork should be noted. Besides being a fort—the strongest on the Great Lakes—Fort Niagara was a very active trading post. It was restored in 1929–34.

Open daily, summer 9–dusk, rest of year 9–4:30, except major holidays: admission

New York City

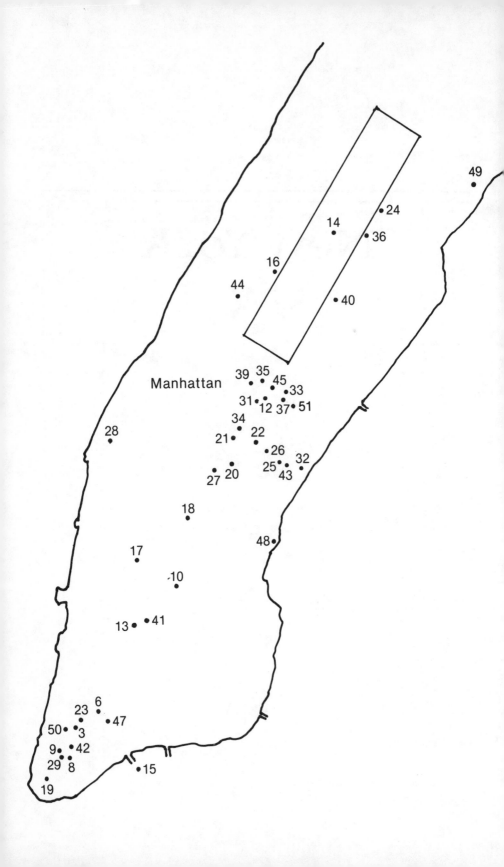

Manhattan

NEW YORK CITY

The buildings in boldface type are of general interest. The others are for the specialist.

1 Billopp House (Conference House—1680)

2 Richmondtown Restoration (17th–19th century)

3 **St. Paul's Chapel** (1764–66)—Thomas McBean

4 **Dyckman House** (1783)

5 **Reformed Protestant Dutch Church** (1793–96)—
Thomas Fardon

6 **City Hall** (1803–12)—McComb and Mangin

7 **Snug Harbor Cultural Center** (Sailors' Snug
Harbor—1831–80)—Minard Lafever

8 **Federal Hall National Memorial** (1834–42)—
Town & Davis and John Frazee

9 **Trinity Church** (1841–46)—Richard Upjohn

10 **Grace Church** (1843–46)—James Renwick, Jr.

11 Green-Wood Cemetery Gates (1861)—Richard M.
Upjohn

12 **St. Patrick's Cathedral** (1858–79)—James Renwick, Jr.

13 **Cast-Iron Architecture in New York City** (mid
to late 19th century)—Bogardus etc.
Remodeled Apartment (1868/1973)—Stephen B.
Jacobs

14 **Central Park** (1859–76)—Olmsted and Vaux
Prospect Park (1867–72)—Olmsted and Vaux

15 **Brooklyn Bridge** (1869–83)—J. A. and
Washington Roebling

16 The Dakota (1880–84)—H. J. Hardenbergh
Alwyn Court Apartments (1907–9)—Harde &
Short

17 Jefferson Market Branch Library (1875–77/
1967)—Frederick C. Withers and Giorgio Cavaglieri

18 Flatiron Building (1901–3)—D. H. Burnham

19 **U. S. Custom House** (1902–9)—Cass Gilbert

20 Pierpont Morgan Library (1903–7)—McKim,
Mead & White

21 **New York Public Library** (1902–11)Carrere &
Hastings
Bryant Park (1884–1934)—Thomas Hastings

22 **Grand Central Station** (1903–13)—Warren & Wetmore, Reed & Stem, W. J. Wilgus

23 **Woolworth Building** (1911–13)—Cass Gilbert

24 International Center of Photography (1914)— Delano & Aldrich

25 **Daily News Building** (1929–30)—Hood and Howells
McGraw-Hill Building (1930–31)—Raymond M. Hood
American Radiator Building (1923–24)— Raymond M. Hood

26 **Chrysler Building** (1928–30)—William Van Alen

27 **Empire State Building** (1929–31)—Shreve, Lamb & Harmon

28 Starrett-Lehigh Building (1929–31)—R. G. and W. R. Cory

29 Irving Trust Company Building (1930–31)— Voorhees, Gmelin & Walker

30 **20th-Century Suspension Bridges in New York City**—Othmar H. Ammann

31 **Rockefeller Center** (1931–40)—Various architects

32 **United Nations Secretariat Building** (1947–50)— Wallace K. Harrison and various associates

33 **Lever House** (1950–52)—Skidmore, Owings & Merrill

34 **Manufacturers Hanover Trust Company** (1953–54)—Skidmore, Owings & Merrill

35 **Museum of Modern Art** (1938–39) **and Sculpture Garden** (1953/1964)—Goodwin & Stone, Philip Johnson

36 **Guggenheim Museum** (1956–59)—Frank Lloyd Wright

37 **Seagram Building** (1954–58)—Mies van der Rohe and Philip Johnson

38 **TWA Flight Center** (1958–62)—Eero Saarinen

39 **CBS Building** (1963–65)—Eero Saarinen

40 **Whitney Museum of American Art** (1964–66)—
Marcel Breuer and Hamilton P. Smith

41 University Plaza (1966)—I. M. Pei

42 **Chase Manhattan Bank** (1957–61), **Marine
Midland Building** (1967–68), **One Liberty Plaza**
(1970–72)—Skidmore, Owings & Merrill

43 **Ford Foundation Building** (1966–67)—Roche &
Dinkeloo

44 Lincoln Center for the Performing Arts
(1959–68)—Various architects

45 **Paley Park** (1967)—Zion & Breen
Greenacre Park (1971)—Hideo Sasaki, with
Goldstone, Dearborn & Hinz

46 **World of Birds Building** (1971–72)—Morris
Ketchum, Jr.
World of Darkness (1969)—Morris Ketchum, Jr.

47 **Police Plaza and Its Buildings** (1968–73)—
Gruzen & Partners
Chatham Towers (1965)—Gruzen & Partners

48 **Waterside** (1970–74)—Davis, Brody & Associates

49 1199 Plaza (1971–75)—Hodne/Stageberg

50 **World Trade Center** (1966–80)—Yamasaki
and Roth

51 **Citicorp Center** (1971–77)—Hugh Stubbins

52 Bronx Developmental Center (1973–77)—
Richard Meier

1 Billopp House (Conference House—1680)
W end of Hyland Boulevard
Tottenville, New York (Staten Island), New York

The Billopp House occupies one of Staten Island's many picturesque sites, here overlooking the Arthur Kill and New Jersey. Reflecting a combination of Dutch and English influences, it was designed and built by its owner, Captain Christopher Billopp. It might be said that its stonework makes up in robustness what the architecture lacks in finesse, a simple ruggedness characterizing the whole. (The wood framing of the attic is very impressive.) The kitchen lean-to was added in the middle of the eighteenth century, the original kitchen having been in the sizable basement. The house was given to the city in 1926, and since then has been fully restored and refurnished by the Conference House Association. Not great architecture but a pleasant and scenic excursion. It was here, incidentally, that Franklin, Adams, and Rutledge met Lord Howe—at British request—with a view to working out a negotiated peace (1776); hence the Conference House subtitle.

Open Wed.–Sun. 1–5, except holidays: admission

2 Richmondtown Restoration (17th–19th century)
Richmond Road at Arthur Kill Road
Richmond, New York (Staten Island), New York

The Richmondtown Restoration, near the center of Staten Island, now comprises twenty-two buildings from the seventeenth to nineteenth centuries, eleven of them occupying their original sites. The Restoration covers 96 acres/39 hectares. The idea for preserving the buildings, which depict "the common life" of the area, was born in the Depression but not incorporated until 1962. It was then that the imminent impact of the Verrazano-Narrows Bridge and a net of interstate highways made preservation efforts essential. The stunned islanders, to paraphrase Santayana, realized that they must keep their eye on their objective and redouble their efforts. With some (but insufficient) financial backing, conscientious scholarship, and land acquisition powers, a representative collection of buildings tracing the heritage of Staten Island is being assembled. The barn-red Voorlezer's House (1690) was used by the Dutch as school, church, and house for the "Voorlezer," or lay teacher. It is claimed to be the oldest elementary school still standing in

the United States. Also in the "Colonial" section stands the picturesque, Dutch-inspired Lake-Tysen House (see photograph), built
around 1740, and moved to its new site (1962) from nearby New
Dorp. Even though not complete, the project offers fine insight into the
non-heroic architecture of the area. In addition to the buildings, there is
a museum with skilled working craftsmen.

Open May–Oct., Sat.–Sun. 2–5; July and Aug., Tues.–Sat. 10–5

---

3   St. Paul's Chapel (1764–66)
Broadway between Fulton and Vesey Streets
New York, New York

THOMAS McBEAN, ARCHITECT

Church architecture in the Thirteen Colonies underwent an evolution of
liturgical mores paralleling that in the mother country. The earliest
churches in Virginia and New England were small-windowed, medieval
affairs (see St. Luke's, Benn's Church, Virginia, and Old Ship Meeting
House, Hingham, Massachusetts). Then with the "new" English fashions of Wren (1632–1723) and Gibbs (1682–1754), who opened up
their churches to snatch scarce sunlight, most churches along the eastern seaboard—as opposed to their contemporaries in the Spanish
Southwest—welcomed the sun as far as their building technique allowed. (The anti-Establishment New England meeting houses—one of
the Colonies' few architectural contributions—also were awash with
light from numerous windows—somewhat strangely, considering their
winter climate.) Yet since Independence, and largely as a result of the
Gothic Revival in the early part of the nineteenth century, we have
tended to avoid luminosity in churches as out of character, hence
disquieting. There are American churches of the last few years which
have virtually no windows at all, relying largely on artificial illumination even in a bucolic setting.

St. Paul's Chapel, which is the only surviving Colonial church in
Manhattan, epitomizes the bright, large-windowed, Gibbs-inspired
church, where because it is 10 degrees latitude south of London's
gloomier weather, it takes on an added atmosphere of cheer plus almost
Baroque exuberance. Gibbs, incidentally, had been McBean's employer
before the latter moved to the New World, and the influence of Gibbs's
St. Martin-in-the-Fields can be seen clearly here on Broadway. This

spirit of light is carried out in the colors of the interior, which range from pinkish walls, to blue-green vaulted ceiling, to white-and-gold-touched pulpit. Note, too, the *Glory* above the altar, carved by Pierre L'Enfant of Washington, D.C., fame. Sparkle is accented by Waterford chandeliers, five down the central aisle with others in the galleries. Here is a setting for a religion of joy: the interior might well indeed be the most genial around. St. Paul's has been little altered since the tower was added in 1793–94 by James C. Lawrence and the portico on Broadway immediately thereafter, the church having earlier had its main entry facing the Hudson River and today's Church Street. A very bright light.

For the antithesis in a nave walk a few blocks south on Broadway to Upjohn's Trinity Church (q.v.). We have in these two a summation of the difference between the Georgian and the Gothic Revival. St. Paul's Chapel, incidentally, is a member of Trinity parish.

Open daily 8–4

---

4   **Dyckman House** (1783)
4881 Broadway at 204th Street
New York, New York

Of all the sights along Broadway, few seem as anachronistic as this nearly two-hundred-year-old Dutch farmhouse. Set in its own small garden, and elevated above the road, it is Manhattan's only Category I house—"of National Importance"—in the Municipal Art Society's

Register. Though the English had long been in control of Manhattan and, subsequent to that, independence had come to the new made U.S.A., Dutch architectural influence was felt along the Hudson River throughout the eighteenth century. The original house on the site—with property which once embraced 400 acres/162 hectares—was erected around 1748 but was burned by the British during the Revolution. William Dyckman rebuilt the dwelling around 1783, in the process salvaging as much material as he could from the old. The gambrel roof carries the characteristic "Dutch" sweep over the front to shelter the porch, and while the lower floor and a half are of local stone and brick, the upper section (for the bedrooms) is of wood clapboarding, as is the extension to the south. (Some historians think that the gambrel roof is more of French Huguenot than Dutch derivation.) The house is neither large nor imposing, but it provides a convenient and unique example of eighteenth-century Dutch farmhouse architecture on Manhattan Island. Moreover many of the furnishings are original, those in the dining room and kitchen being the most interesting. The house and (depleted) grounds were given to the city in 1915 by two descendants of Dyckman and complete restoration undertaken. Not as impressive as the Van Cortlandt Manor (c. 1750) of Sleepy Hollow Restoration, Croton-on-Hudson (q.v.), it is still a sound local representative of its type.

Open Tues.–Sun. 11–5, except holidays: admission

5 **Reformed Protestant Dutch Church** (1793–96)
Flatbush and Church Avenues
New York (Brooklyn), New York

THOMAS FARDON, ARCHITECT

Since 1654 a Dutch Reformed Church has stood on this site, and this, the third, is still very active. Peter Stuyvesant contributed funds to the building of the first (1654—of wood). Its thick gray walls, whose stones were quarried at nearby Hell Gate, came in part from the second church (1699), which was outgrown and replaced by the present structure. In 1886—a confused period in the history of architecture—a polygonal extension was made for choir and organ, and the interior, dominated by its great organ and embellished by Tiffany memorial windows (1889), does not live up to the quiet simplicity of the exterior. Be sure to visit the cemetery. Many of its 385 graves are marked by fragilely slender slabs, and all are shaded by an extensive variety of trees. The bell in the tower has tolled at the death of every President, including George Washington.

Grounds open daily 9–4, church for Sun. service and by appointment

6 City Hall (1803–12)
City Hall Park between Broadway and Park Row
New York, New York

JOHN McCOMB, JR., AND JOSEPH FRANÇOIS MANGIN, ARCHITECTS

New York's famous City Hall is marked by both an outer and inner delicacy. One of its architects—Mangin—was born and educated in eighteenth-century France and hints of Gabriel's Petit Trianon (1762–68) appear in the exterior. Moreover the splendid stair within owes a small bow to Gabriel's Ecole Militaire (1751–82) and to Wardour House in Wiltshire of 1776 (as Clay Lancaster brings out in a perceptive article in the *Journal of the Society of Architectural Historians,* March 1970). But whatever the background, the results at City Hall— Federal Style in statement—are elegant or, as Henry James put it, in "perfect taste and finish." The commission for the building's design was won by competition, but the award-winning project—berated by Latrobe (who obviously lost)—was scaled down because of costs, and Mangin, strangely, took no further part, its completion being carried out by the New York-born McComb.

The entrance hall startles with its geometric counterpoints: the circu-

lar sweep of the twin stairs and the contrast of horizontals (floors, etc.) versus verticals (the Corinthian columns semisilhouetted on the second floor), with a dome climaxing these forces. The Governors' Room on the second floor with five rhythmic roundheaded windows (marked on the exterior above the Ionic entry porch) provides a sunny museum of portraits, many of them distinguished (including one of McComb himself). The delicate interior architecture of this room was completely restored to McComb's original design by Grosvenor Atterbury (1909), and stops just short of being finicky. On the outside, the Justice-topped cupola encounters difficulties in adjusting to its rectangular base, but overall this is one of the city's prizes. A complete restoration, including replacement of all exterior walls (which were disintegrating), was carried out in 1956 by Shreve, Lamb & Harmon.

Open during office hours

---

7   **Snug Harbor Cultural Center** (Sailors' Snug Harbor—1831–80)
Richmond Terrace at Snug Harbor Road
Livingston, New York (Staten Island), New York

MINARD LAFEVER, PRINCIPAL ARCHITECT

The alignment of five interlocked Greek Revival buildings at Snug Harbor produces the most extraordinary parade of temples in the United States. The domed administration building at center (1831–32) opposite the Richmond Terrace Gatehouse (which note), sports eight two-story-high, unfluted Ionic columns of Sing Sing marble. This is accompanied on either side by two narrower units with a simple Classic portico each (1840–42), and these, in turn, are protected by end "temples" with six columns (1879–80) but otherwise similar to the central mass. (The two end wings were added to house additional sailors.) All five are laterally connected by low hyphens. Dormitories occupied the four "side" buildings with chapel and services in separate structures behind. The resulting impression is on the chilly side architecturally—a fact emphasized by the buildings facing north—but nonetheless here stands probably the most ambitious moment of the Classic Revival in the U.S.A. (one curiously slighted by the late Talbot Hamlin in his *Greek Revival Architecture in America*). Much of Snug Harbor can be seen from the road itself, with Manhattan's downtown in the distance—along with Bayonne's refineries across the Kill van Kull. Financed by the will of Captain Robert R. Randall, a boldly

successful privateer in the Revolutionary War, Snug Harbor was built to house over 900 "aged, decrepit and worn-out sailors." Most of Captain Randall's fortune was wisely invested in his Manhattan farm and real estate, and the land rental of some 130 acres/53 hectares of what is now the Washington Square section of New York built and supported Snug Harbor. In 1976, with only 120 "decrepit sailors" in residence, the Harbor moved to new and smaller quarters in Sea Level, North Carolina. The city then purchased the buildings and grounds and has established the Snug Harbor Cultural Center in the structures, keeping the exteriors intact. The facilities include (or will soon include) an Institute of Arts and Sciences, Children's Museum, Botanical Garden, Art Lab, and theater and conference facilities. In addition to the Greek Revival major buildings, there are also fine examples of the Italianate, Victorian, and French Second Empire. Earlier attributed to Martin E. Thompson, the main building is certainly the work of Lafever according to an erudite article by Barnett Shepherd of the Staten Island Institute of Arts and Sciences (*Journal of the Society of Architectural Historians,* May 1976). A prodigious statement of the Greek Revival.

Grounds open Mon.–Fri. 9–5, Sat.–Sun. 12–5: admission to some buildings

---

8 Federal Hall National Memorial (1834–42)
The Sub-Treasury Building
26 Wall Street at Nassau Street
New York, New York

TOWN & DAVIS AND JOHN FRAZEE, ARCHITECTS

There are many individual Greek Revival "temples" in the United States—where, actually, the style attained its most widespread popularity—but few are as pure or as dramatically sited as this. (Note also the siting of nearby Trinity Church just at the end of Wall Street.) A few yards from the New York Stock Exchange, topping the end of Broad Street, ringed with buildings X times its own height, the former Custom House, then Sub-Treasury, maintains its command of identity with total aplomb. And when shafts of sun bore in like searchlights to inch over its Parthenon facade, splashing light and shadow up and down its steps, and wreathing a nimbus on Washington's statue, 26 Wall Street leaps with chiaroscuro. Though designed by those masters of the Greek Revival, Ithiel Town and Alexander Jackson Davis—who won its commission by competition—John Frazee (1790–1852), an early American architect-sculptor and mason, came on the scene and over a period of almost seven years redesigned the building inside and out. As Talbot Hamlin explains, "The Commissioners in charge of the work were perhaps rightly frightened at the lightness of the construction indicated on the Town and Davis plan" (*Greek Revival Architecture,* Oxford University Press, 1944).

The facade rests on a plinth much higher than normal because of the

drop in grade from back to front, necessitating the steep flight of entry steps. Note that this is softened by having the statue of Washington (by J. Q. A. Ward—1883) rise directly from a sidewalk podium. (Washington took his oath as President of the new country at this spot in 1789.) As mentioned, the front of the building is directly modeled on the Parthenon, omitting only the sculpture in the tympanum and metopes. As the New York *Commercial Advertiser* put it, "its general dimensions, compared with those of that ancient temple, are as eleven to twelve" (July 13, 1842). The sturdy development of the Nassau Street side (178 feet/54 meters long) should also be noted. The interior with its strikingly domed rotunda comes as a surprise because of its richness and because of the incongruity of its shallow Roman dome within a Greek temple. (The arch and dome were, strangely, almost never used by the Greeks. Town and Davis' original design had a dome bursting through the roof.) The entire building is fireproof with brick vaulting in both basement, which should be seen, and in dome. Beginning in the 1950s the structure was fully reconditioned and given its new name. One of New York's finest.

Open Mon.–Fri. 9–4:30, daily in summer, except holidays

9   **Trinity Church** (1841–46)
Broadway at Wall Street
New York, New York

RICHARD UPJOHN, ARCHITECT

Of all the Gothic Revival churches in this country, none can match either the dramatic location—terminating Wall Street (which once marked the Dutch wall around the town)—or the immediate church grounds of this intriguing, self-confident house of worship. By virtue of the hoary and beautifully planted cemetery on either side (note the extraordinary variety of trees and shrubs), the church even today has sufficient breathing space to withstand successfully the competition of the towering buildings which encircle it. Ironically, Trinity itself was for forty-two years the tallest structure in New York at 280.5 feet/85 meters, until St. Patrick's—q.v. (The cemetery, incidentally, was a burial ground before Trinity was founded in 1697; its oldest stone carries the date of 1681—for a lad of five.) The first Trinity, built in 1698, burned at the time of the Revolution while the second (1788–94)—with a few spiky Gothic details—was torn down (1839) because of structural weakness. (It is worth noting that domestic Gothic Revival suggestions were evident as early as 1799 in Benjamin Latrobe's Sedgeley Mansion, near Philadelphia, long destroyed.) The present Trinity, the third on the site, was designed by the British-born Upjohn (who later was the principal founder, 1857, then first president of the American Institute of Architects).

Upjohn developed his reputation with St. John's Church in Bangor, Maine, which was finished in 1839, and almost immediately he was called to New York to design Trinity. (Upjohn's Gothic "conversion" was largely due to the work and writings in England of Pugin and the proselytizing of the Cambridge Camden Society.) When Trinity was completed in 1846, it received immense acclaim, inspiring a host of imitations. In effect, it launched the Gothic Revival in the U.S.A. (aided by the same architect's contemporaneous but more remote St. Mary's in Burlington, New Jersey, q.v.). It also launched Mr. Upjohn. The exterior, marvelously blackened by soot, could scarce be improved upon, its dark walls a proper foil to the snows of winter and the bright greens of summer, with the weathered white tombstones engaged in their own pirouette around the brownstone hulk. The interior, unfortunately, does not live up to the fascination of the outside. It is, of course, highly competent, but mechanistically, almost coldly so, an effect which the chancel window seeks vainly to ameliorate. (The stained-glass windows

were among the first in the country and were designed by the architect.) Though Horatio Greenough (1805–52) termed it "the puny cathedral of Broadway" other critics consider this "one of the greatest, if
not the greatest church erected in America" (Wayne Andrews in his
Architecture, Ambition and Americans, Harper, 1955). The reredos
was designed by Frederick C. Withers in 1877. While Upjohn's design
was accepted by the church in 1839, the cornerstone was not laid until
1841, and some feel that changes, mostly influenced by Pugin, occurred
in the final design. All Saints' Chapel, Thomas L. Nash, architect, was
added in 1913.

Open Mon.–Fri. 7–6, Sat.–Sun. 7–4

---

10   Grace Church (1843–46)
Broadway at East 10th Street
New York, New York

JAMES RENWICK, JR., ARCHITECT

Renwick won the competition for Grace Church when he was only
twenty-three and though he went on to design the more oracular St.
Patrick's (q.v.) and the Smithsonian Institution in Washington, D.C.

(q.v.), the Municipal Art Society places the white marble Grace on its list of eight New York City landmarks "which are of National Importance" (St. Patrick's is in Category II). Both churches, it should be noted, rely on steel within their piers; their "buttresses" carry no load from their roof thrust, their ribbing no weight from their (suspended) vaults. This, however, was a product of their eclectic period, and we must regard this sophistry with due restraint. Renwick at Grace Church achieved greater "authenticity," plus more correlation of interior to exterior, than Upjohn did at Trinity, which was finished the same year. As Phoebe B. Stanton wrote in her book *The Gothic Revival and American Church Architecture,* (Johns Hopkins, 1968), "Grace Church is

more tightly knit, less rigorous, and less dry than Trinity." Though the
site is on the slender side (cf. Trinity's), the steeple, its original wood
replaced by marble, was placed so as to be visible up and down Broadway, which angles at 10th Street. Whether the Gothic is appropriate for
Protestant houses of worship—the style having developed in the Middle
Ages for Roman liturgy—injects another question, but for an influential, indeed romantic, example of its Revival visit Grace Church: Renwick himself worshiped there most of his adult life. Note the fine
sense of lateral openness connecting nave and transepts.

Open daily 9–5

---

11   Green-Wood Cemetery Gates (1861)
5th Avenue at 25th Street
New York (Brooklyn), New York

RICHARD M. UPJOHN, ARCHITECT

The Gothic Revival for churches began in earnest in the United States in the early 1840s and continued until the Civil War. After that lamentable conflict, Victorianism or Victorian Gothic became more fashionable. Some churches continued in the "purer" Gothic Revival—some, indeed, are, with comfortable anachronism, being thus built today—but the 1860s marked the climax of the era. Although church building demands a certain sobriety—at least it did until the present hysterical school—the Gothic Revival as a style could also be turned to more emancipated heights. Probably the greatest example of this freedom is this superb 106-foot/32-meter-high gateway (plus offices) by the famous Upjohn's son Richard. Not only is it a splendid example of its period, its play of solids, especially the sculpture of biblical scenes by John M. Moffitt against the tracery by Upjohn, with the whole constrained by the mass of flanking offices, reveals sophisticated know-how and great collaboration between architect and sculptor.

The 478-acre/193-hectare cemetery itself—laid out (1839) by Major David B. Douglass—offers a fascinating mélange of tombs (including those of Samuel F. B. Morse, James Gordon Bennett, Horace Greeley, and architect James Renwick, Jr.). The diligent can probably discover the whole spectrum of architectural history on its rolling site.

Open daily 8–5

---

12 St. Patrick's Cathedral (1858–79)
5th Avenue between 50th and 51st Streets
New York, New York

JAMES RENWICK, JR., ARCHITECT

Renwick's earlier Grace Church (q.v.) is finer, more "organic," in its architecture, but St. Patrick's unquestionably establishes a more commanding urban presence. Actually at the time that the church's location was originally settled upon, it was criticized as being "too far out of town," but never was urban prescience—plus urban lottery—more gratifyingly fulfilled. Thanks primarily to the building of Rockefeller Center in the 1930s, the church now forms part of the core of New York City: for its parishioners, especially the Irish, it is the core. James Renwick, having graduated from Grace Church, pulled out all the stops for St. Patrick's. Renwick, questionably, took Cologne Cathedral as his semiprototype, a church which the famous Banister Fletcher

termed "a conspicuous instance of the adoption of the details of a style, without having assimilated the spirit that created it" (*History of Architecture,* Charles Scribner's, 1896 et seq.). There is, thus, in St. Patrick's a certain dryness, particularly on its exterior fabric (as opposed to its podium setting); it is too "petrified" for the vital Gothic of the Middle Ages. (Incidentally, the "Gothic" got its name from the Italians, who considered it so uncouth that they named it for a tribe of barbarians.)

St. Patrick's interior unfolds its most successful architectural aspect, setting a potent, if for some an overdramatic, stage for worship, a proscenium activated by a constant ebb and flow of people. Much of this puissance stems from remodeling in the early 1900s when Charles T. Mathews pushed out Renwick's originally flat east nave termination, fashioning it into a polygonal Lady Chapel (1901–6). Then in 1941–42 a new High Altar and a 57-foot/17-meter-high, gold-filigreed baldachino by Charles D. Maginnis was added, climaxed by theatrical downlighting to create a numinous setting. The buttresses receive no load from their roof, steel lurks within the piers and vaulting, and the marble within turns to local stone higher up, but what a stage set—and at 330 feet/101 meters what spires! The church's conversation with one avenue and two streets is brilliant. (William H. Pierson, Jr., devotes a long and fascinating chapter to the development of St. Patrick's in his volume *American Buildings and Their Architects, The Corporate and Early Gothic Styles,* Doubleday, 1978.)

Open daily 6:30 A.M.–*9:30* P.M.

---

13   Cast-Iron Architecture in New York City (mid to late 19th century) largely SoHo district: S of Houston Street, N of Canal between Broadway and West Broadway
New York, New York

JAMES BOGARDUS AND OTHERS, ARCHITECTS

Cast-iron architecture developed well over a hundred years ago, initiating a technique which presaged not only today's curtain wall construction but much of the theory of skyscraper design—to say nothing of prefabricated, standardized, demountable, and transportable building. Admitting far more daylight than masonry, cast-iron fronts revolutionized commercial architecture in much of the United States, becoming so popular that shipments of demounted buildings, at least their facades, were regularly made as far as around South America to the West Coast (following the Gold Rush).

The casting of iron was, of course, an early historic development: the Book of Genesis, 4:22, says that Tubal-cain "was the forger of all instruments of bronze and iron"; de Camp in his book *The Ancient Engineers* (Doubleday, 1963) ascribes the invention of cast iron to the Chinese in the fourth century B.C. But until controlled smelting in the Industrial Revolution, cast iron was largely employed for firebacks, balusters, and decorative features because of its friability. The Adam brothers used it often. Norman Davey in *A History of Building Materials* (Phoenix House, 1961) writes that "The first structural cast iron beams by Charles Bage (1774–1822) were used in a five-storey flax mill built at Shrewsbury in 1796 and 1797." William Fairbairn's Iron Flour Mill of 1839–41 was probably the world's first completely iron building. Of three stories and measuring 27×50 feet/8×15 meters it was erected and dismantled in London and then shipped to Istanbul. (Prefabricated, knock-down cottages of wood were

shipped to Australia as early as the 1820s.) In the early nineteenth century rapid technological developments took place in Europe, and cast iron was used frequently as a structural component, particularly as hollow columns, often even for trusses. Paxton's Crystal Palace in London (1851), of course, stunned the world with its cast- (and wrought-) iron unbelievableness. It remained for the Americans, however, to go into large-scale production of whole building fronts of this material, the iron modules of the facade replacing the masonry which once upheld the floors, hence hinting at later skyscraper construction with its completely independent-of-wall columnar grid frame. (Most, if not all, early cast-iron buildings had only iron fronts: sides and backs and often partitions were of masonry. Such was the case with Corlies' and Bogardus' famous—but now destroyed—Harper & Brothers Building of 1854 in New York.) Daniel D. Badger and James Bogardus were leading advocates—and leading rivals—in developing cast iron in this country. Badger was head of the Architectural Iron Works and turned out in his plant an almost endless variety of cast iron; Bogardus, more an architect, was "inventor and patentee," who designed buildings but had others build them. His most stupendous work was a warehouse he sent to Cuba measuring 400×600 feet/122×183 meters!

It is not within the scope of this guidebook to explore further the background of this exotic phase in American architecture: its aim is to point out distinguished examples. However, two more general remarks concerning the "style" might be in order. Cast iron, successful because of the repetitive copies it could turn out in a semifireproof form, possessed as a consequence a "happy adaptability to ornament and decoration." Thus most of its examples—for better if one is a romantic, for worse if a misanthrope—are at times lively with fantastically intricate capitals and decoration. It finally developed such popularity that stone construction began to imitate iron! (The energetic Friends of Cast-Iron Architecture give small magnets to all new members so that they can themselves determine what lurks behind the paint.) Secondly, the nature of cast-iron framing logically developed a sharply defined metronomed beat, at times one of great vitality, thus anticipating the modular construction of today. Cast iron began to meet serious challenges when Carnegie introduced inexpensive rolled steel members, the first of which were used by Jenney in his Home Insurance Building of 1885. Steel has far greater tensile strength, hence greater reliability in spans, could be employed for beams as well as columns, and thus a total structural skeleton of one material, wrapped in fireproofing, was rendered feasible. However, a few examples of cast iron date from the early 1900s. (Like cast iron, exposed steel is vulnerable to fire, but it can be more easily fireproofed than the former. Tile fireproofing for metal construction basically dates from the early 1870s.)

The greatest remaining single monument to cast iron—and now a National Registered Landmark—is New York's former E. V. Haughwout Store at 488 Broadway, northeast corner of Broome Street, by J. P. Gaynor and Mr. Badger's Architectural Iron Works (1856–57). As Paul Goldberger wrote in his extremely useful book *New York, The City Observed* (Vintage Books, 1979), "It is one of those rare pieces of architecture in which everything fits together perfectly and yet with room for passion." The Haughwout Store combines the modular and the rich decoration mentioned above in its two extraordinarily handsome facades, which are largely a copy of Sansovino's library in Venice of 1536. The building is further notable in that Elisha Otis here installed the country's first "safety elevator," with this invention making the skyscraper possible. Beyond Haughwout, so to speak, lies a vast sea of cast iron in an area of wholesale markets, electric supply houses, and—more recently—numerous hopeful artists in a once-forgotten midriff section of the island which the routine New Yorker formerly rarely experienced, sandwiched as it is between the financial district and Greenwich Village. Sir Nikolaus Pevsner calls this SoHo area (south of Houston and bounded by West Broadway and Canal and Crosby Streets) "a veritable museum of cast iron, a greater concentration than anywhere else in the world." In 1973 it was designated a Historic District by the Landmarks Preservation Commission. Here whole streets of smartly profiled cast-iron buildings, many with enormous panes of glass, frame city blocks, their later-added fire escapes (dating from the 1870s following the Chicago fire) only partially blurring the precision of their hundred-year-old proud flair. Greene Street, its sidewalks encrusted with years of detritus, produces several gutsy becolumned facades. Broadway (427 to 654), Broome, and Mercer streets have fine examples, while farther uptown on 23rd Street, a bit west of 5th Avenue (32 to 46), an imposing white-painted former department store lines the south side of the street. For a complete guide to this extraordinary richness contact the Friends of Cast-Iron Architecture, 235 East 87th Street, New York 10028. They are doing a wonderful job in documenting and propagandizing this too little-known lode.

Best seen from the street

An excellent recycling of an old cast-iron building can be seen at Broadway and 11th Street. Designed with Venetian overtones in 1868 by John Kellum, it once housed the McCreery Department Store (among other uses—including a shoe factory). In 1973 the structure was imaginatively remodeled by architect Stephen B. Jacobs to produce 144 luxury apartments. As the side facade is 221 feet/67 meters long, its white-painted four floors of cast iron (a fifth, set back on the top, is new) deliver a sparkling asset to the street. The building's salvation and transformation was initiated by the community, the Landmarks Preservation Commission, and the Friends of Cast-Iron Architecture, and through their petitioning code variances were granted by the Board of Standards and Appeals. Everybody—including the owners—benefited.

14 Central Park (1859–76)
5th Avenue to Central Park West (8th Avenue), between 59th and 110th Streets
New York, New York

FREDERICK L. OLMSTED AND CALVERT VAUX, DESIGNERS

It is important to realize when strolling, sitting, boating, biking, playing, or seeing plays, that Central Park's cornucopia of delights, while seemingly almost spontaneous, has behind its creation just as much functional analysis as goes into the design of a major building complex. Soil conditions, drainage and irrigation, water supply, sewage disposal, classification of circulation (pedestrian, horse, bicycle, vehicular, urban crosstown), provisions for the young, provisions for the old—let alone tree, shrub, and plant characteristics—are merely obvious decision-demanding elements which fashioned the extraordinary heart and lungs of Manhattan Island. As Olmsted wrote, "Every foot of the park's surface, every tree and bush, as well as every arch, roadway and walk has been fixed where it is with a *purpose*" (from Henry Hope Reed and Sophia Duckworth's highly recommended *Central Park, A History and a Guide,* Clarkson N. Potter Inc., 1972).

Central Park was not just a piece of fortuitously available open land in mid-nineteenth-century N.Y.C. which the city simply "fenced off," as Mr. Reed, its former curator, so succinctly put it. It represents landscape architecture at its technical and esthetic peak, the work of a true professional, designing the first significant park in this country. Its 840 acres/340 hectares were municipally acquired in spite of political shenanigans, the infighting of vested interests, and even the objections of many bankers and real estate men. But dedicated civic—and a few political—leaders backed it as an essential component for the rapidly expanding city, William Cullen Bryant leading the clan. The concept was officially approved in 1856, with Frederick Law Olmsted hired to supervise the clearing of the rough, hovel- and hog-infested land, and to drain its swamps. (The site at this time already included the old, rectangular Croton Reservoir, built in 1842, with 106 acres/43 hectares of land for a new reservoir—the present—acquired in 1852. The Arsenal, by Martin E. Thompson, had been completed in 1848.) A competition was then announced (1857) for the design of the new park, but Olmsted, because of his "in-house" position, did not consider entering it until urged to collaborate by and with his friend Calvert Vaux, an English-born architect. (Olmsted also got permission to compete from

his boss.) That theirs was the finest of thirty-three entries was due to Olmsted's passionate, if self-taught, background in landscaping, plus his immense grass-roots knowledge, buttressed, of course, by Vaux's professional know-how and sense of space modeling. Moreover the two had tramped over every millimeter of the acreage. (As background, Vaux had come to the United States in 1850 to work with Andrew Jackson Downing, the famous horticulturist, who died in a tragic accident in 1852. Olmsted himself had studied at first hand Downing's "picturesque" or romantic school of design and expanded his horizons abroad by minutely examining the English school of landscaping from the work of Capability Brown to Repton to Paxton.)

In effect there are two Central Parks, the reservoir (roughly between 86th and 96th streets) nearly cutting it in two with the northern section rougher than the southern and with its topography left more natural. The lower part also has about 50 per cent more land area and far more amenities. The main entrance is at 59th–60th streets and 5th Avenue where it could serve as the gateway for the greatest number of people, for when the park was laid out there were few buildings in its area. This entry also leads to the Mall, double-lined with elms—and one of the few formal elements of the entire design. This promenade is punctuated by the Naumburg Bandshell and climaxed by the Terrace and Bethesda Fountain, which overlook the rowing pond with The Ramble on the far side. The Mall, which is almost .25 mile/.4 kilometer long, lends useful contrast to the picturesque naturalness about it.

So as not to interfere with crosstown traffic—and vice versa—there are four transverse roads (65th–66th, 79th, 85th, and 97th streets) which were mandated by the competition and which Olmsted and Vaux depressed across much of the width of the park. There are, of course, surface carriage and automobile roads which can also be used. (Roads, underpasses, and bridges—the cast-iron ones especially—all merit attention.) With the help of Ignaz Anton Pilat, an Austrian-born botanist, Olmsted and Vaux supervised the installation of several million trees, bushes, and plants (Henry Reed mentions "four or five million" by 1873) representing hundreds of species.

One might say that the only trouble with Central Park is its overwhelming success, for although most physical encroachments have been kept in check, the place is so wonderful it is being almost trampled to death, and with drastic budget cutbacks, a devoted staff cannot now keep up proper maintenance. (Crime and drugs have also become problems.) It is almost impossible to imagine New York City without the park: indeed America's concept of urban living was never the same after it was opened, cities across the country emulating the example. Olmsted took his humanism and technology, his "social democracy" it has been called, as far as California, becoming one of the first advocates of Yosemite Valley and its preservation (1864), a forerunner of the National Park concept which was initiated at Yellowstone in 1872. (He also came back to California to be the landscape architect of Berkeley in 1866, with Vaux, and of Stanford University in 1888, with his son.) Olmsted's concern for man in the wilds or in the city was matched only by his ability to implement this concern: no one has physically enriched the nation more.

Prospect Park (1867–72) in Brooklyn—take the IRT No. 2 to the Eastern Parkway stop—is New York's other great monument to Olmsted and Vaux's skills. Though only 526 acres/213 hectares versus 840/340 for Central Park, it is more felicitously landscaped. Most of its land was left to the city by Edwin C. Litchfield's heirs, plus their 1856 Italianate villa which faces Prospect Park West. McKim, Mead & White's formalistic Brooklyn Museum (1895–1914) is also set in the park off Eastern Parkway at Washington Avenue. In January 1980 it was announced that a thorough rehabilitation of the park would begin. This will include repairs to the Soldiers' and Sailors' Memorial Arch at the entry plus other structures and their landscaping.

Both parks open a half hour before sunrise to midnight

---

15   Brooklyn Bridge (1869–83)
City Hall Park, Manhattan; Cadman Plaza, Brooklyn
New York, New York

JOHN AUGUSTUS ROEBLING AND WASHINGTON ROEBLING,
ENGINEERS

The Crystal Palace in London (1851), the Brooklyn Bridge in New York (1869–83), and the Eiffel Tower in Paris (1889) constitute the greatest spatial conquests of the nineteenth century, as Siegfried Giedion (*Space, Time and Architecture,* Harvard University Press, 1941 et seq.) and James Marston Fitch (*American Architecture: The Historical Forces,* Houghton Mifflin, 1966), among others, have so excitingly shown us. The Palace covered unheard-of spaces with an all-glass prefab (the building was later dismantled and moved to another site: sadly, it burned in 1941); the bridge spanned a staggering horizontal space (1,595 feet/486 meters); while the Eiffel Tower's height of 984 feet/300 meters was unmatched for years—until our own

Empire State Building (q.v.) was finished at 1,250 feet/381 meters (1931—without TV mast). Architecture and architectural engineering would never be the same: the development of the modern movement was inevitable. The study of history is the shape of the tool, and these heroic structures showed man "tools" he had never previously deemed possible.

The Brooklyn Bridge established a scale so gigantic that one gasped —and one still does. A walk even partly along its centrally placed, elevated pedestrian way ranks among the great urban experiences, with the web and woof of the cables weaving the sky together to envelop the astounding backdrop of Manhattan. (The impression by car is disappointing because of the boxed-in structure of the vehicular level.)

John Augustus Roebling (1806–69), who came to this country in 1831 from his native Germany, arrived here with a splendid education and a burning faith in steel suspension bridges. The Chinese had used iron chain spans before the seventh century (Carl Condit mentions A.D. 580), and it is certain that a chain bridge of wrought iron was erected in England by 1741, the 70-foot/21-meter Wynch Bridge. Wrought iron reached its peak with Telford's startling Menai Strait Bridge (1819–26), which still leaps 570 feet/174 meters—"the grandfather of all modern suspension bridges" (David B. Steinman). James Finley and Charles Ellet in the U.S.A. had also done pioneering work, and Marc Séguin in France in 1824 had erected near Tournon the world's first "wire rope" bridge, a foot span still in use. Roebling was, of course, familiar with all of these and the others they inspired, but he had greater and more improbable notions in mind. His first American effort (1845) was at Pittsburgh, and, as he progressed, he developed the concept of "spinning" and tightly binding with a "jacket" the multitude of cables that stretched their catenaries over vast rivers. Previously the cables had been only partially clamped and rarely covered.

The Brooklyn Bridge's center span of 1,595 feet/486 meters was more than 50 per cent longer than the previous record, which was that of the Wheeling Bridge in West Virginia (q.v.). Its double-arched 276.5-foot/84-meter-high Gothic towers may seem quaint today (actually their shapes approximate the mathematical forces), while Montgomery Schuyler felt (1883) that the "disappearance" of the cables into the tower head was an "architectural barbarism." The employment of both vertical and inclined cables as floor stays (to uphold the deck) represented unnecessary complexity—widely "fanned hangers" are today obsolete—but their spreading angles do reach out to clutch, like some giant web, both decking and pedestrians. The bridge, almost needless to add, conquered the world. Tragically, Roebling's foot was crushed soon after the bridge was begun and he died from gangrene. His talented son, Washington, supervised the construction, only himself to suffer from caisson disease (although he did not die until 1926). The Roeblings, father and son, opened the eyes of humanity; their Brooklyn Bridge was not substantially exceeded until the George Washington Bridge of 1931 (q.v.).

---

16   The Dakota (1880–84)
Central Park West at 72nd Street
New York, New York

HENRY JANEWAY HARDENBERGH, ARCHITECT

The first major apartment houses, indeed the first megastructures, in this country were erected by the Pueblos in the twelfth century. At Pueblo Bonito in New Mexico's Chaco Canyon (q.v.) there stands today the semiruin of a five-story, eight-hundred-room complex that housed probably a thousand Indians, and whereas this was the largest of which we have record, there were hundreds of smaller ones in the Four Corners area. In the latter part of the last century our major cities produced another round of high-density accommodations that add a footnote to our architectural development, and though most of them were indifferently planned (even some of the finest), several were outstanding in one facet or another. Among the most successful is The

Dakota—dubbed thus for its then far-out location—a building whose units are so well laid out, constructed, and maintained that it is today avidly cherished by its cooperative owners a hundred years after its completion. Of vague North European architectural ancestry with its steep, multidormered roof and prominent gables—Hardenbergh's first employer-teacher was German-born—its tawny brick walls (with a terra-cotta belt course) are reasonably simple and straightforward. Measuring 204.5×200.2 feet/62×61 meters, it was one of the largest of its kind when built, its seven full floors overly crowding an I-shaped courtyard. (There are two other floors under the roof which originally were intended for servants but which have been remodeled into small flats.) When it opened, an announcement in the New York *Times* called it "One of the Most Perfect Apartment Houses in the World." Hardenbergh went on to design the row houses around the corner from The Dakota (41–49 West 73rd Street), the Plaza Hotel (1907) across Central Park, and the Copley Plaza (1912) in Boston.

For contrast to the basic simplicity of The Dakota, one has only to visit **Alwyn Court Apartments** (1907–9), 180 West 58th Street, by Harde & Short. Its architects took the then highly popular terra-cotta to almost incredible heights: Francis I's salamanders crawl all over it.

Both apartments can be seen only from sidewalk

---

17   Jefferson Market Branch Library (1875–77/1967)
425 Avenue of the Americas at West 10th Street
New York, New York

FREDERICK C. WITHERS, ARCHITECT; GIORGIO CAVAGLIERI, ARCHITECT OF REHABILITATION

Refulgent on the exterior with almost all the architectural trappings which the High Victorian possessed, and highlighted within by parades of original stained-glass windows and doughtily carved black walnut doorways, the Jefferson Market Library offers a nostalgic rallying point for Greenwich Village. (Some of this Ruskin-influenced designing can be traced to the fact that both architects were British-born.) The building did not always establish an amiable forum, for a courthouse (with a few overnight cells) occupied its premises until 1932, while the notorious Women's House of Detention remained next door until 1973,

its cleared site now a cheerful community garden. Threatened with destruction when it became redundant (1958), the courthouse's venerable charms were saved by dedicated friends (including the then Mayor Wagner) to become a local library. Its legal chambers were transformed to bright and lofty reading rooms by the skill and imagination of architect Cavaglieri. He preserved where possible, put in a catwalk to conform to the building code, then accented the dark woodwork with light walls and installed new light fixtures (note that on the circular stair). He also sandblasted the brick vaulting in the basement to turn this once lugubrious spot into a fine reference room (note light fixtures here also). The multicolored exterior was thoroughly cleaned, reinforced where necessary, but left basically as was to let us savor one hundred years later one of the wildest periods of architectural hedonism. The tower, typical—indeed almost mandatory—of its era (note gargoyles), was not mere whimsy; its 98-foot/30-meter-high deck served as fire lookout for the neighborhood with fire bell at hand. One of the delights of a vanishing species.

Open Mon.–Sat.: hours vary—inquire

---

18   Flatiron Building (1901–3)
175 5th Avenue, 949 Broadway, at 23rd Street
New York, New York

D. H. BURNHAM & COMPANY, ARCHITECTS

Daniel Burnham's practice had been overwhelmingly successful—he had for one thing been chief planner and coordinator for the 1893 Chicago Columbian Exposition—when he came to New York to design its then tallest building. With the exemplary Reliance Building in Chicago (q.v.) behind him and Roman shades of the Exposition affecting his tastebuds, he put together one of the city's first all-steel frame skyscrapers: he also draped its twenty floors with a profligate amount of decoration, all arranged in the Classic pattern of attic, shaft, and basement. From the top down we find in layers a balustrade, a bold cornice, a band of maidens peeping out of blocks between windows, two-story roundheaded window framing, and finally a clutch of lions' heads —all in the four floors of the attic. Then come a row of one-story roundheaded windows (all others have flat lintels) and twelve floors of shaft broken by three eight-story vertical bands of slightly projecting windows or oriels. The relatively mild four floors of the "basement" begin with an energetic band of decoration and meet the ground with a sharply incised entry level with proper front door(s). When to the above is added rustication which marks most of the stonework (or terra-cotta), and the triangular plan which the meeting of 5th Avenue and Broadway mandated, it is small wonder that the Flatiron (technically the Fuller) Building was "the most notorious thing in New York, and attracts more attention than all the other buildings now going up put together" (*Architectural Record,* October 1902). The same article, in describing the bowed windows, adds "that the eight-story hanging oriels which diversify his [Burnham's] front are so spaced as on the one hand not visibly to destroy their own purpose of gaining sidelong views out of certain favored offices, and, on the other, as agreeably to diversify the monotony of the wall without impairing the effect of the repetition of its equable fenestration." Lavish decoration aside, the Flatiron was a

local structural pioneer. Perhaps prophetically, its shape is such "that, during a storm, people are sometimes whirled off the side-walk and plate-glass shop-windows shivered" (Baedeker's *United States,* 1909).

Open during business hours

---

19 U. S. Custom House (1902–9)
Bowling Green between Broadway and Whitehall Street
New York, New York

CASS GILBERT, ARCHITECT

For over 350 years this point of Manhattan Island has been occupied by a building of importance. And though the Dutch-built Fort Amsterdam, the earliest (1626), was one of impotence—not firing a shot to

halt the British takeover in 1664—its successors have often been well regarded. Fort George (1714) of modified Vauban design, was one of the best; however, it was torn down (1790) for the erection of the Government House, which burned in 1815, leaving the site empty. The masterpiece of this parade is, of course, Mr. Gilbert's competition-winning Custom House, dating from a time (i.e. before the income tax law of 1913) when customs duties were the federal government's chief source of income. In addition to its function as visual terminus of lower Broadway, the seven-story Custom House and its sculpture form one of our richest examples of early twentieth-century eclecticism. The exterior, framed by Daniel Chester French's *Four Continents,* sets up a compacted luxury of elements. Note, too, the twelve statues across the sixth floor "depicting commercial centers of the world" from Phoenicia to the early part of this century.

The great Rotunda within (135×85 feet/41×26 meters) forms one of our most monumental rooms; in it, until recently, some sixty-five clerks cleared shipping and customs papers. Interestingly, its eight murals by Reginald Marsh were not painted until 1937, and though

Marsh was far more skillful when using tempera and Chinese ink than in these murals, they add a firm chapter to the city's embellishment. (Unhappily the ocher paint of their framing helps neither murals nor room. The skylight was painted out in World War II.) Don't miss the luxuriant Regional Commissioner of Customs office (❋219–220) at the extreme right after entering. It was intended for the U. S. Secretary of State when in town.

The building's functions were moved to the World Trade Center (1973) and its future for a while was uncertain. However, late in 1978 it was announced that the federal government would totally renovate and update mechanically the building with the government occupying the upper floors and the great Rotunda used for cultural purposes. It has been designated a New York City Landmark—exterior 1965, interior 1979—and a National Historic Landmark, so its existence is now assured. In January 1980 the General Services Administration announced the winners of its design competition for the "restoration and renovation" of the U. S. Custom House: they are Marcel Breuer Associates, James Stewart Polshek & Associates, Stewart Daniel Hoban & Associates, and Goldman Sokolow Copeland.

Rotunda open Mon.–Fri. 9–5, Sat.–Sun. 1–5, except holidays

---

20   Pierpont Morgan Library (1903–7)
33 East 36th Street (entry at Annex, 29 East 36)
New York, New York

McKIM, MEAD, & WHITE, ARCHITECTS

In the last score of years of the nineteenth century it became fashionable to unveil wealth, not hide it. As architecture can be an ultimate manifestation of means, the private house from Newport to New York to North Carolina (often for the same families) came alive as never before on these shores. (In Europe domestic ostentation had been a tradition even before Jacques Coeur's house of A.D. 1443; Nicolas Fouquet made Louis XIV so jealous with the elaborateness of his *pied-à-terre* at Vaux that he spent the rest of his life in jail.) Most of New York's domestic extravaganzas are long gone or unavailable to the general public, but the library which Charles Follen McKim, of McKim, Mead & White, designed for Pierpont Morgan remains a special treasure. (The library was built next door to the Morgan house, which since has been

taken down.) Though the design of the library's central portico, with its paired (in depth) columns and its similar dimensions, probably stems from a bay of the arcades that Palladio added to the Basilica at Vicenza (1549), the marble front has a dignity of its own. (Some authorities hold that the upper floor of the Nymphaeum of Pope Julius III, 1487–1555, inspired the entry via McKim, Mead & White's Walker Art Gallery—1893—at Bowdoin College.) Note the flatness of the walls with barely projecting Doric pilasters, then the powerful contrast of the deep-seated entry. Note, too, as the guards are proud to point out, that the stones are so finely fitted that no mortar was needed—shades of ancient Greece.

In plan the building consists of entry hall and two unequal flanking rooms, plus services in the rear. McKim called on several artists to embellish his architecture, and Harry Siddons Mowbray was almost hyperactive in the ceiling of the hall and that of the East Room—both with Roman and astrological motifs. One could say of the lofty main chamber that where there were no books there was Mowbray. (Note the inlaid woodwork of the bookcases: a hidden stair stands behind two sections to give access to the balconies.) The West Room, Mr. Morgan's private study, incorporates the sumptuous sixteenth (?) century ceiling—of strangely unknown provenance—which was purchased in Florence in 1905, dismantled, pieced together, and installed in New York later that year, then "decorated" by James Wall Finn. The rest of the room comfortably acceded to its recessed and polychromed panels.

As the collection of manuscripts, books, master drawings, and book-bindings—started in the 1850s by Pierpont Morgan—continued to grow, J. P. Morgan thought that the library, which had always been available to scholars, should become a public museum and research center (1924). In 1928 a quiet annex, primarily an exhibition hall and reading room, was added on the site of the former house (Benjamin W. Morris, architect); in 1960 a meeting room and additional gallery space were appended to the north (Alexander Perry Morgan, architect); and in 1976–77, an office annex and conference room, much of it belowground so as not to dominate, were put on the northwest corner (Platt, Wyckoff & Coles, architects). Sumptuous books and works of art in a sumptuous setting.

Open Tues.–Sat. 10:30–5, Sun. 1–5, closed Aug.: donation

---

21 New York Public Library (1902–11)
5th Avenue between 40th and 42nd Streets
New York, New York

CARRERE & HASTINGS, ARCHITECTS

The facade of the New York Public Library represents the Beaux-Arts School of architecture at its best, but it is the building's extraordinarily sympathetic relation to the street which is beyond compare—and beyond the veils of any style. Set back 75 feet/23 meters from 5th Avenue (Hastings fought for more), every foot has been carefully developed: note that the planting begins at the sidewalk itself on either side of the gentle steps (and seating alcoves), with E. C. Potter's famous lions (whose heads have never been known to turn) standing guard. We are then introduced to a relaxed parterre which stretches the full length of the 390-foot/119-meter-long building to terminate in well-landscaped retreats at each end. Planting—here backed by good-sized trees—is picked up again to frame the terrace on its inner edge and sof-

ten the flanks of the building. On either side and slightly in front of the triple-arched entry stands a monumental urn, with a fountain set in each angle of the projected portico, adorned by statues of Truth and Beauty by Frederick MacMonnies (1920). The coupled Corinthian columns obviously establish a commanding entrance, but withal this rarely intimidates or becomes too serious, primarily because of the terrace treatment and the invitation extended from the street itself. (The planting is, of course, much finer today than when the library was finished.)

On entering the lobby we are confronted with what many would hold to be the architects' only serious error: to get to the books on the third floor "it was expected that the public would be required to use the stairs"—all seventy-three of them—or wonder and wander down the corridor to find two half-hidden elevators, then walk back to midpoint on the top floor. Flagellating. The great reading room itself is one of the finest spaces in the city, its lofty proportions and the beautifully tempered quality of its bilateral lighting making it virtually a perfect reading and research spot. Moreover it is "undisturbed" by masses of books, having only a modest band of reference volumes around three sides. A service spine divides the room into halves but the spine's height was kept low so as to allow spatial unity—and a full view of a ceiling of prodigious richness. This central service facility is placed directly over the stacks on the lower floors so that efficiency of book retrieval is excellent.

The library, which is privately and municipally supported—and desperately needs more funding—represents the consolidation (1895) of the Astor and Lenox Libraries and the Tilden Trust. Occupying the site of the first Croton Reservoir, the building's design was reached by a two-stage competition (1897), being won by two architects who had formerly worked for McKim, Mead & White (who had also entered the competition and, one gathers, did not relish third place). John Carrere (1858–1911) was unfortunately killed in an automobile accident just a few months before the library was dedicated but it was sufficiently finished for him to appreciate its sterling qualities. G. H. Edgell in his book *The American Architecture of To-day* (Scribner's, 1928) feels that Hastings was not satisfied with the central pavilion, and made a proposal for doubling the single end columns and statues, and elaborating its corners—which Edgell fully illustrates—and "made a provision in his will for the means to carry out the change." This, as can be seen, was never done.

Open Mon., Tues., Wed. 10–9, Fri.–Sat. 10–6, except holidays

Directly behind the library lies **Bryant Park** (1884–1934), Avenue of the Americas between 40th and 42nd Streets. (Open sunrise–9 P.M.) Covering two thirds of a block (9.6 acres/3.9 hectares), the park's simple, symmetrical plan consists of a central greensward surrounded by well-organized trees on four sides. The Lowell Memorial Fountain (by Charles A. Platt—1912) greets one at the west (main) entry, with a statue of William Cullen Bryant (by Herbert Adams—1911) adorning the east. Its modest changes in levels, especially at the quiet east end, the definition of circulation, the degrees of separation of active from passive (note sitting alcoves at east), and the quality of planting, including the use of ivy as ground cover, make this a distinguished small mid-city park. New York's Crystal Palace occupied the site from 1853 until it burned five years later. It became Bryant Park—named for William Cullen Bryant—in 1884. Its scope is of unexpected interest in that it technically wraps around the library and extends to 5th Avenue itself to include the entrance terrace. Thus Thomas Hastings, one of the architects of the library, was also responsible for the park's basic architectural design, notably the raised terrace adjacent to the library at the rear and the two stone kiosks (originally comfort stations) at the west end. Strangely the park encountered neglect beginning in the 1920s, until in 1933 during the Depression, the Architects' Emergency Committee held a competition—limited to unemployed ar-

chitects and draftsmen—for its rejuvenation. This was won by Lusby Simpson, and the landscaping and planting we see today was carried out in 1934 by the Parks Department under its new commissioner Robert Moses, with Aymar Embury II architect to the department. This small bit of urban delight was designated a Scenic Landmark by the Landmarks Preservation Committee in 1974. It is, however, not safe to visit early in the morning or after dusk.

22 Grand Central Station (1903–13)
42nd Street between Vanderbilt and Lexington Avenues
New York, New York

WARREN & WETMORE, REED & STEM, ARCHITECTS; W. J. WILGUS, CHIEF ENGINEER

Grand Central Station—an amusingly egregious title—is far more than a building, it is the most important nodal point and transportation interchange in the city and a fulcrum for the entire East Side. Moreover,

as the multitude of tracks which feed the terminal demand considerable space both lateral and linear, its urban impact has been immense. The first Grand Central (1869–71), with a 200-foot/61-meter-wide arched train shed, was vastly expanded in 1899–1901, both stations having been served by surface steam trains that chugged in and out by the hundreds to make a grimy slash of what was then a very depressing 4th Avenue. In 1902 a smoke-generated accident prompted the state to require electric locomotives for passenger service into the city after 1910, and spurred by the 1901 decision of the rival Pennsylvania Railroad to tunnel under two rivers into Manhattan (it had previously terminated in Jersey City, its Long Island branch in Queens), the directors of the New York Central/New Haven railroads decided on an ambitious new solution. The result was so momentous that Carl W. Condit wrote, "The New York terminals of the Pennsylvania and the New York Central railroads are not only the greatest works of construction ever undertaken anywhere for the purpose of handling rail traffic, they are also the most extensive and most impressive civic projects in the United States built by private capital" (*American Building Art, The Twentieth Century,* Oxford University Press, 1961). This referred, of course, to the time before Rockefeller Center.

The boldness of the new Grand Central concept not only produced an extraordinary terminal, in time it transformed an eyesore—the noisome, open trench of trains on 4th Avenue—into the city's finest residential street. This, in turn, was later rebuilt as the most prestigious office building lineup in New York, with much of the property, incidentally, owned by the railroads via air rights. With its two lanes of traffic divided by a central landscaped mall 4th was appropriately rechristened Park Avenue. Beneath this comely boulevard are nearly fourteen full blocks of tracks—from near Lexington Avenue almost to Madison and from 42nd to 50th streets where they squeeze together—a process which involved a fantastic amount of clearing, excavating, and eventually tunneling. Colonel William John Wilgus (1865–1949), the brilliant engineer, who in four years was responsible for almost all of the rail layout, looped some of the tracks around the terminal itself, so that trains could exit without reversing, and double-decked many of the rest, with express trains utilizing the upper level and suburban commuter trains the lower. Freight and mail—a major post office is adjacent—have their own spurs. In all there are over a hundred platforms, and in the 1940s as many as 600 trains a day used the station: even today they number over 400 with some 500,000 people reputedly passing through the terminal.

On top of this maze of underground rails sits the notable Grand Central Station, the design competition for which was won (1903) by Reed & Stem of St. Paul, Minnesota, architects who had specialized in railroad stations. (Also atop this rail net rises a clutch of office buildings and hotels supported by a veritable forest of enormous steel piers—as Colonel Wilgus envisioned.) According to Carl Condit and his aforementioned book, William K. Vanderbilt more or less forced his cousin, Whitney Warren, along with Warren's partner Charles D. Wetmore, onto the Reed & Stem design team, and when Reed died in 1911, Warren & Wetmore took over and considerably altered the original plans, moreover taking credit "as sole architects of the terminal." (Stem, adds Mr. Condit, sued for damages and collected $400,000. Wilgus, incidentally, had left owing to a disagreement in 1907.) Whoever was chiefly responsible for the final design, it seems likely that the Paris École des Beaux-Arts-educated Warren and the Harvard-educated Wetmore were the prime architects of the main concourse, inside and out. In any case a more than distinguished building resulted, even though it has to contend with an elevated roadway across its front and around its sides. This raised road was designed contemporaneously with the station but not finished until 1920. The former New York Central Building, since 1978 the Helmsley Building, straddles Park Avenue at the 46th Street ends of the two ramps and skillfully accommodates them in its facade. Designed—like the station—by Warren & Wetmore, it was finished in 1929. The building has been thoroughly renovated and brilliantly regilded in the proper places by its new owners. Note, en passant, the pyramidal roof complete with cupola.

The plaque outside Grand Central reads "Completed in 1913 from plans of Warren & Wetmore and Reed & Stem." But whereas the exterior, highlighted by a bravely wing-borne statuary group and clock by Jules Coutan, is merely quietly authoritative in a Classic vein, the main concourse is one of the greatest spaces—anywhere—of the twentieth century, in spite of onslaughts of contemporary advertising. Measuring 120 feet/37 meters wide×375 feet/114 meters long×125 feet/38 meters high, it elevates rail travel, both on arriving and departing, into an almost noble ceremony. Overhead on the barrel-vaulted ceiling—it is suspended from the trusswork—floats Paul Helleu's painting of the heavens which some wags feel represents William K. Vanderbilt's horoscope at the time, while others claim it is merely the ecliptic reversed at the vernal equinox. Note the elegantly embellished lunettes at the window reveals. Not only is the concourse a glorious space, all about it works superbly, which, one might add, a previous N.Y.C. station picturesquely stuffed into a Roman bath did not. Grand Central's clarity and ease of circulation, no matter where one enters, is extraordinary for a structure of such complexity: much of this is probably due to Reed & Stem. In addition it is conveniently connected underground with three subways plus numerous office buildings and hotels. The Biltmore (1913) and Commodore (1916—remodeled in 1980 as the Grand Hyatt) were also designed by Warren & Wetmore. According to Harmon H. Goldstone and Martha Dalrymple, this maze of weather-protected corridors "was the inspiration for the concourse system built later under Rockefeller Center" (see their fascinating *History Preserved,* Schocken, 1976).

Threatened for years either to be demolished or surmounted by a fifty-nine-story skyscraper, Grand Central won a historic reprieve in June 1978, when the U. S. Supreme Court ruled that its Landmark status must not be infringed upon.

Open daily 5:30 A.M.*–1:30* A.M.

---

23   Woolworth Building (1911–13)
233 Broadway at Park Place
New York, New York

CASS GILBERT, ARCHITECT

The Houses of Parliament are the godfathers of this famous "Cathedral of Commerce" (as an amused member of the cloth termed it), because Frank Woolworth, on his many trips to London, admired them extrava-

gantly. When he commissioned this monument to Enterprise, he asked Cass Gilbert to design his office building "in Gothic style." The results startled the world—because of its fifty-eight-story height and structural bravura, not monastic cloaking—and whereas we may now smile at its flying buttresses, gargoyles, and other medieval trappings, the structure represents a conquest of sizable technological problems, for never before had a skyscraper soared to such a wind-exposed height (792 feet/241 meters) on non-bedrock foundations. (The previous tallest building was New York's Metropolitan Life Insurance Building, 1907, by Nicholas Le Brun. This reached 700 feet/213 meters but wind factor was less and the subsoil conditions better.) Gilbert and his engineers, the Gunvald Aus Company, came up with a brilliantly successful result: innovative struts and knee bracing for the wind, 110-foot/34-meter-deep caissons filled with concrete, for the foundations. It was the tallest building in the world from 1913 to 1930, when the Chrysler Building took title for a few months until the Empire State was topped off. Esthetically there is a conviction in the boldness of the tower that transcends its details. Be certain to see the lobby: it is dazzling. A complete overhaul, including replacement of the 4,400 old windows with new aluminum sash (operable), was commenced in 1978.

Open during business hours

---

24   International Center of Photography (1914)
5th Avenue at 94th Street
New York, New York

DELANO & ALDRICH, ARCHITECTS

Few architects of the twentieth century were as much liked—by both clients and fellow practitioners—as William Adams Delano (1874–1960). Delightful personally, he was an admired teacher at Columbia, and impeccable in his Beaux Arts architecture. He and his partner, Chester Holmes Aldrich, also Beaux-Arts-educated, were responsible for a series of distinguished buildings, mostly private houses and clubs, and when they did not use the neo-Georgian they generally turned to seventeenth–eighteenth-century France for basic but never slavish inspiration. Delano's largest commission (besides the original 1939 La Guardia terminal) was the American Embassy in Paris. One of his few structures in New York which is open to the public is the dwelling he designed for Willard Straight. It now houses the city's very active International Center of Photography. Chaste, with commendable scale, and showing some Federal-Style influence, the building bespeaks quiet elegance in both proportion and detail, an ideal city home for its wealthy diplomat and original owner.

Open Tues.–Sun. 11–5, Wed. 11–8: admission

---

25   Daily News Building (1929–30)
220 East 42nd Street
New York, New York

RAYMOND M. HOOD WITH JOHN MEAD HOWELLS,
ARCHITECTS

Raymond M. Hood and John Mead Howells won—with a Gothic-draped proposal—the 1922 competition for the design of the Chicago Tribune Building (q.v.), one of the pivotal international architectural competitions of this century. (There were 260 entries, including 54 from abroad.) Second place went to Finland's Eliel Saarinen and there were many who thought he should have won. In any case as a result Saarinen was invited to this country (1923), where he stayed with his family including his precocious thirteen-year-old son Eero. The American architectural profession was much impressed by Saarinen's entry, plus the squared-off design by Max Taut from Germany, and it seems without question that these two had a particularly strong impact on the pragmatic Raymond Hood. Thus, in 1928, when the New York *Daily News* commission came to Hood and Howells—the *News* being owned by the cousin of the proprietor of the Chicago *Tribune*—the Gothic was

forgotten and a boldly cut thirty-seven-story skyscraper resulted, with Ray Hood in charge of design. The setbacks mandated by zoning laws played their part, but the basic statement of the News Building is all Hood and all very fresh. The white brick verticality with terra-cotta and black spandrels (also of brick)—backed by red Venetian blinds—almost electrified 42nd Street, and it should be pointed out that while only every other pier is structural, the others are filled with utilities. The numerous setbacks—seen later in Rockefeller Center, on which Hood also worked—develop a convincing, well-scaled mass, one that takes off directly from the sidewalk and ends with a squared-off top to conceal elevator housing and water tanks (among the first to do so). As regards the rumor that its "vertical ribbons" of white suggest rolls of newsprint, it is just a canard. (Walter H. Kilham, Jr.'s *Raymond Hood, Architect,* Architectural Book Publishing Company, 1973, gives a fine account of this and Hood's overall contribution.) In any event the News Building ushered in a new phase of high-rise rationality, one liberated from historic cliché and one rightly confident in its geometric statement. As Russell Hitchcock wrote for the memorable *Modern Architecture, International Exhibition* at the Museum of Modern Art in 1932, it "remains the most effective skyscraper in New York." Take a look, too, at the "relief" at the entry and the towering lobby with its dramatically lit, revolving globe. A substantial annex was added in 1958 on the east side (Harrison & Abramovitz, architects).

Lobby open during business hours

The following year and down the same street (330 West 42nd) Hood pioneered another direction when he emphasized the horizontal instead of the vertical, and took the use of color to a new high in the old **McGraw-Hill Building** (1930–31). A partial industrial building in that its lower floors incorporated printing presses (until 1933), the thirty-four-story skyscraper, though economical—and in some respects profiled by the building code (except the Art Deco top)—achieves

high marks, especially its blue-green terra-cotta facing and its lobby. Its neighborhood now being the city's disgrace, and the real estate market concentrating along avenues to the east, the "Green Building," at the age of fifty, faces an uncertain future.

Incidentally, Raymond Hood's first essay in color was the **American Radiator Building** (1923–24), 40 West 40th Street, where black brick for the walls was touched at the top with gilt paint. (The budget would not permit gold leaf.) From the design point of view this use of black was to neutralize the "holes" of the windows "so they wouldn't show" and make the twenty-story, slightly Gothic structure appear more massive.

---

26 Chrysler Building (1928–30)
Lexington Avenue between 42nd and 43rd Streets
New York, New York

WILLIAM VAN ALEN, ARCHITECT

In the century of development of high-rise design probably no sky-scraper has so unabashedly explored (and exploited) a current fashion —here the Art Deco—with such synthesizing success. (Art Deco is a useful vulgarization of the Exposition Internationale des Arts Décoratifs et Industriels Modernes of 1925 in Paris.) That the fashion in the U.S.A. was ephemeral may, indeed, be due to the fact that the seventy-seven-story Chrysler Building said it all: with it the style peaked (as did the Depression). A lance-like finial jabs the clouds above the multiple arcs of the dome which flash in the sun (the topping being 185 feet/56 meters high), then gargoyles of wondrous spread poke from the high corners. Not only did a new material—stainless steel—cap a building, a new esthetic was stamped on New York's skyline. Moreover the Chrysler Building briefly set a new structural height (1,046 feet/319 meters). (Reputedly a miniature of the building's top also crowned Mr. Chrysler's automobile hood.) Glazed enamel white brick (more than 3,500,000) faces the building: note its patterns, its automotive abstractions, and the black striping near top. For at least one generation it was thought only proper to smile wryly at such stylistic exercises, but with the years we have become more tolerant and now regard what was once considered an aberration with avuncular affection. Whether we like it or not—most do—the city's architectural bouillabaisse is far richer for Mr. Chrysler's monument. (Across the top grille of a few of the building's elevator cabs is it too much to suggest the abstracted initials

of Walter Percy Chrysler?) The lobby ceiling is covered with a mural by Edward Trumbull: appropriately, it concerns energy.

The building encountered financial difficulties in 1975 and was taken over by the insurance company which held its mortgage. However, in March 1978 a complete overhaul of the entire structure and its mechanical equipment (air conditioning, etc.) was begun, including a thorough renovation of its handsome lobby and murals. As Paul Goldberger, the distinguished critic of the New York *Times* put it, "There, in one building, is all of New York's height and fantasy in a single gesture" (New York *Times,* August 18, 1980).

Lobby open during business hours

27   **Empire State Building** (1929–31)
     350 5th Avenue between 33rd and 34th Streets
     New York, New York

SHREVE, LAMB & HARMON, ARCHITECTS

The pharos of Manhattan has maintained its civic dignity and provided
its urban function (as radio and TV beamer) for over twoscore years.
It stands as a determined sentinel in a lonely niche of the island, and its
nearly foursquare, stepped-back design (tower seven by nine bays)
rises to meet almost any challenge. The Empire State Building is, in
short, a mnemonic addition to New York's profile, an almost timeless
milestone of distinguished architecture U.S.A. (It was George Washing-

ton who in 1784 reputedly termed the state the "seat of empire.")
That it was also our tallest structure from 1931 to 1971 (when the
World Trade Center, q.v., surpassed it) gave it the useful cachet as
"New York's most distinguished address" (as, of course, was planned).
The building contains eighty-five floors of offices—with primary setbacks at the 6th and 72nd levels—topped by observation platforms at
the 86th and 102nd floors, with a pylon intended (it was claimed) as
a dirigible mooring mast above. This "tower" was extended in 1951–
52—without touching the structural frame below the 102nd floor—to
serve as the consolidated television antenna for all of New York's
stations. (Although never used for lighter-than-air machines, in 1945
a B-25 bomber unfortunately hit the 79th floor while traveling at an
estimated 200 mph/322 kph. It inflicted only moderate damage to the
building.) Total height is 1,250 feet/381 meters, with television
tower 1,472 feet/449 meters. H. G. Balcom was the too little-
recognized structural engineer.

*86th- and 102nd-floor observation platforms open daily
9:30* A.M.*–midnight: admission*

---

28   Starrett-Lehigh Building (1929–31)
26th–27th Streets between 11th and 12th Avenues
New York, New York

RUSSELL G. AND WALTER R. CORY, ARCHITECTS AND
ENGINEERS

"One of the most important industrial buildings completed in the country during 1931" wrote the *Engineering News-Record* (July 7, 1932),
and even today the Starrett-Lehigh's visual boldness and economy of
means carry power. Built over the tracks of the Lehigh Valley Railroad
(and until 1966 incorporating tracks on the ground floor), this nine-to-
nineteen-story, block-square building, which stretches 652 feet/199
meters on its longer side, was designed primarily to accommodate small
(less than 250-man) manufacturing concerns. While it still does this,
there are also fireproof facilities for distribution and sales offices. A single vertical cluster of utilities allows flexible floor space, while elevators
large enough for trucks (which never have to turn around inside) give
them distributional advantages. Trailers up to 50 feet/15 meters long
can be accommodated. The reinforced concrete major section rests on a

three-story steel-framed "base" which accounts for the change in elevation treatment. (The alternate banding of continuous glass and spandrel recalls Erich Mendelsohn's Chemnitz, Germany, department store of 1929.) Yasuo Matsui was consulting architect; Purdy & Henderson consulting engineers. Rarely has a utilitarian building risen to such clean-cut positiveness of statement.

Can only be seen from street

---

29 Irving Trust Company Building (1930–31)
1 Wall Street at Broadway
New York, New York

VOORHEES, GMELIN & WALKER (1931); ADDITION BY SMITH, SMITH, HAINES, LUNDBERG & WAEHLER (1966), ARCHITECTS

Ralph Walker (1889–1973) was one of the early group of architects born in the last century who, though trained in the traditions of the Classic School of architecture (MIT, class of 1911), was continually searching for "non-historic" answers. His inquiring mind was always open to progressive developments—most of them in the 1930s and '40s coming from Europe—and perhaps the chief large building in which he had a firm hand is the handsomely turned fifty-story Irving Trust. With its upper floors stepped in profile to follow zoning regulations, the overall mass is not outstanding (or scarcely visible), but the fluidity and modulation of its limestone-revetted exterior are notable. The Broad-

way (main) facade extends around the corner to Wall Street with sophisticated continuity, while with its spandrels angled in, its lintels angled up, and the three-pane windows slightly angled outward—direct influences of Art Deco—a quiet but arresting pulsation is established that anticipates the current revolt against the taut-skin school of high-rise design. Much of this flair is continued in the sympathetic, thirty-story addition by Smith, Smith, Haines, Lundberg & Waehler, the successors of the earlier firm(s).

Irving Trust's limestone exterior offers little hint of the extraordinary reception room—the Red Room—inside the 1 Wall Street entry. Designed for customers who wish to consult high-level bank officers— the main banking floor was then on another floor (it is now in the new building)—it is one of the country's great rooms, with red, orange, and gold mosaics embracing completely its four walls and ceiling. Bronze accents and framing for the doors and windows (note muntin geometry) complete the scene. The client wanted "an inviting and friendly, rather than austerely monumental or over-impressive" room (*Architecture,* September 1931), and Hildreth Meière, who designed the mosaics, and Ralph Walker, who helped supervise their production in Germany, achieved a brilliant result. Note that the colors are darker near the marble dado and lighten progressively toward the ceiling; note, too, that walls, ceiling, and the shape of the two piers are all irregular surfaces. There are hints here of Ragnar Østberg's Golden Room in Stockholm's Town Hall (1923), but hints only: the Red Room is superb.

Open during business hours

---

30   20th-Century Suspension Bridges in New York City
New York, New York

OTHMAR H. AMMANN, CHIEF ENGINEER

The great suspension bridges of New York City (with the exception of
the Brooklyn Bridge—q.v.), along with those of San Francisco, account for five of the seven mightiest spans in the United States. Moreover, all five show some imprint of O. H. Ammann, who was born in
Schaffhausen, Switzerland, in 1879 and came to this country—like
Roebling before him—because of its almost unlimited opportunities
compared to his native Europe. Not long after he began work with the
Port Authority of New York and New Jersey in 1925, his lyrical monuments could be seen lacing the city together. The Outerbridge Crossing
Bridge (1928) and Goethals (1928), both cantilever; Bayonne
(1931), still the largest arch bridge in the world; and four suspension
bridges—George Washington (1931), Bronx-Whitestone (1939),
Throgs Neck (1961), and Verrazano-Narrows (1964)—all show his
hand, often as chief designer. The bridges in San Francisco, where he
served as adviser, are the Golden Gate (1937—q.v.), and the double-
span San Francisco-Oakland Bay Bridge (1936).

The **George Washington Bridge** first captured public and professional
admiration when the length of its main span (3,500 feet/1,067 meters)
almost doubled that of any other in existence. Comprising over 25,000
individual, parallel wires made up into 61 strands, with its 3-foot/.9-
meter-in-diameter cables (still to be surpassed), this bridge stunned the
world by its technology. Its towers were to have been revetted with
stone but fortunately were spared this fate. Cass Gilbert was the consulting architect. The **Bronx-Whitestone** has, however, captured the eye
of the purist by virtue of the sheer elegance of its towers, for its span
(2,300 feet/701 meters) is much less than that of the George Washington. The sparse mathematics of these pylons are still incomparable. Sad
to relate, however, the boldly honed original deck has been compromised by the introduction of trusses along its upper edge to prevent
wind oscillation. This wind factor has also put a load on other recent
bridges. The **Verrazano-Narrows Bridge** is, as is well known, the
longest in the world (4,260 feet/1,298 meters—just 60 feet/18 meters
more than Golden Gate), and while superb to experience—like any
great span—it does not carry the magic of Golden Gate, due in large
part to the setting of the latter. Structurally it does not represent any
noticeable advance in bridge design over the California example of over
a quarter century earlier, and there is a heaviness at the top of the

towers of the Verrazano Bridge, whose arched portals seem excessive at
87 feet/26 meters deep at center by 28 feet/8.5 meters wide, especially
when compared to the Bronx-Whitestone. As a detail, the Verrazano
lamp standards are of insensitive design. But try all of New York's
bridges; each has its rewards, and each represents a staggering achievement. Moreover the firm of Ammann & Whitney was associated as
structural engineers with architects on a number of the most important
buildings in this book (see Index). Rest in peace, Dr. Ammann
(1879–1965): you have vastly enriched the world by your gossamer
imagination in steel.

---

31   Rockefeller Center (1931–40)
5th Avenue–Avenue of the Americas, 48th–51st Streets
New York, New York

REINHARD & HOFMEISTER; CORBETT, HARRISON &
MacMURRAY; HOOD & FOUILHOUX, PRINCIPAL ARCHITECTS

The essential lesson of Rockefeller Center is its careful grouping of harmonious buildings about a scintillating central focus. This has been so
obvious for so long that it is more than puzzling that subsequent multi-
skyscraper developments have ignored this, including, it should be
added, Rockefeller Center's own expansion westward (post-1940)
across the Avenue of the Americas—the design of which is not relevant
here. The thirteen original buildings are, forty years after birth, a bit
dated with their limestone facing and cast aluminum spandrels, but they
are so mutually respectful, their buildup of scale from six stories to sev-
enty so adroitly handled, and the "waste space" of the sunken plaza
and its promenade so fascinating, that this has become the spontaneous
core of New York City, just as the agora was in ancient Greece, and the
piazza is in today's Italy. The seasonally planted passeggiata from 5th
Avenue down the promenade to the plaza, where the umbrellas of
summer alternate with the ice skaters of winter, where the flags of the
United Nations emblazon the sky (and welcome foreign visitors), together produce a free, non-stop, open-air theater. And however we may
regard Paul Manship's Prometheus in the light of today's sculptural excursions, it furnishes an extremely important visual termination of the
mall axis. Levitating as it does, this gold-leaf figure sparkles in the sun
long after the sun has left in darkness the facades of the skyscrapers

behind it: Prometheus indeed brought fire to man—you can see it glow
any bright day for several hours after twelve noon in Rockefeller Center.

As a group of buildings the Center heralded a whole new concept of
coordinated city development: each building working with the others—
and all to the street. The thirty-three-story 14 West 49 building was
even oriented north-south to cast minimum shadow on the plaza. An
underground pedestrian concourse—which boasts over two hundred
shops and restaurants—ties the entire complex together. (This was
completely refurbished in 1979 by the Walker Group.) From the
design point of view note that part of the original buildings' subtlety
comes from the varying widths of the vertical bands of limestone,
reflecting (generally) the column spacing behind. (The uniform solid-

glass-solid "striping" of the new units across the Avenue of the Americas is lifeless in comparison.) More greenery in the first Center would have been in order, but in its tiny mall and its lively plaza—and in the space celebration between them—we find a few strategic square feet becoming the core for acres of building. Man becomes alive here, a participant, even if vicariously, as he observes, is observed, and absorbs. This imperishable lesson was incredibly ahead of its time.

It is useful to recall that Rockefeller Center was initially planned as a complex based on a new Metropolitan Opera House, the opera having outgrown its quarters on 39th Street. Benjamin W. Morris III and Harvey Wiley Corbett—both architects familiar with large-scale enterprises —made grandiose schemes. The Depression, among other factors, killed this and to salvage the investment in the already assembled land, Mr. Rockefeller developed the beginnings of the Rockefeller Center we see today. L. Andrew Reinhard and Henry Hofmeister are generally credited with its basic scheme, with Raymond Hood contributing significantly to the design of the main buildings.

No discussion of the complex would be complete without mention of its inside mecca, the Radio City Music Hall, a theater which half the nation—and much of the world—either has seen or would like to see: some quarter of a billion have thus far done so. Entering under a low but roomy ticket sale area, one is thrown into a breathtaking lobby 60 feet/18 meters tall and 150 feet/46 meters long, chandeliers dangling, mirrors sparkling, and broad stair tempting at the end. With the entry thus set, one proceeds into the great auditorium to encounter an aurora of semicircular bands of light which spread outward and upward with geometric rapture. There is no theater interior which can match it. The design was in part by the then twenty-nine-year-old Edward Durell Stone, bolstered, one understands, by the Music Hall's impresario, Samuel "Roxy" Rothafel, and his reaction to a sunset at sea. Donald Deskey was responsible for the interior decoration.

In recent years the Music Hall's 6,200 seats were rarely filled and the theater lost vast sums annually. In April 1979 a "master plan" for a completely new entertainment approach was announced—one stressing live productions—relieving fears that the Hall would be closed and the site used for an office block. As a New York *Times* editorial (January 10, 1978) had put it: "If Radio City Music Hall really closes . . . it will be a little like closing New York." A thorough internal restoration of the Art Deco magnificence of the former movie palace (the largest in the world) was also announced, and in June of that year the completely renovated theater reopened to tumultuous acclaim.

RCA Building Observation Roof at 70th floor open daily, except Dec. 25; Apr.–Sept. 9 A.M.*–11* P.M.*, Oct.–Mar. 9–7: admission*

32 United Nations Secretariat Building (1947–50)
1st Avenue between 42nd and 48th Streets
New York, New York

WALLACE K. HARRISON, DIRECTOR OF PLANNING; MAX
ABRAMOVITZ, DEPUTY DIRECTOR; LE CORBUSIER, SVEN
MARKELIUS, OSCAR NIEMEYER, N. D. BASSOV, MEMBERS OF
ADVISORY COMMITTEE

This noble building changed the pattern of skyscraper design in more ways than has been generally recognized. First, the architects—partly under Corbusier's influence—made the building a pure, unflinching slab in form, with no breaks, no setbacks, with its broad sides of glass and its narrow (72 feet/22 meters) ends solidly sheathed with marble. Secondly, they were the first to recognize that the mechanics of air conditioning in a tall structure needed more accommodation than a basement or rooftop could provide. Its designers thus—startlingly for the time—boldly introduced four service floors between roof and ground (sixth, sixteenth, twenty-eighth, and thirty-nineth floors), and expressed them as esthetic and scale assets instead of camouflaged mechanics. Thirdly, they, for better or worse, gave an imprimatur to the curtain wall, a prefabricated skin enclosure totally independent of structure. (Cf. the Hallidie Building of 1918 in San Francisco.) At the UN this curtain wrapping used greenish tinted glass (to screen the sun's heat) and greenish glass spandrels, the two together reflecting the changing skies and the dapplings of sun on adjacent buildings, an effect then unheard of. The features mentioned above are now, a generation or more later, routine, but they were largely pioneered on the banks of the East River by the staff mentioned above buttressed by over a dozen other international consultants. It should be added that Le Corbusier (1887–1965), the Swiss-born French representative on the design team—and probably the greatest architect since Michelangelo—was by temperament not team-oriented, and his sessions with his United Nations confreres were rarely harmonious, in spite of the dedicated efforts of Wallace Harrison. Corbu championed vigorously, for instance, for brise-soleils, or louvers, to protect the broad west side from the hot afternoon sun. This works admirably in semitropical Rio's Ministry of Education (1942), for which Corbusier was consultant and Oscar Niemeyer architect—fine echoes of which can be seen here—and in Le Corbusier's first proposal of brise-soleil (1933) for a project in Algiers. However, movable exterior "blinds" would not be practical with New York's snow and ice, while the sun's heat load could be solved by beefing up the air conditioning on the west side and by the use of tinted glass, as has become standard practice. The final Secretariat Building, the thirty-nine-story nerve center (tombstone?) for the hopes of the world, nonetheless possesses a poetry which even the flaccidity of the Assembly scarce diminishes. Details of the curtain wall and grilles of service floors are fussy by today's tastes—"a Christmas package wrapped in cellophane" wrote Lewis Mumford (*The New Yorker,* September 15, 1951)—and some of the interior decisions regarding office space were questionable. Lamentably, Markelius' proposals for an approach mall westward to connect the UN Building with Lexington

Avenue never materialized. But from the river (one of the finest boat trips available), from the FDR Drive (preferably northbound), or even from the street, there is greatness here.

Tours of the UN complex daily 9:15–4:45, except Jan. 1, Christmas week: admission. Secretariat interior not open to public

---

33   Lever House (1950–52)
390 Park Avenue between 53rd and 54th Streets
New York, New York

SKIDMORE, OWINGS & MERRILL, ARCHITECTS

Lever House, diagonally opposite the Seagram Building (q.v.), was a pivotal skyscraper when built, and though its visual strength has been cruelly vitiated by a 54th Street neighbor's unflattering imitation, Lever's contribution was great. Its chief legacy to the city—and to architecture—lies in its seemingly profligate use of site. As a one-company headquarters (there is no rental space), a certain freedom was built in: SOM seized this opportunity to make this the first "prestige" office block, and to free most of the ground level of enclosure so that the pedestrian could stroll through and under, with an open-to-sky garden court in the center. A one-story computer and stenographic floor stretches across the Park Avenue frontage, airily perched on pilotis. Then soaring above all, a slender slab in form and with pellucid visual detachment from the horizontality below, rise eighteen floors of offices in a precisely rectangular, blue-green glass package that just skirts the flashy. The contrast of the vertical with the horizontal is great, while the "liberation" of the site is superb. Gordon Bunshaft was chief of design; Weiskopf & Pickworth, structural engineers; Raymond Loewy Associates, interiors. One of the generative pioneers.

Ground exhibition floor open during business hours

---

34 Manufacturers Hanover Trust Company (1953–54)
5th Avenue at 43rd Street
New York, New York

SKIDMORE, OWINGS & MERRILL, ARCHITECTS

SOM's reputation for innovative architecture—for years no firm could touch them in this regard—got much of its initial credibility with Lever House (q.v.) and this four-and-a-half-story branch bank. For Manufacturers Hanover not only shattered the then lingering myth that banks must hide behind Roman columns, the architects even took the sacred vault out of the basement and put it almost on the sidewalk. A sheet of .5-inch/13-millimeter plate glass is the only protection provided. Needless to say, this iconoclasm revolutionized the art of bank design—and also elevated vaults into mid-twentieth-century sculpture, here the work of Henry Dreyfuss. In addition, since the working floors are wrapped solely in glass—at the time the largest ever installed at 22 feet/6.7 meters high by 9.8 feet/2.9 meters wide—the interior, being aglow with an unbroken luminous ceiling (of sufficient lumen output to minimize ex-

ternal reflections), extends an invitation for all to enter. The bank's entrance has been criticized as being "incidental," and "not on 5th Avenue," but this is carping: the main item on 5th Avenue is the view of the stainless steel and bronze vault door and the panorama of the banking floor. On the inside, the first floor serves for speedy banking services, while the loftier second, reached by moving stair, is for more lengthy transactions. This upper floor is actually a mezzanine, being inset on the two street sides so that spatially the two public floors are in visual league, and share, actually, the same two-story-tall curtains. This mezzanine is highlighted by a 70-foot/21-meter-long golden sheet-steel screen by Harry Bertoia, a beautiful piece of sculpture which establishes a magnificent partnership with the architecture. The upper floors are occupied by loan offices, bank departments, and boardroom. Charles E. Hughes III won an SOM office "competition" for the initial design; Gordon Bunshaft, as chief of design, carried it through; Eleanor Le Maire was interior design consultant; Weiskopf & Pickworth, the structural engineers.

Open during business hours

35   Museum of Modern Art (1938–39) and Sculpture Garden (1953/ 1964)
11 West 53rd Street
New York, New York

PHILIP L. GOODWIN & EDWARD DURELL STONE AND PHILIP
JOHNSON, ARCHITECTS

When Philip L. Goodwin and Edward D. Stone designed the Museum of Modern Art they revolutionized the self-important, Classical-inspired warehouse concept of displaying art. The museum was designed to show to best advantage its pictures—not itself. Instead of the usual awesome flight of steps followed by a puzzling series of closets for pictures, Messrs. Goodwin and Stone entice the visitor in with a glimpse of a garden behind an all-glass wall, then surround him with art before he knows it. Moreover, this pioneering building—fortified by a series of electrifying exhibitions—was to make "modern" architecture (and art, photography, etc.) acceptable, even fashionable. It played thus an incalculable role in the development of the whole spectrum of contemporary culture in this country. Philip Johnson added the western annex to the Goodwin-Stone core in 1950 (now demolished) and the exquisitely detailed east wing in 1964.

   The Abby Aldrich Rockefeller Sculpture Garden (1953 and 1964), Philip Johnson, architect. The museum trustees from the beginning realized that the "alive" natural light of an outdoor garden would be the most expositive for the display of sculpture. Thus when additional space became available just before the museum opened (May 1939), a quickly designed garden—less than two weeks remained—was run up by the late John McAndrew, the Curator of Architecture, with suggestions from Alfred Barr, the museum's polymathic first director. Philip Goodwin redesigned this in 1942 when he also installed a small garden pavilion-restaurant.

   In 1953 the entire garden was replanned by Philip Johnson, with a hand from the late Director René d'Harnoncourt, as the Abby Aldrich Rockefeller Sculpture Garden in memory of Mrs. John D. Rockefeller, Jr., one of the museum's three founders. An outdoor dining terrace lines the west end to expand the cafeteria behind, with a 2-foot/.6-meter drop-off to give identity. This upper level is continued in an L-shape to create an entrance "surveying" terrace from the main museum floor. (Cf. the contemplation veranda of the fifteenth-century Ryoan-ji at Kyoto.) Ground cover of ivy eases and accents the grade transition.

A 14-foot/4.3-meter-high gray brick wall establishes enclosure along the long north side: note the two grilled openings—one a gate—which give visual relief to the expanse of wall. Two "canals" laterally bisect most of the main sculpture garden level, and are offset so as not to become dominant. Four differently scaled contiguous spaces result in this "roofless room" (see also Johnson's Roofless Church in New Harmony, Indiana). A careful lack of rigidity is evident throughout the garden except for the rectangles of the two pools, one of which carries Maillol's *The River:* note that even the planting areas are irregularly delimited by the Vermont marble paving modules. The predominant tree is the weeping beech.

The result is that sculptured metal, sculptured stone, sculptured greenery are interwoven to mold sculptured spaces, making this not just a garden for art but the most perceptively calculated series of outdoor haunts, lairs, and delights to be seen. Sculpture—interwined with mobile humans—placid waters which sometimes erupt into fountains, quiet nooks, busy bridges, seats in the sun, and seats in the shade are among the elements which garrison this greenery of trees, bushes, and ivy. Each activity, or lack of activity, is carefully plotted, with a modest level change underscoring their division. In spite of limited size (c. 182×100 feet/55×30 meters) there are spatial surprises around every clump of trees as one turns and confronts some of the world's greatest contemporary sculpture. In winter, though the spaces are diminished as the greenery is lost, the sculpture gains new aspects when topped with snow. As Philip Johnson describes his work here, "What I did was to make a processional, using canals to block circulation and preserve vision, greenery to block circulation and block vision too, and bridges to establish the route. Always the sense of turning to see something. The Garden became a place to wander, but not on a rigidly defined path" (*The Sculpture Garden,* a MoMA brochure by Elizabeth Kassler, 1975).

In 1964 the garden was expanded by more than half, at the east end, by an upper 57-foot/17-meter-wide "quiet" terrace elevated 16 feet/4.9 meters. Each level, of course, carries works of art. (The upper terrace rests atop the extended ground-floor gallery—also by Philip Johnson— and can connect with the second floor of the museum.) James Fanning was the landscape architect consultant for the first phase, Zion & Breen for the second.

NOTE: With the building of the Museum's apartment tower (1979–82) the west end of the garden has been closed off and undoubtedly will be altered.

Museum and Garden open Mon.–Tues. 11–6, Thurs. 11–9,

Fri.–Sat. 11–6, Sun. 12–6, closed Dec. 25: donation. The
Summergarden is also open—free—June–Sept., Fri.–Sun.
6 P.M.–10 P.M., often with informal entertainment:
use 54th Street entry

---

36   Guggenheim Museum (1956–59)
1071 5th Avenue between 88th and 89th Streets
New York, New York

FRANK LLOYD WRIGHT, ARCHITECT

Frank Lloyd Wright was early interested in "organic" forms, especially those with a pronounced geometric basis—a heritage, Wright students feel, from his childhood Froebel teaching. Triangles and hexagons can be seen in many projects and some buildings and from these he explored "the ultimate in flexibility—the circle." (FLW was also a great admirer of Buckminster Fuller's geometrically generated work.) Wright's earliest essay with the spiral and "a continuous flow of movement" was probably that for the never-built Sugar Loaf Mountain Planetarium of 1925—a circular ziggurat (cf. the minaret at Samarra)— and continued with his startling proposal for Huntington Hartford's mountaintop country club (1947); while one of his last radius-generated projects was the never-built cultural complex for Baghdad (1957). Wright's Greek Orthodox church near Milwaukee (1956–61—q.v.), however, is one of the important demonstrations of the circle which was built, while the small ex-V.C. Morris shop in San Francisco (q.v.) whirls its own circular ramp. Though the Morris shop was finished (1949) ten years before the Guggenheim, the latter's design with ramp was first presented and published in 1944. (Construction of the museum was delayed by the war and Mr. Guggenheim's death in 1949.) And the circle with ramp, via *Nautilus pompilius,* is, of course, the rationale of the Guggenheim Museum, perhaps with an assist from Baroness Hilla Rebay, the museum's first director, and Rudolf Bauer, Mr. Guggenheim's early artist-protégé. In the museum Wright sought by means of a fantastic expanding helix to create a "reposeful place in which paintings could be seen to better advantage than they have ever been seen" (to quote Mr. Wright in the museum booklet issued by the Solomon R. Guggenheim Foundation, 1975).

There are those who feel that FLW cared little for art, other than a few Japanese prints and pieces, and that this museum reveals his prejudices. Moreover, some hold that he considered the building far more

important than the art. Granted the Guggenheim's walls and original lighting were not always cooperative, the museum itself is so exciting as a sculptured space that people come to experience the building and find themselves captured by the art—art which in many cases the museum has indeed glorified. The progression impact on the visitor is breathtaking as one advances under a purposefully low, even insignificant entrance (a great many of Wright's entries are conspiritously subordinated) to a centrifugal explosion of inner space. Here one is wrapped, almost like Laocoön, in a coil of serpentine spirals that finally leap through the glazed roof—no small museum introduction. Peter Blake, the distinguished architect, editor, and educator, calls this "one of the most beautiful spaces created in this century" (*Architectural Forum*, December 1959). It is also one of the few monumental rooms of our time: somehow we architects have almost lost the art. (The open four-story core of Wright's 1904 Larkin Building—destroyed in 1950—foreshadowed the Guggenheim's heady inner space.) The gallery-goer has the option of strolling up the ramp, or taking the elevator (inadequate) to the top and gliding—a slice of infinity—to the bottom, a process of gravitational advantage but, like walking up, only via a controlled circulation—a very un-Wrightian "path"—not to everyone's liking. Lewis Mumford called it "Procrustean." (One can exit, however, at several levels by means of stairs or elevator.) In the process of unwinding, as it were, the semisilhouettes of the visitors opposite add animation to the interior, while the observer has the pleasure of seeing most pictures both at a distance and close up. The width of the picture-hanging bays, predicated by the building's structural frame, is relatively inflexible for gallery installation, especially for large canvases (cf. the Whitney Museum's total flexibility). The "fins" defining the bays occur at each 30 degrees, thus twelve in plan, and widen as they rise to give lateral structural stability. But on the other hand, art and building become almost one, the building's bays serving as extended "frames" for the pictures, often only one per section, and lending thus preciosity to them. The hanging spaces, in a revolt against the "flat-walled mentality," are angled behind the pictures so that the canvases stand free; they float, hence develop a "liaison" or immediacy with the spectator which other museums with pictures possessed by the walls do not engender. The original lighting was unusual—and ineffective—in that Wright wanted the major source to be natural (but glaring) illumination emanating from the glazed band that rings his continuous spiral, its light bathing the pictures angled against the wall. Upon James Johnson Sweeney's accession as director in 1959 this was supplemented by an angled band of fluorescent lights which wraps around the entire periphery—note the "notches" of the backs of the fins to permit continuity—and by direct incandescent trough fixtures. The domed skylight, it should be noted, bears strong organizational similarity to a Tiffany glass dome designed in 1908 by George B. Post and Sons for the Cleveland Trust Company (and recently restored).

One of the spatial by-products of the Guggenheim's "one-room" design lies in the fact that one always knows where one is and which is the way out, comfortable knowledge not found in labyrinthine complexes that encase much art. And when one looks across the museum, especially from an upper (deeper) bay, the hypnotic continuity of the sweep of the ramp is punctuated by the tangible compartmentation, while the near-horizontal coil of the spiral is visually crosshatched by these short vertical divisions. The interaction of these two geometric determinants creates quiet dynamism in the interior. In addition it is visually refreshing—if hair-raising for some—to look over the parapet (which leans slightly outward) to see the fountain and sculpture on the main floor.

A circular, 277-seat auditorium occupies much of the basement. The Justin K. Thannhauser Collection of seventy-five works was installed in 1965 as a permanent loan in a separate second-floor wing: it greatly expands the scope and depth of the original Guggenheim collection.

The exterior of the Guggenheim has its awkward moments (especially an addition on 89th Street), and a few "junctures" are not only difficult, they are nearly impossible. But as Mr. Wright, with his characteristic wit, exclaimed, "When the first atomic bomb lands on New York [the museum] will not be destroyed. It may be blown a few miles up into the air, *but when it comes down it will bounce!"* (italics FLW— *Architectural Forum,* January 1964). Though faults appear, the Guggenheim is loaded with rewards. George N. Cohen was the brave builder who constructed this difficult masterpiece.

Open Tues. 11–8, Wed.–Sun. and holidays 11–5, closed Dec. 25: admission

---

37   Seagram Building (1954–58)
375 Park Avenue (between 52nd and 53rd Streets)
New York, New York

MIES VAN DER ROHE AND PHILIP JOHNSON, ARCHITECTS

The Parthenon (454–438 B.C.) evolved from a series of prototypes which can be traced back to wood; its first primitive "mock-up" in stone was manifested with the Heraion at Olympia (700 B.C.), contin-

ued at Paestum and Sicily in the 6th–5th centuries B.C., and climaxed on the Acropolis. The same refining process might be said of that Parthenon of skyscrapers, the Seagram Building, for Mies van der Rohe's background in steel—he rarely designed in any other material— seemingly was but preliminary homework for this triumph on Park Avenue. (Mies' never-built project for a glass skyscraper dates from 1921–22, while his twin apartments at 860 Lake Shore Drive in Chicago, 1951—q.v.—are similar in approach to the Seagram.)

Much of the authority of the thirty-nine-floor Seagram Building— Mies' "first major office building"—derives from its 100-foot/30-meter setback from Park Avenue and from its side streets, lending it imperial detachment together with elegant monumentality. (The building occupies only 52 per cent of its site.) Then the "openness" of its precisely double-height ground floor adds airiness to the entry, which if "solid" would be dead. (It is fair to say that Mies' work must always be raised or partially raised aboveground, as here, to develop transparency or lightness, otherwise it will stifle. His famous one-story Crown Hall in Chicago, q.v., and the Farnsworth House achieve this by being transparent themselves.) The low granite-paved podium on which the

Seagram Building rests—and which adjusts to Park Avenue's slight change in grade—creates dominion, while fountains and a pool on either side keep matters from becoming too serious; a touch of greenery also helps. Behind rises the pure and incredibly dignified building. (At least it is "pure" on the front and two sides: on the back the geometry of the massing becomes complicated and is far less satisfactory.) The Seagram also proclaims more eloquently than any other skyscraper before or since the ultimate expression of the divisible cube; that is total flexibility in office partitioning behind a cage facade. Far more than a proclamation, however, it is a poem. An office floor provides an open work space which may or may not demand subdivision, and the Seagram exterior says just this. Other tall buildings may stress the vertical or the horizontal: the Seagram states neutrality, but neutrality with éclat—and, of course, within the verticality of 516 feet/157 meters height. However, the five-by-three structural bays of the tower (which are not expressed) meet some difficulties in accommodating the utility core on each floor.

The architects of the Seagram Building pioneered several features which have now become part of the skyscraper vernacular: the "prestige" concept of a plaza with building rising behind, the plaza here actually flowing into the lobby, thus allowing the shaft of the tower to rise without setbacks (cf. the Lever House's different use of site, diagonally opposite); brown tinted glass to reduce sun load within and lend a solemn majesty without (its first use); bronze mullions and bronze-colored Muntz metal spandrels—a rash of "dark" skyscrapers has arisen in imitation; and floor-to-ceiling windows made feasible by utilizing a new low-profile (11 inches/28 centimeters high) air-conditioning unit. As regards the bronze exterior, building codes demand fireproof construction (which unprotected metal cannot meet); therefore the structural frame of the Seagram is steel encased in concrete—as is routine—the whole wrapped in a skin of metal and glass of meticulous detail (note corners especially). "God is in the details," wrote Mies: He is obviously no stranger to 375 Park. The Four Seasons Restaurant and bar, which were designed by Philip Johnson, take interior elegance to a new high. Kahn & Jacobs were associate architects; Severud-Elstad-Krueger, structural engineers. In toto incomparable.

Note that the building sets up an entertaining colloquium with McKim, Mead & White's Racquet & Tennis Club (1916–19) directly opposite (not open to public); the latter expresses the useful formalism of the Italian Renaissance.

Lobby open during business hours

38 TWA Flight Center (1958–62)
John F. Kennedy International Airport
via Van Wyck Expressway
New York (Queens), New York

EERO SAARINEN & ASSOCIATES, ARCHITECTS; AMMANN &
WHITNEY, STRUCTURAL ENGINEERS

Expressionism in contemporary architecture is somewhat questionable, and we are not likely to produce again a building as boldly loaded with expressionistic takeoff as this TWA Terminal. But as Eero Saarinen said: "I wanted to catch the excitement of the trip": he did. For contrast it is useful to quote Mies van der Rohe: "I am, in fact, completely opposed to the idea that a specific building should have an individual character" (Peter Carter, *Mies van der Rohe at Work,* Praeger, 1972). The space within TWA's sprawling, crablike shell sparkles with excitement. It is, as Edgar Kaufmann, Jr., wrote in *Interiors* (July 1962), "a festival of ordered movements and exhilarating vistas." The morphology of the enclosure uses four angled carapaces for the roof, each separated by a band of skylight; these strips of light not only make graspable the complicated structure by dividing it into components, they liberate any potential oppression of being under a shell. Ribbons of sunshine dart back and forth across the interior. The four roof vaults fuse into four extraordinarily powerful Y-shaped columns without, and cantilever at the ends in an impressive act of concrete engineering. As one progresses into the terminal, the changes of level play an important visual role. Moving up a broad flight of low steps to the departure area, one finds a climax in the red-carpeted "conversation pit" placed in front of and just below those headed for their planes, yet allowing a good view through the window-wall of the field for those waiting in the pit. Overhead near the center of the terminal an angled bridge connects the upper sections of the two ends (restaurants), adding another three-dimensional element to this vast "room," one which ranks among the most spirited spaces of our time. Space, however, dwindles on the trip down either of the two long, windowless tunnels to one's departure lounge. When one deplanes they perhaps deliver an impact by contrast, squeezing one into a tunnel, and then bursting one into the freedom of the terminal, but some travelers laden with carry-ons find these long, narrow passages irksome. Expansion of flight facilities has proved difficult with the unexpected acceleration of air traffic, but with few ex-

ceptions the architects, engineers, and TWA have achieved a beautifully constructed major adventure into an architectural direction that is always dangerous but here so exciting that it gives its client identity, and—more important—delights cash customers. Kevin Roche was co-designer.

A pedestrian shelter 330×22 feet/101×6.7 meters was added to the roadway in front in 1978. This concrete and Plexiglas canopy efficiently separates and shelters arriving and departing passengers while being respectful of the terminal. Witthoefft & Rudolph were the architects.

39 CBS Building (1963–65)
51 West 52nd Street at Avenue of the Americas
New York, New York

EERO SAARINEN & ASSOCIATES, ARCHITECTS

Understatement has never been so totally stated: the granitic solemnity of this thirty-eight-floor skyscraper—the only skyscraper the late Eero Saarinen designed—stands out with forceful character amid the tinplate and slick spandrels around it. Inset from the avenue and the two side streets that mark its site, with a sedately landscaped terrace providing breathing space, the tower (of reinforced concrete frame) rises unflinchingly uniform as though extruded from the mysterious depths of the earth, an impression intensified by the fact that the entrance lies five steps down from street level. There is, forsooth, an aloofness vis-à-vis its three streets which is on the reserved side. Today the "active" functions of the window in skyscraper design have been made largely obsolete by air conditioning and fluorescent lighting (always kept on during working hours), and Saarinen was one of the earlier architects to state this in the fenestration of this building. With occasional visual relief now being the window's chief claim to attention (although operable sash will always be useful in an emergency, as brownouts prove), Saarinen at CBS alternates window and wall, each with a 5-foot/1.5-meter module, instead of wrapping a strip of windows around the complete floor. To accommodate air-conditioning ducts and other utilities, he made these "solid" modules into structural utility triangles, with outer faces at 45 degrees, creating a saw-toothed exterior that vibrates visually as the pedestrian moves by, the wall calmly opening and closing as he goes. He then clad these right-angle triangles and the spandrels between with thin slabs of dark gray granite (running into unresolved problems on the corners). In these are set frameless panes of plate glass. On the interior, the flat (i.e. office) face of these piers is flush, facilitating movement of partitions. Moreover, there are no columns between outer wall and central service-elevator core, thus divisions can be made at any 5-foot/1.5 meter interval. The use of reinforced concrete bearing columns on 10-foot/3-meter centers—instead of wide-bay steel construction—was quite new when Saarinen tried it, with the enthusiastic collaboration of Paul Weidlinger as structural engineer. The result is a concrete bearing wall rather than a bearing frame. As the exterior

walls are based on continuous (and uniform) piers from top to bottom, the module of 5 feet/1.5 meters was adopted so as to be flexible with office partitioning and also provide space for revolving doors at entry. The pedestrian's impression of the exterior is of sobriety; it is only when one views the building from on high from one of its neighbors that its deeply grained character stands out amid the riffraff of the skyscraper world about it. In the restaurant and bar (by Warren Platner of the Saarinen office) one can sample the elegance at first hand: it's worth every shilling. After Eero Saarinen's death (1961) the building was completed by Kevin Roche/John Dinkeloo & Associates.

Only the restaurant, bar, and bank open to public

40 Whitney Museum of American Art (1964–66)
945 Madison Avenue at 75th Street
New York, New York

MARCEL BREUER AND HAMILTON P. SMITH, ARCHITECTS

As one approaches the Whitney, its upside-down, stepped pyramidal form might well conjure esthetic juggling: in actuality, the shape grew from a logic so programmatic that its form was in effect self-generating. Museum "identity," Breuer feels, should be expressed, but within the parameters of reason: "sculpture with rather serious functional requirements" as he put it (Cranston Jones in *Horizon,* Summer 1967). The generating mandate of the Whitney's Board of Trustees insisted—wisely —that an open sculpture court be incorporated in the museum's design, with maximum gallery areas above; exposed sculpture would subconsciously "tease" people into the museum. Inasmuch as the amount of land available was severely limited, the open court was placed a full floor below street level and across the front of the lot with only a curtain of glass separating it from the enclosed exhibition space directly behind. This "moat" is imaginatively bridged to inaugurate a stimulating parade to the museum—a "ritual," it has been called—while the sunken sculpture court issues constant invitations to the passersby to come in. (It was once visited by 25,000 in two weeks to see a modular house.)

The entrance lobby, which occupies most of the front of the ground floor, contains ticket and sales counter and checkroom under a ceiling with too much visual agitation, a nervousness which fades into serenity as one enters the galleries on the three upper floors. These totally flexible, largely column-free spaces, especially the extra-high one (17.5 feet/5.3 meters) on the fourth floor, are scintillating exhibition areas, which is, after all, what a museum is about. An open eggcrate grid of precast concrete on 2-foot/.6-meter squares is suspended from the ceiling: its waffle reticulation contains continuously wired tracking which allows complete freedom in the placement of spotlights. Partitions 4 feet/1.2 meters wide (with aluminum core) are like the lights in that they can be affixed to the grid where needed to subdivide the spaces. As most of the Whitney shows are temporary, such flexibility is essential. Partitions and walls are painted to reflect the needs of each exhibition. In addition to the major spaces on the three floors, there is a more intimate, more "domestic" gallery on the north side of two floors which not only provides a different kind and texture of space for difficult (and semipermanent) exhibits, but makes for greater perceptual stimulation,

via its variety, for museum-goers. The largely concealed fifth floor houses museum offices. Below the sculpture court, lower gallery, and restaurant there is a full working basement. The vertical circulation of the museum is not altogether sufficient—more could have been made of the stairs—and its hooded windows are personal, but in its essential object-displaying function under extremely cramped conditions, the Whitney is hard to beat: its fourth floor is unequaled. Its only problem is its overwhelming success. Michael H. Irving was consulting architect.

Open Tues. 11–9, Wed.–Sat. 11–6, Sun. and holidays noon–6, closed Dec. 25: admission except Tues. 6–9

---

41   University Plaza (1966)
100 and 110 Bleecker Street, 505 West Broadway
New York, New York

I. M. PEI & PARTNERS, ARCHITECTS

Though these three towers are almost identical in plan and height (thirty stories), they are so well designed and juxtaposed that they complement each other instead of being monotonous. Indeed the merit of the module and the spaces that are green conspire to produce one of the few civilized answers to urban living that one will encounter in New York. Two of the buildings are owned by nearby New York University, while the third (on West Broadway) provides 175 middle-income housing units under the Mitchell-Lama Act. Across the northern edge of the plot, along Bleecker Street, stand four rows of trees set in a lawn that gives definition and identity to the university's apartments, and allows close vehicular access (but no parking) to all three buildings. The Mitchell-Lama block can also be reached on foot from the west. In the center of the circular access drive flourishes an outsize (60 tons, 36 feet/11 meters high) *Bust of Sylvette,* designed by Picasso and executed (1968) in folded-plane, sandblasted concrete by Carl Nesjar, a talented artist who pioneered sandblasting Picasso's monumental works in concrete in his native Norway. The statue's height, angled sides, and forceful lines act as a spirited catalyst to knit the three towers spatially together. The towers themselves, reminiscent of Pei's earlier Society Hill development in Philadelphia (q.v.), combine that quality of beehive and plain wall, of glass and solid, that gives distinction to his high-rise work. Their "projected" ends make the compact forms seem slender as they rise above a neighborhood that could well stand more attention.

The plans of the buildings, a stretched pinwheel in shape, allow for a variety of sizes of apartments from one bedroom to four, with all end apartments having two orientations. Note the trim slanting windowsill with air intake (for optional air conditioning) concealed beneath. Two underground garages take care of the automobile. Playgrounds stand adjacent. By combining one subsidized unit with two conventionally financed ones with 350 apartments, economies were realized which brought distinguished design to Mitchell-Lama cooperative housing and reduced costs to the university for its two buildings. However, the university apartments were pared down in room sizes and storage space to meet Michell-Lama standards. A lack of communal facilities is also evident.

Grounds open daily

42   Chase Manhattan Bank (1957–61)
1 Chase Manhattan Plaza: Nassau Street between Pine, Liberty, and William
Marine Midland Building (1967–68)
140 Broadway between Cedar and Liberty Streets
One Liberty Plaza (1970–72)
165 Broadway at Liberty Street
New York, New York

SKIDMORE, OWINGS & MERRILL, ARCHITECTS

Downtown Manhattan boasts three skyscrapers by SOM, all more or less aligned, and all making contributions to the evolution of postwar high-rise design. Two of the three are enriched by outstanding pieces of sculpture, the third by a small park.

The Chase Manhattan Bank virtually "saved" the financial district by staying downtown and reestablishing the area's pre-World War II importance (a decision urged by David Rockefeller in 1955). It also injected via its new building a hard-edged profile into the mélange of turrets, domes, crockets, and finials which bedeck most of its older eclectic neighbors. Chase was the first of downtown's "slab" skyscrapers and its logically arrived-at boldness stands out. Its two-block site was assembled by a trade-off with the city, whereby the city permitted the bank to close (and build over and under) one block of Cedar Street, and the bank gave the city sidewalk perimeters on much of four sides so that street widening could be carried out, the city giving a bit more than it received. The architects then took this challenging site and established a podium over all but one corner (occupied by Chase's former headquarters). On this sweeping terrace, which also equalized the drop-off in grade down to William Street, they erected the 280-foot/85-meter-long skyscraper, running it up without breaks for sixty floors. The result is not only extraordinarily powerful visually—the building's "arcaded" meeting with the horizontal is masterful—it was far more economical to construct than a series of setbacks. Note that the structural frame is expressed on the exterior, its great piers giving both scale and vitality to the long facades and effecting an uninterrupted wall within for flexibility in partitioning. (The two rows of inner columns are encased in the elevator and service core down the middle for further ease of office division. The core is offset, with open floor

width being 40 feet/12 meters on the south side and 30 feet/9 meters on the north.)

To give identity to customer banking operations, which occupy the lower level off William Street, the terrace has a large circular opening which enables all using the building to gaze into the banking floor and to look down onto a landscaped pool by Isamu Noguchi. The opening also permits views into this pool area for those on the banking floor. The crowning touch of the plaza is the 42-foot/13-meter-high walk-through *Group of Four Trees* by Jean Dubuffet, installed in 1972, a work of both strength and delicacy. This "closes" the space of the podium when approaching from Nassau Street—it had previously leaked out—acts as an intriguing magnet from Pine and William streets, and establishes the territory of the terrace with élan. The sculpture is constructed of epoxy-coated fiber glass and aluminum over a steel frame. The interior works of art are equally distinguished. Gordon Bunshaft was partner in charge of design; Weiskopf & Pickworth, structural engineers.

In **Marine Midland** SOM sought to create a building which would not impinge on or be in conflict with Chase Manhattan across the street. They therefore evolved a dark, smooth-skinned (black anodized aluminum and bronze glass) skyscraper rising straight from the ground. To give its fifty-two-story height breathing space (and to enable it to rise without setbacks) more than half of the site was treated as a plaza and

paved with travertine. This terrace is made eloquent on the Broadway side by Noguchi's brilliant orange-red cube (28 feet/8.5 meters on a side)—which, like Chase's Dubuffet, is one of our finest pieces of urban sculpture—and given accents by circular seater-planters on Cedar Street. Briefly challenged by a slightly irregular trapezoidal street pattern, the architects came up with a symmetrical trapezoidal shape for their building, avoiding awkward street relationships and maximizing office space allowable. The main banking floor is on the second level (cf. PSFS's pioneering with this in Philadelphia in 1932), and its extra tallness (18 feet/5.5 meters) tends to push the lower entry floor into the ground: here the building suffers in comparison with Chase Manhattan. The treatment of the top of the building, by contrast, with an inset marking the utility level, is unsurpassed. For an economical commercial office block Marine Midland is hard to equal. Gordon Bunshaft was chief of design.

The startling quality of the fifty-four-story **One Liberty Plaza** lies in its incredible exposed steel framework. There is a brooding yet confident virility in its great spandrel girders which no other high-rise has approached. (The girders are approximately 52 feet/16 meters long on the three-bay ends and 47 feet/14 meters on the five-bay sides, with both measuring 70 inches/1.8 meters deep.) Its structural development was arrived at after almost a year of collaborative exploration between

U. S. Steel (which owns much of the building), the architects, and the engineers—Paul Weidlinger and Weiskopf & Pickworth. U. S. Steel's Applied Research Laboratory felt that there were new structural possibilities in skyscraper design, particularly the ability to express steel more vividly, and the result—after a minute examination of the pros and cons of nine potential means—resolved upon the solution seen here. (Weight of steel versus cost of enclosing it, free bay size versus weight of steel—these were only two of the considerations.)

The most extraordinary aspect of the exterior, both technical and esthetic, can be seen in the exposed spandrels mentioned, for steel, of course, buckles when subjected to intense heat unless it is properly fireproofed—as the building code requires—and yet there is visible metal here. What the architects and their consultants did was to develop a flame shield for the built-up girders, wrapping their flanges first with insulation then with 14-gauge steel but leaving the deep web almost totally exposed on its exterior face. Moreover, the shield's width was extended some 8 inches/20 centimeters beyond the spandrel girder's flange to deflect outward any fire which might occur—and also to give greater sun protection (2.3 feet/.7 meter overhang) to the vertically pivoted windows. (The client-requested operable sash is a U. S. Steel design to facilitate window washing.) The proposal for flame-shielding the exposed steel structure required considerable testing with a full-size mock-up before it was accepted by the New York City Board of Standards and Appeals. Another unusual facet of the building's design can be seen in the fact that the solid and void are almost precisely equal, making the exterior half steel (all exposed) and half glass.

There is, however, a disappointing note concerning One Liberty Plaza and that is its meeting with the ground. The building's main approach is from Broadway and because of the pronounced grade falloff the setback entrance is lower than the street, while the entry floor is far less high than the second (banking) floor, so that the structure seems to be subsiding into the ground, an effect intensified by its somber color and dark gray glass. (The west side terraces down to Church Street.) It is reported that the architects initially wanted to leave the entire ground level unenclosed except for the elevator lobby, but this exciting notion gave way to rental considerations. In plan the building is framed directly from outer periphery to inner circulation-and-service core, producing a column-free interior. The landscaped park opposite the Liberty Street side (still—but not permanently—partially occupied) was acquired so that the building could rise without setbacks. Ernest Flagg's forty-one-story Singer Building (1908)—the tallest in the world when built (also the tallest to be demolished, 1967)—previously stood on the site of One Liberty Plaza. Roy O. Allen was partner-in-charge; Paul Weidlinger and Weiskopf & Pickworth were joint structural engineers.

All three open during business hours

---

43 Ford Foundation Building (1966–67)
320 East 43rd Street
New York, New York

KEVIN ROCHE & JOHN DINKELOO, ARCHITECTS; DAN KILEY, LANDSCAPE ARCHITECT

Man's initial experience in a garden got off to a shaky start, but the rewards of embracing nature are obviously tempting. Eden was momentous while Babylon is imperishably hailed as one of the Seven Wonders. However, it is doubtful that any designer has achieved so much in so

little space as in this dramatic garden in this stronghold of philanthropy. As one enters the building from the shadowy main (43rd Street) entrance—it can be approached from 42nd Street—the unexpected confrontation with a sun-dappled forest ensorcells. Municipal zoning laws require that a certain proportion of a site (the proportion depending on the building's height) be kept open; when Roche & Dinkeloo proposed an enclosed garden instead of an open-to-the-street court to meet this code requirement, the firm was logically granted a "variance" to permit the building to be so designed. The structure is almost precisely square in plan, with its working area concentrated in an L-shape that enfolds the garden on the north and west sides. Except for the offices facing 43rd Street, most of the remaining ones open (literally) onto the enclosed court for their full ten-story height. The eleventh floor, however, completely frames the court on four sides, but allows the space of the courtyard to burst through in the center to vanish in the great skylight that caps its ceiling 160 feet/49 meters above. The eleventh floor contains the chairman's office, a small conference room, and the executive and employees' dining rooms. From the ground floor to the tenth, the east and south sides enclosing the garden are largely of glass, through which the sun pours by day, and thus lights the offices on the court side; by dusk the court is internally spot-lit and thus delights the passersby on the street. The three granite-faced parallelograms poking from the east and south sides (angled to provide a better view of the East River) contain fire stairs (the two near the office wings) and air-conditioning discharge pylon (on the corner).

The garden court is conditioned to keep a year-round temperature of a low of $50°$ F/$10°$ C in winter to a high of $85°$ F/$29°$ C in summer. Heating coils along the window-walls keep the glass-conducted cold of winter in control. The garden is, of course, interconnected with the air-conditioning system of the entire building. Comprising a mere third of an acre (.13 hectare), the garden deploys an intriguing series of levels (it steps down 13 feet/4 meters from 43rd to 42nd streets), so that its exploration produces new and unexpected vistas at almost every turn: it is not a two-dimensional layout, but a bountiful bit of landscaped witchcraft. The earth colors of the Cor-Ten weathering steel and the granite give the greenery a sympathetic background. Among the trees are a magnolia, eucalyptus, Japanese cedar, etc., plus a vast assortment of shrubs, vines, and flowers. There are numerous planting zones—all in a temperate growing belt—each automatically watered and nourished with liquid fertilizer by underground piping. Some of the planting has not lived up to expectation, and bugs are a problem at times (there being no birds), but this patch of greenery still refreshes all who see it. In addition to providing a visual focus, the garden acts as a cohesive agent for the foundation staff in that it makes a "family" of all the glass-walled offices, including those of the president. All are working for the common goal—to dispense monies wisely; thus most of the staff enjoy offices which partake of a mutual—and stunning—collective space. The garden court ties man to fellow man and both to nature. From the imagination of concept, to the boldness of realization, to impeccable detailing, the building is superb. The Ford Foundation has never made a more wonderful, or more lasting, bequest to the city —and indeed to all of us.

Garden court open to public during working hours

44   Lincoln Center for the Performing Arts (1959–68)
    62nd–66th Streets at Columbus Avenue (Broadway) and
        Amsterdam Avenue
    New York, New York

ARCHITECTS AS LISTED

Avery Fisher Hall (1962)—Max Abramovitz, architect; remodeled by
Philip Johnson (1976); New York State Theater (1964)—Philip
Johnson and Richard Foster, architects; Vivian Beaumont Theater
(1965)—Eero Saarinen & Associates, architects; Metropolitan Opera
House (1966)—Wallace K. Harrison, architect (and director of Board
of Architects); Juilliard School of Music (1968)—Pietro Belluschi,
Eduardo Catalano, and Westermann & Miller, architects.

Guided tours daily, except some holidays

45 Paley Park (1967)
3 East 53rd Street (just E of 5th Avenue)
New York, New York

ZION & BREEN ASSOCIATES, LANDSCAPE ARCHITECTS

Niagara is higher, Victoria wider, but for urban impact nothing equals
this minipark's waterfall, a mere 20 feet/6 meters high and 42 feet/13
meters across, cascading into a pool 6 feet/1.8 meters wide. The rush
of waters over its pebbled wall provides visual fascination as it sparkles
and fades in the sun, while equally importantly its "white" sound
muffles the rudeness of the street. Here is a retreat for the neighborhood,
the passerby, the visitor—even in winter when delicate snow limns its
ghostlike chairs and the then spindly trees. Twelve honey locusts,
planted at 12-foot/3.6-meter intervals in alternate rows of two and

three, "roof" this minuscule area (42.9×100.3 feet/13×30 meters), while walls of simple gray brick, flourishing with ivy, delineate the two sides. Movable pots of flowers, on a floor of pink granite blocks, serve as accents. Five additional trees frame the entry and cleverly extend the park onto the sidewalk while heralding its approach. Simple refreshments are available except in January and February. The park was presented to the city by William S. Paley as a memorial to his father Samuel Paley, 1875–1963.

New York has on the same street and within a block of each other two supreme twentieth-century tiny parks: Paley is introspective and its comfortable retreat cossets from the outside world. At the Museum of Modern Art garden by Philip Johnson (q.v.), the museum itself supplies the rewards and the pleasures reside largely in what one finds. Both are marvelous, but Paley's functional use of a few square feet provides an empyrean urban retreat: pure poetry. Albert Preston Moore was consulting architect.

Open Mon.–Sat., 8–7 in summer, 8–6 in winter; closed in Jan. and Feb. and major holidays

At 217 East 51st Street, between 2nd and 3rd avenues, stands another welcome gift to the city, **Greenacre Park** (1971), designed by Hideo Sasaki of Sasaki, Dawson, Demay Associates. (Open Mon.–Fri. 8–8, Sat. 9–8, except major holidays.) Park and its upkeep were made possible by the generosity of the late Abby Rockefeller Mauzé. Goldstone, Dearborn & Hinz were the architects.

---

46 World of Birds Building (1971–72)
Bronx Zoo
Pelham and Bronx River Parkways, Bronx Park
New York (Bronx), New York

MORRIS KETCHUM, JR. & ASSOCIATES, ARCHITECTS

Rejecting the caged prison for birds, the architect, in consultation with the Zoo staff, has created instead an unfettered, natural environment that sets an exciting milestone in ornithology. It is quite likely that the birds enjoy it as much as the humans. One approaches the Lila Acheson Wallace World of Birds from either the Bronxdale parking

field or the Concourse entrance—it lies only a short distance west of the former and south of the latter—to find a provocative collection of strange ellipses and "cylinders" crowning a rocky hillock. These varyingly sized, rounded forms, clustered together in lopped combinations, set an intriguing introduction as they state clearly that the whole is made up of a series of separate but coordinated exhibits within. A central approach leads to the entry, while on each side ramps swoop down from behind the building, that on the right rising again and jutting back in airy fashion. (The ramp at left is the main exit, the one at right a midpoint exit.) Circulation within the building is also largely ramp- and bridge-controlled, at times whisking one from the ground to the very treetops of a rain forest. The resulting one-way flow pattern moves the visitor—at his own pace—through twenty-five bird habitats, ranging from desert to tropical forest, each setting (marked by one of the lopped cylinders mentioned) creating with impressive fidelity the microculture of the birds which fly merrily about within their diorama world (which the rounded forms facilitate), complete with living plants. A natural environment—not a jail—was sought for each of the two hundred species and over five hundred birds. Five of the aviaries are completely open: in two of the largest the uncaged public walks through the habitat with birds flying freely overhead. In the rain-forest section there are some one hundred birds flying about, made quite at home by occasional artificial rain, lightning, and thunder, plus, of course, proper temperature and humidity control. Small screens with continuous projections explain such themes as courtship, mating procedures, nest construction, and ecology. Banks of separately controllable artificial lights outside and above each cylinder deliver the proper amount of illumination to each habitat, with excellent quality of light within. Developed closely with the staff of the New York Zoological Society (a private organization), the World of Birds has opened an exciting new future for ornithological education and pleasure. Brilliant.

World of Darkness (1969), at the southerly end of the Zoo, was also designed by Morris Ketchum, Jr. & Associates. This reverses day and night so that the visitor can see in "our" daylight hours some of the activities of that 60 per cent of the animal world which moves mostly after dark. The building housing this expresses on its own exterior the mysterious dusk within by means of its blackish, angular, pebble-concrete panels (note varying heights) which enclose its three-quarter doughnut shape. The sunken central court exposes the original glacial rock surface. The exhibits inside invert the life cycle of the animals by using strong artificial light during exterior darkness, and red light, which is invisible to most nocturnal animals, during our daylight. Thus they and their life-style can be observed. Morris Ketchum, Jr., was partner-in-charge of both buildings.

Open Mon.–Sat. 10–5, Sun. 10–5:30: admission

47   Police Plaza and Its Buildings (1968–73)
via Centre Street at Manhattan end of Brooklyn Bridge
New York, New York

GRUZEN & PARTNERS, ARCHITECTS AND PLANNERS; M. PAUL
FRIEDBERG & ASSOCIATES, LANDSCAPE ARCHITECTS

With what the *Architectural Record* termed "A Firm, New Edge for New York's Chaotic Civic District" (November 1974), a distinguished slice of pedestrian territoriality via a plaza and several fine buildings have been established amid the previous urban turmoil near the Manhattan end of the Brooklyn Bridge. The triple arches of McKim, Mead & White's episodic twenty-five-floor **Municipal Building** (1909–16) form an introduction to the plaza and also double in tying the new buildings to the old. (It was designed, as competition winner, by the younger partners of the firm, primarily W. M. Kendall and T. J. van der Bent.) There then unfolds a landscaped mall, some 380×75 feet/ 116×23 meters, crowned by the stalwart nine-story brick cube (atop three-story base of pinwheel plan) called **One Police Plaza** (1973). Its lobby contains an unusual brick mural by Josef Twirbutt, while the Assembly Room is colorful with banners by Sheila White Samton.

Overall plaza planning and landscaping were evolved by the architects and the landscape architect, and crucial to the success of the entire area was the suppression and bridging over of Park Row, a busy street which exits from the Brooklyn Bridge (no minor civic undertaking). The landscaping proper employs several small changes in levels to help define circulation—walking versus strolling versus sitting, or simply gazing at the fascinating silhouette of lower Manhattan to the south. Honey locusts, benches, retreats, and a dominant 30-foot/9-meter-high sculpture of weathering steel by Tony Rosenthal set the stage either for brisk pedestrian movement or relaxed sight-seeing.

On the left (north) side of the Plaza beyond **St. Andrew's Church** (1939) stands the **U. S. Attorney's Office** with the **Metropolitan Department of Correction** directly behind, the two separated by a previously existing transit substation. Both were designed in 1974 by Gruzen & Partners. The Attorney's Office and the Correction Building (primarily for prisoners awaiting trial) are linked by overhead passages to Cass Gilbert's and Cass Gilbert, Jr.'s 1936 **U. S. Courthouse.** To the right is a public garage for 478 cars plus police services: it is well integrated with the various levels with which it has to deal. Behind this

rises the seven-story **Murry Bergtraum High School for Business Careers** (1975), entrance on Madison Street (ground floor open during school hours); like the others it came from the office of Gruzen & Partners. Note its non-authoritative massing and respect for neighbors; its brickwork, especially in the circular stair towers, is excellent. It accommodates 2,500 pupils—with security and flexibility—attracting students from a wide range of the city's population.

Altogether planning, landscaping, and buildings work together to create a splendid urban setting, one which also acts as a link between officialdom on one side and housing to the east and southeast on the other. Jordan Gruzen and Peter Samton were the principals-in-charge.

Plaza always open, building lobbies open during office hours

Almost immediately to the north across Pearl Street rise the twenty-five-story twin buildings of **Chatham Towers** (1965) by Gruzen & Partners. This forms an imaginative medium-income cooperative housing venture in part made possible by site assemblage under Title I (the city buying the land, using condemnation if necessary, and reselling it to a limited-profit developer). Only 15 per cent of the site is covered with buildings. Chatham Towers contains 240 apartments, ranging from efficiencies to three bedrooms: half of them open onto balconies and it is the rhythmic grouping of these which lends the buildings their special cachet. The quiet, outdoor sitting area at the nexus of the two was largely created on the roof of the garage with an active play space adjoining. M. Paul Friedberg was the landscape architect.

48   Waterside (1970–74)
FDR Drive at 25th–30th Streets (take 23rd Street exit southbound)
New York, New York

DAVIS, BRODY & ASSOCIATES, ARCHITECTS

Waterside is almost a world apart for New York City habitation: it puts housing where it belongs but where it is rarely seen—on the water. Although the motorist along the FDR Drive (on the western edge of the site) senses only a walled-off series of towers, for those who live there Waterside provides a private, elevated retreat with handsomely spaced apartments framing a quiet plaza on three sides with the East River sparkling on the fourth. Much of the city's bustle is forgotten in this urban aerie. The tops of the distant Empire State and Chrysler buildings give hint of the workaday world, and there is some noise from the Drive, but the sense of detachment, and the escape via the river, embrace and reward one warmly. It is only tragic that almost all of our water-placed cities (except Chicago—and increasingly Boston, Baltimore, and Jacksonville) devote their river and lake edges to commerce with few spots for the implementers of that commerce.

Waterside's development—plagued by inexcusable city delays—imaginatively transformed a derelict pier area into 1,471 apartments in one 34-story and three 40-story towers, plus a row of 20 duplex town houses aligned atop the shopping area. (The complex rests on 2,400 piles driven to bedrock.) Though most of its rental apartments cater to middle-income families, 370 are subsidized. The design of the four towers represents a conscious attempt to mold the high-rise apartment into a profile of sculpted elegance instead of an inexorable series of anonymous, punch-card boxes. Its architects have long sought to humanize housing and here they have attained their most sophisticated result.

The plan of the towers takes a near-symmetrical pinwheel layout with ten apartments per floor (twelve in the north, subsidized tower), enabling the corner units to be "projected," thus breaking out of rigid rectangles, while the corners of intermediate floors are chamfered to develop better three-dimensionality and external grace, leading also to more apartment planning options. Terraces lead down to the river's edge at several points, garaging for nine hundred cars is underneath the well-elevated "podium," while a pedestrian bridge gives connection with 25th Street. Some esthetic juggling can be seen but altogether Waterside represents a most encouraging new direction. The elevated

plaza, incidentally, is much used for a wide variety of activities (exhibitions, concerts, etc.). Robert Rosenwasser Associates were the structural engineers. The low white building on the site is the UN School, designed by Harrison & Abramovitz (1972).

Elevated public plaza open daily

---

49 1199 Plaza (1971–75)
1st Avenue between 107th and 111th Streets
New York, New York

THE HODNE/STAGEBERG PARTNERS INC., ARCHITECTS

1199—sponsored by Local 1199 Drug and Hospital Union, and constructed under the Mitchell-Lama Act—probably provides the most ingenious large-scale, moderate-income shelter in the city. Stepping up from the FDR Drive on the East River, its dense complex is arranged in four near-identical U-shaped buildings and represents a welcome advance over the dreary clusters of equi-spaced, equi-faced boxes of housing characteristic of much urban development. It contains 1,590 cooperative apartments at 450 people per acre. Almost unbelievably a

competition—generously sponsored by the Ruberoid Company—was held for its design (1963) and was won by Hodne Associates of Minneapolis. (Their project was substantially revised later.) Perhaps its most accomplished features are its "river-seizing," its fraternizing with the view and its sweep of waters, the vibration of its balconies (over half the apartments have one), followed by its outstanding development of scale. There is a buildup from the five-story units—all duplexes and nearest the river—to the thirty-one-story towers at rear: their interaction, augmented by a clever stepped profile and offset building relations, creates a dynamic grouping. Moreover its height on the avenue side gives identity and a statement of security. The views from the apartments, low and high, facing eastward are all rewarding, while even those on the westerly side are largely set back from the avenue. A health center, day-care center for 110 children, two gymnasiums, community room (smallish), 683-car garage, and a band of shops (off 1st Avenue) complete the group. There are 156 efficiency apartments, 620 one-bedroom, 546 two-bedroom, 197 three-bedroom, and 71 four-bedroom units in the development, 394 being duplexes. Each building —of flat slab reinforced concrete—has 6 common room terraces. If only the development could have bridged over the FDR Drive. Robert Rosenwasser Associates were the structural engineers; Herbert Baldwin, landscape architect.

Grounds open daily

50 **World Trade Center** (1966–80)
Church Street between Liberty and Vesey
New York, New York

**MINORU YAMASAKI & ASSOCIATES AND EMERY ROTH & SONS,
ARCHITECTS; SKILLING, HELLE, CHRISTIANSEN, ROBERTSON,
STRUCTURAL ENGINEERS**

Unflinchingly stalwart, this pair of foursquare, sheer towers has
changed—probably forever—the madcap profile of lower Manhattan.
At 110 stories in height (1,350 feet/411 meters) the twins surpass the
Empire State Building's long, long record by 100 feet/30 meters (but
were in turn outstretched by Chicago's Sears Tower, q.v., in June
1973). The Trade Center's fourteen-block site was chosen because it
contained virtually no buildings of architectural merit, while three subway lines and the PATH train (Port Authority Trans Hudson—to New
Jersey) could be incorporated within the structure on the concourse
level, with a fourth subway (the Lexington Avenue line) only a block
or so away on lower Broadway. Though transportation logistics have
been extremely well handled, there are still some forty-five to fifty thousand workers a day who pour in and out of these great towers at appointed hours.

   To arrive at the size of the projected building, the Port Authority calculated the number of square feet of office space which they thought
would be required by the various firms and organizations concerned

with world trade, plus offices which New York State requested (almost one quarter of the total), and a new U. S. Custom House. This worked out to be approximately 9 million square feet/836,000 square meters. To house this economically and efficiently the architects proposed two identical towers, measuring 209 feet/63.7 meters on a side, a conclusion which in effect automatically called for a 110-story height after subtracting for elevators and other core services. This opting for two towers instead of a single mammoth one was brilliant, and the overall concept was further advanced when a plaza in front of the towers was suggested with 8-story buildings giving edge definition and scale transfer. As Yamasaki wrote: "The real opportunity at the Trade Center was to open up one area of our largest urban concentration and provide a great outdoor space, shielded from vehicular traffic, easily accessible to pedestrians and which could bring pleasure to the occupants, visitors and people who work in and around the Trade Center site." He adds, this is a place "to give [man] a soaring feeling, imparting pride and a sense of nobility in his environment." Incidentally, the two buildings which frame the entrance to the plaza from Church Street (WTC 4 and 5) serve a rental function in that their net floor area (and potential for double-height rooms) is much larger than a single tower floor, hence can readily accommodate the commodities exchanges and the brokerage house which now occupy them.

The next problem was the specific design of the (then) tallest buildings in the world on a totally exposed site, partially of landfill, where winds of 140 mph/225 kph must be reckoned with. The "squared tube" concept which evolved, it is important to note, was advanced by the architects and its details worked out jointly with the engineers. Though there might be disagreement concerning the esthetics of the World Trade Center (primarily—to some—the lack of exterior scale and the treatment of the public spaces), there has been only praise for its superbly engineered structure. Before discussing the towers themselves, it should be mentioned that though the Port Authority of New York and New Jersey, which built the Center, is a bistate, semigovernmental organization, a status which frees its architecture from New York City building code restrictions as regards setbacks etc., the project either met or exceeded code requirements.

The excavation process and the foundations were incredibly difficult because almost half the site was, as mentioned, filled land while an underground railroad and a subway tube both had to be accommodated without interrupting service. A "slurry trench" foundation method of construction, first perfected by Italian engineers, was used (and the engineers imported for the job). This was carried out by using a clamshell bucket to dig a connecting series of trenches 3 feet/.9 meter wide and 22 feet/6.7 meters long around the periphery of the site, and filling the trenches with slurry (bentonite clay and water) as the earth was removed. Each trench extended to bedrock and was notched into it: steel reinforcing cages were then lowered and anchored, and the concrete poured, displacing the slurry, which was drained off. This system permitted erecting the 65-to-100-foot/20-to-30-meter-deep foundation walls without excavating on either side—and with the Hudson River next door. When the entire foundation periphery was complete the inner section was excavated—probably the largest hole in the ground Manhattan has seen—and cleared for construction. The excavated earth and rock were used to create landfill for the nearby site of the proposed Battery Park City.

Routine skyscrapers consist of a cage of steel or concrete bays with the exterior in effect hung onto the framing structure: load (e.g. weight and wind) is carried throughout the building primarily by a series of columns and braces. In the World Trade Center each of the four sides of the towers is built up of closely spaced columns welded to substantial spandrels to become an enormous load-bearing and wind-resisting wall for the full height of the building, a construction system technically known as a Vierendeel truss after the Belgian engineer who invented it in 1896. The only interior columns are those framing the elevator-service core. As the brochure says, "Most of the steel is on the outside, instead of inside." With the towers formed as an uninterrupted squared tube—on a scale never previously approached—the enclosing fabric is composed of built-up steel wall columns (for the most part 14 inches/36 centimeters square), which were insulated for fireproofing and to minimize temperature differential. These were then wrapped in a special alloy aluminum (outside width 18.75 inches/47.6 centimeters) and set 40 inches/102 centimeters on center (which permits great flexibility in office partitioning). These columns alternate with window openings, typically 21.3 inches/54 centimeters wide, with glass measuring 19.3 inches/49 centimeters, thus in cross section solid and void are almost precisely equal. (Compare Saarinen's CBS Building with concrete bearing walls and identical window/wall width of 5 feet/1.5 meters and SOM's adjacent One Liberty Plaza where window and structural spandrel are equal but horizontal.) The wall sections of the WTC were prefabricated in two- and three-story-high panels framed horizontally by 52-inch/1.3-meter-deep steel spandrel plates. The vertical alternation of narrow solid and glass—as seen also in the new west buildings of Rockefeller Center—produces an unusual scale on the exterior, while on the inside it totally transforms the routine horizontal sweep of large-pane fenestration. There are, however, advantages in this, among them (as Yamasaki has often pointed out) being a freedom from the acrophobia that for some attends vistas from most high buildings. Moreover the slender glass panes are recessed from the framing

edge 11.5 inches/29.2 centimeters, effecting a reduction of sun load, thus saving energy and cutting glare. (Glass comprises about 30 per cent of the outside skin.) The appearance within the offices, with windows almost flush with floor and ceiling, is extraordinarily bright and airy. There are, incidentally, 43,600 standard windows in the towers, all of which are washed by unmanned automatic machinery which runs on built-in stainless steel tracks. (Ford & Earl Design Associates were responsible for the Port Authority's offices.)

Spans between the outside bearing walls and the interior service core are of steel truss construction 30 inches/76 centimeters deep: as mentioned, no intermediate columns are necessary. The inner face of the outside walls is flush. The elevators are divided into three zones each served by its own "skylobby." These are located on the concourse (one floor below plaza level at the subway-PATH convergence) and at the 44th and 78th floors, with high-speed express cars, capacity fifty-five persons, providing direct service to each skylobby and also non-stop to the 107th floor restaurant (WTC 1) and the observation platforms atop WTC 2. Local floors are served by local elevators from the skylobbies and thus have to take care of only one third of the buildings' height: in effect three local elevators operate within a single shaft.

Perhaps the chief architectural criticism which has been leveled at the World Trade Center is the fact that the two mid-building service floors —the 44th and 78th levels mentioned—are camouflaged on the exterior to a large degree, thus vitiating scale. It is only with an oblique light that these floors become semiprominent, and it is then that the towers have more assertiveness. (Compare the "banded" United Nations Building in this regard.) In addition their almost Venetian-Gothic meeting with the plaza is not to everyone's taste. It should be added, in defense, that there is a welcome "transparency" at the towers' base, while the melding of a triad of upper columns to produce one wide bay at ground level was necessary to create sufficient intercolumniation for entries, not to mention the desirability of stating and lighting the tall (and slightly fussy) lobbies.

The 5-acre/2-hectare plaza in front of the towers, and bounded with sensitive irregularity by the eight-story Custom House, the two plaza buildings, and (in 1981) the hotel (WTC 3), acts "to set off the buildings facing it and to create an environment totally for pedestrians, away from automobiles—an oasis, a paved garden where people can spend a few moments to relieve the tensions or monotonies of the usual working day" (Yamasaki). However, as matters now stand, the paving of this vast plaza is unrelieved, except by sculpture and fountain accents, and makes one yearn for the type of bold geometric mosaic "floor" which gives such scale and life to Siena's Campo and Rome's Campidoglio. The sculpture consists of a potent black granite pyramidal grouping by Masayuki Nagare (34 feet/10 meters long) holding down the entry, with Fritz Koenig's spherical bronze sculpture and fountain shining in the sun at center, and James Rosati's *Ideogram* at left background. At the west entrance to WTC 1 is a fine red stabile by Alexander Calder. The hotel mentioned above has 829 rooms in its twenty-two stories and was designed by Skidmore, Owings & Merrill.

The six levels below the plaza provide parking for almost two thousand automobiles, plus PATH and subway lines, a plethora (some fifty) of shops, and a wide variety of dining facilities. At the other end —the top—there are two spectacular observation platforms in the south tower, one enclosed and one open, while the Windows on the World Restaurant (expensive) in the north tower is superb: Warren Platner & Associates were the interior architects. Controversial or not, the World Trade Center is an extraordinary document on the New York skyline and a brilliant chapter in high-rise engineering. As Henry Wright, a distinguished architect and editor, put it, "The WTC wall is not only structurally unique; there are reasons for considering it the first truly rational skyscraper envelope" (*Architecture Plus,* January– February 1974).

Observation deck on Tower 2 open daily, 9:30–9:30: admission; restaurant atop Tower 1 open Mon.–Sat. for lunch, Mon.–Sun. for dinner—reservations required

51 Citicorp Center (1971–77)
Lexington Avenue between 53rd and 54th Streets
New York, New York

HUGH STUBBINS & ASSOCIATES, ARCHITECTS; LeMESSURIER ASSOCIATES/SCI AND THE OFFICE OF JAMES RUDERMAN, STRUCTURAL ENGINEERS

Citicorp Center represents a brilliant extension of the commercial possibilities of very expensive midtown real estate beyond nine-to-five office usage. (It was the most costly block acquisition in New York history.) Thus in addition to providing 1,800,000 square feet/167,200 square meters of rental office space (some, of course, occupied by Citibank itself) the Center contains a marvelous three-story shopping arena called the Market, featuring a non-stop series of intriguing restaurants and shops deployed around a skylit central court—tempting with trees, plants, chairs, and tables—plus a major housewares emporium on two levels, and a freestanding church in one corner. St. Peter's Lutheran Church was, indeed, the begetter of the elevated office tower, for its previous home was an eclectic Gothic building (1905) on this site and it would only sell if its dedicated parish could rebuild on the same spot. Today it sits comfortably accessible (visitors welcome Mon.–Thurs. 9–6, Fri. 9–5, Sun. 8:30–7:30), perhaps a unique proclaimer of today's religion under the benevolent arm of capitalism. Its handsome sanctuary, one level down, is temptingly visible from the street.

With the church's provocative requirement in the contract, the architects and engineers elevated the great bulk of the office tower on 115-foot/35-meter-high piers, left the northwest corner of the site free for the new church, created a small sunken plaza, a busy galleria, and the broad array of restaurants and shops mentioned. Further shopping, and some office space, are accommodated in the seven-story extension (of overly complex juncture) which projects eastward to 3rd Avenue. So successful has the dining/shopping excursion been that the Center is often more crowded on Saturdays and Sundays than on weekdays. It should be pointed out that the covered pedestrian ways and the bright central agora represent "incentive" zoning trade-offs with the city whereby greater building area was allowed if the public amenities and circulation referred to were incorporated in the overall design.

The most striking statement of the Center is, of course, its extraordinary skyscraper—the world's seventh highest at 914 feet/278 meters —a silver, soaring object tiptoeing down Lexington Avenue and barely

touching it. In simplified terms the lower structure upholding this dazzling high-rise is based on four "legs" 25 feet/7.6 meters square (and also enveloping stairs and services) placed at the midpoint of the 152-foot/46-meter equal-sided building where, together with the concrete inner core, they uphold a 26.8-foot/8-meter-deep trussed "platform." (Note that these legs have a slight chamfer which plays an active role in reflecting the sun when low.) On this thirteen-story-high elevated platform rises the sleek-skinned, superbly fabricated, unbroken shaft of the office tower, its forty-eight floors divided into six structurally independent "tiers" of eight floors each triangulated by internal framing. Primarily because of the expense, this "chevron" triangulation was enclosed by the aluminum skin: it can be traced through the fenestration. This resourceful framing is integrated with horizontally triangulated floor bracing, almost eliminating the need for internal columns. Four 5-foot/1.5-meter-wide "mast columns," one per side, provide the chief vertical supports for the tower, forming extensions of the "legs" below. On top a 400-ton/363-metric-ton "tuned mass damper" of reinforced concrete can be actuated to minimize building sway in a high wind. The 45° angled roof was designed from the beginning to give a distinctive profile to the Center (cf. the Pennzoil Building in Houston), and initially it was hoped that one hundred luxury flats could be incorporated within it but Citicorp could not get the zoning variance needed. It was later considered as an experimental solar collector—it faces southward—but the estimated benefits were less than the projected costs and this was abandoned, at least for the present. But in spite of this theoretic loss, the Citicorp Building is extremely energy-efficient with double-glazed windows and thickly insulated aluminum spandrels.

St. Peter's Church, which traces its founding back to 1861 and twenty-three German immigrants, was also designed by Hugh Stubbins & Associates, and achieves polygonal personality in spite of its towering neighbor. The interior is unusual yet provides a reverent background for worship, highlighted by a 2,150-pipe boxed organ made by Klais Orgelbau Inc. of Bonn, Germany, and by a spider web of a circular stair in one corner. Vignelli Associates were responsible for the colorful and flexible furnishings except in the Erol Beker Chapel, which was decorated by Louise Nevelson (and is on the agitated side). Emery Roth & Sons were consulting architects; Sasaki Associates, landscape architects.

Hugh Stubbins wrote the bank in 1970 saying that "We must use the resources of big business, reinforced by moral and social ideas, to develop a new generation of office buildings planned for the community and expressive of the humanity of the individuals who use them. By revitalizing urban development with an emphasis on people, we could produce a more enjoyable place in which to live and work" (quoted in the *Architectural Record,* June 1978). As a consequence of this thinking, Citicorp Center is an exhilarating urban experience.

Office building open during business hours, the Market open
10–10 daily

52   Bronx Developmental Center (1973–77)
1200 Waters Place—from Manhattan take Hutchinson River Parkway E to Westchester Avenue exit, first L then first R
New York (Bronx), New York

RICHARD MEIER & ASSOCIATES, ARCHITECTS

Utilizing technology perfected for airplanes and advanced engineering, the architects have developed here an innovative series of panel modules to enclose the Bronx Developmental Center. By standardizing proportionally related sizes for solids, windows, and vents, and by using gasketed, round-cornered openings, they have with economy and flair given an enormous push toward a new-generation building technique. The Developmental Center was initially planned to house over seven hundred mentally retarded and physically handicapped residents of all ages. However, before the building was finished the program was drastically changed to make it a multipurpose treatment center, and though there are today fifty to sixty in-house residents they are not considered to be there permanently. The new philosophy of the BDC seeks to create as many linkages as possible with the community, thus stressing

outpatient services. In addition to various therapies and training in "life skills" (the simple acts of taking care of oneself), there is a school program for the multihandicapped which, it is pertinent to add, is under the direction of the Board of Education. And as there are extensive hospital facilities in the immediate vicinity, much of the initially large infirmary has been adapted for educational purposes.

Fortunately the plan had enough built-in flexibility so that these substantial programmatic changes could be accommodated architecturally. It should be added that new philosophies and techniques for treating the retarded—or the afflicted of any kind—will continue to be developed. In addition to the basic sociocultural changes mentioned, another factor affected the building: a substantial cut in budget late in construction. Thus some interior finishes are skimpy (no acoustic ceilings in public rooms, etc.), and some furnishings are on the minimal side (roller shades instead of Venetian blinds), while even the marquee at entry is awkward because it was initially designed to span the road.

The building that evolved was planned with three basic divisions around a U-shaped court: a four-story administrative and instructional unit stretching 563 feet/171 meters across the front; recreational facilities (swimming pool and gymnasium) closing the short south end; and four identical four-story apartment blocks of pinwheel plan and irregular disposition stepped as an articulated residential wing forming the east side (and visible from the Hutchinson River Parkway). The court within, which has a grade differential of 12 feet/3.6 meters, provides a multilevel play area—it even has a small stepped arena—permitting outdoor, in-touch-with-nature (and some concrete) recreation with, it should be added, wind shelter and considerable privacy. At midpoint, a tri-level covered passageway bisects the court and connects the two long wings of the U while a small "bridge" joins the north ends.

The Developmental Center is an extraordinary technological and esthetic achievement that hopefully will meet the many changes which undoubtedly lie in its future. It has encountered opposition from those who do not find it "homelike"—a curious disapprobation considering much of the neighborhood—but for many its gleaming, cheerful architecture and facilities will indeed help provide "a decent life in the Bronx community for the severely handicapped." The Bronx, the dedicated staff, and the architects should all be proud of this achievement.

Visitors welcome Mon.–Fri. 9–4: telephone Public Relations in advance for guided tours—(390) 430-0811

Pennsylvania

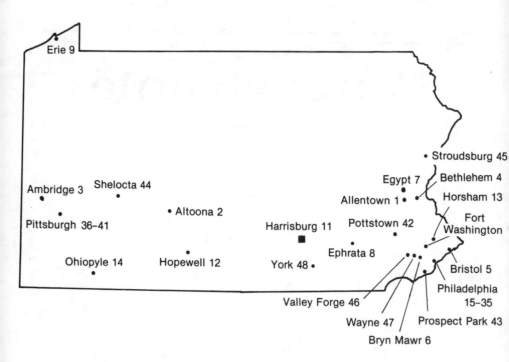

Erie 9

Stroudsburg 45

Egypt 7   Bethlehem 4

Ambridge 3   Shelocta 44

Allentown 1   Horsham 13

Altoona 2

Pittsburgh 36–41

Fort
Washington

Harrisburg 11   Pottstown 42

Ohiopyle 14   Hopewell 12   York 48   Ephrata 8

Bristol 5

Valley Forge 46

Philadelphia
15–35

Wayne 47   Prospect Park 43

Bryn Mawr 6

PENNSYLVANIA

The buildings in boldface type are of general interest. The others are for the specialist.

Allentown	1	Trout Hall (1768–70)
Altoona	2	Baker Mansion (1844–48)— Robert Cary Long, Jr.
Ambridge	3	**Old Economy Village** (1824–31)
Bethlehem	4	**Historic Bethlehem** (1743–68)
Bristol	5	**Pennsbury Manor** (1683–99/ 1939–46)
Bryn Mawr	6	Erdman Dormitories (1962–65)— Louis I. Kahn
Egypt	7	**Troxell-Steckel House** (1755–56)
Ephrata	8	**Ephrata Cloister** (1740–46)
Erie	9	Old Custom House (1839)— William Kelly
Fort Washington	10	Hope Lodge (c. 1750)
Harrisburg	11	Olivetti Corporation of America Factory (1970)—Louis I. Kahn
Hopewell	12	**Hopewell Village National Historic Site** (1770–1883) Cornwall Furnace (1742–1883)
Horsham	13	**Graeme Park House** (1721–22/1739)
Ohiopyle	14	**Fallingwater** (1936–37)—Frank Lloyd Wright Visitors' Center (1978)—Paul Mayén/Curry, Martin & Highberger
Philadelphia		See also Bryn Mawr, Horsham, Prospect Park, Valley Forge, and Wayne.
	15	**Christ Church** (1727–44)

16 **Independence Hall** (1732–56)
17 **Fairmount Park, Its Water Works, and Its Houses**
18 **Powel House** (1765)
19 **Cliveden** (1763–67)
20 **Second Bank of the United States** (Old Custom House—1819–24)— William Strickland
21 **Andalusia** (1798/1836)— Thomas U. Walter
22 **Founder's Hall** (1833–47)— Thomas U. Walter
23 Cast-Iron Buildings (1857)
24 **City Hall** (1872–1901)—John McArthur, Jr.
25 **Pennsylvania Academy of the Fine Arts** (1872–76)—Furness and Hewitt
26 **Philadelphia Saving Fund Society Building** (1929–32)—Howe & Lescaze
27 **Beth Sholom Synagogue** (1959)— Frank Lloyd Wright
28 **Alfred Newton Richards Medical Research Building** (1957–61) **and Biology Laboratory** (1962–64)— Louis I. Kahn
29 Guild House (1960–63)—Venturi & Rauch
30 **Society Hill Apartments and Town Houses** (1962–64)—I. M. Pei
31 **Downtown Redevelopment** (1965–75)
32 Central Atlantic Headquarters, Prudential Life Insurance Company (1970–72)—The Kling Partnership
33 **INA Tower** (1974–75)—Mitchell/ Giurgola
34 **Franklin Court** (1975–76)— Venturi & Rauch

1 Trout Hall (1768–70)
414 Walnut Street
Allentown, Pennsylvania

Compact in form, sturdily built but delicate in detail (note pediments), Trout Hall is a good example of an eastern Pennsylvania interpretation of Georgian architecture. Originally built as a summer place in the country—it was named for the fishing—it is still surrounded by magnificent trees though it stands just east of the downtown area. The house until its purchase by the city (1908) was used by Muhlenberg College. Restoration was undertaken (1916–18) and all later additions removed from the original dwelling. Subsequent renovations took place as funds became available. Though the city still owns the property and maintains the exterior, the interior has been leased to the Lehigh County Historical Society, which fully restored the interior for the bicentennial (1975–76, Benjamin L. Walbert 3rd, architect), and furnished it as of the late eighteenth, early nineteenth century.

Open Tues.–Sat. 12–3, Sun. 1–4, except holidays: admission

2   Baker Mansion (1844–48)
Baker Boulevard at 35th Street, 1 block N of Logan Boulevard
Altoona, Pennsylvania

ROBERT CARY LONG, JR., ARCHITECT

Although almost isolated in the Alleghenies—the nearby Phila-delphia-Pittsburgh line of the railroad was not completed until 1854—the Elias Baker House on the south edge of the city is a surpris-ingly competent example of the Greek Revival (although its architect was eventually fired). Its carefully quarried blocks of warm gray lime-stone give proper contrast to the six white Ionic columns (with slightly overlarge capitals) that stand across its front. The grounds and the fa-cade reflect the solidarity of its ironmaster owner's position in the com-munity. The back of the house—which also provides the entry—is marked by six square semi-Doric piers which uphold a second-story porch. The Blair County Historical Society acquired the house in 1922—the Baker family having occupied it until 1914—and has care-fully furnished it in the mid-nineteenth-century style. The music room and the Belgian furniture are outstanding.

Open June–Oct., Thurs.–Sat. 1:30–4:30, except holidays: admission

3   Old Economy Village (1824–31)
    Church Street between 13th and 14th (facing PA 65)
    Ambridge, Pennsylvania (c. 17 miles/27 kilometers NW of
    Pittsburgh)

The Harmony Society, which built Old Economy, comprised a group of
German Pietists that evolved from Philipp Jakob Spener's late-seventeenth-century movement in Frankfurt. (They were also heavily
influenced by Jakob Böhme—1575–1624.) The Harmonists, however,
went further than Spener and spurned established religion to found a
community of dedicated souls who sought brotherhood, peace, joint
property ("Christian communism"), communal work and rewards—
and which favored celibacy, upheld the Bible strictly, and anticipated
an almost immediate Second Coming. Finding Germany restrictive,
these pilgrims, with George Rapp (1757–1847) as their leader, first
settled (1805) in Harmony, Pennsylvania, but after ten years the entire
group of about 750 betook themselves to Harmony, Indiana. Ten years
after this (1825) they sold their well-established community to Robert
Owen and his Owenites (see New Harmony) and moved back to Pennsylvania. They settled less than a score of miles south of the first Harmony (now partially restored and the site of a museum), acquiring a
substantial site on the bank of the Ohio River, a plot which they
selected for its transportation advantages. The Harmonites set about establishing the village we see today and soon created an extremely successful industrial and farming center. A grid plan was used for the new
town with, refreshingly, a large garden that borders the river as its
center instead of an urban square. Moreover, the garden was formally
planted with vegetables as well as flowers. The major communal buildings enframe the garden with the Great House at the head on the main
street and the church opposite. Smaller dwellings, then the factories
and farm units, fanned out from this core. As a planned community for
a planned society, and as an early expression of urban development in
the United States, Old Economy stands as an illuminating achievement.
The architecture of the minor buildings shows hints of the German
background of most of its inhabitants, but much of the village reflects
an austere or "Economy Federal" variation of the Colonial, especially
the Great House. This building and the Feast Hall (mostly used as
town hall) are the most important structures but the entire village is
well worth exploration. Frederick Rapp (1775–1834) is thought to
have been the architect.

Open Mon.–Sat. 8:30–5, Sun. 1–5, except holidays: admission

4 Historic Bethlehem (1743–68)
West Church Street
Bethlehem, Pennsylvania

The sedate string of Moravian buildings which line Church Street just east of Main gives us a good row of early Germanic-inspired structures. The Bethlehem pioneers were akin to the German settlers in the west-of-Philadelphia area, but they came largely from Saxony (the movement had originated earlier in what is now Czechoslovakia), were basically urban, often upper-class, and were definitely church-organized. Like the Quakers they came to do good and were particularly helpful to the Indians, their "red brothers." Their architectural contribution will be found more in clusters of buildings than in isolated dwellings and farms. With the exception of the Gemeindehaus, whose square hewn logs were clapboarded for greater weather protection in

the middle of the last century, the buildings we see today stand largely as constructed except that their original heavy tile roofs have been replaced. The earliest is the Gemeindehaus (1743), which with the others forms a picturesque open U-shape: its small chapel (1751) stands directly behind, the Bell House (1749) is parallel to the street, with the Sisters' House (1744, 1752, and 1773) beyond. The Brethrens' House (1748) and the Widows' House (1786) are across the street. Cast in a simple, almost elementary mold, these quiet buildings frame a peaceful avenue. The Gemeindehaus, which was recently turned into a museum, is the only major unit open to the public. It is, incidentally, possibly the largest log building (of white oak) still in use in this country. Note, on the exterior, the delicate upswing of the roof at the eave. The subsequent buildings, harmoniously organized, are of local limestone with thick walls, small brick-arched shuttered windows, and with shed dormers on the roof. The great buttresses shoring the buildings on either side of the Bell House add a nice touch, an informality accented by the more than casual roof-line junctures of these buildings. The belfry atop the Bell House is typical of Moravian buildings in Europe.

Open Tues.–Sat. 1–4, except holidays: admission; tours available at 66 West Church Street

5 Pennsbury Manor (1683–99/1939–46)
c. 5 miles/8 kilometers NE of Bristol via US 13 and Brodentown-Ferry Road (c. 25 miles/40 kilometers NE of Philadelphia, c. 7 miles/11 kilometers S of Trenton, N.J.) near Bristol, Pennsylvania

Pennsbury Manor was the late-seventeenth-century country estate of William Penn and comprises house and numerous outbuildings, plus a splendid command of the Delaware River. Its site, originally 8,431 acres/3,412 hectares, was selected by William Markham, Penn's deputy governor, in 1681, a full year before Penn himself arrived to set up his land grant and governmental structure. Penn was committed to country living and considered Pennsbury Manor to be his principal and most beloved residence. Construction probably began in the fall of 1683 and seems to have been personally supervised by Penn. When, in 1684, Penn returned to England, he sent a flurry of instructions to his steward regarding outbuilding construction, garden layout, and interior features of the manor house. Financial and political problems in England prevented his return to Pennsylvania until 1699—to find his estate finished and his colony thriving. Continuing political pressures in England, however, cut his second visit short, and in 1701 Penn set sail for his native land, never to return again. His son, the wayward William Penn, Jr., managed the plantation for a short time (1704–5), but preferring the pleasures of city living, he remained in the colony for less

than a year. After William Penn's death in 1718, the estate had a series of overseers and a small staff, but in 1750 it appears to have been abandoned. The manor house was in ruins by 1826, and the last original structure on the site, Penn's Brew House, was demolished in 1864.

To help celebrate the 250th anniversary of Penn's landing (1932), the Warner Company, which owned the land, presented almost 10 acres/4 hectares to the Commonwealth of Pennsylvania and with the help of the Depression-created Works Progress Administration, the Pennsylvania Historical Commission began a total reconstruction. After considerable research—Penn's original instructions being invaluable—and after probing for foundations, the cornerstone of the manor house was laid in 1938, with most of the structures completed the following year. However, because of World War II, refurnishing and completion of the gardens was delayed until 1946. The interiors, though somewhat hypothetical, are handsome. Note that the river (i.e. front) half of the house is of brick, the land side of wood, a bifurcation probably selected by Penn. The bricks for the original house were fired on the site by brickmakers sent from England for that purpose. Dr. Donald A. Cadzow was responsible for the archeological excavations; R. Brognard Okie was the historical architect; and Dr. Warren P. Laird was the consultant.

Open Tues.–Sat. 9–5, Sun. 12–5, except holidays: admission

---

6 Erdman Dormitories (1962–65)
Bryn Mawr College
Merion Avenue
Bryn Mawr, Pennsylvania

LOUIS I. KAHN, ARCHITECT

With a subdued palette, combined with an unusual geometry, the architect has put together a sophisticated basically black and white building. Virtually all of Kahn's work is based on interacting geometric forms—an approach which never fails to be exciting in his hands if, at times, it becomes formal. Here he has evolved a plan of three separate "hollow" squares attached at their diagonal corners and strung across the brow of a small hillside. The understated, almost difficult-to-find main entrance is via the central square, with dining room and kitchen to left, lounges to right. The central cores, two stories high, form the major interior spaces, and are wrapped by minor ones. (Cf. Kahn's Unitarian church

in Rochester, N.Y.) The second floor of each square comprises bedrooms on four sides, leaving the central open space forming "a molecular structure that looks for the light." Because of the site gradient some bedrooms—of which there are 150—are on the lower level. The fenestration in the bedrooms—two slender windows at the extreme ends of some rooms alternating with one recessed central window in the rooms adjoining—approaches the arbitrary, as does the extension of the slate walls to form the roof parapet. However, its use of a difficult site and its scale make the building interesting to architects, and the surprising variety of its interior spaces makes it eagerly sought by the students for residence.

Visitors should check with Admissions Department

---

7   **Troxell-Steckel House** (1755–56)
     Reliance Street (6 miles/9.6 kilometers N of Allentown on PA
        145, L on PA 329)
     Egypt, Pennsylvania

The Troxell-Steckel dwelling and the barn facing it constitute prime examples of the rural vernacular of eastern Pennsylvania of two hundred years ago. Although most of the region's settlers came from western Germany and Switzerland, hence were more accustomed to constructing with half-timbering and brick than with stone, the limestone ledge which runs just below the soil of the eastern part of Pennsylvania

proved an irresistible material. It is this lovely stone—sometimes naively employed (few arches or corbels)—the direct geometry of its use, and its frequent conjunction with red-painted wood that make this area the home of the finest autochthonous farm buildings in the country. The steep roof of the house with its doubled trusses, half-timbered interior walls, and oversized fireplaces suggest medieval German influences in its design. The gray exterior walls are of the limestone mentioned—quarried in the vicinity—and needed no restoration. However, new shakes have been put on the roof and on the "pent" roof that marks the top of the ground floor (and helps protect its windows), while the interior has been recently completely redone. The property was acquired by the Lehigh County Historical Society (1942) and restored by them (1943), with John K. Heyl, architect. It is one of the few farm groups in the Pennsylvania Dutch country accessible to the public. (The "Dutch" misnomer arose either from a garbled "Deutsch" or from the fact that most of the German immigrants to Pennsylvania in the eighteenth century left for the New World from the port of Rotterdam.) The stone lower floor of the barn, the vibrant red paint on the upper wooden section, and the *Hexenfoos* decoration—here indicating propitiation for rain—are typical of the region. (*Hexe* means "witch" or "sorceress" in German.) House and barn are now a most welcome museum.

The barn buff will find other examples in the area, though they are not open to the public. PA 143 and PA 662 provide reasonable hunting for examples which can be seen (only) from the road.

Open June–Sept., Sat.–Sun. 1–4, except holidays: admission

8   Ephrata Cloister (1740–46)
632 West Main Street
Ephrata, Pennyslvania

The Ephrata Cloister is one of the country's major indigenous architectural groups of the eighteenth century and, reputedly, the earliest Protestant monastery in the United States. Fortunately some of its major buildings, which date from the 1740s, survive and have been carefully restored to give us a revealing index of Palatinate-inspired architecture. They reflect the northwest German homeland of Johann Konrad Beissel, who in 1732 founded Ephrata—the biblical name for the Bethlehem of the Holy Land—as a religious, primarily celibate

community for the German Seventh-Day Baptist Church. The society prospered and in addition to running a successful farm, tannery, and several mills also founded a noted choral school and established one of the finest printing presses in the fledgling Colonies. The most compelling single building is the three-story Saron, or Sisters' House (1743), with steeply pitched roof, shed dormers (instead of gabled ones), vertically lapped shakes, and tiny windows. The attached Saal, or chapel (1741), stands at right angles, creating a fine medieval, almost Hanseatic, group. Note the projecting framing beams of the Saal capped against the weather.

The interiors, meticulously restored, reflect the frugal life of the community. In what might be termed architectural masochism, the halls are lengthy and narrow to suggest the only path to heaven, the doorways are low to encourage humility by requiring constant stooping, and the wooden beds were made too short to allow indulgent rest. The Sisters' House and most of the smaller buildings are of wood (several have vanished), but the Almonry, where not only alms were distributed to the poor but where bread was baked and grain stored, is of local stone. The Saal is of half-timbering and stone. Celibacy, factionalism, and the changing socioeconomic pattern of America's development occasioned the demise of the communal society and in 1814 it was incorporated into the German Religious Society of the Seventh-Day Baptists, which used the buildings until 1934. The Pennsylvania Historical and Museum Commission took over in 1941 and restored the surviving buildings. A unique and illuminating group of ethnic structures.

Open May–Oct., Mon.–Sat. 9–4:30, Sun. 1–4:30; Nov.–Apr., Tues.–Sat. 10–4:30, Sun. 1–4:30 except holidays: admission

---

9   Old Custom House (1839)
409 State Street
Erie, Pennsylvania

WILLIAM KELLY, ARCHITECT

A good example of textbook Greek Revival by the little-known William Kelly and based on the Theseion in Athens. Built as the U. S. Bank of Pennsylvania, and now hemmed in by downtown Erie (and three blocks from Perry's rebuilt flagship *Niagara*), the white Vermont mar-

ble building has been recently refurbished. It is today rarely open, but the exterior is the more important part architecturally.

Open only on special occasions

---

10   **Hope Lodge** (c. 1750)
    Bethlehem Pike (PA 309), W of Camp Hill Road, immediately S of
      PA Turnpike
    Fort Washington, Pennsylvania

A Pennsylvania Georgian house given interest by its setting and several unusual details. Although brick graces its formal facade, the other three walls and the outbuildings are of stuccoed stone. A brick stringcourse gives horizontal emphasis which is accentuated by the white shutters on the outside of the ground floor (whereas they are inside on the second). An unusual blind brick arch surmounts the door. Each of the large rooms, four main ones per floor, has a fireplace in a prominently paneled wall. Saved from destruction in 1922 by Mr. and

Mrs. William L. Degn, the house was fully restored by them and given to the state in 1957.

Open Wed.–Sat. 10–4:30, Sun. 1–4:30, except holidays: admission

---

11 **Olivetti Corporation of America Factory** (1970)
2800 Valley Road, S side of IS 81, just E of Progress Avenue exit
Harrisburg, Pennsylvania

LOUIS I. KAHN, ARCHITECT

An understated manufacturing facility lifted above the routine by thoughtful landscaping (note berms at rear to conceal parking), and given accents in the building itself by unusual detail, especially the blue

hooded skylights that pepper the roof. Administration and production areas are purposefully undifferentiated externally to minimize distinction between white-collar/blue-collar work. The interior of the office section tends to the gray side but the exposed stainless steel utilities add visual vitality. The most interesting feature of the plant is its structural system of octagonal inverted concrete "umbrellas," which are placed 60 feet/18 meters on center for maximum manufacturing flexibility. They were evolved with Dr. August E. Komendant and the Keast & Hood Company as structural consultants. The square openings in the roof formed by the intersection of the octagons serve to bring in daylight and fresh air and to exhaust stale air. These openings are covered by complex skylights made of small aluminum channels and a number of pyramids of glass-fiber-reinforced plastic. The skylights were designed in consultation with Renzo Piano.

Reception area open during business hours

12   Hopewell Village National Historic Site (1770–1883)
10 miles/16 kilometers NE of Morgantown intersection of PA
Turnpike (IS 76); E on PA 23, N on PA 345 (c. 15 miles/24
kilometers SE of Reading)
Hopewell, Pennsylvania

There are not many examples of industrial architecture remaining from
the late eighteenth and early ninetenth centuries, and this iron-making
village is one of the most complete. It comprises not only the furnace
and its related dependencies, but also the iron master's house, the barn,
and tenant dwellings. All of these have been put back into excellent
condition as a National Historic Site under the National Park Service.
The iron-making process of the day, one based on charcoal, has been
convincingly simulated, with demonstrations and tape recordings filling
in the details. The furnace (built 1770–71), casting house, and sheds
have the industrial looks and scales which reflect directly if somewhat
primitively their respective functions. This businesslike layout, which
seems smallish to us today (although it consumed an acre of trees a day
for fuel), was capable of turning out cannon during the Revolution. Its
stoves, also, were famous, some eighty thousand having been manufac-

tured. Look, too, at the barn opposite the furnace; this stabled the horses needed for hauling supplies to the furnace and its products to the market. The barn's whitewashed stone base and red-painted, cantilevered wood sides are, as we have seen, typical of the region. With the introduction in western Pennsylvania of anthracite coal instead of charcoal for smelting, and then the large-scale Bessemer process for making steel from pig iron, Hopewell declined and closed shop in 1883. It was acquired by the federal government in 1935.

Open daily 9–5, except Jan. 1, Dec. 25

Of related interest is the **Cornwall Furnace** (1742–1883), about 35 miles/56 kilometers west of Hopewell just north of the Pennsylvania Turnpike via US 322, southeast of Lebanon. (Open Tues.–Sat. 9–4:30, Sun. 1–4:30, except holidays: admission.) A Tuscan mansion (private) holds down one end of the town, the gutsy furnace (remodeled in 1856) retains the middle, while rows of workers' stone houses stretch eastward. The furnace, which ceased operation in 1883, was supplied with the famous magnetite ore from mines which line the nearby valley. Charcoal and limestone were also closely available. The mines themselves remained active until 1973. In 1931 Mrs. Margaret C. Buckingham gave the Cornwall Furnace to the state of Pennsylvania with an endowment for upkeep. It is now administered by the Pennsylvania Historical and Museum Commission, forming a fine chapter in the state's industrial history.

---

13 Graeme Park House (1721–22/1739)
.9 mile/1.4 kilometers W of US 611 on County Line Road, 3.2 miles/5.1 kilometers N of
Horsham, Pennsylvania

Graeme Park mansion and barn, with duck pond, trees, fences, and well-tended lawn, compose the complete early-eighteenth-century country gentleman's estate. The exterior of the house, which was originally built for distilling spirits, reveals its utilitarian character in its more than casually dressed fieldstone, its prominent mortar joints, and its lack of finesse in detail. However, the interior was totally transformed in 1739 when the building was changed into a residence upon the marriage of the stepdaughter of the original owner to Dr. Thomas Graeme. Richly paneled partitions and large fireplaces were installed in the three

ground-floor rooms, which were unusually laid out in that there was no central hall.

The nearby barn should be noted, especially the juxtaposition of its massive stone ends with the wooden south projection—to provide an open-air sheltered work space. Notice, too, the neatly turned white-washed pillars and, on the stone north side, the ramp to the upper floor. Part of the barn's lower floor has been converted to administration quarters of the Commonwealth of Pennsylvania, which acquired the property in 1958 and is fully restoring it.

Open Tues.–Sat. 10–4:30, Sun. 1–4:30, except holidays: admission

---

14 Fallingwater (1936–37)
PA 381, 3.5 miles/5.6 kilometers N of
Ohiopyle, Pennsylvania

FRANK LLOYD WRIGHT, ARCHITECT

Nature and architecture, embraced and embracing, are here: and unless man works intimately with and respects the environment—as Wright did—the one will wither as the other immolates itself. Pyrrhus is

the name. This is no perfect house: perfection on terms of domestic choice and complexity does not exist, but Fallingwater stands on a pinnacle in its interlock, indeed its clannish conspiracy, with its setting. Providentially this house and the Robie in Chicago—two of Wright's greatest works—survive and are open to the public even if some formalities are necessary to enter each.

Fallingwater, or Bear Run as the family called it, is approached via a winding path which reveals mere snatches of the house through the trees. It is only upon crossing a modest bridge that we see the whole building and perceive the waters which tumble and swirl at its feet. The dominant elements which one first grasps are the pale ocher concrete cantilevered terraces, resembling enormous shallow boxes, the upper set at right angles to the lower and jutting with magnificent authority over the falling waters.

The house itself, its local sandstone walls, its glass, and the slender cantilever of its roof then materialize, all of its elements agitating and complementing each other, and then the space games begin. The waters gurgle and splash—"the noise of which is presumably welcomed by the occupants," an irate critic once remarked—while above this the tensions of the terraces, intensified by the vibrancy of their right-angle placement, take over and contrast first with nature and then as counterpoint with the other man-fashioned components, fieldstone and glass. Space is embraced, and stone, concrete, and glass dance. Within, the music continues with Wright's famous "free plan," wherein, as the Italian critic Bruno Zevi perceptively remarked, "the same tendency is apparent: to amalgamate the rooms, to animate the building as if it were a continuous spatial discourse rather than a series of separate words." The boundaries between man and nature are architecturally slender here—and purposefully so; rooms flow outward onto terraces and almost evaporate in the mists of the waterfall, while the boundaries between one room and the next are almost non-existent. No room in this smallish house is a foursquare box, the major ones do not even have a single-plane ceiling. A certain fracturing of space can be said to result, and in the living room a lack of focus is apparent even with the potent accent of the great fireplace and the living rock that rises through the floor and nestles against the chimney-breast. But no more quibbling: see this stone and concrete poem—and see, too, the Guest House (1939) on the small ridge behind the main dwelling. As the Museum of Modern Art's 1965 exhibition and catalog entitled *Modern Architecture U.S.A.* said, "in no other building, even by Wright, do poetry and technique fuse in a vision so hypnotic."

Built for the late Edgar J. Kaufmann as a weekend retreat from Pittsburgh, some 60 miles/97 kilometers to the northwest, Mr. Kaufmann's son, Edgar Kaufmann, Jr., gave the house and its extensive grounds (1,543 acres/624 hectares) to the public (1963) with an endowment to keep it up. It is now open to the public under the Western Pennsylvania Conservancy. The Conservancy has since added considerable more ground to safeguard the watershed, and in 1976 completed a major restoration of the property dwelling. As to its background, FLW himself wrote: "The Gale House built in wood and plaster in 1909 was the progenitor, as to general type, of Fallingwater, 1936" (*A Testament,* Horizon Press, 1957).

A **Visitors' Center** was built (1978) to accommodate the numerous visitors to the house. Designed as a series of "pods" projecting from a central open but covered information core, it provides a "display pod" illustrating the background of Fallingwater, its geology, flora, fauna. There is also a toilet pod, a children's pod (those under twelve cannot visit the house), and a service pod. Well separated from the house, the Center has been carried through with "invisibility" in mind plus sharp attention to detail. Paul Mayén was the designer, with Curry, Martin & Highberger the architects.

Open Apr.–mid Nov., Tues.–Sun. 10–5: advance reservation required; telephone (412) 329-8501

---

15   Christ Church (1727–44)
2nd and Market Streets
Philadelphia, Pennsylvania

Christ Church represented the most accomplished and urbane development of religious architecture in the Colonies at the time of its completion in 1744 (tower and steeple 1754). Its basic design comes straight out of London, Gibbs's St. Martin's-in-the-Fields (1721–26) being most frequently mentioned as its inspiration although its interior, especially, is tamer than St. Martin's. Christ Church's red brick walls, projecting chancel, and balustraded and urned parapet show by their exuberant articulation full development of Georgian architecture. This finds climax in the 209-foot/64-meter-high wooden steeple which rests easily upon its brick base. (Note the carved heads on this tower.) The richness of the exterior appears within in the chancel with its enormous Palladian window—which the church claims is the first of its size in America—and by the ornate entablature. The Tuscan columns with impost blocks that parade down the nave are virtually a Gibbs trademark. From these columns spring the arches which carry the elliptical ceiling. The great window behind the altar is, unfortunately, of clear glass instead of translucent, its chromatic Victorian predecessor having been recently replaced, permitting a distracting view of the commercial

buildings across the street, while the aisle windows are—equally unfortunately—*not* of clear glass (they are Victorian).

As the founding Episcopal church (1695) in Pennsylvania—the colony of Quakers—Christ Church's first shelter was probably also of brick; in 1727 work was begun on the building we see today. Dr. John Kearsley, a physician, vestryman, and amateur architect who was born (c. 1684) and educated in England, is generally credited with the church's design, though some feel James Porteus, whom William Penn brought from Scotland in 1682, was responsible. In any case the church prospered greatly and was by the mid-eighteenth century the most fashionable in Philadelphia. It was here also in 1789 that the Protestant Episcopal Church in America was born, severing ties with the Church of England. Though interior changes were made during the last century it stands basically as designed, a significant landmark in our Colonial architectural heritage. Seven signers of the Declaration of Independence are buried in its churchyard and nearby graveyard (Arch Street at 5th).

Open daily 9–5

16   Independence Hall (1732–56)
     Chestnut Street between 5th and 6th
     Philadelphia, Pennsylvania

Independence Hall is so intertwined emotionally with our nation's origin that we often neglect its architecture. It is—in parts—architecturally superb, its two chief components of excellence being the design
of its massive tower and the quality of its interior. The brick tower, it
should be mentioned, was not even started until 1750, and the first
wooden steeple was so poorly built that it had to be removed (1781).
This was rebuilt with major alterations (10 feet/3 meters higher, more
elaborate) by William Strickland in 1828—perhaps our earliest Colonial restoration. Without tower and steeple, the Old State House, to use
its original name, would be a competent but dullish building—"a modest brick edifice," Mr. Baedeker called it. Tower and the treed square on
the south side save all, and it is worth noting that the tower itself is almost exactly as wide as each flank. From the north (Chestnut Street
side) the building is horizontally prominent; from the south it seems
vertical. Its "park," on the south, which was once enclosed by a 7-
foot/2.1-meter-high brick wall, provides a respectful bosky setting for

this Palladian-descended group. (The same distinction cannot be claimed for the mall to the north, which has been cleared of earlier buildings and landscaped.) On either side of the Old State House and connected to it by triple open arcades (originally solid) are two curiously scaled office wings (1736), which have been built and rebuilt (once by Robert Mills) until the final restoration of 1898. Standing as separate entities on either side of these wings are the Congress Hall (and former County Court House) at west (1787–89) and Old City Hall—temporary U. S. Supreme Court (1791–1800)—at east (1789–91). Their exteriors are basically as originally built but inner arrangements have been altered on several occasions.

The interior of the Old State House is, as suggested, splendid in scale and in the detailing of its woodwork. It is divided by a central hall into two equal (but unequal-appearing) rooms. One of these accommodates the Supreme Court of the Province (arched and open to the hall) and the other, to east, the Pennsylvania Assembly (behind door) where the Declaration of Independence was signed. Both number among our great early chambers. The second floor, reached by an impressive tower stair, is dominated by the Banquet Hall. Edmund Woolley, a master carpenter, designed the building aided by Andrew Hamilton (c. 1676–1741), a talented lawyer and amateur architect. Some feel that James Gibbs's *A Design for a Gentleman in Dorsetshire* (1728) was of influence. After neglect following the removal of the federal capital to Washington in 1800, then a slight sprucing up for the centennial in 1876, the entire group of Independence Hall, Congress Hall, the Old City Hall, and the square were restored early in this century. At one point the state legislature had voted to tear it down! In 1951 the buildings came under the watchful protection of the National Park Service.

Tours daily 9–8

---

17 Fairmount Park, Its Water Works, and Its Houses
Philadelphia, Pennsylvania

Philadelphians claim that Fairmount Park (Penn's Faire Mount) is the largest city park in the United States (presently 4,319 acres/1,748 hectares). Starting at John F. Kennedy Plaza almost in the middle of the city, it heads for the Schuylkill River, which it warmly embraces on both banks, then meanders northward up Wissahickon Creek for a total distance of some 10 miles/16 kilometers. Size, however, pays homage to quality, for this is one of the loveliest spreads of urban greenery to

be seen, one accented by the placid river which flows between its largely unspoiled banks. Even from the windows of the Metroliners this carefully tended, rolling series of hills and plains, treed areas, and playing grounds (and, unhappily, the Schuylkill Expressway—IS 676) refreshes. The riverside **Water Works**—suggestive of a templed landscape by Poussin—form a more than engaging group of Greek Revival buildings. Built between 1812 and 1815 they were designed by engineer Frederick C. Graff (*Architectural Record,* July 1927)—probably with help from Latrobe or Mills. (Benjamin H. Latrobe and Graff in 1799–1801 designed the city's first waterworks system, their neat, domed pumping house being torn down in 1827.) The enormous museum on the hill was designed by Zantzinger, Borie & Medary together with Horace Trumbauer (1916–28).

The historic houses open to the public in the park, five on the east bank and three on the west (where the Centennial Exposition was held), range in date from around 1721 to 1798. On the west side of the river are **Cedar Grove** (c. 1721—open daily except holidays 10–5:

admission), the only house to be moved to the park from its original countryside location and one which reflects its rural origin; the Adam-Style **Solitude** (c. 1785—open daily except holidays 10–5: admission); and **Sweetbrier** (1797—open daily except Tues. and holidays 10–4:30: admission), a formal Early Federal Style mansion. The houses on the east bank (from S to N) are **Lemon Hill** (c. 1770—open daily 10–5: admission), whose three handsome ovoid rooms atop one another are clearly expressed on the exterior; **Mount Pleasant** (1761–62—open daily 10–5, except holidays: admission), a rich, indeed very rich, Georgian example with two dependencies (unusual north of Virginia) in front—one of the most famous houses in the city and the finest in the park; **Laurel Hill** (c. 1760—open daily except holidays 10–5: admission), Georgian with Federal addition from 1810; **Woodford** (1756—open Tues.–Sun. 10–5: admission), with typical southeast Pennsylvania pent roof; and **Strawberry** (c. 1798—open Tues.–Sun. 10–4, except holidays: admission), whose original grace was marred in the 1830s by the addition of dominating end wings.

An extraordinary facet of these houses in Fairmount Park is that four of them and their acreage became part of the park province well over a hundred years ago. In 1867 the city purchased the area for recreation, condemning almost four hundred properties (many of them stream-side industrial contaminators), an act facilitated by the fact that serious pollution and odors from the dammed-up river had already caused many families to leave. The Fairmount Park Commission then began a cleanup process which climaxed in the Centennial International Exposition of 1876. All eight houses mentioned are beautifully maintained. The park is, of course, one of the glories of Philadelphia.

Houses open as indicated

---

18 Powel House (1765)
244 South 3rd Street
Philadelphia, Pennsylvania

Rescued—like the entire area of Society Hill—from the slum pall which began to creep upon this once desirable section of Philadelphia after people of means moved away from the nearby river, the Powel House stands as eloquent witness to architectural salvation. When deterioration set in, the house was used by boarders, then as an office; finally when threatened (1930) with almost immediate destruction it was saved by the Herculean efforts of a group which then formed the Philadelphia Society for the Preservation of Landmarks. (The Society also maintains the nearby **Hill-Physick House,** 1786, at 321 South 4th Street, and **Grumblethorpe,** 1744, at 5267 Germantown Avenue—both open same hours as below.) In spite of the uses and misuses of the Powel House through the years, the mansion today stands in pristine restoration, one of the handsomest Georgian dwellings in the city. Two of its finest rooms were purchased by and removed to the Philadelphia Museum of Art and the Metropolitan Museum in New York—at the time acts of kindness—but these have been meticulously restored. Though the main dwelling is only 31 feet/9.4 meters wide by 46 feet/14 meters deep, a long "back building" for kitchen and offices attaches to the rear, with a "period" garden adjoining. The dark red brick of the chaste exterior (probably white at one time) is enlivened by the Colonial ivory woodwork of its entrance and shutters and by the light marble keystones above each window plus the usual stringcourse. It is within the house that lavishness takes over. The two major rooms of the second floor—the front drawing room-ballroom and the back parlor—are elegant achievements both in overall harmony and refinement of detail. The front room, which extends the width of the house, is unusual in that its walls are wainscoted all the way up to the finely carved cornice that encircles the chamber. A delicately ornamented ceiling tops all. The designer of the Powel House is unknown but the English archi-

tectural "text" books of the day were obviously of importance for the decoration. Very superior.

Open Tues.–Sat. 10–5, Sun. 1–5, to 4 P.M. *in winter, except holidays: admission*

---

19 Cliveden (1763–67)
6401 Germantown Avenue (US 422)
Philadelphia, Pennsylvania

Withdrawn behind a walled lot and surrounded by magnificent trees (especially the tulipifera), Cliveden sets a patrician stage as the summer home of Chief Justice Benjamin Chew (1722–1810). Its design was basically the justice's (his somewhat primitive drawings were recently found), aided by the various books available, notably those on Palladio's works, the whole put together by a local master carpenter and a skilled mason-contractor. The estate consists of the main dwelling with two setback dependencies which were already on the land but which were enlarged for kitchen and laundry when the house was built. The kitchen (at left) was then attached to the house by a curved colonnade—Chew's pride. In appearance Cliveden's dressed stone facade (the sides and rear are stuccoed), with slightly projecting pedimented entry bay, and rich cornice bear resemblance to Mount Pleasant (see Fairmount Park) a few miles away and a few years earlier. But in plan Cliveden uses a luxurious lateral hall with stairs set dramatically behind four rich Doric columns instead of the more usual central hallway. With its 12-foot/3.6-meter height it forms an imposing entry. (This T-shaped entry can also be seen in Carter's Grove in Virginia—q.v.—and in the Chase-Lloyd House in Annapolis—q.v.) On either side of the hall are the reception rooms, of which the drawing room, or parlor, is the finest (note detail of door and fireplace), with the dining room almost equally distinguished. The furnishings, many of them museum pieces, are almost all from the Chew family, and add greatly to the quality of the interior—and to its livable atmosphere.

Cliveden played a major role in the Battle of Germantown (1777),

when some 3,000 men under Washington tried to move back into Philadelphia but were repulsed by 120 British soldiers holed up in the house. That the mansion survived the bombardment—scars still abound —is miraculous; it also speaks well of John Hesser, its mason-builder. The house's purity, however, was compromised in 1856 when additions were made at the rear and atop the colonnade to the kitchen.

The dwelling, contents, and 6 acres/2.4 hectares of land were acquired by the National Trust for Historic Preservation in 1972. The furnishings were given by members of the Chew family, whose forebears had occupied the house for over two hundred years. It is one of the Trust's finest properties. Meticulous restoration is in process.

Open daily 10–4, except Dec. 25: admission

---

20   Second Bank of the United States (Old Custom House—1819–24)
420 Chestnut Street between 4th and 5th
Philadelphia, Pennsylvania

WILLIAM STRICKLAND, ARCHITECT

The Second Bank is one of the key buildings in the development of the Greek Revival—a revival which had such marked influence on the design of public buildings in the United States in the first half of the nineteenth century. Strickland won the commission for the bank via a competition (1818), and though some feel that Latrobe's entry, which placed second, subsequently modified Strickland's design, most authorities attribute the building completely to young Strickland and to the English books on ancient Greece which he possessed. (Strickland had earlier worked with Latrobe.) The bank's gabled ends were directly inspired by the Parthenon without the sculpture—as Strickland himself proclaimed—but its sides, because of interior space demands, lack the fifteen lateral Doric columns which embrace the home of the virgin Athena. Actually the competition itself called for "a chaste imitation of Grecian architecture," and the result is the earliest "pure" example of this style which we have. The main banking room, which occupies the entire center of the building extending from side to side, is a well-proportioned chamber with freestanding Ionic columns upholding a vaulted ceiling. Note on the exterior the arched windows on the sides.

In 1836 the Federal Charter for the Second Bank expired and its renewal was vetoed by President Jackson. A State Charter was granted for a private bank which operated in the building, but in 1841 the bank

failed, and from 1844 to 1932 the building was used by the federal government as a customhouse. For the bicentennial it was transformed into a portrait gallery of the nation's leaders from the 1775–1825 period. The bank forms a major asset to the Independence National Historical Park.

Open daily 9–5

21 Andalusia (1798/1836)
off State Road, .5 mile/.8 kilometer beyond Tennis Avenue, c. 13
miles/21 kilometers NE of
Philadelphia, Pennsylvania

THOMAS U. WALTER, ARCHITECT OF THE RENOVATION

A superb Greek Revival remodeling (1834–36) of an earlier farm
manor house (1798), to create the finest mansion along the upper
banks of the Delaware River. Nicholas Biddle, the owner, himself had
a hand in its design. The grounds edging down to the tidal waters are
not only immaculate, they are highlighted by a romantic grotto, also
designed by Walter, plus a marvelous double-deck Greek Revival
pavilion containing a billiard room on the ground floor and "temple"
card room (for the gentlemen) above. The finely chiseled Doric
remodeling of the manor is impeccable on the exterior, but within it
is somewhat strangely divided into two longitudinal rooms instead of
one airy chamber overlooking lawn and river. The Empire furniture,
made in Philadelphia, and the sculpture are outstanding. House,
pavilions, and grounds make a memorable group.

*Open May–Nov., Wed. and Sat., 10:30, 12, and 2—by
appointment: call Cliveden (215) 848-1777*

22 Founder's Hall (1833–47)
Girard College
Girard and Corinthian Avenues
Philadelphia, Pennsylvania

THOMAS U. WALTER, ARCHITECT

Founder's Hall was designed by the Philadelphia-born Walter when he was twenty-nine, with precise instructions from Girard's will, which stipulated length "at least one hundred and ten feet [33 meters] east and west, and one hundred and sixty feet [49 meters] north and south . . . It shall be three stories in height, each story at least fifteen feet [4.6 meters] high in the clear from the floor to the cornice: It shall be fire proof inside and outside." And so the will goes, down to details such as wall thicknesses and stair details. There were probably suggestions also from the Hellenophile Nicholas Biddle, whose Greek Revival Andalusia (q.v.) Walter was designing at roughly the same time. Moreover Pierre Vignon's Paris Church of the Madeleine (begun in 1806) must have been of influence, each being of temple form with eight Corinthian columns across the front. In any event Girard College forms one of the monuments of the development of the Greek Revival in this country, a substantial step in scope beyond Strickland's Second Bank (q.v.).

With its four flanking buildings, two per side, the Hall initially constituted the complete "college" for "poor male white orphans . . . born in the City of Philadelphia . . . in any other part of Pennsylvania . . . the City of New York . . . the City of New Orleans." (Girard first landed from his native France in New York, while New Orleans was the first port at which he traded as "first officer, and subsequently as master and part owner of a vessel." Stephen Girard, 1750–1831, was subsequently enormously successful as merchant and banker.) However, the "simple, chaste and pure architecture of the ancients" which Walter used encountered difficulties in housing a school for young boys, and problems of heating, humidification, and acoustics arose at every turn; these recurred during the following sixty-six years until other buildings more appropriate for school purposes were erected. As Robert Dale Owen, chairman of the Building Committee for the Smithsonian Institution, put it, "So serious are the obstacles presented by the rigid and uncomplying forms of the classical school, that internal convenience is often sacrificed upon the altar of antique taste" (*Hints on Public,* 1849, De Capo reprint 1978). The second and third floors were —and still are—divided into four rooms (formerly for classes), a low,

precisely calculated vault covering each with the top four (now closed off) being skylit. Since the early part of this century the main building has been used as a memorial to its founder, with a museum and recreational and social facilities occupying the remaining space. With its authoritative massing at the head of the street, abetted by the bold scale of the columns of Founder's Hall (54.5 feet/16.6 meters high), this group of five buildings—"the most sumptuous example of the Greek Revival in the country" (Agnes A. Gilchrist)—exerted a powerful architectural influence on the nation.

Originally limited by Girard's will to orphan lads, "functional male orphans" (not receiving adequate care from one or both of their natural parents) were admitted in 1977, while "whiteness" previously had been ruled unconstitutional in 1968. Some three hundred students (capacity to five hundred) receive free boarding and tuition. Some enter in the first grade and can stay through high school—or, indeed, remain for 365 days a year if there is family need. Extraordinary.

Can be seen from entrance gate and visited by appointment

---

23   Cast-Iron Buildings (1857)
Arch Street at Front
Philadelphia, Pennsylvania

These two five-story cast-iron buildings—originally a continuous line—are good souvenirs of the waterfront structures that once characterized much of mid-nineteenth-century Philadelphia. Though at present this

area is somewhat dilapidated, at least one block is in the process of restoration. In design module they are similar to the Grain Buildings of the Architectural Iron Works catalog of 1865. Note the scale progression from ground floor to those above, each floor slightly less in height than that underneath. The far building was originally occupied by the Smythe Stores, its cast iron coming from the Tiffany & Bottom Ironworks.

Can only be seen from street

---

24   City Hall (1872–1901)
Market Street at Broad Street
Philadelphia, Pennsylvania

JOHN McARTHUR, JR., ARCHITECT

Pride of city fathers has never been more exuberantly expressed than in this glorious mastodon, this "tasteless pile," which dominates downtown Philadelphia. (One might add that questionable city-county finances and patronage have rarely been more conspicuously monumentalized.) Pelion on Ossa pales beside it, the Capitol in Washington reputedly could fit inside with ease. Ambition has been matched by performance. The central bays are splendiferous, the corners magnificent —all in a late Second Empire "Louvre" Style—and the tower outrageous, so outrageous in fact that the building took thirty years to complete. The 511-foot/156-meter tower (without statue) claims

to be the tallest all-masonry construction (i.e. with no steel) achieved by man, its tremendous weight demanding walls 22 feet/6.7 meters thick at the bottom. (It is, in fact, 45 feet/14 meters lower than the Washington Monument, which, however, was not finished until 1885. Moreover, City Hall's tower is of brick and masonry up to the level below the clock, its upper stages being of cast iron painted to match the gray granite.)

Mr. William Penn, all 37 feet/11 meters and 53,348 pounds/24,200 kilograms of him, surveys from his vantage point atop the tower the legacy of his enlightened leadership that did so much to plant the city's seed of growth in "the virgin settlement of this province." The building stands on the precise spot selected for it by Penn in 1683. Binoculars are recommended here to study William and the smaller sculptures which leap from every cranny of the outside. All continents, all races, and practically all animals can be seen, carved by Alexander Milne Calder, who, like the building's architect, was a Scot immigrant. (Calder's late grandson and namesake, of course, ranked with the most noted sculptors of the twentieth century.)

In plan City Hall describes a hollow square with all rooms facing either outward or onto the inner courtyard. (The evidence also seems conclusive that Thomas U. Walter had a hand in the design of the tower and inner decoration, for in 1865, upon resigning as Architect of the Capitol, he returned to Philadelphia and joined forces with John McArthur, Jr.) The interior perhaps attains greatest architectural impact in the six-story-high open stairwells located at the four corners. The Council Chamber, its "Conversation Hall," and the Mayor's Reception Room in all their glory should also be seen. There will never be another city hall like this one. Fortunately a 1957 committee of the American Institute of Architects, in strongly recommending renovation over destruction and "modern" replacement, said "City Hall is perhaps the greatest single effort of late-nineteenth-century American architecture" (quoted by John Maass in an excellent article in the *AIA Journal*, February 1965).

Tours Mon.–Fri. at 10, except holidays; Observation Tower open daily except holidays 9–4

---

25   Pennsylvania Academy of the Fine Arts (1872–76)
Broad Street at Cherry
Philadelphia, Pennsylvania

FRANK FURNESS AND GEORGE W. HEWITT, ARCHITECTS

Frank Furness (1839–1912)—"fearless Frank" he has with reason been called—was probably the gutsiest architect who ever walked the North American continent. His extraordinary buildings, of which, sadly, only a few remain, apotheosize boldness, exude power even when small in size, and clearly anticipated what is now called the New Brutalism: they are preposterously wonderful. The buildings are, indeed, like the man himself, who won the Congressional Medal as Captain Frank Furness of the 6th Pennsylvania Cavalry for carrying a

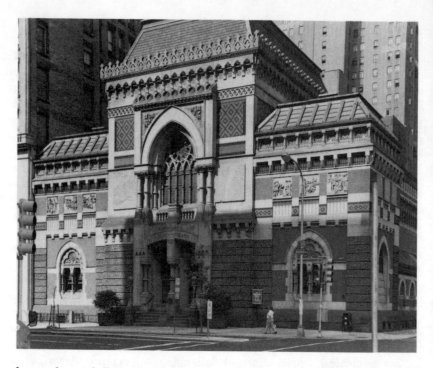

heavy box of live ammunition to a beleaguered outpost, an action which necessitated directly exposing himself to enemy fire. He is probably the only architect in the U.S.A. to win the nation's highest military honor. Furness, who was born in Philadelphia, worked for the famous Richard Morris Hunt in New York before returning home, thus acquiring a practical, French-influenced background. (Interestingly the young Louis Sullivan worked briefly for Furness until the depression of 1873—the two reputedly became great friends. Sullivan, it should be added, was also undoubtedly influenced in Philadelphia by William J. Johnston's eight-story plus cupola Jayne Building of 1849–51, then probably the tallest structure in the world. It had a materials hoist but no passenger elevator. The building was destroyed in 1958.)

Furness' architecture in his heyday was an amalgam of late Victorian Gothic plus the Queen Anne Style, with a bit of Richardson, his contemporary, in the background. The writings of Ruskin (*The Stones of Venice*) and of Viollet-le-Duc were also influential. However, Furness manipulated and sublimated these fashionable facets with the force of a pile driver, achieving an intensity and "compaction" rarely seen. His greatest surviving building is that for the Pennsylvania Academy of the Fine Arts, the oldest institution of its kind in the country (founded in 1805), combining a distinguished art school (on the lower floor) with a first-rate museum. Its commission was won by Furness and George W. Hewitt through an invitation competition. Though Hewitt left Furness a year after the Academy was finished (to set up an office with his brother William D.), his contribution to its design perhaps has been underplayed. For Hewitt's work—including some fifty churches—reveled in the polychromatic neo-Gothic style which is apparent in the Academy, particularly in the stunning stair hall. Observe on the building's facade—probably largely by Furness—that although each element is prodigiously detailed, the whole has been orchestrated with tremendous authority, while the interior is almost phosphorescent with its newly renovated richness. Robert Venturi in his provocative book *Complexity and Contradiction in Architecture* (Museum of Modern Art, 1966) wrote of an equally "violent" but now destroyed Furness building that "it is an almost insane short story of a castle on a city street"!

Hyman Myers, an architect and Furness scholar working with the firm of Day & Zimmermann, was responsible for the total restoration of the building: it has been sumptuously carried out (1974–76). The building was built for the nation's Centennial Exposition in Philadelphia; let us hope that it graces our three hundredth birthday.

NOTE: A comprehensive book on *The Architecture of Frank Furness* with text by James F. O'Gorman and outstanding photographs by Cervin Robinson was published in 1973 by the Philadelphia Museum of Art.

Open Tues.–Sat. 10–5, Sun. 1–5, except holidays: admission

---

26 Philadelphia Saving Fund Society Building (1929–32)
Market Street at South 12th
Philadelphia, Pennsylvania

HOWE & LESCAZE, ARCHITECTS

The superb thirty-six-story PSFS Building was one of the germinal office towers in the country. Considered by many as the most important tall structure from the 1890s to the 1930s, it was our first truly "modern skyscraper" (*Architectural Review,* May 1957), and one which influenced subsequent buildings for years. The evolution of its design is elusive but there is more than a hint of the European International Style in it. (The late William Lescaze was himself born in Switzerland.) Neutra's office building of c. 1925 for Rush City Reformed had similar cantilevered horizontal bands of fenestration in front and vertically expressed structure on the side. However, PSFS stands as an advanced and magnificent building in its own right. Its tripartite sections are functionally and eloquently stated: banking floor in base (but not at street level); firmly cantilevered office slab with exposed structure; and, at rear, service spine sharply differentiated by both color and shape. Placing the banking floor on the second level with access by moving stair—and thus being able to rent the ground floor—was rare and daring in its day and, of course, has been much copied since. Reputedly it was the building's "practicality" which sold its then very advanced

design to the bank. Note, in this regard, the low (and expressed) twentieth floor which houses air-conditioning equipment. Air conditioning—here only the second installation in a high-rise in the U.S.A.—made the building far more attractive to potential tenants. The narrow band of fenestration of the mechanical floor, moreover, gives subtle scale to the facade. Not only is the exterior of great merit, the interiors down to the design of the clocks and the colors used are admirable. The rounded-corner base might be considered mannered today, and there is some fussiness at the top, but PSFS will always remain prominent in the hierarchy of office buildings and in the development of modern American architecture. (William H. Jordy in the fourth volume of *American Buildings and Their Architects*—Doubleday, 1972—has an excellent chapter on PSFS and its architects.) The Society, incidentally, was founded in 1816, and is now the largest savings bank in the country.

Open during business hours

---

27   Beth Sholom Synagogue (1959)
**Old York Road just N of Church Road (c. 11 miles/18 kilometers
    N of downtown)
Philadelphia (Elkins Park), Pennsylvania**

FRANK LLOYD WRIGHT, ARCHITECT

Crowning its hill and dominating it by day like some gigantic biblical tent perched on a Pennsylvania Sinai, shining forth at dusk through its translucent roof, Beth Sholom—House of Peace—commands all approaches day and night. The structure of the building is based on an equilateral triangle with a heavy concrete parallelogram-shaped pier anchoring each point. However, the glazed walls (above the solid entry base) angle outward on each side to make a modified hexagon of the plan. The mighty ridge beams, which then rise from the three points, lean inward and upward from their foundations to their truncated pinnacle, producing a towering monumentality. The panels of these roof-walls are double-thick with wired glass on the exterior and plastic within forming, so to speak, a translucent tent, "a lighted mountain." (Wright's original sketch was less open.) The seven crockets on the ridge beams which uphold this fabric recall the seven-branch menorah, hence the seven days of the Creation. The "tent" rests on an angled tan

concrete base with symbolic laver at entrance. One reaches the sanctuary via either of two straight flights of steps, angled like the facade, an arrangement carefully calculated to permit only tantalizing views upward under the magnetic canopy of the roof. This space-light trip epitomizes Wright's concern for three-dimensional exploration, space and light having always characterized his architecture. However, the focus of this journey—the sanctuary—does not altogether match the brilliance of the exterior. It is not sufficiently cohesive to hold down visually the vast panorama of 1,016 seats in front of it. Moreover for some there is a fussy quality in the strangely neo-Gothic grilles on the sides of the sanctuary. Note, however, the prominent—and striking—multicolored glass chandelier over the nave. Details aside, there is magnificence in this great translucid prism—Wright's "Manlight." A chapel and lounges fill the lower floor. Rabbi Mortimer J. Cohen of Beth Sholom worked closely with Wright in developing the basic concept.

Open Tues., Thurs. 1–3, Sun. 12–4: services Fri. 8:30 P.M., *Sat. 9:30* A.M.

28 Alfred Newton Richards Medical Research Building (1957–61) and Biology Laboratory (1962–64) Hamilton Walk, next to Medical School Philadelphia, Pennsylvania

LOUIS I. KAHN, ARCHITECT

The Richards Research Building and the slightly later conjoined Biology Lab number among the influential buildings in the development of mid-twentieth-century architecture. The Museum of Modern Art in a special brochure termed Richards "probably the single most consequential building constructed in the United States since the war" (1961

—Wilder Green). The reasons for this accolade lie in the conceptual, humanistic, and technical achievements of its architect. First of all he sought the "humanity" of clusters of smallish labs instead of an impersonal attenuated corridor plan. He then stated—some feel overstated—the division of what he called the "served" spaces from the "servant" to emphasize their differing functions. (Frank Lloyd Wright had closely studied and expressed "servicing requirements" in his long-destroyed Larkin Building of 1904.) The scientists and professors who work in Richards use a number of noisome gases and fumes, but instead of treating the necessary air-change and air-dissipation problem as an embarrassing nuisance to be swept under an architectural rug, Kahn seized upon it as the rationale of the whole building. To this end he designed four separate but coupled eight-story blocks comprising three "served" laboratory towers grouped around and plugged into a windowless concrete "servant" unit which houses animals used in research plus mechanical services. On the south side of the servant unit are attached four dramatic brick air-intake stacks whose sheer and solid walls rise two stories above the roof. Pure air is taken in near the bottom of these stacks, then conditioned and ducted to the distribution shaft on every floor and piped into the laboratories. Fumes and exhausted air from each lab are voided high above the roof by ventilating ducts rising in brick towers attached to the laboratories. On the opposite side of each laboratory block is affixed a similar brick "tower" containing emergency stairs. The 45-foot/14-meter-square laboratories, with their air-exhaust stack and fire stairs on the outside, are thus completely free of vertical obstruction, hence can be subdivided as needed. Altogether there are eleven ten-story stacks, four intake, four exhaust, and three emergency stairs, clutching the eight-story servant and three served towers—the most romantic group of towers big and small since San Gimignano. (Kahn had spent 1950–51 at the American Academy in Rome.) The dynamic force of these equal-height, blank-walled stretched verticals and their oscillation with the glassy horizontality of the laboratories rightly set the architectural world on fire. (They provided in the process a design quarry in which not a few of today's practitioners have dug.) The structure of the laboratory towers—which was closely worked out with Dr. August E. Komendant and the Keast & Hood Company as consultants—consists of an ingenious framework of both prestressed and post-tensioned concrete beams, designed, fabricated, and put together with imagination and precision, as can be seen at the entry. The open "webbing" of these 3-foot/.9-meter-deep floor trusses enables the extensive pipe runs to be woven through as needed. Note also the drop-off in the size of members as the spandrel beams cantilever to the corners: beautiful.

The Biology Laboratory, respectfully tied to Richards, was constructed several years later and shows more finesse, especially in window detailing, and also more economy. Lacking the soaring grandeur of Richards, it is nonetheless impressive, one of its most sensitive features being the fact that one wing of its ground floor is raised on pilotis, which not only lets the southern sun stream through to give life to the northern (and entrance) facade, but also provides visual contact with the garden beyond.

Richards has not been without critics. Some of the professors like it very much, others not. The perceptive Reyner Banham terms it "picturesquely heroic" (*Architectural Review*, March 1962). Many of the complaints stem from changes made after original construction cost bids came in substantially over the budget and the building was completed economically without reducing its size. Some of the building's users feel that there is too much visual intimacy between labs in one tower and the one adjacent, and too much aural intimacy within one's own tower (over the partitions and through the trusses) and not enough flexibility to accommodate change. Moreover there have been problems with sun control—which have been largely corrected in the Biology Lab. But with any complex undertaking, there are bound to be problems; when the effort is a pioneering one, such likelihood increases. Richards' contribution, however, shines and here is where we all benefit: it is a brilliant demonstration of turning the utilitarian, the architectural nuisances, into logical and vital elements of design. And, perhaps equally important, it was an act of liberation by this "prophet of the suppressed generation."

Ground floor only open to public: best seen from south side

---

29   Guild House (1960–63)
Spring Garden Street near 7th Street
Philadelphia, Pennsylvania

**VENTURI & RAUCH, ARCHITECTS; COPE & LIPPINCOTT,
ASSOCIATE ARCHITECTS**

Here is no routine building nor is its designer (Robert Venturi) a routine architect. Venturi's thesis is that "Boring is Interesting and [the] Extraordinary is Ordinary," a philosophy allied to the Pop Art approach which seeks to "reveal" the "dumb and ordinary" about us. He is, as Vincent Scully writes, "consistently anti-heroic," adding at the same time, "the essential point is that Venturi's philosophy and design are humanistic." Venturi's buildings thus tend to be architecturally Mannerist, scenographic, and rationalized, occasionally puzzlingly so. They even espouse "ornamented structure." However, do not brush off this paradoxical man, for he is incredibly learned (Phi Beta Kappa at Princeton; Prix de Rome) concerning the great historic buildings of this world and in probing and juxtaposing their essence, as can be seen in his book *Complexity and Contradiction in Architecture* (Museum of Modern Art, 1966). Venturi & Rauch's buildings, whether we are sympathetic to them or not, are among the most provocative of our time, and, it should be added, they all evolve from the spirit of their immediate environment.

Guild House for the Aged with its "billboard" of glazed white brick blazoning the entrance, its oversized lettering, its outsized granite column, and its fanlike neo-Palladian window at top (matching the width of the splayed entry) sets out to provoke, intellectually, Establishment architecture. (One wonders if the window was not partially inspired by a similar one in Latrobe's Burd House of 1802, also in Philadelphia.) The fact that the stringcourse at the fifth floor deliberately does not align with the window heads or bases is merely another design stiletto. But these seeming inconsistencies, which focus on

understatement, orchestrate, if they do not harmonize, to produce a sophisticated, "naive" building which will intrigue many, vex a few, and baffle the rest. With a scale and character "respecting" the street and with a plan that places the maximum number of rooms on the southerly side, there is more here than meets the hasty eye. In any case the cognoscenti of the various paths of contemporary architectural development in this country will find the enigmatic flair of this tensioned building ineluctably on their list. The House provides a retirement center of ninety-one apartments and a reception room (behind arced window at top) for elderly men and women who lived in this neighborhood before reconstruction of the area, and who wanted to remain. It was built under the aegis of the Friends.

Lobby only open to the public

---

30 Society Hill Apartments and Town Houses (1962–64)
2nd and Dock Streets
Philadelphia, Pennsylvania

I. M. PEI, ARCHITECT

Philadelphia was born at the water's edge in the autumn of 1682 when William Penn stepped ashore from the *Welcome* with a charter to establish a planned city of harmony and delight. The site, near the confluence of the Delaware and Schuylkill rivers, earlier had been casually occupied by Swedes, Finns, and some Dutch, but Philadelphia itself did not become a reality until Penn's ship dropped anchor. He had sent Thomas Holme, a surveyor, some months before his own arrival to select the actual site and lay out the future city's street pattern—which Holme did with probably a good deal more rigidity than Penn had envisioned. For years the city was the country's greatest port and the Delaware River, consequently, the place to be near, but through the generations the town's burgeoning size pushed its epicenter inland, between the rivers, a shift given finality in the last century by the westward relocation of the railroads. The old waterfront area declined, many of its buildings collapsed, and though only a short stroll from Independence Hall and the business and shopping world, this once proud section crept into slumhood. To resuscitate the area—which Penn had sold to the Free Society of Traders, hence the name Society Hill—the Philadelphia Redevelopment Authority conducted in 1958 an invitation

competition among developers and their architects. Webb & Knapp with I. M. Pei as their designer won out. Their concept stressed tower apartments rather than slabs which would have seriously cut off the river from downtown. The preservation and restoration of old town houses was also part of the Pei plan. The result is one of the most sensitive-to-neighborhood and most agreeable-to-eye revitalizations in the country. Three thirty-one-story towers, accommodating 720 apartments, and two sets of three-story town houses comprise the undertaking. (Five towers were originally anticipated.) Row or town houses are, incidentally, an old Philadelphia tradition, the earliest probably dating from 1691 and the best from the drawing board of Robert Mills (Franklin Row, 9th Street between Locust and Walnut, 1810—the only one of ten left). The Society Hill towers offer spectacular views of the city, and put middle- and upper-bracket taxpayers within walking distance of work and play. Well spaced and well related to each other (though somewhat unprotected from the wind), they form a model urban nexus. Their relation to the street pattern is excellent and it should be noted that one of the three identical buildings is at right angles to the other two, greatly enhancing their urban profile. Observe, too, that the depth of the module of their wall-bearing, poured-in-place concrete construction gives good sun protection to the inset windows. A garage for four hundred automobiles lies underneath and a shopping complex stands adjacent. When Penn's Landing Project along the nearby Delaware River is completed, and the Interstate highway bridged over and landscaped, the area will be even more attractive and valuable.

Grounds and lobby only open to public

The **Town Houses** (one group adjacent, the other on 4th and Locust) provide elegance in town-house living that is difficult to match— and also help translate stylistically the scale of the towers to that of the neighborhood. These low buildings focus inward on a paved courtyard of non-upkeep trees and sculpture, with each house enjoying its own walled garden. All of them offer more space and higher ceilings than in the FHA-limited towers. Kitchen and dining occupy the ground floor, living room and library the second, and three bedrooms—marked by the continuous band of windows—the top. Both towers and town houses take their scale, Flemish bond brick, and even their arched doorways and window proportions from the basic module of the historic houses of the neighborhood and from the nearby refurbished market. (The 1765 Powel House, q.v., is just around the corner.) As a result of this farsighted urban salvage operation and the exemplary quality of its land usage and architecture, this entire section of the city is being rapidly upgraded via private initiative. Some seven hundred surviving eighteenth- and early-nineteenth-century houses have already been restored: Philadelphians are moving back to the city. The whole Society Hill Historic District is listed in the National Register of Historic Places.

31   Downtown Redevelopment (1965–75)
     Philadelphia, Pennsylvania

PHILADELPHIA PLANNING COMMISSION, PLANNERS; EDMUND N.
BACON, EXECUTIVE DIRECTOR; BUILDINGS BY VARIOUS
ARCHITECTS

Once stagnating Philadelphia has done more than any major city in the
United States to replan and revive its aged downtown core. (Boston
and Baltimore have also made commendable progress.) It is also safe
to say that until and unless our other cities, major and minor, do more
in this regard—and do it with farsighted intelligence—they will virtually perish by rot or self-strangulation, particularly as regards urban
movement. With many of our urban decision-makers fleeing to the
delights of carefree suburban living, hence too little confronted by the
acid problems of downtown, the hope for the future is not encouraging.
New York, for instance, demolished structures along avenue after avenue but rebuilt with little foresight or enlightened land usage. New
York City's recent development of Roosevelt (ex-Welfare) Island—
probably the world's most spectacular urban building site—is architecturally pusillanimous and politically compromised. Chicago, which
did so much in the earlier part of the century to embrace the lake—as
opposed to Cleveland, which did nothing then and too little today—
boasts a number of exciting recent buildings but almost no coordinated
central development and, like all the others, has too little mass transportation. Detroit ruthlessly wiped out square miles of buildings, and
much of it is still wiped out. Atlanta is making a pressure cooker of its
CBD. San Francisco operates primarily on a piecemeal basis. (Los An-
geles, rudderless for decades, is now awakening.)
    Philadelphia's downtown planning began in the early 1950s when the
downtown Broad Street Station (1881) and its sixteen lines of elevated
railroad tracks—locally known as the Chinese Wall—were removed.
Most cities would probably have put a reduced-size station and fewer
tracks underground—as Philadelphia did—and forgotten the invitation
of the rest—which Philadelphia did not. Bacon and his cohorts had
been making long-range plans for the area years before they could actually be implemented, so with the removal of the station and the tracks
they were ready and able to turn a blight into an asset. Penn Center
Plaza, stretching three blocks, was the prime result, with well-spaced
(but unfortunately architecturally undistinguished) office blocks lining

its sunken pedestrian mall. A new park was created to the north and a new transportation hub at the west end, with extensive parking facilities near the expressway. Although Penn Center did not materialize into the cohesive Rockefeller Center it hoped to be—largely because of the dullish quality of its new buildings—it has had a profound effect on the life and economy of the central business and shopping district, yet is only one chapter of the city's planning activity. The Market Street East development (1978)—on the other side of City Hall from Penn Center —is of definite interest. The glass-topped Gallery at Market East with over a hundred shops is sparkling in architectural terms and very successful financially. (Bower & Fradley were the architects, succeeded by Bower Fradley Lewis Thrower.)

The city then went on with the rehabilitation of other areas, primarily the Independence National Historical Park and Independence Mall (not exalted), areas which were financed by city, state, and national funds, and the Society Hill renovation (q.v.), mostly privately financed. The ten-lane Delaware Expressway (Interstate 95), which parallels the river, until recently semi-isolated the as yet unfinished 37-acre/15-hectare Penn's Landing Project. Under the conditions (obsolete wharves to be removed plus an ancient, little-used street pattern), this was probably the only location where this highway could be placed. The expressway has been bridged over (1978) to the water's edge in the historic area, which is now under development to the river. Target date for completion of Penn's Landing with a host of facilities is the early 1980s.

Altogether Philadelphia has over 11 square miles/28 square kilometers under restoration, a good part of which is contiguous. This acreage, however, is not as important as the fact that the rehabilitation is being done under a farsighted, unified plan. It is a plan, moreover, which seeks to preserve every salvageable historic building possible: no bulldozer approach here. Much of the impetus for this high level of looking at the city and its future came from the Citizens' Council on City Planning, which put on a tremendously successful, privately financed "Better Philadelphia" show in 1947, an exhibition designed by the late Oskar Stonorov. This challenging exhibit at Gimbel's Department Store was seen by 400,000 people, creating that essential citizen and political awareness and excitement which led to the support of the work by the professional planners and architects. If you want a better city, you have to work like the devil for it—Philadelphia did.

32   Central Atlantic Headquarters, Prudential Life Insurance Company
(1970–72)
N off Exit 27 of Penn Turnpike (IS 276) or take PA 611 direct
from downtown
near Philadelphia (Dresher), Pennsylvania

THE KLING PARTNERSHIP, ARCHITECTS

A particularly handsome, well-thought-out suburban regional headquarters along the north edge of the Pennsylvania Turnpike. Astute
advantage was taken of the change of grade of the 82-acre/33-hec-
tare site, its unevenness prompting two four-story, unequal-sized inter-

connected units to meet these changes with optimum efficiency—and to produce a non-authoritarian scale. A 70-foot/21-meter, three-story glass nexus connects the two sections, its transparency providing visual animation to the entry court. The building envelope is of exposed, precast concrete and glass which is given relief by the outrigging of bronze anodized aluminum louvers which shield the windows from the sun on the east, south, and west sides. Such use of solar protection is strangely absent from too many buildings in this country though the thermal and esthetic benefits of such louvers are obvious.

The main entrance lies off the angled courtyard mentioned, with a one-story 625-seat cafeteria projecting at right adjacent to a pond with a sunken garden which is much used for a lunchtime break. The lofty lobby provides a spacious introduction to the building; a retail shop for the staff of 1,700 lies directly adjacent. The cheerful interiors were designed by the architect. The interaction of the rhomboid shapes of the buildings, their pronounced horizontality punctured by vertical stair and utility towers, the handling of the space between the two structures, and their adaptation to the rolling terrain are first-rate. Parking for 1,400 cars is distributed in lots on the periphery.

Grounds and lobby open during business hours

---

33   INA Tower (1974–75)
Arch Street at 17th (just W of Kennedy Plaza)
Philadelphia, Pennsylvania

MITCHELL/GIURGOLA, ARCHITECTS

An unusual, highly successful twenty-seven-story office block, the rationale of which—like many of Mitchell/Giurgola's buildings—stems from that well-known friend and enemy of man, the sun. To deal properly with this bane or blessing, the architects analyzed the potential solar considerations of heat and light, of exclusion and extraction, on each facade and designed them accordingly. The north wall (on Arch Street) is almost all glass; the south side, on the other hand, has shielded strip windows at top but cleverly opens with large panes below where the narrow street (Cuthbert) enshadows and light is needed. The east and west strip windows are set back and properly protected by inner-curved overhangs. From the design point of view there is an obvious danger that the building will not hold together visually, that it will

sprout four facades in search of a home, but there is a fine family coordination here, effected by the smooth enameled-aluminum skin and
greenish plate glass, plus coordination of sills and expert corner detailing. The dramatic, angled indentations at mid-height of the north
and south sides are intakes for air conditioning, while the stale-air ex-
hausts are smartly tailored on the east and west facades. Square in plan,
the building offers a basically unencumbered U-shape space for offices,
surrounding the elevator and utility core. It is an original, keenly
analyzed skyscraper. The tower is attached—the juncture is good—to
the 1923 headquarters of the Insurance Company of North America
(founded in 1792), Stewardson & Page, architects.

Lobby open during business hours

34 Franklin Court (1975–76)
Market Street between 3rd and 4th
Philadelphia, Pennsylvania

VENTURI & RAUCH, ARCHITECTS, WITH JOHN MILNER AND THE NATIONAL HERITAGE CORPORATION

Erecting a "ghost" frame of Benjamin Franklin's house and printing-press shop provides us with an inventive solution to a difficult reconstruction problem. Franklin's former residence once stood on the site but was torn down in 1812 for a street-widening program. (The archway—for a carriage—leading to the house is, however, original.) As the architects knew from drawings the basic pattern but not the specifics of several of the houses Franklin had built, this mauve-painted steel frame, its members made of 12-inch/30-centimeter-square tubing, ingeniously gives us the concept if not the substance. Moreover, it enables the small area available today to be an open garden court (marked by robust detail to withstand crowd abuse). Archeological excavations established the plan and amusing concrete viewing hoods enable one to

view the foundations, privy, and ice pits. Room layout is indicated by different-colored paving stones.

Expanding beneath all this, and reached by a long ramp, is a theater and frisky museum of the multifarious activities of our famous statesman, printer, scientist, master of aphorism, etc.—the son of a Boston soapmaker and one who dropped out of school (but obviously not out of studying) when ten years old. De Martin-Merona-Cranstoun-Downes Associates designed the museum installation. The buildings on Market Street—in front of the courtyard—include a post office and Postal Service Museum—thoughtful mementos of the former postmaster general—and were reconstructed by the National Heritage Corporation, specialists in historic restoration. The complex is now under the wing of the National Park Service.

Open daily 8:30–5, except Jan. 1 and Dec. 25

---

35   Robin Hood Dell West (1975–76)
Parkside at 52nd Drive
Philadelphia, Pennsylvania

JOHN H. MacFADYEN AND ALFREDO DE VIDO, ARCHITECTS

Robin Hood Dell West stands as a structurally svelte shed for the summer home of the Philadelphia Orchestra and related music groups. (Compare MacFadyen, Knowles & De Vido's famous Wolf Trap, a similar open-air concert hall-theater at Vienna, Virginia.) This new facility is situated away from street and highway noises yet is convenient to the motorist. As it rests in a natural amphitheater overflow crowds can be accommodated on the sloping ground yet maintain visual contact with the stage. There are seats for 3,810 in the orchestra, 815 in the balcony, with benches for approximately 5,000 under the stars and a like number on the lawn. (The original Robin Hood Dell, built in 1930 in East Fairmount Park, is still in use, primarily for jazz and rock concerts.) The dramatics of the new building lie in its great roof, 263 feet/80 meters wide, 260 feet/79 meters deep, and 107 feet/33 meters high, with full-width balcony lightly hovering in space. The pared bridged ramps to the balcony form a key element of the design. The internal construction—and its sight lines—are made possible by a 32-foot/9.8-meter-deep king-post truss system of lightweight steel. This abuts the 100-foot/30-meter-high stagehouse, which also contains dressing rooms, administrative offices, box office, and public toilets, the

latter two facilities duplicated at the upper end of the site. Note on the outside the meeting of structure and Terne-coated stainless steel roof with the low brick stylobate. Adjustable natural-wood acoustic panels line the interior of the stagehouse. I. Demchick was associate architect; Charles H. Thornton of Lev Zetlin Associates, structural engineer; and A. Melzer, acoustician.

Open for performances: exterior visible daily

---

36   Allegheny County Jail and Court House (1884–88)
436 Grant Street between 5th Avenue and Forbes Avenue
Pittsburgh, Pennsylvania

HENRY HOBSON RICHARDSON, ARCHITECT

Strength in American architecture reaches its apogee in these Allegheny County conjoined buildings, Richardson's and the era's masterpiece. We find here an ultimate in stone construction—guts with sophistication: the lessons of the cut-stone masonry in the Jail are imperishable. The more formal Court House, which shelters an elaborate quota of functions (and was finished a year later), is handsome, however more routine. But the Jail, attached to the Court House by its Bridge of

Sighs (on Ross Street), recalls, appropriately, Piranesi's *carceri* series as it rises as an unfractured bastion to fill its block. Its wall, broken only by an elegantly grilled entrance and a few windows in front plus a service gate on the side (see photograph above), wraps masterfully about the semitriangular block as it envelops the three-armed jail and its yard. No base, no cornice jars this wall's stupendous authority. The junctures of the wall as it rises flush to fair into the ends of the jail wings and as it meets the towers provide one of architecture's greatest statements in undressed ashlar granite. Here, indeed, is the primeval strength of the inner earth.

The Court House, though somewhat fractured on the exterior, except for a superior tower, achieves strength within, especially in the two entrance halls, where parades of arches uphold the floors above. Note, too, in the entry the vitality of the main stairs and the variety of capitals atop the columns. The design of the Court House—which was won by competition—is of interest in that it was planned so that its high and wide courtrooms alternate with narrow "double-decked" judges' rooms, most of which are marked by the half-round turrets of the exterior. Thus the problem of public versus private scale has been imaginatively handled. With a continuous corridor on each of its five floors encircling the open courtyard of the center, a very functional building results. Incidentally, step into this courtyard to see the rhythm of the window and wall arches there. The yard itself was refurbished (1977) with new brick paving, a fountain, a number of planting boxes with trees, and sixteen teak benches. The great tower which rises above yard and building was designed for storage of legal documents and—an advancement for the time as well as a reflection of the city's atmosphere—as fresh-air intake for the whole building. Richardson, the building's genius, saw only the Jail section of his masterpiece completed: he died in April 1886 at the age of forty-eight just two years before the Court House was opened. The supervisory work was completed by Shepley, Rutan and Coolidge. One of the greatest buildings of the nineteenth century.

Court House open Mon.–Fri. 8:30–4:30, except holidays

---

37   Chatham Village (1932/1936)
   Bigham Street, Virginia Avenue, Olympia Road, and Pennridge
   Road in the Mount Washington area
   Pittsburgh, Pennsylvania

   CLARENCE S. STEIN & HENRY WRIGHT, SR., PLANNERS; INGHAM
   & BOYD, ARCHITECTS

The Buhl Foundation built the 45-acre/18-hectare Chatham Village as low-cost rental housing at the depth of the Depression: it is still a model, full of lessons for the developer and architect. Its three rows of

houses reflect directly the steep topography, and every change of level
has been used functionally and for visual variety. Services are confined
to the periphery while groups of attached houses form a ring around
beautifully landscaped and scaled central "greens." Unobtrusive yet
convenient garage "compounds" accommodate many cars with other
parking incorporated under some of the individual houses when grade
permits. The first section of 129 simple red-brick, modified Georgian
two-story houses was completed in 1932 (R. E. Griswold, landscape
architect), and the second phase of 68 more in 1936 (T. M. Kohankie,
landscape architect). A former mansion (1844) is used as a clubhouse
with a small group of shops occupying the northeast corner. Recreation
facilities abound; a public park lies adjacent. Chatham Village is admirable—and a highly successful private undertaking. It was purchased
by its devoted tenants as a cooperative in 1960.

Grounds only open to the public

38 Land Usage in the Gateway Center Development (1952–69)
Gateway Center between Liberty and Duquesne Streets
Pittsburgh, Pennsylvania

CLARKE + RAPUANO, LANDSCAPE ARCHITECTS; IRWIN CLAVAN, ARCHITECT

Pittsburgh's Gateway Center with the adjacent Point State Park form the city's famous Golden Triangle at the meeting of the Allegheny and Monongahela rivers (exeunt as the Ohio). Though its land usage is excellent, its buildings are not of the same caliber or homogeneity— while its public transportation and private parking are both inadequate. And in spite of a sizable hotel, lifelessness begins to creep in late in the day. However, the space between the key buildings is exemplary

and the pedestrian is master of the ground and can stroll unthreatened by the automobile down allées of oak and sweet gum with flowering plants and fountains on all sides. The landscaping which interprets and guides this urban freedom is more than refreshing: would that every business district boasted such amenity. Gateway Center's core forms, indeed, the closest approximation of Le Corbusier's *ville radieuse* (promoted in 1922) that one will encounter in the United States— office buildings in a parklike setting, classified circulation, and even cruciform-plan skyscrapers (the three earliest of Gateway being of twenty and twenty-four floors). In 1969 the tenth and final skyscraper in the Gateway Center complex was dedicated, and in the contrast between what stands there today with the dilapidated small industries and burned-out railway facilities which had previously blighted the area lies a major element in the salvation of the city of Pittsburgh. (The entire point of land was imaginatively and bravely transformed following the establishment of the Urban Redevelopment Authority in 1946 by Mayor David L. Lawrence. Altogether there are 59 acres/24 hectares, 23/9 in Gateway Center and 36/14 in the state park.) Though financed with private funds, the city used the right of eminent domain to assemble the land, which it then resold, with the Equitable Life Assurance Society acting as builder and operator. When walking through the Center luxuriate in the space where buildings cover only 20 per cent of the site, regard the trees, smell the flowers, and most of all consider their microcosmic lesson for all cities. It is very important.

Clarke + Rapuano and GWSM Inc. collaborated on the design of the adjacent Point State Park.

---

39 Mellon Square (1956) and the Alcoa Building (1952)
William Penn Place, Oliver Avenue, Smithfield Street, 6th Avenue
Pittsburgh, Pennsylvania

SIMONDS & SIMONDS, LANDSCAPE ARCHITECTS OF MELLON SQUARE; HARRISON & ABRAMOVITZ, ARCHITECTS OF ALCOA BUILDING

Mellon Square forms the most verdurous roof of a midtown garage that one will see. If all parking facilities were so topped, our central business districts would be vastly more pleasant. Taking advantage of a sharp level change between the upper and lower parallel streets which demark the Square, a 1,200-car, five-level underground garage has been shoehorned into the slope by architects Mitchell & Ritchey. Simonds & Simonds then transformed its roof into a garden with honey locusts set in raised boxes—raised to ease roof problems and to give better protection and visual change—with linden, gum, and other trees framing the periphery and giving dimension to the open center. A major flower planter adds color, with a water basin as central focus, and cascading fountains escort one to the lower street, soothing the passage with their "white" noise. Kenneth Snelson's *Forest Devil* adds its tensioned sparkle. Some of the details, as in the fountain, are heavy but the whole is a haven. The architectural firm of Mitchell and Ritchey is now Deeter, Ritchey, Sippel Associates and the landscape architects Simonds and Simonds are The Environmental Planning and Design Partnership.

The thirty-story **Alcoa Building** (open during business hours) stands at the northeast corner of the square. When completed in 1952 this "aluminum envelope" pioneered an imaginative new direction in "clip-on" metal curtain wall design, here in 6×12 foot/1.8×3.6 meter prefabricated aluminum panels. Moreover these were installed and fastened completely from the inside, thus obviating the need for scaffolding. Its heat-resistant windows—note their appropriate small size—are reversible for cleaning. The diamond pattern of the panels reflects sun and shadow and, of course, produces stiffening. The four-story-high glass entry seemingly is tacked on but the main building makes an important contribution. Altenhof & Brown, Mitchell & Ritchey were associate architects; Edwards & Hjorth, structural engineers.

---

40 U. S. Steel Building (1970)
600 Grant Street
Pittsburgh, Pennsylvania

HARRISON & ABRAMOVITZ AND ABBE, ARCHITECTS; SKILLING, HELLE, CHRISTIANSON & ROBERTSON AND EDWARDS & HJORTH, STRUCTURAL ENGINEERS

Fire protection has always dictated via building codes that the steel frame of multistory buildings must be encased in concrete, masonry, or asbestos to prevent the steel from buckling in a conflagration. The steel frame of this extraordinary sixty-four-story skyscraper, however, is fully exposed, achieving its necessary fireproofing by having its exoskeletal hollow-box columns filled with water—and antifreeze. Exposed steel is both structure and finish. This ingenious technique has, of course, opened new structural and visual possibilities in high-rise design, and the architects have taken bold advantage of it in this show-case for the U. S. Steel Corporation. It should be added immediately, however, that the exoskeleton came before the water-filled columns: by having the structure on the outside a column-free interior, subdivisible at will, would result. The first studies of an exoskeleton had columns on 13-foot/3.9-meter centers and engaged to the building at each floor. This evolved into the 39-foot/11.8-meter spacing used with a three-story-high "lift" or section, the largest that the fabricator, American

Bridge, recommended. The columns were made as sizable as feasible
for esthetic reasons and to accommodate the water which is used both
for fireproofing and, by circulation, to minimize temperature changes
on opposite sides of the building. The resulting exterior framework produces consequently a new and very imposing scale. (Compare the more
modest vertical three-bay expression of Jenney's Second Leiter Building
in Chicago of 1891.) The two intermediate floors of U. S. Steel's three-
floor division do not frame into the exterior steel columns (six per
side), but are supported internally by two-story columns which are
upheld by each "primary" floor. The skin of the building is set back 3
feet/.9 meter from and completely independent of the exoskeleton, the
air space contributing to the fireproofing. Both framing and walls are
made of Cor-Ten, a weathering, self-protecting special steel which
needs no upkeep—and was developed by U. S. Steel.

Not only is the building innovative in structural concept, its plan,
which was determined only after considerable analysis, forms an unu-

sual equilateral triangle notched at the corners. Though this might prove awkward in a smaller building—its office space is exceeded only by that in the Pan Am and Port Authority buildings in New York—it works readily here, providing three contiguous column-free rectangles of office area each 221×45 feet/67×14 meters, quickly (overnight) divisible at will, with all services and vertical circulation in an inner triangular core. This idea-full and handsome building epitomizes steel construction, as three blocks down Grant Street, Richardson's County Court House and Jail heralded the zenith—and the swan song—of masonry.

The 62nd floor Top of the Triangle Restaurant is open for lunch and dinner, Mon.–Sat.

---

41   Student Union (1967)
Duquesne University
Centennial Walk (mid-campus)
Pittsburgh, Pennsylvania

PAUL SCHWEIKHER, ARCHITECT

A tough, powerful building with well-modulated facades (and, perhaps, an overmonumental entrance ramp). Its plasticity stems from the boxed outrigging which on front and back stands largely free of the building, and by its projections not only shades the windows from too much sun, but plays visually with light and shade throughout the day. The raw concrete of the building contrasts with the slick plate glass of the fenestration and the natural-finish oak of the doors and mullions. The Union has four floors on the entry side and, because of sharp falloff in grade, six on the far side. The entrance level contains publication, administrative, and miscellaneous student offices, while the major space above, reached by either the external ramp or inside stair, contains the great "hall" with student lounges and dining facility. It also serves for concerts, exhibitions, assemblies, and as ballroom. The hall is best reached via the off-center ramp which takes one up the switchback of the incline under a low and narrow entry to burst into the three-story hall. This space, with two solid-faced stepped-back balconies, finds climax in the ceiling, which pours forth natural light throughout the day from five sizable roof monitors. Lounges occupy the main level, with a thousand-seat student dining room and serving pantry/kitchen on the first bal-

cony, the top balcony catering to special events, faculty facilities, departmental offices, and conference rooms. More chromatic liveliness in the furnishings would be welcome but space and light are dramatically handled. A central kitchen, bookstore, and recreation area occupy the two lowest floors.

Open daily, 7 A.M.–midnight

Directly facing the Student Union across Centennial Walk stands the **Richard King Mellon Hall of Science** by Mies van der Rohe (1970), representing the steel antithesis to Schweikher's concrete expressionism.

---

42   Pottsgrove Mansion (1752–54)
West King Street (PA 663) just E of PA 100, and W of
Pottstown, Pennsylvania

The eastern Pennsylvania manor house with its local fieldstone walls, wood shakes, pent roof over much of the first floor—the whole trimmed with white shutters and girdled by white fences—has for over

two hundred years formed a comely regional addition to American domestic architecture. Generally starting with a small rectangular nucleus, such houses often expanded with the owner's fortune and family with the result that a rambling picturesqueness, as opposed to a formal Georgian symmetry, characterizes many. Pottsgrove Mansion, as the house of a wealthy ironmaster, falls into this pattern. The original front toward the Schuylkill River is of dressed reddish sandstone and is not particularly appealing, being somewhat rigid, but the rest of the exterior, its additions clearly marked by roof breaks and variations of stone dressing and stone color, makes the house well worth a visit. In 1940 the building, having served as a hotel for years, was purchased by Potts descendants and in 1941 given to the Commonwealth of Pennsylvania and the Pennsylvania Historical Commission. In 1952—the bicentennial of its commencement—it was opened to the public, having been completely restored and refurnished—note period furniture, colors, and Scalamandré fabrics—and its flower and herb garden replanted. G. Edwin Brumbaugh was architect of the restoration (1941–52).

Open Tues.–Sat. 10–4:30, Sun. 1–4:30, except holidays: admission

43   Morton Homestead (c. 1654/c. 1698)
100 Lincoln Avenue
Prospect Park, Pennsylvania

A restoration of a Swedish log cabin employing a number of existing timbers: it is probably the earliest surviving house in the state. (The Swedes were the first Europeans to settle in Pennsylvania.) The right side, of squared timbers, was built initially, then forty to fifty years later the left was constructed, the two being joined by the stone-fronted center and a common roof in the eighteenth century. The interiors accurately portray the primitive originals.

Open Tues.–Sat. 10–4:30, Sun. 1–4:30, except holidays:
admission

44 Keystone Generating Station (1964–68)
1.7 miles/2.7 kilometers SW off US 422 on PA 156
Shelocta, Pennsylvania

GILBERT ASSOCIATES, ENGINEERS

Gigantic power plants are among the most awe-inspiring engineering works to be seen, and this Keystone installation with 1,700,000-kilowatt capacity is one of the largest in North America. It is also the largest minehead (actually near mine) station in the country. Moreover it not only welcomes visitors, it provides a strategically placed overlook, complete with snack bar, rest rooms, and information. Two 800-foot/244-meter-high stacks, 67 feet/20 meters in diameter at base and 34 feet/10 meters at top, dominate the landscape, with four mathematically profiled cooling towers (325 feet/99 meters high, base diameter 247 feet/75 meters, top 142 feet/43 meters) adding inferno accents. These towers cool 560,000 gallons/2,120,000 liters of water per minute from 118° F/48° C to 90° F/32° C. The coal arrives both from conveyor belts from nearby mines and by truck; 650 tons/590 metric tons are burned per hour, with electrostatic precipitators cleaning the smoke. The plant's transformers are the largest ever built. Seven utility companies own the installation in proportion to their power requirements.

Open May 15–Sept. 15, 1–8

45 Administration Building of Unity House (1972)
   Exit 52 off IS 80, NE on US 209 to Bushkill, L (N) at blinker,
   about 17 miles/27 kilometers NE of
   Stroudsburg, Pennsylvania

PRENTICE & CHAN, OHLHAUSEN, ARCHITECTS

Unity House is a summer resort on a 1,000-acre/405-hectare plot in
the Pocono Mountains, founded (1919), built, and sponsored by the
International Ladies' Garment Workers' Union as a non-profit escape
from the city (primarily NYC). Though preference is given ILGWU
and AFL-CIO members, the non-affiliated are also accommodated
(generally on a weekly basis) if there is room.

The new Administration Building (replacing one that burned in
1969), set amid a collection of older structures, combines reception,
lounge, dining rooms, bar, snack bar, and recreation rooms. Angled to

embrace the view and to keep it from architectural insistence among the smaller-scaled units, and focused on two broad terraces which step down invitingly to the lawn, the handsome new building forms the spontaneous meeting ground for the entire complex. An amusing ramp spirals upward around the main lounge (at left by entry) to provide sun terraces at top. An atmosphere of cheerfulness and festivity—with taste—characterizes both exterior and interiors.

Open June–Labor Day

---

46 **Washington's Headquarters** (c. 1758) **and Valley Forge National Historical Park**
off PA 23 at W end of Valley Forge State Park, reached by Pennsylvania Turnpike (IS 76) via Exit 24
Valley Forge, Pennsylvania

Washington's headquarters was built as a small house for a gristmill owner and is of simple architectural merit. However, due to its historical importance, it has been carefully preserved through the years with many of its original features intact, even to the floors. Moreover, the

period furnishings are excellent and are arranged to communicate the building's military use during the cruel Valley Forge encampment of 1777–78.

The park itself is being fully restored as the military camp it once was, with a number of soldiers' huts rebuilt on their original foundations, while other buildings on the site include a 1705 school, Varnum's Quarters (a fine eighteenth-century stone house), and a new Visitor Center (1978—Eshbach, Glass, Kale Associates, architects). The National Park Service took charge of the park in 1977, and has instituted a thorough, technical survey of the area using aerial infrared photography, soil-penetrating radar, and other devices to get "primary" data.

House and Visitor Center open 8:30–6 in summer, 8:30–5 in winter, except Dec. 25

---

47   St. David's (Radnor) Church (1715–18+)
S of US 30 on Valley Forge Road at Darby-Paoli Road
Wayne, Pennsylvania

A tiny (27×44 feet/8.2×13.4 meters) missionary church engulfed in ancient trees and surrounded by a picturesque cemetery. The simple fieldstone structure with arch-head windows was largely built by the first parishioners themselves, most of whom were of Welsh origin. (St. David is the patron saint of Wales.) Although the exterior was largely completed within a few years of the cornerstone laying (1715), the interior was not altogether finished until early in the twentieth century, when the Georgian-Style paneling was inserted (1893–1912). The distinctive exterior stone staircase was built in 1771, and the large chancel window added in 1786. The chancel itself was placed in its present position in 1830. The lich-gate leading to the church was designed by T. Mellon Rogers (1901). Though not architecturally a masterwork, St. David's, Radnor, is useful in documenting its periods of construction. It was placed in the National Register in 1978.

Open daily 8 A.M. to dusk

---

48   **Golden Plough Tavern** (c. 1741), **General Gates House** (1751), **and Barnet Bobb Log House** (1812)
West Market Street at Pershing Avenue
York, Pennsylvania

The Golden Plough Tavern and General Gates House comprise two conjoined mid-eighteenth-century buildings. Though they are not to be compared to architectural developments at this time along the Atlantic seaboard—Williamsburg, for instance, was at its peak of elegance—they give us a picture both of frontier conditions and of direct European influence. York was laid out in 1741, about the time that this tavern was constructed. Almost all of the early York settlers were German, and the Black Forest origin of Martin Eichelberger, the innkeeper-builder of this tavern, is clearly seen in its medieval *Fachwerkbau* or half-timbering, its brick infilling being here facilitated by the local abundance of suitable clay. (Long rows of red brick houses became an early York trademark.) Both exterior and interior of the tavern have been carefully restored. The adjacent Gates House, built a decade later by Joseph Chambers, reveals the more sophisticated background of its English-born owner in the eastern Pennsylvania vernacular. Note, on the interior, the panels showing the original framing. The two-story Bobb Log House, of unusual size for log construction, was

moved behind tavern and house in 1968, and gives a good idea of the
wood country idiom that was also common in the area. The building's
design and decor are basically German, but English influence is evident. All three buildings have been put back in excellent condition, a
fine credit to the Historical Society of York County.

*Open Mon.–Sat. 10–4, Sun. 1–4:30, except major holidays:
admission*

Rhode Island

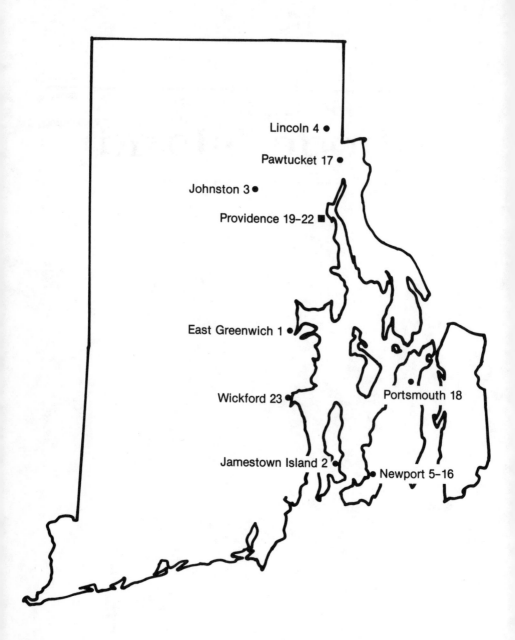

RHODE ISLAND

The buildings in boldface type are of general interest. The others are for the specialist.

East Greenwich   1 East Greenwich High School (1968)—TAC

Jamestown Island   2 Jamestown Windmill (1787)

Johnston   3 **Clemence-Irons House** (c. 1680)

Lincoln   4 **Eleazer Arnold House** (c. 1687/ mid-18th century)

Newport   5 **Trinity Church** (1725–26)— Richard Munday
                          Newport Historic Districts
                       6 Old Colony House (1739–41)— Richard Munday
                       7 **Hunter House** (c. 1748)
                       8 **Redwood Library** (1747–50)— Peter Harrison
                       9 **Touro Synagogue National Historic Site** (1759–63)—Peter Harrison
                      10 Brick Market (1762–72)—Peter Harrison
                      11 **Samuel Whitehorne House** (c. 1800–10)
                      12 Château-sur-Mer (1851–52/ 1870–74)—Seth Bradford and R. M. Hunt
                      13 **Marble House** (1888–92)—R. M. Hunt
                      14 **The Breakers** (1893–95)—R. M. Hunt
                      15 **The Elms** (1899–1901)—Horace Trumbauer
                      16 **Rosecliff** (1899–1902)—McKim, Mead & White

Pawtucket

17 **Old Slater Mill** (1793–c. 1830)

Portsmouth

18 **Chapel, Portsmouth Priory School** (1961)—Pietro Belluschi

Providence

See also Johnston, Lincoln, and Pawtucket

19 **First Baptist Church** (1774–75)—Joseph Brown

College Hill Historic District

20 John Brown House (1786–88)—Joseph Brown

21 The Arcade (1827–29)—Bucklin & Warren

22 The Athenaeum (1837–38)—William Strickland

Wickford

23 **Old Narragansett Church** (1707) and Main Street East

1 East Greenwich High School (1968)
300 Avenger Drive
(SW of town, 1.8 miles/2.9 kilometers from US 1 via South Pierce
Road, Middle Road, S on Avenger)
East Greenwich, Rhode Island

THE ARCHITECTS COLLABORATIVE WITH ALBERT HARKNESS AND PETER GEDDES, ARCHITECTS

The East Greenwich School is distinguished by spaces flowing laterally and trees growing vertically within its courtyard. The building frames an open quadrangle whose uneven grade and every shrub were carefully preserved. Even when approaching the school one can see and feel in contact with its bucolic core because the entry wing is raised on stilts. Cafeteria and auditorium, which can be combined for community functions, stand at left with gymnasium at right. The library faces the entry from the center of the far side of the courtyard, with general-purpose classrooms flanking it, science classes to right, and music room and shop on the northeast side. All classrooms are thus in touch with unspoiled nature, a contact further encouraged by the covered walk recessed into the building and wrapping around much of the central courtyard. Construction is of reinforced concrete and red brick.

Grounds open during school hours

2   Jamestown Windmill (1787)
.7 mile/1.1 kilometers S of RI 138 on North Road
Jamestown Island, Rhode Island

The windmill buff will enjoy seeing this restored example, now in working shape, just off the Jamestown Road (and visible from it). The mill
is of the smock type, so called because its rotating domed head or cap
faintly recalls the garment. Introduced by the Dutch in New Amsterdam (i.e. Manhattan), windmills spread over much of the Northeast
but few examples are now extant. The great cogged wheels of the grist
machinery at Jamestown (now of iron gears instead of the original oak
pegs) and the substantial 25-foot/7.6-meter windshaft will reward a
look. The exterior was restored in 1957, the interior three years later.
It is listed in the National Register of Historic Places.

Open late June–Labor Day, Wed.–Sun. 1–4: donation

3   **Clemence-Irons House** (c. 1680)
    38 George Waterman Road (RI 128)
    (Apply at 43 Waterman for admission)
    Johnston, Rhode Island

Dominated—like the Arnold House (q.v.)—by its great fieldstone double chimney (left side rebuilt) which almost fills the west wall, this
small house, just west of Providence, provides a venerable example of a
little-known regional species. Moreover, it is one of the few dwellings
of its time known to have been built all at once. The house underwent
complete restoration in 1938 by the notably careful Norman M. Isham,
including new roof (probably thatched originally) and new clapboarding (which abuts without corner boards), plus the removal of several
nineteenth-century additions and the replacement of its latter-day large
windows. There is still a newness about the exterior which belies the
building's age, but its years are fully revealed within, especially in the
sharply pitched half floor under the gable. Here the original beams and
rafters are fully exposed—if one can squeeze up the tiny stair by the
chimney to see them. Even some of the interior sheathing is original.

The rest of the interior has been properly attended to and the furnishings reproduced under Mr. Isham's direction. It is owned by the Society for the Preservation of New England Antiquities.

Open by appointment; telephone (617) 227-3956: admission

---

4   Eleazer Arnold House (c. 1687/mid-18th century)
449 Great Road (RI 123), W of intersection with RI 126 (c. 3
**   miles/4.8 kilometers NW of Pawtucket)**
Lincoln (Lonsdale), Rhode Island

A fetching primitiveness characterizes the two-and-a-half-story, four-room Arnold house; however, some authorities feel that the restoration of 1952 was highly questionable in parts. A Herculean, unpunctured fieldstone wall (original) steadies one entire end of the structure and anchors it against northwest winds, fairing into a splendid chimney at

top. The rest of the house—called a "stone-ender" in Rhode Island—
appends this wall, clutching it for stability and barely attaining such.
Narrow, unpainted clapboards, tiny diamond-paned casements, and
studded front door (all restored) mark the exterior, with the long lean-
to of an ell at the rear, indicating the widened four-room plan of the
mid-eighteenth century. The brick chimney was added at the same
time. The interior, some of it original, reveals the medievalism of its
early Colonial day, its substantial summer beam bisecting the "hall"-
kitchen in typical fashion, with unpainted boarding (all new) lining the
walls. When the house was restored the greatest changes took the exterior back to its seventeenth-century appearance and, within, replaced
rotted timbers. A lack of funds, presumably, prevented restoration of
the gable which once graced the front, and whose original valley framing beams are still in place. In 1918 the dwelling was acquired by the
Society for the Preservation of New England Antiquities.

Open June–Oct., Tues., Thurs., Sun. 1–5, except holidays:
admission

---

5   Trinity Church (1725–26)
141 Spring Street, at Church Street
Newport, Rhode Island

RICHARD MUNDAY, ARCHITECT

Richard Munday designed Trinity Church, or, as has been said, "made
a copy in wood of Boston's Old North" (Hugh Morrison in *Early
American Architecture,* Oxford University Press, 1952). Unmistakably
London-derived on the interior, the outside is sheathed in beaded white
clapboards, its wide sides given a lilt by the double row of roundheaded
windows. This is accentuated by the scale relation of the narrow-width
clapboarding and the "30 over 24" panes of the windows. The exterior
is also marked by a first-rate steeple (spire and cupola inspired by Old
North) with supposedly the first church bell to ring in New England.
An open square—dedicated by Queen Elizabeth II in 1976—sets off
the whole. The interior was based, as mentioned, on the just completed
interior of Christ Church (i.e. Old North—q.v.), but Trinity is longer
than the former, having been sliced in half and had two additional bays,
totaling 30 feet/9 meters, added in 1762. (Note the unusual super-
imposed square columns upholding gallery and vaulted ceiling in each

building.) Trinity has otherwise been little touched through the subsequent years even to the extent of having real candles in the chandeliers that hang down the aisle aligned with the prominent wineglass pulpit, whose axial location—and superb sounding board—successfully blankets the altar: almost unheard of in an Anglican church. The interior is colorful with light green walls and ceiling, white woodwork, and seasonal vestments.

Open mid-June–mid-Sept., daily 10–5; rest of year by appointment

Newport is one of the most rewarding cities in the United States as regards seventeenth- and eighteenth-century architecture and streetscapes. Reputedly it contains over three hundred pre-Revolutionary buildings. It is suggested that the visitor get one of several local guidebooks to facilitate an exploration of the Historic Districts and the late-nineteenth-century work.

6 Old Colony House (1739–41)
Washington Square
Newport, Rhode Island

RICHARD MUNDAY, ARCHITECT

The Old Colony House, or the Old State House, was once the capitol of Rhode Island, the second oldest capitol in the United States (after Philadelphia's Independence Hall, q.v.). For a time it was the largest—and certainly the most ambitious—building in Rhode Island. The location prominently terminates the head of Washington Square with Peter Harrison's Brick Market (q.v.) at the west end. The facade, which shows Dutch influence, displays what might be termed a rustic originality as it sprouts a strange pediment, its truncated triangular shape recalling the gable ends of the building, the whole topped by a balustraded flat deck with octagonal cupola. Every door and window (and even the clock) have received lavish attention, with sandstone quoins emphasizing their shapes in the red brick walls (the city's first major use of brick). The stringcourse, too, is of sandstone. Competing with the pediment is the combined entry and balcony, which with the multiplicity of other elements produces a facade of some agitation. However, the "one-room"

main floor, measuring 40×80 feet/12×24 meters and with a central row of six square Doric columns, makes a substantial meeting hall. As the noted historian Antoinette Downing has written concerning the second floor: "The Senate Chamber, enlarged one bay in 1841, has fine floor to ceiling bolection paneling dating from 1740. The Assembly Room, which took its form c. 1841–1845, has excellent mid-19th Century paneling, coffered ceiling and furnishings. The room was designed by Russell Warren, who was responsible for the Providence Arcade." The Old Colony House was used as a hospital during the Revolution but it was restored in 1785. In 1917 Norman M. Isham carried out a second restoration, in the process opening up the ground floor, which had been partitioned through the years. The whole building is now in excellent condition.

Open June 15–Aug., daily 9:30–12, 1–4, rest of year except. holidays 9:30–12

---

7   **Hunter House** (c. 1748)
   54 Washington Street at Elm
   Newport, Rhode Island

As one of the finest examples of the Colonial period in the country, the Hunter House merits a visit even if fleeting. More time is amply repaid. The house faces Narragansett Bay so that its original owner could watch his ships enter the harbor, a body of water which has seen a busier and tidier past. The dwelling—earlier known as the Jonathan Nichols House—experienced declining fortunes, then serious alterations, beginning in the latter part of the nineteenth century. It first served as a convalescent home and later sheltered the Sisters of St. Joseph. Originally the most elaborate entry was on the waterfront side but this disappeared at the time a porch was added (c. 1872). When recently discovered in a nearby rectory the retrieved door was placed in front of the house because of the now unimportant water approach: a duplicate was made for the rectory. The beaded clapboards establish a neutrality which emphasizes the garlanded, broken pediment of the entry, one of the period's most regal doorways. But it is within that the chief richness lies. On each of the two main floors there are four rooms, all small in size though the central halls are spacious. The rooms on both floors at the northeast corner (right on entering), with their fireplaces verged on each side by shell cupboards, and with pilasters that fill and turn the corners, are noteworthy, but the wainscoted halls

and the other rooms are outstanding. All has been beautifully restored (1949) and refurnished by the Preservation Society of Newport County, a dedicated group organized in 1945 which fomented the "saving" of the area's architectural wealth. (See Antoinette F. Downing and Vincent J. Scully, Jr.'s admirable *The Architectural Heritage of Newport, Rhode Island,* Harvard University Press, 1952/Clarkson N. Potter, Jr., 1967, for the historic background.)

Open May–Oct., daily 10–5; April, Sat.–Sun. 10–5; winter by appointment: admission

---

8   Redwood Library (1747–50)
50 Bellevue Avenue (between Old Beach Road and Redwood Street)
Newport, Rhode Island

PETER HARRISON, ARCHITECT

Palladio's S. Giorgio Maggiore (1560) in Venice was the double-pedimented great-grandfather of the Redwood Library, but its direct parentage, as Fiske Kimball first pointed out, was Hoppus' *Fourth Book of Andrea Palladio* (1736). The skillful, British-born and

-educated Harrison, though a sea captain and merchant by trade, and later a Royal Customs Collector, was a knowledgeable architectural amateur who had the Hoppus book in his library, plus works on Inigo Jones, Lord Burlington, etc. For the Redwood Library Harrison mulled the possibility of combining several vocabularies—at that time architecture in America was still largely a vocabulary art—and came up with this accomplished, if derivative, result possibly in association with his brother Joseph. It vaunts, moreover, one of the earliest portico and temple facades in the Colonies following the much larger one on the second St. Philip's (1710–23) in Charleston, a church which Harrison saw when in that Southern port. (Harrison also used a portico in his later King's Chapel in Boston—q.v.) The Classic Revival expression of the library is given greater verisimilitude to its European prototypes by its precise imitation in wood of ashlar construction, even to sanding the paint to resemble stone. Some feel that Harrison's use of the Classic was the forerunner of Jefferson's.

A transverse wing by George Snell with octagonal cupola was added to the library in 1858; a larger wing, designed by George C. Mason, was added at the rear in 1875; smaller additions were made in this century. Thus when viewed from the side—and only from the side—there is an accretive and even awkward quality to the building. The facade, however, is superb. The interior, in spite of the additions, is surprisingly homogeneous, lofty and dignified. In addition to its rare books— almost half the original collection survives—the Library has an important assemblage of paintings, including one of Abraham Redwood, for whom the building is named. Note the eighteenth-century octagonal gazebo in the garden which formerly graced the Redwood House: it is attributed to Harrison.

Open Mon.–Sat. 10–6 (10–5 in Aug.) except holidays

---

9   **Touro Synagogue National Historic Site** (1759–63)
85 Touro Street at Division Street
Newport, Rhode Island

PETER HARRISON, ARCHITECT

Congregation Jeshuat Israel's Sephardic forebears had been attracted to Rhode Island by Roger Williams' espousal in the 1640s of religious tolerance—that startling concept in the early Colonies. They built in Newport what is now the oldest synagogue in North America. Peter Harrison, convenient and talented, and with his Redwood Library just up the street, was chosen as its architect. The synagogue's beige exterior, highlighted by a small portico, stands calmly on its open site, its unusual angle to the street arising from the necessity to have the ark face east.

After the reticence of the outside the closely packed architectural activity of the interior hits one with suprising force: it is one of the most accomplished rooms in the American Colonies. Slightly longer than wide (approximately 40×30 feet/12×9 meters), the temple's modest size is impacted on three sides by the balconies for the women, and by the prominent bema and sanctuary which occupy much of the central floor space. The men of the original congregation sat only on wainscot benches along the sides under the balconies, not in the center. The galleries are supported by twelve columns—Ionic below, Corinthian above —which, of course, recall the twelve tribes of Israel. Columns, balustrade, and entablature are precisely detailed, the balusters around the bema and sanctuary repeating those defining the balconies. Most of these architectural elements, including the basic inner form, were freely adopted from English books with many details inspired by Gibbs, but they were incorporated with an innate feeling for both space and detail. Some authorities feel that Bevis Marks, the Spanish and Portuguese synagogue (1701) on Heneage Lane, London—the oldest in England and a building which Harrison had almost undoubtedly seen—was influential in the Newport building, particularly the interior.

The synagogue experienced difficult days after the Revolution (as did Newport itself) and the congregation almost in toto dispersed to New York: for much of the nineteenth century the temple was closed. If it had not been for the thoughtful generosity of the sons of the first rabbi, Isaac Touro, who left funds in their wills for the preservation of the synagogue—hence giving it the popular name it now carries—the building would have vanished. Today, fortunately, it stands in excellent shape, and is in use for services by an active congregation.

Open June–Labor Day, Mon.–Fri. 10–5, Sun. 10–6; rest of year Sun. only 2–4

---

10   Brick Market (1762–72)
Washington Square at Thames Street
Newport, Rhode Island

PETER HARRISON, ARCHITECT

For this market Harrison adopted the design of Somerset House by Inigo Jones and John Webb published in *Vitruvius Britannicus,* Volume I (1715–25). (See *Peter Harrison, First American Architect* by Carl Bridenbaugh, University of North Carolina Press, 1949.) Instead

of a five-bay frontal design, the Newport version is a three-by-seven-bay freestanding building 33×66 feet/10×20 meters in size. Thus Harrison, in this his last major work, as in his first (the Redwood Library—q.v.), was heavily dependent upon his "phenomenal" collection of architectural books, a not unreasonable turn seeing that he was, as mentioned, an architectural dilettante. The Brick Market, though built for the transaction of goods—its ground floor was originally open in the approved market fashion, while its upper two contained offices—was remodeled as a theater (1793), then from 1853 to 1900 used as the city hall. The exterior was restored (1928) and the interior rebuilt (1930), as the plaque outside proclaims, under Norman M. Isham through the generosity of John Nicholas Brown. The building is owned by the city of Newport.

Open daily except Sun. and holidays 10–5

---

11 **Samuel Whitehorne House** (c. 1800–10)
414 Thames Street at Dennison
Newport, Rhode Island

The architectural ancestry of the Whitehorne House lies primarily in the work of Bulfinch and McIntire (see Index)—but what finer inspiration could one have in the domestic field in the early years of the nine-

teenth century? Mr. Whitehorne was a shipping merchant who unhappily went bankrupt when two of his vessels were lost at sea; as a result he also lost his house. Though an elegant three-story brick structure amid more plebeian clapboarding, decline set in as the years rolled by and a one-story closed porch with shops was built across the entire front in the mid-nineteenth century. The dwelling was being used as a tenement for eight families when it was acquired by the Newport Restoration Foundation in 1969. Under the expert eye of Francis Adams Comstock, former professor of architecture at Princeton, the entire house was stripped of appendages and has now been completely restored and superbly furnished. It must be added that of necessity much of the restoration is conjectural and thus to some experts questionable.

Note on the exterior the uncommonly delicate carving of the cornice (the cupola dates from 1858), and on the interior the bountiful use of very superior eighteenth-century furniture, almost all of which had been made locally (with several highboys of unbelievable value).

The Newport Restoration Foundation was established and funded in 1968 by Miss Doris Duke—a longtime summer resident—to save at least some of the city's rapidly vanishing examples of its early architectural heritage (Newport was founded in 1639). Miss Duke's further wish was to make Newport "a more pleasant place to live in." This non-profit organization has purchased some eighty houses and one farm, of which thirty-six houses have thus far been restored and rented —not sold—so that control over their destinies can be maintained. Scattered throughout the city, these restorations have exerted an immense influence in upgrading the entire town. Like all of the Newport buildings in this guide, the Whitehorne House is listed in the National Register of Historic Places.

Open Apr.–Nov., daily 10–5; winter by appointment: apply at 415 for admission ticket

---

12   Château-sur-Mer (1851–52/1870–74)
Bellevue Avenue between Leroy and Shepard Avenues
Newport, Rhode Island

SETH BRADFORD, BUILDER OF ORIGINAL HOUSE; RICHARD MORRIS HUNT, ARCHITECT OF RENOVATION

The stern exterior of Château-sur-Mer—the property originally extended to within 50 feet/15 meters of the coast—is granitically imposing. Seth Bradford, a local contractor (and possibly an architect), probably abetted by William S. Wetmore, its owner, designed it. Twenty years later, spatial inadequacies being apparent, this early Victorian hulk was partially gutted within and expanded without by Mr. Hunt. As regards the interior, Hunt immediately realized the need for spatial "release" and so opened the hall right through three stories and topped it with a painted glass skylight 45 feet/14 meters above. Having thus liberated the inside, he enlarged the northeast wing, added a porte cochere, and proceeded to develop within the existing walls a series of richly embellished rooms. The finest of these are the library and dining room, which were worked out with collaboration beween architect and the talented Luigi Frullini of Florence, whose carved walnut ceiling and

woodwork are masterful. Hunt, some years later, designed Newport's unbelievably lavish Marble House (1892) and the Breakers (1895 —both q.v.), but his reputation as an architect and that of Newport as a summer resort gathered momentum behind the plain granite walls of Château-sur-Mer. John Russell Pope redesigned the entrance in 1914. In 1969 the Preservation Society of Newport County saved the house from demolition and now guards it with its usual careful attention.

Open Apr.–Oct., daily 10–5; Nov.–Mar., Sat.–Sun. only 11–4: admission

---

13 Marble House (1888–92)
Bellevue Avenue and Cliff Walk
Newport, Rhode Island

RICHARD MORRIS HUNT, ARCHITECT

The Colonial inheritance of Newport, samples of which we have seen, was in the late nineteenth and early twentieth centuries overshadowed by villas of proper Veblenian presumption. Quaintly called "cottages,"

Newport's summer houses find no equal in the Western world: their interiors, indeed, must be seen to be believed. Fortunately the most pretentious are open to the public during much of the year. Hunt's Marble House for William K. Vanderbilt—its name reflecting the unrelenting use of its material—recalls with its Corinthian columned and balustraded shape the garden facade of the Petit Trianon (1762–68) at Versailles, except that Hunt's projected portico and roundheaded windows lack the compact authority of Gabriel's earlier building. But Hunt, who studied for nine years at the Paris Ecole des Beaux-Arts—the first American to do so—and who afterward worked at the Tuileries in Versailles, put together a highly skillful small palace. Chastely white on the exterior, and impeccably detailed, the house within erupts with unrestrained hedonism. The Neronian richness of the dining room is established by roast beef-colored marble walls, while the ballroom—the Gold Room—projects its aureate charms from panels gilded in red, green, and yellow gold and set off by wondrous chandeliers and by gold-leaf and bronze mantel. And so it progresses, from entry gates (which should be noted) to the black walnut and silk details upstairs—where almost all major bedrooms unaccountably face the land. The architect himself is remembered by the grateful owner with a bas-relief on the stairs—he should be.

In addition to designing several of the most sumptuous houses in the United States, plus the facade of the Metropolitan Museum and one of the first skyscrapers with elevators (the 230-foot/70-meter-high, wall-bearing Tribune Building, 1875, in New York), Richard Morris Hunt —by helping also to establish the American Institute of Architects— fathered professional architecture in this country.

Open Apr.–Oct., daily 10–5; Nov.–Mar., Sat.–Sun. only 11–4: admission

---

14   The Breakers (1893–95)
Ochre Point Avenue at Ruggles Avenue
Newport, Rhode Island

RICHARD MORRIS HUNT, ARCHITECT

Marble House, which Mr. Hunt finished three years before The Breakers, was the ultimate in French-inspired late Renaissance. At The Breakers, with affluence spread more widely and with even more studied casualness, we find a North Italian inspiration which matches any

palazzo in sixteenth-century Genoa. The house is staggering. But whether we like it or not—and it is impossible not to be impressed—the fact remains that for his client and his supposed needs/desires the architect produced a masterpiece. (However, Leonard Eaton, a renowned historian, calls it "an incredible display of tasteless vulgarity" —Society of Architectural Historians *Bulletin,* February 1979.) The building also commands technical respect because, remembering the fire which had destroyed the previous house on this site (1892), Mr. Hunt built it entirely of masonry and steel, no wood being used in its construction. The plan, incidentally, is based on that of the original house. Moreover, in spite of its complexity and detail it was designed in one year and built in a little over two. The exterior was modeled, as mentioned, on late Renaissance palaces of Genoa, but these elegant *palazzi* were tight city dwellings built around a courtyard. The "transplanted" Breakers thus sits a bit lonely on its wide, ocean-facing lawn. Only a slender terrace stretches forth to act as intermedium between free waters and domestic refuge, no pavilions set up spatial rhythms amid all that grass. Nature and man simply confront each other, they do not embrace. (Originally there were formal parterred gardens on the south side but not the ocean front.)

But The Breakers' exterior is of secondary importance; it is the seventy-room interior which stuns. And it is well to keep in mind that we must regard the house not by today's standards but as a product of a time of riotous eclecticism and maecenean (and tax-free) wealth. The soaring Great Hall, 45 feet/14 meters high, forms a proper introduction with probably the most fantastic cornice known to man—note, too, the alabaster capitals. An inspired Grand Staircase leads past a hooded Italian fireplace and porphyry vases to the balcony with a tapestry 24×18

feet/7.3×5.5 meters—woven in 1619—supervising the landing. The Grand Salon was designed by Richard Bouwens Van der Boyen and made in France, dismantled, and then shipped to Newport and reassembled. However, it is the two-story dining room which is the most unbelievable; as the official booklet states, "It is doubtful if any of the state apartments in the palaces of Italy and France are more ornate than this room." Room after room offer a visual feast on every side— anything that money could buy, money bought. Not to be missed. Be sure to see the Queen Anne playhouse on the grounds between side gate and house.

In 1948 Countess Gladys Vanderbilt Szechenyi leased—for one dollar—The Breakers to the Preservation Society of Newport County. The countess died in 1965 and in 1971 the Preservation Society purchased the property outright.

Open Apr.–Oct., daily 10–5: admission

---

15   **The Elms** (1899–1901)
Bellevue Avenue between Bellevue Court and Dixon Street
Newport, Rhode Island

HORACE TRUMBAUER, ARCHITECT

Though removed from the sea (and questionably close to the avenue) The Elms establishes intimate contact with nature on its garden side through its Le Nôtre-inspired landscaping by C. H. Miller and E. W. Bowditch working in close cooperation with the architect. The gardens are probably the finest to be seen in Newport. The house itself achieves a stylistically "correct" eighteenth-century French château mantle though the result might be said to be on the dry side. The little-known Château d'Asnières (1751, on the southwest edge of Paris), built for the Marquis de Voyer d'Argenson, is mentioned as inspiration—as indeed it is—but Trumbauer, who had never even been to France at that time, cut its wings to four bays and added a pediment. The interior of The Elms, beginning with its foyer and entry hall, rises with relaxed opulence (note the murals) and even excitement, with its elaborate furnishings carried out by two French decorating firms. The resulting impression, however, tends to be of a series of highly furnished, almost competitive rooms. One of the most sophisticated houses of the early twentieth century, it had been scheduled for demolition and its furnish-

ings had been sold when the Preservation Society of Newport County raised enough money to purchase it (1962) and to collect and borrow sufficient furnishings to refit it in proper style. In summer there are often evening concerts in the garden.

Open May–Oct., daily 10–5; Nov.–Apr., Sat.–Sun. 11–4: admission

---

16 Rosecliff (1899–1902)
Bellevue Avenue at Marine Avenue
Newport, Rhode Island

McKIM, MEAD & WHITE, ARCHITECTS

Restrained grace, as opposed to inescapable opulence, characterizes Rosecliff. This "decorative confection," as it has been called, is also, more than any other "cottage" in Newport, highly livable, with almost all major rooms in visual contact with the sea and with light and air coursing through the ballroom, which forms the "bar" (appropriately) of its H-shaped plan. This sunny chamber ranks with Newport's finest. Stanford White—the partner-in-charge—in designing the mansion recalled—freely—J. H. Mansart's Grand Trianon at Versailles (1688) but added a second floor and extended the end wings.

Open Apr.–Oct., daily 10–5: admission

---

17 Old Slater Mill (1793–c. 1830)
Roosevelt Avenue, just S of City Hall
Pawtucket, Rhode Island

With its modest size and cupola complete with bell (added around 1830), the Slater Mill might be mistaken for a Colonial town hall rather than the earliest cotton mill in the country. Rising directly at a dam across the Blackstone River, and garnished with a variety of trees, the mill furnishes a restful contrast to the recent urban redevelopment about it. The city fathers and planners wisely preserved the building and abetted its restoration. It was this mill, designed by Samuel Slater, a brilliant young English émigré, which transformed the home spinning of cotton in the budding U.S.A. into a water-powered industry. The results sired New England's mill future. The English-developed, mid-eighteenth-century machine for the preparation of yarn, especially Arkwright's inventions on which Slater had worked as a lad of fourteen, established the "factory" and indeed the Industrial Revolution. Slater, in effect, brought the revolution (small "r") to America: the Cotton Centennial of 1890 properly celebrated the December 1790 opening of his first successful operation. The two-and-a-half-story Pawtucket mill initially measured only 43×29 feet/13×8.8 meters (the section back of belfry), but it was expanded in 1801, 1823, and c. 1830. The building, which had suffered through the years, was

purchased in 1923 by the Old Slater Mill Association and restored, and in 1955 was remodeled as a museum tribute to the New England textile industry. In addition to historic background it contains an intriguing quota of operating machinery. In the early 1970s the area was expanded as the Slater Mill Historic Site with the acquisition and restoration of the Wilkinson Mill (1810–11; tower and bellfry c. 1840) and the Sylvanus Brown House (1758). Altogether an exemplary insight into early-nineteenth-century industrial beginnings in the U.S.A.—and a fine attraction for downtown Pawtucket.

Open June–Sept., Tues.–Sat. 10–5, Sun. 1–5; rest of year Sat.–Sun. 1–5; closed Dec. and Jan.: admission

---

18   Chapel, Portsmouth Priory School (1961)
W off RI 114 via Cory's Lane
Portsmouth, Rhode Island

PIETRO BELLUSCHI, ARCHITECT

Beginning with his pioneering efforts in Oregon, Pietro Belluschi has designed notable religious buildings over a wide span of years. Few, however, can match this chapel for 180 boys and 60 Benedictine brothers. Its use of wood and local stone, its sympathetic scale, its embracing liturgical plan and religiosity, and its deft provisions for monks as well as lads combine with its outstanding art to give us a marvelous religious building. The plan—an octagon and abutting rectangle—provides a focused worship room for boys and visitors with retrochoir for the monks, who sing or chant here seven times each day. Quiet side chapels for the monks, each private yet each in visual touch with the main altar, are set in the facets of the octagon on both main floor and gallery. The high altar acts as fulcrum between nave and chancel. Above the altar Richard Lippold's brilliant crucifix radiates throughout the sanctuary, its gold and silver wires interacting and supporting a small Christ in such a fashion that its minute height is communicated throughout much of the church. This is one of the finest examples of twentieth-century religious art to be seen. The upper part, or lantern, of the octagon is enclosed with strips of colored glass—largely greens and blues with accents of red—alternating with wood mullions in a design by H. L. Willet and the architect that brings subdued vitality to the nave. Much of the furniture, including altar, pews, and stalls, was designed by George Nakashima. The art work, including the front door

with its masterfully incised ancient Roman lettering, was by Father
Peter. Anderson, Beckwith & Haible were associated architects.

Open daily during school year

---

19 **First Baptist Church** (1774–75)
75 North Main Street at Waterman
Providence, Rhode Island

JOSEPH BROWN, BUILDER-ARCHITECT

Roger Williams, that admirable gladiator for religious freedom ("soul liberty") of the early Colonies, founded not only this "the First Baptist Church in America" and served as its short-term pastor, but the city in which it stands (1636). The latter was named by him for his deliverance after banishment from Massachusetts. Williams died in 1683, and in a way this splendid church, though completed almost a century after his death, can be considered his metaphoric memorial. Joseph Brown, of the still famous Rhode Island family (see also John Brown House), remains the acknowledged designer—he was a merchant by profession —but James Gibbs, late of London, was vicariously by his side via his 1728 *Book of Architecture.* The elegant steeple of the church was indeed basically copied from Gibbs's book. Incidentally, the spire's 185-foot/56-meter height was raised into position from within the church by means of telescoping sections, one James Sumner in charge. An excellent Tuscan portico adds the other distinguished note to the facade. The body of the First Baptist is in the New England wooden tradition with sand-colored clapboarding, quoins in imitation of stone, and double row of unshuttered roundheaded windows. The interior, which measures approximately 80 feet/24 meters square, suggests a plan compromise between the short-axis Meeting House and the long-aisle Church of England. In any case it lives up to the promise of excellence of the outside, its restrained exuberance revealing its late Colonial date. An elaborate Waterford chandelier (1792—its Irish provenance is not authenticated) hangs from the center of the vaulted nave, a richness expanded by the well-detailed sanctuary wall. The church, which seats eight hundred on the main floor and six hundred in the balconies that encircle three sides, was made larger than necessary for its congregation so that commencements for nearby Brown University (until 1804 Rhode Island College) could also be accommodated. The building, from foundation to spire, was beautifully restored with funds provided by John D. Rockefeller, Jr., who taught Sunday school in the church when he was a student at Brown.

Open daily except holidays; guided tours Apr.–Oct., Mon.–Fri. 10–3, Sat. 10–2, Sun. following worship

On the hill behind the church stretches the **College Hill Historic District,** which well merits a walk. Benefit Street, once a semislum along many blocks, has been superbly reconditioned under the aegis of the Providence Preservation Society and constitutes a model of neighborhood rehabilitation. The area is now a National Historic Landmark. The Brown University campus also has many architectural rewards.

20   John Brown House (1786–88)
52 Power Street at Benefit
Providence, Rhode Island

JOSEPH BROWN, BUILDER-ARCHITECT

Most of the great houses of Providence are privately occupied, hence
not open to the public. However, this handsome box-shaped Georgian
dwelling (with subsequent Federal additions) was given in 1942 to the
Rhode Island Historical Society by the late John Nicholas Brown, a direct descendant of the original owner, and is now open throughout the
year. In addition it serves as the Society's headquarters. Georgian elements can be seen in the narrow pedimented projection of its central
bay, in the balconied portico (with strangely "arched" Palladian win-

dow), and in the generally liberated detail. Federal (really Federal Revival) touches in the portico date from a renovation (c. 1902) by architect Marsden Perry. (The rear wing was also enlarged by Mr. Perry.) The house is perhaps more impressive across the lawn from the Benefit Street side than from the front. Within, the formal hallway should be noted, as should the fireplaces and cornices, which are outstanding for the elaborateness of their carving.

Open Tues.–Fri. 11–3, Sat.–Sun. 1–4, except holidays: admission

---

21   The Arcade (1827–29)
130 Westminster Street and 65 Weybosset
Providence, Rhode Island

J. C. BUCKLIN AND RUSSELL WARREN, ARCHITECTS

The multistory arcade, as an urban link and adjunct, enjoyed only sketchy beginnings in the early nineteenth century in the United States in spite of the successful examples of the Royal Opera (1790) and Burlington (1819) arcades in London. Structural demands and the necessity for substantial panes of glass inhibited widespread use here until a bit later. Among the pioneers in this country is this affirmative arcade in Providence, 216 feet/66 meters in overall length. Introduced at each end by a stalwart line of granite Ionic columns—for years the largest monoliths (22 feet/6.7 meters high and weighing 13 tons/13.2 metric tons each) in the U.S.A.—this Greek Revival arcade provides to this day a pleasant milieu for shopping. Note that the Westminster end has a pediment while the other does not. Some feel that arcade shops anticipated the department store and that this Rhode Island example was one of the first enclosed shopping centers in America. Its lateral tightness and modest dimensions deny it the grandeur of the much later Arcade in Cleveland (1890—q.v.), but it is a pleasure to find a weather-protected "street" (recently reconditioned) where one can stroll and shop at leisure in the fast-moving turmoil of downtown Providence. It is also rewarding to see that contemporary architects and planners, impressed by such elderly prototypes, are recognizing the delights of top-lighted covered spaces—as many of today's covered mall shopping centers attest.

Open during business hours

22 The Athenaeum (1837–38)
251 Benefit Street
Providence, Rhode Island

WILLIAM STRICKLAND, ARCHITECT

As this is William Strickland's only New England essay, it will particularly interest in Greek Revivalist. Measuring 48×78 feet/14×24 meters and with an inset porch (distyle in antis), it forms a compact, well-proportioned example of its style. Numerous alterations have been made in the interior, the first by J. C. Bucklin in 1868. A small wing was added (1914) and an addition in 1978, but in general this remains a simple, dignified period piece. Incidentally, the granite for the additions is identical to the original. Strickland got the job, in spite of being a Philadelphian, because Russell Warren (one of the architects of the Arcade—as, of course, was Bucklin, who redid the interior) was in Nova Scotia.

Open May–Sept., Mon.–Fri. 8:30–5:30, Sat. 9:30–5:30;
Oct.–Apr., Mon.–Sat. 8:30–5:30, except holidays

---

23 **Old Narragansett Church** (1707) **and Main Street East**
60 Church Lane
Wickford, Rhode Island

Wickford, once a thriving little port on Narragansett Bay, eventually lost out in importance to the more strategically situated Newport on Rhode Island Sound. Having thus been bypassed, the town has remained largely unspoiled—at least in its non-commercial sections. Among its pleasures are the Old Narragansett Church, or St. Paul's Episcopal as it is more properly known, and Main Street East, a fine avenue of eighteenth-century clapboarded houses. (The church is on Church Lane one block north of Main.) Reputedly the oldest still-standing Episcopal church north of the Potomac, Old Narragansett was built in 1707 (compare St. Luke's in Virginia of 1632). It originally stood several miles away but was moved to its present site in 1800. Though earlier attributed to Richard Munday, current historians discount this. Extremely simple, almost severe, it suggests a Puritan meeting house more than the Church of England. Indeed if it were not for its roundheaded windows it would suggest a dwelling more than a meeting house. The lack of steeple accentuates this feeling, as, within, does the entry, which is on the long wall opposite the pulpit with galleries on the three sides (added in 1723). Both setting and the quaintly proportioned doorway relieve this austerity. It should be mentioned that a steeple was added onto the church shortly after it was moved (in 1811) but "it fell down on a clear calm night in the winter of 1866" and was never replaced. The church was deserted in 1848 for the new St. Paul's, but early restoration was undertaken beginning in 1870 while complete restoration was carried out in the 1920s under the direction of Norman M. Isham. It has been kept in shining condition since although services are limited to two summer months. The church is owned by the Episcopal Diocese of Rhode Island.

Open July and Aug. for Sun. services and Fri.–Sat. 2–4

The east end of **Main Street** deserves a detour by itself, its somewhat prim lineup of highly similar houses freshened by chromatic changes and by the penetration of treed spaces about the buildings.

Vermont

Brownington 1

Burlington 2–4

Richmond 10

Shelburne 12

Montpelier 6

Middlebury 5

Strafford 13

Plymouth Notch 9

Windsor 15

Rockingham 11

Newfane 7

West Dummerston 14

Old Bennington 8

VERMONT

The buildings in boldface type are of general interest. The others are for the specialist.

Brownington	1 **Old Stone House** (1834–36)
Burlington	2 First Unitarian Church (1815–16)—Peter Banner
	3 Billings Student Center (1883–85)—H. H. Richardson
	4 IBM Facility (1970–72)—Curtis & Davis
Middlebury	5 **Congregational Church** (1806–9)—Lavius Fillmore
Montpelier	6 **State Capitol** (1833–38/1859)—Ammi B. Young
Newfane	7 **Windham County Court House** (1825–26)
Old Bennington	8 **First Congregational Church** (Old First—1804–5)—Lavius Fillmore
Plymouth Notch	9 **Plymouth Historic District** (19th century)
Richmond	10 **Old Round Church** (1812–13)
Rockingham	11 **Rockingham Meeting House** (1787–1800)
Shelburne	12 **Shelburne Museum**
Strafford	13 Justin Smith Morrill House (1848–51)
West Dummerston	14 **West Dummerston Covered Bridge** (1872) Covered Bridge, Woodstock (1968)
Windsor	15 Windsor-Cornish Covered Bridge (1866)

1 Old Stone House (1834–36)
c. 3 miles/5 kilometers E of Orleans exit of IS 91
Brownington, Vermont

Vermont is the nation's chief producer of granite (and also of marble) and here a few miles off the Interstate—and just south of the Canadian border—is a "house" which irrefutably exalts this granular crystalline rock. The Old Stone House was built as a dormitory for the Orleans County Grammar School, the sparse population and severe winters encouraging a central place of instruction. Besides sheltering 154 boys and girls of fifteen to sixteen years of age, it also held the required classrooms. The ground floor contained commons, kitchen, and music room, the second floor was for the girls, the third for boys, with two classrooms and an assembly in the attic. Abandoned as a school building (1859) and later used as lodgings, the building was threatened with destruction in 1916 but was purchased by the Orleans County Historical Society. Over the years it has been restored as funds became available. The exterior walls and sash are in pristine condition, but the present tin roof (note the well-angled gables) needs replacement and the interior requires considerable freshening. None of the original furnishings having survived, the house is being refitted with gifts from individuals and donations from the Orleans County townships. It is now used as a summer museum. The building, which measures 36×66 feet/

11×20 meters, was built—almost without help—by the Reverend
Alexander L. Twilight, the school's headmaster and reputedly the first
black American college graduate (Middlebury College in 1823). He
rightly christened his academy "Athenian Hall."

Open May 15–Oct. 15, daily 10–5: admission

---

2 First Unitarian Church (1815–16)
Church Street at Pearl
Burlington, Vermont

PETER BANNER, ARCHITECT

For over 160 years the First Unitarian Church (originally First Congregational Society) has punctuated and terminated Church Street, its brick mass providing a strong dominant and vertical accent for the downtown area. At one time it was thought that Charles Bulfinch "reviewed" Peter Banner's design: documentation (in church vestibule) shows that each had been asked to plan the building and that each had been paid. Banner, however, received the commission and it seems unlikely that Bulfinch played any role at all in the final design. Banner, it should be added, had been "associated" with Bulfinch as early as 1806.

The church when erected stood in a lonely pasture and the village population was only two thousand. The tower and facade remain as built (except the side doors are now closed), but the interior has suffered. The original barrel-vaulted ceiling had to be eliminated in 1845 so that lateral tie rods could be installed (for stability). In 1868 the chancel windows were blocked out (fortunately from the glare standpoint) because of the addition of the parish house. Other interior changes involved removal of the box pews and the old pulpit, and—on the good side—the replacement (c. 1925) of the inevitable Victorian stained glass of 1894 with clear panes. There is a laudable movement to "restore, insofar as is practical, the original colonial simplicity of the church."

Open daily 8–12 except some holidays

---

3 **Billings Student Center** (1883–85)
University of Vermont, Main Campus
via Colchester Avenue on University Place
Burlington, Vermont

HENRY HOBSON RICHARDSON, ARCHITECT

The Richardson buff will want to see the Billings Student Center (ex-library) on the ridge overlooking the main campus mall. One of five libraries HHR designed, it combines almost all his trademarks: pivotal tower jostling vertical with horizontal, large arched entrance almost demanding that one enter (cf. Wright's often hidden entries), strip and gathered windows, and polygonal (here octagonal) end bay, the whole pulled together into a rosy sandstone mass. The interior has been restored to its original condition and, with the library stacks removed, the full glory of Richardson's interior design is revealed. As part of the restoration, furniture designed by Richardson specifically for this building

has been repaired and refinished or, in some instances, replaced with custom-made duplicates. The building now serves as a student center, and the ground-floor rooms serve as lecture and concert halls and for small student, faculty, and public gatherings. The tower room, open from floor to roof beams, is occasionally used for student theater productions.

Lobby open weekdays 7:30 A.M.*–11* P.M., *weekends 9* A.M.*–10* P.M. *during school year*

---

4   IBM Facility (1970–72)
Robinson Parkway (E off VT 2A, c. .5 mile/.8 kilometer S of junction with VT 15)
Burlington (Essex Junction), Vermont

CURTIS & DAVIS, ARCHITECTS

Occupying a comely site (200 acres/81 hectares) on a bend of the Winooski River with natural stands of birch and pine along the banks, and cooperating thoroughly with nature, this administrative, research,

and manufacturing facility represents an enlightened approach to industrial architecture. A flat, dull landscape would have sufficed, and probably cost less, but there are values here in pride and satisfaction which undoubtedly make this a wise investment. The facility comprises an older (pre-Curtis & Davis) one-story manufacturing plant (to left on entering) with a new three-story administrative office block adjacent to this and a long two-story laboratory and research building stretching to the right and tied to the offices by a low entry lobby. All units are connected by glass-enclosed knuckles or bridges. The site of the administrative block was raised slightly to make its entry floor level with the previously existing low manufacturing buildings to which it is tied, and also to increase its focal advantages in the grouping. The two floors of lab and research wing follow the grade, with offices along the outside and laboratories and exhaust spine down the middle. All new buildings are of tannish brick with black, metal-framed, dark glass fenestration, pared in detail. The multilevel garden behind the lobby should also be seen.

Grounds and reception lobby open during business hours

---

5   **Congregational Church** (1806–9)
    The Common (US 7)
    Middlebury, Vermont

    LAVIUS FILLMORE, ARCHITECT

Lavius Fillmore's masterpiece, the Congregational Church, was carefully located to face the town green and also to be seen obliquely from two of its main streets. For many observers the finest church in the

state, it epitomizes, outside and in, one's concept of a New England urban house of worship of the early nineteenth century. The projected, column-less entry and pediment are almost identical to the Old Bennington church (q.v.) which Fillmore had just finished. However, the tower, belfry, and spire at Middlebury are more accomplished and better tied to the mass of the building, only the setting being less prepossessing. The steeple is composed of square on square, octagon on octagon, with short spire atop. The interior, too, resembles the Bennington church but is larger and it no longer has the original box pews. Like its predecessor, it is light, airy, and dignified. An unusual feature of both churches can be seen in the four semifreestanding Ionic columns that edge-support the balcony and rise uninterruptedly to fair into the ceiling vaults. Note in the Middlebury example the painted ceiling with its symbolism of the cross surrounding the orb of the world. Altogether a gracious setting for worship.

Open June–mid-Oct., daily 8:30–4:30; rest of year Sun. service only

---

6   State Capitol (1833–38/1859)
     State Street (US 2)
     Montpelier, Vermont

AMMI B. YOUNG, ARCHITECT

An appealing competent statehouse for the nation's smallest capital.
The original building, designed by Mr. Young in 1833, burned in January 1857, but it was soon rebuilt largely on the same lines though with
a bay added at each end and at the rear, plus a higher dome. Thomas
W. Silloway was for a year the architect of the reconstruction, followed
by Joseph R. Richards. The scale of the projected Doric portico—
which survived the fire and which is more or less straight from Athens'
Theseion of 465 B.C.—tends to overwhelm even the extended side
wings and dome. However the spacious elm-shaded lawn in front, the
spritely, gold-leafed dome topped by the 14-foot/4.3-meter statue of
Ceres, and the backdrop of trees on the hill behind make one soon
overlook any discrepancy of parts. Close at hand the excellent detailing
takes over. The Capitol's granite construction, its careful upkeep, and
what must be its pollution-free environment make it appear minted yes-
terday in spite of well more than a century of use. On the interior the
D-shaped House of Representatives with 150 seats is a bit crowded, but

the Senate (at east end), with Corinthian columns and ovoid domed ceiling, carries atmosphere. Ammi Young went on to become the first Supervising Architect of the U. S. Treasury Department following the famous Robert Mills, who had been Federal Architect.

Open July 1–Labor Day, Mon.–Fri. 9–4:15, Sat.–Sun. 1–5; rest of year, Mon.–Fri. only

---

7   **Windham County Court House** (1825–26)
Village Green (VT 30)
Newfane, Vermont

A dozen or so miles (20 kilometers) northwest of Brattleboro stands a little-known but delightful Greek Revival courthouse, one of New England's finest. Set back on the Village Green, it is flanked on one side by an ancient (1787) and excellent inn, and on the other by two not so ancient and not so excellent churches. The spaces between are first-rate, with the Green on one side of the highway and the common on the other. The courthouse fronts the Green with a correct portico of four Doric columns and the proper pilasters down the sides. An unusual fea-

ture of both front and sides can be seen in the two rows of round-headed shuttered windows with "fan" inserts. (The open shutters play a geometric game with the closed ones and the fans above.) Town offices, not of architectural interest, occupy the interior. The architect is unknown.

Open during business hours

---

8 First Congregational Church (Old First—1804–5)
W end of Main Street (VT 9), on Monument Avenue
Old Bennington, Vermont

LAVIUS FILLMORE, ARCHITECT

Girdled by a fence of spirited sweeps and urns, and facing a tree-lined double street, Old First enjoys a synoptic New England setting. The adjacent cemetery, with tombs dating from 1762, the Revolutionary Battle of Bennington, and down to Robert Frost, completes the scene. Designed by the Connecticut-born Fillmore, the church's tower, facade, and plan show considerable "inspiration" from the work of his contemporary, Asher Benjamin, whose book *The Country Builder's Assistant* (1796) was, as earlier mentioned, influential in much of New England.

In fact, for some time First Congregational was ascribed to Benjamin. (Benjamin's most successful other book—all of them going through numerous editions—was his *The American Builder's Companion,* 1806, which shows everything from stair details to courthouses.)

The interior of the Bennington church, though altered through the years, was completely restored in 1936–37 by Denison B. Hall and the original enclosed box pews, which seat 650, reinstated. The pulpit is reached by the typical airy twin stairs. A shallow dome fills the center of the ceiling, the columns upholding it, we are told, each cut from a single tree of white pine. The overall effect is joyful. Be sure to stroll through the cemetery. The church's first congregation gathered in December of 1762.

Open Memorial Day–June, Sat. 10–5, Sun. 1–5; July–Oct., Mon.–Sat. 9–5, Sun. 1–5; Sun. services throughout year

---

9   Plymouth Historic District (19th century)
W off VT 100A
Plymouth Notch, Vermont

This minute collection of buildings folded in the central Vermont hills offers a capsule vignette of Green Mountain village regionalism. The church was completed in 1840 (dedicated in 1842, interior Gothicized in the 1890s); the store dates from around 1835, and the attached dwelling where former President Calvin Coolidge (1872–1933) was born was built about 1840. The Coolidge homestead across the street (c. 1876), the cheese factory (1890), the school (c. 1890), and a handful of other houses are politely scattered yet coherently gathered. No architectural expertise will be found in the details but the whole transcends the parts and is very sympathetic. The Coolidge homestead, its several elements articulated in northern New England fashion against winter chill and snows, was given to the state in 1956 by Mr. and Mrs. John Coolidge and is now operated by the Vermont Division for Historic Preservation. It has been restored in all respects to that early moment of August 3, 1923, when Mr. Coolidge's father, as notary public, swore in his son as President.

The Memorial Center (1971–72) by the parking lot offers a museum on the President's life, while the nearby Farmers' Museum contains agricultural memorabilia of the region.

Open Memorial Day–mid-Oct., daily 9–6: admission

---

10   Old Round Church (1812–13)
c. 1 mile/1.6 kilometers SW of Exit 11 of IS 89
Richmond, Vermont

San Stefano Rotundo (A.D. 470) in Rome helped start the circular vogue, and today all up-to-date church architects espouse the round plan at least once. This wooden edition, a combination meeting house and church, though not radius-generated (it has sixteen sides), stakes out an early New England claim with geometric conviction. Its white clapboard sides are punctured by dark, sharply cut windows and doors in each facet, three doors and thirteen windows on the lower rank, sixteen windows above. An octagonal belfry crowns its shingled roof. The original deed for the building stipulated a town "meeting house" but it was also used by five Protestant sects with early ecumenicalism. Church use gradually phased out late in the last century but the town still gathers there for meetings. A complete restoration took place in 1978–79. The master builder of the church was one William Rhoades, who, some feel, had seen similar meeting houses in his travels.

Open only occasionally: interior can be seen through windows

---

11   Rockingham Meeting House (1787–1800)
   on hill above village, off VT 103 (1.4 miles/2.3 kilometers NW of
   Exit 6 of IS 91)
   Rockingham, Vermont

When regarded as an isolated structure the Rockingham Meeting House stands as a well-proportioned white clapboard box with auxiliary entries and stairs at each end. Measuring 56×44 feet/17×13 meters, it carries the proper number of windows on its four sides and exhibits a good main door. However, when studied in relation to its hilltop site and its adjacent cemetery (1782) and even its frail picket fence, the whole, to paraphrase Valéry, almost bursts into song. (It is a rare building which can be properly assayed out of its environmental context.) The meeting house, which is the oldest in the state and the second for its congregation, reflects the straightforward characteristics of its contemporaries in remote areas, following cautiously architectural developments along the seaboard. For years, in the usual tradition, it was used for both religious and secular offices. After the Civil War the building, which had long ceased to serve as a church (1839), was abandoned as a town meeting hall (1869), but early in this century—

the interior having been vandalized—it was fully restored (1906), and rededicated the following year. The interior, which when locked can be glimpsed through the windows, exhibits little more elaboration than the spartan white pine exterior. A highlight can be seen in the box pews of natural wood with delicately spindled tops (restored), those around the periphery being slightly higher than those toward the center. The usual balcony surrounds the three sides above.

This chaste house of worship is lifted above routine interest by its proportions, its sweeping command of the countryside, and its very vibration with nearby tombs. As regards its location, "In voting to place the Meeting House on a hill, the town carried out the usual custom of early days of locating such buildings on some eminence, where they could be seen for miles around, and where, in addition, they would be strategically located for defense from hostile Indians" (*The Old Rockingham Meeting House,* Lyman S. Hayes, 1915).

Open mid-June–Labor Day, daily 10–4

12   Shelburne Museum
off US 7, SW of
Shelburne, Vermont

One of the largest and most enlightening collections of late-eighteenth-
to-early-twentieth-century American vernacular building and artifacts
will be found in this open-air museum a bit south of Burlington. With
thirty-five New England buildings—plus a side-wheel lake steamboat
(1906), a covered bridge of around 1845, and a 1914 steam locomo-
tive—a panoply of structures and artifacts is laid out in a 45-acre/18-
hectare planned landscape near Lake Champlain. It is beyond the
scope of this guidebook to more than sketch a few of the individual
structures, but collectively they provide a prolific unfolding of building
types and related memorabilia, much of which would not otherwise
have survived without the efforts of Mr. and Mrs. J. Watson Webb,
who built the museum between 1947 and 1960. One reaches the collection via the 168-foot/51-meter-long, double-lane wooden bridge (Burr
truss) mentioned, and the scene is immediately set: the Stagecoach Inn
(c. 1783) is found at right after leaving the bridge, with two late-

eighteenth-century houses—the Dutton House and the Vermont House—
flanking the path in front that leads to the Charlotte Meeting House (c.
1840). The oldest building at the museum is the Prentis House (c.
1733), a saltbox moved from Massachusetts, while the newest is the
Webb Memorial (1967). In between lies a vast array of buildings and,
within them, an impressive variety of primitive and academic paintings,
dolls, kitchen utensils, toys, folk artifacts, etc., plus a staggering collection of tools—all of which give an illuminating and highly valuable insight into too-long ignored aspects of Americana.

Open mid-May–mid-Oct., daily 9–5: admission

---

13   Justin Smith Morrill House (1848–51)
Main Street, S edge of town (N off IS 89 on VT 132)
Strafford, Vermont

Vermont does not possess many Gothic Revival buildings and this
small house in the north-central hills of the state will interest the spe-
cialist. It was designed by Senator Morrill, who drew heavily from
Andrew Jackson Downing's book *Cottage Residences: or, A Series of
Designs for Rural Cottages and Cottage Villas. And Their Gardens and
Grounds. Adapted to North America* (1842). Recently spruced up and
painted pink, the house is operated by the Vermont Division of Historic
Preservation. Senator Morrill, incidentally, was the author of the Land-
Grant College bill of 1862.

*Open Memorial Day–Labor Day, Tues.–Sat. 9–12, 1–4:30:
admission*

14 West Dummerston Covered Bridge (1872)
off VT 30, c. 7 miles/11 kilometers NW of Brattleboro
West Dummerston, Vermont

This fine covered bridge is the longest (280 feet/85 meters) wholly within Vermont (see also the Windsor-Cornish Bridge). Vermont claims to have more covered bridges in active use—a bit over one hundred—than the rest of New England put together. (R. S. Allen in his admirable books *Covered Bridges of the Northeast* and *Covered Bridges of the Middle Atlantic States,* Stephen Greene Press, Brattleboro, 1957 and 1959, writes that Pennsylvania has "nearly 400 covered

spans within her borders. The nearest competitor is Ohio with 271"—figures which of course diminish with the years.)

The West Dummerston Bridge is of two spans which pause and gather strength on a single granite pier in midstream. Its Town lattice truss (named after Ithiel Town, its architect-inventor) can be partially seen through the longitudinal openings at each end, openings which ease the transition from light to dark. Six small diamond-shaped "windows" admit additional illumination toward the middle of the span. One of the area's finest covered bridges, it is marred only by its metal roof. Caleb B. Lamson constructed the bridge when he was only twenty-two.

With great satisfaction Vermont in 1968 dedicated a *new* **covered wooden bridge** at picturesque Woodstock, a 150-foot/45-meter span at Union Street that replaced an unsafe steel bridge! Wood (fir timbers, cedar shakes), here complete with sprinkler system, was cheaper than steel and far more comely. The sprinkler, incidentally, saved the bridge from total destruction when teenage vandals set it afire.

---

15 Windsor-Cornish Covered Bridge (1866)
Bridge Street, S edge of
Windsor, Vermont

The Windsor-Cornish Bridge leaps the Connecticut River to join Vermont and New Hampshire (which state through a quirk of law had to pay for most of the costs), and its span at 460 feet/140 meters makes it probably the longest covered bridge now in use in the United States. Thanks to a complete structural overhaul, it is also one of the best maintained, serving today as a very active vehicle carrier. The central stone pier, verily streamlined on the north face, still upholds the center, but the end supports have been buttressed by or replaced with reinforced concrete. The roof, regrettably, is corrugated tin. The unusual paucity of windows, here neatly hooded, produces a dark passage which necessitates headlights for automobiles. This closed quality also lessens from the design standpoint the "invitation" extended by the West Dummerston Bridge. Structurally, however, Windsor-Cornish is a great achievement. Its heavily reinforced Town lattice construction was designed by James F. Tasker, who made many bridges in New Hamsphire and Vermont, assisted by Bela J. Fletcher.

Glossary

abacus	The topmost, blocklike element of a capital, that on which the architrave (i.e. beam) rests
acropolis	Literally a city on a hill, the most famous example being in Athens
acroterion	A small pedestal at ends and/or on top of a pediment to hold a statue (Greek or Roman temples); the word often includes the figure(s); also commonly an eave ornament
Adam/Adamesque	Influenced by the Scot Robert Adam (1728–92) and his brother James (1732–94), the most important British architects of their time
adobe	Sun-dried brick generally mixed with straw binder
aggregate	Gravel or crushed stone mixed with cement and water to form concrete
agora	An open square or marketplace in ancient Greece generally surrounded by a peristyle
allée	An avenue of trees
anthemion	Foliated leaf pattern in clusters in Greek and Roman friezes
architrave	The bottom part of an entablature—that which rests on the columns
archivolt	The outside molding of an arch; also the ornamental molding on the face of an arch
Art Deco	The "jazzed," zigzag design approach popular in the late 1920s and the 1930s. Its name stems from L'Exposition Internationale des Arts Décoratifs et Industriels Modernes of 1925 in Paris, also known as Moderne
ashlar masonry	Stone cut in rectangles: it can be smooth or rough-faced, aligned or random
atrium	An open inner courtyard in a Roman house generally surrounded by a colonnade
baldachino	The canopy supported over an altar. Also called a ciborium
balloon frame	Framing of precut light wood studs, generally 2×4's, often two stories long and spaced less than 2 feet/.6 meter apart
baluster	The upright supports of a railing
balustrade	The railing around the head of stairs or atop some buildings
band course	See stringcourse
barge board	A decorative, often scroll-cut board at gable ends
batten	A narrow board nailed to cover the joint of two vertical boards

bay	A vertical wall module (as between structural columns in a skyscraper)
belt course	See stringcourse
bema	A raised platform from which religious services are conducted, generally applied to synagogues
berm	A man-made low earth "boundary"
betonglass	Thick faceted glass (1 inch/2.5 centimeters generally)
blind arcade	An "arcade" indicated by pilasters applied to a wall surface
blind arch	A relieving arch built into a wall to distribute overhead weight
bolection mold	The prominent roll mold which covers the juncture of door panel and frame
box girder	A rectangular, hollow girder usually of steel
brackets	Angled supports, often elaborate, to uphold overhang
brise-soleil	Exterior louvers, fixed or movable, to control sun load on a building
cartouche	A shield or coat of arms used as a decorative panel on a wall
cavetto cornice	An outward-curved, usually quarter-round, cornice used in Egyptian Revival
CBD	The Central Business District of a city
cella	The inner room(s) of a Classical temple, primarily the sanctuary
chamfer	A beveled edge at the meeting of two planes
chancel	The (east) end of the church, the part reserved for the clergy
Chicago window	A large fixed central pane of plate glass flanked by sash windows
ciborium	See baldachino
clapboard	A covering board thin on inner (upper) edge, thicker at butt; the boards are overlapped horizontally for weather protection. Sometimes called weatherboards
clerestory	The topmost windows of a church nave, those above the aisle roof, thus any high band of windows
console	An elaborate bracket, often scroll-shaped
coquina	A soft limestone of marine origin found in Florida; it hardens on exposure to air
corbel	A (series of) cantilevered short projection(s) supporting an overhang
Corinthian Order	The richest of the Greek and Roman orders, the capital representing stylized acanthus leaves; at

	ten diameters its column is the most slender of all
cornice	Technically the top and most projected element of an entablature; in contemporary buildings it refers to the entire projecting eave
cortile	A small courtyard
crockets	Ornamental decorations, usually vegetation-derived, on Gothic members
cupola	A domed accent on a roof with either round or polygonal base
curtain wall	An enclosing wall or wall panel independently attached to the frame of a building
dendrochronology	Dating of a wooden building by counting annual tree rings in a beam cross section or core. The method was developed by Professor A. E. Douglass of the University of Arizona
dentils	A continuous line of small blocks in a Classical molding just under the fascia
dependencies	Smaller buildings symmetrically placed on either side of a major one: flankers
distyle in antis	Two Classical columns set between end walls
dogtrot	A breezeway separating two sections of a (log) house, early popular in Southern vernacular
Doric Order	The oldest and simplest of the Classical orders. The Greek Doric column is fluted and has no base
drum	The (circular) base and support of a dome
Eastlake Style	The Eastlake Style, named for the English architect C. L. Eastlake, was popular toward the end of the nineteenth century. It helped popularize the Stick Style
ell	An addition to a house making an L-shape
English bond	A brick pattern with alternating rows of headers (brick ends) and stretchers (brick sides)
entablature	The horizontal element which tops Classical columns. The lowest part—that resting on the columns—is the architrave, the middle (and often decorated) the frieze, and the top the cornice
entasis	The slight swelling profile curve of a Greek or Roman column as it diminishes upward (an optical correction)
exedra	A semicircular (or rectangular) niche, often half-vaulted and with seats
extrados	The outside face or edge of an arch
facade	The face of a building, usually the main elevation

fanlight	A window over an entry, either semicircular or semielliptical
fascia	The flat band(s) of an entablature; also the flat top edge of a building
Federal Style	The planar, tightly restrained yet elegant style which budded in the U.S.A. following the Revolution. Found largely in the Northeast, it lasted until the 1830s
fenestration	The disposition of the windows of a building
flankers	Flanking wings or dependencies usually symmetrically disposed about the main building
Flemish bond	Alternate brick headers and stretchers in the same row
Four Corners area	The juncture of Utah, Colorado, New Mexico, and Arizona
frieze	The mid-member of the three-part entablature (architrave, frieze, cornice), often with decorative panels
furring	Inner blocking of an exterior wall to create air space with inside wall
gable	The (triangular) upper wall established by the roof planes
galleria	Typically a glass-roofed urban passageway
gambrel roof	A roof with two slopes on each side, the lower sharply pitched. It stems from the French Mansard roof
Georgian architecture	In the U.S.A. the period of increasing architectural richness beginning under the reign of George I (1714–27) to the Revolution. Symmetry and Classically derived details are characteristic
ghorfas	A series of long, mud-brick paraboloid "warehouses" (like horizontally piled cigarettes) found in south Tunisia
girder	A major horizontal supporting beam
girt	A heavy beam at the ends (and often flanking the chimney) of a Colonial house to receive upper floor joists and sometimes the summer beam
Greek cross	A (church) plan with all four arms of equal length
Greek Revival	A style based on Greek architectural prototypes or details, popular in the first half of the nineteenth century
hall	The name given to the living room of a seventeenth-century New England house

hammer beam	A short cantilevered beam or bracket supporting a timber roof arch
hatchment	An escutcheon with armorial insignia
headers	Bricks laid with their ends facing out
hexastyle	Having six columns at one end
hip roof	A roof with four sloping planes, at times meeting in a flat roof-deck
hogans	The traditional semirounded, earth-covered log dwellings of the Navajo
Howe truss	A (bridge) truss made up of a series of X-frames; similar to Long truss but with vertical wrought-iron or steel tie rods
hyphen	A connecting link between the main house in Georgian architecture and the flanking dependencies
impost	The springing point or block of an arch
in antis	The end of a (Classical) building with columns between the side walls
International Style	The first organized architectural movement against Academism: it dates largely from the 1920s and '30s
intrados	The under surface or soffit of an arch
Ionic Order	One of the major Classical orders; its capitals are immediately identified by their volutes or scrolls
IS	Abbreviation of Interstate Highway
jalousies	Slatted exterior blinds, often adjustable to control light and air
jerkin-head	The small triangular nipping off of the gable end of a roof
joist	The parallel secondary beams upholding a floor
lantern	A small geometric structure atop a roof, most frequently glazed and usually for appearance only
lights	The panes of glass of a window
lintel	A beam over an opening, or over two or more vertical members (post-and-lintel)
Long truss	A bridge truss composed of continuous boxed X-panels
lunette	Small round or half-round window generally in a gable
Mansard roof	Like the gambrel roof (q.v.), a roof with two sloping planes per side, the lower much more sharply pitched. Named for François Mansart (1598–1666)
mastaba	A flat-roofed, slope-sided tomb from Egypt's Old Kingdom
metope	The panel between the triglyphs of a Doric frieze, either plain or sculptured

Moderne	See Art Deco
modillions	Small scroll brackets, larger and wider than dentils
mortise	A cut-out hole in a beam or member which receives a tenon
mullion	The vertical division between windows (and windows and doors)
muntin	The pane divider within a window frame
oculus	A circular opening in the crown of a dome
oriel window	A bay window projecting on brackets or corbels
P/A	The abbreviation of *Progressive Architecture* magazine
Palladian	Architecture influenced by the Italian architect Andrea Palladio (1508–80). Characterized by majestic symmetry often with flanking dependencies. Palladian windows have a broad arched central section with lower flat-headed side portions
passerelle	A footbridge
pavilion	A projecting center section—for prominence—of a (usually) symmetrical building
pediment	The triangular space of the gable end of a building; also at small scale used over doors and windows—triangular, segmental (curved), and "broken" pediments
pendentive	A triangular spheroid section used to effect the transition from a square or polygonal base to a dome above
pent roof	A small "attached" roof used over first-floor windows
peripteral	Having columns completely surrounding a temple (or building)
peristyle	A colonnade surrounding a building on the outside or a court inside
piano nobile	The main floor of a mansion, generally elevated a full floor above grade
pilaster	In effect a column reduced to a thin rectangle to establish wall divisions; an engaged pier
pilotis	Columns which uphold the upper floor(s) of a building leaving ground level largely open
plate	The top horizontal member of a wood-framed wall: the rafters spring from the plate
platted	Surveyed and laid out, as of a town
plinth	The square block under a column; also the base for a statue
portal(es)	The covered porch or veranda fronting a Spanish building

portico	A columned shelter at entry; a porch
post-and-lintel	Construction by vertical uprights supporting horizontal beams
prestressed concrete	Reinforced concrete whose end-threaded steel bars or cables are prestretched to develop extra strength
purlin	Secondary horizontal beams supporting roof rafters
quadriga	A representation of a four-horse Roman chariot used as decorative feature
Queen Anne Style	A late-nineteenth-century, almost frantic mélange of styles, often with prominent triangular gable
quoins	Prominently beveled stones (or wood in imitation of stone) used to give emphasis to corners: from French *coins* or corners
rafters	The (generally) angled framing members which directly support the roof
raised basement	A "basement" partly or totally above grade
random ashlar	Miscellaneously sized, non-aligning, rectangular stones
reredos	An ornamental screen placed on the wall behind an altar
retable (retablo)	The niches and shelves behind a Spanish altar (in Gothic architecture often an encased shrine)
return	The carrying of a molding partly around a corner, often on gabled ends
reveal	The depth of inset from the wall face of a window or door
ridgepole	The topmost horizontal roof member receiving upper ends of rafters
rinceau	A low-relief vine-like running ornament
riser	The vertical measure between stair treads
roundel	A small circular opening or window
rustication	Exaggeration of joints and/or surface of stone or wood imitating stone
saltbox	The name for a New England cottage with rear addition and assymmetrically extended roof
segmental arch	A partial arch over a window
shaft	The part of a column between base and capital
shakes	Hand-split shingles, generally large and thick
sheathing	Boards or panels enclosing a structural frame
shed roof	A one-slope roof
Shingle Style	A late-nineteenth-century domestic style using (unpainted) shingles on walls as well as for roof;

	a term made popular by Professor Vincent Scully
sill	A wood (or metal) member atop and fastened to foundation walls to which the upright framing is attached
single-loaded	Rooms on one side only of a corridor
soffit	The underside of an arch or overhead beam
spandrel	In high-rise construction the enclosing panels between window head below and windowsill above; the solid bands between rows of windows
spire	The tapered section of a steeple
steeple	A church tower and its spire
stepped gable	A gable whose slope or rake is stepped rather than straight (or curved). Also called crow-foot and Dutch gable
stereotomy	The art of stone cutting and placing
Stick Style	A middle-late-nineteenth-century style of complex projections, roof, and wood outrigging
stile	The vertical framing member of a door or window
stretchers	The long sides of bricks laid facing out
stringcourse	A generally flat band of minute projection horizontally stretching across a brick facade. Also called a belt course or band course
studs	The (secondary) upright members of a wood-framed wall, often 2×4's
stylobate	The base, usually stepped, for a columned building or colonnade
summer beam	A heavy intermediate beam, mainly used in seventeenth-century New England, which carries floor joists and is itself supported by chimney and end girts
tache	Literally a spot, used here as a wall accent
temenos	A sacred confine
tenon	A projection on a wooden beam designed to fit the mortise in another beam to effect juncture. The two are fastened with a dowel
tholos	A round building, especially Greek
tie beam	A horizontal beam connecting the ends of rafters to make a truss
Town truss	A lattice panel truss with alternate closely spaced diagonals
trabeated	Post-and-lintel construction
tread	The step of a stair
triglyphs	The rectangular blocks in a Doric frieze with

	two vertical channels and half channels on edges
truss	A combination, generally triangulated, of wood, concrete, or metal members to span a space and provide structure for supporting the roof
Tuscan Order	A Roman adaptation of the Greek Doric without fluting but with base; the frieze is plain
tympanum	The framed (triangular) inner area of a pediment; also framed semicircular panel above door
vermiculated	Grooved stone imitations of worm tracks
vigas	The projecting roof beams in Indian pueblo and Spanish Colonial architecture
volutes	Spiral ornament as on an Ionic capital
voussoirs	The wedge-shaped stones or bricks which make up an arch
wainscot	The paneled protective wall lining of a domestic interior, usually not to ceiling
weatherboard	Lapped horizontal wood siding using boards often of parallel faces—as opposed to radial-cut clapboards which they resemble

Index

State abbreviations are the U. S. Post Office Department designations—i.e. Connecticut is CT, New York is NY, etc.

KIDDER SMITH is an architect and Fellow of the American Institute of Architects who has devoted most of his professional life trying to make architecture a more significant part of our culture. Supported by a number of major foundation grants, he has produced a series of distinguished articles, books, and exhibitions on the architecture of twenty-four countries. He has also lectured on four continents, often under the auspices of the Department of State. Mr. Smith received the ENIT Gold Medal from the Italian Government for his *Italy Builds,* and he and the late Philip L. Goodwin were decorated by the Brazilian Government for their *Brazil Builds* book and exhibition for the Museum of Modern Art. His *New Architecture of Europe* and *New Churches of Europe* were published in the U.S.A., England, Italy, and Germany; his *Pictorial History of Architecture in America* was one of the major books at the Moscow International Book Fair of 1979. He has also contributed to the Encyclopaedia Britannica. The twelve-year undertaking which produced these volumes on *The Architecture of the United States* represents his most ambitious effort.

Mr. Smith was born in Birmingham, Alabama (1913), and received his A.B. and M.F.A. from Princeton University. He and his wife, Dorothea, live in New York City, with one son teaching in California and the other in Switzerland.